COMMEMORATING PUSHKIN

Commemorating Pushkin

RUSSIA'S MYTH OF A
NATIONAL POET

Stephanie Sandler

STANFORD UNIVERSITY PRESS
STANFORD, CALIFORNIA 2004

Stanford University Press
Stanford, California

© 2004 by the Board of Trustees of the
Leland Stanford Junior University. All rights reserved.

Printed in the United States of America
on acid-free, archival-quality paper

Library of Congress Cataloging-in-Publication Data
Sandler, Stephanie, date-
   Commemorating Pushkin : Russia's myth of a national poet / Stephanie Sandler.
      p.   cm.
   Includes bibliographical references and index.
   ISBN 0-8047-3448-8 (alk. paper)
   1. Pushkin, Aleksandr Sergeevich, 1799–1837—Appreciation—Russia (Federation)   2. Pushkin, Aleksandr Sergeevich, 1799–1837—Criticism and interpretation. 3. Pushkin, Aleksandr Sergeevich, 1799–1837—In literature. I. Title.
PG3355.5.S26 2004
891.71'3—dc21   2003009140

Typeset by Integrated Composition Systems in 10/12.5 Sabon

Original Printing 2004
Last figure below indicates year of this printing:
13   12   11   10   09   08   07   06   05   04

For Austin and Benjamin, with love

Contents

List of Illustrations	ix
Acknowledgments	xi
Introduction: Transformative Myths and Acts of Possession	1
1. Pushkin Is Dead: The Elegies of Mikhail Lermontov, Vasily Zhukovsky, and Evdokia Rostopchina	26
2. The Making of Museum Culture: The Poet's Spirit and the Work of Remembrance	47
3. Solid Gold Pushkin: Anniversary Commemorations and the Time Lines of a Story	85
4. Document, Fidelity, and the Cinematic Image	136
5. Anna Akhmatova's Pushkin: Allegories, Ethics, Grieving for the Dead	175
6. Marina Tsvetaeva's Pushkin and the Poet's Identities	214
7. Andrei Bitov and the Mystifications of Self and Story	266
Afterword: Ending / Beginning with Andrei Sinyavsky / Abram Tertz	301
Notes	313
Index	407

Illustrations

1. Cover Photograph, *Latin Quarter*, 1990 — 8
2. Cover Illustration, *Citizens of the Night*, 1990 — 11
3. Vasily Zhukovsky Drawing, Pushkin in His Coffin, 1837 — 32
4. Zhukovsky Drawing, Floor Plan of Pushkin's Apartment at Moika 12, 1837 — 33
5. Display of Posters Showing Nazi Destruction at Mikhailovskoe — 60
6. Sign with Pushkin's Poetry at Mikhailovskoe — 74
7. The Sisters' Room in the Moika 12 Museum — 77
8. S. I. Galberg, Death Mask of Pushkin, 1837 — 78
9. Inside Cover, *The Star*, 1937 — 86
10. Pushkin Manuscript Page with Sketch of a Gallows, 1826 — 124
11. Child's Sculpture of the Helicopter *Pushkin*, Still from the 1987 Film *Let's Fly Away!* — 125
12. Lev Melikhov Photograph of the Moscow Pushkin Statue, 1999 — 133
13. O. A. Kiprensky Oil, *Pushkin*, 1827 — 152
14. Actor Posing as Pushkin, Still from the 1990 Film *Side Whiskers* — 153
15. Pushkin Manuscript Page with Drawing of a Woman's Leg, 1834 — 157
16. Trees Inscribed with Writing, Still from the 1987 Animated Film *My Favorite Time* — 158
17. Rezo Gabriadze Drawings of Pushkin, 1990 — 161
18. Pushkin Manuscript Page with Drawing of a Moor at Court, 1823 — 162
19. Pushkin's Death Mask, Still from *My Favorite Time* — 164
20. Pushkin in the Marketplace, Still from *My Favorite Time* — 166
21. A. A. Naumov Oil, *Pushkin's Duel with d'Anthès*, 1884 — 217
22. E. I. Geitman Engraving, *Pushkin*, 1822 — 218

Acknowledgments

I should preface this book about the long life of the Pushkin myth in Russian culture by admitting that Pushkin has sustained my own writing and thinking for a great many years. I began with a dissertation on his historical writings under the wise direction of Victor Erlich and Peter Demetz. I came to that topic because of a seminar with William Mills Todd III, and I began to think about the interrelationship between Pushkin's poetry and prose in courses with Omry Ronen. These teachers inspired me, and they have continued to stand in my mind as exemplary scholars. It is a pleasure to thank them for all that they taught me. As a graduate student, I had no idea that Pushkin would come to occupy such a large place in my life as a writer and teacher, and I probably began to explore topics related to this book as a way to understand my own fascination.

Through the years of work on *Commemorating Pushkin*, friends and colleagues both here and abroad have helped me in countless ways, and I am happy to have the chance to thank them. In the libraries and archives of the Institute of Russian Literature (Pushkin House), Tatiana Krasnoborodko, Valentina Zaitseva, and Liubov Timofeeva were tremendously helpful. Sergei Fomichev arranged my memorable trip to Boldino, where I was well cared for by Galina Gumennaia in Nizhny Novgorod and then by the marvelous staff members of the museum in Boldino. In St. Petersburg, I benefited from excellent conversations with Igor Nemirovsky, Elena Rabinovich, and Maria Virolainen, and with Natan Eidelman, Mikhail Gillelson, and Vadim Vatsuro, whom it was an honor to know. My friends Elena and Sergei Antonov, Marietta Turian, Konstantin and Svetlana Azadovsky, and, in Moscow, Inna Babyonysheva and the late Yuri Krutogorov shared with me their insights into the Pushkin myth and into the world of Russia more broadly.

In the United States, Tatiana Babyonysheva regularly sent new material my way. Vladimir Padunov made me copies of several Pushkin films, and both he and Susan Larsen helped me know better how to write about film. Catherine Ciepiela, John Malmstad, and William Mills Todd III put their own work aside to read this book as I was writing it, and I am grateful for their extensive comments, as well as for the warm encouragement and friendship they have given me.

Fellowships from the National Endowment for the Humanities and the Social Science Research Council funded leaves of absence for writing and research, and two IREX awards allowed me to live in Russia and continue my research there. I am grateful to several Amherst deans of faculty for supporting my work and for their assistance through the college's Faculty Research Award Program: Richard Fink, Ronald Rosbottom, and Lisa Raskin. On nearly a daily basis, Jeanne Stolarski provided help with photocopying and many other details. As I was finishing the book I changed jobs, and I was grateful to receive continued research support from Harvard University. Emily van Buskirk provided splendid research assistance and Natalia Reed proofread the Russian quotations.

Topics from this book were discussed in lectures at Williams College, Brandeis University, Wellesley College, Yale University, University of Wisconsin–Madison, Wesleyan University, Stanford University, Keele University, Harvard University, and the University of North Carolina–Chapel Hill; I thank colleagues and students for inviting me to speak and for their challenging and helpful questions. Parts of several chapters appeared in earlier versions, and permission to use that material here has been granted by the University of Wisconsin Press, Slavica Helsigiensia, Stanford Slavic Studies, University of California Press, *Slavic Review*, *Slavic and East European Journal*, and *Canadian-American Slavic Studies*. Illustrations appear courtesy of the St. Petersburg National Pushkin Museum, the Moscow Pushkin Museum, Viktor Kulle, and the journal *The Star (Zvezda)*. At Stanford University Press, Rob Ehle, Kim Lewis Brown, and Mariana Raykov were extremely helpful in all stages of the book's production. What a pleasure to work again with Barbara Mnookin, whose scrupulous editing I very much appreciate. And what a loss that Helen Tartar, whose good advice and patient encouragement benefited so many humanities scholars, is no longer at Stanford University Press—I all the more appreciate her initial work with me on this project.

My friends in and beyond the world of Slavic studies have shared many conversations with me about Pushkin and his modern legacy, and about the challenges and pleasures of writing books. They have lifted my spirits over the years and set high standards for me by the example of their work: Catherine Ciepiela, Andrew Kahn, Laura Engelstein, Caryl Emerson, Joan Dayan, Helena Goscilo, Cathy Popkin, and Rosalina de la Carrera. Last, I thank my family—above all Austin, who somehow always convinced me that I would finish this book. He and Ben indulged me in conversations about what to call it (Ben's suggestion, *Pushkin Who Is Always in Our Hearts*, could not have been bettered), and they have helped me keep a balance between work and play—which is, in the end, quite Pushkinian.

A brief note on conventions. I have used a modified Library of Congress system in the transliteration of Russian names, Anglicizing them throughout except in the bibliographic citations in the Notes. Unless otherwise noted, the translations are mine and the emphasis is in the original.

COMMEMORATING PUSHKIN

Introduction

TRANSFORMATIVE MYTHS
AND ACTS OF POSSESSION

> The love for Pushkin, which is incomprehensible to foreigners, is the true sign of a person born of Russian culture. You can like or dislike any other Russian writer; that's a matter of taste. But Pushkin as a phenomenon is obligatory for us. Pushkin is the pivot on which Russian culture turns; he connects the past to the future. Take away the pivot and the connections will disintegrate.
> —Lydia Ginzburg

"Pushkin Lives!" announces a street banner that outlived Soviet communism into the twenty-first century. Two hundred years after his birth, Alexander Pushkin is more than just a monument: the example of his life and work gives meaning to Russia's identity and to the culture of its people. This myth was articulated well by the conservative critic Stanislav Rassadin: "We who seem to have lost everything there is to lose—above all, ourselves as a nation and as a people—we possess a hope of remembering our face and suddenly repossessing our soul *when we look at Pushkin*."[1] When Russians "look at Pushkin" in the way Rassadin describes, they see all that they hope to be, they see the integrity, creativity, and spiritual values they hold dear, and they see a dynamic, liberating mind that challenges all that seems stultifying or intolerant elsewhere in their culture. Rassadin speaks as a supporter of national ambitions that inform his language of hope, nostalgia, and fervent affection. Although he reminds his readers that he stands at a historical moment of disarray (the early 1990s), his hopes for Russia are meant to be timeless. Pushkin lives for Rassadin outside time; the contemplation of his image and achievements offers the possibility of reacquiring a soul, a timeless notion of identity and spirit.

Compare words spoken from a less centrist cultural position by the Petersburg poet Elena Shvarts. Writing at about the same time, she focuses on death, not life, and on myth-making, rather than on national self-understanding. Shvarts also sees the historical figure of Alexander Pushkin outside any specific temporal frame, but because of cultural processes: "To a certain extent all poets are mythological figures. There is nothing real about Pushkin or Baratynsky. The real person dies and the myth is all that's left." She adds, "the greater the poet, the more inescapable the myth."[2] Shvarts points us toward a new question: how a myth comes into being. She sees the poet as trapped by the processes of myth-making and, unlike Rassadin, she does not celebrate its benefits for ordinary Russians. What matters is how the moment when "the real person dies" figures in the poet's "inescapable myth." The myth is as inescapable as human mortality, and it makes of Pushkin a mortal man rather than the godlike figure imagined by Rassadin. Myth begins where life ends, so, for her, the Pushkin myth draws its energy from the premise of his death.

I believe that the positions taken by both Rassadin and Shvarts are needed to understand Russia's enduring fascination with Pushkin. Several kinds of oppositions, only some of which are captured in these two quotations, will come into play throughout my study. Both the official and the marginal, the national and the personal, the visual and the verbal, the present and the past—these seeming contrasts are invoked by many different kinds of cultural artifacts, and one of my goals has been to understand how Pushkin can have generated what seem to be entirely contradictory reactions. The place from which I begin, death, is itself a source of paradox. Pushkin's death has fascinated Russians in every generation since 1837, the year he died in a duel. Death, "the most meaningful event in his biography," centers Russia's myth of a national poet.[3] Pushkin lives, but he thrives beyond a death that Russians have loved to contemplate. Perhaps this is not unique—most national heroes win their cherished status only in death. Nina Tumarkin begins her book on the Lenin cult with a visit to his tomb. He looked, in her view, "neither dead nor alive,"[4] and her ambiguous description may well remind us of the cliché that "Pushkin is immortal." But Pushkin is not only experienced as a divine being whose existence has no endpoints. His life seems deeply human to Russians, and its high drama and final tragedy have brought him close to every generation that has followed him. Yet he *became* Pushkin only when he died in a duel, and those who believe that "Pushkin Lives!" have never stopped exploring the circumstances and symbolic meanings of his death. He has been imagined as both alive and dead, one state sustaining the other; he is animated into a present that mourns his absence. I shall argue that we need both these points of view, Pushkin as tragically dead and Pushkin as endlessly alive, however much traditions within the Russian intelligentsia may try to separate them. The paradox of their coexistence is itself constitutive of Russia's myth of a national poet.

Who precisely has built Pushkin's legacy? Shvarts implies that the myth was created inevitably, and as if anonymously. One project of this book is to give names and histories to poets, novelists, artists, actors, writers, filmmakers, scholars, and museum designers who have worked with Pushkinian themes and biographical realia. I want to see how they have made the Pushkin story theirs, how they have imprinted their own stories on his, and how their ideas of Pushkin are shaped by the culture around them. For Rassadin, the viewer, the reader, and the museum visitor make the myth: every time a Russian sees into his or her soul by contemplating Pushkin, the myth is given new life. I will examine extant documents about these private encounters, which tend not to be so idiosyncratic, since they are formed by the myths of the poet as we know them. The divergence between Shvarts's and Rassadin's points of view, though, also has a history, suggesting for Pushkin two identities. The first, Pushkin as the founder of a culture, takes him as a praiseworthy public figure, as someone whose achievements can be studied.[5] The second, Pushkin as the cherished object of affection, brings devotees into closer contact with him. It is personal, even intimate. It permits identification and self-exploration, whereas tribute to his cultural primacy seems to come not from individuals but from *Russia*, undifferentiated and united in the ways symbolic nations always are.

The dispute over "my" vs. "our" Pushkin has existed at least since his death, when he was mourned as a symbol of Russia and as an immensely beloved friend. At times the two sides have coexisted, although polemics about Pushkin have often been based on one side's outrage at the attitudes of the other. I believe that Pushkin has maintained his powerful hold on the Russian cultural imagination because he has been able to seem "our" Pushkin as well as "my" Pushkin.[6] Rassadin's Pushkin, for example, is largely a shared national cultural figure, yet each individual seems free to contemplate the poet's meanings alone and with private reverence. Shvarts, too, works from the premise of a public figure, one who is made into a myth; yet she, like others in the more dissident camps of the Russian intelligentsia, implies that only an individual's view of the poet is legitimate.

Often, and in significant ways, this idiosyncratic appropriation of the poet has been expressed as a form of love. The nineteenth-century poet Fyodor Tiutchev wrote, "Like a first love, / The heart of Russia will not forget you" ("Tebia zh, kak pervuiu liubov', / Rossii serdtse ne zabudet!").[7] Tiutchev's idea of a national romance occasioned many later poems, essays, and cultural fantasies. The theme of Pushkin has been productive not only because of its intrinsic interest and complexity, but also because of the loyal, loving perceptions it has drawn from so many creative men and women. Love has generated insight, revealing beliefs about words, images, and national identity. Pushkin's writings and the quickly emergent legends about his life enabled others to write, paint, sculpt, film, and dramatize ideas that had great powers of national definition. He created modern Russian culture, not because he gave things their names, like some Slavic Adam, but because he himself remains the poet Russians most love to contemplate. His specific individual traits have assumed larger-than-life significance, but he is also the symbol of the poet; he stands for all that poetry is meant to be.

To say something similar in the language of psychoanalysis, as it has been rephrased by Adam Phillips, the figure of the poet is "a highly valued internal object, and one who is often linked . . . with fantasies of freedom and independence: the poet represents the apotheosis (at least for some people) of self-becoming, of individuality, of difference wrought to a distinctive pitch through style."[8] A number of different people may occupy this symbolic pride of place in a given culture, and in Russia others have taken on this role in different generations (one thinks of Velimir Khlebnikov, Osip Mandelstam, and Joseph Brodsky, for example), but Pushkin was exemplary for each of these poets and, indeed, for countless ordinary Russians. In the words of Lydia Ginzburg, as cited in the chapter epigraph, Pushkin is obligatory. That obligation translates, I believe, into an intense emotional investment that accompanies any glance in his direction.

Love, then, has many complexities: it can involve anger, possessiveness, poor judgment, and projection. A first love is often the source of embarrassment and error. Through the decades, love for Pushkin has been tempered by irritation, bickering, and a desire for distance. During his lifetime (1799–1837) and for at least two periods of debate (the 1860s and the 1910s), images of Pushkin were hotly contested; many voices proclaimed his irrelevance against those who championed his status as Russia's national poet. In the 1990s, tempers flared once again, and those praising Pushkin often let cynicism and criticism inform their encomia. During earlier periods of social change, critics felt special impatience with Pushkin's writings they deemed excessively private or intimate. Their high-minded vision was in turn attacked by irreverent anecdotes about Pushkin, a resilient countercultural response that took the playful image of Pushkin from his lyceum days as its point of departure and found further support in the energetic obscenity of some of his writings.[9] From every side, Pushkin and his writings have been passionately possessed, and they have become vehicles for ardent self-expression and determined argumentation. These emotional personal responses have contributed to larger cultural debates about what it means to be Russian, what role the poet is fated to play in the drama of national self-definition, and how all who live after Pushkin's death can comprehend themselves as Russians through and against his experience.

This process continues in Russia today, even at a moment (I write these words in 2002) of difficult and prolonged national transition. One would think that other, more urgent needs might take priority, and of course in many forums they have, but Russians still argue about Pushkin. Recent essays dispute the political implications of reading him as uniquely Russian, quarrel about the religious meanings of his poems, and put forth differing versions of why he still matters in these days of chaotic change.[10] In 1999, Russia mounted a grand celebration of Pushkin's bicentennial, which in turn generated more writing and arguing about his legacy. No story has offered the promise of greater national coherence than has Pushkin's, and the allure of some remnant of shared national self-definition propels many ongoing disputes and dialogues.

Aspects of the Pushkin Myth

The disputes over Pushkin have often turned on an argument about myth, a term I use to name several things.[11] First, myths as we know them from ancient cultures are explanatory narratives, tales that tell us how the world has come to be, how nature's forces change, or how human actions are ordained by the gods. Myths point to origins, offering us explanations of how something came into existence. The Pushkin story is a myth in this sense—a narrative in which modern Russia sees signs of its own beginnings. For example, Pushkin is taken as the first modern Russian writer because he worked in a European and not purely native context, or because he was a professional writer trying to earn his livelihood through his work. These aspects of his experience become symbolic stages in the culture's emergence into modernity.

Mythic origins are also sacred origins, a fact not diminished by narratives about secular and national beginnings. Russian culture has a special affinity for the doubled faith (*dvoeverie*) that intermingles Christian with pagan, and anthropologists have long studied the way in which even modern cultures create "'mythical' beings" who are "excluded from everyday life and relegated to the vague and frightening zone where everything that was an object of religious belief was assumed to belong."[12] Legends of gods and heroes who inhabit this other zone can play powerful roles in the cultural attitudes of modern people: attitudes, preferences, and appropriate forms of behavior may be modeled on them. Since 1837, Pushkin has inhabited this special zone, and it has long been unclear how much his standing there depended on his own piety, Orthodoxy, or sense of spiritual quest. Particularly in the 1990s (reprising a concern found a century earlier, but in harsher tones), arguments over the broad question of Pushkin and Christianity raged, a symptom of the culture's larger anxiety about how to reclaim its own religious traditions in the post-Soviet era.

Myths in the modern world also suggest a third meaning: explanatory systems that are false. A myth can be an erroneous belief, something widely shared and buttressed by official ideologies and the interests of the powerful; one studies such myths by identifying the designs and the blind spots of those who use them.[13] This aspect of the Pushkin story complicates the simple elevation of him to quasi-divine status, since false stories about him and his work have clearly been generated for purposes one cannot easily approve, and since the boundaries around the false stories or the reprehensible purposes are not always clear. It is insufficient to declare that a Pushkin cult has perniciously distorted his reputation, even though such a cult has harmfully existed (for example, during the Stalin period, itself an era of the "cult of personality"). Stories about Pushkin have from the beginning set up false images about the poet that the dedicated seek to tear down. The fear that someone has created a false image of Pushkin has kept alive a passion for the "real" Pushkin, always just beyond reach. Which aspects of the Pushkin story are worth fighting over differ: for some the central questions are political, for others religious, and for still others as mundane as the question of whether Pushkin loved his wife, slept with his sister-in-law, and fathered a child by one of his serfs. It is not accidental that these domestic questions stir deep interest, nor is it insignificant that they turn on sexual questions long suppressed in official debates about the poet.

Some aspects of both Pushkin myths can, then, be named, for they have recurred across the decades since his death, subject to repetition, resistance, and revision. The first myth is that Pushkin was a beacon amid the seeming morass of Russian history, a spot of light and clarity that promises to illuminate the future as well as the past. Russian self-consciousness, after the Romantic period (in which Pushkin lived), after the nationalist debates of the 1840s and 1860s, and after the highly charged proclamations of turn-of-the-century thinkers, has often turned on an image of shared national tragedy and apocalyptic rhetoric. When Russia's influential writers, poets, and philosophers take up the task of defining their nation, they speak in tones of prophecy and lament, and they comment on Russia's history of destruction and loss. Dostoevsky articulated these ideas in words so powerful that he has come to represent them in most people's minds, but Dostoevsky does not stand alone, as exemplified in works as different as Nikolai Berdiaev's *Russian Idea*, Roman Jakobson's essay "On a Generation that Squandered Its Poets," and the essays of Joseph Brodsky. Against this tragic national self-image, some (including Rassadin, quoted earlier) would seem to say that Pushkin has offered Russians hope. His role has been restorative, palliative, and spiritually enriching.

Yet for every Russian who beams happily at the thought that Pushkin once lived and wrote, another finds in him the very national tragedy he is imagined as curing. Tragic tales of Pushkin abound. Many of them focus on his death, an event through which Russians proclaimed themselves unified in their grief. Some of his writings have seemed retrospectively to speak to these themes. Dostoevsky made excellent use of *The Gypsies* (*Tsigany*, 1824) and "The Prophet" ("Prorok," 1826) in his Pushkin speech in 1880, and others have found tragic notes in Pushkin's historical writings, including his problematic and brilliant play *Boris Godunov* (1825) and his late tale *The Captain's Daughter* (*Kapitanskaia dochka*, 1836). The variety within Pushkin's oeuvre has meant that any amount of serious, disturbing writing could always be balanced by what Victor Erlich calls Pushkin's "sacred play," just as those who sought purely political justifications for their admiration for Pushkin could point to one set of poems and stories, whereas others interested in aesthetic complexity could point to another.[14]

In addition to these quite different views of Pushkin's place within Russia's tragic self-definition, there is a third position, distinguished by its rejection of the tragedy altogether. It was well expressed in the work of Yuri Lotman, who saw Pushkin's life and work as a brilliant form of adaptation to potentially repressive social mechanisms. Lotman's impact on contemporary thinking about Pushkin remains considerable, as can be seen in the voluminous republication of his writings and in collections like *Cultural Mythologies of Russian Modernism*, edited by Boris Gasparov, Robert P. Hughes, and Irina Paperno (1992) and *Legends and Myths About Pushkin* (*Legendy i mify o Pushkine*, 1995), edited by Maria Virolainen. For these scholars, Pushkin's life and work are tightly bound to each other, and the very idea of the Pushkin myth grows more lively and more varied. One other large group of late-twentieth-century writings about Pushkin deserves mention in this context—the works of Andrei Sinyavsky (writing as Abram Tertz) and Andrei Bitov, where a love of parody combines with a self-conscious rejection of the Pushkin myth as inherently tragic; particularly in the experiments of the 1990s, these trends were newly instructive, influencing postmodern poets like Timur Kibirov and Dmitri Aleksandrovich Prigov, among many others. An early almanac of this avant-garde poetry movement, *Latin Quarter* (*Latinskii kvartal*, 1990), had as its cover photograph a picture of a Pushkin monument encased in scaffolding (Fig. 1); this irreverent image was surely meant as a parody of the term *restructuring* (*perestroika*), and contributors to *Latin Quarter* presented themselves as reinventing Russian culture. They were the poets who would rescue Pushkin from the confining structures of scaffolding and liberate Russian culture for future glory.

This variety of responses to a Pushkin myth begins to answer the question of why *Pushkin* (and not Lermontov, Dostoevsky, Tolstoy, or Gogol—or, for that matter, Baratynsky, mentioned by Shvarts as an equivalent figure) became Russia's national poet, but there are other reasons as well. The timing is enormously important. Pushkin appeared at that moment early in the nineteenth century when post-Napoleonic Romantic nationalism made

FIGURE 1. Cover photograph for the poetry almanac *Latin Quarter* (*Latinskii kvartal*), 1990. Courtesy of the editor, Victor Kulle.

it seem as if every nation needed its native genius. The only other writer and poet who might then have fit the bill was Mikhail Lermontov. He, too, had a short, intensely lived life (Lermontov died even younger than Pushkin: his dates are 1814–41, Pushkin's 1799–1837). But Pushkin's having written with authority and "clarity" (a cliché in Pushkin criticism) in every genre, and his having died in a duel marked by romantic intrigue, rather than the all-male dispute of Lermontov's duel, helped him become the more appealing figure. He also preceded Lermontov, if only by a few years, and his death was itself a poetic subject that catapulted the young Lermontov to fame (we will study his poem about Pushkin's death in Chapter One).

The circumstances of Pushkin's death were especially conducive to the myth-making process. Contemporaries saw his death as a time of coming together, and their belief in a national reaction to tragedy became a foundational moment in myths of Pushkin.[15] Nicholas I's government recognized the magnitude and danger of the response at once: Pushkin's body was wheeled out of Petersburg in the dark of night to be buried at the distant Sviatogorsk Monastery. The absence of the body enabled an especially spiritual aspect of the Pushkin myth, although his meager property was treated with a reverence that belied any absolute denial of the material. The relics of his life include his library, sanctified by Pushkin's gesture of farewell to his books as he was dying, as well as the expected paraphernalia of death that can still be seen in Russian museums: death masks, the waistcoat with its bullet hole, the dueling pistols, the divan on which he lay.

The removal of Pushkin's body was brought about by political considerations (the tsar's informers claimed that the crowds would get out of hand, and the very idea of such attention being paid a mere writer, and one whom they also found politically untrustworthy, was not to be borne), with the result that the death itself came to seem politically meaningful.[16] Pushkin had died from a duel motivated by a gentleman's sense of family honor, but the tsar's intervention into the funeral arrangements reminded friends that he might have prevented the duel altogether. Lermontov's widely circulated poem blamed Russian high society. Particularly when compared with other elegies on Pushkin's death, Lermontov's offers a vividly disembodied poem, and it initiated the politics of Pushkin as state martyr in a way that required this negation of the body.

As it turned out, one hundred years later, when Stalin urged Russians to commemorate the anniversary of Pushkin's death, the 1937 Pushkin jubilee coincided with the height of the purges, a time when the body became an object of terror and destruction.[17] Some fifty years after the first of their kind, monuments as sites for a kind of Pushkin worship proliferated in the wake of the 1937 and 1949 Pushkin anniversary celebrations,[18] repeating a small number of iconographic poses in ways that fix images of Pushkin declaiming his verse, relaxing on a park bench, or standing contemplatively, head bowed. The monuments' stillness and similarity well represent for us the attitude of official Pushkin myths, as constituted by literary, religious, philosophical, and political culture.[19] These myths produce a static rather than dynamic Pushkin, also disembodying him. How ironic that these monuments now seem to incarnate an official and slightly dishonest myth of Pushkin: erecting a monument to a private person in 1880 was actually quite a daring thing to do in a nation that previously so honored only autocrats and generals. But the monuments are consonant with a disembodied version of the Pushkin myth where there is no place for stories and legends of the poet that suggest bodily energy, erotic inventiveness, transgressive desire, and physical difference. This myth long shaped the inherited canon of Pushkin's writings, expurgating letters and lyrics and keeping obscene texts, like *Gavriliad* (*Gavriiliada*, 1821), almost entirely out of the hands of readers.[20] But like all myths these, too, have generated resistance. Opponents include Vladimir Mayakovsky, Marina Tsvetaeva, and Andrei Sinyavsky; the creators of popular legend and endless anecdotes; and filmmakers who have developed techniques for enlivening the public image of Pushkin. Perhaps the best example of the anecdotal rejection of Pushkin as a monument comes in the expression "Who's going to do that, Pushkin?" (in this rhetorical question, the verb is endlessly replaceable by activities of daily life—sweeping, mending, laundering). Another almanac cover from the perestroika period brought this expression to life with its picture of Pushkin innocently holding a broom, ready to sweep (Fig. 2).[21] The wish to bring Pushkin down from his monument reacted against mindless elevations of Pushkin in official discourse, at the same time that it reinvigorated and renewed affection for him.

A vivid sense of the range of Pushkin's public images emerges in the best-known clichés about him. He was a "radiant name" ("eto svetloe imia") from the beginning, a "happy name" ("veseloe imia") to Alexander Blok in the early twentieth century, the "sun of Russian poetry" ("solntse russkoi poezii"). These names share metaphorical references to light and to gaiety, and they reflect an optimism that has long had many Russians defending him or his image from apparently sullying commentary, as in the controversy over Sinyavsky's *Strolls with Pushkin* (*Progulki s Pushkinym*, 1975). The light-filled aura of Pushkinian presence has him illuminating Russia as the sun lights the earth, but it also lends impermanence and fragility to his image. Pushkin's death was described as the setting of the sun ("solntse nashei poezii zakatilos'") as early as 1837, and the metaphor persisted, as in Osip Mandelstam's essay on Pushkin and Scriabin (1915–20), which evoked "the poet's sun-filled body" and placed the sun "in its coffin at night."[22] Mandelstam's "night sun" reminds us of the tragedy hidden in the bright light of official cheer (and refers to the dark time when Mandelstam lived).

In the early Soviet period, another cliché about Pushkin began to seem more appropriate: Apollon Grigoriev's 1859 assertion that "Pushkin is our everything" ("Pushkin—eto nashe vse").[23] This emphasis on unity compares Pushkin to a vessel able to contain any experience shared by Russians. The quotation from Rassadin given above, as will be obvious, draws on

FIGURE 2. Cover illustration for the almanac *Citizens of the Night* (*Grazhdane nochi*), 1990.

both the exaggerated rhetoric of Grigoriev and the implicit hope expressed by images of Pushkin as bright sunshine. The word *our* is important in the phrase "our everything": Grigoriev emphasizes that Pushkin absorbed fully Russia's being, its spirituality. "Pushkin is our everything" implies a leveling in which all of the experiences held in the vessel *Pushkin* have equal value and equal meaning. Grigoriev's claim lifts Pushkin out of history into an absolute realm where heroes do not change and where nations are defined by their heroes. The association of Pushkin with light is ahistorical because of its grounding in the world of nature, but the association of Pushkin with "everything" goes further, obliterating distinctions like nature vs. culture, past vs. present. It contemplates Pushkin in an emotional rather than rational way, demonstrating by its own extravagance that attitudes toward Pushkin properly exist in the superlative.

These verbal formulas, and one could include others, exemplify a shared perception of Pushkin as light-filled and clear, as capacious and profoundly Russian. Through them, he becomes as inevitable as sunshine, as all-encompassing as the world around us. The clichés concentrate a number of the implicit myths: the national poet whose brilliant achievements demonstrate the greatness of the nation that produced him; the protean writer in whom successive generations of Russians saw themselves (and their political or aesthetic agendas); the martyr whose early death helped a nation understand its own tragic fate and showed the ruthless power of the state; and the integrity-filled man of genius, an inspiring example to later generations of artists, thinkers, and citizens. Now, over a hundred and fifty years after Pushkin's death, it is difficult to read any of his texts without this mediating interpretative activity, without these myths.

One way in which Pushkin, then, remains distinctive among Russian writers is the density of this activity of myth-making. That is not to say that there are not myths of Tolstoy and Dostoevsky, of Mandelstam and Mayakovsky, for of course there are. Their myths also pushed others in new directions, as, for example, when Tolstoy's description of his childhood shapes later Russian writings on this theme (as Andrew Wachtel has argued), or when the myth of Mandelstam as charismatic poet (wonderfully assessed by Gregory Freidin) models self-creation for contemporary poets as different as Prigov and Brodsky.[24] The difference is in the multifaceted, indeed contradictory nature of Pushkin myths, in the love and repetition they have generated, in the sharper focus on contrasts of death and life, and in the greater capacity for Pushkin's story to seem the story of Russia itself.

The late twentieth century saw the discovery of the Pushkin myth as a scholarly theme. Marcus Levitt has published a definitive study of the 1880 Pushkin celebration as well as an essay on the 1899 celebration; anthologies from Petersburg and Moscow include excellent critical introductions that place writing about Pushkin in the larger philosophical traditions of Russia.[25] Paul Debreczeny has written an absorbing monograph on Pushkin's impact on his readers.[26] Others have begun to write critically of official Pushkin culture, particularly of the role played by visual representations of

Pushkin, Pushkin monuments, and the professionalization of Pushkin scholarship.[27] And many studies of Pushkin's influence on subsequent writers exist, some of them examining the ways in which his career served as a model for others.[28] My own work is thus part of ongoing work that will continue for years to come. Its contribution is not meant to be definitive. Rather, it attempts to show how foundational texts and cultural institutions have created myths of Pushkin around paradoxes of life and death, of the individual and the national group; how thinking about Pushkin has been a vehicle for self-expression and self-discovery; how Russia's national culture has emerged through myths of Pushkin as friend, prophet, and national genius; and how intense feelings have informed poems, speeches, films, fictions, polemics, museum exhibits, and commemorations of Pushkin throughout the twentieth century.

The Shape of This Book

The first part of my study presents literary texts and cultural institutions that established and maintained Pushkin's elevated status in Russian culture. Chapter One treats three immediate responses to Pushkin's death in 1837; elegies by Vasily Zhukovsky, Mikhail Lermontov, and Evdokia Rostopchina use the conventions of poetic lament for national as well as personal self-definition. It is the one chapter devoted to Pushkin's contemporaries. It examines critically the hallowed status accorded those who "knew" Pushkin, and it identifies the first forms of love with which he was mourned. The poems by Zhukovsky and Lermontov will frequently be invoked by subsequent writers, so a deeper knowledge of these famous elegies is useful. Rostopchina's elegy, by comparison, was received indifferently. This is a response her poem ironically predicted; it also offers insight into the ways in which expectations about women's and men's emotional differences will be played out in all subsequent forms of love and grief for Pushkin.

Chapter Two looks at museums that memorialize Pushkin, drawing on new studies of the cultural politics of the museum. The chapter focuses on two former estates, Boldino and Mikhailovskoe, where major Pushkin museums have evolved. They use theatrical effects in different ways and show their own histories differently to visitors. The shrines indirectly ask what it means to remember Pushkin, and not just to honor or love him; many poetic testimonies by minor poets exemplify the power of Boldino and Mikhailovskoe to suggest that Pushkin's spirit lives in these pastoral places. The chapter includes literary texts that conjure up the specter of Pushkin past, as well as those that parody museums altogether.

Chapter Three studies Pushkin celebrations as a set of cultural practices.

Each anniversary fashions a new Pushkin, sometimes via memorable literary, artistic, and cinematic texts. Given the solid scholarship on the nineteenth-century celebrations, I begin in the twentieth century, when the culture of celebration itself changed. The commemoration of 1921 featured eloquent speeches about the perceived end to traditional Russian culture in the post-revolutionary era, but the 1924 gatherings were a new beginning for Soviet culture. The 1937 jubilee used Pushkin material to distract from the horrors of Stalin's purges, and some of the Pushkin texts created for the jubilee powerfully reflect the traumas of the age. The 1937 events were formative for later perceptions of Pushkin as Russia's official national poet, and for the remainder of the century, most commemorations followed its patterns even as they tried to distance themselves from its violence. In 1999, the only twentieth-century anniversary to seek the grandeur of 1937, and the only one to be so fully entwined with the project of national identity, open weariness with official activity was juxtaposed to an astonishing variety in forms of commemoration. Films and art exhibits merit special attention in 1999, a sign of the rise of visual culture in the late twentieth century. In all the anniversaries of the twentieth century, remarkable men and women participated even in events they found questionable; in Chapter Three, work by Vladislav Khodasevich, Vladimir Mayakovsky, Alexander Blok, Mikhail Bulgakov, Daniil Kharms, and others will thus be important.

Chapter Four turns to film as a medium that has the potential to buttress but also critique official Pushkin myths. All five films discussed here challenge conventions of realism, the dominant aesthetic paradigm during the Soviet period. One movie, *Keep Me Safe, My Talisman* (*Khrani menia, moi talisman*, 1986), takes place in Boldino, where it transposes into the modern era motifs from Pushkin's life and works. I look at a biographical film, *The Last Road* (*Posledniaia doroga*, 1986), that questions the strict division between official and unofficial culture; in its decision not to include an actor playing Pushkin in the story of his death, it also addresses a central problem of Pushkin films, how to represent him. *Side Whiskers* (*Bakenbardy*, 1990) resolves that question with a dizzying array of Pushkin lookalikes, and it also recalls the politically charged questions of jubilee celebrations with its aggressive attack on the idea of a Pushkin cult. The brilliant animated films of Andrei Khrzhanovsky, collected as *My Favorite Time* (*Liubimoe moe vremia*, 1987), show that motion pictures can go beyond commemorating Pushkin, seeming to replicate his creative process. Mikhail Shveitser's *Little Tragedies* (*Malen'kie tragedii*, 1980) is informed by a desire to bring Pushkin himself to life; like Khrzhanovsky's cartoon, it seeks to understand the work of creating poetry, allegorized in the film's acts of improvisation and performance.

After these first four chapters, I turn to the literary readings that make up the second half of this study. The object of mythic adoration becomes the subject of many kinds of stories, poems, and essays. I concentrate on three writers who devoted a significant portion of their work to Pushkin and who do so in ways that are interestingly self-revealing. It is no accident that two, Marina Tsvetaeva and Anna Akhmatova, are poets, or that when I turn to the third, Andrei Bitov, a fascination with poetry-writing seizes even this accomplished writer of prose. An Afterword looks at a fourth writer, Andrei Sinyavsky, placing him last because his writings so well summarize the themes of this book and suggest ways in which Pushkin myths might evolve in the future.

Chapter Five argues that Akhmatova writes about Pushkin from a position of grief, which informs even her earliest lyrics about him. In her essays, she takes up the tale of his death with a rare intensity; she lets this readiness to mourn coexist with a stringent ethical attitude toward the silences, lies, and distortions that she sees as the cause of his tragic demise. That dishonesty marked public discourse in Akhmatova's lifetime, too, and her Pushkin essays offer occasions to hint at parallels; his standards of behavior and his creation of an identity as a professional writer inspire Akhmatova as she seeks, in the essays, models for her own reactions to difficult times. She is like the Pushkin scholars of her age in her fascination with the drama of his death, although she is also focused on the sexual transgressions that were a part of that drama. The chapter suggests strong continuities between Akhmatova's poems, early and late, and her prose about Pushkin. Although I believe that it was her own autobiography that Akhmatova wrote in her Pushkin texts, I give equal weight to her methods as a scholar—the ways in which she uses evidence, the intonations and repetitions of her writing, and the kinds of themes to which she was most often drawn.

If Akhmatova was fascinated by documents and the uncovering of secrets, then Tsvetaeva by comparison cared more about the emotions and physical sensations of the people who knew Pushkin. In her earliest lyric poetry, she creates fantasies of encountering Pushkin. She writes about him from the position of both child and adult, and we rightly value her poems and essays for what they tell us about him (she was daringly insightful even when fabulously wrongheaded). Her identifications with Pushkin and with Natalia Nikolaevna Pushkina tell us more than any confession could. Tsvetaeva came to share Akhmatova's interest in the tale of Pushkin's death, but not so as to explain the machinations that caused it. Everything in Tsvetaeva's world is symbolic, and through symbolic similarities (rather than through the allegories favored by Akhmatova), she fills her Pushkin essays with lyrical passion. There is no reining in of the personal in her essays or in her lyrics, nor does the poet slight larger political themes. On the contrary, when she defines Pushkin's position as emphatically marginal and identifies him with the rebel Emelian Pugachev, rather than with the Empress Catherine II, Tsvetaeva is simply reversing the terms for what counts as Russian. She does not let us forget her own marginal position (she writes her major Pushkin texts in exile), and she never loses sight of the importance of writing about him as a woman. She contemplates the effects of gender difference in all her Pushkin writings, creating a convergence of sexuality and nationality. The line between celebration and lament is often blurred, and the project of declaring oneself a poet worthy of Pushkin's legacy is embedded in meditations on self, sex, childhood, and loss.

In Chapter Seven, I take up Andrei Bitov's essays and story about Pushkin and his novel *Pushkin House* (*Pushkinskii dom*, 1978). Bitov's bemused demeanor offers a sharp contrast to Tsvetaeva's passion. He can treat Pushkin with scholarly clarity, like Akhmatova, but always with complex mystifications. Bitov has an elusive, playful presence as a writer, yet he asks serious questions about the chronology of Pushkin's writings, the ways Pushkin sought inspiration, and the challenges of his last year. He offers a psychologically rich portrayal of Pushkin, one that in turn enables a view of Bitov himself as a less self-absorbed or pedantic writer than he might otherwise seem. The impersonations of his essays and the fantastic variegations of his fictions betray an anxiety about how to write about Pushkin, and the nervousness intensifies when he considers writing poetry or writing as if he were Pushkin himself. Quoting others is a Bitov trademark, yet the ante is upped when he considers quoting Pushkin—and he quotes Pushkin quite a lot. The resulting fascination with various forms of transgression can approach the concern for ethics found in Akhmatova, and like hers, the fascination works through historical failures for Russia as a nation along the way. Pushkin prompts Bitov to dig deeper into himself, and into his view of his culture, and it is a topic that he seems unwilling to relinquish entirely.

Only one contemporary writer matches Bitov's insight into Pushkinian playfulness with identity, and that is Andrei Sinyavsky, the subject of the Afterword. Sinyavsky's exuberant account of Pushkin's sexuality, his unorthodox treatment of Pushkin's death, and the combination of the two themes, sex and death, in the image of the vampire elicited a hate-filled reaction from Russian nationalists that made Sinyavsky himself out as someone who hated Russia. Nowhere does one see more powerfully the deployment of the Pushkin myth to fight highly charged battles over national self-definition, although it is not unusual for cultural artifacts that refuse to elevate Pushkin to receive angry labels as inappropriate or vulgar. By ending with Sinyavsky, I conclude with a writer who, for many, exemplified the most prized Pushkinian values: a capacity for playfulness combined with integrity, a legacy of work that spans and crosses several genres, and a self-image as anything but monumental.

Back to Pushkin

Before concentrating on texts about Pushkin by others, I want to look briefly at Pushkin's thoughts about himself, his reputation, and the creative process in two poems: "The Prophet" ("Prorok," 1826) and "I have built myself a monument" ("Ia pamiatnik sebe vozdvig nerukotvornyi," 1836).[29] Mentioned often in later chapters, they are excellent texts for studying Pushkin's habits of self-mythologization. One gives a violent account of the creative process and the transformation of an ordinary person into a god-like poet; the other shows Pushkin considering how he might himself become the subject of cultural myth-making. Pushkin's self-mythologizing writings lift the story of the poet out of time and biography, creating not the legends of a historical man who lived, loved, and wrote his poems, but the ever-shifting impression of a godlike figure whose most inspired creation was his own self-image. This is not to dismiss the impact of lived experience and historical circumstance on Pushkin's work, or to ignore the fact that Pushkin himself turned to historical writing in the 1830s and then began to offer much more prosaic accounts of himself as a writer. But the most influential tales of self that Pushkin left us emphasize his uncanny ability to retell the circumstances of his life according to his own design and desire.[30] Many different works show the traces of this self-creation, from fragmentary sketches to masterpieces like *Eugene Onegin* and *Boris Godunov*. In his short poems about the poet, of which there are more than a dozen, Pushkin concentrates on the experience and the consequences of creating poetry.[31]

It is distinctive that so many of Pushkin's acts of self-mythologization would take the form of lyric poems, and it is also striking that he focused on three themes—the image of the poet, the creative process, and the imagined response of readers and subsequent poets. His lyrics create an ideal poet, for example in the sonnet "To the Poet" ("Poetu," 1830) and, most famously, "The Poet" ("Poet," 1827), which begins "Until the poet is called" ("Poka ne trebuet poeta"). Virtually missing is an interest in the death of the poet, a surprising fact given the importance of such poems in the early nineteenth century, and an ironic one, given how much was made of Pushkin's own death.[32] Pushkin's admired contemporary Evgeny Baratynsky wrote "On the Death of Goethe" ("Na smert' Gete," 1832) and "When your voice, o poet" ("Kogda tvoi golos, o poet," 1843), among other elegies, that were statements of his poetic credo, but Pushkin wrote of death as a personal loss, as in his response to the death of his friend Baron Anton Delvig.[33]

In "The Prophet," Pushkin gives us a poet attached to no particular biography. The setting seems a biblical wilderness, and Pushkin chooses elevated diction for this dramatic poem, which draws its images from chapter

6 of the Book of Isaiah.³⁴ It rewrites a terrifying visitation from a messenger of the Lord rewritten as the encounter between poet and muse.

The Prophet

Parched by a spiritual thirst,
I was dragging myself through a gloomy wasteland,
And a six-winged seraphim
Appeared to me in the crossroads;
With fingers light as a dream
He touched my eyes:
The prophetic eyes opened wide,
Like those of a frightened eaglet.
He touched my ears,
And filled them with sound and ringing:
And I heard the shudder of heaven,
And the angels' flight on high,
And the underwater movement of sea creatures,
And the vegetation of the earth's vines.
And he leaned into my lips
And tore out my sinful tongue,
Its idle talk and cunning.
And into my stilled lips
He inserted the fang of a wise serpent
With his bloody hand.
And he cut open my breast with a sword,
And took out the throbbing heart,
And inserted a coal, burning in flame,
Into the open breast.
I lay in the desert like a corpse,
And the voice of God called out unto me:
"Arise, prophet, and see, and hear,
Fulfill my will,
And, traveling the seas and the land,
Ignite the hearts of men with words."³⁵

Пророк

Духовной жаждою томим,
В пустыне мрачной я влачился,
И шестикрылый серафим
На перепутье мне явился;
Перстами легкими как сон
Моих зениц коснулся он:
Отверзлись вещие зеницы,
Как у испуганной орлицы.
Моих ушей коснулся он,
И их наполнил шум и звон:

И внял я неба содроганье,
И горний ангелов полет,
И гад морских подводный ход,
И дольней лозы прозябанье.
И он к устам моим приник,
И вырвал грешный мой язык,
И празднословный и лукавый,
И жало мудрыя змеи
В уста замершие мои
Вложил десницею кровавой.
И он мне грудь рассек мечом,
И сердце трепетное вынул,
И угль, пылающий огнем,
Во грудь отверстую водвинул.
Как труп в пустыне я лежал,
И Бога глас ко мне воззвал:
«Восстань, пророк, и виждь, и внемли,
Исполнись волею моей,
И, обходя моря и земли,
Глаголом жги сердца людей».[36]

The six-winged seraphim replaces the poet's eyes, ears, tongue, and then heart. The first two substitutions make him able to attend to nature's movements as if for the first time, but only the new capacity for speech and feeling can make the poet a prophet. He lies ready, barely alive—after the operations are over, the poet describes himself as a corpse in the desert.[37] The seraphim has killed him, or killed an old self, so that now he can hear the voice of the Lord telling him to rise up and go forth to speak with new passion.

Nothing in this remarkable poem left it more open to distorted readings than this final command. Many readers have wanted to supply the prophet's imagined message.[38] Written in 1826 during what was to be the end of Pushkin's five-year period of exile, the poem seems poised to set out a new self-description.[39] Such moments of self-transformation were always problematic for Pushkin (and probably for any poet), as one senses in a more intimate lyric, "Autumn" ("Osen'," 1833). Both poems stop short of announcing the nature of the poet's newly inspired work.[40] In "The Prophet," we hear God's commands to change, not the poet's "new" voice. Charged to burn fire into the hearts of his listeners, the poet has lost his heart for a burning piece of coal, suggesting that he burns with the same fire as his prophetic words.[41] Pushkin carefully tells us only that the poet, lying like a corpse after all that has been done to him, *hears* a voice telling him to rise up and fulfill the will of God. The poet's passivity is suggested throughout "The Prophet": in active but grammatically reflexive verbs like "I was dragging myself" ("vlachilsia"); in syntactic forms where the poet is the object of the action, not its agent; and in sentences where the poet is the indirect, dative object—these are the most striking—when something is done to a part of his body. If "The Prophet" tells a tale of poetic inspiration, then it does so by dramatizing how the poet is chosen by forces over which he has no control. Prophetic status is laid on him, rather than being presented as a form of election.

The best counter to such an observation about "The Prophet" comes in the poem itself, its sound orchestration and rhythmic organization so fine as to prove that the encounter with the Lord's messenger has been brought about by a great talent.[42] The poem's peculiar authority ought to come from this magic fusion of sound and song, but that is not the case. It derives almost entirely from an aspect of the poem's reception that surely would have produced a shudder in Pushkin as significant as what ripples through the heavens in the poem: generations of readers have simply wished to see Pushkin himself as a prophet, and thus found it immensely appealing to think that he announced himself as such at the age of twenty-seven. Nikolai Gogol, a man of no small prophetic inclinations himself, announced Pushkin to be "the Russian man as he might be expected to appear two hundred years hence" ("russkim chelovekom v ego razvitii, v kakom on, mozhet byt', iavitsia chrez dvesti let").[43] Fyodor Dostoevsky definitively made Pushkin the seer of modern Russia in his 1880 speech, where he praised the receptiveness, humility, and passivity of Pushkinian heroes, as exemplified by the way in which prophetic status was thrust on the poet in "The Prophet."[44] After his speech, he recited the poem twice.

I will return to "The Prophet" in connection with the discussion of Pushkin films in Chapter Four: it is heard in the only Pushkin film to confront the violence of Russia's national self-image (*Side Whiskers*). *Side Whiskers* features the physical violence a nation inflicts on its citizens (or, more precisely, the violence that an ideology demands from its followers), but in "The Prophet," Pushkin explores the violence done to one who takes on the burdens of creative work. In other poems, Pushkin glorifies the poet, making him the sacred servant of Apollo or a kind of tsar, and of course it could be said that glory also comes to the poet in "The Prophet" when he is sent forth to bear the word of God. But the poet is laid low in this poem, literally horizontal as he drags himself across the wilderness and as he rests prostrate, like a corpse, hearing the Lord's commands. Being transformed from one who is lost in obscurity and emptiness (suggested by the "gloomy wasteland," "pustynia mrachnaia") into one who can fathom God's words is an entirely physical experience, and, as ears, eyes, tongue and finally heart are ripped out and replaced by newly acute organs, the poet becomes ready to speak in ways that will burn straight through to the hearts of his listeners.

Both processes are violent, then, the poet's transformation and the hearers' reaction; both are felt in the body as a jolt of force that leaves one scorched by the sheer intensity of the encounter. In that intensity, I believe, Pushkin gives us the searing experience of the present, not an anticipation of some greater future. He refuses to behave like a prophet (who tells of what will come) and insists that he is, through it all, a poet (who speaks of what is).[45]

In an earlier version of the poem, the first line described the poet as tormented not by a "spiritual thirst," but by a "great loss" ("velikoi skorbiiu").[46] Perhaps Pushkin changed the line to steer readers away from any personal reference the image might have; indeed his substitution stresses the spiritual nature of the quest that takes the poet into the desert. But loss or grief (another meaning of *skorb'*) has a place in this poem, a rare place, considering that Pushkin tends not to write of the poet's death. What is lost in the course of the poem is something physical. Indeed one reader has gone so far as to say that the poet must lose his heart entirely in this transformation, which makes the prophet literally heartless and thus inhuman.[47] The poet's body becomes symbolic, rather than a physical object whose meanings can be understood in the prosaic world. Like the later poem in which Pushkin imagines himself as a monument, "The Prophet" contains the fear that in order to be a genuine poet, one must cut ties to the world of day-to-day life. We know that Pushkin did nothing of the kind, and that his writings frequently affirm the poet's pleasures in the physical and domestic world. But like other poets reared on Romanticism, he betrays a nervousness about this topic, and for those who create Russia's myths of Pushkin, there has been something very attractive about keeping him far from the messiness of daily life.

No lyric poem facilitated that reading of Pushkin more powerfully than "I have built myself a monument." Based on Horace's last ode,[48] it remains the most intensely canonized of all Pushkin's poems, partly because it appeared to predict the terms of his future fame.[49] It well describes the reverential pose of those who claim possession of "our" Pushkin, although its language evidences Pushkin's anticipation that his readers would feel for him the affection of individuals. Its steely nerve has been taken as his poetic credo, and its nearness to his death has added irony to the poem's prediction of immortality. Irina Surat, in a discerning essay on Pushkin's death and on the concept of death in his works, finds the poem posthumous in its feel, as if written from the other side of the grave.[50]

> Exegi monumentum
> I have built myself a monument not made by human hands,
> The people's path to it will not be overgrown,
> It rises, its head unsubdued, higher
> Than Alexander's column.

No, I shall not wholly die—the soul in its sacred lyre
Will outlive my dust and escape decay—
And I shall be famous so long as in this world beneath the moon
    Lives even a single poet.

News of me will pass through the whole of great Russia,
And every language in her realm will speak my name:
The proud Slavs' descendant, the Finn, the wild
    Tungus, and the steppe-loving Kalmyk.

And long shall I be loved by the people
Because I awakened kind feelings with my lyre,
Because in my cruel age I sang the glories of freedom
    And was calling for mercy to the fallen.

Be obedient, o Muse, to the gods' will,
Not fearing insult, not demanding a wreath;
Heed praise and blame indifferently,
    And do not quarrel with a fool.[51]

                  Exegi monumentum.
Я памятник себе воздвиг нерукотворный,
К нему не зарастет народная тропа,
Вознесся выше он главою непокорной
    Александрийского столпа.

Нет, весь я не умру—душа в заветной лире
Мой прах переживет и тленья убежит—
И славен буду я, доколь в подлунном мире
    Жив будет хоть один пиит.

Слух обо мне пройдет по всей Руси великой,
И назовет меня всяк сущий в ней язык,
И гордый внук славян, и финн, и ныне дикой
    Тунгус, и друг степей калмык.

И долго буду тем любезен я народу,
Что чувства добрые я лирой пробуждал,
Что в мой жестокий век восславил я свободу
    И милость к падшим призывал.

Веленью божию, о муза, будь послушна,
Обиды не страшась, не требуя венца;
Хвалу и клевету приемли равнодушно,
    И не оспоривай глупца.[52]

    This poem lays out the terms for shared national admiration of Pushkin with uncanny prescience. The poet describes a path trod by all the people of his nation, and his fame spreads to neighboring nations as well. He contrasts his own monumental individuality to these groups of admirers, his unbowed head rising higher even than a column that symbolizes the tsar. Pushkin has substituted Alexander's column for the measure of the pyramids found in Horace (and in Gavriel Derzhavin's 1795 version of Horace);[53] scholars have rightly emphasized the provocative reference to a monument at whose opening Pushkin refused to be present. Attention might also be drawn to the way Pushkin personalizes the reference with his own first name,[54] thus heightening the contrast within the rhymed pair "people's path" ("narodnaia tropa") and "Alexander's column" ("Aleksandriiskaia stolba"). As Renate Lachman has observed, the choice of the adjective "Aleksandriiskii" rather than "Aleksandrovskii" makes the epithet all the more prominent: it refers us to Alexandria, a North African place-name that may suggest Pushkin's self-consciousness about his African heritage; and it calls to mind the verse form known as Alexandrines, whose mixed iambic form with masculine rhyme structures this poem.[55]

Pushkin continues the equation between his identity and his poetry in the third stanza, where he, like Derzhavin before him, mentions specific features of his own work. Where Derzhavin sought honor for having glorified Catherine while telling her the truth and for having been the first to write such poems in Russian, Pushkin points to his call for mercy toward the fallen and emphasizes the gentleness and kindness of his poetic speech.[56] In noting this contrast, scholars often have urged the political significance of Pushkin's change, arguing that these lines specifically refer to the Decembrists.[57] Yet the emotional tenor could not be further from the civic rage practiced by Decembrist poets. Pushkin associates "kind feelings" ("chuvstva dobrye") with his lyre.

Valentin Nepomnyashchy has urged a religious reading of Pushkin's poetic mission, stressing compassion as fundamental to Pushkin and to Orthodox Christianity.[58] The poet's image has struck other readers of that persuasion as profoundly Christ-like. The epithet "not made by human hands" is the foundation of this interpretation, for it refers conventionally to an icon of the face of Jesus, and by extension, to churches honoring that icon or to the church Jesus promised to build for man.[59] Just as such churches or icons were thought to have been created by God, not by man, so the poet's monument assumes divine provenance.[60] These arguments can be as tendentious as the politically driven interpretations of "I have built myself a monument" and "The Prophet," and one suspects that they gained currency in the post-Soviet period because they had been suppressed for decades and thus seemed fresh. An exceptionally sensitive account of the poem's philosophical and religious underpinnings was given by the poet Olga Sedakova in a 1999 essay, where she calls attention to the "fool" in the poem's last line.[61] Her dazzling analysis of Pushkin's ideas of foolishness, madness, and reason opens the poem to new readings that can incorporate Christian underpinnings without rendering it deadly pious. Alongside Christian nuances in the poem's diction, it should be added, are refreshingly pagan notions deriving from the ancient Latin source and a worldview where monuments incarnate the spiritual power of the dead and poets speak to muses of the gods' power.

Let me, in turn, emphasize the poem's secular understanding of human history and of the poet's place in his culture. Pushkin predicts that people will long feel for him an affectionate inclination: I have translated "liubezen" as "loved," although it is a less intensely emotional word than *love* might connote in English. Indeed, "liubezen" has the same gentle tonality of the "kind feelings" in the next line, suggesting that Pushkin hopes not for fervent adoration but for something milder, more a part of daily life in the same way that words like *liubeznyi* and *dobryi* are.[62] In that choice of words, Pushkin imagines a relationship to his readers quite unlike the overpowering act of recreation in "The Prophet." But there are stronger emotions implied by "liubeznyi," which can mean dear, beloved, or a person to whom one feels a heartfelt attachment. In the nineteenth century, these more emotional meanings were common, and although Pushkin does not have them principally in mind, they reverberate in the poem.[63] The meanings inform the myths of Pushkin as they have developed over the years, myths that are defined by a love for him that can range from the affections of daily life to a deeper and more complicated heartfelt attachment. The final stanza of the poem maintains this more intimate feel in its address to the Muse. Pushkin speaks as much to himself here, wanting to ignore criticism as well as praise, and thus not to waste his breath in argument with a fool. A poem that begins with grand images of a monument—and with the elevating epithet "not made by human hands" ("nerukotvornyi")—comes down to a quite human level, then, speaking of the people who will read the poet as informed by feelings of tenderness for him, and speaking of himself as needing the gentle reminder that foolish reactions merit none of his attention. That last point is strongly marked in the poem because it is not found in either Horace or Derzhavin: their poets asked for crowning laurels, whereas Pushkin's commands the Muse to expect no glory, indeed to accept praise and blame with equal indifference.

Readings of the poem have understandably stressed moments where Pushkin departs from the Horatian model or where he translates Horace very differently from his predecessors (who included Mikhail Lomonosov, Alexander Vostokov, Vasily Kapnist, and Derzhavin). Such an approach has sought the distinctively Pushkinian part of "I have erected a monument" in discrete verbal elements, arguing that Pushkin gave Horace's poem his own meaning by changing words, images, and terms, but assuming that he kept Horace's larger project, signaled by the Latin epigraph, of creating a poem that describes the timeless and towering monument of the poetic legacy. But some lines or images now most deeply associated with Pushkin do not stray very far from the original (except that they are in Russian, not Latin) or from Derzhavin's translation, which most influenced Pushkin. Of particular significance is the beginning of the second stanza, "No, I shall not wholly die" ("Net, ves' ia ne umru"); compare Derzhavin's "So I shall not wholly die" ("Tak, ves' ia ne umru") and Horace's "I shall not wholly die" ("non omnis moriar"). Pushkin changes next to nothing here (he substitutes "No" for Derzhavin's "So" in the start of the line, which makes the contrast to the preceding stanza stronger but little changes the already firm claim of the sentence that follows).

I take this often-quoted line to be important because the poem has always been read with Pushkin's death soon afterwards in mind.[64] The poet's prediction of immortality, a possible cliché, seems proleptically to console his mourners. One scholar has suggested that Pushkin did not write the poem for public recitation or publication, but intended it to be found in his papers (which in fact is what happened).[65] The soul will live longer than the decaying flesh, Pushkin writes, and the place where the soul lives is the poet's lyre, which is to say, his poetry. This poem creates a blueprint for Pushkin's legacy, mentioning two expectations that were to shape it: death and the absence of laurels to recompense his labors. The poem also sets out an image of the poet who cared equally for freedom and mercy. But the blueprint suggests an edifice that might be built with entirely different features. The final strophe puts forward a poet not fully in control of his legacy. His poems will be read, reread, distorted, and reinvented, and the readers may include fools or those who bestow laurels. The only thing that counters his feeling of powerlessness is the claim of immortality through verse. The poems live as long as poets live. Their interpretations, their poems, will long thrive.

"I have built myself a monument" balances Pushkin's legacy between the human and the divine. Empowered to raise monuments and create myths, Pushkin also elicits popular affection in a very human way. The mix of humility and glory found in "The Prophet" recurs in "I have built myself a monument," as if Pushkin were both a monument that towers over his culture and no greater than the people who trod its paths. Pushkin's poems set up attitudes toward his legacy that range from the gentle to the reverential, from the argumentative to the adoring. His poems could not foresee how the poet would actually be mourned, nor the intensity with which he would be loved. Chapter One turns our attention to poems on Pushkin's death written by three of his contemporaries, and with this material we begin to study the way Russians built their myth of a national poet.

1 Pushkin Is Dead

THE ELEGIES OF MIKHAIL LERMONTOV, VASILY ZHUKOVSKY, AND EVDOKIA ROSTOPCHINA

> . . . his face is always young,
> Burning with the radiance of immortality,
> It shines like a sun that is eternally gold,
> Like the first dawn over Eden.
> —Wilhelm Küchelbecker

> . . . лицо его всегда младое,
> Сияньем бессмертия горя,
> Блестит, как солнце вечно золотое,
> Как первая эдемская заря.

Wilhelm Küchelbecker writes in these lines as if Pushkin could never die. Similarly, Fyodor Tiutchev named Pushkin as Russia's first love, but both were writing elegies on the death of Pushkin. Poems of loss have shaped Russia's myth of a national poet.[1] Modern Russian letters built its foundation on a scene of loss; in many poems, the mourned absence was converted into a presence, most effectively by conjuring up the body of the deceased. We would expect later poets to lament that they could not share the special knowledge of those who saw Pushkin alive. That gap between expression and emotion became constitutive of Russia's relationship to Pushkin. In fact, signs of the gap emerged almost immediately after he died.

Judgment, Rhetoric, and Violence (Lermontov)

Mikhail Lermontov's "The Death of the Poet" ("Smert' poeta," 1837) is the obvious place to start. The poem was penned instantly, perhaps as Pushkin lay dying. Copies circulated widely. Written when Lermontov was twenty-three, the poem brought him immediate fame, as well as the special notoriety reserved for victims of state repression (it led to his first exile to the south).[2] For at least this reason, "The Death of the Poet" made Lermontov into Pushkin's heir apparent.[3] He defined Pushkin's death as an act of social and rhetorical violence and created a powerful discourse about Pushkin's death based on moral judgment.

> The Death of the Poet
>
> The poet has perished!—a prisoner of honor—
> He fell, slandered by rumor,
> With a bullet in his breast and thirsting for vengeance,
> Hanging his proud head!..
> The Poet's soul could not endure
> The shame of petty offenses,
> He rebelled against the opinions of high society
> Alone, as before ... and was slain!
> Slain!.. of what use is this weeping now,
> The futile chorus of empty praise
> And the pitiful babble of justification?
> The sentence of fate has been carried out!
> Was it not you who from the beginning meanly
> Rebuffed his free, bold gift
> And for your own amusement fanned
> The flames as soon as they had died out?
> You may celebrate, then ... but he could not bear
> The final torments:
> The wondrous genius has gone out like a candle,
> The triumphal wreath has withered.
>
> His murderer cold-bloodedly
> Took aim ... there is no escape:
> His empty heart beats evenly,
> The pistol did not tremble in his hand.
> No wonder ... from afar,
> Like hundreds of other runaways
> Seeking fortune and rank,
> He was tossed our way by the will of fate;
> With a laugh, he impudently scorned
> The language and customs of this foreign land;
> He could not spare our glory;
> He could not understand in that bloody moment
> Against what he was raising his hand!..
>   And he was killed—and taken by the grave,
>   Like that unknown, beloved singer
>   Who was taken down by empty zeal
>   And whom he had celebrated with such wondrous power,
> Struck down, like him, by a merciless hand.
>
> Why did he leave peaceful languors and heartfelt friendship
> To enter this society, envious and stifling
> To a heart of free and fiery passions?

Why did he extend his hand to worthless slanderers,
Why did he believe their hollow words and false kindness,
    He, who had always understood his fellow man?..

And, having taken off his former wreath, they placed
A crown of thorns entwined with laurel on him:
    But the hidden thorns cruelly
    Pierced his noble brow;
His final moments were poisoned
By the insidious whispering of mocking ignorants,
    And he died—vainly thirsting for vengeance,
Secretly vexed by hopes deceived.
    The sounds of wondrous songs fell silent,
    They will never again resound:
    The singer's refuge now is gloomy and confining,
    His lips are sealed.

    And you, the arrogant descendants
Of fathers known for their baseness,
Who crushed with slavish heels
The ruins of families hurt by fortune's game!
You, standing by the throne in a rapacious throng,
The executioners of Freedom, Genius, and Glory!
    You hide yourselves under the cover of law,
    Judgment and truth fall silent before you!
But there is also God's judgment, you intimates of debauchery!
    There is a terrible judgment: it awaits.
    It is unaffected by the clink of gold coins,
And it knows your future thoughts and deeds.
Then you shall resort to slander in vain:
    It will no longer help you,
And you will not wash away with all your black blood
    The righteous blood of the poet!

Смерть Поэта[4]

Погиб поэт!—невольник чести—
Пал, оклеветанный молвой,
С свинцом в груди и жаждой мести,
Поникнув гордой головой!..
Не вынесла душа Поэта
Позора мелочных обид,
Восстал он против мнений света
Один, как прежде... и убит!
Убит!.. к чему теперь рыданья,
Пустых похвал ненужный хор
И жалкий лепет оправданья?

Судьбы свершился приговор!
Не вы ль сперва так злобно гнали
Его свободный, смелый дар
И для потехи раздували
Чуть затаившийся пожар?
Что ж? веселитесь... он мучений
Последних вынести не мог:
Угас, как светоч, дивный гений,
Увял торжественный венок.

Его убийца хладнокровно
Навел удар... спасенья нет:
Пустое сердце бьется ровно,
В руке не дрогнул пистолет.
И что за диво?.. издалека,
Подобный сотням беглецов,
На ловлю счастья и чинов
Заброшен к нам по воле рока;
Смеясь, он дерзко презирал
Земли чужой язык и нравы;
Не мог щадить он нашей славы;
Не мог понять в сей миг кровавый,
На что́ он руку поднимал!..

   И он убит—и взят могилой,
  Как тот певец, неведомый, но милый,
    Добыча ревности глухой,
 Воспетый им с такою чудной силой,
Сраженный, как и он, безжалостной рукой.

Зачем от мирных нег и дружбы простодушной
Вступил он в этот свет завистливый и душный
Для сердца вольного и пламенных страстей?
Зачем он руку дал клеветникам ничтожным,
Зачем поверил он словам и ласкам ложным,
  Он, с юных лет постигнувший людей?..

И прежний сняв венок—они венец терновый,
Увитый лаврами, надели на него:
  Но иглы тайные сурово
  Язвили славное чело;
Отравлены его последние мгновенья
Коварным шепотом насмешливых невежд,
  И умер он—с напрасной жаждой мщенья,
С досадой тайною обманутых надежд.
  Замолкли звуки чудных песен,
  Не раздаваться им опять:
  Приют певца угрюм и тесен,
  И на устах его печать.

>   А вы, надменные потомки
> Известной подлостью прославленных отцов,
> Пятою рабскою поправшие обломки
> Игрою счастия обиженных родов!
> Вы, жадною толпой стоящие у трона,
> Свободы, Гения и Славы палачи!
>   Таитесь вы под сению закона,
>   Пред вами суд и правда—всё молчи!..
> Но есть и Божий суд, наперсники разврата!
>   Есть грозный суд: он ждет;
>   Он не доступен звону злата,
> И мысли и дела он знает наперед.
> Тогда напрасно вы прибегнете к злословью:
>   Оно вам не поможет вновь,
> И вы не смоете всей вашей черной кровью
>   Поэта праведную кровь!

Pushkinian echoes are heard in this poem,[5] but Lermontov's authority comes from his anger. The poem cries out in rage from its first line. "The Death of the Poet" seethes with hatred of the society against which Pushkin stood alone, an all-powerful social world that passes judgments and carries out executions. Lermontov has Pushkin living in a world where social groups can kill by the sheer force of their hatred—thus the first sentence shows the poet felled by rumor. Later in the poem, these same evildoers change the poet's laurels into a crown of thorns, and their perfidious whispers poison his last moments.[6] Lermontov's references to slander, whisperings, gossip, and betrayal make verbal wrongdoing the true evil done to Pushkin. Gossip is a privately expressed sentiment that, when it is repeated and spread, comes to have the force of a public judgment.[7] Lermontov indicts Pushkin's killers for murdering him with their evil words,[8] and he seeks revenge in kind when he uses his words to prophesy their doom.

In his prophecy, Lermontov also invokes the moral order with a vocabulary of crime and retribution. He makes Pushkin's death the result of a conflict between the forces of good and evil. Nearly every phrase in "The Death of the Poet" describes either the poet or those who caused his death, creating an absolute division between the victim and his killers. Words of location or time are largely relative and abstract. The death is neither narrated nor grounded in specific historical circumstances. Pushkin has no proper name in the poem—he is "the Poet." The duel is not mentioned, and the poem's possible comparison of Pushkin's death to the demise of André Chénier (stanza 2) mutes the differences between the times of the French Revolution and the age of Nicholas I, and between an executed poet and one who died in a duel. Placing Pushkin's death on the moral ground of judgment in effect removes it from temporality, from particular historical or even political circumstances.⁹

Lermontov's dependence on a universal, moral vocabulary also reveals to us something crucial about the poem's anger. As the legal scholar Robert Cover influentially argued, law's diction about wrongdoing conceals a state's use of force to make good on law's threatened sanctions.¹⁰ A comparable concealment occurs in Lermontov's poem. It talks about both the laws that govern his society and a higher, divine law that will someday condemn Pushkin's killer and slanderers, but it elides the violence and pain of Pushkin's death.¹¹ One has little sense in "The Death of the Poet" that a flesh and blood body has met its demise, which completes the logic of the poem's figures—the poet is killed by rumors, not bullets.¹²

Body parts appear in "The Death of the Poet" as passing metonymies, all of them poetic commonplaces. The bullet is lodged in the poet's breast, and death bows his head; his killer acts with an empty, evenly beating heart, and his hand is steady and unpitying. The act of murder is imaged as the killer's raised hand, the death as a seal on the poet's lips and wounds to his noble brow. In the nostalgic interlude about the poet's mistaken trust in these slanderers, his heart is described as free, and his acts of trust are figured as an extended hand. Any one of these images would seem an insignificant turn of phrase taken from the standard vocabulary for nineteenth-century odes and elegies, but the strange enumeration of body parts, in a poem whose title speaks of death, emphasizes the way in which the bodily attributes most pertinent to the poem have been excluded altogether. Only the blood, mentioned in the final two lines, could undo this exclusion, but Lermontov is careful to call it the poet's righteous blood ("Poeta pravednuiu krov'!"), turning a physiological detail into a reiteration of ethical rightness (thus the killer's blood is black, evil). For Lermontov, it is not the body but the law that is at stake, law in its broadest sense: the language that regulates bodies. His poem has lamented the loss of Pushkin by means of a particular attitude toward language—words killed Pushkin, and now Lermontov's words will in turn label the evil of his killers. Lermontov's example will forever be tied to this redemptive view of language, which also means that one possibility for lamenting the death of Pushkin inherently ties his loss to the condemnation of others, and to the martyrdom of Russia itself.

Identifications and Reversed Projections (Zhukovsky)

Lermontov's ahistorical, moral tone and his rhetorical turn away from the dying poet's body would seem to be reversed in the writings of Vasily Zhukovsky (1783–1852). Zhukovsky recorded the specific circumstances of Pushkin's death in several prose accounts, and he wrote a short poem that looks intently at Pushkin's dead body. Here, several texts will

FIGURE 3. Line drawing by Vasily Zhukovsky of Pushkin in his coffin, 1837. Reproduction from E. V. Pavlova, ed., *A. S. Pushkin v portretakh* (Moscow: Sovetskii khudozhnik, 1989), vol. 1, p. 130. Courtesy National Pushkin Museum, St. Petersburg.

concern us, which marks an important departure from the singularity with which "The Death of the Poet" rises from Lermontov's oeuvre. The documents include letters to the chief of police Aleksei Benckendorff and to Pushkin's father, giving fairly full accounts of Pushkin's duel and death; some more cryptic notes about the events that led up to the fatal duel; and a line drawing of the dead Pushkin, a visual complement to the verbal description found in the poem to Pushkin (Fig. 3).[13] The letter to Pushkin's father was accompanied by a schematized drawing of the layout of Pushkin's apartment (Fig. 4), a document so precise that it helped twentieth-century restorers of the building.

In the poem, Zhukovsky modulates his emotions by adopting a discursive tone, but he reveals the entire history of his friendship with Pushkin through rhetorical tropes. This complex personal history also offers a vivid contrast to Lermontov's moral discourse. Zhukovsky memorializes Pushkin in a densely written and slow-moving lyric that proceeds across Pushkin's features like a camera, trying to compare what it now sees with a remembered image of the poet's living face. Repetition is the poem's central trope, rather

The Elegies of Lermontov, Zhukovsky, and Rostopchina 33

a strange thing for a poem so brief, and the static quality of the diction looms larger because of the exceptionally free quality of the poem's meter.[14] Given his drawings and other writings about Pushkin's death, and given that some details in those writings also appear in the poem, we might say that repetition was Zhukovsky's way of mourning Pushkin. He expressed his grief by tracing the same ground repeatedly, realized in the lexical, imagistic, and phonic repetitions of the poem.

> He was lying without movement, having lowered his hands
> As if from hard work. Head peacefully inclined,
> I stood over him alone for a long time, looking attentively
> At the deceased right in the eyes; the eyes were closed,
> His face was so familiar to me, and it was striking
> What was expressed on it—in life

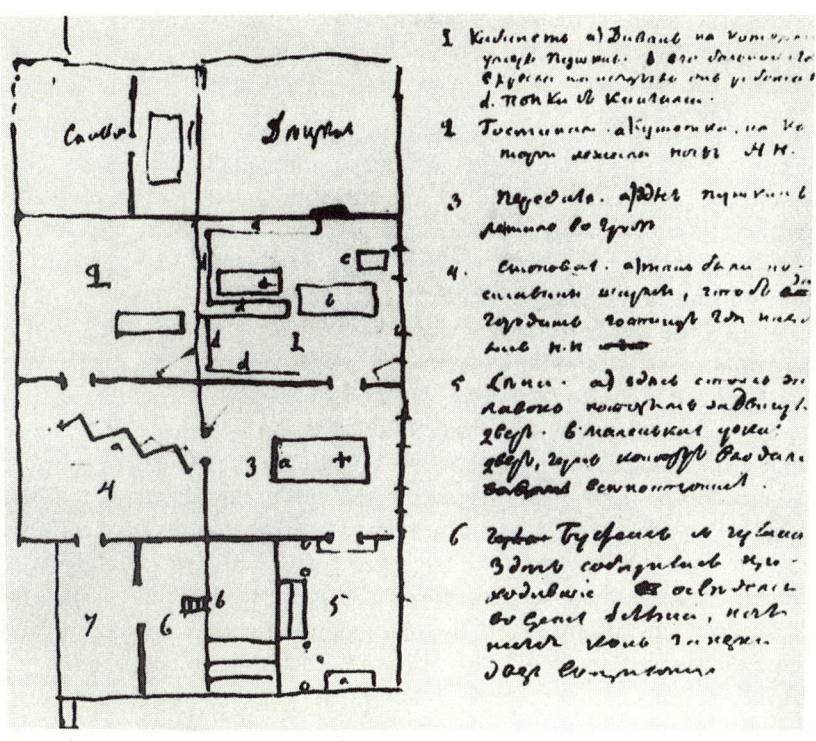

FIGURE 4. Line drawing by Zhukovsky of the floor plan of Pushkin's apartment at Moika 12, 1837. From *Muzei-kvartira A. S. Pushkina na Moike* (Moscow: Sovetskaia Rossiia, 1989), p. 18. Courtesy National Pushkin Museum, St. Petersburg.

> We never saw such an expression on this face. The flame of
> Inspiration did not burn on it; his keen mind did not shine;
> No! But some kind of thought, a deep, lofty thought
> Had enveloped it: it seemed to me that at this moment
> It was as if some kind of vision lay at hand,
> Something was taking place above him, and I wanted to ask:
>   what do you see?

> Он лежал без движенья, как будто по тяжкой работе
> Руки свои опустив. Голову тихо склоня,
> Долго стоял я над ним, один, смотря со вниманьем
> Мертвому прямо в глаза; были закрыты глаза,
> Было лицо его мне так знакомо, и было заметно,
> Что выражалось на нем,—в жизни такого
> Мы не видали на этом лице. Не горел вдохновенья
> Пламень на нем; не сиял острый ум;
> Нет! Но какою-то мыслью, глубокой, высокою мыслью
> Было объято оно: мнилося мне, что ему
> В этот миг предстояло как будто какое виденье,
> Что-то сбывалось над ним, и спросить мне хотелось:
>   что видишь?[15]

Although its repetitions suggest a calm or static quality, this poem seems troubled by several things, including the very repetitions that it permits. The final line poses an unanswerable question about similarity across death's boundary. How can this body correspond to a person of such mental liveliness and inspired thinking? Zhukovsky's poem, like his drawing of the dead poet and his letter to Pushkin's father, raises a larger question of referentiality—to whom does his pronoun "he" (*on*) refer? To the live poet or to the dead body? In the poem Zhukovsky muses over whether the body can "be" Pushkin. He moves urgently toward spiritual questions, and we might read the intensity and speed of that move as a wish to escape the physical uncertainties that press themselves on him. As the editors of a volume on *Death and Representation* have pointed out, the corpse is always uncanny, seeming to lie just before its viewer but also to be located nowhere, neither of this world nor absent from it.[16] This perspective relies on the work of Maurice Blanchot, for whom the space of literature was one of remove.[17] I sense that remove in Zhukovsky's poem, both in the gap between the poet and the dead man he contemplates and in the gap that widens within the poet himself.

Based on the time that Zhukovsky sat alone with the dead Pushkin,[18] the poem fixes on that moment of transition between life and death. Thus its glance typifies the Romantic urge to peer into the experience of death. Indeed, *looking* is its only action, emphasized by the way that Zhukovsky looks right into Pushkin's eyes, by his eyes being closed, by the imagination of his vision, and by the final question of what he sees. Only the verb *to be* is as frequently invoked, also in various forms (*byt'*, *sbyvat'sia*, *kak budto*). The emphasis on seeing and being opens up an ambivalence about death, and in his wish to know what the dead man sees, the poet almost treats him as if he were alive. Almost, I say, because the poet does not engage the dead man as interlocutor; he merely records his wish to ask the question, "What do you see?"

In its focus on what *is*, the poem compares what is seen with what is hidden. Being and seeing are reversed in the poem as absence and mystery (and it is in this way that the poem's rhetorical figures confront the reality of death). Reversal structures Zhukovsky's mourning of Pushkin as powerfully as does repetition (he noted that Pushkin died on January 29 [o.s.], his birthday, and, in a letter to Ivan Dmitriev, he called Pushkin's death an inversion of their roles).[19] But the crucial reversal has to do with their positions as master and pupil, which the poem transmits as a visual image, one poet standing over another.

Throughout the nearly two decades in which they knew each other, Zhukovsky represented himself as Pushkin's mentor and as a father figure.[20] His famous portrait inscription of 1820, presented to Pushkin when he completed *Ruslan and Liudmila*, had already predicted the reversal of their teacher-student relationship: "To the conqueror-student from the conquered teacher on that solemn day when he finished his poem." As is well known, Zhukovsky was a teacher in other important relationships, including his affection for the young Masha Protasova, whom he loved but was not allowed to marry,[21] and his role as tutor to the Russian imperial family, where he provided instruction for the Empress Alexandra Fyodorovna and the future Tsar Alexander II. But with Pushkin, Zhukovsky's tutelage inevitably involved blurred lines of authority and ambivalence about his superiority. The young Pushkin learned from his poetic innovations, and no doubt received important guidance and protection. As Pushkin matured, Zhukovsky intervened on his behalf in times of crisis.[22]

Pushkin sought his help, but he wanted the influence and protection without the fatherly advice. Zhukovsky wrote in a letter to Pushkin in 1825: "My God, how I would like to live with you for a little while, in order to say sincerely what I think of you, and what I need from you. I have a right to this more than many another, and you should trust me."[23] The letter condenses a whole history of emotional connection, tender reproach, and perhaps unanswered demands as well. Particularly in the 1830s, Zhukovsky and Pushkin had few such moments of intense contact. Their poetic practices diverged, and Pushkin turned more toward prose.[24] By the 1830s, Pushkin had outgrown the pose of schoolboy: he was married, father to a growing family, and founding editor of a literary journal. He sought to support himself and his family with the income from his writing (which made him the first professional man of letters in Russia, as William Mills Todd III has discussed).[25] Zhukovsky seems not to have known what to do with this development. His final letters protest almost pathetically that Pushkin had been avoiding him; Pushkin indeed concealed his plan to duel with Georges d'Anthès.[26]

At Pushkin's death, Zhukovsky's frustrations would have been replaced by the shock of loss and mourning. Unlike Lermontov, he writes not in anger but in melancholy. He seeks the meaning of the death, not the meaning of separation from Pushkin (which was the great theme of Prince Pyotr Viazemsky's elegy "In Memoriam," "Na pamiat'," 1837). For Zhukovsky, the loss cannot be transmuted into other emotions (which would be a normal elegiac substitution),[27] and this melancholy state also explains his ceaseless repetitions.

Zhukovsky does, however, identify with the dead poet, as often happens in poems on the death of a poet. (Joseph Brodsky, among others, has shown how such poems almost always become self-portraits.)[28] In identifying with Pushkin, Zhukovsky puts aside the superiority he might have had as an authority figure in their relationship. He seems to ponder what it would be like to *be* Pushkin, and we sense his strong connection to him in his letter to Benckendorff. There, instead of reporting on the required inventory of Pushkin's papers, he defends Pushkin's integrity, as if feeling new kinship with a writer harassed by government surveillance.[29] In his letter to Pushkin's father, he changes the poem's descriptions in ways that trace the path of his identification: in the letter, the inclined head (l. 2 of the poem) describes the dead poet.[30] In the poem, too, the peacefully bent head seems momentarily to belong to Pushkin, who is described as motionless, but after a line break, we see that the head belongs to the speaker (l. 3). He stands, head inclined as if after labor as burdensome as that which has slowed the poet to the stillness of death. A thought hovers above the poet, the dead man's thought, but it is Zhukovsky's thought as well. These symmetries enable one final act of identification, an exchange of methods of seeing.

The vision hovering over the dead poet is presumably an insight into life eternal, which accords with Zhukovsky's religious and mystical convictions. In his poem on the death of Andrei Turgenev (1803), for example, he exclaims hopefully, "We will meet again; / Fate has arranged a meeting in the grave for us!" ("Uvidimsia opiat'; / Vo grobe nam sud'boi naznacheno svidan'e!").[31] When he writes about Pushkin, however, Zhukovsky exudes no such certainty. The spiritual movement of the poem brings him to a question, leaving open the possibility that Pushkin sees nothing, only the void that is death. This tentativeness makes sense, for Pushkin's blasphemies irritated Zhukovsky, who doubted his young friend's piety.[32] The spiritual drift of the poem counters something psychological in Zhukovsky as well.

He cannot console himself in this poem, or in any of the formats he chose to write about Pushkin's death. He remains fixed in the state of melancholia, not mourning, to use Freud's terms, displaying a resistance to solace that Jahan Ramazani has found typical of modern elegies.[33]

I do not mean to suggest that the poem was anachronistic, although it did not play the role in the social imagination of Pushkin's death that, say, Lermontov's lyric did, nor could it, since Zhukovsky wrote it in a notebook that once belonged to Pushkin, along with eight other short poems that mostly speak of death. The act of inscribing these lines in Pushkin's notebook was one last intimacy, and Zhukovsky went on to present the notebook to Countess Evdokia Rostopchina, who in turn wrote her own poem to Pushkin (a poem that explicitly takes up the themes of inscription and self-comparison; we turn to it shortly). Zhukovsky's poem was published only in 1867, when its subject and style surely seemed irrelevant to the dominant debates within Russian literature. Most striking of all might have been the stripped-down and intensely personal tone of the poem: in the 1860s, when a social vision of Russian culture mattered so much, this quietly personal poem to Russia's national poet would have seemed strangely dissonant. Only in the twentieth century has Zhukovsky's poem been regarded as significant, perhaps because its tone is so modern. Zhukovsky writes of *his own* Pushkin, as twentieth-century writers (from Briusov to Sinyavsky) were to do; those who demand only a shared national poet, "our" Pushkin, cannot help reacting with consternation. Zhukovsky made Pushkin's death a nationally shared, symbolic tragedy in his other documents, but in his poem we sense the loss of a dear friend, and it is a loss for which there is no consolation.

Although he was rightly perceived as Pushkin's very close friend, Zhukovsky's precise activities at the time of his death tell a more complex story: he reported to waiting crowds on the Moika embankment; he persuaded the tsar to award Pushkin's widow a pension; he ordered a death mask, distributed Pushkin's possessions as gifts to friends; and he safeguarded and catalogued the dead poet's papers.[34] He became the manager, the arranger of circumstances and ceremonies. It is from this perspective that one comprehends Zhukovsky's effort, in several genres and formats, to fix on paper the story of Pushkin's death. Of the various documents, the letter to Pushkin's father has the most complicated and revealing history.[35] It is also extraordinary as an artistic document.[36] Clearly, Zhukovsky was not just recording facts: exaggerations of Pushkin's devotion to Orthodoxy and to the tsar were calculated to improve things for his widow and children.[37]

Particularly when set against the denunciations of Lermontov's poem, Zhukovsky's letter demonstrates how a writer can maneuver around the dangers of writing about Pushkin's death: words that mourn become an occasion for celebrating the generous tsar who permits such mourning. That movement from setting the historical record straight to praising Russia, even when such praise involves distortions of the historical record, was to be reenacted in ever more vulgar fashion during the Soviet jubilee celebrations for Pushkin in 1937 (which, in fact, learned a great deal about the rhetoric of good and evil from Lermontov's poem). One point to note about Zhukovsky's letter, then, is that the impulse to record truths for posterity was modified by historical circumstances in unavoidable ways: he felt the need to rehabilitate Pushkin's image not alone for the benefit of his family but also for posterity. He wanted Pushkin's many unpublished works to reach readers. He saw that, if he was to tell his story at all, it would have to be couched in terms that made the tale of death seem patriotic and illustrative of the nation's fate at large.

For all the ways that Zhukovsky inscribes his own psychological portrait into these accounts of Pushkin's death (especially in the elegy), still he writes with a sense of future readers who will want to know specific details and physical attributes. With his varied documentations, he restores history to the public literary account of Pushkin's death, not as an impersonal record, but as a fluid, powerful set of events that he can already shape toward immediate ends. In the imagistic focus of his poem and in the attention to physiological detail in his letter, Zhukovsky also restores the poet's body to the account of Pushkin's death (although not in a way that is unequivocal or unproblematic: the body with which he sits becomes symbolic and spiritual; the first published version of his letter excluded concrete physical details, although for reasons out of his control). Last, Zhukovsky's ability to write from personal knowledge and to write without repressing his own desires as a poet presents us with a model for reacting to Pushkin's death that sharply diverges from Lermontov's. Many poets were to follow Zhukovsky's example of letting their own emotions and ambitions show through their writings about Pushkin.

Gender, Romance, and Irony (Rostopchina)

Countess Evdokia Rostopchina (1812–58) did not know Pushkin well, and she wrote about him with much less authority than Zhukovsky did. Well published during her lifetime and moderately respected for her poetry and prose, she was neither a central figure of literary culture nor the best representative of a poetic school, as both Lermontov and Zhukovsky were; in fact, Rostopchina worked within the vocabulary of Romanticism, which was waning in Russia when she began to be published in 1831. It is not she so much as her poem "Pushkin's Notebook" ("Chernovaia kniga Pushkina," 1838), then, that merits attention. It anticipates the process by which

Pushkin's life and death became a series of textual figures, that is, the ways in which biographical facts become the stuff of books. The poem also exposes the barriers to writing unselfconsciously about Pushkin. It asks implicitly whether the Pushkin tradition in Russian literature was and is a male tradition—a question that is unusually important because two of the most significant modern writers about Pushkin are Anna Akhmatova and Marina Tsvetaeva.

Rostopchina also wrote about Pushkin in "Two Meetings" ("Dve vstrechi," 1838, 1839). A two-part poem, it tells of seeing him first at a crowded Moscow festival and then at a ball. She is a child in the first part, relegated to the periphery; in the second part, where she dances with Pushkin, her relationship to him is sexualized. Both experiences—being peripheral, being eroticized—are relevant to modern writings about Pushkin by women. Rostopchina gives us the same persecuted poet found in Lermontov's poem, as the following excerpt shows, but her description is more grounded in the social world.[38]

> In *his* uneven features,
> In his Southern eyes,
> In his exhausted smile,
> I unmistakably read
> That our inspired one had felt
> Much bitterness,—and felt love,
> And scorn, and hatred;
> That high society had offended him all too often,
> That fate had painfully wounded
> His heart, that in vain
> A treacherous dream of false hopes
> Had lured him, that fame
> Had come to him at a price
> Both fateful and dear!..

> В *его* неправильных чертах,
> В его полуденных глазах,
> В его измученной улыбке
> Я прочитала без ошибки,
> Что много, горько сердцем жил
> Наш вдохновенный,—и любил,
> И презирал, и ненавидел,
> Что свет не раз его обидел,
> Что рок не раз уж уязвил
> Больное сердце, что манил
> Его напрасно сон лукавый
> Надежд обманчивых, что слава
> Досталася ему ценой
> И роковой и дорогой!..[39]

Not unlike the way in which Zhukovsky studies the dead Pushkin's visage for signs of spiritual knowledge, Rostopchina closely reads Pushkin's face, searching for the signs that he is playing a painful social role. This focus makes physically precise her abstract rhetoric of social injustice, a theme she would have learned from Lermontov's "Death of the Poet." She has none of Lermontov's jagged, rage-filled diction, however; indeed, Rostopchina was known for a smooth style, a style that in her less successful poems could sound formulaic. Here, she makes the description of a seemingly usual male Romantic hero more interesting because readers know that she describes Pushkin.[40] Moreover, she gives him a grand entrance, so grand that one expects the tsar: "Suddenly everything got crowded, and with / A single headlong wave of movement / The crowd rushed forward ... / And they told me "*He* is coming" ("Vdrug vse stesnilos', i s volnen'em, / Odnim stremitel'nym dvizhen'em / Tolpa rvanulasia vpered ... / I mne skazali: "*On idet*").[41] The scene itself is presented as a popular festival where boundaries between the classes are broken down. The poet, seeing this all for the first time, remembers it as opening up the possibility of a future for her, a time when she would enjoy the pleasures of society. Yet her interpretation of the great poet as suffering also imagines a different future, one where she too might feel "offended," "wounded," and "lured" by false hopes. The barriers break down just enough during this festival for the child to witness the poet's arrival and to dream a similar future of fame and injury. In the second part of "Two Meetings," Rostopchina is more grown up, and she presents herself to Pushkin as a poet. She feels no fear or shame when she whispers her poems to him as they dance. The scene projects the romance that might have been (and such fancies reappear in later women poets' dreams of having met Pushkin).

By comparison, "Pushkin's Notebook" leaves one with the impression that Pushkin lived by and in the book, and that Rostopchina chooses to meet him on exclusively poetic ground. That difference makes it all the more interesting, given the effort it takes for a woman to imagine that she comes to Pushkin not as a potential beloved but as a poet, perhaps even an equal.

"Pushkin's Notebook"*

For Vasily Andreevich Zhukovsky
Sic transit gloria mundi!..
Motto of Louis XIV

I look, feeling agitation and tender sadness,
At the book-orphan, at its blank pages,
Where our deceased planned to inscribe
Songs and dreams with his inspired hand;
Where, at the height of his powers, he wished
To collect the wondrous creations of his ripe imagination ...
Now taken to an early grave,—

He did not manage to write a single word here!..
I look and think: fickle destiny
Had intended such a blessed, elevated and glorious fate
For these empty pages!
How many lofty creative ideas,
How many radiant thoughts, priceless revelations
He would have entrusted to them ... And the grave laid waste
   to it all!!.
Heir to the legacy of a departed friend,
The melancholy witness of his mortal illness,
Another inspired, meditative poet
Looked with pain at this mute testament,
   And his breast tightened with fear ...

"Has it been long," he thought, "so long ago, that he stood
   before me
In the full flower of youth, healthy,
And he dreamed about the future, made plans, worked?..
And now he has disappeared from my sight forever!..
No! Enough looking into the distance!.. Not by means
   of my pen,
Book, will you come alive in spirit!.."

And now to me, to me comes this gift! To me, weak,
   unworthy,
My confessor of the heart came to entrust it,
He ordered that my timid, naive, unharmonious song
Take the place of the miraculous verse of Pushkin!..
But it is not for me to fulfill such a task,
Nor for me to attain the desired heights!
Not all the sources of living poetry,
Not all subjects are accessible or given to me:
I am a woman!.. In me both thought and inspiration
Must be fettered with humble modesty!

April 1838
Petersburg

---

* Pushkin ordered a notebook for himself. After his death, it came into the possession of V. A. Zhukovsky, who wrote several unfinished poems in it and then gave it to me as a gift, with the instruction that I add to the notebook, finish it.

Черновая книга Пушкина*
   Василию Андреевичу Жуковскому
      Sic transit gloria mundi!..
         Devise de Louis XIV
Смотрю с волнением, с тоскою умиленной
На книгу-сироту, на белые листы,

Куда усопший наш рукою вдохновенной
Сбирался вписывать и песни и мечты;
Куда фантазии созревшей, в полной силе,
Созданья дивные он собирать хотел...
И где, доставшийся безвременно могиле,—
    Он начертать ни слова не успел!..
Смотрю и думаю: судьбою легконравной
Какой удел благой, возвышенный и славный
Страницам сим пустым назначен прежде был!
Как много творческих высоких помышлений,
Как много светлых дум, бесценных откровений
Он им поверил бы... И гроб все истребил!!..
Приняв наследие утраченного друга,
Свидетель горестный предсмертного недуга,
Другой, восторженный, мечтательный поэт
Болезненно взирал на сей немой завет,
    И сердце в нем стеснялось от испуга...

«Давно ли,—думал он,—давно ли предо мной
Он, в полном цвете лет, здоровый, молодой,
Мечтал о будущем, загадывал, трудился?..
И вот он навсегда от глаз моих сокрылся!..
Нет! Полно вдаль смотреть!.. Не под моим пером
Ты, книга, оживешь духовным бытием!..»

И мне, и мне сей дар! Мне, слабой, недостойной,
Мой сердца духовник пришел ее вручить,
Мне песнью робкою, неопытной, нестройной
Стих чудный Пушкина велел он заменить!..
Но не исполнить мне такого назначенья,
Но не достигнуть мне желанной вышины!
Не все источники живого песнопенья,
Не все предметы мне доступны и даны:
Я женщина!.. Во мне и мысль и вдохновенье
Смиренной скромностью быть скованы должны![42]

Апрель 1838
Петербург

---

*Пушкин заказал себе черновую книгу. Она, после его смерти, перешла к В. А. Жуковскому, который написал в ней несколько недоконченных стихотворений и потом подарил ее мне, с наказом дополнить и докончить ее.

Whereas Zhukovsky's poem had described the physical presence of the dead poet's body, Rostopchina's poem has in mind a different physical object, the dead poet's notebook. Unlike him, she gives a footnote to elucidate both the genealogy of her poem and the symbolism of the notebook.[43]

Rostopchina draws Zhukovsky's poem into her own text. (It was inscribed in the notebook when he presented it to her.) In the second stanza, she "quotes" the poem, giving a paraphrase that preserves his central metaphor (seeing), his reference to Pushkin's labors, and, perhaps most instructively, the underlying sense of Pushkin's youth and promise, as opposed to Zhukovsky's feelings of failure. Thus, she has Zhukovsky sigh with frustration that he cannot bring the book to life: she alludes both to the desire for animation in his poem and to the ways that his guilt and grief collide. For all her claims of naiveté and limited imagination in the final stanza, she has incorporated an insightful critique of Zhukovsky, casting him as patron and literary impresario.

Why, though, does Rostopchina make so much of his aegis in this poem? Zhukovsky's having given her the notebook and the order to write in it has lowered but not removed the barrier of gender: to borrow words meant to describe nineteenth-century English poetry, "the literary images available to women all demonstrate to them their unfitness for poetry."[44] The work of Slavists Barbara Heldt, Catriona Kelly, Wendy Rosslyn, and Judith Vowles has extended that judgment to Russia's women poets.[45] By citing Zhukovsky's injunction to write, Rostopchina shows that she has earned the right to be treated as a poet. His testimony to her skill and intuition also appears in the first version of the poem (published in *The Contemporary* in 1839), where a "Letter from V. A. Zhukovsky to Countess E. P. Rostopchina, upon sending her the notebook of Alexander Pushkin" precedes the poem. It reads in part:

You will complete and finish this book of his. It has now reached its genuine destination. I would have written all of this in verse in times gone by, and the poems would have been good because they would have been about you and your poetry; but poems no longer flow as they once did. I will end simply: do not forget my exhortation. May this year of solitude be a truly poetic year in your life.[46]

Zhukovsky's letter shows his wisdom but also his need for a successor. Rostopchina, one is to assume, will replace him, writing about Pushkin as he no longer can. His letter also hints at another difficulty facing Rostopchina: when he says that his former, good poetry would have been about her and her poetry, he reminds us that the proper role of women in poetry was to be its subject. Moreover, the "year of solitude" that he hopes will be "poetic" was caused by her pregnancy and confinement, as the poet Vladislav Khodasevich later noted.[47] Khodasevich asserts that she typically wrote nothing while pregnant, but she in fact wrote more than a dozen poems over the years 1837–39, during three pregnancies—not a lot, but not nothing. Khodasevich's comment would be beside the point, but it reflects the continuing prejudices against women's fitness for writing that Rostopchina faced in her lifetime. In the words of the prose writer Elena Gan (1814–42), a woman writer was seen as "a peculiar creation, a deformed caprice of nature—or, more precisely, a deformity of the female gender."[48]

Rostopchina wrote with clarity and wit about the representation of women poets in her culture. In "How Women Are Supposed to Write" ("Kak dolzhny pisat' zhenshchiny," 1840), she figures women's writing as light and heat:

> Yes, a woman's soul should give off light in the shadows,
> Like the hidden ray of a lamp in a marble urn,
> Like the moon, seen through enveloping clouds at dusk,
> And, giving warmth to life, unseen, it should glimmer.
>
> Да, женская душа должна в тени светиться,
> Как в урне мраморной лампады скрытой луч,
> Как в сумерки луна сквозь оболочку туч,
> И, согревая жизнь, незримая, теплиться.[49]

A woman's poetry is to be like her sanctioned physical presence: a concealed source of light illuminating others. Rostopchina imbues the lines with a special irony by using images of pregnancy (the vessel) and child-rearing (the light that lets others shine). Earlier in the poem, she writes of the pleasures of women's poetry, with no distancing irony undercutting her sentiments: "every line of a woman's verse / Moves my heart" ("kazhdyi zhenskii stikh / Volnuet serdtse mne").[50]

What view of women poets might Rostopchina have found in Pushkin's writings? He could be quite forthcoming about the subject:

People complain about the indifference of Russian women toward our poetry, explaining it by their ignorance of the linguistic patrimony: but what kind of lady could possibly not understand the poetry of Zhukovsky, Viazemsky, or Baratynsky? The problem is that women are everywhere the same. Having endowed them with subtle intellect and the most impressionable sensibility, nature virtually denied them a sense of refinement. Poetry glides past their ears and does not reach their souls; they are insensible to its harmony; note how they sing fashionable romances, how they distort the most natural verses, break up the measure, destroy the rhyme. Listen carefully to their literary judgments, and you will be astonished at the misshapenness and even coarseness of their understanding ... exceptions are rare.[51]

Probably written in 1827, these lines compliment women's sensitive intelligence, but they are unequivocal in their assertion that women are "dull" to the resonant pleasures of poetry.[52]

Certainly, the portrait of women as writers in Pushkin's works is more complicated than this—indeed, the topic merits a serious reassessment.[53] As in other aphoristic comments by Pushkin, an opinion that is not necessarily the author's is introduced ("People complain about the indifference of Russian women toward our poetry"). His response begins as a rhetorical question, then becomes firmer. The dismissive tone ("women are everywhere the same ... exceptions are rare") suggests a condescending attitude toward women readers untempered by Pushkin's frequent self-irony. Nature and culture collide in this judgment: "nature" has denied "a sense of refinement" to women, who "sing fashionable romances." A view of women's talent and literary taste is inextricable from women's presence in society, but Pushkin suggests that they are born deficient, not made that way by a distorting social order.

Although Pushkin's views are more subtle and ambiguous in other writings, this strong statement usefully shows us an attitude that Rostopchina would have faced. The impression that she made as a woman dominates accounts of her. In the words of one of the most influential women of her time, Sophia Karamzina (daughter of the historian Nikolai Karamzin), she "was far from deserving her reputation as a beauty; true, she has large dark eyes, but her skin is also dark and oily, her facial features are large, and she is small and insignificant in stature."[54] Even an admirer of her poetry, Yakov Grot, sought to find out what she looked like and how old she was.[55] Others have chosen to remember her salon, and these memoirs often include complaints that she imposed on visitors by reciting her own works at length.[56]

Yet it was precisely in terms of her written work that Rostopchina wanted others to know her, not unlike the sentiment expressed by many poets of her age, Pushkin included. In 1853, she wrote to Mikhail Pogodin that "work is increasingly becoming the indispensable condition and highest need of my spiritual life."[57] Such a self-conception is at the center of "Pushkin's Notebook": the poem hinges on a comparison between her possession of the notebook she received from Zhukovsky and its former ownership by Pushkin. Rather than a world of social relations and physical charms, Rostopchina suggests that the words written down by women and men are what matter.

Her poem begins by contemplating the notebook's blank pages and imagining the "songs and dreams" Pushkin might have inscribed there. Poets are brought down to the product of their labors—history and biography seem for the moment not to matter, since poets live by and for the book. The only entity with a lived experience is the book itself: thus Rostopchina thinks about the "elevated and glorious fate" the pages ought to have met, the "radiant thoughts" that they were meant to contain. This passage in the poem is long enough for us to note its function as more than a passing thought; it is, as the title suggests, at the poem's center. Thus Rostopchina calls Pushkin's notebook a "book-orphan," repeating the act of animation that she will attribute to Zhukovsky. But she also suggests that

Pushkin's death orphans poetry itself. It becomes a loss felt by the language and expressed in a symbolically blank notebook.

When she talks about the poems she will not write, her tone and argument shift. Pushkin's range, foreclosed by his death, then Zhukovsky's, implicitly limited by his age and will, are realities against which Rostopchina's "timid, naive, unharmonious song" and the requirements of "humble modesty" are meant to sound preposterous. The world draws poetry back into the sphere of social relations and physical limitations, no matter how one seeks to live by the book. Rostopchina might long, though, to suffer only the limitations of advancing old age or death, rather than the false appearances and extreme modesty required by her social role as a woman.

Her poetry has been described as a "chronicle" of her rich interior life.[58] The image of Rostopchina as recording the intimate impressions of domestic life finds considerable support in her own words (one poem, for example, praises "the poetry of domestic life").[59] The description may elide too easily into a notion of the poetry appropriate for women, yet the domestication of poetry's lyricism shows how far we have come from the view of Pushkin's death held by Lermontov. He made Pushkin into a symbol of moral purity and a martyr to undying integrity. The impersonal monumentality of his poem is out of Rostopchina's reach, as she tells us herself in the end of "Pushkin's Notebook." Her sense of irony, however, may make one wonder why that reach is valued in the first place. Lermontov makes Pushkin's biography into a public symbol and transforms the tragedy of one poet's death into a national occasion for mourning and outrage. Zhukovsky would agree that such transformations are appropriate and necessary, as demonstrated by his letter about the duel. Yet he chooses in his poem about Pushkin to write a terse description of physical presence and absence that encodes his complicated relationship with the poet. Rostopchina writes more directly about her own position with regard to Pushkin, perhaps because the feminine self that she projects is itself an obstacle to writing.

These three poems created myths about Pushkin's death that grow out of metaphors of law and morality, of the body in history, of the writer and language. The lament for Pushkin draws on the familiar poetic vocabulary of the 1830s, although each poet's lament is imprinted with a life story and a sense of social position. Their combinations of self-reference, self-effacement, moral judgment, and emotional reversal set the parameters for lyrics to and about Pushkin, many of which will go beyond the theme of death. In the next chapter I turn to poems set in places where Pushkin lived.

2 *The Making of Museum Culture*

THE POET'S SPIRIT AND THE
WORK OF REMEMBRANCE

> It would appear that most people find it difficult to remember without having access to mementos, images, and physical sites to objectify their memory.
> —John R. Gillis

The elegies composed by Pushkin's contemporaries appear prophetic when we view them from the twentieth century: they created lasting categories within which Russians still contemplate Pushkin, and their confident apprehension of him as a definitive figure for modern Russian culture proved true. Lermontov, Zhukovsky, and Rostopchina mourned Pushkin, and they began to imagine their culture in terms of this loss. In contemporary Russia, Pushkin's importance is most deeply felt where his absence is marked. This chapter considers the places he haunts, the museums, preserves, and shrines to his memory.

A large and complex system of Pushkin shrines (*Pushkinskie mesta*) emerged in the twentieth century. As significant cultural institutions, these shrines offer visitors historical information and dramatic visualizations of Pushkin's world. They number at least twenty-five, and they differ widely. They stand in the places Pushkin visited, like Kishinev, Arzrum, Ukraine, the Caucasus, and Crimea; in the Volga, Ural, and Tver regions, where he traveled and sought historical information; in a village near Pskov, where he lived for two years in exile; in Moscow, where he was born and often visited; and in Petersburg, where he lived most of his life and fought his fatal duel. Add to this countless memorial plaques, the houses of his friends, museums about his literary characters, and fully 291 monuments listed in a 1993 tally, and you get a sense of how greatly Russia's landscape is marked by Pushkin's life and works.[1] Museums have played an obvious pedagogical role in spreading national myths of Pushkin. They act as elaborate stage sets for an encounter with Pushkin, although most museum creators, even in the Soviet period, chose religion, not theater, as the metaphor to describe their work.

Amid this geography of Russia's cult of Pushkin, two shrines are the most important for their great symbolic value, the former family estates of Mikhailovskoe and Boldino; the Petersburg apartment on the Moika canal, where Pushkin died, is a close third. All Pushkin shrines invite visitors to find a more intimate, personal connection to Pushkin, often expressed as a search for his spirit. For Mikhailovskoe and Boldino, and, to a lesser degree, Moika 12, we have a legacy of written testimony from visitors who have "found Pushkin" there and, in the process, found themselves. A formidable literary culture has grown up around Mikhailovskoe and Boldino, and the resulting memoir and poetic texts will help us see how they have worked as cultural institutions.

Mikhailovskoe and Boldino as place-names are almost exclusively associated with Pushkin. One can hardly escape the linkage of Boldino to fall, of Mikhailovskoe to exile.[2] Both are country estates, which has determined their hallowed place for modern urban intellectuals. This seeming pastoral atmosphere has made them special sites for poetic inspiration. How that inspiration in the present draws on a sense of the past, however, is different in the two places, since the past includes the institutional history of each museum. In proposing a theory of why Pushkin places have been significant, I look beyond Boldino and Mikhailovskoe to other places where visitors are invited to be in touch with Pushkin's "spirit," particularly the museum at Moika 12. In what sense does the invitation to authentic emotional and spiritual experience depend on successful theatrical effects? And how much do visitors play a role when they come to these places? Before turning to questions of authenticity in the public's response, let me sketch out the history and present state of the two rural house-museums.

Remembrance in Mikhailovskoe

Part of a large estate that came into the family of Pushkin's mother, and, like Boldino, a tsar's reward, Mikhailovskoe was bestowed on Abram Gannibal in 1742 by Peter the Great's daughter Elizabeth. According to the 1744 census, Gannibal held forty-one villages in the area and over eight hundred serfs.[3] Subsequent divisions diminished the holdings, but when the village came to Pushkin's generation (he, his brother Lev, and his sister Olga inherited it on the death of their mother in 1836), it included a landowner's home and a park laid out in late-eighteenth-century style. Pushkin visited Mikhailovskoe twice before his exile, and several times thereafter, but his longest stay was in 1824–26, when it was still his mother's property. These were the last two years of his exile, a paradoxically liberating time for Pushkin, before the onset of worries about family, money, and plans for a journal. He wrote extraordinary things here—parts of *Eugene Onegin*, some of his best-known lyric poems, and the play *Boris Godunov*. An idea of Pushkin's rural and productive life at this time is an attractive feature for visitors, but the proximity of his site of burial, in Sviatogorsk Monastery, has also made Mikhailovskoe a destination for pilgrimage.

Along with the nearby Osipov-Wolf estate of Trigorskoe, Mikhailovskoe began drawing visitors by the end of the nineteenth century, particularly after the 1899 jubilee celebrations.[4] At that time, an account of an 1859 visit was published: it attested to earlier pilgrimages and gave visitors further impetus to travel there. This timing tells us something about the causes of increased attention to Mikhailovskoe, for the late nineteenth century saw an increase in tourism and a curiosity about specifically Russian national sites that was a legacy of the broader European trend of nationalism.[5] (Public shrines to English Romantic poets also appeared.)[6] After the October Revolution, the substitution of literary shrines for disappearing destinations of religious pilgrimage drew more attention to Mikhailovskoe.[7] Both the national and the religious impulses affected the choices of those who preserved and refurbished Mikhailovskoe, which created some tension between the experiences visitors were officially expected to seek (a reaffirmation of their status as Soviet citizens) and those that many wanted for themselves (a kind of spiritual self-discovery).

Several early visitors left memoirs that reveal emerging attitudes toward this first Pushkin shrine. They typically begin by describing the trip as a fulfillment of long-cherished dreams. One 1902 guest wrote, "At last I succeeded in bringing about my long-standing desire to visit the place where the ashes of our eternal poet Alexander Pushkin had his final resting place, and to visit that 'corner of the earth,' the village Mikhailovskoe, where, as Pushkin put it, he 'spent two unnoticed years as a hermit.'"[8] P. M. Ustimovich, later much involved in the transformation of Mikhailovskoe into a museum-preserve, began his memoir of a first visit in a similar way: "From the time that I sat on my Gymnasium bench, I had dreamed that someday I would visit the little nook where our great poet spent virtually the best two years of his life, in the company of simple, kind, and sympathetic people."[9]

Such memoirs helped to foster public desire to emulate the pilgrimage. They also document the emergence of nostalgia for a Mikhailovskoe presumed gone. Even in 1859, less than twenty-five years after Pushkin's last visit to the area, a visitor noted how little had been preserved:

We went into the entryway, opened the door to the room. . . . No, it's better not to look in there! Romantic desires—like the desire to be in the same room, relax in the same chair where Pushkin used to sit, where lively conversation with his friends took place, where he used to listen to the folk tales of his nanny—these desires have no place in our severe, destructive climate. We are not England, Pushkin is not Burns;[10]

in England, his armchair would be preserved like a holy relic, the window pane on which he scratched a quatrain would be worth hundreds of pounds sterling and remain the property of the house-owner for generation after generation. We are too properly brought up to treasure such trifles: in our nature, beyond laziness, there is also practicality; we require furniture in town, in someone's house, not in the wilderness where no one will see it; logs are needed at the mill, forests provide firewood rather than repairing a historic roof. And so twenty-two years after the poet's death the roof has collapsed, the beams are rotten, the ceiling has caved in beneath the rafters. At the intersection of two stakes in the corner sits an owl, emblem of wisdom, the only poetical object to be found in the poet's dwelling.[11]

This visitor cared most for the condition of Pushkin's house, but others were eager to find scenery from his poems, especially the three pine trees of "... Once again I visited" ("... Vnov' ia posetil," 1835). A 1924 book includes a haunting photograph from the 1880s of a dead remnant of one tree, along with speculative explanations why the other two did not survive.[12] (In fact, a small remnant is still to be seen in the museum.)

One account of Mikhailovskoe from the years of the First World War is worth examining at some length. The memoirist was Varvara Timofeeva, who usually published under the pen name O. Pochinkovskaia and also wrote an account of her years as a secretary to Dostoevsky. She lived in Mikhailovskoe between 1911 and 1917, when it was a residential colony for elderly writers. She recorded in some detail the struggle to preserve the estate as a place associated with Pushkin:

> As to the estate, with its wealthy forests, there remained only the widely held conviction that one could rob it under various pretexts, openly and in secret, without any fear of reprisal. The builders of "state" buildings and bridges successfully filled their pockets here, while the local people, embittered and made wild, were arrested and even imprisoned for every last log taken from "the gentlefolks' parks." And these self-same people were already threatening "to come with their axes, chop it all down and set it aflame."[13]

Timofeeva astutely observed two threats to Mikhailovskoe: economic development (the "builders") and political unrest (the people threatening destruction). She saw destruction begin just before the First World War:

> People started to talk about war, about building railroads for strategic purposes ... Every day, from all around one heard axes resounding through the forest. Chopped-down tree stumps ached pitifully, and age-old tree trunks fell with a moan, just as people were falling then on the fields of battle. The healthiest, the mightiest fell. They were carted away to build bridges at the front, floated by river for sale; they were stolen and plundered by anyone so inclined. History will one day tell this tale.[14]

Timofeeva wants to save these trees, not only because it seems cruel to fell the "healthiest" and the "mightiest," and not only because of her pacifist analogy to people dying in the First World War. These trees are living symbols of Pushkin's life and age; they are vessels of not completely defined meaning—of ancientness, of eternal youth, of the essence of poetry:

> From the age-old, wide-branching fir trees, from the fragrant, heat-saturated pines, wafted something from the ancient past, primordial, as if seen in a dream or in early childhood. The sweet reveries of youth, the curative poetry of eternal life were there ... as if precisely in these groves there remained some living trace of Pushkin. And one's heart believed that this sorcerer, this enchanter had thought up and breathed life into his captivating dreams, his magical tales, there, for all time. His dreams, his hopes, were narrated by all these old, precious trees. Miraculous symphonies, chorales, hymns, and serenades were heard there spring and fall, winter and summer. And, suddenly, oh horror! they begin to cut them down! These miraculous trees, these treasured firs of Pushkin![15]

Timofeeva's statement that "in these groves there remained some living trace of Pushkin" ("ostalos' chto-to zhivoe ot Pushkina") articulates an often unspoken idea behind post-revolutionary enthusiasm for Mikhailovskoe. The natural scene is alive, hence her comparison of the destruction of trees to soldiers dying on a field of battle, and her complex personifications ("age-old tree trunks fell with a moan," "his dreams, his hopes, were narrated there by all these old, precious trees"). Timofeeva creates the illusion that Pushkin has animated the trees, as if he magically made it possible for the land he inhabited to tell his tales once he was no longer there.

The thought that Pushkin enabled the powerful emotional response to Mikhailovskoe felt by successive generations depends on an old literary topos, as old as the sentimental groves of "poesy," and it will reappear in arguments for creating a national preserve. Timofeeva tells us her story of how the idea for a national preserve originated:

> As I thought about ways to defend [this land], a happy thought occurred to me. In the early 1900s, I was fortunate enough to spend time in Altdorf, Switzerland, the native land of William Tell. There I saw his grove, a national preserve. No citizen of the Swiss Republic has the right, under threat of punishment, to cut down so much as a twig, nor can one carry off even a flower or a tree branch ... Why shouldn't we, in our Soviet Republic, follow their example? I thought this to myself, and in 1920 I sent my first proposal for preserving the estates of Mikhailovskoe and Trigorskoe as historical monuments of our past glory to the Opochka department of public education, with the firm condition that the government would recognize them as *permanent preserves*. The project was taken under consideration, and I was instructed to oversee the preservation of the "Pushkin Nook" ["Pushkinskii Ugolok"].[16]

By 1924 the story was already codified rather differently. Two scholars from Pushkin House in Leningrad, under whose authority the (newly established) preserve fell, claimed that a local committee for the protection of Mikhailovskoe had formed during the most difficult moments of the civil war; they name Timofeeva as a member.[17] This version of the story suggests the nascent mythification of Mikhailovskoe's emergence as a Pushkin shrine as a matter of popular will. Timofeeva's role soon ended by all accounts. She concluded her 1924 memoir by saying that she had to hand over responsibility to someone more able-bodied; elsewhere, she says she left out of frustration that the area was being destroyed.[18]

Timofeeva's frustration would have been fueled by the events of the civil war. Mikhailovskoe was burned to the ground on February 19, 1918; among the valuables lost were the carriage that carried Pushkin's body to Sviatorgorsk Monastery and his billiard set, and all the buildings on the premises were destroyed. Trigorskoe had been burned down the previous day, February 18.[19] By the time Mikhailovskoe was declared a national preserve in 1922, the place was in ruins, as all memoir, epistolary, and official accounts from the period attest. A visitor who came only weeks after the fires died down in 1918 wrote that "everything has been laid to waste and burned, only the chimneys remain."[20] A 1924 visitor saw "a heap of stones in the place where there had been a house, now overgrown with burdock and nettles. The broad staircase leading down to the river had crumbled and was overgrown with bushes that concealed the view of the river and the lake."[21] Elizaveta Sadova, a Petrograd teacher and librarian, brought students eager to see the landscapes associated with Pushkin. She begins her 1921 letter about the trip with a forthright acknowledgment of how little they found:

we already knew about the destruction wrought by time, . . . but we did not anticipate how, during the last two decades, virtually everything that spoke of Pushkin had disappeared. The earth where his feet walked remained, as did the sky and the River Sorot that he and Iazykov described so vividly and poetically, but nothing else.[22]

Sadova is angrily emphatic when she describes Pushkin's grave ("*The hill . . . is steadily collapsing, crumbling. What will happen to the monument in another twenty or thirty years?*"),[23] and shocked and disappointed on seeing the ruins of the Mikhailovskoe house:

The main house and its surrounding buildings stand some distance from the settlement of Mikhailovskoe, just beyond a lovely grove. We walked several versts through it without noticing the distance, so enjoyable were the views; suddenly we came upon the main house. Disillusion awaited us: to know that nothing remained there from the life of Pushkin is one thing, to see it with one's own eyes is another.

In a large open space, thickly overgrown with weeds and flowers, surrounded by overgrown trees, we caught sight of the remains of the manor house, a brick foundation. The bricks had collapsed and were left there; the walls were long gone.[24]

All these accounts suggest how few tangible signs of Pushkin's distant presence remained in early-twentieth-century Mikhailovskoe.[25]

A daunting task, then, must have faced those determined to make the place a shrine to Pushkin. P. M. Ustimovich, assigned responsibility for the preserve when it came under the protection of the Academy of Sciences, confirms that chaos reigned. He describes how run down the place was before repairs began; so bad was the state of Pushkin's grave in Sviatogorsk Monastery, he explained, that the coffin was exposed to view.[26] The most famous visitor to record his impressions was Anatoly Lunacharsky, who came in 1926.[27] He was shocked at the destruction and at the widespread belief there that the homes at Mikhailovskoe, Trigorskoe, and elsewhere were burned on government orders.[28] Like Sadova and many others, he wrongly assumed that the building destroyed in the civil war was the house in which Pushkin lived in 1824–26; it was not. Pushkin's son, Grigory Aleksandrovich, had replaced the original in 1866; then, when the replacement burned down in 1907, he built a new house in 1911 to more closely resemble the one in which Pushkin lived.[29] It was this 1911 structure that was burned down during the civil war.

Yet even after all this destruction, in 1922 Mikhailovskoe was made a national preserve by government decree, along with Trigorskoe and Sviatogorsk Monastery. Local intelligentsia participated in this move, some from the colony for elderly writers and widows established on the estate in 1911 (this was where Timofeeva lived). A Pushkin society also existed through the 1920s. After 1922, the Petrograd academic community played the major role. Mikhailovskoe emerges in official cultural life in 1924, in connection with celebrations that June of the one hundred twenty-fifth anniversary of Pushkin's birth and later, in August, of the hundredth anniversary of his arrival in exile. Before the 1937 jubilee, the territory of the preserve was enlarged, a new home was built on the old foundation,[30] and a rudimentary museum was established. During the Second World War, German soldiers occupied the area; buildings were again burnt to the ground, and mines were laid in the monastery.[31] Restoration recommenced in anticipation of the 1949 Pushkin anniversary. Further renovation of the grounds, and work on Trigorskoe and Petrovskoe (the Gannibal estate, restored in 1977) have continued ever since.[32] In 1967, a yearly poetry festival was instituted,[33] and substantial numbers of visitors now come to the area, particularly in summer and fall. All these marks of success contrast sharply with the devastation that befell Mikhailovskoe in the first years of Soviet rule. How success was declared on the grounds of such loss is our next question.

The Argument for a Pushkin Preserve

When Mikhailovskoe opened to the public in 1924, virtually nothing tangible that could be linked to Pushkin remained, so how was the act of preservation conceived? Was it nothing more than belated homage? A more complex answer can be found in the speech inaugurating the Pushkin shrine in September of that year. It was delivered by Benjamin Semyonov-Tian-Shansky (1870–1942), a member of the Academy of Sciences and a renowned geographer. More than fifty years later, the speech still seemed valuable (it was republished in 1979), perhaps because it distinctively offered a theory of the reasons for preserving the area. "What," he began by asking, "is a preserve? It is a place where people have agreed never to touch a tree, a bush, or blade of grass, to let them grow and flourish as nature herself intended."[34] Semyonov-Tian-Shansky makes a crucial point here: to preserve is to leave unchanged, to resist improving and to prevent defiling. He teases out the metaphor of purity when he implies that his contemporaries will leave no trace on this land, only draw inspiration from its remnants of Pushkin's distant presence: "what is preserved . . . is a part of that original, untouched natural setting, which urged . . . Pushkin toward his greatest creative images and ideas"; "the visitor involuntarily and thus very vividly and clearly experiences in this natural setting everything that once surrounded the great man."[35] The landscape becomes a "pure crystal" through which all the greatness of Pushkin's achievements and of the human spirit can be glimpsed.[36] Yet Semyonov-Tian-Shansky wants to articulate the uniqueness of monumental land preserves at the same time that he seems determined to neutralize any sense of the work performed by those who do the preserving. The landscape around Mikhailovskoe is represented as pure, unchanged by post-Pushkinian visitations, despite a history of destruction, neglect, and reconstruction.[37]

Those who would preserve Mikhailovskoe as a monument to Pushkin needed to argue, then, that the land in and of itself could evoke his presence and his glory. Semyonov-Tian-Shansky's speech does this by means of its metaphors. He suggests the purity of the place by reference to its crystalline form, rendering Mikhailovskoe a transparency through which Pushkin is magically glimpsed. It becomes a kind of optical piece that reveals some aspects of the Pushkinian past but not others. Semyonov-Tian-Shansky emphasizes simplicity and clarity, usual epithets to attach to Pushkin here made interesting because they describe the place, not the poet's words: "The soil is weightless, dirtless. All of nature is equally light, soft, pure, just as it is described in Pushkin's verse."[38] In this notion of Mikhailovskoe as pure and undefiled, one stumbles over a small problem: the implication that it is virgin soil or wilderness territory does not work well with the requirement that the place preserve Pushkin. Visitors are meant to feel the power of nature, but, more specifically, the achievements of one famous human intruder—only Pushkin's presence left an imprint on Mikhailovskoe. To insist that one remembers only Pushkin is to wish away the human events after his burial in 1837, the consequences of historical crises, and, more mundanely, the labor of gardeners, restorers, and tour guides. With this emphasis on purity, the land is characterized as unmarked by present-day (1920s) viewers in search of some authentic trace of Pushkin. An odd assumption, but it follows quite logically from early Soviet cultural politics.

The political logic was borne out in the history of the 1920s. Mikhailovskoe emerged comparatively early among nascent Soviet cultural institutions. By comparison, the lyceum in Tsarskoe Selo was opened as a museum in 1949, and the adjoining All-Union Pushkin Museum in 1967 (it closed in the late 1980s, and its holdings were transferred to the house on the Moika). Pushkin House received its permanent building in 1927, and it was constituted as the Institute of Russian Literature in 1930.[39] The other exception, besides Mikhailovskoe, was Moika 12, opened to the public for a commemoration of Pushkin's death in February 1925 and declared a state-protected site in 1927.[40] It is no coincidence that Moika 12, the site of Pushkin's death, was important early on: sites to memorialize Pushkin were easier to construct or preserve in the earliest days of Soviet rule, perhaps because rituals associated with death have in general greater cultural importance for Russia than those associated with birth (Easter, for example, being more important than Christmas). The first exhibit at Moika 12 was designed to make an emotional impact on visitors, to present the apartment as a site of death.[41]

We might read Mikhailovskoe with this cultural emphasis on death in mind. It is a place where things no longer are to be found. Its most important "authentic" detail is Pushkin's grave, which, like all graves, is a marker of loss and absence. Rather than a museum that collects whatever has been preserved (we know that remarkably little was left), Mikhailovskoe becomes a place where the absent objects and ideas are to be recalled. Pushkin himself consistently represented Mikhailovskoe as a site for memory, and those who made it into a shrine often used his words as a source of authority in their decisions. Timofeeva, for example, asks: "Isn't this precisely what the poet dreamed of when he was exiled here?" She proceeds to quote from the poem "When I wander down noisy streets" ("Brozhu li ia vdol' ulits shumnykh," 1829), where Pushkin hopes that life, in its youth and playfulness, will be felt at the site of his grave. She concludes, "We can only greet with joy such a deep accord in the fulfillment of his dream."[42] Timofeeva's heartfelt sense of accord (*edinodushie*) presumes that in setting aside Mikhailovskoe as a preserve, modern cultural leaders are fulfilling Pushkin's desires. The strategy is risky: it imputes motivations and intentions to a historical subject in a way one cannot prove, and it takes on a potentially harmful authority of its own.[43] But the recourse to Pushkin in this case also has an undercurrent of truth, as his writings about Mikhailovskoe uncannily demonstrate.

Pushkin's Views of Mikhailovskoe

Pushkin has left us a wonderfully nuanced reading of the role of memory in perceiving a landscape. These poems offer new angles for understanding why cultural and political leaders turned Mikhailovskoe into a preserve in the 1920s. "... Once again I visited" and "The Countryside" ("Derevnia," 1819) show the relationship Pushkin imagined between the Mikhailovskoe landscape and the act of remembrance. He reads the landscape as a text in these two poems, implicitly undercutting any sense of the countryside as a natural phenomenon devoid of human markings. For Pushkin, Mikhailovskoe first became a site of memory in 1824, when he completed "To the Sea" ("K moriu," 1824) on arriving there: the poem ends with a cognitive embrace of the remembered pleasures of the south's seascape.[44] Pushkin's famous love poem cast in the form of a recollection, "I remember the wondrous moment" ("Ia pomniu chudnoe mgnoven'e," 1825), was also written in Mikhailovskoe, furthering the image of the place as a site of memory. In more private comments, he structures his thoughts about Mikhailovskoe as contrasts within memory. In a notation dated November 19, 1824, for example, he recalls an earlier visit: "I remember how I rejoiced in rural life—the Russian baths, strawberries, etc.—but my pleasure was short-lived. I loved and to this day love noise and the crowd and I agree with Voltaire that the countryside *est le premier*...."[45] (This note also reveals Pushkin's ambivalence about life in the country, something advocates for rural preserves play down.)

Pushkin's best-known poem about Mikhailovskoe is "... Once again I visited," a lovely lyric in blank verse written during a six-week stay in the fall of 1835.[46] Pushkin lived in the neighboring estate of Trigorskoe during this stay, but in "... Once again I visited" he unmistakably evokes the landscape of Mikhailovskoe, its sloping fields and distant windmill, sights that could again be seen there in the late twentieth century, when I last visited. (Pushkin first made these sights emblematic in "The Countryside.") The central cognitive act of "... Once again I visited" is remembrance.[47] Pushkin reviews previous visits to Mikhailovskoe, as if wanting to catch himself in a moment of recollection:

> Here is the forested hill, above which
> I used to sit motionlessly and gaze
> At the lake, remembering with sadness
> Other shores, other waves ...

> Вот холм лесистый, над которым часто
> Я сиживал недвижим—и глядел
> На озеро, воспоминая с грустью
> Иные берега, иные волны...[48]

The entire poem (it is fifty-five lines long) shows how the memories evoked by this landscape affect the poet: "here again / The past embraces me vividly" ("zdes' opiat' / Minuvshee menia ob"emlet zhivo").[49] Just as the present inspires recollections in the poet, so the past brings to his mind moments when he was lost in his memories.[50] The present moment is a repetition, which itself will be repeated in the poem's final vision. A moment in Mikhailovskoe is always a moment of remembrance, both in Pushkin's experience as he represents it in the poem and in the future he imagines for others. The poem attributes to the land a capacity to inspire endlessly repeating moments of retrospection. Pushkin suggests that even when the past seemed filled with authentically experienced present moments, still it was given over to recollecting the past. "... Once again I visited" invites its readers into this endless experience of remembrance: for Pushkin, memory is an infinite process where what is remembered is itself a moment of remembrance and what is imagined for the future is no less a part of this endless sequence of mutually referential moments.[51] We note Pushkin's fine perception that nostalgia for the past is easily transformed and transferred onto some fictive descendant. The poem suggests, in its closing invocation, that a future visitor will hear in the whispers of Mikhailovskoe's tall trees the background music for a memory of Pushkin.

Thus, when Pushkin projects future visitors, he does not imagine that their moment of remembrance will be personal or introspective. He writes:

> But let it please my grandson
> To hear your inviting sounds, when,
> As he returns from an evening with friends
> Filled with gay, cheerful thoughts,
> He will pass by you in the darkness of night
> And remember me.

> Но пусть мой внук
> Услышит ваш приветный шум, когда,
> С приятельской беседы возвращаясь,
> Веселых и приятных мыслей полон,
> Пройдет он мимо вас во мраке ночи
> И обо мне вспомянет.[52]

Pushkin so fully projects his image onto this descendant that he has him repeat his own activities (earlier in the poem Pushkin also rides past the three trees and remembers having ridden past them previously). When the descendant moves through the landscape, however, he remembers Pushkin, not his own earlier visits to the place. And in that substitution, Pushkin predicts the focus on him to be felt by future visitors to the preserve.[53]

Mikhailovskoe has been so thoroughly imprinted by his verbal representations of his stays there that visitors in a sense "remember" Pushkin. This is precisely the logic of the preserve: visitors are not there to appreciate the beauty of nature or to indulge in personal introspection; instead, they are to call to mind images of Pushkin, perhaps aided by recollections of his verse, but in any case focused on perceiving what it meant for him to live in the isolation and quiet of Mikhailovskoe. It is ironic that we would find some confirmation for this modern decision in Pushkin's poetry, since his writings otherwise show how problematic was the plan to make Mikhailovskoe a preserve. Pushkin not only suggests that what one remembers may well be nothing more than the memory of a memory, thus urging us to note the transitory and not essentially "authentic" quality of remembrance as an experience; he also affirms the universality of change—in nature, and in people. The preserve's fundamental idea, that nothing has changed since the 1830s, was undermined even by Pushkin himself. The beauty of "... Once again I visited" is that he articulates both the inevitability of change and his own deep desire for sameness: the contrast between past and present lies at the poem's center.[54] These are obvious things to say about the poem, but worth making explicit given the correlation between progress and stability in the Mikhailovskoe preserve. A sense of change is felt in the poet's mournful comment that his nanny has died, and in his more hopeful observations that a new generation of trees has begun to grow near his three pines.

Pushkin may seem to try to take control of this natural flux in the poem by his projection into the future, but the poet's disturbed awareness of fluidity as temptation and as threat is formidably there from the start, represented most vividly in the division of verbs in the first part of the poem into statements of stasis or assertions of movement.[55] A sense of this divided attitude toward temporality in "... Once again I visited" should change our reading of the poem's conclusion, where Pushkin's desire to see himself in the landscape is balanced by the descendant who represents both continuity and change.

Such an ambiguous temporality is probably too much to expect in the 1920s. The revolution and civil war were too recent, the negative implications of stability too overwhelming, for writers to see Mikhailovskoe as a remnant of nineteenth-century culture refashioned for twentieth-century use. And yet Timofeeva and Sadova sense that preserving Mikhailovskoe conflicts with the goals of the revolution. Timofeeva describes the destruction that the First World War worked on industry and farming; Sadova records the sad sight of Pushkin's house reduced to a foundation. If one looks across the decades, then, the difficulties of preserving Mikhailovskoe become still more obvious: the rebuilding efforts of the 1920s and 1930s were completely obliterated during the Second World War.

I mention these political hostilities as the major encroachments also with an eye back toward Pushkin's own writings. For Pushkin's first text about

Mikhailovskoe, "The Countryside," finds that every landscape is always political. The poem moves from an idyllic rhapsody about the pleasures of looking at a country landscape to the disquieting revelation that whatever beauty may be here has been created by the labor of enserfed workers.[56] This lesson, taught so powerfully by "The Countryside," ought not to be ignored as we study Mikhailovskoe in the 1920s. It lets us see that Semyonov-Tian-Shansky's dream of an inviolate tract of land was impossible, for even before the violence of revolution and civil war, Pushkin saw how fundamentally any image of rolling hills and patterned fields concealed social patterns of force, domination, and expropriation.

"The Countryside" also teaches that scenes from nature are made beautiful by human labor. Any restoration of Mikhailovskoe can be achieved only with immense human labor. To render that labor invisible, even in the hope of making Pushkin's distant presence more vivid, not only contradicts the principles of the revolution; it contradicts Pushkin's most fervent writings about all landscapes, and this landscape in particular. The rhetoric of labor is of course not foreign to official Soviet rhetoric, but I have in mind here something other than praise for the patriotic acts of protectors or restorers of historic sites. Immense ideological work has gone into the reconstruction, as have countless decisions about how to tell the Pushkin story and about what made the nineteenth century an era of change and transition.

Unfortunately, official descriptions and the oral presentation of the museum by tour guides omit any frank account of historical change or ideological work. A striking example emerges when a guide comes to the burning of Mikhailovskoe during the civil war, an event that during the Soviet period was likely to be passed over in silence. When I first visited (in 1986), my guide answered questions about the fires truthfully, but his discussion to that point had simply described the house as the fifth version on its foundation. A 1984 guidebook more deceptively includes some history, but not much: "By 1917 Pushkin's former estate was in pitiful condition. The Great October Socialist Revolution made the people the owners of this Pushkin shrine. As early as the first years of Soviet power, the Pskov Regional Party Committee worked at reconstructing and restoring this extremely valuable monument of Russian culture."[57] Another guidebook follows the same narrative pattern with slightly more extravagant language, concluding: "Only after the Great October Socialist Revolution did a genuine and caring owner come into this Pushkin shrine—the Soviet people."[58] A more personal account by Alexander Savygin reveals the destruction of 1918, but he claims that the fires were laid by hooligans passing through the area: "You could call them visiting young people who were a bit overly enthusiastic in warming their hands," he writes, resorting to euphemism.[59]

This heroic rhetoric returns in descriptions after the Second World War.

FIGURE 5. Display of posters showing the extent of Nazi destruction at Mikhailovskoe. Author's photograph, 1986.

The Germans occupied the area, the scene of heavy fighting, with considerable damage.[60] It is characterized as a form of desecration in descriptions of Pushkin's grave, Sviatogorsk Monastery (mined as well as bombed), and Mikhailovskoe itself.[61] This interpretation extends beyond tour guides' words and published descriptions: visitors see a huge outdoor display on the side of a building about Nazi destruction (Fig. 5). One is meant to perceive the labor that produced this museum as heroic. The various memorial rooms mix contemporary copies and period pieces, but the display offers little comment on design choices or themes.[62]

Allegory in Mikhailovskoe

A dual temporality is at work in Mikhailovskoe.[63] Both past and present create Mikhailovskoe as a legible text. The idea of reading it as a text is not new: one of its best-known curators, S. S. Geichenko, has already suggested the metaphor of the place as a legible, familiar book.[64] In his reading, the figure of the book decodes simply, since all signs refer to Pushkin's writings and his life.

Yet even for Geichenko, Mikhailovskoe works as an allegorical text. The landscape, by its history, "says other" to its visitors, becoming a geographical instance of the rhetorical trope. It displays not mere trees, hills, river, and buildings, but natural views described in Pushkin's writings and said to have inspired them. Stephen Greenblatt has noted that "allegory arises in periods of loss, periods in which a once powerful theological, political, or familial authority is threatened with effacement."[65] The turn to allegory here emerges, then, as a reactive strategy, a way to preserve fragile connections to Pushkin. The allegorical sign functions by pointing to something other than itself, and to itself as well. Allegory will always do both at once but not without making readers sense how the two referents (past and present or other and self) are so different as to make the act of linkage that is at the center of any rhetorical figure seem nearly impossible. In allegory, a tension between two meanings endures. That is the crucial difference between allegory and analogy, since the latter establishes parallels of meaning between entities that resemble each other.[66]

Mikhailovskoe in 1924 (and, with different details, in its present state) points backward toward an era when Pushkin visited, was exiled, and was buried. As a preserve, it keeps telling that story of the past. Excursion guides use objects in the landscape and restored interiors to pull this narrative out of the silent scene. Yet even without these interventions of verbalization, a visitor who knows Pushkin's poems, which means nearly every visitor, can feel as if the surroundings "speak." The views are familiar from Pushkin's descriptions in "The Countryside" and "... Once again I visited." Buildings, even modern reconstructions, create a background against which past events may be imagined. Mikhailovskoe stands as an allegory of a national myth, and because of its proximity to Pushkin's grave, it seems to convey a remarkably full sense of his life story despite his having spent relatively little time there.

The nearness of Pushkin's place of burial is crucial (and it is one of the most important distinctions between Mikhailovskoe and Boldino): it makes Mikhailovskoe into a self-conscious memorial that bespeaks the contradictions of Pushkin's fame. The transport of his body, secretly and at night, was to become an emblem of martyrdom. The interpretation of his death as a court intrigue with political implications was a central moment in the Soviet appropriation of Pushkin as a national poet (as is seen more fully in Chapter Three; Chapter One noted Lermontov's role in initiating this view). Pushkin's grave, modestly marked, remote from Petersburg, proximate to the place of his northern exile, helped Russians interpret him as a martyr. The motifs of exile, of deep political commitment but limited political involvement, of hard creative work done in retreat from the false pleasures of Petersburg, of closeness to the "real" Russian people personified by his nanny, Arina Rodionovna, of tragic early death—these all can be drawn from the landscape of Mikhailovskoe and, particularly in official versions of Pushkin's life and works, they have seemed to tell almost the whole story.

Mikhailovskoe cannot, however, tell an entire story about his life and writings. It can continue to work as a memory, in which case one must also acknowledge that memories are partial, that acts of remembrance select moments from the past to invest them with feeling and meaning. One wants to challenge not the emergence of Mikhailovskoe as a preserve but its transformation into a monument, with the concomitant monumentalization of Pushkin himself. Even in the best possible reading, the transformation of a place of exile into a monument to Pushkin is a transformation, an act of substitution that should not be allowed to disappear before our eyes. Alternatively, there is much to be gained from a more visible sense of the other half of the allegory at Mikhailovskoe, the state of post-Pushkinian politics and desires. Preserving and reconstructing Mikhailovskoe are an achievement of the twentieth century, one fraught with complicated reversals, one that should not be subsumed under a glorious idea of progress, Socialist or otherwise. If a preserve can, as allegory, point the visitor's attention to what has been preserved, by whom, and at what price, then the labor of preserving can be made visible. Mikhailovskoe can then become apparent to us as a collection of artifacts both genuine and invented, assembled to honor a man who personified his nation's past. Remembrance in Mikhailovskoe could then be seen as properly social, if not political; it can teach us not only about Pushkin but about how his legacy has been preserved, which is to say changed, forgotten, recreated, remembered.

I have been measuring Mikhailovskoe against time, asking how it presents an idea of temporality and suggesting that it does so allegorically. In returning to the descriptive language about the land, I will now shift literary terms. The pastoral mode structures discourse about rural Pushkin shrines, and although it will also shed new light on Mikhailovskoe, the focus of attention will now be Boldino.

Pushkin Shrines and the Pastoral

Both Mikhailovskoe and Boldino were country estates, retreats from the stress of Petersburg life and a source of income that made city life possible. Tour guides in both places will tell you how Pushkin longed to leave Petersburg in the 1830s for one or the other (each, with pride, will claim primacy). This view can be disputed, for example, by citing his desire to gain acceptance and distinction in court circles,[67] but it retains an imaginative power that is hard to vanquish. Mikhailovskoe and Boldino themselves contribute to that attractively pastoral image, since even today they attract thousands of visitors who seek the calm and beauty of rural views. This is particularly true of Mikhailovskoe, which has hotel space in the nearby village Pushkinskie Gory. Boldino, by contrast, has a decided lack of amenities and is harder to reach. But the image clings to Boldino as well, especially when seen from afar: in glorious photographs, nearly all in tones of gold, often reproduced in handsome albums, and in the film *Keep Me Safe, My Talisman* (*Khrani menia, moi talisman*, 1987), which was shot on location and is discussed in Chapter Four. Mikhailovskoe and Boldino are sites of pastoral retreat today, as they are imagined to have been for Pushkin.

The pastoral evokes images of fertile rural landscape and a shepherd trilling away on his reed-pipe. Seen always from some distance, pastoral scenes produce a longing for a golden age. In an excellent discussion of why the countryside retains its hold on popular and intellectual imaginations through many changes in historical and economic circumstances, John Rennie Short has argued that "the countryside is the nostalgic past, providing a glimpse of a simpler, purer age."[68] His view of pastoral as ideology is historically and politically specific: "For the past four hundred years the idealized countryside has been contrasted with the rise of the city and the power of the market. The two are often joined in the contrasting image of the evil city dominated by the love of money, a moral cesspit to be contrasted with the fresh air, moral purity and good life of the country."[69] In Russia under Bolshevik rule, this description of a city's capitalist accumulation might seem inappropriate, but for city-dwellers, home was associated with labor and with the demands of public life. Many took to the countryside at every opportunity. Cleaner air, trees, and perhaps a riverbank offered escape from the intensely ideologized spaces of urban life.

Nostalgia had its rewards in a weekend in the nearest meadow, and an excursion to an "architectural monument" from pre-revolutionary times could also offer a momentary return to a golden age. It is in this sense that Pushkin shrines work as pastoral retreat, conceptualized not just as nature but also as culture. The gold-toned leaves in Boldino pictures (the reconstructed house is even painted gold) work as a visual pun on this golden hue of the pastoral, and a verbal pun on the naming of Pushkin's lifetime as the golden age of Russian culture. A wild suggestion, only half-humorous: if Pushkin's family had no country estates, it would have been necessary to establish some relevant rural site, so much has the pastoral moment been built into the Pushkin myth. It feels fated that he would be experienced by Russians in this context, especially given the nature of pastoral as a literary mode.[70] The shepherd's piping and his way of life were valued for their simplicity, a term strongly associated with Pushkin. Other pastoral heroes derive their elevated status from such simplicity (notably Joan of Arc and most other saints, also Lenin); Pushkin's simplicity was reiterated by the clarity and seeming accessibility of his writings. Another term, harmony, also often figures in platitudes and in serious works about Pushkin, and it too fits the pastoral pattern. The pastoral also looks back on a supposedly harmonious relationship between land and work from a time of greater tension and complexity. William Empson best described this harmony when he said that "the essential trick of the old pastoral" was "to imply a beautiful relationship between rich and poor."[71] Empson emphasizes the economic aspect, and we should keep that in mind as we review the history and present state of Boldino.

It is located in the Nizhegorodsky region, which makes Nizhny Novgorod (Gorky for most of the Soviet period) its closest major city. You can get there from Nizhny Novgorod in six hours by bus, or one hour in a rickety eight-seat plane. Along with nearby Kistenyovo, Lvovka, and other smaller villages, Boldino belonged to the Pushkin family beginning in the early seventeenth century. They received the land as a reward for loyal service during the Time of Troubles. The villages were a substantial and wealth-generating reward; Bolshoe Boldino was also called Bazarnoe Boldino because it was a center of trade. But by the end of the eighteenth century, the land and the serfs were mostly mortgaged.[72] The villages became typical scenes of neglect and corruption, suffering from decades of noble owners who preferred to live in the capital and left them in the hands of managers who were careless or dishonest, or both. Pushkin's father and his uncle, the poet Vasily Lvovich Pushkin, inherited the land in 1790. In 1830, when Pushkin announced his intention to marry, his father gave him Kistenyovo with its two hundred serfs. Pushkin came in 1830 to Boldino, the site of the main house, to sort out the finances of the estate and to register the transfer of Kistenyovo. He found a confused record of debt, subdivision, and diminished income. By the time of his trips in 1833 and 1834, he was sanguine about the disastrous economic conditions (in 1834 his father also gave him responsibility for his share of Boldino), and he continued selling off some parts of the estate, renouncing others to avoid the encumbered debts.

Poverty marks Boldino. It distinguishes it from Mikhailovskoe significantly, as does its greater remoteness. Things happened more slowly and more modestly in the history of its emergence as a Pushkin shrine. In contrast to the destruction wrought at Mikhailovskoe after 1917, Boldino peasants voted not to burn down Pushkin's house.[73] Boldino was made a preserve in 1929, although on a very modest scale. Even as late as 1949, when a Pushkin museum was finally established, it was sited in what had formerly been a hut for the supervisor of the serf laborers across from the main house. That changed in the 1960s, when the main house was restored.[74] The new museum combines rooms set up like nineteenth-century living quarters with those organized around the display of illustrative material.[75] The exhibits, redesigned in the 1980s, intelligently use the paucity of available material to leave quite a lot to the imagination of visitors.

A virtue was thus made of necessity: because the museum lacked extensive original furnishings and a vast library, and because it had meager financial resources, there was little temptation to ornament the rooms. The museum was conceived as a place of poetic inspiration. One designer of the exhibits explains that she and her colleagues "foresaw a home that was clearly a country home, not richly ornamented, not especially comfortable, since that is how it was when Pushkin visited, a home that became a temporary refuge for a poet."[76] They used one of Pushkin's drawings of his writing table to replicate his desk arrangement in the corner of one room;[77] they included a couch nearby because Pushkin wrote lying down. In another room, whose purpose is no longer known, they set up simple period furnishings and displayed material relating to the poet's second trip to Boldino, in 1833.[78] The most striking aspect of these rooms is the use of Pushkin's manuscripts. The designers had facsimile copies of his manuscripts drawn by a Leningrad artist, using paper from Pushkin's lifetime, and scattered them throughout the rooms that he would have inhabited in the 1830s (some parts of the house represent later additions and are used to different ends). The plan was to have visitors struck by the profusion of manuscripts, which would "serve as an embodiment of the creative process."[79]

Beyond all this, the exhibit designers sought, by the very openness of their design, to bring the out of doors into the museum. They left the windows uncovered and unshuttered, inviting the eye outward to contemplate the landscape scenes assumed to have inspired Pushkin. Visitors could wander through the small park, with its charming arched bridge across the pond, again with the idea that they would experience the natural environment as Pushkin felt it.[80] For some visitors, as we will see, the landscape also inspired *them* to write.

The final rooms along the exhibition route show documents, portraits, and objects relating to the history of Boldino after Pushkin's death. These include an 1837 letter from Pushkin's widow to the overseer of Boldino, Penkovsky, asking that any of his things left in the house be sent to her. The letter explains why so few of Pushkin's possessions remained in the house and illustrates the care with which Natalia Nikolaevna attended to such matters (in general, the museum shows a remarkably kind view of Natalia Nikolaevna, including a portrait of her Pushkin might have brought during his 1833 trip).[81] The rooms tell of Pushkin's brother's inheritance of Boldino, and how his family lived there after his death in 1852, and they do so largely by means of family portraits. The heirs made certain additions and changes during their occupancy and finally sold the house to the government in 1911. By including the documents and portraits of these rooms, the Boldino museum brings its own history into a visitor's view.[82]

In discussing the more dramatic transformations of Mikhailovskoe, we compared its twentieth-century state to descriptions found in Pushkin's writings. It is useful to do the same with Boldino. We must turn to Pushkin's writings in any case because we have little else: unlike the wealth of memoir accounts of early visitors to Mikhailovskoe, the Boldino literary heritage is relatively sparse. Just as a certain poverty has defined the museum, so the discourse about Boldino is limited. All the more reason to look closely at Pushkin's words.

Pushkin's Descriptions of Boldino

Compared with Pushkin's elegies about Mikhailovskoe, his poetic treatment of Boldino seems strikingly unlyrical. The poems are bleak and unsentimental. One poem, a quick portrait of bare trees and deserted yards, includes a peasant carrying his child's coffin for burial. Untitled, it begins "My ruddy-faced critic" ("Rumiannyi kritik moi," 1830), and mixes pathos and informality. Here is its descriptive portion:

> Look at the view here: a row of wretched huts,
> Behind them black earth, a steep-sloped ravine,
> Above them a thick band of gray clouds.
> Where are the radiant fields? the dark forests?
> The stream? In the yard by a low fence
> Two poor little trees gladden the eye,
> Only two little trees, and one of them
> Has been utterly stripped this rainy fall,
> And the leaves on the other, soaked and yellowing,
> Will become litter in a puddle after the merest wind
>   of Boreas.
> That's it. In the yard there's not a single dog.
> True, there's a peasant man, and two peasant women
>   following him.
> He wears no hat; he carries a child's coffin under his arm
> And from afar he bids the priest's lazy child
> To get his father and open the church.
> Hurry up! I've no time to wait! I should have done
>   the burying long ago.

> Смотри, какой здесь вид: избушек ряд убогий,
> За ними чернозем, равнины скат отлогий,
> Над ними серых туч густая полоса.
> Где нивы светлые? где темные леса?
> Где речка? На дворе у низкого забора
> Два бедных деревца стоят в отраду взора,
> Два только деревца, и то из них одно

> Дождливой осенью совсем обнажено,
> И листья на другом, размокнув и желтея,
> Чтоб лужу засорить, лишь только ждут Борея.
> И только. На дворе живой собаки нет.
> Вот, правда, мужичок, за ним две бабы вслед.
> Без шапки он; несет под мышкой гроб ребенка
> И кличет издали ленивого попенка,
> Чтоб тот отца позвал да церковь отворил.
> Скорей! ждать некогда! давно бы схоронил.[83]

Pushkin's sad description flies in the face of pastoral expectations, self-consciously when he asks after the expected fields, forests, and stream—the very attributes of Mikhailovskoe, in fact. Instead, he gives us nearly denuded trees surrounded by rain, dirt, and blowing wind. The landscape shows movement only when a peasant man appears, carrying the coffin of a child: this incursion of death, especially the death of a child as if all future has been cut off, intensifies the desolation.

These lines are only occasionally cited in accounts of Pushkin's visits to Boldino.[84] The poem more readily associated with the estate is "Autumn" ("Osen'," 1833), a long and intriguing meditation with more potential for nostalgia.[85] Its opening stanza paints a livelier picture but rewrites "My ruddy-faced critic," down to the barking dog who wakes the slumbering oak trees. The poet compares autumn, the least appealing season, to an unfavored child who is all the more loved by an outsider, and then to a consumptive girl whose face still shows her wish to live. Here is the second of these two comparisons, which begins by commenting on the poet's unlikely affection for autumn:

> How to explain it? I like it
> As you, perhaps, sometimes like
> A consumptive girl. Condemned to death,
> The poor creature droops without complaint or anger.
> A smile is seen on her faded lips;
> She does not sense the grave's gaping abyss;
> A crimson hue still plays on her face.
> She is alive today, but gone tomorrow.

> Как это объяснить? Мне нравится она,
> Как, вероятно, вам чахоточная дева
> Порою нравится. На смерть осуждена,
> Бедняжка клонится без ропота, без гнева.
> Улыбка на устах увянувших видна;
> Могильной пропасти она не слышит зева;
> Играет на лице еще багровый цвет.
> Она жива еще сегодня, завтра нет.[86]

Pushkin next offers two exclamations that condense all the paradox of his response to this autumn landscape: "A melancholy season! A delight for the eyes" ("Unylaia pora! Ochei ocharovan'e!"). He describes the land in terms that are in constant conflict with each other:

> Your beauty pleases me as it bids farewell—
> I love the sumptuous fading of nature,
> The forests clothed in crimson and gold,
> The noise of the wind and the fresh breeze
>   in their canopies,
> And the skies covered with undulating mist,
> And that rare sunbeam, and the first frost,
> And the distant threats of hoary winter.

> Приятна мне твоя прощальная краса—
> Люблю я пышное природы увяданье,
> В багрец и в золото одетые леса,
> В их сенях ветра шум и свежее дыханье,
> И мглой волнистою покрыты небеса,
> И редкий солнца луч, и первые морозы,
> И отдаленные седой зимы угрозы.[87]

Pushkin thus invests the desolate landscape with attractiveness, a paradox that would be lost if one saw only the land's beauty, as if the consumptive young girl were not dying on the morrow or the child singled out in a strange family not unloved by its own kin.[88]

Some scholars read "Autumn" as mainly celebrating Pushkin's pleasure in the season and its capacity to inspire him.[89] The poem allows this emphasis when the poet comments that every fall he "blossoms anew" ("rastsvetaiu vnov'"), another paradoxical juxtaposition but one that rejoices in the poet's creative growth in this desolate season. That theme takes over "Autumn" as the fragment ends. Two of the most remarkable stanzas Pushkin ever wrote give a riveting description of how inspiration physically enters the poet's body and moves him to write:

> And I forget the world—and in the sweet silence
> I am sweetly lulled by my imagination,
> And poetry awakens within me:
> My soul is gripped by lyric excitement,
> It trembles and resounds, and searches, as if in a dream,
> For release at last in free expression—
> And an invisible throng of guests approaches me,
> Old acquaintances, the fruits of my fancy.

> And thoughts seethe bravely in my mind,
> And airy rhymes race to meet them,
> And my fingers cry out for a pen, the pen for paper,
> In a moment poetry will freely flow.

> И забываю мир — и в сладкой тишине
> Я сладко усыплен моим воображеньем,
> И пробуждается поэзия во мне:
> Душа стесняется лирическим волненьем,
> Трепещет и звучит, и ищет, как во сне,
> Излиться наконец свободным проявленьем —
> И тут ко мне идет незримый рой гостей,
> Знакомцы давние, плоды мечты моей.
>
> И мысли в голове волнуются в отваге,
> И рифмы легкие навстречу им бегут,
> И пальцы просятся к перу, перо к бумаге,
> Минута — и стихи свободно потекут.[90]

One can hardly blame scholars, museum workers, or those who just read Pushkin with pleasure for taking these exquisite lines as the poem's central point;[91] the best readings explore the interrelationship between the poet's state of mind and the descriptions of nature. In an animated film that vividly captures Pushkin's creative process, Andrei Khrzhanovsky's *My Favorite Time* (*Liubimoe moe vremia*, 1987), the actor Sergei Yursky reads the lines with wonderful resonance. But he continues, as does Pushkin, with the poem's uncertain final image:

> Thus a ship slumbers motionless in motionless water,
> But, hark! — suddenly the sailors swing into action and
> Climb up and down the masts, and the sails are filled with wind;
> The hulking mass moves forth and cleaves the waves.
>
> It sails. But where are we to sail? . . .
> . . . .
> . . . .
>
> Так дремлет недвижим корабль в недвижной влаге,[92]
> Но чу! — матросы вдруг кидаются, ползут
> Вверх, вниз — и паруса надулись, ветра полны;
> Громада двинулась и рассекает волны.
>
> Плывет. Куда ж нам плыть? . . .
> . . . .
> . . . .

The last line of "Autumn" asks a question: the vessel of poetry is ready to set sail, but without a destination. The inspired poet does not know what to write.[93] The poem breaks off in demonstration of that uncertainty, substituting two-and-a-half lines of ellipses for poetry that cannot be written. The imagery intensifies the uncertainty by giving several ideas of inspiration (is it the sight of a dying girl? an unseen swarm of guests? wind filling sails?). "Thoughts" and "airy rhymes" awaken the poet's mind and soul, fingers reach for a pen, the pen for paper, but, through all this movement, the poet is grammatically passive, no longer the subject of any sentences once he has forgotten the world and been lulled to sleep by his imagination.

Pushkin makes the poetic process all the more mysterious by seeming not to control it or to be able to reason through its steps. And the process is incomplete: "Autumn" demonstrates an imagined fragmentariness, as one scholar has noted, recalling the ending of *Eugene Onegin*.[94] But whereas *Onegin* plays with fragmentary forms within a large and rewarding text that fully develops its plot and characters, "Autumn" races from one metaphor to another, succeeding marvelously in capturing the feel of poetic creation but postponing any commitment to what the created poem might be about.[95] In its last magnificent image, "Autumn" renders Pushkin's creativity as a great hulking vessel sailing for unknown waters. The poem leaves the impression that the creative process is determined by nature's whim (the onset of autumn, the coming of nautical winds), returning the poet to the vulnerability associated with a sick girl at the start of the poem. The poet awaiting his muse is no more in control of his fate than the girl is of hers.

Inspiration in Boldino

How to show visitors this mix of success with vulnerability, especially when they are likely to know about Pushkin's phenomenal productiveness in 1830 and, perhaps, his second visit in 1833, with its smaller number of important texts, including "Autumn." Some twentieth-century Russian texts represent Pushkin's achievements as an unrepeatable, mythic exploit, and this view has affected popular notions of his stay in Boldino. The museum too privileges success over failure, but it still manages to suggest a complex view of Pushkin's time there. The manuscript facsimiles convey an idea of how much he wrote; one room presents a chronology of his Boldino writings, certainly a staggering sight to behold when one reads through the long list of poems and stories completed in 1830 and 1833; that room features the poem "Autumn"—an enlarged text of the poem hangs on one wall. The more frustrating fall of 1834, when Pushkin wrote just *The Tale of the Golden Cockerel* (*Skazka o zolotom petushke*), like his later 1830s visits to Mikhailovskoe when he found himself almost entirely unable to write, poses special problems for the museum. It represents the meager output of the 1834 visit with some subtlety. Pushkin was in Boldino for only two-and-a-half weeks, during which he lived in his overseer's office.[96] This small hut, separate from the main house where exhibits emphasize Pushkin's creativity, is where the estate's accounts were once done; the exhibit can show signs of the financial worries that dominated Pushkin's 1834 visit.[97] This decision tempers the pastoral myth of Pushkin magically able to write brilliantly merely because he was in the countryside, reminding us that his genius did not always yield its riches, and that the countryside signified very practical concerns to him as well. The museum relegates that failure to a separate, lesser building, but it does not exclude it. The museum's success across all its exhibits derives in large measure from its consistent use of understatement. Each object draws intense attention because there are so few of them, which allows something so simple as an abacus in the overseer's office, juxtaposed to the manuscript facsimiles that appear in the main house, to convey dramatically how different Pushkin's life was in 1834 from his visits in 1830 and 1833.

The paucity of displayed objects, then, corresponds to the poverty of the area and diminishes its potential for pastoral escape. In Boldino, there was no economic harmony, no "beautiful relationship between rich and poor"—not in Pushkin's day, and not now. The serfs in Boldino, Kistenyovo, and Lvovka were terribly poor, even by the standards of nineteenth-century peasants. Pushkin's short poem about the bare landscape ("My ruddy-faced critic") evokes this sad truth. Neither Pushkin nor his heirs found a way to make the estates profitable. Boldino exemplified the decay of a feudal order in Marxist readings of its nineteenth-century conditions; in the supposed glory days of Stalinist collectivization, its prosperity was severely limited, despite the rhetoric of utopian agricultural wealth popular in the 1930s.[98] If, to some, it has seemed to exemplify the pastoral because of all that Pushkin wrote here, and because it kept him far from the harms imputed to court life,[99] then one achievement of the museum is to undermine, very quietly, this pastoral ideal. Instead, it conveys Pushkin's immense efforts at recreating himself in this setting, and although the work of the museum staff does not call attention to itself, it does suggest implicitly that labor need not be hidden behind a wall of "naturalness"—not the museum workers' labor, and not Pushkin's.

Pastoral in Mikhailovskoe

Given the limits to reading Boldino as pastoral, we might return briefly to Mikhailovskoe to see how the mode has been used there. Pastoral simplicity certainly clings to the image of Pushkin's time at that estate. Many accounts emphasize his acquaintance with simple Russian folk and folk customs. He walked around the marketplace listening to peasant speech, sometimes dressed in peasant garb.[100] This kind of legend also clings to Boldino, but less tenaciously, in part because visitors came to Mikhailovskoe earlier and could interview peasants who knew or had heard of Pushkin. Stories about Pushkin and the *narod* might have emerged during the Soviet period anyway, since an affinity with the people was counted as an ideological necessity. The 1824–26 stay in Mikhailovskoe had unusually high potential for such tales: Pushkin's companion was Arina Rodionovna, his peasant nanny, who is said to have told him Russian folktales. Her tales were attested in letters and poems by Pushkin and other contemporaries, and she figures prominently in his life in many accounts of Mikhailovskoe. Perhaps her importance is emphasized unduly, especially by writers who contend that she was more like a mother to Pushkin than his own mother,[101] but her warmth and care need to be taken into account in any readings that would paint a happy picture of 1824–26, since these were also years of exile and relative isolation.

A second element of the pastoral, its evocation of a golden age in the past, also appears in the discourse about Mikhailovskoe. Pushkin's exile, the bulk of his time in Mikhailovskoe, was a time of enormous growth and courageous change as a writer, but it came at some cost to a poet who felt imprisoned.[102] The golden hue of Mikhailovskoe in the literature has also been colored by Pushkin's own landscape descriptions. In the 1819 poem "The Countryside," he describes the land in nearly idyllic terms at first, but the poem comes to reject this beauty. His initial description of the landscape as calmly lovely, seemingly appropriate to poetic inspiration, yields to a thunderous conclusion where the hidden ugliness of serfdom is revealed. The poem's climax more or less dispenses with a pastoral model for interpreting any Russian landscape where the work was done by forced labor.

"The Countryside" also eerily forewarns of the discord that marked the transition to a museum-preserve in the twentieth century. Some of this disagreement was discussed above, in terms of the destruction that occurred during the civil war. A much longer history of disputatiousness afterward occurred in connection with the parks. The private correspondence and official reports about Mikhailovskoe and Trigorskoe reveal complications in the plan to create a national preserve. Reports of illicit logging were frequent. Some trees were cut down during the First World War,[103] but more regularly local peasants simply helped themselves to much-needed firewood. Arguments over their rights to cut down trees and to graze animals on what was soon declared a land preserve continued almost to the end of the 1920s. There were court cases, fines, appeals to higher ministries, attempts to hire additional guards, and yearly tree counts.[104]

We can conclude from this prolonged dispute that competing economic interests shaped the debate about forming a Pushkin preserve in the early years of Soviet rule. Land was removed from struggling farmers and peasant families scavenging for enough firewood to heat their homes. Whatever this is, it is not the world of pastoral harmony; there is no beautiful relationship between those who made decisions about the preserve from the capital and those who saw it as their land.[105] Even less well than it fits Boldino's emergence as a Pushkin museum, the pastoral model cannot finally be brought to describe accurately what happened in Mikhailovskoe.

None of which is to say that visits to these country estates are without their pleasures, including the pleasures of a certain kind of nostalgia. This is especially true in Boldino, where there are few cars, and farmers can still be seen riding slowly on carts pulled by massive work horses. Animals walk down the street or are tethered to the ground near every small house. The museum itself is done up with great simplicity. Its most notable feature is the total absence of glass display cases, something that marks every other Pushkin museum I visited (even when they display only copies). The museum is staffed by a small group of phenomenally humane and intelligent people. Some local schoolchildren were taking tours of the house when I was there in 1990, and it was stunning to see the kindness with which they were treated by museum staff, especially as compared with the snappish tones of their counterparts in urban literary museums. Yearly conferences (*Boldinskie chteniia*) provided this museum a vital link with the outside world: they brought Pushkin scholars to this faraway place, and particularly in the 1970s and early 1980s, they produced some remarkably interesting scholarship, including fine interpretations of the poetry.[106] The staff at Boldino will tell you proudly how they fought to have these conferences and to publish the results; a few days in their company produced in me, at least, the impression that I had visited an outpost of Russian culture that had successfully resisted a great deal that is false and self-important in modern appropriations of the Pushkin myth. I had also spent time in the presence of people who were interested in something other than their own career advancement, and although the extremely difficult economic circumstances in which they lived means that one ought not to idealize their lives as some sort of remote idyll, Boldino still offered a world of intellectual and ethical values that was difficult to find in post-Soviet Russia in the 1990s—or for decades before that.

Local people do not make for such an experience in Mikhailovskoe. With over half a million visitors yearly,[107] the local hotel had the usual rude staff and broken-down rooms as at the end of the Soviet period. The museum-preserves at Mikhailovskoe and Trigorskoe, even if you wander around the parks on your own without a tour guide, try aggressively to structure your experience. Little signs with Pushkin's poetry are posted outside, and a peculiarly heroic version of Pushkin emerges because of the selections (see Fig. 6). There is a curious object displayed in the main house in Mikhailovskoe that inadvertently symbolizes the museum's attitude toward the natural surroundings in the area: a piece of one of the original pine trees, enclosed in plexiglass, sits like some precious bit of petrified wood. One contemplates it as if it had the holy status of Pushkin's clothing or dueling pistols, dis-

FIGURE 6. One of several signs with Pushkin's poetry at Mikhailovskoe. The quoted lines are from an ending of "... Once again I visited" that Pushkin discarded: "...Sacred Providence / Safeguarded me here with its mysterious shield, / Poetry, like a consoling angel, / Saved me, and my soul was reborn." Author's photograph, 1986.

played in the apartment at Moika 12 where he died, and it too seems a symbol of loss. But if what is lost is some authentic replication in nature of the landscape through which Pushkin moved, then how is one to experience the large wooded area that surrounds the house? As it turns out, the walk from Mikhailovskoe to Trigorskoe can be lovely, even restorative, in part because one can forget entirely about Pushkin (as soon as the poetry selections thin out).[108] Similarly, the museum at Petrovskoe, with its picturesque two-story gazebo near the lake, can be enjoyable to visit. Less frequented than the house in Mikhailovskoe, it benefited from the idiosyncratic independence of its director, Boris Kozmin.

The calm of the places is also associated with the higher spiritual values that Pushkin himself is thought to have embodied, and visitors are variously invited to appreciate specific sights because he wrote about them. Boldino and Mikhailovskoe are cultural memorials, meant to work not just as nature preserves, but as shrines, as sites of the spirit, as places to elicit experiences of national and cultural memory. By way of concluding this chapter, I want to consider how the idea of creating access to Pushkin's spirit has evolved, in particular how it emerged from something so insistently material as a system of museums.

Spirit and Recovered Identity in Pushkin Shrines

A contemporary writer, Andrei Bitov, has described Russia's relationship to Pushkin in terms of loss, but a loss that is bridged by the crossing of spirits from the dead:

Pushkin is our eternal loss. And the eternal memory of this loss. Our apprehension of him is nothing but a kind of remembrance—of a contemporary, a dear relation, someone we have lost in an untimely way, a beloved, a person who is real to us. Every Russian summons his spirit, and his spirit never tires of appearing to us. We feel him incarnated, we sense vividly that he is right there, we have only to turn around to see him.[109]

Bitov believes that Pushkin's spirit will appear tirelessly to those who seek him. Others share this belief, and Bitov's words help us see how faith in Pushkin's indomitable spirit, especially when it is put in terms of loss and love, is sufficient to motivate the Russians' enduring attraction to Pushkin shrines.

Several meanings of the word *spirit* (*dukh*) intertwine here. In one sense, Bitov means Pushkin's soul, that essence of his earthly existence that inhered in his being and has eternal life in religious terms. Spirit in this meaning is emphatically nonmaterial (hence its etymological association with breathing, evident in the Russian and in the Latin root of the English word, *spirare*).[110] In this insistence on that which is not matter, spirit suggests the will, the thinking, the consciousness of Pushkin, and it reminds us of why his writings are often described as interchangeable with the essence of his being. Second, spirit means ghost. The supernatural beings associated with a particular place, a place they haunt, emerge as a category into which Pushkin also falls, particularly when Bitov describes visitors ready to turn around and see him. In contrast to the first meaning, spirit in this sense almost becomes matter, hence Bitov's use of the word *incarnation*, as the ghost seems about to materialize.

Bitov's use of "spirit" thus hovers between its materiality and its ephemerality. Precisely that paradoxical duality informs Pushkin shrines. The shrines are, of course, themselves insistently *material*— museums where objects are preserved as tangible proof of a distant past. The fascination, even obsession, with *reproducing* such objects emerges from this focus on the material. Because the originals are nearly all gone, it is not the authenticity of the objects that finally matters (not the original house, not the original furniture, not the original trees), but the aura of authenticity, the capacity of the object to evoke an association with Pushkin and thus to set in motion the chain of expectations and desires that he will himself appear out of the forest or from behind a door.[111] For visitors intent on finding the "real" Pushkin in Mikhailovskoe or Boldino, an imaginative turn to his spirit seems so powerful that many claim it to be physically palpable. Thus the longtime director of Mikhailovskoe, Sergei Geichenko, pointed to the spiritual nature of material things associated with Pushkin:

> When people depart, their possessions remain after them. The possessions wordlessly bear witness to an ancient truth, that they are more long-lived than people. There are no inanimate objects, only inanimate people. Without Pushkin's possessions, without the natural sights of Pushkin shrines, it is difficult to fully comprehend his life and work.... Today Pushkin's things are in preserves and museums. Here they live their own, mysterious life, and the curators read their secret alphabet.[112]

Geichenko links the mysteriously alive objects in the preserve to an expectation that Pushkin also lives there. He urges visitors: "When you visit Mikhailovkoe, go out some evening to the outskirts of the estate, face the little lake and cry out loudly, 'Alexander Sergeevich!' I can assure you that he will answer without fail 'Hee-ee-re! I'm coming!'"[113]

To have this experience, a visitor needs some prodding, either in a book like Geichenko's that can be read in advance or from a guide who accompanies one through the visit. Yet one museum experience teaches a kind of reflex response for subsequent visits, and most museums know well how to elicit reactions almost wordlessly. As Nina Popova, the former director of the house on the Moika, put it, the museum does its work on the basis of a kind of triad: historical documentation, original possessions, and the devices of a theater director.[114] That third component, theatricality, might not be the first explanation that comes to the lips of someone like Geichenko, himself a great advocate of mystical language to help in the conjuring of spirits, but it aptly describes the role Geichenko takes on in his writings—right down to the moment of directing visitors to go out into the woods and speak their lines.

Theatricality is at once the most effective and the riskiest device that a museum designer can turn to, and we have seen it subtly at work in the decisions about exhibits in Boldino. In the post-1987 version of the house on the Moika, for example, a stunning innovation was to use a storage passageway for hundreds of facsimiles of the unsold copies of Pushkin's *History of Pugachev* (*Istoriia Pugacheva*, 1834) and his journal, *The Contemporary* (*Sovremennik*). The designers had some basis for this invention (the *History* had sold badly, and the restorers of the building discovered this pas-

FIGURE 7. The sisters' room in the Moika 12 museum. The stacks of copies of Pushkin's journal *The Contemporary* (*Sovremennik*) that can be seen through the doorway were later removed. Reproduction from *Muzei-kvartira A. S. Pushkina na Moike* (Moscow: Sovetskaia Rossiia, 1989), p. 75. Courtesy National Pushkin Museum, St. Petersburg.

sageway leading from the room used by Natalia Nikolaevna's sisters), but it was certainly an invention. When I visited in 1987, the corridor was a striking part of the exhibit, perhaps the one eloquent reminder of Pushkin's struggle to support himself as a writer (Fig. 7).[115] But the design was controversial from the start,[116] and this detail was especially problematic: the passageway was accessible through the sisters' room, and some objected to such a dramatic reminder that Natalia Nikolaevna's sisters, one of whom was married to Pushkin's killer, had lived in the apartment. The directors of the museum soon backed down. When I returned in 1990 the unsold books were gone.

The room full of unsold books, a defiantly theatrical gesture but also an insistently material, physical way of telling Pushkin's story, may simply have been *too* material.[117] And it provided a sharp contrast to the display of Pushkin's own vast library of books in his study, the room that is the museum's centerpiece.[118] Such dramatic inventions risk clashing with the spiritual truths (and thus authentic experiences) that are said to stand behind

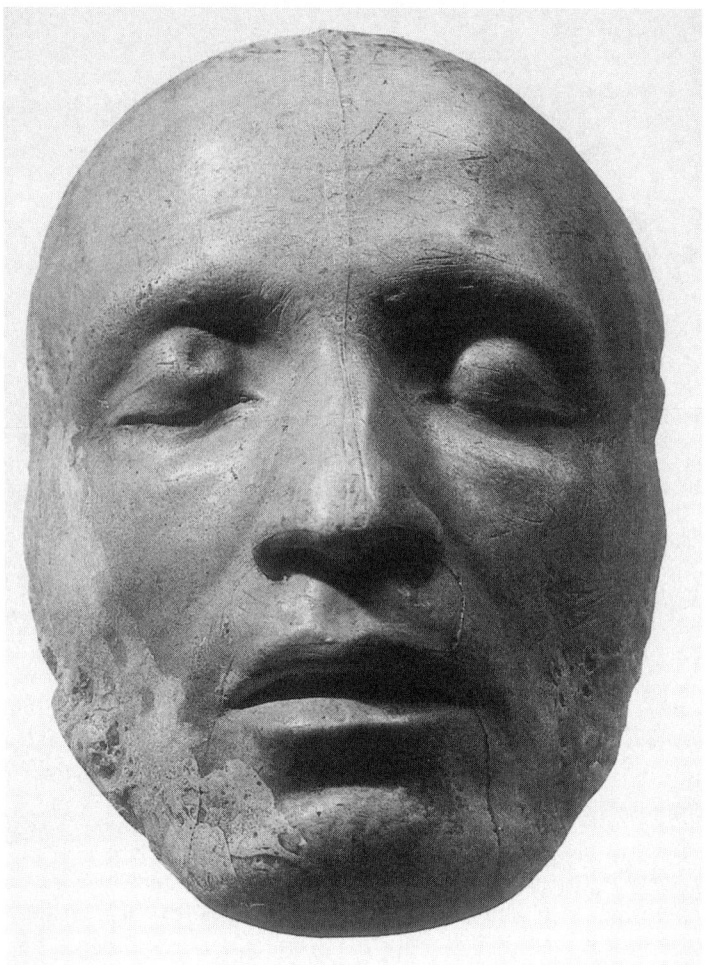

FIGURE 8. S. I. Galberg's death mask of Pushkin (1837) in the Moika 12 museum. Reproduction from E. V. Pavlova, ed., *A. S. Pushkin v portretakh* (Moscow: Sovetskii khudozhnik, 1989), vol. 1, p. 127. Courtesy National Pushkin Museum, St. Petersburg.

many of these museums. The museums that have gained cultural acceptance seem to have found their niche in part by mediating between the spiritual and the material—and by investing displayed objects with spiritual qualities. In the Moika exhibit, the displays that work best do precisely this. The mere sight of (copies of) Pushkin's books in his study makes the room seem to come alive with his intense attachment to them, and if you do not know Pushkin's life and legend well enough to remember that he bade his books farewell from his deathbed, then the guide is there to recite his words for you.[119] The house on the Moika displays one of the original death masks, an exhibit that all but brings Pushkin's face into the room (Fig. 8). This object is handled very theatrically—on my first visit, I remember the guide whisking away a tiny curtain that protected the mask from sunlight, revealing Pushkin's deathly face as if she were a prestidigitator pulling a rabbit out of a top hat. In the post-1987 exhibit, the mask was in a hallway, resting beneath A. A. Kozlov's portrait of Pushkin on his deathbed (*Pushkin na smertnom odre*, 1837), which created the illusion that not just the face, but the entire dead body had been imported into the apartment, lying in state for all who pass by to see. That, too, was subsequently changed.

Some recent discussions of museums have noted the potential sublation from the material object to a spiritual experience. As Boris Groys writes, this kind of museum offers the experience of transcendence, but it is an illusory transcendence of time itself:

A secularized historical transcendence, one of whose forms is the preservation of things in museums, creates only the illusion of cultural immortality: its material nature signifies both its extreme vulnerability to all sorts of accidents, its dependence on too many external factors, and, in the final analysis, its condemnation to inevitable ruin in some more distant future.[120]

Groys would have us experience the museum as the kind of allegory I have discussed above in connection with Mikhailovskoe. The difficulty of allegory comes in keeping before a visitor's mind its dual temporality, which Groys invokes by telling us that displayed objects are as much exemplary of time's power to destroy things as they are defiant by their mere survival. He is perhaps more right than he can have known, when we realize how many items displayed in Pushkin shrines are copies, making them testimony to lost or absent originals. The buildings themselves are often copies (although as we have seen, not all histories of the museums tell the truth about the reconstruction), and some, like the house on the Moika, have been very extensively rebuilt.[121]

In a sense, Pushkin shrines try to exist outside a concrete frame of chronological reference. Time can be made to seem to stop in these places, so that one can concentrate entirely on the moment when one is there. Some Pushkin museums attempt to fulfill this wish for time to stand still, not just by trying to make the present moment seem suspended out of context, but also by trying to recreate the past. Thus, electrical poles are kept out of tourists' view in Mikhailovskoe.[122] In the house on the Moika, all clocks are stopped at 2:45 P.M., the hour of Pushkin's death, including his own pocket watch—rather a grotesque touch when you think about it. Visitors to all "house-museums" will surely feel a chronological jump as they view period furnishings and a living space recreated from an earlier era.[123] When asked, they may stress this aspect of their visit. As one Moika visitor wrote, "Walking through these quiet rooms, you literally feel the spirit of Pushkin's epoch. Every exhibit plays a role in the picture, which recreates the spirit of the time."[124]

This comment returns us, by its diction, to the question of Pushkin's spirit, as might the remark of another Moika visitor: "This apartment of the great poet is filled with his spirit. It seems that any moment you will hear his steps, and the master will enter the room."[125] I quote this remark not because it is compelling or even plausible (so powerfully does the house on the Moika mourn Pushkin's death, that it seems unlikely to me that anyone there would actually start to think him alive and walking through the rooms), but because it reflects the kind of personal response that Pushkin shrines may induce in their visitors. Some articulate this belief quite simply, as in Viktor Bokov's poem, "I see Pushkin alive, / Powerfully life-size" or, more lyrically, a poem by Raisa Akhmatova, "I imagine that your Nanny will blow out the candle, / And you will slowly emerge onto the porch."[126] Other poetic responses can be more narrative, detailing whole chunks of Pushkin's life and often drawing on his writings.[127]

The strongest claims that Pushkin yet lives in these places come as paeans to nature. One writer has put it quite emphatically:

He lived here. Here is a chair, a table, a goose quill. Things raised to the level of symbol. But these things are silent. One must seek the spirit of the poet elsewhere. In the open spaces of land, in nature, nature that brought us into the world and will lead us out into darkness. . . . Pushkin is more than anywhere else in this grove, Luchinnik, in this spring, in these recently plowed fields. Here you don't have to ask any questions, Pushkin will fly toward you together with the light wind.[128]

Others share this urge to move out of doors, as if nature had some more authentic trace of Pushkin (recall the decision in Mikhailovskoe to enshrine a piece of a tree from Pushkin's age). The most productive and revealing genre for these writings has been the lyric, with its opportunity for the poet to overlay an intensely subjective experience of a place with the apprehension of a renewed, or altogether new, appreciation for Pushkin.

Dozens of poems have been written about Pushkin shrines, especially Mikhailovskoe and Boldino;[129] many of them describe the landscape in ways that make it the special repository for Pushkin's spirit. Vladimir Sokolov, in "Boldino Autumn" ("Boldinskaia osen'"), uses a pun on the word *leaves* (*list / list'ia*) to make the pages of Pushkin's writing seem a part of nature: "leaves were flowing, / Leaf after leaf, into eternity."[130] Alexander Figaret's poem "Pushkin's Birch Trees" ("Berezy Pushkina") has as its central image Pushkin writing on birch bark.[131] For many of these poets, the landscape is spiritually pure, recalling Semyonov-Tian-Shansky's claim in 1924 that even the soil in Mikhailovskoe was clean.

The poetry nearly always points to itself as the happy result of this inspiring purity. Boris Pilnik's poem "The little leaves again have droplets" ("Vot opiat' listochki zakapali") includes these stanzas:

> After all, I'm also waiting for something ...
> Droplets of leaves and droplets of peace ...
> I want my hand to touch
> Thoughts never thought before.
> . . .
> Let the inspiration of fall in Boldino
> Fall upon me,
> With its early frost, early dew
> In these almost final days.[132]

This poet searches for poetic inspiration, and for a way to transcend the physical environment toward a rewarding spiritual experience. Sokolov, in his poem "Boldino Autumn," cited above, seeks the purity of soul that he attributes to Pushkin: "Oh, if only I, smallest of the small, / Could cleanse my soul in the same way."[133]

For these poets, Pushkin shrines are a site of pilgrimage and tourism. The analysis of John F. Sears, writing about nineteenth-century American tourism, is altogether apt:

Both tourism and the pilgrimage provide escape from anxieties (and comforts) of everyday life; freedom from ordinary social relationships, hierarchies, and restraints; and hence evoke playfulness and a feeling of liberation. They both promise spiritual renewal through contact with a transcendent reality.[134]

Sears wisely refuses to leave this description of "contact with a transcendent reality" without some historical and political grounding. He refers specifically to the context of the United States:

Nineteenth-century American society was composed of a wide variety of religious sects; ... tourist attractions, however, are the sacred places of a nation or people, not a sect. Their religious meaning was broad enough to appeal to people of any persuasion. In a pluralistic society they provided points of mythic and national unity.[135]

The Soviet Union too sought that "mythic and national unity." After the 1917 revolution, it sought to create a feeling of national unity for its people. The new Soviets had to find replacements for the two belief systems that seemed natural, "taken for granted": religious community and dynastic realm, as Benedict Anderson has named them.[136] Pushkin's story, among others, offered a narrative through which one could experience oneself as a citizen. This was more true for Russians than for members of other nationalities, but translations of Pushkin and the sheer force of Russian ideological dominance in the Soviet Union meant that he was made to serve these purposes broadly. He could seem to those who visited his estates as if he were their distant ancestor, their progenitor, the one who had made them who they were. And they, in turn, could become that metaphorical descendant whose visit opens out Pushkin's memories in ". . . Once again I visited" toward a broad and welcoming future.

How do we know that Pushkin's story actually worked in this connection? One measure is the sheer intensity of feeling that he could arouse from so many different kinds of Soviet citizens (officials, dissidents, poets, filmmakers, museum creators, etc.). That measure, although it is the subject of this book and something I obviously take seriously, might in fact elicit skepticism: after all, the system of command culture meant that Pushkin was decreed to have central importance, something we have seen in the evolution of Pushkin museums (and will be still more apparent in the next chapter, on anniversary commemorations). But it requires a very narrow approach to society and culture to take this skepticism as the only truth about attention to Pushkin. That is, we would have to see visitors to the shrines as dupes, as only plodding members of a group excursion; once in Boldino or Mikhailovskoe (or Moika 12 or the lyceum), they feign expected emotions and insights or they exude the indifference they feel, but it is little noted. The poets who celebrate these places, whether or not they are hack writers, would be composing on themes that suit their patrons, not their own desires. Some of the poetry is mediocre, to be sure, but it is not uniformly false. And although thousands of the visitors to Mikhailovskoe were undoubtedly brought there on factory excursions or family outings not of their own design, the evidence suggests that a great many of these visitors found *something* in the visit that was moving.

I read their reactions more moderately because I do not think that people are such unresisting fools. My middle path seeks to expose the myth-making aspects of cultural institutions (as in the discussion of Mikhailovskoe) but also to acknowledge the successful, theatrical reproduction of Pushkin's world (as in the discussion of Boldino and some aspects of the house on the Moika and the surroundings in Mikhailovskoe). It leaves open the possibility that visitors to any Pushkin shrine will come away with some new insight about him and also about themselves.

Let me offer myself as an example. Mikhailovskoe was a site of indescribable disappointment. I had heard so much about it, seen it, in a way, in my own mind as I read Pushkin's writings from and about the place, that I was more than ready to find inspiration there. Instead, I found guides who vacantly intoned their lines, Intourist rules that made clear the profitability of Pushkin's shrine when the visitors were foreigners, and an overwhelming sense of the place as an official institution. But in Boldino I saw a completely different side of the Pushkin shrine, as I described above, and that lesson taught me something about my own tendency to find a way to feel superior to these mass scenes for tourists. I had that lesson repeated to me when I went back to Mikhailovskoe a few years later. The place was little changed, but my encounters were different. I made the acquaintance of a friendly, middle-aged Russian woman as I was walking between Mikhailovskoe and Trigorskoe. She came there every year from Petersburg to walk in the woods and see sights now quite familiar to her. She was not unlike other amateur Pushkin enthusiasts I have met over the years—people often of erudition and discernment, or sometimes people of little knowledge but considerable passion—that is, people for whom Pushkin occupies a place in their emotional and intellectual lives. This woman stared uncomprehendingly at my attempts to criticize Mikhailovskoe, not because she disagreed but because these things did not matter to her. She hated the little signs with poetry, too; she knew that the guides had the history wrong; and she saw the distortions large and small. But she did not care. None of it could stand in the way of her pleasure in walking along a path Pushkin himself once trod, perhaps saying to herself his poems or perhaps not, reveling in the simple and lovely sights of meadow, field, farm, and stream.

I am sorry not to remember this woman's name, but perhaps it is more appropriate that way. Let her stand in for any number of people for whom these shrines endure as special, important places.[137] It would be too restrictive to say that this affection or loyalty to a place is born just of deep national pride, but it would be silly to ignore the connection to a larger community and a nation's history that visitors may feel. In a country where, for many decades, purely political monuments and shrines (like Lenin's mausoleum) required that visitors show their adulation, Pushkin shrines seemed "natural" and (for all the political elements of their codification, detailed above), somehow beyond Soviet politics. This is another form of transcendence that the shrines invite, and although we can certainly deconstruct this apparent spiritual value as another politically useful entity, the fact remains that in many people's experience there is genuine emotion beneath the veil of trickery. In part that is because of Pushkin himself—for those who know his writings, he will always provide an interesting and subtle view on just about anything, including the shrines that mark his place in Russian culture today.

Let me not end on a note of such high lyricism, since the reaction to these places has been as ambiguous as the places themselves. A contemporary writer whom Pushkin deeply touched, Andrei Bitov, penned this sarcastic commentary (speaking through a fictional hero): "I have never been in Mikhailovskoe. Oh, that's an entirely separate subject, how many times I have not been in Mikhailovskoe!"[138] More pungently, Sergei Dovlatov's novella *The Preserve* (*Zapovednik*, 1983) gives a wonderfully skeptical account of the place. He writes his tale from the point of view of a tour guide.[139] His hero arrives from the city, at once an outsider and someone who needs quickly to know the place from within. This narrative device, especially as the hero is learning what to say during his tours, lets him ask naive questions that expose the values and assumptions of Mikhailovskoe as an institution.[140] Dovlatov's tale constantly deflates the high rhetoric used to describe Pushkin, as when one young women intones, "Here everything lives and breathes Pushkin ... literally every twig, every path. You just expect that he'll emerge right now from around the curve ... his top hat, morning coat, familiar profile ... ," to which the narrator responds, "But, from around the bend emerged Lyova Gurianov, an informer from my university days."[141] In other passages his hero criticizes the Disneyland-like additions to Mikhailovskoe of recent years, calling them the "idiotic ideas of Comrade Geichenko."[142] When the sense of harmony and beauty at last strikes him, the hero is on a drinking binge, inebriated almost to incoherency.[143]

Dovlatov's novella exposes the potential for Pushkin shrines to seem laughable, themselves parodies of what one associates with Pushkin. The remarkable thing about the shrines is that parodies cannot entirely displace the deeply felt memoirs by visitors for whom the place transcends all place and time. Even for Dovlatov, Mikhailovskoe disappoints because it is inescapably *Soviet*, and in the worst senses of the word—a site of false rhetoric and distorted history, where informers lurk in the forest, and KGB majors invite you in for a little chat. Neither pastoral nor retreat, the Pushkin preserve of Dovlatov's novella shows all the signs of the world that created it. He writes a fictional version of what the Formalists called the "laying bare of a literary device" (*obnazhenie priema*), as he takes us backstage to see how the experience of visiting the preserve is produced. An exaggerated, parodic tale, *The Preserve* is a telling meditation on the place of Pushkin shrines in Russian culture: a place of staged preservation and spiritual quest; a place where material objects are invested with meanings by each new generation of visitors; and a place where guides, restorers, museum officials, tourist industry workers, and writers together try to create the illusion that one crosses over into a time and space that was inhabited by Pushkin, and that indelibly bears the trace of his life.

3 *Solid Gold Pushkin*

ANNIVERSARY COMMEMORATIONS
AND THE TIME LINES OF A STORY

> ... this strange figure of the moment in which memory of
> the past is seized in the present, in which recognition takes
> place always coincident with irretrievable disappearance.
> —Carol Jacobs

When we look back across the decades that separate us from Pushkin's lifetime, the long span of years is delineated by historical events and, perhaps more significantly, by the anniversary years 1880, 1899, 1921, 1924, 1937, 1949, 1987, and 1999. Nearly all marked "round" numbers of years from the times of Pushkin's birth or death, and they occasioned public rituals of remarkable continuity. Some were elaborate and nationwide, others small but unforgettable because of their famous participants. Anniversary years stand in self-conscious relation to one another, to cumulative effect; amid much repetition, the ceremonies respond to historical change and to new political and cultural pressures. Some commemorations have questioned their relevance to the contemporary world.

Anniversary dates are thus abstractly valuable, a narrative device that organizes the Pushkin story in Russian culture. They segment its chronology and serve as markers along the time line that began with his life. They cluster a large number of responses to Pushkin in a single day or month or year, urging writers, thinkers, and public figures to note their attitudes and reflections on particular texts. These statements and images in turn drive a more generally intensified attention to Pushkin among the larger population. The anniversary appears not to be an artificial occasion—its timing is determined by a fateful repetition, the day when something important happened fifty or a hundred years ago. Yet there is rich artifice in any commemoration, particularly in the elaborately coordinated events of the twentieth century. This paradox of a natural, powerful love for the poet made manifest in a centrally organized celebration is a constituent feature of the Pushkin myth in Russia.

I will concentrate on the celebrations in 1921, 1924, 1937, and 1999, which show vividly the consequences and contours of this paradoxical

FIGURE 9. Inside cover of the literary monthly *The Star* (*Zvezda*), no. 1 (Feb. 10, 1937). To mark this first number as a commemorative issue, the editors captioned the picture: "One hundred years 'after the death of Alexander Sergeevich Pushkin, great Russian poet, creator of the Russian literary language, and founder of the new Russian literature, who enriched humankind with his immortal creations in artistic language.'" The internal quotation is from a directive of the central committee of the Communist Party (Dec. 16, 1935).

attitude. The most dramatic contrast was in 1937, with its centralized control of jubilation against a background of hidden terror. It is also the best test case against an either-or theory that would see all official celebrations as false, unworthy of those who "truly" love Pushkin. Even in 1937, remarkable individuals participated and important new views of Pushkin emerged. No official imposition of a mandated approach could ever be wholly successful, and each anniversary shows interesting fractures of belief and commitment. Commemorations typically include a great range of events, and within this broad diversity one finds unexpected consistency in Pushkin's ability to help Russia invent itself over time. All these celebrations reveal a transitional society using public rituals for the purposes of cultural exploration and stabilization.

More than the dates of birth and death were marked. To give two examples, in 1923, the hundredth anniversary of Pushkin's arrival in Odessa in 1823 was celebrated, and, in 1926, a Moscow evening and a book commemorated the publication of Pushkin's first volume of poetry in 1826.[1] Still, the most ambitious commemorations noted Pushkin's birth in 1799 or his death in 1837, with greater emphasis on the date of death.[2] Such anniversaries announced their own time lines with date notations like "Pushkin 1837–1937" or "Pushkin 1837–1987" (see Fig. 9). These notations subliminally reorganize the endpoints of the Pushkin story, turning a life lived from 1799 to 1837 into a myth begun in his lifetime and culminating in the present.

Anniversary celebrations are thus in some sense always about time. They shuttle between a remembered past event and an often confusing and demanding present, which accounts for the enormously self-conscious rhetoric. In 1937, for example, powerful contrasts were drawn between average Russians in 1837, enserfed and illiterate, and those of 1937, described as proud workers able to read Pushkin for themselves. As this example shows, a self-conscious glance did not bar shocking distortions (we might characterize many workers in 1937 as more scared than proud). Unlike some museums, the celebrations do not try to erase the years separating readers from Pushkin's lifetime, but attention to the present moment can be oblique. More than one twentieth-century Russian writer has told a story of contemporary Russia through allusion to Pushkin, which they learned from Fyodor Dostoevsky's speech in 1880.

Origins of the Pushkin Jubilees

The three-day June 1880 commemoration held just after Pushkin's birthday that year (May 26, o.s.) did not mark a round date, but it laid the basis for the spectacles of the twentieth century, and many subsequent anniversaries referred to it.³ The gathering celebrated the opening of the Moscow monument to Pushkin. Monuments have remained crucial; indeed a major anniversary for any great writer is likely to yield some public statuary. But no other writer has been honored so often: between 1917 and 1987, 257 monuments to Pushkin were erected on the territory of the former Soviet Union.⁴ They act as what Pierre Nora has called "lieux de mémoire," by which he means a wide range of sites, objects, events, and artifacts that keep alive a memory that risks disappearing. Nora calls them the markers of "commemorative vigilance,"⁵ an apt term for twentieth-century Pushkin anniversaries. The 1880 celebration was also an occasion for national cultural validation. In the words of Marcus C. Levitt, it was "a brief, intoxicating moment when it seemed as if the long and painful conflict between state and nation would be happily and peacefully resolved, the moment when modern Russian national identity consolidated around its literature, with Pushkin as its focus."⁶ Levitt clarifies the important connection between celebration and emerging national identity, using ideas also associated with the work of Benedict Anderson. We might say that there was more imagining than genuine community in 1880: in Levitt's terms, the moment of celebration was "brief" and "intoxicating," when it "seemed" as if a firm national identity had been achieved. The anniversary permitted a fantasy of cultural coherence, one that held the attention of subsequent observers. We look back with some nostalgia to the 1880 celebration. Just imagine a Pushkin celebration where Dostoevsky and Turgenev spoke, and one marked by Tolstoy's proud absence. Our nostalgia will be intensified if we accept Levitt's analysis of the 1880 celebration as the creation of a cultural middle ground, a meeting place for intellectuals and common people that permitted a less polarized vision of national identity. As Levitt's subsequent work shows, this common meeting ground was soon to disappear; the 1899 celebrations were divisive, with most writers refusing to participate in the official celebration.⁷ The perceived split between official (false) spectacles to honor Pushkin and individual (authentic) tributes to him continued through the Soviet era, often as a contrast between émigré attitudes and those of official organizations, but also within the country, where resistance to "commemorative vigilance" persists to this day.

The 1880 celebration would seem to predate such anxieties. The participants appeared indifferent to any official view, which in turn lent their speeches that air of authenticity so important to later commemorations hoping to emulate their ardor. The defining speech was delivered by Dostoevsky. He called Pushkin a moral hero whose characters were passionate in their suffering. In a gesture to be repeated in all subsequent commemorations, Dostoevsky praised Pushkin for idiosyncratic qualities that proved fatefully national. His words were prophetic, but he also saw Pushkin as a prophet, opening his speech with these words: "'Pushkin is an extraordinary phenomenon and perhaps the most singular manifestation of the Russian spirit,' observed Gogol. And I would add: he is a prophetic phenomenon."[8] Dostoevsky recited Pushkin's poem "The Prophet" and became associated with the poem. Many anniversary activities, whether self-consciously religious, as in 1899 and 1999, or not, have aimed to copy Dostoevsky's elevated rhetoric. The claim that Pushkin saw Russia's future lets an orator see the future as well, typically in order to predict greatness for a nation flailing in chaos.

Dostoevsky's speech had one other rhetorical trait that others followed: his deep conviction that the ideas he was expressing were true and eternal, and that they must be expressed in only this form. He sounds like one of his own melodramatic characters when he confesses, "I know, I know only too well that my words may seem excessively fervid, exaggerated, fantastic. Be that as it may, I do not regret having uttered them."[9] Dostoevsky adds that he has said nothing new, and this combination of insistence on his rightness with an intimation that he is merely repeating others' views distinguishes his speech. Later commemorations will occasionally repeat the combination. His specific views, of Pushkin's artistic genius as a function of his salvation, of his incarnation of the chosen nature of suffering Slavic peoples, of the essentially passive nature of his heroes, were not kept fully intact, and their religious underpinnings disappeared during the Soviet period. But the claim for Pushkin's heroic status remained, as did the aspiration of any speaker who invoked it to a lesser heroism by association. Diagnoses of Russia's condition also often followed Dostoevsky's example. Some speakers used this tactic as a form of resistance, saying that Russia was losing touch with Pushkin. This fear was felt palpably in 1921, when the Pushkin commemoration also marked the beginning of post-revolutionary culture and the symbolic end of imperial Russia. By 1924, speakers were more anxious to establish a break with a discredited past, or, if they had emigrated, more anxious about the disappearance of a valuable past. It is to these two commemorations that I now turn.

The Sense of an Ending in 1921

In February 1921, a group of Petrograd writers and cultural activists resolved to make January 29 (o.s.; February 11 n.s.) a nationwide day of mourning for Pushkin.[10] They saw his death as a point of origin for Russian culture: "Modern Russian literature begins with Pushkin. Before Pushkin our literature was a hothouse plant giving pleasure to a few collectors; on the day after Pushkin's death it was a shared phenomenon of primary importance and power, inspiring automatic respect."[11] They created a committee to organize future yearly celebrations, seeking to make Pushkin the equal of other writers (the committee would award prizes from a special fund, similar to those honoring Tolstoy, Turgenev, and Korolenko). They wanted to raise his international stature, too; future anniversaries, they promised, would feature lectures on his influence on foreign literature. There were plans for new publications, and the Institute for the Study of Books (Institut knigovedeniia) organized an exhibit.[12]

None of this could have been very smooth, given the chaos of Petrograd life at the time, and in fact when we think about the 1921 celebration, we hardly recall prizes, publications, and exhibits. February 11, 1921, is remembered for the people who graced the stage, and for the words they spoke; the evening initiated a series of four such gatherings, with new speakers added each time. Many agreed that Alexander Blok was the star, but Blok was in extraordinary company: Vladislav Khodasevich, Nikolai Gumilev, Mikhail Kuzmin, Anna Akhmatova, Anatoly Koni, Boris Eikhenbaum, Pavel Shchegolev, and Boris Modzalevsky spoke, read poetry, or presided. Because Blok died in August of that year, his public appearance was all the more memorable in retrospect, as was his eerie diagnosis of Pushkin as having died not from the bullet fired by d'Anthès but from a lack of air. It soon seemed as if Blok had explained and predicted his own imminent death, enacting a moment of prophecy of the sort Dostoevsky had exemplified.[13] August 1921 also saw the execution of another speaker, Nikolai Gumilev (an ominous early signal of the new Soviet state's treatment of poets), so that the fine words of February looked in retrospect all the more like a last tribute to Russia's Silver Age. Khodasevich would leave for Europe in 1922, as would Marina Tsvetaeva (from Moscow); Velimir Khlebnikov died in 1922; and Soviet repressions would begin variously to affect Mandelstam, Akhmatova, Kuzmin, Kharms, and many others.

The first point about 1921, then, is that it set a twentieth-century standard to which no later commemoration could rise.[14] In that sense, it replicated something of the magic of the 1880 gathering, and it, too, came to represent an ending more than a new beginning in Russia's cultural memory. The public statements made in February 1921 echo with the fear that the values of Golden Age Russian culture were endangered, if not entirely lost.[15] Some speakers reached for a more optimistic if inevitably shaky note. Robert P. Hughes observes that images of Pushkin were formed in an "experience of disorder and dislocation."[16] But only a few of the speeches register the cultural surroundings as inchoate. I suspect that the world looked darkly clear to many who spoke in 1921, although not all were entirely pessimistic.

A. F. Koni (1844–1927), a law professor, former judge, and memoirist, gave the most optimistic speech. He self-consciously set the terms for the celebration but also revealed the paradoxes of the event. His pompous rhetoric should stop us from unduly idealizing the 1921 commemoration. Indeed when we recall grand perorations like his, the uneven quality of the event becomes a more reliable predictor of festivities to come: "The present gathering witnesses the birth of nationwide, all-Russian funeral celebrations of Pushkin, which shall not be marked by passing bursts of feeling or temporary manifestations of sympathy toward one who died young. Rather they shall be constant, yearly, nationwide, repeated with the immutability of a well-known moral law, and they will be a widely understood and recognized holiday for all thinking Russian people."[17] Koni's inflated claims of universal and constant deference were repeated in subsequent twentieth-century anniversaries.

But Koni also had enough insight to be disturbed by the commemoration's unsettling focus on death. He found the juxtaposition of loss and celebration a telling detail:

Death delineates a poet, it draws certain conclusions about him. Finally, and very important, death strikes at the heart with much more force than does birth. Death unites everyone who valued the deceased into a single feeling of grief; death concludes his existence and resounds as the final accord.... With death comes a genuine birth of Russian literature in its genuine sense, the birth of the Russian language in its genuine magnitude and beauty.[18]

The language lapses into repetitive largesse once again, but in a way that explains the emotional value of anniversaries of death. Koni exemplifies the feeling-laden quality of Russia's attention to Pushkin, and, perhaps more important, he turns this death into a birth. This transformation also shows his attitude toward the year 1921, where he sees not the end of an era, as Khodasevich and Blok did, but rather a time for optimism and hope. Koni compares Pushkin to Peter the Great, a symbol of innovation and renewal in Russian culture, and, without saying so explicitly, he suggests that his own time holds a similar promise of greatness: "In his memoirs Dal writes that when Pushkin was dying, he said to him, 'Raise me up, raise me higher, still higher.' And in fact, since then Pushkin has been rising higher and higher, and in the present he has risen in our consciousness to an enormous height. We shall help this, we shall raise him still higher, as high as we physically can."[19]

The metaphor of elevation is subtly different in the speech given by the scholar Boris Eikhenbaum (1886–1959). Unlike Koni's forgotten words, Eikhenbaum's "Problems in Pushkin's Poetics" ("Problemy poetiki Pushkina") continues to be read for its analysis of Pushkin and as an exemplary Formalist text.[20] It chiefly explores Pushkin's connections to eighteenth-century Russian literature. For our purposes, the comments that frame this argument are most important. Apparently he added them to make his essay more like an anniversary speech. Eikhenbaum begins:

It is not accidental, although it is sudden, that Pushkin Days have sprung up here. Life moves through a struggle of contradictory opposites. The renunciation of the past and the revolt against stable traditions urge one to look back, to see if some of what was left behind, abandoned, and forgotten as unnecessary is not close to us and actually quite necessary.[21]

Eikhenbaum goes on to argue that what seems distant is in fact near at hand. He assumes that Pushkin is still loved and that Russians care deeply about preserving that love, but he documents the anxiety that accompanies this affection: "After all that we have lived through in life and in art, everyone is anxious about the question of whether Pushkin is alive or not. And if he is, then what has he become for us?"[22] Eikhenbaum believes that "everyone" worries over this question, so he hardly imagines that Pushkin is *not* "alive."[23]

Eikhenbaum notes a persistent attachment to what might otherwise seem distant. His language pairs opposing descriptive terms (near/distant, new/old, alive/dead, preserved/discarded) but uses them as points of potential similarity. He finds situations in which these opposing terms can come down to the same thing. For example, he remarks that the increasing distance from the early nineteenth century brings Pushkin into sharper focus: "Have we moved so far away that we already see him poorly, or is the distance that separates us from him precisely what is needed in order to see things in their entirety, without losing the details?"[24] This technique persists in the body of the essay. Pushkin's connections to the eighteenth century, and thus to a "classical" period, actually link him more profoundly to the present, where Eikhenbaum finds a new classicism in the poetry of Mandelstam, Akhmatova, and Kuzmin.

Eikhenbaum also claims that Russia's very nearness to Pushkin has until now actually obscured him from sight. This extreme proximity has reduced him in size: "Pushkin has become not a monument, but a little gypsum statue."[25] The reference to a statue is common in anniversary speeches,[26] but Eikhenbaum uses the image idiosyncratically. He says that the Futurists rightly urged throwing Pushkin off the ship of modernity, if, that is, they had in mind the Pushkin reduced to pitiful insignificance by writers like Vissarion Belinsky (who, for all his admiration of Pushkin, is seen by Eikhenbaum as formulaic and inflexible in his thinking).[27] Eikhenbaum suggests that Russians must learn to recognize a different side of Pushkin. Others will soon argue that Pushkin's political beliefs can make him pertinent in the post-revolutionary period, but Eikhenbaum's rescue is insistently apolitical and aesthetic. He saves Pushkin by reference to poets whom the new regime will target as despised.

Eikhenbaum's speech, like Koni's, was based on a belief that Pushkin was valued in Russia in 1921, but public opinion was divided on this point. Journalistic accounts solidly document the split. Although one literary newspaper noted a new yearning for culture created by the revolution and an unusual interest in Pushkin, another reported on a debate in Vladikavkaz about whether Pushkin was a bourgeois or counterrevolutionary writer.[28] Pushkin's politics were already in question in the 1920s.[29] In the 1921 declaration making the Pushkin celebration a yearly event, the organizers used an incipiently political analysis of literary process and of government involvement in culture.[30] Their perspective echoed and extended the utilitarian aesthetics advocated in the nineteenth century by Nikolai Chernyshevsky and Dmitri Pisarev (the very terms Eikhenbaum was challenging when he named Belinsky as his target). They had also resounded, albeit in somewhat different tones, in Futurist manifestos. These acts to rescue Pushkin were forward-looking and in several senses progressive. Not so the speeches of Khodasevich and Blok.

The words of the poet Vladislav Khodasevich (1886–1939) combined a much more appealing rhetoric and style than Koni offered with as keen a knowledge of Pushkin as we find in Eikhenbaum. As John Malmstad has noted, Khodasevich's speech, "The Swaying Tripod" ("Koleblemyi trenozhnik"), seemed especially intense just after Eikhenbaum's dispassionate analysis (and it attacked the Formalists, including Eikhenbaum).[31] Khodasevich agrees that attitudes toward Pushkin have changed, but his approach to the changes is more capacious. The rich semantic possibilities in Pushkin's writings enable, he says, a bewildering range of responses. And it is these responses, rather than Pushkin's words, that Khodasevich urges us to consider.[32] The most valuable responses come from those whose turn of mind resembles Pushkin's, which nicely privileges Khodasevich's views, given his aesthetic similarity to Pushkin,[33] but it also yields an uncomfortable criticism of Mikhail Gershenzon's book *Pushkin's Wisdom* (*Mudrost' Pushkina*, 1919) as the work of someone with a vastly different cast of mind. (Khodasevich's affectionate memoir about Gershenzon reveals his esteem.)[34]

When Khodasevich adds that "Gershenzon must be seen as standing on that unseen boundary with which history divides epochs,"[35] he suggests the more general discontinuity of Russian history that marks his speech, and he reveals a profound awareness of the cultural break that his age constitutes. Russia's historical time line is broken by ruptures that have the power to change the way we view the world:

Our history has made such a leap that the result is a kind of void between yesterday and today, as psychologically unhealthy as an open wound. And everything around us has changed: not only the political order and all social relations, but also the external order, the rhythm of life, its shape, our way of life, and style. We have new habits, customs, clothes, even, if you will, fashions. The Petersburg that we walk through on our way home today is not the Petersburg of the recent past. The world surrounding us has become something different.[36]

Khodasevich rejects the idea of a return to the past: "The Petrine and Petersburg period of Russian history has ended; no matter what lies ahead, the old will not return. A return is unthinkable both historically and psychologically."[37] This last point puts him into conflict with the return-oriented thinkers of the Silver Age, well described by Irina Paperno.[38] He stresses not the cyclical nature of time, but its brokenness, its segmentation into periods that hold the possibility for complete rupture.[39] He fears that his age marks the end of a time connected by signs of similarity to the age of Pushkin.

Khodasevich sees around himself rising incomprehension of the Pushkin period and ignorance of its basic vocabulary. "It may happen that the general twilight of our culture will clear," he suggests, but a doomed future seems to him more likely: "What I have called the eclipse of Pushkin will stretch out for a long time and it will not disappear without a trace. The historical break with the previous Pushkin epoch will push Pushkin into the depths of history forever. That closeness to Pushkin within which we grew up shall never be repeated."[40] Khodasevich sees his age as a moment when it may not yet be too late. This chronological diagnosis responds to the obviously paradoxical situation in which he places himself. Among his benighted contemporaries, he is one of the few who exemplifies increased attention to Pushkin. He uses that paradox of attention to do two things common to anniversary speeches: to meditate on Pushkin's face and to restate the salutary effects of love.

But never will Russian culture's permanent, blood tie to Pushkin be broken. It will merely take on a new hue. Like us, our descendants will never cease to trod the land they will inherit from Pushkin, because we have nowhere to go from this land. But it will be divided up and many times over plowed again and in different ways. And the very name of the one who gave this land and watered it with his blood will at times be forgotten.

Cast aside into the "haze of centuries," Pushkin will arise there in a colossal image. National pride will be molded into indestructible bronze forms because of him, but future generations will not know our immediate nearness or that heartfelt tenderness with which we loved. This happiness will not be given to them. They will no longer see Pushkin's face as we saw him. This mysterious face, the face of a demigod, will change, as at times it seems as if the bronze face of a statue changes.[41]

For Khodasevich the world is changing, even the face of Pushkin himself, creating the most memorable image in an essay brimming with metaphors. Khodasevich predicts, in a different arrangement, the question posed by Stanislav Rassadin in the 1980s (discussed in the Introduction): his concern is not what happens to us when we look at Pushkin, but how is the face of Pushkin changing beneath our gaze. By likening it to the changing face of a statue, Khodasevich invokes the Pushkinian image of a monument come to life (in *The Bronze Horseman, Mednyi Vsadnik*, 1833, a poem Khodasevich mentions, and in *The Stone Guest, Kamennyi gost'*, 1830).[42] Pushkin's statues can be threatening, even apocalyptic, and Khodasevich, too, sees the changing face as a terrifying end point when a loving contemplation of Pushkin is no longer possible.

He concludes with a last metaphor, that of a word with magical powers:

Perhaps the lively interest in the poet of the last few years has come from a sense of foreboding and urgent need: a need to understand Pushkin before it is too late, before the connection with his time is completely lost, and a passionate desire to feel his closeness as we live through its last hours. Our desire to make the day of Pushkin's death into a popular [*narodnyi*] celebration has been prompted in part, I think, by the same foreboding: we are deciding what name to use as a password, how to call out to one another in the gathering gloom.[43]

These beautiful lines anticipate a bleak future when the name "Pushkin" becomes a password that can be called out by those hoping to recognize kindred spirits in the dark. Khodasevich accepts the burden of cultural preservation and social connection, saying that it is "we" who choose the words to call out as night falls. He would go on to write prolifically about Pushkin, but from a distance, both geographical and spiritual. As in Blok's speech, an imminent future seems predicted by Khodasevich's words.

As it happens, Khodasevich did not give this speech on the first evening of the commemoration. He was an observer that night, February 11, when Gumilev came late and left early, and Akhmatova, Koni, Kuzmin, and Shchegolev sat at the presidium. Perhaps because he was not performing, he left a vivid memoir of the evening, from which we learn that he was greatly impressed by Blok's speech.[44] He heard it as "deeply tragic" and perhaps as an act of "repentance" for Blok's earlier enthusiasm for the revolution. He wrote: "The author of *The Twelve* bequeathed to Russian society and Russian literature a duty to preserve Pushkin's last legacy: freedom, even if only 'secret' freedom. While he was speaking, one felt how the wall between him and the audience gradually fell down. In the ovations that accompanied his departure, there was that radiant joy that always comes with a reconciliation with someone one loves [*liubimyi chelovek*]."[45]

This description resembles Khodasevich's views of Pushkin in the image of rapturous adoration. He also has Blok deliver part of Pushkin's inheritance, as if they were so similar that Blok can tap into the same mysterious freedom. The similarity recalls the premise of "The Swaying Tripod," that to speak truthfully of Pushkin, one must be like him.[46] Pushkin is not, then, merely a password to be called out in the dark, but also a poet to emulate. For all the pessimism of Khodasevich's speech, he believes that modern poets and critics may yet resemble Pushkin. Subsequent anniversary events may not state this premise so categorically, but they will live out its logic. Khodasevich's passionate, self-referential words forewarn of the inclination of twentieth-century poets to inform their poems and essays about Pushkin with their own autobiographies.

To turn now directly to Blok's speech, "The Poet's Calling" ("O naznachenii poeta"), I begin by noting how it condenses and sharpens many of the images and rhetorical assumptions of other 1921 speeches. Blok displaces their basic time lines, particularly the contrast between "old" and "new" that motivated Khodasevich, Eikhenbaum, and Koni. When he uses a word like *new,* he does so without reference to place or history. He writes in the absolutist terms of Symbolism, where time is not so much divided among past, present, and future as between apparent movement within the present and the truer movements of the cosmos. Blok writes about eternity, and in leaving behind the time lines of an anniversary occasion, he sets an example for later work by poets like Mayakovsky and Tsvetaeva. He has his own predecessor in this tradition, Dostoevsky, once again building on the 1880 speech.

Blok writes about the poet as a different order of being. "What is the poet? A person who writes in verse? No, of course not. He is called a poet not because he writes in verse; rather, he writes in verse, that is, he brings words and sounds into harmonious relation because he is a son of harmony, a poet."[47] When Blok describes the process by which poetry is created, he quotes Pushkin and seems to follow him in having the poet nearly deified by the act of turning sounds into poems. This poetic act wills the chaotic world into harmonious order:

Harmony is the consonance of universal forces, the order of the universe's life. Order is the cosmos, in contrast, disorder is chaos. From chaos the cosmos is born, the ancients taught. . . . Chaos is the primordial, elemental anarchy; the cosmos is ordered harmony, culture. . . . The poet is the son of harmony, and he is given a certain role in world culture. Three tasks are placed on him: first, to free sounds from the native anarchic element in which they originate; second, to bring these sounds into harmony, to give them form; and third, to bring this harmony forth into the external world.[48]

Blok makes the poet a god who can bring order from chaos, but with some down-to-earth, daily points of reference. Recalling Robert Hughes's characterization of 1921 as a period of chaotic cultural and social change, we can read Blok as referring allegorically to his immediate world.

Tragically, poets cannot bear the burden Blok describes for very long. Even Pushkin had his limits, as the most quoted passage in the speech suggests: "And it absolutely was not d'Anthès's bullet that killed Pushkin. He was killed by the absence of air. And his culture was dying with him."[49] The third of these three sentences, less often cited, shows Blok adding to the poet's responsibility and burden. For when the poet cannot breathe, when harmonious sounds cannot be drawn out from the chaos of sound, then the entire culture is fated to perish. Here Blok's most dire prediction resounds. It had been heard, fleetingly, at earlier moments in the speech, for example, when he traced a word to its specific Pushkinian meaning and added warily that "a Pushkin dictionary will clarify this matter—if Russian culture is reborn," or when he wondered whether ever-greater obstacles would soon be placed in the poet's path.[50]

Blok has little faith in Russian culture to bring about this rebirth, and his final three commonsensical reminders, merely by needing to be spoken, emerge as a scathing commentary on the post-revolutionary world: "Art has no special properties; one should not give the name 'art' to that which is not to be called 'art'; in order to create a work of art, one must know how."[51] Here, as in Eikhenbaum's attack on Belinsky, Blok unerringly zeroes in on pieties that will soon be Soviet doctrine. What he saw in 1921 was not only that Russia's poets would die from oppressions of many kinds, but that modes of thinking about poetry and art were changing. Past Pushkin anniversaries had celebrated eternal values that were now endangered, as Blok saw it. Within three short years, in 1924, the shift he feared would begin. Still, some moments of insight and affection persisted, in a pattern true of all anniversary celebrations. I turn now to two Soviet commemorations, 1924 and 1937, one struggling to establish a different new era, the other aiming to fulfill its promises, and to cover over the terror being established as the Soviet way of life.

The Founding Rituals of 1924

In 1924 Anatoly Lunacharsky, the commissar of education, predicted that "in a short period of time, Pushkin will not only shine like a star in the skies of earthly and eternal values, but also those of cold and distant values. He will live as an instance of the present and a great teacher of the new life."[52] If the 1921 anniversary was marked by the fear that a valued cultural order was ending, then the 1924 events seemed a fine new beginning. In 1922 the Pushkin days were moved from February, the time of his death, to his birthday in June (in the new calendar style), which fit the one hundred twenty-fifth anniversary approaching in 1924. The new Soviet cultural order was consolidating. The celebration coincided with a year of hard struggle for a "peacefully organized and wisely functioning social economy," as one newspaper had it.[53] Pushkin seemed less dear to the hearts of his readers in the aftermath of revolution and civil war, and Tolstoy's status as the preeminent national literary figure was now firmer.[54] The Futurists' rejection of Pushkin as old-fashioned and the Proletarian poets' dismissal of him because of his aristocratic class position created some problems for Soviet cultural leaders.[55] They began to recreate Pushkin as a hero for the new order. A much reprinted statement by Lunacharsky and similar editorials laid the foundation for a positive political reading of his life and works. They emphasized the democratizing sentiments of poems like "The Upas Tree" ("Anchar," 1828) and *The Bronze Horseman*. Pushkin's way of grounding himself in the here and now was read as a kind of cheerful materialism; the final lines of Pushkin's "Bacchic Song" ("Vakkhicheskaia pesn'," 1825), which would be cited obsessively in 1937, seemed to prove this point.[56] At least one newspaper had the courage to describe this kind of reading as utter nonsense, expressing horror that Pushkin had practically been turned into a Communist.[57]

To bolster this faltering logic, some journalists appealed to authority. Hence the prominence given Comrade Sosnovsky's 1924 essay "Why Lenin Loved Pushkin," which claims that Lenin *resembled* Pushkin—in his simplicity, optimism, love for nature, and respect for common people.[58] It was not an easy case to make, since Lenin wrote no essays on Pushkin, and he apparently preferred Tolstoy (a 1918 decree listing candidates for new monuments has Tolstoy first among writers, Pushkin fourth; Tolstoy's Moscow house came under government protection in April 1920, two years before equivalent status was conferred on Pushkin's Mikhailovskoe).[59] Creating a Soviet Pushkin faced challenges, and the first significant commemoration, 1924, in many ways lacked coherence. Its tentativeness exposed the way rituals to honor Pushkin were selected, codified, and made to seem authoritative.

Many 1924 events concentrated on Mikhailovskoe and nearby Sviatogorsk Monastery and Trigorskoe, an emphasis facilitated by new memoirs and guidebooks about the area.[60] Some programmatic statements stressed the importance of the region to Pushkin personally.[61] On June 6, the preserve officially opened with a gathering at Sviatogorsk Monastery and a procession on foot to Mikhailovskoe. A tourist station displayed wreaths that had been laid at Pushkin's grave in 1899 and some old photographs (presumably as the area looked before the destructions of the civil war). These events were attended by scholars, writers, and educational workers from Moscow and Leningrad brought by special excursion. Among the treats planned for them was a local school performance of "Pushkin in Mikhailovskoe Village," where guests from the region and local peasants joined them.[62]

Conditions in Mikhailovskoe were far from ideal. The tourist station erected for the special exhibit, for example, resembled an army barracks.[63] The estate showed the remains of what had been destroyed, not a shrine to what had been preserved. A 1923 observer had lamented "the frightening and bitter fact of the destruction of the Pushkin nook, which transformed the poet's beautiful estate into 'nothing,' and pushed the estate into the *irretrievable past*."[64] Another described the site of Pushkin's former house as "a pile of stones overgrown with burdock and nettles. The broad stairs down to the river have fallen apart and are overgrown with bushes that obscure the view of the river and lake. To the right, if you look toward the river, you see something that isn't exactly a barn, and isn't exactly a gazebo as landowners used to have. On the left is the slightly cleaned up little house of Pushkin's nanny, and to the rear are two barely standing houses for writers."[65] The official speeches took place in a converted barn, with benches brought in for the guests.[66] Visitors from Leningrad and Moscow took turns sleeping on the few beds (and wrote poems to commemorate the one who ended up on the floor).[67] The opening ceremonies went on for several days. One scholar found the sessions "tolerable"; another said they gave grounds for a migraine.[68] Ideas for a monument to Pushkin cropped up, and proposals and competitions were discussed in the newspapers (but a monument was not to be erected until 1959).[69] Dreary as some found the occasion, official accounts in 1924 were predictably positive, and they announced a name change of the sort that came to characterize Soviet commemorations—the hills of Sviatye Gory, where the Sviatogorsk Monastery is located (and where Pushkin is buried) became Pushgkinskie Gory.[70]

The June events had their echo within two months when further celebrations marked the centenary of Pushkin's arrival in exile in Mikhailovskoe in August 1824. An inaugural Pushkin conference (*Pushkinskie chteniia*) was held. At the end of August 1924, parks were being cleaned and ponds readied for the anticipated guests.[71] Another special train excursion brought visitors from Leningrad, including some who had attended the June events, and also the poet Anna Akhmatova.[72] Events again featured a ceremony at the grave, a walking excursion, and an evening of poetry. Some additions showed a nascent urge to centralize control over ideas about Mikhailovskoe (a talk on excursion methodology, a political meeting for delegates and workers, a meeting on the fate of the preserve).[73] One Proletarian poet, on returning from the celebration, enthused about the genuine feeling of connection between the literary representatives and local peasants: "The peasants experienced Pushkin in their emotions for the first time. Many of them said that if they had known earlier who Pushkin was, then neither his home in Mikhailovskoe nor the estate in Trigorskoe would have been burnt down."[74] As if to substantiate this new enthusiasm for Pushkin, a society for friends of the preserve was formed (not unlike the Pushkin Society of the 1910s that had struggled to have Mikhailovskoe declared a state preserve), and readers of the Leningrad newspaper were told how to join up.[75] Yet, as we know from the previous chapter, debates about the fate of Mikhailovskoe extended well past 1924. Land continued to be wrested from peasants, illegal logging and poaching went on and was punished, and officials kept changing plans for the Pushkin preserve.[76]

There were also official gatherings in Leningrad and Moscow in June 1924, close in design if not in spirit to the 1921 evenings. The Writers' Union was more efficiently in charge in both cities. Speeches included news of archival finds; among the poets who read Pushkin's work and their own were Akhmatova, Nikolai Kliuev, Mikhail Kuzmin, Konstantin Vaginov, and Vladimir Piast (in Leningrad) and Sergei Esenin and Sergei Gorodetsky (in Moscow).[77] A surprising inclusion among the speech-makers in Moscow was the Symbolist poet Viacheslav Ivanov—surprising because he seemed so much a part of pre-Soviet culture.[78] But where in 1921 many of the speeches were published in a book within a year, and a Petrograd newspaper ran several of them in full, the record of the 1924 celebrations in the two principal cities is relatively sparse, and perhaps the presence of so many "holdover" cultural figures accounts for that.[79] We may never know which poems these poets read, or whether they chose them themselves. Might Kuzmin have read his 1921 poem about Pushkin? Akhmatova probably did read the third poem in her 1911 cycle "In Tsarskoe Selo" ("V Tsarskom Sele") that evokes a youthful Pushkin.

Outside official events, however, the anniversary elicited two reactions from poets that are quite telling. The first was exemplified by Vladimir Mayakovsky (1893–1930). If Mayakovsky was "the deadest Russian poet of the twentieth century," as a 1994 *Times Literary Supplement* review stated,[80] the writer of this outlandish claim was only giving Mayakovsky a taste of the hyperbolic style that he himself perfected. Such a poet would not participate modestly in anniversary gatherings. Yuri Karabchievsky called him the only poet to base his work on blood and force: Mayakovsky "always applies force to an object in order to make it expressive; he uses the same force with his words."[81] But it is too easy to conclude that Mayakovsky flatly resisted the mythic adoration of Pushkin that anniversaries required, or that he substituted violence for admiration. In fact, his aggressive language typically reveals deep feelings of affection, and the man who signed the 1912 Futurist manifesto urging that Pushkin be thrown off the ship of modernity comes close in 1924 to speaking of him as Russia's "first love."[82]

In "The Anniversary Poem" ("Iubileinoe," 1924), Mayakovsky speaks in direct address to Pushkin. After a formal introduction, he mixes tender reassurances with commanding assertions and a fantastic plot: Mayakovsky removes the Pushkin statue from Tver Boulevard in Moscow and takes the poet out for a little chat.

> I am dragging you.
>   You are surprised, of course?
> Did I squeeze you?
>   Does it hurt?
>   Pardon me, my dear.
>
> Я тащу вас.
>   Удивляетесь, конечно?
> Стиснул?
>   Больно?
>   Извините, дорогой.[83]

With none of the violence of the sort that Karabchievsky and others have noted, the poet's will exerts inordinate pressure on all events in this poem, beginning with the removal of the statue. The tone, typically Mayakovskian in its declarative authority and forward propulsion, also contributes to an image of a powerful speaker in full control of the poetic act. He does not really engage in conversation with Pushkin;[84] nor is he the involuntary recipient of a visit from Pushkin's ghostly presence, as other poets have portrayed themselves. It would be too strong to say that Pushkin is hardly present in the poem (in fact, Mayakovsky includes images from *Eugene Onegin* and biographical motifs, like the last duel), but his presence works solely to facilitate Mayakovsky's own monologue. He wonders whether he will be next to Pushkin when he too is dead, "M" coming near "P" in the alphabet, and he considers other contemporary poets who might join them. This long speculation seems to be one of the poem's central points, a sort of mental riffling through the poets of the present. "My country / is all too poor / in poets" ("Chereschur / strana moia / poetami nishcha"); and, later in the poem, "but we have, / alas, / no poets" ("Tol'ko vot / poetov, / k sozhalen'iu, netu").[85]

How we hear these two assertions determines our response to Mayakovsky's poem. Is the poet simply blind to others, filled with self-love to the point of narcissism?[86] Or do these comments resound with tragedy and loss, with a sense that the land of the Soviets is impoverishing itself of poets? I think that Mayakovsky might well want us to take the former tack, to be so impressed with the poem's verbal pyrotechnics that we see it as focused on himself, but there are powerful emotional contradictions in the poem, and its aftereffect is remarkably sad. For all the bombast, Mayakovsky writes a tender, tragic love poem to Pushkin, despite his claims to be free from love: "I / now / am liberated / from love / and from posters" ("Ia / teper' / svoboden / ot liubvi / i ot plakatov").[87] The liberation from love refers to his own final break with Lilia Brik and makes the poem's tragedy personal. The thematic interweaving of love's language into "The Anniversary Poem" creates the springboard from which Mayakovsky's self-assertions propel themselves. What he most wants to say to Pushkin comes in an irreverent paraphrase from *Eugene Onegin*:

> What was it
>   you had
>   Olga saying?..
> No, not Olga!
>   it's from the letter
>   Onegin wrote to Tatiana.
> He says,
>   your husband
>   is a fool
>   and an old gelding
> I love you,
>   be mine, without fail,
> I must know
>   with certainty this morning
> that I will see you again this afternoon.
>
> Как это
>   у вас
>   говаривала Ольга?..
> Да не Ольга!
>   из письма
>   Онегина к Татьяне.
> —Дескать,
>   муж у вас
>   дурак
>   и старый мерин,
> я люблю вас,
>   будьте обязательно моя,
> я сейчас же
>   утром должен быть уверен,
> что с вами днем увижусь я.[88]

Without mocking Pushkin's poem, Mayakovsky pokes fun at the intense familiarity of its language and readers' knowing reactions. No educated Russian could attribute Onegin's passionate letter to the predictable Olga; and readers will also recognize the transposition of the dream scene here (Onegin says "Mine!" to Tatiana in her nightmare, not in his tender, pleading letter). The lines ridicule newly literate readers of Pushkin, whose garbled accounts of *Onegin* and other texts would have mixed genuine uncertainty with a confusion of details. Mayakovsky recapitulates Pushkin's words so that he may himself speak them back to the poet, and as in Bakhtin's account of parody, he thereby endows his own speech act with greater verbal authority.⁸⁹ Yet tremendous humility emerges in the self-comparison to Onegin: he likens himself to a man who learns too late what it means to love, and he exposes his vulnerability in confessing a need, like Onegin's, to know each morning that he will see his beloved by day's end.⁹⁰

When he characterizes d'Anthès, he speaks mockingly, mixing contemporary references and down-to-earth spoken Russian. All humility has vanished when Mayakovsky calls d'Anthès a son of a bitch, and says, "We would ask him, / 'And who were *your* parents?/ / What did you do / *before* 1917?'" ("My b ego sprosili: / —A vashi *kto* roditeli?/ / Chem vy zanimalis'/ *do* 17-go goda?").⁹¹ The echo of Soviet interrogations of citizens' class origins has an implied threat of violence typical of Mayakovsky's way of resorting to force in his poetry.⁹² But there is also a desperate quality to the offer of police interrogation as an expression of his bond to Pushkin. You can tell that he has gotten too close to the bone with these lines because he makes fun of them immediately: "But / what kind of blather! / It's practically spiritualism" ("Vprochem, / chto zh boltan'e! / Spiritizma vrode").⁹³ Mayakovsky thinks about how Soviet cultural institutions might draw him nearer to Pushkin, imagining that he could get Pushkin a job as an editor at *Lef*, even trusting him to do agit-prop work with his "swell style" ("khoroshii slog").⁹⁴

Mayakovsky notes ruefully that "it's just great here / in the Land of the Soviets. // One can live, / one can work with friendly ease" ("Khorosho u nas / v Strane sovetov. // Mozhno zhit', / rabotat' mozhno druzhno").⁹⁵ The references to agit-prop work, *Lef*, and the secret police (and, elsewhere in the poem, to the GUM department store, the "Koopsakh" sugar cooperative, the central committee, and the police) draw Soviet daily life into this fantastic poem.⁹⁶ These realia are typical of Mayakovsky's poetry, and they poignantly rub against the poem's earlier claim to take place in a time called eternity ("I, / and you, too, / have all of eternity in store. // What's it to us / to lose / an hour or two?!"; "U menia, / da i u vas, / v zapase vechnost'. // Chto nam / poteriat' / chasok-drugoi?!").⁹⁷ Like Blok, Mayakovsky wishes to speak outside time, reaching across the centuries to bring Pushkin back to life; or, more precisely, he speaks against time, pointing to his solitude and his disdain for the very social institutions that fix his poem in temporality.

This "Anniversary Poem" stands in self-conscious proximity to anniversary commemorations. It omits public rituals from the list of new Soviet phenomena, positing a private conversation between the two poets, one that is in sufficient violation of social norms to require that the poet replace Pushkin's statue on its pedestal before the police notice the theft. Mayakovsky sets his relation to Pushkin in contrast to what others in his society are doing, as a kind of crime. The very choice of the monument as the object of his transgression and as the embodiment of Pushkin puts this poem into a public context. Like Khodasevich in "The Swaying Tripod," Mayakovsky wills the monument to life, as if the culture that erected it has left Pushkin for dead; he disparages the treatment of Pushkin at every turn. He warns him to beware of the "Pushkinists" (a term that for him means both scholars and public officials), and he announces, "Perhaps / I / alone / really regret // That today / you are not among the living"("Mozhet / ia / odin / deistvitel'no zhaleiu, // chto segodnia / netu vas v zhivykh."[98] When Mayakovsky so strongly singles himself out, he invokes the cultural commemoration of Pushkin as a contrasting and diminished background. He has penned an idiosyncratic anniversary poem, but in its declaration of a unique relationship with a misunderstood Pushkin, "The Anniversary Poem" recreates an authentic love for him. Mayakovsky declares, "I love you, but alive, not as a mummy. / They've given you an anthology gloss" ("Ia liubliu vas, / no zhivogo, / a ne mumiiu. // Naveli / khrestomatiinyi glianets").[99]

Vladislav Khodasevich, after emigrating in 1922, wrote two short poems in 1924 that also reinstated an absent love. His "Romance" ("Romans," 1924) extends and completes a Pushkin fragment, "The night is silent, and in the heavenly expanse" ("Noch' tikha, v nebesnom pole," date uncertain, between 1827 and 1836).[100] It was published by the journal *Russia* (*Rossiia*) to lead off its section "Pushkin 1799–1924."[101] After five lines taken from Pushkin,[102] the poem tells of inner sadness and isolation. Pushkin described an old doge with a young wife, from which Khodasevich spins the tale of a couple living in separate emotional worlds; the doge's attempt to take his wife's hand, to reach out to her with affection, leads only to further retreat. Romance turns to silent withdrawal. The sense of isolation may refer to Khodasevich's attitudes toward Russia, and the final lines ordering a homeward return suggest a wished-for return. The poem associates return with renewed attention to a shared cultural heritage; poetry resounds through the quiet Venetian night, when the gondolier sings Tasso (with whom Pushkin identified during his exile), and poetry has the power to renew emotions and hopes even if the renewal is in vain.[103] Two others had completed this poem: A. N. Maikov, in 1888 ("The Old Doge," "Staryi dozh") and S. Golovachevsky, in 1906. Ought poets "complete" someone else's work? That question animated an argument, and Khodasevich excluded the poem from collections of his verse.[104] We know from his "Swaying Tripod" speech that Khodasevich believed strongly that one should speak about Pushkin from the perspective of similarity. To complete a Pushkin fragment would risk an arrogant claim that one could write with his simplicity and perfection, and perhaps Khodasevich felt "Romance" did not live up to Pushkin's standards.

The second poem, "He left his carriage at the gate" ("Ostavil drozhki u zastavy," 1924), imagines the emotions Pushkin might have felt on what was to be his last birthday, and it, too, enacts a return, this time to a place, Mikhailovskoe, itself a scene of return in Pushkin's writings (in "... Once again I visited"). The poem is filled with reminders of impending death. It is structured as a retrospective (Pushkin's) within a retrospective (Khodasevich's):

> He left his carriage at the gate,
>   He strolled pensively on.
> Here, look now: the oak groves
>   Stand encircled around.
>
> Until recently he had dreamed of going there,
>   To his own fields!
> Now the groves, the peasant women, and all the land around
>   Are unbearable.
>
> Now he is stuffed to the gills
>   With the lofty and the low,
> And only to the shades beyond Styx
>   Does the soul fly off.
>
> Now both dreams and life itself are a burden
>   That is too much to bear.
> Be silent, Parca! That will do, Muse!
>   Enough from you all.

> Оставил дрожки у заставы,
>   Побрел пешком.
> Ну вот, смотри теперь: дубравы
>   Стоят кругом.
>
> Недавно ведь мечтал: туда бы,
>   В свои поля!
> Теперь несносны рощи, бабы
>   И вся земля.
>
> Уж и возвышенным и низким
>   По горло сыт,
> И только к теням застигийским
>   Душа летит.
>
> Уж и мечта и жизнь—обуза
>   Не по плечам.
> Умолкни, Парка! Полно, Муза!
>   Довольно вам![105]

Khodasevich comes close to repudiating "... Once again I visited" with this poem. His meter tightens and seems to break up Pushkin's graceful iambic pentameter, and his rhymes accentuate the sharp breaks. He has Pushkin leaving a carriage at the gate to walk, as opposed to Pushkin's memory of riding horseback or sitting dreamily; he gives us an oak grove with bushes intolerable to the eye, whereas Pushkin's well-known pine trees nurture seedlings beneath their heights. The new trees inspire not disgust but hope in Pushkin for the pleasures they will bring to future descendants (we might hear an echo of those pine trees, *sosny*, in Khodasevich's epithet that means "unbearable, intolerable," *nesnosny*). And rather than Pushkin's tender reference to Arina Rodionovna, his companion in Mikhailovskoe, Khodasevich mentions peasant women (*baby*), whose appearance is oppressive. (They recall more precisely the peasants who appear in "My ruddy-faced critic," "Rumianyi kritik moi," 1830.)

Pushkin ends "... Once again I visited" with a calm acceptance of death and the hope of future visitors to create continuity. Khodasevich's poem exudes neither equanimity nor hope. Anger fills the last lines, where life at present and dreams for the future bring pain. Is Khodasevich writing a biographically accurate account of Pushkin's last birthday? The answer has to be no. Pushkin was on Stone Island (Kamennyi ostrov), living in a summer dacha with his family on May 26, 1835. He arrived from Moscow on the evening of May 23, only hours after his daughter Natalia was born. Pushkin expressed joy at Natalia Nikolaevna's safe passage through childbirth and at their new daughter, and in the following days he had renewed visits with friends and paid some attention to publication details of the second and third issues of *The Contemporary* (*Sovremennik*). On May 26 he went to some bookstores, and his brother and sister joined in a family celebration at the dacha.[106] Khodasevich may not have known every one of these details (I have culled them from S. L. Abramovich's scrupulous 1991 account), but he generally knew the facts of Pushkin's life well, and he would hardly have imagined him depressed so soon after the birth of his daughter, since his affectionate happiness in his children is well attested.

Khodasevich writes, then, not so much about Pushkin as about a returning poet, about the backward glance of a birthday, and about the fearful look ahead to an impending end. Again, we may read allegorically to note Khodasevich's projection of his own anxieties. It may not be irrelevant that his birthday came in May (May 28 n.s.), and that in some of his other poems from this period, he says that he has reached the halfway point in his life, and that he feels abandoned in some profound way.[107] His other 1924 anniversary statement argues that Pushkin's poetry was autobiographical, and that all poetry shares this autobiographical project; the same argument informs his book-length study, *Pushkin's Poetic Economy* (*Poeticheskoe khoziaistvo Pushkina*, 1924).[108]

"He left his carriage at the gate" also makes a more broadly cultural and historical point. Khodasevich says not that one cannot go back, but that going back brings one face to face with the hopelessness of the present and the impossibility of a future. After the moment of return, Khodasevich suggests, comes death. The only movement possible in such a revisitation will be the soul's flight toward death. In that observation, this birthday poem also offers us a final thought about the public commemoration of a poet's birth date. Khodasevich implies that the transfer of anniversary celebrations from the date of death to the date of birth in 1924 had no effect beyond its timing. The occasion is still marked by death, as is the myth of Pushkin. To look back at Pushkin is to look back upon a scene of loss, and aside from the falsely optimistic journalistic accounts in 1924, there are few texts from the period that suggest anything else.

The "Great" Jubilee: 1937

More than other rituals celebrating the consolidation of Soviet power, the 1937 jubilee was significant for its forceful recuperation of an episode from the imperial past.[109] The national poet was seen anew, transformed into a hero that the new Soviet man could admire, if not emulate. David Brandenberger has rightly noted that "Pushkin was more useful alive than dead," and a poet who had seemed an aristocrat with European sensibilities in the aftermath of the revolution now provided the first test for a new style of "mobilizational politics."[110] As another scholar, Arlen Blium, has put it, "The regime needed a certain legitimization, and the great ghosts of the past were perfectly suited to this task."[111] A "mythologized, heroic view of the past" was created, and the 1937 anniversary provided the perfect occasion to elevate Pushkin, his "'shining image'... singled out as a model for 'the new Soviet man.'"[112] Pushkin's ability to see himself as Russian and to envision a different future for his nation was crucial.[113] He was well suited to this new role, despite his class background, which was at times discussed but always in order to show that his love for Russia's language and people (*narod*) overcame the liabilities of being an aristocrat.[114] And his writings were consonant with the spirit of vitality, energy, and optimism required of the new Soviet hero.[115] They were praised for their simplicity and clarity.[116] The new slogan of realism was stretched to fit the emerging canon of Pushkin's writings. Censors and party officials kept a tight watch on quotations from the political writings, ensuring that they could not be misread as anti-revolutionary and that inferences about Pushkin's changing political views could not be easily drawn.[117] More easily available and readily cited in academic journals and the popular press were his historical writings and lyrics with social content, such as "My ruddy-faced critic," with its understated description of life in poverty.[118]

Yet it was not a grim Pushkin whom the Soviets emphasized, far from it. Among his most widely reprinted poems was "Bacchic Song," with its rousing last line "Let the sun shine forth, let darkness be hidden!" ("Da zdravstvuet solntse, da skroetsia t'ma!").[119] Praise for the light of day and denunciation of excess when reason should flourish were themes that resonated well with public discourse in the mid-1930s. The tenor of public celebration in a time of hidden arrests is now easier to assess: a revealing set of newsreels from the 1930s became available in 1999 in Pavel Gromov's film *Three Songs of Pushkin* (*Tri pesni o Pushkine*). Its first "song" is about the Stalin period and bears a telling Pushkinian title, *Feast in Time of Plague* (*Pir vo vremia chumy*, 1830). Gromov interprets the 1937 jubilee as a false celebration in a desperate time. Pushkin may remain, as one observer put it in 1999, the writer who could withstand any jubilee,[120] but the celebrations of 1937 put him to a strenuous test. When we think of Russia in 1937, we rightly recall its dark-of-night arrests and distant deportations, its public show trials and private violence.

That historical experience of collective trauma lay just beneath the public performances of happiness and achievement. The Pushkin jubilee provided a blanket cover of optimism beneath which individual Russians suffered terrifying injustices. The cover, however, painfully repeated patterns observed in the hidden traumas of millions. The grim humor that could link overt happiness to private pain produced some remarkable jokes from the late 1930s, one of which has Stalin observing that if Pushkin had lived in the twentieth century, he would still have died in a year ending in "37."[121] Repetition is the key to this joke, 1837 turning into 1937, the tragedy of one poet's death in a duel reimagined as an execution at the hands of the Soviet state.

The only rhetorical trope more prominent than repetition in 1937 was hyperbole, perhaps because the experience of loss was as heightened as the language designed to cover it. The grand, puffed-up rhetoric of the celebration is not lost in translation: 1937 was one hundred years "after the death of Alexander Sergeevich Pushkin, great Russian poet, creator of the Russian literary language, and founder of the new Russian literature, who enriched humankind with his immortal creations in artistic language," announced the central committee of the Communist Party.[122] The word *great* (*velikii*) resounded constantly. It described Pushkin, elevating him to heroic status,[123] but also the new Soviet state, the jubilee, and Stalin himself. Lest anyone miss the way that greatness joined the political leader and the literary hero, any number of public places and ceremonies provided reminders; in the vestibule of the restored Moika 12 apartment in Leningrad, for example, busts of Stalin and Pushkin were placed alongside each other.[124] In Moscow's grand celebration, Pushkin's portrait hung in a row alongside pictures of Marx, Lenin, Stalin, and Politburo members.[125]

The commemoration also emphasized unity. Unity of perception—

claims that everywhere in the Soviet Union *all* people would turn their attention to Pushkin—suggested that all of culture could be signified by a single symbol, Pushkin.[126] Unity was realized as ideological conformity; the Writers' Union forbade organizations to use Pushkin material without its permission.[127] This emphasis on unity was not entirely new,[128] but no commemoration had attempted to unify so many events across so long a time. It is difficult to grasp the extent and scope of events leading up to February 10, 1937 (the anniversary of his death, by the new calendar). An article in *Pravda* could proclaim that Pushkin had never been so loved as he was in 1937 because there had never been so many literate people in Russia.[129]

The jubilee seemed to have no end, and the beginning was difficult to pinpoint. Discussion of the jubilee was to be found in nearly every issue of 1936 literary newspapers, and not infrequently in 1935. Some references were mere reports of planned events or publications, and some were pro forma criticisms of inadequate preparation.[130] As part of the general move to industrialization and intensified economic production, the Pushkin commemoration was used to put more books in schools, to prepare teachers better, to cut illiteracy, and to spread an ideological message.[131] So some preparations had little to do with Pushkin. But many scholars, writers, and poets were publishing their Pushkin-related work in advance of the date, and commemorative events had plenty of "rehearsals." In June 1936, for example, there was a huge gathering in Mikhailovskoe (officially 13,500 people, although an eyewitness put the crowd closer to 30,000).[132]

Things reached a fever pitch as the jubilee drew closer. During the four months before February 1937, there were 1,495 paid lectures and 1,737 presentations by artists in Leningrad, purportedly heard by some 700,000 people.[133] Similar events took place in thousands of cities, towns, farm villages, schools, factories, and political institutions across the vast territory of the Soviet Union.[134] Pushkin's writings were republished in huge quantities. One émigré newspaper reported that every fifth book in a Soviet library was by Pushkin.[135] The total volume of Pushkin jubilee editions to be published had been set at 13.4 million copies.[136]

In January and February, every major journal and newspaper covered the jubilee extensively.[137] Almost every newspaper or journal, in fact, no matter what its focus (agriculture, statistics, film, or steel-working), turned its attention to Pushkin—if only for the moment.[138] The January issues of literary journals were all about Pushkin. Articles on Lenin's love for Pushkin were common, and the canon of Russian literature typically included Pushkin, Tolstoy, Mayakovsky, and Gorky. (Until 1991, the emblem of *The Literary Gazette* [*Literaturnaia gazeta*] was a double-profile, Pushkin and Gorky; thereafter, only Pushkin remained.) On February 10, 1937, official gatherings were held in the Bolshoi Theater in Moscow and the recently renamed Kirov Theater in Leningrad, and in similarly prestigious forums in every major city. The central committee ordered other theaters to organize a concert or dramatic spectacle based on Pushkinian themes.[139] The official Bolshoi commemoration was recorded for radio transmission across the country.[140] Commemorative speeches were reprinted in newspapers, as were relevant decrees of the central committee.

When the jubilee did occur, it was less a culmination than a very significant event in an apparently endless series. Most journals continued their special coverage through the year. The name Pushkin multiplied before the eyes, and it appeared in new and unlikely spaces: seven sites were renamed by the central committee during the jubilee, including Bolshaia Dmitrovka in Moscow turned Pushkin Street, the former town of Detskoe Selo (before that Tsarskoe Selo), now the town of Pushkin, and the Leningrad Academy Theater become the Pushkin Academy Theater.[141] Dramatic and musical spectacles that premiered during the "Pushkin Days" continued in repertoire during the year (except those that were closed for ideological reasons), and exhibits in various museums extended well into 1937.[142]

The experience of rereading all the newspaper accounts decades later is a revelation, not just because the context for commemorative events changed dramatically over the years 1934–37, but also because in the repetitiveness of newspaper rhythms one begins to sense how large Pushkin must have loomed in daily life.[143] It was not that you just read about him on the front page of every paper; you went to Pushkin reading groups in your place of work, you organized Pushkin plays in your apartment buildings, you criticized new Pushkin-related art in your regional party gatherings. Mikhail Zoshchenko, in his brilliant feuilleton "During the Pushkin Days" ("V pushkinskie dni," 1937), recorded the confusion and hilarity of two barely educated new Soviet men trying to speak at Pushkin gatherings in their apartment buildings.[144] The first speech begins with the boast that a six-ruble, fifty-kopeck volume of Pushkin has been purchased for all apartment-dwellers to share; a bust of the poet now adorns the building supervisor's office; a portrait graces the building's exterior. These objects are meant by the speaker to evidence the building's superior participation in the Pushkin festivities, although Zoshchenko undercuts the sense of achievement by making each acquisition seem shabby. The speaker quickly descends into an unfortunate mix of misquotation and misguided commentary about those who live in the building with him, and, like the speaker who follows him, he suffers the interruptions and corrections of an audience impatient with his digressions. They prod him to return to the subject at hand, that is, to speak *about Pushkin*. They repeat the command of the culture. Both speakers wander from the topic, speak of themselves and their neighbors as much as of Pushkin, confuse Pushkin with Lermontov, or *Eugene Onegin* with

"The Queen of Spades," reflecting the errors of a public on whom the requirement to speak about Pushkin was imposed. Zoshchenko, always quick to note speech patterns and narrative devices that revealed hidden anxieties, here presents the performance of adulation for Pushkin at its most theatrical.[145] Weariness and ignorance show through (as does a wish to use any public gathering to air petty grievances against one's neighbors: the satirist misses no opportunity to record what people were allowed to squabble about in those troubled times).

A different kind of news account may have been just as mind-numbing: the ever-increasing tales of arrest and sabotage. Newspapers in January and February of 1937 featured two stories that received equally intense coverage: the trial, sentencing, and execution of Karl Radek, Yuri Piatakov, and fifteen others; and the Pushkin celebration. Front-page parallel treatment was common.[146] Arlen Blium cites an example of this parallelism at its most paradoxical, from *The Literary Gazette*: a quotation from Pushkin's famous monument poem that says he will be remembered for having urged mercy toward the fallen appears opposite a banner headline insisting that "Trotskyist traitors and murderers be wiped from the face of the earth."[147] The public campaigns invoked Pushkin's legacy to justify cultural and political reforms, including purges within literary organizations. As a report from the Writers' Union plenum that concluded the February jubilee put it:

Particularly in light of the political events during the last year, an orientation toward the Pushkinian heritage helped the plenum define more precisely the watershed dividing the basic core of Soviet literature . . . from the small number of little groups and individuals who are trying to separate themselves from the basic questions of reality with their nonsensical, mumbling lies or to hide their confusion and ruins beneath a mask of false innovation (which in fact is nothing more than concealed formalism).[148]

We note here all the earmarks of pejorative labeling used against writers who did not share the state's view of "the basic questions of reality" or who dared to value "innovation," false or otherwise. Purges within organizations like the Writers' Union and the newspapers and journals covering the purges meant that accounts of the Pushkin commemorations were repeatedly marked by criticism, self-criticism, and news of the replacement of writers, journalists, and culture workers. The social processes of a cultural commemoration and a country undergoing violent transformation were inevitably fused. As the celebration itself began, demands for critical vigilance did not subside, and virtually no speech, publication, film, play, exhibit, ballet, or musical performance, even when positively reviewed, escaped critical commentary.

Despite this watchfulness, the 1937 commemoration was sometimes surprisingly varied.[149] And this may be its most remarkable trait. The unevenly textured intellectual life during the Terror was well described by Lydia Ginzburg:

> People wrongly imagine the disastrous epochs of the past as occupied only with their disasters. These periods consisted of a great deal else—chiefly, that which generally makes up life itself, although against a certain, unmistakable background. The thirties were not just defined by labor and fear, but also by many talented people with a will to realize their talents.[150]

Ginzburg's comments invite us to imagine educated Soviet men and women seeking to go about their business in the 1930s. She herself exemplified this behavior, as we can tell from her lively notes from this period and from her contribution to the Pushkin celebrations—a fine discussion of Pushkin's lyrics under the innocuous title "Pushkin's Realism," in which she lucidly showed that his poems moved away from "poetical" epithets toward ordinary, prosaic words.[151]

Yet it would be false to imagine that the version of Pushkin's life and legacy produced in 1937 was entirely resistant to the pressures that made up daily life during the Terror. The discourse of death and punishment, deviously renamed in the show trials, is transferred onto the narrative of Pushkin's death as a form of martyrdom. Trotsky's "hirelings" (*naimity*) who deserve death for their treason are named with the same word as the foreign "hireling" (d'Anthès) who murdered Russia's national poet. Xenophobia linked the two stories, and both told tales of death. Many texts from the 1937 jubilee, in fact, retell Pushkin's death, often in ways that refer as well to the deaths of Soviet citizens every day.

Mikhail Bulgakov's controversial play *The Last Days* (*Poslednie dni*) well exemplifies the fascination with Pushkin's death. Written in 1934–35, intended for performance in 1937 in Moscow's Vakhtangov Theater, the play was halted in production, and it was first seen only in 1943. The delay attests to the jubilee's atmosphere of nervousness and unpredictability. The stakes were especially high in the theater, and calls for successful dramatic work on Pushkin themes were shrill, frequent, and apparently futile. Bulgakov does not interpret Pushkin's death much differently from other writers at the time.[152] Most were influenced by Pavel Shchegolev's 1927 book, *Pushkin's Duel and Death* (*Duel'i smert' Pushkina*), although Bulgakov also engaged in his own research and had the collaboration, at least for a time, of Vikenty Veresaev.[153] Like others, he presents Pushkin's death as a near-conspiracy among his enemies, the secret police, and to some extent his ineffectual friends (he especially derides Zhukovsky). The death is a tragedy, although contemporary critics found Bulgakov's play insufficiently tragic.[154]

It is an open question whether *The Last Days* succeeds as drama. Some critics extolled its subtle and precise reproduction of Pushkin's era; others fixed on jarring historical inaccuracies.[155] Structured by citations from Pushkin's poetry rather than by his biography,[156] the play risks incoherence and obscurity. Even admirers have seemed uncomfortable with the play's virtual exclusion of Pushkin from the action (he fleetingly appears twice and is mentioned often, but does not figure actively in the unfolding drama of his death). Bulgakov apparently believed that including Pushkin would be vulgar,[157] and there is something of a taboo suggested in the sentiment that no actor could satisfactorily represent him. Pushkin's energy is sensed in the play by the effects he has on others, as Colin Wright has observed,[158] but this transference means that attention shifts away from him. He becomes the passive victim of the intrigues of others. (The same structure and strategy inform a 1987 film, *The Last Road [Posledniaia doroga]*, suggesting that Bulgakov's historical interpretation has had lasting consequences.)

I can see a different reason for Bulgakov's wish to keep Pushkin off the stage in *The Last Days*, however, a reason that is all the more paradoxical when we recall that his own name for the play was *Alexander Pushkin*. Bulgakov, I believe, was bent on keeping Pushkin out of the contemporary picture altogether, which is to say, the picture of the years of the Stalinist crackdown. His play becomes a mirror held up to his own historical era, reflecting an image he cannot bear for Pushkin to see. Whereas others were hiding their horror at what their culture was doing to his image, Bulgakov turns that sense of revulsion around. His play acts out an acute sense of shame at the world to which it would be performed, and the allegory of that world that his play presents nostalgically yearns for a possible alternative in which Pushkin, at least, would not have to know the nightmare of Stalin's Terror.

The nightmare permeates the play at all levels of its action—its combinations of players, its language, its atmosphere of heightened anxiety and impending doom. It begins in Pushkin's apartment, where Alexandra Nikolaevna Goncharova contends with moneylenders, an ailing Pushkin, and her headstrong sister. We move to the Saltykov salon, a ball at the Vorontsovs, a dark government office, the Heeckerens' apartment, the site of the duel, and back to the Pushkin apartment, before the play ends in a station master's house on the road to Sviatogorsk Monastery, where the dead Pushkin is to be buried. The action is furiously paced, as if it cannot move fast enough toward the terrible, known ending. Alexandra Nikolaevna says to Zhukovsky that she feels as if she is standing over an abyss; and Pushkin's dark poem "Winter Evening" ("Zimnii vecher," 1825) is a leitmotif in the play, with several echoing references to winter storms.[159]

Nature's violence seems almost calm, however, in comparison to the representations of human force. An example occurs in the most bizarre scene in the play, one that otherwise seems an incomprehensible aside. In his salon, Saltykov tells two disturbing tales, one familiar from Pushkin lore (that Pushkin was whipped by the gendarmes), the other utterly idiosyncratic (that Saltykov had shot a horse rather than sell it to the tsar). Both stories are told with uncanny calm. Saltykov speaks to two writers, Kukolnik and Benediktov, in company with others, telling them that a fellow writer, Pushkin, was recently flogged in the Third Division. His wife finds this outrageous.

> *Saltykov:* Please, my friends, keep eating. (*to Saltykova*) A pity that you react to this so indifferently, you too could be flogged.
> *Dolgorukov:* Well, they say it's true. I heard the same thing, although long ago.
> *Saltykov:* No, I have just heard it. I was riding past the Chain Bridge and I heard someone yelling. I asked, what was going on? Oh, my Lord, that's Pushkin being thrashed.
> *Bogomazov:* Oh, Sergei Vasilievich, this is Petersburg folklore!
> *Saltykov:* Why folklore? Once I too was very nearly flogged. The Emperor Alexander wanted to buy my horse and was offering a good price, ten thousand rubles. But in order not to sell the horse I shot it with a pistol. I put the pistol up to his ear and shot him.[160]

Saltykov rides around the city and hears the cries of someone being flogged; when the story is dismissed as an invention, he tops himself, now telling of a horse that he shot through the head. The passing rebuke to his wife that she, too, could be whipped, like the claim that he was almost thrashed over the horse incident, makes this strange violence pervasive and unpredictable.[161]

The moment of overhearing the cries of a man being beaten betrays a fascination with what goes on behind the walls of official institutions. The play is obsessed with the workings of the secret police; their conversations and decisions occupy center stage in one long scene, and individual agents appear in Pushkin's apartment several times. We watch a spy, Bitkov, at work impersonating a clockmaker, insinuating himself into Pushkin's household, observing at an alarmingly intimate proximity the sufferings, death, and transport of the dead poet. We see others confer, make decisions about how much to reward one spy versus another and about whether to intervene to stop Pushkin's duel. The investigation of those who control the fates of others behind the scenes reveals an ugly sense of the self-importance (from the tsar and Benckendorff down to Dubelt and the invented Bitkov). In a play written during a time of tyranny, we watch a tsar lash out at a courtier who speaks with insufficient deference about the tsarina; we hear Dubelt effectively close off any path of resistance to the police presence in Pushkin's apartment by making Zhukovsky's protestations sound unpatriotic; we watch a policeman penetrate Pushkin's apartment while he is alive, then others swarm in once he has died. The sense that the state can invade a family's scene of grief has a special sting in a play written in 1934–35 (when, for example, Bulgakov had learned of Mandelstam's exile in 1934 and had just survived a period of immense fear of going out in public himself).[162]

The play is strangely fascinated by the character of d'Anthès, but with flat results.[163] With Pushkin absent from the action, our attention turns inevitably to the perpetrator of the crime, and the fascination is an effect of Bulgakov's general interest in evil at the time.[164] He was working intensely on *Master and Margarita* at this point, and *The Last Days* has some of the same concerns as the greater novel: who is to be held responsible for the demise of a truly heroic individual, one who will not act in his own behalf? Can one apprehend the inner qualities of someone who has committed a great sin, a sin that offends not just an individual but an entire culture? Unlike the novel, Bulgakov's play does not try to answer the latter question. He does not much explore d'Anthès's affections, leaving viewers uncertain whether he loves Natalia Nikolaevna, whether his loyalty to Heeckeren is genuine and perhaps based on an erotic bond, or whether he cares only for his own career. The longest speech he gives is about Petersburg's dismal weather. Bulgakov shows a banal side of evil, a man who commits an act he cannot comprehend nor, as a result, much intend.

This portrayal is complemented by the police spies in *The Last Days*, since they, too, commit acts of evil. Indeed, their responsibility is greater. Bitkov, Dubelt, and Benckendorff have privileged knowledge (it is their business to collect knowledge), including prior information about the duel. When they talk of stopping it but do not act, they become the real murderers. Bulgakov spreads responsibility for Pushkin's demise far beyond d'Anthès, then, and in doing so he follows the script first set forth by Mikhail Lermontov in "The Death of the Poet." Bulgakov has the poem recited outside the Moika apartment where Pushkin has died, in a scene of utter pandemonium. The poem was standard fare in the 1937 jubilee; it was among the most reprinted texts about Pushkin, and its moral outrage resonated successfully with the angry rhetoric of 1937. Bulgakov turns the poem in a different direction, however, not by diminishing the anger, but by using its recitation to reveal a popular response to Pushkin's death and to the state's control of its citizens. The lines of the poem transfix the policemen who are supposed to arrest the student who recites it. An officer rises above the crowd and shouts, "My fellow citizens! What we have heard just now is all too true. Pushkin was killed deliberately, intentionally. And our entire people is insulted by this loathsome murder. . . . A great citizen has perished because unlimited power has been given over to the unworthy. They treat the people as prisoners [*nevol'niki*]."[165] These words safely repeat Soviet views of tsarist Russia as responsible for Pushkin's death and as indifferent to the fates of its people, but they also more dangerously suggest a contemporary world in which citizens are prisoners and the state's power is unlimited.

It may seem as if I am suggesting that Bulgakov's play was a completely rational allegory of the insane world of the Terror. His world was obsessed with evil, crowded with police spies, and built on forms of violence that were unmentionable but horribly pervasive. But, in his decision to exclude Pushkin from the play's action, I believe that Bulgakov goes beyond such a rational or allegorical model of drama. As the *New York Times* noted on February 11, 1937, "All Moscow was Pushkin-mad today on the hundredth anniversary of the poet's death."[166] It is the "Pushkin madness" that Bulgakov's play manages to reproduce. For in addition to conveying the insane conditions of daily life in the 1930s, Bulgakov reveals a lunatic reality about the jubilee itself. Like his play, it is a performance from which Pushkin was virtually absent. The events whirled around other interests and different obsessions.

Aftereffects of the 1937 Jubilee

The 1937 jubilee required a hardening of soul and spirit to its violence, distortions, and genuine dishonesties. One cannot overestimate the irony that a commemoration, which is after all a public experience that has the potential to *heal* trauma and to be a positive moment of national self-definition, itself became the occasion for further injury and pain.[167] But traumatic it was, a seemingly endless experience that defied absorption, thinking, reaction, and action. The automatized behaviors and benumbed survival strategies of the Stalin period were repeated in the commemoration itself, and the remaining Pushkin commemorations of the twentieth century, even those that occurred after the Stalin period, bore the burden of overcoming this trauma. Put another way, no later commemoration could much put the nation in touch with the loss of Pushkin himself, so powerfully did this trauma stand in its way. It did not help matters that the next occasion for commemoration was in 1949, when events were again compounded by a national spectacle, the recovery from the Second World War.[168] The other side of this inability to do justice to Pushkin was that commemorations in the middle of the twentieth century did an enormous amount of nation-building work, at the expense of building a sense of citizenship and national identity among the Soviet people. They showed the now solid state recreating nineteenth-century heroes for twentieth-century purposes, and they gave the populace opportunities to fashion themselves as interested citizens in this new era. There were many ways to express this love, and even at the height of Stalin's purges, (grim) humor was a response of some, as the Zoshchenko feuilleton demonstrates well. It also showed that self-fashioning could occur by resisting the command to celebrate Pushkin. Consider the following example, by Daniil Kharms.

The short anecdotes about Pushkin Kharms includes in his "Incidents" ("Sluchai," 1939) recall Zoshchenko in their mix of humor with strangely revealing truths. Rather than the jubilee's grand claims about greatness, Kharms's anecdotes revel in deflated rhetoric: "Pushkin was a poet and he was always writing something."[169] Kharms offers not a Pushkin of heroic exploits, but one with deficiencies (he cannot grow a beard). His Pushkin sleeps, throws stones, and breaks his legs. He does not thrill to the culture of simple peasants: he signals to them that they smell foul. Rejecting the long-winded discourse of anniversary commemorations, Kharms created stories of a single paragraph or a few sentences with sparse dialogue. His minimalist recreations satirize the project of commemorating a legend, but without attacking Pushkin himself. The last of his seven stories tells of Pushkin's four sons, all of them idiots falling off their chairs, one after another. Perhaps here Kharms allows himself not just his usual absurd non sequiturs but also a bit of allegory, where it is the generations that came after Pushkin who are fallen.[170]

Kharms implicitly asks what it meant to listen to Pushkin. He gave a tentative answer to this question in a story he did not finish, one that takes up the scene in which Pushkin read his verse to Gavriel Derzhavin at the Tsarskoe Selo lyceum.

Words flew into Derzhavin's ears, into his eyes and his nostrils. One word even flew by the scruff of his neck and hit hard against the old man's back. Derzhavin put his hand under his shirt and caught the word and tried to smash it with his nails against the table. But the word tore out of Derzhavin's old fingers and skipped away. Derzhavin listened. His eyes filled with tears. Every word seemed wonderful.[171]

Anthony Anemone is right in emphasizing that, for Kharms, signifier could wander very far from signified (and thus, when we read of the four idiot sons, the name Pushkin points well beyond the biography of a poet who had two entirely sane sons).[172] In the lyceum reading scene, the names and some details suggest powerfully the recitation of "Remembrances in Tsarskoe Selo" ("Vospominaniia v Tsarskom sele," 1814) as Pushkin was to record it, as in the errant word that "skipped away" (in Pushkin's recollection of the reading, it is the poet who slips away at the end).[173] But the attack of words on the listener is pure fantasy, a Kharmsian delight in showing us the futile attempts of any listener or reader to capture a poet's words, to make of them what he will. When the word escapes, Derzhavin listens. And then his eyes fill with tears of recognition, and he listens on with pleasure. The pleasure intensifies precisely because the words cannot be captured, because the meanings cannot be grabbed and held.

This unfinished text, not destined for publication, found only when scholars ferreted it out of the archives some fifty years later, would seem the very opposite of the traumatic artistic texts I have singled out as conveying the lived experience of a jubilee observed in a time of terror. Kharms offers instead the scene of one poet listening to another with pleasure. We might read that opposition as fantasy, as Kharms's escape from the grimmer realities of Soviet life in the late 1930s, as a retreat to another world in which the critical audience for an artistic work would be someone of the stature of Derzhavin, and one in which assaults on the body were performed by words, not blows. One has only to read Kharms's diary for the late 1930s to see how dreadfully he suffered the deprivations and constraints of Soviet life (January 21, 1937: "I am dying. I am dying as matter, and I am dying as a creative artist"),[174] and thus how strong might have been the desire to imagine some magical alternative. But even fantasies of escape are marked by the world they would flee. We might also read this tale, like the other "Incidents," as a bit of narrative that has been fractured by trauma.[175] Coherent, meaningful, sequential narratives can no longer hold (or, if they can, they are flattened into self-parody, as in Kharms's children's tale "Pushkin," to which the Derzhavin scene has a connection). The bits of story fly off, like the words Derzhavin tries to capture, and there is no holding them together. And where there is no story, there is also no narrating subject. As Mikhail Iampolski has put it, referring to "Incidents," "The disappearance of the word is a sign of the disappearance of subjectivity."[176] Kharms substitutes the disappearance of the word for Pushkin's tale of the poet's flight from the word ("they looked for me, but I was nowhere to be found"), but the result is to make the tale of disappearance all the more compelling. Nothing holds against such centrifugal force. Soviet officials may have succeeded in their wish to rehabilitate Pushkin for modern use by means of public commemoration, but Kharms shows how futile was the aim to construct a new Soviet subjectivity in this process. Rather than a new hero with whom to identify, Pushkin as sign and symbol is nearly overwhelmed by repetition and hyperbole. His idiot sons fall down, rising up, we might foresee, with every new Pushkin anniversary, at best to announce that once again the rites of celebration have not completely covered over the pain and disaffection of the seemingly joyous public.

One later anniversary, in 1987, might have had the potential to escape the shadow of 1937. It occurred at the height of perestroika before the Soviet Union collapsed. Its significant achievement was the complete reconstruction of Pushkin's apartment on the Moika into a twentieth-century museum ready to serve a more modern public. Such institution-building seemed possible in the late 1980s. The brief experience of a common meeting ground that characterized the 1880 commemoration might, in fact, be an appropriate way to imagine the 1987 events, and the kind of ambitious plans spoken in 1924 were again heard. Many of these plans never came to fruition. A number of dissenting writers and public figures emerged from the shadows in 1987, including Fazil Iskander, Andrei Bitov, and the medievalist Dmitri Likhachev, who was a kind of Andrei Sakharov to the Leningrad intelligentsia.[177] The weekly magazine *The Spark* (*Ogonek*), a leader in the glasnost movement, had a telling mix for its Pushkin issue, notably, a lead article by Likhachev; excerpts from the then unpublished diaries of Pavel Luknitsky, which recorded Akhmatova's passing comments about Pushkin in the 1920s; portions of Khodasevich's 1921 "Swaying Tripod" speech and archival excerpts never previously published; Kuzmin's 1921 poem "Pushkin"; and an essay by the collector Ilya Zilbershtein about Serge Lifar's Pushkiniana collection.[178] The symbolic glance back to the Silver Age and across to the world of the emigration was typical of the late 1980s and felt immensely significant to the intelligentsia, promising a kind of integrity and authenticity in the Pushkin commemoration that had long been absent. Considerable hope that a complete Pushkin edition, with commentary, would appear by 1999 was heard. That was not to be.

Two Hundred Years of Commemoration

The city of Moscow spent some four million dollars on the 1999 bicentennial of Pushkin's birth.[179] Another five million was allocated for restoring the three Pushkin museums in the Pskov region.[180] Money, lots of it, became the measure of respect for Pushkin in the last commemoration of the twentieth century. One recipient of a Pushkin medal hoped (in vain) that the medal would come with a cash award.[181] Despite worries that the crumbling Russian economy would never support a sufficiently lavish celebration, it was quickly obvious that Pushkin, having survived the Stalin Terror in the 1937 jubilee, would do fine in the era of financial default.[182] His image was put to good commercial use, resulting in several memorable advertising campaigns. "Pushkin knew how to put words together into a poem. We know how to assemble an excellent automobile," promised one company. Another did a direct mailing that began "Dear Muscovites! We congratulate you on the two-hundredth anniversary of the birth of Alexander Sergeevich Pushkin! If you want to rent a cottage in the country, please call us," followed by phone, fax, and pager numbers.[183] The DeBeers diamond monopoly published a handsome catalogue trumpeting its role in returning to Russia various memorabilia from émigré collections for its exhibit of July 30–September 5.[184] Another exhibit, which compared Pushkin and Goethe (1999 was also the two hundred fiftieth anniversary of Goethe's birth), provoked a splendid riff by the postmodernist poet Lev Rubinshtein on "Pushkin as an object of kitsch." He laughed at the symbolism of Pushkin appearing on a plebeian vodka label, whereas Goethe was used to sell brandy; when he saw Goethe's image on a package of women's stockings, he found it regrettable that Pushkin's name was not put to the same use—after all, Pushkin famously celebrated women's legs in *Eugene Onegin*.[185]

Russian commentaries predictably found the commercialization of their national poet and the show business atmosphere tremendously off-putting. There was loud condemnation of supposedly wrongheaded views in books or films or exhibits. In the Petersburg journal *Neva*, Evgenia Shcheglova attacked Yuri Druzhnikov's book about Pushkin called *Russian Myths*.[186] Grigory Anisimov's tale "What's in My Name?" ("Chto v imeni tebe moem?" 1999) was demolished by Andrei Turkin in *Film Art (Iskusstvo kino)*.[187] Valentin Nepomnyashchy took on the English film *Eugene Onegin* (directed by Martha Fiennes). He found the utterly implausible Liv Tyler a successful Tatiana because she seemed older than a girl but not quite a woman.[188] Nepomnyashchy used the review for large and rather stale ideas of his own about Western vs. Russian art, another grand gesture very much in the jubilee tradition.

Some critics praised the spiritual purification of the jubilee, observing that public complaints about the vulgarity of various events showed that the masses kept their instinctive good taste.[189] Faith in the *narod* was thus apparently intact. Most publications implied that past commemorations had been better in all senses and more significant in shaping attitudes toward Pushkin; one vehicle for doing this was an article about some earlier commemoration, often the 1899 jubilee.[190] The television station Kultura aired a new documentary, *The Bronze Pushkin: Seven Jubilees or the Holy Week (Mednyi Pushkin: sem' iubileev ili Strastnaia Sedmitsa)*, about previous Pushkin jubilees.[191] All this nostalgia for commemorations past idealized them, and for a few commentators the nostalgia sweetened the bitter cynicism of some coverage. The prominent Moscow critic and editor Natalia Ivanova fled to St. Petersburg, still many Russians' fantasy site for a closer connection to imperial Russian culture, where she was gratified to find an atmosphere of happy celebration: "Surprising as it seems, it all worked."[192]

What made it work, though, if that is what happened, is a strange mix of commerce, incomplete planning, and a steadfast capacity to find meaning in the vast range of events, publications, art exhibits, and films. The end of censorship meant that almost anything was possible, including a remarkable slew of errors that had even vaguely knowledgeable Russians laughing. Grigoriev's dictum "Pushkin is our everything" was attributed to Boris Yeltsin (still president of Russia in 1999); a famous aria from Tchaikovsky's opera *Eugene Onegin* was given as an example of a beloved Pushkin line on Radio Russia; a television reporter announced, "As is well known, Pushkin said that 'we have all come out from under Gogol's overcoat.'"[193] A poll asking for a favorite line of Pushkin produced one emblematically fantastic result: Lermontov's "I go out alone onto the road" ("Vykhozhu odin ia na dorogu").[194] Television in particular played an enormous role in setting the tone, conveying information, and exemplifying modes of celebration. A camera man for channel ORT stopped people on the streets to recite a line from *Eugene Onegin*, and a stanza was given every night in these different voices and faces. One critic called the participants tourists who had turned up in the land of Pushkin on cheap excursion tickets.[195] But vast numbers of responses, much in the tradition of factory workers and farmers reciting Pushkin across the Soviet land, remain a tradition, imitating an idea of democratic "leveling" and broad access to high culture. Television coverage itself became an object of commentary. One anniversary joke parodied the television station NTV for its daily announcement of how many days were left before the jubilee: "A homeless man is brought into the police. 'Name?' 'Don't remember.' 'Place of birth?' 'Don't remember.' 'Any living relatives?' 'Don't remember.' 'Is there anything that you do know?' 'I remember that there are seven days until the birthday of Alexander Pushkin.'"[196]

In this atmosphere of messy celebration, the possibility for carnival was vast, and one critic noted that the real motivation for the large-scale public events was the urge to celebrate something, anything.[197] Various "balls" were announced for the public squares in Moscow, collectively named "Love! Russia! Sun! Pushkin!" Sergei Penkin blasted out his rock-and-roll version of an intimate Pushkin lyric ("I Loved You," "Ia Vas liubil") on Moscow's Manezh Square.[198] In Sochi, where the Kinotavr film festival coincided with the jubilee, audiences vastly preferred listening to the pop band Na-Na outside rather than the official commemorations inside. In Moscow, thirty-three men bearing the name Alexander Sergeevich marched to meet the thirty-fourth at a new monument to Pushkin.[199] Contributing to the celebratory atmosphere where there could be more than one Alexander Sergeevich were newspapers, who joined in the foolishness with mockeries of their own. The literary supplement to *The Independent Gazette* (*Nezavisimaia gazeta*), *Ex Libris*, treated Pushkin as a contemporary writer, listing him in its masthead as a contributor and featuring an interview with him. Questions were asked by Gogol, and Pushkin offered candid views of writers (Victor Pelevin's writing is boring, he confides) and of his critics ("half-ladylike tearful sighing nonsense," he says, with only Sinyavsky's *Strolls with Pushkin* and the works of Yuri Lotman as exceptions). Several Pushkin texts were "reviewed" as if just published by the imaginary "Our Everything" ("Nashe vse") press in Moscow, with laments that his prose had received neither the Booker nor the Anti-Booker prize that year.[200] In another high-brow publication, the scholar and cultural critic Andrei Zorin published a spicy story long ago told him by the director of Mikhailovskoe, Semyon Geichenko, about how Pushkin once accidentally used a page of *Eugene Onegin* for toilet paper.[201] Geichenko takes obvious pleasure in sprinkling his story with obscenities, which the newspaper prints, and in reminding his young listeners that such a story could never pass the censors. Zorin, without comment, demonstrates to his post-Soviet audience how times have changed.

Such irony and self-consciousness marked a striking departure from Soviet anniversaries. *The Literary Gazette* has long trumpeted its direct link to the Pushkinian tradition with his famous self-portrait in profile on its front page along with a banner announcement that the paper was founded in 1830 with the participation of Pushkin, then "renewed" in 1929. True to form, the *Gazette* had an entire section and front-page coverage of the jubilee in its June 6, 1999, issue, but on the front page of its next issue, it had a small boxed epigraph, just under the profile, quoting a letter from Pushkin to his wife: "I am sitting out all these festivities at home."[202] The most vibrant mix of homage and verbal irreverence may have been the collection *Pushkin's Overcoat* (*Shinel' Pushkina*, 2000), with its brilliant introduction by Andrei Zorin describing Pushkin as the modern incarnation of safe sex for Russia: "rarified pleasure practically guaranteed without the slightest undesirable consequence."[203] Zorin concluded that Pushkin's relevance to Russian self-definition had conclusively been proven by the 1999 commemorations: he was an equally appropriate national hero for tsarist, Soviet, and commercially self-obsessed post-Soviet Russia.

The tone was often different, then, but much in 1999 was the same, varying the themes and adding players from the rising generation of the intelligentsia but keeping many old favorites. Andrei Bitov, who had just been gaining official recognition when the 1987 ceremonies were held, now organized the Petersburg festivities attended by Ivanova and played a major role in television and print commemorations. Dmitri Likhachev, prominently featured in the 1987 commemoration, was on the front page of *The Literary Gazette*, answering predictable questions in an editorial questionnaire. The very use of a questionnaire was emblematically familiar.[204] In *The Literary Gazette*, the practice of drawing disparate voices together juxtaposed the now elderly Likhachev, an esteemed member of the Academy of Sciences, to a neoclassical Petersburg poet, Alexander Kushner, and a humorous prose writer, Evgeny Popov, among others. Their mix of informal commentary and ideological aside was familiar: Kushner said that Pushkin's anti-Semitism was not really so anti-Semitic; Popov compared the droning on about Pushkin in the schools to deadening speeches about Lenin. Other questionnaires were little different. The interesting journal *The Banner* (*Znamia*) asked whether Pushkin was still a useful model for artistic innovation at the end of the twentieth century, with responses from the poets Maxim Amelin, Timur Kibirov, Alexander Kushner, and Lev Rubinshtein and two fiction writers, Andrei Dmitriev and Anton Utkin. But the result was simply boring: the writers either challenged the premise of the question by defining Pushkin in familiar ways or repeated platitudes about innovation, post-Soviet realities, and the Pushkinian tradition.[205]

Perhaps to avoid such platitudes, the journal *Film Art* asked its questions in an acidic tone and also gave multiple-choice answers to set an example of clever jocularity. The result was the reverse of what the editors sought: filmmakers and actors alike answered with expressions of love for Pushkin. They challenged the journal's assumption that the era of reading was over or that contemporary readers would not feel any deep emotion about Pushkin's anthologized heroes, and most found the invitation to name the Pushkin of the twentieth century ridiculous (some, though, responded with alternatives: Prigov, Brodsky, Vysotsky).[206] They especially resisted any condemnation of the jubilee itself: as the director Gleb Panfilov put it, better a campaign about Pushkin than a presidential campaign.

New poems to Pushkin were less prominent than in earlier commemorations, as if the genre were almost too retro for renewal. Several poetry publications involved a form of recycling. Bella Akhmadulina gathered all her writings on Pushkinian themes in *Enclosed in Winter* (*Zimniaia zamknutost'*, 1999), subtitled *An Offering for the Two-Hundredth Anniversary of A. S. Pushkin*, but her volume attracted little attention. More interesting was Genrikh Sapgir's completion of Pushkinian fragments, written in 1985, quietly published in 1992, and made widely available in the journal *The Peoples' Friendship* (*Druzhba narodov*) in May 1999, with an admiring introduction by Andrei Chernov. Sapgir chose little-known Pushkin poems for completion, although he includes the famous line "And like a fool, I could have been ... " that Pushkin wrote above a sketch of a gallows in his notebooks (Fig. 10), long taken as a contemplation that he might have shared the fate of five hanged Decembrists.[207] Sapgir did three poems based on this broken line, keeping the context of the gallows but amplifying it with references to dance, and layering Pushkin's intonation of fear and regret with notes of pride. The three poems subtly increase in possible violence, creating a successful if entirely inadvertent resonance with the chaos of daily life in Russia in 1999.

Another republishing project, also poetry, was Dmitri Aleksandrovich Prigov's 1992 rewriting of *Eugene Onegin*.[208] It appeared in 1998, a "facsimile" edition of the only surviving part of the project, the preface claimed, the fruit of Prigov's wish to copy out this "sacred" text of Russian culture. He changed the novel's epithets to either "insane" or "unearthly" ("bezumnyi," "nezemnyi"), choices that made the text more Lermontovian, he

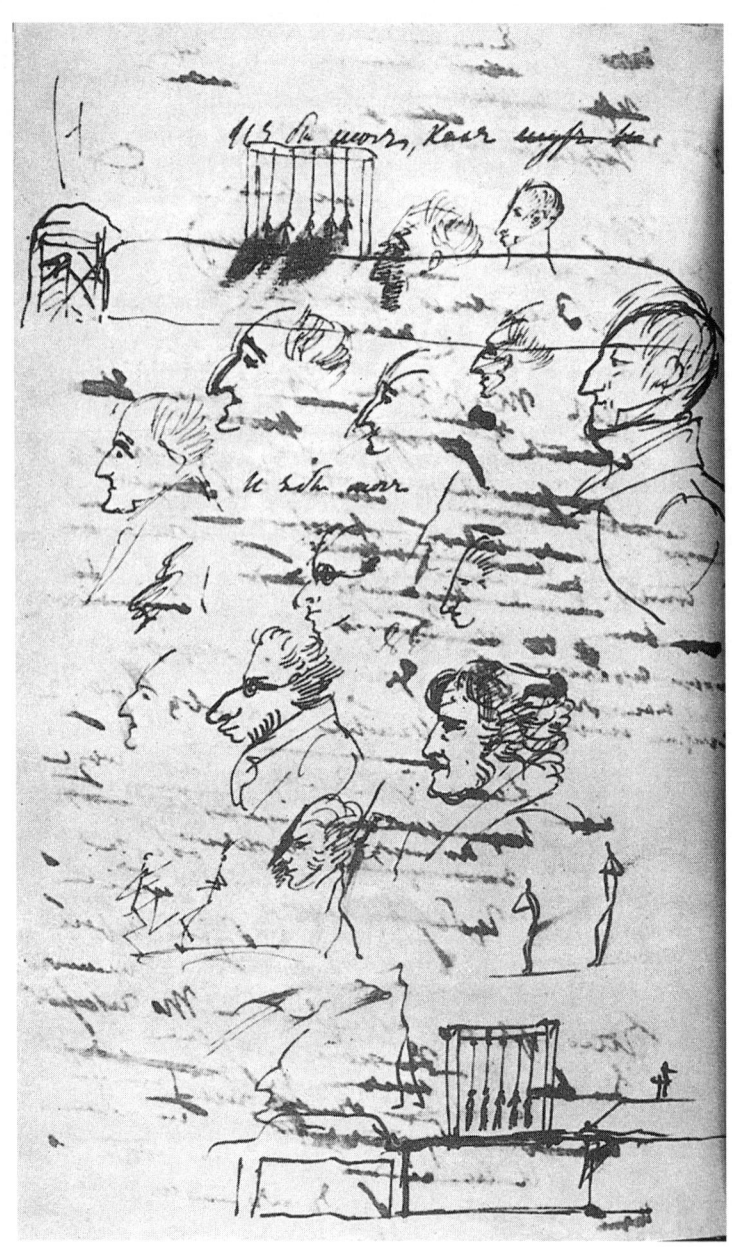

FIGURE 10. Pushkin sketch on a page of *Eugene Onegin*, chap. 5 (1826). At the top of the page, he wrote that he, too, might have been hanged, "like a fool." Reproduction from *Mir Pushkina* (Moscow: Sovetskaia Rossiia, 1990), p. 99. Courtesy National Pushkin Museum, St. Petersburg.

said.²⁰⁹ The changes are more interesting than that, however, substituting "bezumnyi" for many parts of speech and rendering the familiar text truly otherworldly and insane. In the 1998 edition, illustrations by Alexander Favorsky add a quaintly loony touch (the bottom right corner of each page features a line drawing of Pushkin, with top hat and cane, just enough different from one page to the next that if you flip through the pages you get the effect of an animated image of him doffing his hat). Because the "facsimile" pages are imitations of *samizdat*-era typescript, there is something nostalgic about the entire production, despite its use of clever formatting and good-quality paper to reproduce the effect of tissue-thin *samizdat* pages.

As in the past, the 1999 anniversary offered films about Pushkin to Russian audiences. The documentaries were perhaps more interesting than the feature films, but they were sadly ignored. Andrei Khrzhanovsky's two small Pushkin films were screened to a negligible audience at the Sochi film festival and a few other festivals.²¹⁰ Both include excerpts from his earlier Pushkin films (discussed in Chapter Four). The short films, each under half

FIGURE 11. Sculpture of the helicopter *Pushkin* in the children's exhibit "Pushkin Again," featured in Andrei Khrzhanovsky's 1987 film *Let's Fly Away! (The Pushkin Can Now Take Off)*.

an hour, are enigmatic and charming, particularly the second, the nearly wordless *Let's Fly Away! (The Pushkin Can Now Take Off)* (*Davai uletim! [Pushkinu vzlet razreshen]*).[211] Its title comes from a helicopter sculpture with Pushkin's face as its front window (Fig. 11), and from a real helicopter named *The Pushkin*.

Let's Fly Away! focuses on an exhibit that opened in October 1998, featuring thirteen soft and kinetic sculptures created by children.[212] It begins with the Russian flag fluttering in the wind and a flower bed with blossoms laid out to form Pushkin's profile and the words "Well done, Pushkin" ("Ai da, Pushkin"), a quotation from one of his letters that became a slogan in 1999. The film intercuts many images from that commemoration: buildings draped with banners showing Pushkin's face or body; shop windows with Pushkin's name or image on boxes of chocolates; shopping bags with "Pushkin 200 Years" imprinted on them; billboards with words like *passion*, *love*, and *beauty* alongside Pushkin's face; and Pushkin rugs, with the selling price visibly marked. As such, the film is an excellent documentary compilation of visual imagery from the jubilee, and a fine demonstration (mercifully, without voice-over narration) of how Pushkin was marketed to the new Russia.

Let's Fly Away! preempts the cynical inference that one might draw from this commodification of Pushkin—that his "image" has lost all value—when it lingers over the sculptures in the children's exhibit, entitled "Pushkin Again" (a title with its own irony). By showing the process of making the sculptures, Khrzhanovsky indulges his favorite cinematic moment, showing how art is created. We see the application of lips to face, of red paint to the lips, of extra pieces of tape to hold things together, which means that we see the pleasure and efforts of the young creators as vividly as we see the final product. The editing and camera work denaturalize the sculptures, using extreme close-ups and rhythmically repeating shots to make the faces grotesque. They are already grotesque, in several instances, with disproportionate lips or eyes and garish colors thickly applied. An early sequence has one of the sculptures carried by unseen people through the streets, with a stop-start action: the filmmaker suggests that Pushkin's ghost walks the streets of the city that commemorates his birth. In and of itself, this is not a new idea; other films, like Gromov's *Three Songs of Pushkin*, use the Moscow Pushkin monument this way, and with less subtlety. Khrzhanovsky, by comparison, has several Pushkins in this watchful role—the artworks of children, the images on billboards and shop windows that look out onto the Moscow scene, and a small Pushkin monument unveiled at the end of the film that looks as if it is made of wax and is also the work of a child. All defamiliarize Pushkin, a remarkable feat in a film that shows how exceedingly familiar his image was in the 1999 celebrations.

Moving the Pushkin sculpture through the Moscow streets almost makes it seem to come alive. Again, it is a familiar idea, Pushkin's own, but recreated here through a device from animated film (Khrzhanovsky's usual medium), where a still object is made to seem mobile. The movement is not naturalized: the puppet remains an object, manipulated by filmmaker and viewers. The same is true of the art objects in the exhibit "Pushkin Again": some can be activated by visitors, for example, a chair shaped like Pushkin's body (his arms are the chair's arms). Others have motors, like the helicopter, or internal mechanisms. One mattress-like face invites children to lie on its cheeks, making the face move. An eerily beautiful wire sculpture, seen from several angles, casts its shadow on a wall. But the real suggestion of movement in these images is not human movement; it is flight. The reality of Pushkin's never having left Russia and his various experiences of limitation are as important as his legendary verbal dynamism, for example, when images of Pushkin are shown behind the bars of a shop window—the film's first words are Pushkin's "I am imprisoned behind bars" ("Sizhu za reshetkoi") from "The Prisoner" ("Uznik," 1822). How to liberate Pushkin? asks the film. The answer is shamelessly romantic: put him in the hands of children, let the imagery be grotesque and irreverent and loving, let him soar if only in our imaginations.[213]

Somewhat less successful among 1999 films is Gromov's *Three Songs of Pushkin*, but it is a valuable film for its historical retrospective and use of documentary footage. Like the Dziga Vertov film from which it takes its title, *Three Songs of Lenin* (*Tri pesni o Lenine*, 1934), *Three Songs of Pushkin* is a compilation, mixing documentary footage from newsreel and other sources to re-create historical moments from a past that seems distant. It is didactic in the extreme, as was Vertov, using relentless voice-overs to hammer home its message of the lasting evil of Stalin's regime. Its first "song" interprets the 1937 jubilee as a terrible celebration in a desperate time. It intercuts several excerpts from Mikhail Shveitser's film version of *Feast in Time of Plague* (in his film *Little Tragedies*, *Malen'kie tragedii*, discussed in Chapter Four) to make this point emphatically, and its real subject becomes Stalin, just as Vertov's subject was Lenin. As the film moves forward in time, it tries to do the same with Khrushchev and Brezhnev, but less exclusively, and much of the footage about the 1960s and 1970s shows the young poets who emerged at that time. The film's last "song" is titled "On the Ruins of Autocracy" ("Na oblomkakh samovlast'ia") from Pushkin's poem to Chaadaev, "Love, hope, and quiet fame" ("Liubvi, nadezhdy, tikhoi slavy," 1818), and it looks at what has been built on the ruins of the past in contemporary Russia. Signs of commercialization are shown, the most expressive a Pushkin matryoshka lined up next to one of Bill Clinton with his saxophone. People on the street are asked about Pushkin, one responding with more clichés than the next. At the end of the film, old footage from earlier in the movie is intercut with contemporary street scenes, suggesting that past Pushkins live into the present, which means, in this film's view, that the Pushkin created in 1937 cannot be displaced.

If you take that image as a residue of violence and autocratic excess, then the one 1999 feature film based on Pushkin's works proves Gromov's point: the epic production of *The Russian Uprising* (*Russkii bunt*), directed by Alexander Proshkin. This self-described "big-budget" film reflects its creation during the disorganized advent of capitalism of the 1990s, when the collapsing command culture made for ambiguous financing.[214] The premiere was postponed and, although trumpeted in the press during June 1999, *The Russian Uprising* was released in Russia in the fall of 2000. Shown at the Berlin Film Festival, it was awarded prizes in Sochi, including a prize for the best male lead (Sergei Makovetsky as Shvabrin).

The result is hard to watch, an aesthetically confused film more bloody than Pushkin's *The History of Pugachev* (*Istoriia Pugacheva*, 1834) and considerably more romantic than his fictional tale about the same period, *The Captain's Daughter* (*Kapitanskaia dochka*, 1836). Like Soviet film adaptations that turned Pushkin's restrained writings into over-the-top spectacles, *The Russian Uprising* has some good acting (Makovetsky most of the time, and Vladimir Mashkov as Pugachev), and it cares more about costumes and sets than about historical interpretation. In that preference, *The Russian Uprising* reflects the tastes and mores of the era in which it was produced. Playing to newly rich viewers, the film pauses for scenes of aristocratic luxury, knowing its audience is curious about the details of daily life in the royal household. It shows Catherine on a carnival sleigh ride, and it offers a tour of her palace, letting the camera move viewers through one room after another as if in search of decorating ideas. The violence in the film corresponds to the tastes of those for whom bloodshed is a new business tool: a severed head is delivered to Russian officers when Belgorsk fortress is stormed, bodies of just-hanged men twitch in the agony of death, and the camera lingers on battlefield injuries and assaulted peasants. The captain's wife, Vasilisa Egorovna, is improbably made to witness more than her fair share of these injuries, including the severed head, which she unwittingly removes from its cloth cover for all to see. As in Pushkin's tale, she finds her husband hanged, but Proshkin adds a camera shot of her pendulous breasts as she rips her shirt in mourning, just before she is felled by a pistol shot. Women and their sexuality are meant to bring life to the film, as when Masha Mironova and the young Grinev nearly have sex in a threshing barn, with close-up shots of spilling grain unsubtly duplicating Masha's eager sexuality. (The scene reminds one of nothing so much as Uma Thurman's portrayal of Cecile in Stephen Frears's film *Dangerous Liaisons*.)

Never mind that such an encounter, especially at Masha's initiative, was unthinkable for the characters Pushkin created in *The Captain's Daughter*, where an epigraph stresses the point of honor.[215] It makes some sense for the film to pile on details about Catherine's decadent life at court, but Pushkin did not imagine his young heroes, Petya Grinev and Masha Mironova, as similarly dissolute. When the film's Shvabrin forces himself on her, Masha's sense of honor and her personal revulsion are equally important as she resists his advances. He responds by ripping open her shirt for another gratuitous flash of women's breasts.

For whom are these bodies on display? *The Russian Uprising* shows women's bodies to an overseas audience as well as to Russians at home. The same income could be generated in the 1990s by a single showing on European television as by an entire year of revenues in the Russian market.[216] Films keyed into the desires and expectations of a foreign audience, and *The Russian Uprising* is no exception.[217] For every idealizing shot of countryside loveliness meant to stir hearts nostalgic for a landscape destroyed by Soviet ecological disasters and urban growth, the film provides an allegory of the "Russian soul" as the West has come to fantasize it. Passionate excess and visual pleasure combine, for example, in the too-long sequence of dancing and drinking Cossacks, led by Pugachev, who cuts his hand and waves it as he dances, dripping blood. The insane *khorovod* of men performing a mix of pleasure and fear holds up to the West a vivid and blood-red image of self-mutilation, of abasement before power, and simulated pleasure in a dance before death. In the end, the film knows that its audiences, both of them, prefer eroticism to sheer force, so a lascivious Catherine II has a young lover at her side when she offers her pardon to Masha Mironova, and says that she does so because the only thing that matters in life is love.

In an astute review of *The Russian Uprising*, Anastasia Arkhipova criticized its deviations from Pushkin and its incoherent historical vision.[218] The director, perhaps anticipating such criticisms, tried in interviews to make the film seem less about the past than about the moral effects of the past on the present. He claimed that his goal was ethical, meant to expose the cruelty of such national heroes as Pugachev and Stenka Razin, and the cruelty of the government's reaction to them. Proshkin compared Pugachev's uprising to the war in Chechnya: "We live in a society where we are daily shown blood and dead bodies on TV. We have grown accustomed to the sight of death."[219] Whatever one thinks of the film, then, its director's ambitions follow the jubilee tradition of using Pushkinian material for contemporary commentary, and of taking on issues no less significant than the nature of good and evil. All that implausible talk about love is meant to serve this lofty end, although *The Russian Uprising* largely does not live up to these ambitions.

It is no less challenging to do this in fictional prose. Let me offer only one example, also tellingly flawed: Vladimir Krakovsky's strange novella *One Fate for Us All* (*Odin nad nami rok*, 1999), which appeared in the August issue of the mainstream Moscow journal *October* (*Oktiabr'*). Krakovsky, an established Soviet writer born in 1930, recreates a familiar Soviet fiction of labor and masculine friendship but with a quirky change: the workers have names like Pushkin, Viazemsky, d'Anthès, and Natashka Goncharova. Familiar biographical details (Pushkin shoots a gun at d'Anthès, Pushkin is the most talented worker, Natashka is a beauty to end all beauties) are brought into distorting new contexts (Pushkin is put into a mental hospital for shooting d'Anthès; he is a leader in production at the factory and the key to the collective's success). The time of the story is seemingly post-Soviet, with the factory workers coming up with one economic adventure after another. When they hit it rich, the workers spend all their money on conspicuous consumption and foreign travel. The use of Pushkinian names makes a temporal mishmash in any case, but the confused temporality is motivated by a longing not for the Pushkin era but for the days before the government fell apart. Krakovsky's narrator feels nostalgic for the old days, the period before the post-Soviet "economic collapse, when the bosses were seized by the new fashion of not paying salaries."[220] The complexity of daily life in the psychiatric hospital is compared by Pushkin to the intricacies of capitalism.[221] The loosely structured story features vignettes of everyday life in the 1990s, with the workers insisting that they are not anti-Semitic as they force a Jew to admit he changed his first name ("We tried to catch him in his lies, but in vain. You can't catch a Jew").[222]

With its emphasis on the chatter and survival strategies of daily life, *One Fate for Us All* cares less about Pushkin than it does about Russians' views of themselves in the late 1990s. The narrative parodies the very idea of Pushkin's relevance in two scenes in which the workers try to decide why Pushkin is superior to them. Magical hands, goes one explanation; a brilliant mind, goes another; a gift from God, suggests still another, this last especially ignored because the workers are atheists. The plot, such as it is, turns more on why Pushkin shoots d'Anthès: his fellow workers think they can get him released if they show he had a logical motive. Eventually, Pushkin explains that, like all internationalists, he hates one people, in his case, the French. D'Anthès soon reveals his genealogy—he's Italian, not French, and his name is a corruption of "Dante" with the "s" (for "sir") added at the end. Pushkin's motive for shooting is now wiped away, and he is freed from the mental hospital in the process. The workers celebrate with a "ceremonial kiss between Pushkin and d'Anthès,"[223] and, at the end of the story, Pushkin is sharing d'Anthès's palace—all an absurd resolution to a conflict that had generated so much of Russia's national identity, the story suggests.

Pushkin plays a small, comic role in the tale of contemporary life, where romantic confusions and violent actions are wished away by implausible explanations. The Pushkin story gives daily life no added coherence and is all too ripe for parody.

Before concluding with some comments on 1999 art exhibits, let me briefly mention the publications in Pushkin scholarship, where successes and failures again very much reflected the mixed state of the Russian national psyche and economy. The lamentable failure to produce a complete Pushkin edition was seen as a sign that such an edition might never be produced in Russia. Two hundred copies of the first volume were printed at the expense of Pushkin House, so that the scholars would have something to show for their efforts.[224] Less ambitious scholarly goals were reached, however. Among the most significant was a splendid one-volume encyclopedia of films about Pushkin or based on his works (*Pushkinskii kinoslovar'*, 1999), whose appearance was enabled by a special presidential grant.[225] The encyclopedia maintained high standards of accuracy, completeness, and principled organization; its success suggests the importance of film as a medium for exploring Pushkinian themes. Samples of the full-scale Pushkin encyclopedia in progress, under the direction of Irina Chistova, appeared in the Petersburg journal *The Star* (*Zvezda*) in every 1999 issue.[226] At this writing, the encyclopedia has yet to appear. And, in the new technological spirit of 1999, not one but two companies produced full editions of Pushkin on CD-ROM.[227]

Andrei Bitov, with the help of a major bank (Vneshekonombank, which marked its own seventy-fifth anniversary on the opening pages of the volume), assembled an impressive book, *The Intention to Live 1836* (*Predpolozhenie zhit' 1836*, 1999), with all of Pushkin's writings from the last year of his life, a facsimile of the rare 1837 edition of *The Captain's Daughter*, and Bitov's own long essay "The Intention to Live." The Pushkin texts are scrupulously annotated by Maria Virolainen of Pushkin House, and the book effectively combines fine scholarship with a fiction writer's imagination and vision. Natan Eidelman and others had long ago assembled a volume of the Boldino writings from 1830, offering the reader an opportunity to read the poems and prose pieces in the order in which Pushkin wrote them.[228] Bitov does something similar here, and with an equivalent emphasis on Pushkin's own fertile imagination. It is no accident that he called his essay, and the volume, *The Intention to Live*, for he wishes to celebrate Pushkin's life, not to mourn his death. He also produced a self-conscious collector's item, a volume with fine paper and stylish format.

Republications remained important, continuing the earlier glasnost-era fascination with forgotten classics. Perhaps the most significant was a completion of earlier work: the four-volume chronicle of Pushkin's life and works, based on Mstislav Tsiavlovsky's work begun in 1938.[229] Interest in Tsiavlovsky himself led to an extremely useful and well-annotated volume of his essays and diaries.[230] The deaths of Yuri Lotman and Natan Eidelman in the 1990s renewed attention to their work, as did the death of Vadim Vatsuro in 2000, along with new editions and reissues of works by Boris Modzalevsky, Larisa Volpert, and others.[231] The year 1999 was also the Nabokov centenary, and one publication that was meant to honor both Pushkin and Nabokov was the 1998 translation into Russian of Nabokov's massive commentary on *Eugene Onegin*.[232] Oleg Proskurin's valuable book on Pushkin's poetry was praised on the front page of *Ex libris* for its hands-off attitude toward the celebrations.[233] His book makes a fittingly paradoxical icon for Pushkin scholarship in 1999: the work of a native Russian who has taught in American universities, it argues with (at times imaginary) phantoms of postmodernism, only to use the best lessons of postmodernism very well. It treats influences on Pushkin, not the more expected topic of how Pushkin affected others.

Reversals were everywhere in the 1999 events, actually. In one of the most successful artistic productions that year, Kama Ginkas's play *Pushkin. Duel. Death* (*Pushkin. Duel'. Smert'*), three actors held tiny binoculars up to the audience, reversing the theater audience's inspecting gaze to suggest that a production about Pushkin's life or death is as much about those in the audience as it is about the players on the stage.[234] Ginkas's play was praised as one of the most successful artistic productions of 1999.[235] *Pushkin. Duel. Death* cannot have reached a very large audience, since it was shown at the Moscow Theater for Young Viewers (TIuZ), a tiny theater designed for an audience of forty. And nothing, it would seem, is more ephemeral than a staged play. But the lesson of Bulgakov's play, which was not seen in fact by anyone in 1937 given its postponed premiere, is that the least accessible events and artifacts may have the greatest impact.[236]

Art exhibits during the jubilee were also both ephemeral and potentially lasting, some strikingly self-conscious about the issues of value and permanence. At the prestigious Moscow gallery of Marat Guelman, Irina Waldron showed seven tapestries under the title "Fuck you, d'Anthès." The works were as dramatic as the title, mingling words with animals and faces, scandalous images with Pushkin's expressions of grief and outrage. The gallery's website directed attention not just to Waldron's mix of high and low but to a historical moment when all values were being reassessed, when Pushkin remained perhaps the only shared national language.[237] The Constructivist Yuri Avvakumov chose a more direct indicator of his interest in the question of value in his exhibit "Pushkin and Money" ("Pushkin i den'gi"), which opened at XL Gallery in Moscow on January 29, 1999 (the old-style day of Pushkin's death). Avvakumov used graphic works and

FIGURE 12. Lev Melikhov, untitled photograph, *New Literary Review* (*Novoe literaturnoe obozrenie*), no. 37 (1999), p. 267. One of four views of the Moscow Pushkin monument published in the journal's jubilee issue, all using odd camera angles or unusual juxtapositions.

computer-generated voice-over, relying entirely on what Pushkin himself said about money, always a complaint about need.[238] The voice-over was meant to bring Pushkin's presence into the exhibit, but the graphic works were stylized, changing the handwriting and lettering to suggest a personal letter, a desperate note, or an announcement. Pushkin is himself the nation's currency; he is solid gold to those who value him but pure exchange value to his cynical detractors. Avvakumov suggests that Pushkin was as vulnerable to the difficulties of getting money as he was apt to become used as if he were himself made of coin.

What is permanent about these exhibits? The existence of the Internet lengthens and widens access to representations of artists' work, although not to the physical objects they create. If one uses permanence as a measure, then surely monuments are meant to stand as the most lasting and more imposing symbols of a jubilee. Here, too, confusion coexisted with creativity in 1999. Two new monuments were unveiled, both featuring Pushkin and his wife, a first in Pushkin commemorations and a sure sign of not only the continuing fascination with his marriage, but also the ebbing tide of criticism toward the woman who married him. One was raised near the church where they were engaged, the other near the house on Arbat where Pushkin first brought Natalia Nikolaevna after their marriage.[239] In Petersburg, an odd proposal to erect a chapel on the site of Pushkin's duel surfaced, but it was linked to a wish to demolish the obelisk now there. A letter signed by the head of the Union of Russian Writers, Valery Ganichev, repeated an old Petersburg rumor that the obelisk placed on Chernaia Rechka by the Soviets in 1937 had been illicitly taken from someone's grave.[240]

The idea that Pushkin monuments might be tainted by some secret or might themselves contain a secret is old, as old as Pushkin's own writings, where a monument (to Peter the Great) turns out to have terrifying magical powers in *The Bronze Horseman*. Mayakovsky in his 1924 poem had a Pushkin monument come beneficently to life, and many years later, in 1970, Bulat Okudzhava wrote a gentler song about a family having its picture taken with a Pushkin monument in the background. Representations of monuments, then, remain as significant as the objects themselves—indeed in some ways more significant, since the second version is already an interpretation, a suggestion of an attitude toward the monument that can make it less frozen into stillness. That was shown dramatically by a series of photographs in a 1999 issue of a prestigious Moscow literary theory journal: four photographs by Lev Melikhov of the Moscow Pushkin monument used the style of Soviet Constructivist photography to distort the familiar monument by using extreme close-ups (of Pushkin's hat and the drape of his coat), odd camera angles, or, in the example I reproduce here (Fig. 12), placing the monument into the background, with a man's head seen from the rear in extreme close-up in the foreground. The man wears earphones and watches a hand-held television that is nearly obscured from view. A woman to his right watches as well. Pushkin is truly relegated to the background, guarding over a man absorbed in the technological innovations of the late twentieth century. Yet in the layout of the photograph, the monument seems to arise from the man's head. Is one to infer that whatever he watches on his tiny screen also has to do with Pushkin?

Pushkin's words and ideas were used in films, stories, advertisements, dramatic spectacles, and popular festivals at anniversaries across the twentieth century. Individual Russians continued to find his words and his image compelling despite an atmosphere that routinized or demeaned them. From the top down, there was every attempt at self-importance, but in 1999 there were voices to answer in many tones, including lightness: as the theater director Kama Ginkas put it, Pushkin never goes out of Russian consciousness precisely because of his unbearable lightness.[241]

4 Document, Fidelity, and the Cinematic Image

> Art is tightly bound up with questions of moral responsibility and has a much more fully expressed moral pathos than does science or scholarship. Film has a special place here: it does not tell by means of words; it creates the illusion of a "secondary reality," and so the filmmaker powerfully influences the intellectual and, more important, the emotional and volitional aspects of a person's identity.
> —Yuri Lotman and Yuri Tsivian

Commemorations of Pushkin as Russia's national poet have long appeared on film. Cinematic treatments of Pushkin balance their lament at the tragedy of his death with pictures of his creative process as a poet, often using the technique that the Formalists identified as exposing artifice (*obnazhenie priema*) to put interpretation and self-conscious commentary into ironic double play. Writers can do this, too (Bitov and Sinyavsky, for example), but film directors can mix a fullness of period detail with poetic and visual quotation, and evocative music as well. As a result, the films are often incredibly beautiful in a way Western viewers have found in, say, the work of Ismail Merchant and James Ivory. These films can have similar elements of nostalgia, and, because of Pushkin's elevated status in Russian culture, the nostalgia evokes both a fragile sense of national identity and an anxiety about losing the authenticity he once promised. Following Svetlana Boym's definitions, I find two types of nostalgia here, one that is "reconstructive and collective," the other "ironic, fragmentary, and singular."[1] Some Pushkin films create the illusion that Pushkin lives, that he writes his poems and stories before a viewer's eyes. Their nostalgia is reconstructive, their pleasures are collective. Others create more ironic forms of nostalgia, always about loss as they show over and over again that Pushkin is irrevocably, tragically gone.

Russians have been making movies about Pushkin since the advent of cinema, beginning with *The Life and Death of Pushkin* (*Zhizn' i smert' A. S. Pushkina*, 1910).[2] More pre-revolutionary films based on the classics were inspired by Pushkin than by any other writer, the earliest instance of which was *Boris Godunov* (1907).³ It is striking that the new art form would turn to Pushkinian material from its inception, and that the earliest reception of cinema in Russia would have had, as Yuri Tsivian has argued, a quality of estrangement (*ostranenie*, to cite another Formalist term), giving viewers the "uncanny feeling that films somehow belonged to the world of the dead."⁴ Pushkinian material fit extremely well into the new art form of cinema—it was in a sense already uncanny.

As cinema became a more routine part of Russian and Soviet culture, Pushkin films struck out into new areas. These included biographical films, typically focused on his death; narrative films based on his writings; fictional films inspired by elements of his life or work; and documentaries. In this chapter, I will not treat the last, although questions of documentary fidelity occur in all Pushkin films, and scholarship on documentary practice has been very useful to me. Guided by Bill Nichols's work, I define Pushkin films by their appeal to an audience presumed to know about Pushkin already.⁵ Assumed familiarity means that the epistemology of Pushkin films, as in much art, literature, and journalism about him, depends on repetition. In anniversary celebrations, we saw how press accounts have worked less to give new information than to intone familiar facts and recast known images. The risk of this repetition is that it can ritualize praise, and anything memorable or new can get lost in the well-known details. In film, directors nostalgically present familiar words and images, hoping to offer a new angle on old material; some filmmakers seek more innovation and denounce routinized cultural appreciation and the cult it creates.

Pushkin films exude confidence in conveying his words (typically by having him or others seem to declaim the texts), but they are nervous about representing him visually. His saintly aura makes it potentially transgressive to represent him in film (as on the stage). Two films confront this risk of representation directly: Pushkin is virtually absent from Leonid Menaker's biographical film *The Last Road* (*Posledniaia doroga*, 1986), whereas the image of Pushkin's body, especially his face, proliferates in the fictional fantasy *Side Whiskers* (*Bakenbardy*, 1990). There, the filmmaker suggests that the more pervasive Pushkin's visible image is, the less presence he actually has in the culture. Two other films avoid having an actor pretend to be Pushkin by focusing on the poet's creative process. *Little Tragedies* (*Malen'kie tragedii*, 1979) is a television adaptation of the four plays of 1830, bound together by passages from Pushkin's poetry and fiction. It is a long period piece, carefully re-creating historical and atmospheric details with all the documentary fidelity of biographical films. *Little Tragedies* also presents an allegory of the creative process, establishing intriguing parallels between the director's vision and that of Pushkin himself. Directed by Mikhail Shveitser, *Little Tragedies* is one of the best screen adaptations of the late Soviet period, embodying Russia's reverence toward its classics and its ways of adapting them for contemporary use. A very different film will conclude the chapter, Andrei Khrzhanovsky's *My Favorite Time* (*Liubimoe moe vremia*, 1987). Based on Pushkin's drawings, which it animates, this film offers the pleasure of cartoons to engage the viewer's imagination and fantasy. It takes us back to childhood, yet the director also evokes the complicated adult world in which Pushkin created his best work.

These are, then, enormously different films, not just in type but also in the ways they find viewers (television, movie theaters, film festivals) and in the ways they contribute to Russia's myth of a national poet. I begin with a film that adds still other forms of difference to this mix: *Keep Me Safe, My Talisman* (*Khrani menia, moi talisman*, 1986), which just barely qualifies as a Pushkin film. Precisely because of this gentler use of Pushkinian themes, it delicately asks the question of relevance. How can a film director adapt Pushkinian techniques? What does a viewer learn from Pushkin? What magic, in other words, can his world work for the screen?

Film and 'Talisman'

In 1825, Pushkin wrote several poems to Countess Elizaveta Vorontsova (1792–1880), whom he had known and loved in Odessa.[6] Of them, the melodic "Keep Me Safe, My Talisman," is especially well known. The poet asks that an object, given to him by a woman he treasures, protect him. The poem never names the magic object; Pushkin's sister said in her memoirs that it was a signet ring, a gift from Vorontsova that matched one in her possession. In the poem, the talisman shelters the poet in the ocean's storm, eases the loneliness of foreign travel, and lessens the terror of armed struggle, but it cannot erase the pain associated with his beloved, who gave it to him on a day of sadness. Both she and the talisman are associated with sweet deception, betrayal, and the poison of memory.[7]

The film *Keep Me Safe, My Talisman*, takes its title from the refrain of this poem, and its story and images explore similar emotions. They inhere in the film's melodramatic love plot: a journalist, Aleksei Dmitriev, and his young wife Tanya encounter a peculiar man, Anatoly Klimov, during a trip to Boldino. Klimov pursues Tanya, and Aleksei challenges him to a duel. This outcome recalls Pushkin's fatal duel: Klimov's self-conscious behavior copies d'Anthès's odd infatuation with Natalia Nikolaevna, and Klimov even tries to discuss the behavior of d'Anthès and Pushkin with Aleksei.

The Pushkinian context lends this story both its comedy and its near tragedy. Aleksei and Tanya are in Boldino for an anniversary celebration. Familiar sights—the Boldino house, the white bridge over the small pond, the statue of Pushkin in front of the house—appear throughout the film, imbuing present-day events with meanings from the past. A mime troupe is rehearsing in the wooded setting, offering glimpses of costumed actors made up as Pushkin, Natalia Nikolaevna, and others. As these players wander through the landscape, they create the illusion that Pushkin and his wife mix with present-day visitors. (It is bizarre to show Pushkin here with his wife, since his visits to Boldino were all without her; the filmmaker presumably indulges this error so that the couple can fill out the background for the troubled relations between Aleksei and Tanya.)

Another visitor, the poet and singer Bulat Okudzhava, feels that Pushkin is alive in Boldino, that he might appear in the landscape. This is a commonplace in talk about Pushkin museums, but the film gives the comment fresh credibility by attributing it to Okudzhava; Pushkin is alive to him as a creative force. Okudzhava articulates unofficial and idiosyncratic views about Pushkin in the film, and three of his songs are heard. The actor Mikhail Kozakov, renowned for his recitations of Russian poetry including Pushkin, also appears, playing himself, as does, fleetingly, a Pushkin scholar, Sergei Fomichev. These men lend authenticity to the film's Pushkinian themes, and their presence gives *Keep Me Safe, My Talisman* the occasional feel of a documentary (also emphasized when we see Aleksei, a journalist, "interview" Okudzhava and others).

Something equally documentary emerges in a long set-piece that comes about halfway through the film. It is a late-night gathering for Kozakov, Okudzhava, Aleksei, Klimov, Tanya, and the museum director, Aleksei's good friend Mitya. It helps along the love plot, because Klimov dances in the background with Tanya, and some interesting Pushkin talk occurs in the foreground.[8] All the participants express views about what response contemporary Russians can make to Pushkin's life and work. The conversation begins with Kozakov's inebriated insistence that Pushkin cannot be represented on the screen, because an actor cannot play a genius. His words largely misfire, and his reiterations are overplayed, so much so that one realizes that Kozakov, a talented actor, is likely giving an exaggerated version of himself (his first appearance in the film, in broad daylight but with equally slurred speech, seems more genuinely a "caught" moment, although one never knows).[9] His comments are symbolically important, bespeaking a widely held conviction that Pushkin should not be played, a view that will also animate *The Last Road*.[10] Okudzhava gently puts aside Kozakov's claim that there is a difference between a genius and a normal, everyday person, implying that this is the wrong place to begin, even if it is true. The film in effect has Kozakov espousing an official view of Pushkin as elevated and mythic, and Okudzhava demonstrating that this monolithic perspective has harmful effects. He recounts an old idea for a film script, to show the aftermath of Pushkin's last duel from the point of view of d'Anthès and to locate all the action in d'Anthès's rooms. D'Anthès would come to recognize that he has killed someone extraordinary. The film idea got nowhere, he tells his friends, and his comments show how hard it can be to introduce alternative interpretations of Pushkin to a wider public. In Okudzhava's next anecdote, a scholar, Liubov Kraval, cannot get her interpretations of Pushkin's drawings published.[11] Both these moments align the film with views of Pushkin that are risky.[12]

The film generally associates itself with Okudzhava's views. Gerald Smith describes Okudzhava as "a poet who for most of his active life had been, at best, tolerated by the Soviet cultural establishment," who had remarkably little official public exposure, and who had been "subjected at times to vicious negative criticism," a poet "whose work had circulated for the most part on illegal tape recordings" or abroad.[13] This reputation may be one reason why the film makes Okudzhava more important than his few minutes on camera would suggest. His music begins and ends the film, first with the song "The past cannot be brought back" ("Byloe nel'zia vorotit'") and then with the song "A visiting family takes its picture near the Pushkin monument" ("Priezzhaia sem'ia fotografiruetsia u pamiatnika Pushkinu," 1970). The latter song includes the observation that contemporary silliness and petty crimes become charming when seen against the background of Pushkin ("How charming / (for those in the know) / are all our foolish mistakes and petty evil deeds / against the background of Pushkin!"; "Kak obaiatel'ny / (dlia tekh, kto ponimaet) / vse nashi gluposti i melkie zlodeistva / na fone Pushkina!").[14] That sentiment is tested in *Keep Me Safe, My Talisman*: Aleksei's duel with Klimov is both petty and filled with ridiculous details. Okudzhava's song and the film more generally treat this bit of petty evil with good humor, the comic details serving to make the characters seem silly but in a tender sort of way. A sharper interpretation could be offered, however: the misdeeds of the present are small compared with the graver sins of the past, and the present, even in its errors, is not worthy of the past.

Okudzhava reads one other poem, which he left unfinished because he felt that he was simply repeating Pushkin. That is an illusion, though.

> Taking advantage of other rights,
> Let me repeat after you,
> Keep me safe, my talisman.

> Into our souls, stealthily,
> Crawls first evil truth, then deception.
> While not everything is lost
> Keep me safe, my talisman.[15]

Okudzhava repeats the line "Keep me safe, my talisman," and Pushkin's rhyme words, and he takes the phrase "other rights" from Pushkin's 1836 poem "(From Pindemonte)," but his point is not mimicry. He contrasts his era to Pushkin's: now is a time when nearly everything is lost. These lines echo notes of dissatisfaction that run through the film, particularly in the "evil truth" and "deception" that crawl into the soul. The film's director, Roman Balaian, has said that he wished to show that "we are wonderful, subtle, smart, and so perceptive, but we are not what we take ourselves to be."[16] This statement suggests a film about hypocrisy, but critics who agreed that the film contained important social criticism were more inclined to see it as a comment on honor. One found few options here for honorable behavior by a man whose wife has been seduced.[17] Another agreed, seeing "an intelligent and noble man who comes up against the reality of an unceremonious encroachment on the foundations of his family."[18]

The film thus derives its meaning in some part from a comparison with Pushkin's behavior during his duel with d'Anthès; it attempts "to create a contemporary, compact model of the situation 'Pushkin—Nathalie—d'Anthès.'"[19] But does the tragedy of Pushkin's last duel remain, or does the film turn it into farce? Much of the film plays as farce, particularly in scenes of Aleksei and his friend Misha clowning around with a kind of mock combativeness. We might read this playful fighting as the innocent underside of genuine fighting (or dueling), but the duel between Aleksei and Klimov is also performed with ridiculous mockery. Klimov poses under an umbrella, whistling and turning in profile as Aleksei takes aim to shoot him, but Aleksei faints without getting off a shot, the kind of behavior one associates with theatrical ladies, not men determined to settle a score. Klimov then dances through the motions of pouring muddy water on Aleksei's face to revive him. He bows deeply and disappears into thin air.[20]

The film counters such silly scenes with an enormous dose of seriousness, and it especially takes the Pushkinian context seriously (as in the heated exchange between Kozakov and Okudzhava). In ways that occupy perhaps too much screen time, the hero focuses fiercely on his feelings of betrayal. And he gets those around him to pay attention to his feelings, too, by allowing them (and us) to believe that he has killed Klimov—Balaian delays the presentation of the duel scene, eventually shown as a dazed dream or flashback. Critics reacted sharply to this device, one speculating nervously about what motivates it. (Does Aleksei mislead Tanya to make her suffer? Does he lie out of shame that he was too weak to kill Anatoly? Is he by nature a "mystifier"?)[21] My own view is that the delay has less to do with the psychology of the hero, who seems desperate and out of control, than with the film's turn toward melodrama.

Peter Brooks, who shaped late-twentieth-century scholarship on melodrama, has pointed out that "the final act of melodrama will frequently stage a trial scene . . . in which the character of innocence and virtue is publicly recognized through its signs, and publicly celebrated and rewarded, while the villain is bodily expelled from the social realm: driven out, branded as evil, relegated to a space off-stage and outside the civilized world."[22] When Klimov disappears from the duel scene, he indeed seems a villain who is "bodily expelled from the social realm." And Aleksei seems the positive hero. It is he, for example, whose name is derived from Pushkin's initials (he is Aleksei Petrovich, a change from Rustam Ibragimbekov's film script, where, in an ironic twist, the character who became Klimov was named Alexander Sergeevich). The actor who plays Aleksei, Oleg Iankovsky, has said, "My character proved to be a man with surprisingly thin skin," one who "equates his honor and the purity of his love with life itself"; such men are "our defense against vulgarity, coarseness, and self-satisfaction."[23] Alexander Abdulov, who plays Klimov, describes Anatoly as the classical bearer of evil, the one who destroys.[24] In the film script, the prototype for Aleksei, Kirill, also associates this enemy with a kind of banal immorality that has the power to do immense harm. Tellingly, he says, "I want to kill you for Pushkin, because people like you once pushed him to his death."[25] But can Aleksei embody the moral force that counters such evil? One could find him, rather, to be pathetic and weak,[26] especially in the film's conclusion, when he maintains neither consciousness nor conscience.

A test of Aleksei's goodness is to consider not just his words and decisions, but also his physical presence, the language of his body. The film's affinities with melodrama especially urge this approach. As Brooks observes, "the melodramatic body is a body seized by meaning," which means that we need to read carefully its "aesthetics of mute expression."[27] *Keep Me Safe, My Talisman*, with its inclusion of a troupe of mimes, invites such a reading by showing actors whose entire communicative apparatus is in their bodies. The mimes even teach Tanya some of their movements (and Klimov intently observes Tanya copying these gestures in her awkward way—he finds her enchanting, and he copies these movements as if in a trance). In one dance scene, the mimes mix with Boldino visitors to further integrate them into the film. Aleksei also uses his body to express something that requires no words, although he always imitates emotions in an ironic way. When he first sees his friend Misha, the two greet each other with a limping walk, where each mirrors the other as if they were two men with wooden legs. It is a ritual that they must have done often in the past and that well expresses the intimacy of their connection, but the scene also has them turn mockingly physical, pretending to punch or shove combatively. A more memorable and consequential mix of clownishness with aggressiveness occurs when Aleksei, in a performance he believes is only for Tanya, squats and struts like a hunchbacked dwarf.[28] But it turns out that Klimov witnesses this show, and I cannot help thinking that the real reason Aleksei challenges him to a duel is that he feels ashamed by his antics, especially before a man who emerges from a bedroom where his wife sits in tears. Duels were their own form of ritualized humiliation—making a man stand before you while you aimed a pistol at him, making him hide his fear because of the rules of honor—and Aleksei wishes to impose such a punishment on Klimov.[29]

Klimov is not shamed, of course. His clowning around never makes him look ridiculous, even during the duel. In the tea-drinking scene, he stealthily and surely dances with Tanya in the dark background. His body moves confidently through space for the film's duration. He often waits and watches, whistling expressively to himself or contorting his face in secret reaction to what he has seen. He follows Tanya and Aleksei with his eyes, staging his encounters with them. In one meeting that has no chance about it, he stands in the foreground of the scene, and we hear the couple coming up in the background; he turns around to meet them face on. Klimov is in fact something of a camera (one wonders if his name was meant to remind viewers of the Soviet director Elem Klimov, who was especially popular and increasingly powerful in the late 1980s), and like a camera, he has good control of what comes in and out of his field of vision. He is not the film's only observant player. Pushkin, shown as the statue in the park and as a portrait, watches over Klimov's pursuit of Tanya, and the camera emphasizes the fixity of his gaze. His impassivity reflects badly on Klimov, whose acts of watching become increasingly malevolent. Klimov vanishes when the duel ends, departing from the scene mysteriously when the film is over.[30] This may add to his evil aura—he resembles no one so much as a Mephistophelian demon, with the demon's charm, not unlike the consultant in Bulgakov's *Master and Margarita*. Abdulov, in fact, playing Klimov gives the most interesting performance in the film.[31]

This comparison of how the two actors appear bodily on the screen complicates any view of Klimov as evil, Aleksei as good. All the clowning around was added by Balaian to Ibragimbekov's script, where the dueling figures were compared to pieces on a chessboard,[32] a more serious metaphor, and where the Klimov figure is far more objectionable. He behaves deceptively and in an offensive way, luring the couple to a dinner where they are uninvited guests and then provocatively stirring up conversation about d'Anthès. Balaian lightens many elements of the film script in this way (changing its claustrophobic settings of ship and urban apartment to Boldino, for example), in part from his wish to imitate the light, improvisational quality he associates with Pushkin.[33]

How Pushkinian is it, though? A critic who insists that the main theme of the movie is "Pushkin and us, as we are today," concludes that the theme is never elaborated, in part because the director mixes pathos with sarcasm, tastelessness with silliness.[34] This criticism may be based on a dislike of the film's playfulness, and perhaps a lingering Soviet aesthetic preference for firmer delineations between good and evil, especially when it comes to Pushkin. But it is not enough to say that the film is insufficiently Pushkinian because it fails to rise to the level of his seriousness; rather, one wants to know what precisely the film wishes to say about the relevance of his life and work to modern-day Russians. That in fact seems to be its goal: can a modern man, faced with a family situation in some ways like the one Pushkin found himself in the late 1830s, learn anything from his example? For all its idyllic evocation of the Boldino landscape and museum, *Keep Me Safe, My Talisman*, believes that the answer is no. Pushkin's sense of honor does not translate into the late Soviet context. Family life, masculine identity, and patterns of communication have all changed too much.

Balaian offers another criticism by transposing the theme of fidelity, usually represented in film as historical fidelity. *Keep Me Safe, My Talisman*, instead explores marital fidelity, a topic that is uncomfortably pertinent to Pushkin's last duel. In so doing, the film shows not that Pushkin's life experiences can model contemporary behavior, but that the travails of modern life offer new ways to understand the age of Pushkin. Okudzhava's song lyrics imply that there can be no loyalty to Pushkinian principles or ideals, and for Balaian there is not much loyalty within marriage, either. The film's atmosphere of nostalgia is permeated by irony and loss, yielding a cinematic experience that is fragmentary and uneven. I turn now to a movie made at the same time, where a more unified presentation of similar themes strives for deeper nostalgia.

Pushkin's 'Last Road'

The Last Road seems a straightforward biographical film. It reenacts the days of Pushkin's duel and death, but without Pushkin as a player on the screen. His absence is cast as a species of documentary fidelity. The director, Leonid Menaker, did not want an actor to "be" Pushkin, and his coauthor, the writer and editor Iakov Gordin, made it a condition of his participation in the project that Pushkin would not be shown on screen.[35] A historical film that enjoins the conventions of realism to create the illusion of Petersburg in 1837, *The Last Road* features key players in the drama of Pushkin's last days, with special attention to Zhukovsky, Danzas, and Viazemsky. Each displays the expected emotions: regret that they did not do more to save him, guilt at their participation in his demise, astonishment that he could be dead. Heeckeren, played by the great actor Innokenty Smoktunovsky, represents the evil indifference that many would say killed him. It is an interpretation straight out of Lermontov's 1837 poem "The Death of the Poet."

The actors all have a strong, vital physical presence in the film, which is signaled in an opening sequence that announces the techniques and themes of *The Last Road*. A servant calls for the carriage of each guest. In this film about endings, the players are all seen leaving a ball; they walk toward carriages and are driven off, evoking the sense of both finality and movement in the film's title. The gathering they depart also becomes a leitmotif in the film, where high society is glimpsed through windows and doorways indulging in its destructive pleasures. The roll call begins with political figures who play important roles in the drama, and it ends with Pushkin. As each name is called, the film's audience sees the face and upper body in close-up. As Yuri Tynianov noted, close-up shooting enlarges the actor's body out of proportion to the viewer's sense of scale and invites curiosity about the actor's transformation for this role.[36] In this film, the acting of Alexander Koliagin as Zhukovsky and Smoktunovsky as Heeckeren is enhanced by this technique. Two other players are also remarkably well chosen, Irina Kupchenko as Vera Viazemsky and Sergei Sazontiev as Konstantin Danzas. In contrast, the role of Natalia Nikolaevna is played by the less well-known actress Elena Karadzhova, and rather melodramatically at that, a choice that reflects Natalia's diminished status in a film more concerned with Pushkin's male friends and antagonists.

The few seconds in which Pushkin is seen walking to their carriage with his wife reveal a great deal about the poet's position in this society and about the filmmaker's decisions in representing him. Tellingly, the request for the carriage of "Mr. Pushkin" ("Gospodin Pushkin") elicits a query from the coachmen, "Which one?" Is it the Count? they ask. The doorman bellows back, "No, the writer" ("sochinitel'"), emphasizing the descent in rank from "His Excellency, the Minister," with which the announcements began. Pushkin and his wife are seen from the rear, she turning around as if to bid someone farewell, so that we see her lovely face. But we barely glimpse the actor (Yuri Khomutiansky) made up as Pushkin. The positioning of Pushkin and his wife is to some degree based on N. P. Ulyanov's hideous painting *Pushkin and His Wife Before a Looking-Glass at a Court Ball* (*Pushkin s zhenoi pered zerkalom na pridvornom balu*, 1936), where Pushkin and his wife look at themselves in a mirror that reflects the glittering social scene behind them. This opening sequence, with its reference to a famous portrait, is emblematic of the film's relationship to source material: whenever possible, known documentary sources are evoked in *The Last Road*.[37] Together, they reinforce the film's fidelity to artifacts that have codified public views of the poet.[38]

The film also shows many familiar images of Pushkin's demise, for example, the clock hands stopped at 2:45, the waiting crowds outside on the Moika embankment, the broken fence at the snowy scene of his duel. These sequences fill the screen with people and objects that compensate for the absence of Pushkin himself. Well-known verbal formulas are heard as well, many from his poems, memoirs by his friends, and poems about his death. Some sound natural, like Viazemsky's statement that he is turning his face away from the Pushkin family, but others are odd: Zhukovsky is ludicrously made to compose out loud his poem on Pushkin's death as he emerges from the study; Lermontov's poem "The Death of the Poet" is read by police officials as they receive their agents' reports and, peculiarly, by d'Anthès, who finds the characterization of him amusing. The oddity of these quotations accentuates the film's insistence on their inclusion, as if they need to be there at whatever cost to the movie's unity of style or psychological realism.

In these moments the film plays to its pedagogical mission and its historical status. *The Last Road* creates the illusion of familiar history with ornamental sets and well-known phrases.[39] It presents itself as producing no new knowledge, merely putting onto film known facts from literary and historical documents. But the impression of repetition is false, for *The Last Road* has an interpretation to offer of Pushkin's death, one that we readily see if we compare it to its obvious precursor, Bulgakov's play *The Last Days*. Bulgakov, as we saw in Chapter Three, interprets Pushkin's death as a conspiracy among the tsar, his officials, and evil aristocrats like Count Nesselrode. The play suggests that Pushkin's wife was guilty of infidelity, pairing her suggestively with both d'Anthès and Tsar Nicholas. Bulgakov analyzes Pushkin's death in a way that is fully consonant with the 1930s, when the emphasis was placed on conspiracy, betrayal, and intrigue among the powerful.

The Last Road invites comparison to *The Last Days* by the echo of its title and by its similar decision to leave Pushkin out of the action. Excluding him allowed Bulgakov to show that Pushkin's death was a drama played out by other people. He died because of their deeds, not because of his own actions, in effect. But the film's version of social intrigue is significantly different: he was betrayed by his *friends*, the film suggests, and emphasis is laid on Viazemsky and Zhukovsky, particularly when they discuss Pushkin's difficulties during a carriage ride.[40] Zhukovsky, whose ties to the imperial court merit frequent reference, orders Pushkin's servant to see to it that his master appears at court functions in his Gentleman of the Bedchamber uniform, and the disloyalty of this directive is underlined when the servant nearly dresses the dead poet in the humiliating costume. Pushkin died, the film argues, not because his enemies plotted against him (as in Bulgakov's play), but because his friends failed him.[41]

In its dramatization of a failure of loyalty, *The Last Road* enacts one of the central problems in the veneration of Pushkin—how the love for him is narrowed to loyalty, which requires watchfulness against possible disloyalty. We might say that the film adopts its ethos from Pushkin's lifetime, when strong bonds of friendship among aristocratic men had the cultural importance to make them the subject matter of poetry and public discourse.[42] *The Last Road* criticizes Pushkin's friends for their inability to act out of true devotion. Zhukovsky tells Viazemsky that he has "no one, except for all of you. No wife, children. You, and Pushkin," but later neither man can part with his own concerns long enough to do what is needed to save Pushkin. A failure of loyalty makes Pushkin's death inevitable, and on this point the film is unsparing in its criticism. It is filled with blame.[43] In vulgar contrast, *The Last Road* presents the circle of friends surrounding d'Anthès, particularly in the scene when he reclines wounded after his duel and they dramatically fear for his health. *The Last Road* also alludes to Heeckeren's erotic attachment to d'Anthès, for example, when d'Anthès charges him with being jealous of Natalia Nikolaevna and with not understanding or caring for women, and when Heeckeren looks all too tenderly at the officers who come carousing to their apartment; one of these officers somewhat resembles d'Anthès. All their scenes together are tinged with an air of predation and decadence.

Small wonder, then, that Pushkin does not appear on screen. He is a minor figure in the drama of his own death. *The Last Road*, like *The Last Days*, makes him a martyr, and the film's idea of his martyrdom depends on the absence of his body. Martyrdom and disembodiment are not unrelated, as Natalia Ivanova noted in a controversial essay about Russian nationalism.[44] That is not because martyrdom, as in saints' lives, does not involve bodily injury—it almost always does—but because the rhetoric of martyrdom has stressed spiritual suffering. Ivanova is principally interested, then, in the political consequences of disembodiment, and the film I consider next, *Side Whiskers*, links embodiment to nationalist aspirations. Here, the question is more complexly psychological and historical: *The Last Road* does not show Pushkin's body, but it uses words to refer to it, creating a verbal narrative about pain when the sufferer cannot be seen. One of the clichés about the forty-six hours when Pushkin lay dying of an abdominal gunshot wound is that they were hours of torment and courage. In the film, Dr. Arendt describes Pushkin's condition with the following: "It is a rare soldier who can withstand such pain."[45] Zhukovsky answers that Pushkin is "fearless" and rare ("nam ne cheta").[46] The servant Nikita brings Konstantin Danzas Pushkin's gun, at his orders, with the apparent request that Danzas come in and shoot him (in Danzas's memoirs, Pushkin had concealed the gun in his bed in order to shoot himself because the pain was so bad, but Danzas found out about the gun and took it).[47] Both tales emphasize Pushkin's pain and suffering, worsening the tragedy of his demise while keeping the suffering body off screen. *The Last Road* cloaks Pushkin in near-invisibility, making a mystery of the man who issued a challenge, fought a duel, fell to the snow, and lay in his bed dying. Just as scenes iconographically refer back to paintings and known artifacts, creating a kind of *mise en abyme* where an image refers back to another image, so the Pushkin story in *The Last Road* refers back to often repeated stories and documents. There can be no act of reference that could take us back to Pushkin himself; we are forced to interpret his death through others' impressions and opinions.

How, then, to end the film? I surmise considerable uncertainty on this score, based on the strong departure from the final scenes in the film script, where Pushkin's possessions are auctioned off. The film shows instead the pawnbroker who held items of silver and jewelry against fifteen thousand rubles he had lent the poet, the objects themselves now laden less with financial than emotional value. They make the pawnbroker feel guilty, as does Zhukovsky, who comes in to say that he need not worry, the debt will be paid. Zhukovsky had just gone through Pushkin's papers with Dubelt, another moment when objects from the poet's life come to have a different value and when Zhukovsky rants against the power and indifference of the state. There is embarrassment and shame all around, it seems—Zhukovsky's, the pawnbroker's, the young cavalry officer who keeps turning up. The film then ends with a juxtaposition of scenes, including those that show Pushkin's coffin being transported to Sviatogorsk Monastery for burial. Beginning with the title, *The Last Road* has used the imagery of the road as a unifying device.[48] One of the few strong technical interventions of the editing process occurs at this point, with scenes of the carriages and police escort intercut with other events. The very final image shows the site of the duel, with a peasant repairing the broken fence; the duel sequence too, had been given in segments, and it is now concluded. But the fence repair does not connote some broader form of reconciliation or healing. The music is a grinding waltz, also heard in scenes that show the players of high society enjoying themselves, and it continues as the credits roll. The film hopes to send its viewers out of the theater feeling outrage.

A final image intercut into this sequence is the creation of Pushkin's death mask.[49] The sculptor's hands tap at the mold, then pull back the layer of plaster cover to show a last semblance of Pushkin's face. We see an object produced with strict fidelity to facial features because of its imprint technique, thus a splendidly chosen symbol of the film's own aspirations to historical fidelity. In the death mask, however, we also see a subject turned into an object. Subjectivity seems for an instant to be most intense as it is vanishing: one seems "to trace the lineaments of the singular biographical subject as he appeared at the moment of death."[50] This is also the moment when the identity of the person known as Pushkin is transformed into the myth of Russia's national poet. The film in general seeks to trace the process of Pushkin's transformation into a cultural symbol, which explains the otherwise odd conjunction of objects in the final scenes. We see Pushkin's papers sorted by Zhukovsky and Dubelt, the silverware and jewelry at the pawnbroker's, and the death mask, all soon-to-be-fetishized objects that bring into sharper focus the earlier glimpses of clock, dueling pistols, fancy court uniform, and the like. In its compulsion to record the sight of these objects, the film acts as a museum and provides its viewers a glance at something nearly lost. In that impulse, *The Last Road* is not unlike other historical films about Pushkin, which use the realia of his period as a legitimating device. It points to an absence in *Keep Me Safe, My Talisman*, where we expect a film that was shot in Boldino and that has "talisman" in its title to hold up the objects of the place as treasured exhibits. But the interior of the Boldino house is seen once, quickly, and in a shot that focuses on the hero, not the setting. *Keep Me Safe, My Talisman*, does not believe in the magic of objects, for it shows how magic can no longer save a lost soul. *The Last Road* holds to a deeper nostalgia, one that inheres in its project of taking viewers back to the era when Pushkin lived and when he died.

One other object that is said to have belonged to Pushkin deserves mention in *The Last Road*, a black shawl. When the pawnbroker displays the silver and gems to his wide-eyed spectator, the sad cavalry officer from d'Anthès's regiment, he mentions that he also has that famous black shawl. The film's viewers will recognize it, perhaps aided by the two lines from Pushkin's poem by that title ("Chernaia shal'," 1820) sung when the servants await news of his health; and, earlier, the poem is performed during a night of card-playing and drinking. The poem is brilliantly chosen for this film, for, as we know from the melodies that set the poem to music, as well as the enormous influence it had on the Russian ballad, "The Black Shawl" came to hold a special cultural status.[51] That status is as if proleptically thematized in the poem itself, which opens and closes with descriptions of the shawl that remains after the poet's lover has died (at his hand, no less); "The Black Shawl" also sings of jealousy, violence, and loss, themes that *The Last Road* plays out in its way. The shawl seems more of a talisman than anything in *Keep Me Safe, My Talisman*.

As different as *The Last Road* and *Keep Me Safe, My Talisman* are, they share a fascination with Pushkin's duel and death. It is no accident that an early, melodic Pushkin poem of love and betrayal figures in each film. Both want their viewers to have some (but not much) sense of Pushkin as poet; thus both cite a well-known poem, use the combination of music and poetry to intensify the emotional response to the poetry, and rely on poems in which Pushkin seemed to write of his own powerful feelings. In the end, though, the two films are more interested in the psychology and ethics of their players, whether they be the contemporary fictional heroes of *Keep Me Safe, My Talisman* or the historical figures of *The Last Road*. We turn now to a film configured instead around politics, both the politics of national myths and the power relations between individuals who are joined by the bonds of friendship.

Sex and Power in 'Side Whiskers'

Side Whiskers (*Bakenbardy*, 1990), directed by Yuri Mamin, tells the story of a Pushkin club in the fictional town of Zaborsk. The action takes place during what we now recognize as the chaotic end of perestroika, whose waning ethos it mocks; this was a time when it was daring to lampoon Komsomol officials. The film uses pseudo-documentary technique in including a television news reporter played by the director. Mamin's strong credentials as a film satirist mean that we should expect him to turn his camera against a rapidly changing society.[52] But the real target of *Side Whiskers* is Russian fascist nationalism, whose power was ominously on the rise. The nationalist Pushkin club is formed to eradicate a free-spirited collective of young rebels called Capella. The music and dancing of Capella give the film much of its energy, and not just because the dancing is lewd. Mamin resists the pattern of pornographic representation that Russian cinema was then exploring avidly, and instead models his Capella street scenes along the lines of Bakhtin's notion of bodily pleasure and carnival inversion.[53] Women's breasts and swaying hips are displayed with audacious abandon, but the real target of revelation and parody is the phallus, inventively mocked in the song "Organs," a paean to male sexual organs and a send-up of the Soviet organs of police surveillance. Phallic objects are mocked by castration games practiced on a cucumber, by a young man who uses a dildo as a microphone, by a young woman who uses her dildo-microphone as a whistle, and by a crowd-pleasing game where phallic balloons race like programmed rats.

The director shows that he values the ethos and aesthetics of Capella by giving them all the best scenes, and by having the Pushkin club later perform a pallid nightclub act that suggests how much was lost by the rout of Capella. Capella's performances are self-consciously and happily theatrical.[54] They stage machine-gun murders that end when the "dead" stand up and laugh, but the Pushkin club's violence is all too real. Shrieking scenes of "Pushkintsy" chasing members of Capella through the streets and viciously beating them are a form of pogrom. Thanks to Capella's antics, the visual representations of *Side Whiskers* are focused on the body: in the Capella scenes, bodies fill the screen with energy and movement. The Pushkin club also exists according to the logic of the body, since it has all members masquerade as Pushkin. The side whiskers of the film's title are sported by the members, dozens of young men (and one woman, Valkiria). The club members bear the imprint of Pushkin's profile on their chests. A bizarre scene of branding redoubles the logic of the body, so that members strive both to be like Pushkin and to express their devotion to him by bearing his mark. In a revenge scene against the journalist who introduces the film, they brand him, too, after a desperate chase scene where one expects them to beat him up. The film prepares the viewer for Pushkin club violence and instead supplies a Capella-like joke.

The Pushkin club is led by Victor Ivanovich, and it is with his face that the film opens. Even before the opening credits roll, the film shows an extreme close-up shot of Victor's face, filling the screen. He looks warily to each side—his head is still, only his eyes move—[55] and then looks straight into the camera and begins declaiming Pushkin's poem "The Prophet." As the scene unfolds, an air of gaiety yields to palpable doom. The camera pulls back from his face to reveal that he speaks into a portable loudspeaker in Leningrad before Kazan Cathedral, a gathering place for extreme right-wing political groups like Pamiat. Victor is taken off by policemen, and a loud, intense march plays during the opening title sequence. He then goes to Zaborsk with his friend Sasha, and together they go on to form the Pushkin club, eradicate Capella, and lead the club to new heights. They create the Pushkin Jugend, put up a massive poster of Pushkin with an outstretched Seig Heil salute, and fix up a personalized train with Pushkin's profile as the emblem. The night they wipe out Capella is called The Night of the Long Canes, another evocation of Nazism (recalling the 1934 Night of the Long Knives, when the storm troopers of the S.A. were purged in several days of bloody violence).[56] *Side Whiskers* is not, then, particularly subtle in making its political point, a denunciation of Pamiat and other extremist groups who mix anti-Semitism with nationalism. The mode is excess. Most plot segments or images are repeated in the film in some way, for example, when the Pushkin club members come upon an opposing group of Lermontov clones (called Mtsyri), but then later in the film they morph into a terrifying band of Mayakovskys on the march.

Are these other cults meant to suggest that the choice of Pushkin in the first place is arbitrary? To answer that question one needs to consider how his poetry, life story, and visual image are deployed by the Pushkin club. The poetry is intoned like rap music, a pounding rhythm that organizes the group's calisthenics. After you have heard their recitation, you will never experience the opening lines of *Eugene Onegin* in their iambic innocence again. The first poem chosen for this treatment is an excerpt from Pushkin's 1818 poem to Pyotr Chaadaev, "Love, hope, and quiet fame" ("Liubvi, nadezhdy, tikhoi slavy"); its theme of loyal friendship is implicitly invoked

FIGURE 13. O. A. Kiprensky, *Pushkin* (1827). Tretyakov Museum, Moscow. Reproduction from E. V. Pavlova, ed., *A. S. Pushkin v portretakh* (Moscow: Sovetskii khudozhnik, 1989), vol. 1, p. 98.

by the Pushkin club. But friendship here is subject to convenience and ambition, especially between Victor and Sasha. They recite the poem with their canes poised as batons, looking little like the usual serious poets of Russia. The treatment of Pushkin's life is also distorted. Victor tells a maudlin and garbled version of the duel with d'Anthès that has him protected by a bulletproof vest, bringing tears to the eyes of the one woman club member, Valkiria.

How the film handles representations of Pushkin is more complicated. The visual signs of Pushkin would seem to be profligate: club members dress up as Pushkin, and pictures of him, both well known and in kitschy derivations, abound. In one scene, these two impulses (to mime Pushkin's looks, to reproduce known pictures of him) come together: Victor hangs the Kiprensky portrait of Pushkin in the studio of Sasha's uncle Pasha, just after he has placed a bust of Pushkin on an end table (Figs. 13, 14). When Uncle Pasha and a friend ask Victor why he idolizes Pushkin, he answers first with platitudes (including Apollon Grigoriev's statement, "Pushkin is our everything"). But then he pauses, and invites the artists to contemplate his face. "Is it possible that you don't see it?" he asks, wondering at their lack of visual imagination. With the Kiprensky portrait visible in the background, Victor strikes its pose, draping his bath towel to copy the tartan plaid Pushkin wears. It is a remarkable resemblance, he tells them, something that only happens once in 150 years.

The scene ridicules Victor, making him look silly with his bath towel, but

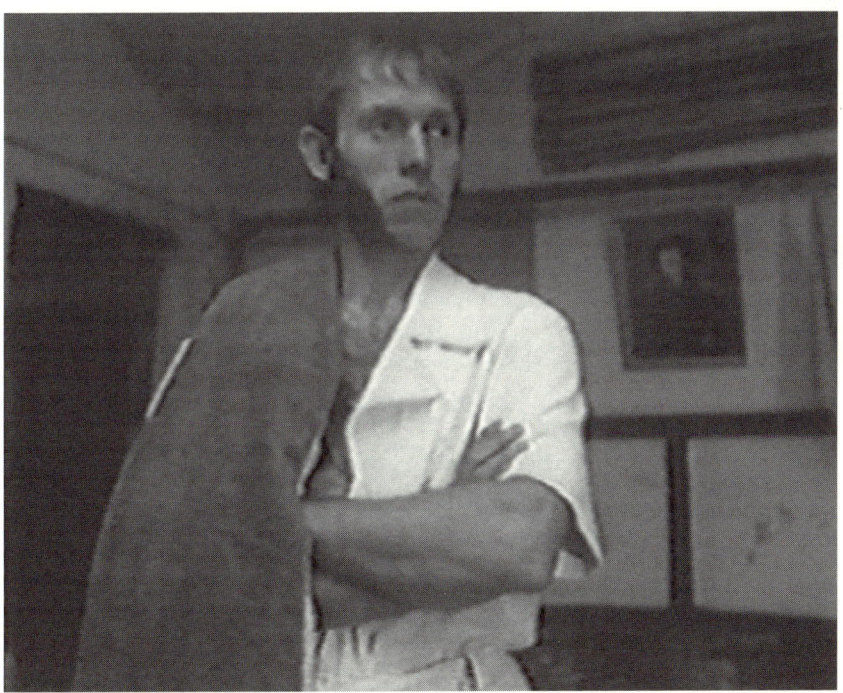

FIGURE 14. Victor (Viktor Sukhorukov) in the film *Side Whiskers* posed like Kiprensky's portrait *Pushkin*, a reproduction of which hangs in the background.

he departs the room with a frightening warning that no one should dismiss him as mad. His gesture reveals the logic of organizing a club around a collective act of masquerade. He dangerously thinks he is as godlike as Pushkin. In a later scene, when he is donning a bullet-proof vest, Victor says that his life does not belong to him, it belongs to Russia. (Wearing the bullet-proof vest, however, links him to d'Anthès, not to the Russian national hero Pushkin, according to his version of the final duel.) In another early scene, Sasha tells a recruit that Victor is an extraordinary person, but he knows little about him, not even his age. Victor's class background is revealed (or Victor's version of it—he's from a poor family), but this detail is an empty Soviet convention. Victor strives to live outside his prosaic, everyday existence in the world of myth where his idol Pushkin resides.

There can be little doubt that the film perceives the veneration of Pushkin, as Victor practices it, as a dangerous form of cult worship; members of Capella observe that Victor reminds them of "Uncle Joe" (Stalin). Consider the scene when Uncle Pasha's sculptor friend makes a bust of Pushkin by slapping clay onto a Lenin sculpture in progress. With a few deft additions and reshapings, the bald, smooth face of Vladimir Ilich is transformed into a troubled, curly-haired Pushkin. The Lenin cult, with its factories turning out Lenin busts, stands as a model for the Pushkin cult that will replace it, and Uncle Pasha will end up supervising a workshop for the manufacture of Pushkin toys.

The other indication that the cult is dangerous comes in the film's ending: the Pushkin club is routed by the police, although the rout relies on the humorous, theatrical violence typical of Capella—the worst indignity is having their side whiskers shaved off. Victor Ivanovich's writhing protest makes it seem as if real pain is being inflicted, and one suspects at that moment that his public career has come to an end. But Victor is dauntless. The film ends as he leads a band of Mayakovsky clones to a new march through the streets. Their shaved heads ominously evoke the skinheads of right-wing youth culture.[57] The ending is nothing short of apocalyptic, and in that sense it resembles the end of *The Last Road*, or Mikhail Shveitser's *Little Tragedies*. But its interpretive reach is more ambitious than in those two films, whose concern is principally the Pushkin period. Mamin takes the largest possible mandate in answering the question of Pushkin's relevance to contemporary Russia, and his film is meant to show how details from his life and works, which leaders know will be recognized, have the potential for dangerous misuse. It is terror that distinguishes his film, and once again, we can see that difference by considering the Pushkin poem that fixes its tone: "The Prophet." Where the romantic lyric and romantic ballad are central in *The Last Road* and *Keep Me Safe, My Talisman*, *Side Whiskers* chooses a poem in which Pushkin dramatically describes the creative process. Mamin lets the poem set the tenor of his film. No Pushkin poem about the creative act matches the violence of "The Prophet," with its image of a poet's heart ripped out to make way for the burning coal of creative inspiration. And the ending of that poem, with its famous imperative to the poet that he burn the hearts of his listeners with his word, renders the poet's work as more aggressive than the gentle imprecations of a poem like "Keep Me Safe, My Talisman." To some extent that violence enlivens "The Black Shawl" and thus *The Last Road*, but it has Pushkin as its target. In *Side Whiskers*, the poet is not a martyr. Instead, the filmmaker insists that such a view of the poet is itself dangerous: the will to idolize a poet, or to elevate political leaders to cult status, makes citizens into hyper-obedient and all-too-malleable followers. In the leader's name, they can do unthinkable violence, and thus threaten the future of the nation they claim to love.

Mamin's film, then, shows us a danger in the forms of fidelity that mark Pushkin films in general. It exposes this danger without emulating or repeating that theme. In fact, all its acts of apparent loyalty, as when a Pushkin poem is recited or when a familiar visual image of the poet is cited, are heavily layered with mockery. *Side Whiskers* has been called a "potentially inflammatory social satire," and it smartly adapts the exaggerations and social criticism of satire.[58] More than any other Pushkin film, it poses questions of national self-definition, well exemplifying the comment by Stanislav Rassadin discussed in the Introduction linking acts of national self-definition to the moment when one "*looks at Pushkin.*" Given the visual intensity of cinema, the medium offers a splendid opportunity to think about this connection between looking at Pushkin and national self-definition. One might imagine, for example, that Russians already numbly perceive Pushkin everywhere, so frequently is his image invoked and so often have his words entered into everyday conversation. *Side Whiskers*, with its multiplication of Pushkin lookalikes, gives a vital dramatization of this consequence. In a context of near-automatic (and thus dulled) perception, film can also offer an intense alternative gaze. The intensity comes from the way film is viewed—in a darkened room, with magnified and projected images moving before the viewer and with sound filling the room.[59] Because films show simulations of Pushkin, they can draw attention to this artifice, but for the vast majority of Pushkin films, realism reigns. A fairly urgent verisimilitude is found in *The Last Road*, and, although *Side Whiskers* offers a fanciful alternative, it, too, uses the conventions of realism in its allusions to film documentary and in its political concerns. For a dramatic rejection of realist cinema, we turn to an animated film that favors expansive visual pleasures. The chapter will then conclude with a live-action film that tempers the conventions of realism in other ways.

Animating Pushkin

The cartoon that we come to now grew out of three short films with titles taken from Pushkin's poetry, made between 1977 and 1982.[60] They were assembled as a sixty-five-minute animated film, *My Favorite Time* (*Liubimoe moe vremia*), which was shown on Soviet television in 1987. The filmmaker is Andrei Khrzhanovsky;[61] the artwork is by Yuri Norshtein, a premier animator in the former Soviet Union; the music is by the late Alfred Schnittke, a brilliant innovator in classical music; and the voice of Pushkin alternates between Innokenty Smoktunovsky (who played Heeckeren in *The Last Road*) and Sergei Iursky, a stage and film actor highly regarded for his comic talents and one who often read from Pushkin's writings at one-man concerts. The seemingly modest project of a cartoon, then, drew together some of the most talented artists and performers of their generation, and *My Favorite Time* remains universally praised, a rare Pushkin film that long retains its ability to intrigue an audience. Khrzhanovsky was retrospectively awarded a UNESCO prize in 1998 and Russian prizes in 1986 and 1999 for the film, testimony to this sustained admiration.

My Favorite Time has no plot that can be summarized. It progresses chronologically from Pushkin's southern exile to his death, but frequent repetitions and transpositions twist the narrative line. It does create miniature narratives when it matches screen images to recited poetic texts. The images may enact the poem—galloping horses, dancing devils, clusters of men and women in high society—but they are as likely to embellish or contrast the words. The film's most compelling narrative is that of the imaginative act, recreating Pushkin's writing, drawing, doodling, and improvising witticisms in conversation with his friends. Perhaps this fascination with his inner world accounts for the pleasure of the film, but given the pervasiveness of melodrama and tragedy in Pushkin films, and given the trajectory of *My Favorite Time* toward death, our first question needs to be how this film exudes happiness without sacrificing the gravity of its subject.

Considerable aesthetic pleasure comes from the film's layering of sights and sounds. There is always a lot happening on the screen—for example, drawn figures in motion, an overlay of diagonal lines to suggest rain, quick lighting changes between black and white background that seem to electrify the screen, the sound of rain, a spoken text from Pushkin's writings, and orchestral music that first intensifies, then contrasts the sequence's mood. One cannot overestimate the impact of music in this film. Schnittke, rightly regarded as one of the most interesting composers of the late twentieth century, had mixed feelings about his work in cinema, which largely provided him financial security.[62] In *My Favorite Time* we have an excellent resource for approaching Schnittke, whose own performances can be heard in some

FIGURE 15. Pushkin's sketch on his manuscript page for the poem "Autumn" ("Osen'," 1834). Reproduction from T. G. Tsiavlovskaia, *Risunki Pushkina* (Moscow: Iskusstvo, 1980), pp. 28–29. Courtesy National Pushkin Museum, St. Petersburg.

of the film's piano music. Throughout, we hear the remarkable range of his musical experimentation: choral compositions, stylized waltzes, "landscape" music for strings, dissonant passages that mix jazz rhythms with folk melodies. Few films offered Schnittke so apt a showcase for his creative method of poly-stylistics.

Still, for all the different things to watch and hear in *My Favorite Time*, a powerful unifying force in the film is indicated by its subtitle, *Pushkin's Drawings* (*Po risunkam Pushkina*). The look of Pushkin's drawings, often overlapping with objects on top of one another or with writing across drawing, provides the model for the film's layered format. The animated drawings hold a viewer's attention, whatever else happens onscreen. *My Favorite Time* brings to movement familiar self-portraits, sketches of women's bodies and especially their legs and feet, the faces of friends, literary characters, historical figures, horses, landscapes, and so forth (see Figs. 15 and 16 for examples of Pushkin's drawings in manuscript pages; also see Fig. 10, in Chapter Three).[63] *My Favorite Time* includes other artistic material as visual

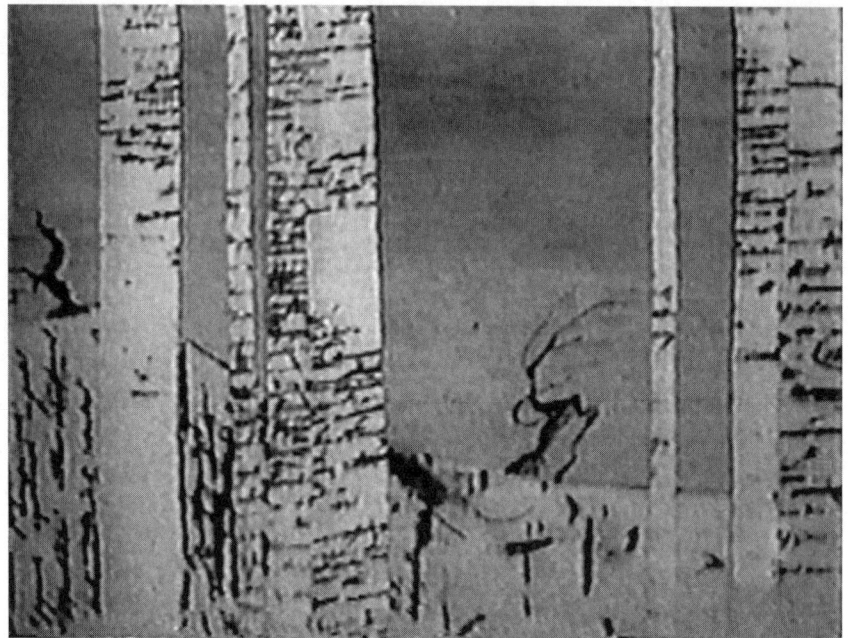

FIGURE 16. Collage of trees inscribed with Pushkin's handwriting, in Andrei Khrzhanovsky's film *My Favorite Time*.

counterpoint, like well-known portraits of tsars, etchings of Petersburg facades, and photographs of landscapes near Boldino. These may occur as interesting compositional elements, but they are typically subordinate to figures based on Pushkin's drawings.

The director, Andrei Khrzhanovsky, has said of these drawings that they show Pushkin's ability as a graphic artist to reconstruct and to be reincarnated as the object when he drew it.[64] The object has mystical properties in Pushkin's drawings, he suggests, and his role as filmmaker is to convey that magic. Other aspects of the film have seemed to work similarly. Thus one critic has suggested that Khrzhanovsky's decision to make lines of writing into rain, waves, snow, and floodwaters literalizes the elemental force of Pushkin's poetry.[65] Both these ideas revert to a pagan belief in Pushkin's magical powers, as if film has made the technology of animation work so effectively *because* of the potential magic of Pushkin's own creative acts. The poet who wrote of statues that come to life (in *The Bronze Horseman* most notably, a poem of which *My Favorite Time* makes good use) is a fitting subject for a film based on the technology of animation.[66] This technology creates the illusion of movement by a fast sequence of frames in which nothing, of course, moves at all.[67] Russians call animated films *mul'tiplikatsionnye fil'my*, using a mathematical metaphor to indicate the medium's capacity, in increasing the number of images before a viewer, to create the illusion of movement, but when we think of this film, the inherent pun in *animated films* remains: in Russian, to animate is to give an object a soul (*odushevit'*), and just as Pushkin is said by Khrzhanovsky to have breathed his own life into the objects he drew (and, of course, others would say that he does the same thing with words), so this film takes on the task of bringing Pushkin's world to life.

Another quality of his writing that the film copies is his creation of fragments and his famous ability, with only one or two lines, to conjure up an entire image or plot. Thus, for example, four lines from Pushkin's 1825 "Scene from *Faust*" ("Stsena iz Fausta") push the film's drawings off into an incredible fantasy of infernal revels; similarly, lines from the foot digression in *Eugene Onegin* motivate beautiful, swirling images of women's feet, and a later stanza conjures up the ballerina Evdokia Istomina. As in Pushkin's writings, the film exudes confidence that a viewer's knowledge of a poem or biographical event can fill out a few lines or a single sketched profile, and this laconic quality has an informal, spontaneous feel.[68] Able to rely on a knowing viewer, *My Favorite Time* dispatches abrupt bits of cinematic montage to elicit split-second emotional reactions. At times, entire poetic or epistolary texts are read, and the film seems to slow down as it savors Pushkin's "Elegy" ("Elegiia": "Bezumnykh let ugasshee vesel'e," 1830), "Lines Composed During a Night of Insomnia" ("Stikhi, sochinennye noch'iu vo vremia bessonitsy," 1830), "God grant that I not go out of my mind" ("Ne dai mne Bog soiti s uma," 1833), and nearly all of "Demons" ("Besy," 1830) and "Arion" (1827). These extended readings can be unnerving, particularly when they are paced unexpectedly. Some pause ominously and at length for eerie music and strangely animated drawings just before they end, and because so many of the texts are fragments, the return to a poem's last lines can come as a surprise, as if we were not expecting the film to give us the entire text. This happens in the performance of "Arion."

Other passages of the film are entirely wordless, governed by the moods of Schnittke's music and the inventive camera work. At times, the camera moves across still images as if with the rhythm of our own contemplation; the lens zooms in to draw us closer to a pained self-portrait or pulls us back from a seductive line drawing; the manuscript page itself turns, rocks, and shakes (as if in response to the text being read, for example "Arion"). These segments sometimes strive to replicate Pushkin's creative process, as when we hear the first line of *Gypsies* (*Tsigany*, 1824) change from its first to its final versions. We also follow Pushkin's mental changes as he draws, sometimes sketching in a self-portrait only to cross it out. Two-thirds of the way into the film, after many of the self-portraits have been shown at a glance, the animation process returns to them, adding in the lines of one after another, so that we seem to see Pushkin drawing his own image again and again. At other times, we hear the scratching pen as it transfers words from mind to page. A striking example is part of the unfinished sentence "And, like a fool, I could have been ..." ("A ia by mog, kak shut ..."), penned near drawings of a gallows, just after Pushkin has written the initials of five hanged Decembrists (shown in Fig. 10). This act of writing comes at the end of the recitation of "Arion," and its iambs sound almost as if they continue the poem. Moments like these let the film direct our attention to texts we think we have long known (both the poem and the unfinished sentence are quite famous). It is another example of *ostranenie*, the defamiliarization that film can do so well, and that this particular Pushkin film relies on heavily.

These sequences animate Pushkin's handwriting, which is a marvelous technique for replicating the creative process.[69] Every kind of mark that he made when he put pen to page is in fact used: the numbers found on some pages, for examples, are given as his mental calculations of debt; ink blots and strikeouts across a face are reenacted to show Pushkin's dissatisfaction with the images we now have. His written words are treated as compositional elements, shown on the screen as the dark rings that mark some birch trees, turned into moving droplets of rain and snow, and wittily deployed as an undulating wave of water that races up to kiss a woman's seductive feet.

Thus the film explains the pun of its title: late fall was Pushkin's favorite time of year, and references to autumn come at spaced intervals in the film, but Pushkin loved autumn because he associated it with his capacity for work, as in the Boldino autumn of 1830. The film makes his most cherished periods of time the hours when he sat, pen in hand, wrote, and drew pictures.[70] This aspect of *My Favorite Time* calls to mind the writing of Andrei Bitov: often in his essays and fictions the fantasy of a man at his desk is an organizing principle. The association is based on more than this fantasy, though: in 1999, the collaborative work of Rezo Gabriadze and Andrei Bitov was the subject of a ten-minute film by the young Ekaterina Sokolova, *Autumn Has Arrived* (*Nastupila osen'*).[71] Sokolova's work was supervised by Khrzhanovsky and Norshtein. Many years before that, Bitov and Gabriadze had shared in a project of imagining what would happen if Pushkin had been free to go abroad, the first fruit of which was *Pushkin in Spain* (*Pushkin v Ispanii*). Gabriadze's free, spirited drawings in that volume resemble Pushkin's own drawings in *My Favorite Time* (see Fig. 17). In both cases we find attempts to place the "official" Pushkin into a freer and more celebratory context. Gabriadze and Bitov liberate him from the confines of

FIGURE 17. Rezo Gabriadze's drawings of Pushkin as he might have appeared had he been free to travel to Spain. The inscription is to Andrei Bitov, who copublished several sequences of these drawings with him. Published in Gabriadze and Bitov, "Freedom to Pushkin!" *Sintaksis*, no. 27, 1990, pp. 168–69.

Russia's borders, and their work initiated the *Sintaksis* series "Freedom to Pushkin!" ("Svobodu Pushkinu!").[72]

Gabriadze and Bitov give us many Pushkins, and so does *My Favorite Time*. In particular, the film splits Pushkin into two consciousnesses, two drawn figures, and two voices (clearly one reason why two actors read Pushkin's lines, although some scenes use the same voice for both parts); the result is dialogical performance, even in moments of introspection.[73] In some passages, we see a taller, conventionally dressed (with various fabulous hats) poet conversing with a short and rotund other self. This figure (in Fig. 18), identified by scholars as a "Moor at court" ("pridvornyi arap"), plays a Sancho Panza–like companion in some segments, a servant in others. He is not, in any sense, a servile inner self—quite the opposite, he is a joking and feisty alter ego.[74] The filmmakers here rely on Pushkin's well-known identification with his Ethiopian great-grandfather, Abram Gannibal, a "Moor" at the court of Peter the Great. In one charming sequence, this chubby figure recreates Pushkin's "Imagined Conversation with Alexander I" (1825). The film reproduces its parody of autocracy and his self-parody by having the Moor play both parts, switching back and forth clumsily so as to deflate tsar and poet at once.

In the hat scene between the two Pushkins, the tall, slimmer figure of the poet in a frock coat tries on various hats from a tall, wobbly stack held out by his rotund companion. The idea for the scene surely comes from the scattering of hats found in Pushkin's drawings and from his self-portraits in various hats. They are gathered together here irreverently, a comic diversion

FIGURE 18. Sketch of a Moor at court on a page from *Eugene Onegin*, chap. 2 (1823). Reproduction from T. G. Tsiavlovskaia, *Risunki Pushkina* (Moscow, Iskusstvo, 1980), p. 342. Courtesy National Pushkin Museum, St. Petersburg.

between the two conversations with a tsar (first the imagined one, then the actual one in 1826). But the hat scene has its grim side, since it is prompted by the arrival of the police to take Pushkin off to the tsar, which was almost a form of arrest (and certainly others feared he had been arrested). That mood, which mixes humor with a fearful contemplation of imperial power, continues in the representation of the "real" conversation between tsar and poet.[75] Here Pushkin is again shown both as the tall and dignified figure and as the Moor, who blurts out something irreverent, only to be snatched away by the seemingly more noble version of the poet. Tsar Nicholas is represented by a full-body portrait, where his formal military attire makes him the incarnation of state power, although chickens scratch at the ground just below in splendid disrespect.

When the film turns to Pushkin's death, this same mix of moods obtains. The turn comes quickly, with no pause for his final duel or for his marital difficulties (all references to his marriage emphasize his love for Natalia Nikolaevna, quoting from his letters to her). The only preparation for the death sequence is in the *Bronze Horseman* section, which directly precedes it, a scene marked by foreboding imagery and dramatic music. There is the sound of a pistol shot as well, and as the music grows more ominous, inserted photographs of a rising river and the Peter and Paul Fortress. One of Pushkin's self-portraits in profile is now seen, but it rests flat on the screen: this suggestion that the poet is lying down leads visually to the death sequence. Minor-key folk music is chanted as a horse is seen trotting through a "forest" of upright columns of Pushkin's handwriting. Then, for a very few moments, the death mask is shown, and the screen fills with many self-portraits, as if compensating in advance for the loss of Pushkin's life with a multiplying presence of his face. These profiles are stacked in still rows, the camera moving from left to right across them, arriving last at the Moor, who removes his hat solemnly. The figures (the profiles, the Moor) have all been shown in white lines against a black background. Images associated with Pushkin's death follow—the clock, his books, a candle, his desk, and the music switches to a somber melody played on the organ. Four lines from one of his "Songs of the Western Slavs" ("Pesni zapadnykh slavian," 1834) are heard, lines that end "the goblet is drunk down to the bottom" ("charka vypita do dna").[76] This choice of text is unexpected, a little-known poem that has no association with his death—indeed a collection of folk stylizations usually admired by poets more than by a popular audience. Throughout the film, one realizes, folk elements in image and music have appeared in atypical ways, not to suggest that Pushkin was himself "of the people," as would be a Soviet norm, but to give to the film itself a warmer and more prosaic quality.

The film now returns to the death mask. It is perhaps the most clichéd

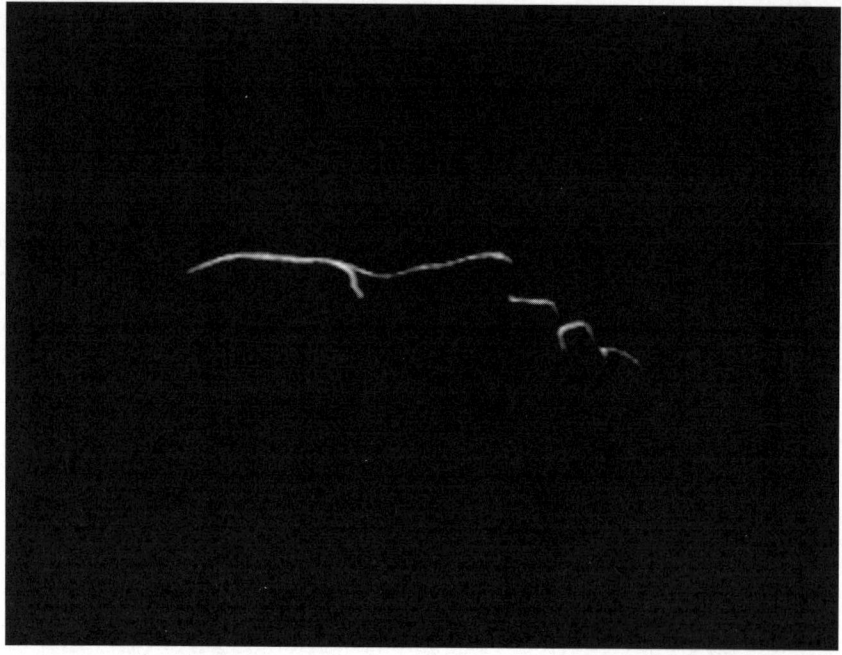

FIGURE 19. Pushkin's death mask, barely lit, shown at the conclusion of Khrzhanovsky's *My Favorite Time*.

image for his death, familiar to us from the end of *The Last Road*, but *My Favorite Time* handles the death mask as it has treated Pushkin's drawings and handwriting—as a compositional element, turning it into a kind of line drawing that shows only the profile. This is achieved by lighting the mask from above, and it looks like an eclipse of the face (Fig. 19). The film makes the mask a profile, rather than offering an *en face* contemplation of the face straight on: that follows Pushkin's own nearly uniform preference for representing himself in profile, thus looking away. It is another brilliant moment of defamiliarization. After a full hour of animated high spirits in a film that constantly changes its moves and moods, viewers who stare at the wavy white line on a black screen rightly expect it to move, to curl up, to turn itself into a flourish of handwriting or galloping horses. The mournful voice-over and stately organ music remind us that other films use the death mask as an icon of despair, making viewers gaze long and hard at the plaster replication of a dead man's face, and Khrzhanovsky keeps that same tempo (this is one of the few visually static moments in the film, and its pace suddenly slows). A light comes on over the mask, illuminating it in profile with a very slightly flickering light, as if to suggest the movement of thought, which is the subject matter of the voice-over: Vasily Zhukovsky's wish to ask Pushkin, "what do you see?" (We hear Zhukovsky's letter to Pushkin's father, which resembles his poem on Pushkin's death.)

Zhukovsky's words bespeak, perhaps, the viewers' wish to see the world as if from Pushkin's perspective, something the film has sought to reproduce by miming his mental and creative processes. *My Favorite Time* testifies to the cultural fantasy that Pushkin himself is always looking at us (compare the apparent gaze of the Pushkin statue in Boldino in *Keep Me Safe, My Talisman*, for example, or the death mask that ends *The Last Road*). But here, Pushkin is shown *looking away* (literally above himself), staring at something beyond his own life that the film invites the reader to contemplate as well. The ethereal suggestions are brought back to earth as images from Pushkin's actual work appear. This return to the words and pictures of his manuscripts allows the film one last loving comment on them. A few lines from the poem "André Chénier" (1825) follow, lines in which Chénier speaks of his belief that his manuscripts contain "his entire life"—"hopes, and dreams, and tears, and love." Chénier, about to be executed, directs his friends to preserve his manuscripts, to assemble and read his verses, and to say that he is those words. He promises: "And I, forgetting the grave's dream, / Will arise unseen and sit among you, / I will listen in."[77] The film suggests that Pushkin, too, lives in his manuscripts, and that he is "present" when his words are read. He predicts the desire for his presence, and, in this ending, *My Favorite Time* goes beyond history as the story of events and written texts to show how myths seem to originate in the creative acts of their subject. It shows us as well that there is no greater pleasure for those who believe in any part of the myth than the active contemplation of these creative acts. *My Favorite Time* luxuriates in the pleasure of its own artifice. It makes drawings move before our eyes, but rather than a motion picture in which we suspend disbelief and watch something pretending to be real life, *My Favorite Time* simulates the work of the imagination.

Let me close not with the death sequence,[78] but with an earlier section where Khrzhanovsky also shows the Pushkin legend in the making. He returns to the overworked theme of Pushkin and the *narod*, but in a way that emphasizes how the folk participated in creating Pushkin myths: it presents the recollections of a peasant who "looked at" Pushkin.[79] The passage evokes an image of Pushkin moving through a marketplace, quoting a peasant's memoirs and having the poet act out the peasant's story (for example, when he peels and eats oranges). The technique of animation for this sequence is different: the camera moves across a stack of still images of Pushkin's drawings, stylized imitations of Pushkin's drawings, and traditional Russian *lubok*, and it shows the figures of Pushkin and others ambling between these layers (Fig. 20).[80] By keeping some drawn or painted

FIGURE 20. Shot of Pushkin seen in a crowd at the market in Khrzhanovsky's *My Favorite Time*.

images still, the film lets us appreciate the animation of moving images more intensely, as when Pushkin lifts his head or the speaking tradesman's arm moves. The rich coloration of these scenes, unfortunately lost in my black-and-white still, adds to the intensity.

This sequence returns us to the question of how the familiar is presented in historical films. Khrzhanovsky successfully makes a well-known story about Pushkin sound new, I think, by the defamiliarizing replication of halting, barely educated speech, and by the visual montage of popular art forms. Of all the sequences in *My Favorite Time*, this one may most haunt viewers.[81] To some extent, that is because of Schnittke's wildly alive music, which uses folk melodies and choral singing, but the verbal score is also impressive: the tradesman recalls that he "had the pleasure of catching sight of Alexander Sergeevich Pushkin"; Pushkin observes that he had turned the isolation of exile in the countryside into pleasure in listening to Russian folktales. And, visually, one watches Pushkin moving, disappearing, coming back into view. He seems free in his movements, idiosyncratic in his dress and gustatory pleasures (this is the gist of the peasant's recollection of him, the *barin* who ate so many oranges), but also caught by the crowd of images around him. It is a splendid illustration of what it means *to look at*

Pushkin—and of how, when we look, we are always seeing the layers of speech, images, and sounds that come between us and him.

Cinematic Realism and Embodied Inspiration in 'Little Tragedies'

All the films discussed so far have been in various ways about Pushkin, but there have also been many cinematic adaptations of his writings, and they, too, participate in Russia's myth of Pushkin as national poet. In Mikhail Shveitser's 1979 version of *Little Tragedies* (*Malen'kie tragedii*), two issues central to biographical films—how to convey a sense of Pushkin's world and how to recreate a moment of Pushkinian inspiration—reappear. An admixture of the biographical diminishes the film's more realist aspirations in favor of allegorical representations of creative work. The director's interpretation of Pushkin's writings (he includes other texts beyond the four tragedies as framing and interpolated material) are often innovative, and his unusual cinematic decisions offer stimulating ideas about artistic inspiration and the creative process. This film, then, like *My Favorite Time*, returns us to Pushkin's writings and presents a very good opportunity to see how they were interpreted for the screen in the late Soviet period.

The director, like Balaian, Menaker, Mamin, and Khrzhanovsky, is little known outside the former Soviet Union, but well known within. He became especially famous in post-Soviet Russia when his always popular 1968 film, *The Golden Calf* (*Zolotoi telenok*), enjoyed a tremendous revival. Born in 1920, Shveitser lived in Moscow until his death in 2000. He graduated from the prestigious VGIK film institute in 1944, where he studied with Sergei Eisenstein. He became an established and successful Soviet filmmaker specializing in literary adaptations.[82] His work is often praised for its gentle humor and strong pathos; a mix of comedy with serious drama makes his films more human than many other period films. Shveitser resisted the temptation to make his historical work into allegorical commentary and, although some measure of self-reference is inevitable, he consistently focused on the historical material itself.[83] In filming *Little Tragedies*, he immersed himself in the worlds of the four little plays, and in Pushkin's own world as well.

We deal, then, not with the monumental turn to Pushkin by an auteur-filmmaker who purports to offer a blockbuster version of the chosen text (which is one way to describe a film like Sergei Bondarchuk's 1986 *Boris Godunov* or Alexander Proshkin's 1999 *Russian Uprising, Russkii bunt*). In *Little Tragedies*, Shveitser chose material that was itself already a form of adaptation. His creative imagination was, I suspect, liberated by the example of Pushkin's having transformed others' ideas into four idiosyncratic and wonderfully shaped little plays. Rather than a straightforward adaptation of the four plays into filmed format, *Little Tragedies* builds an interpretation on framing texts, music, and cinematography, and the transposition, cutting, and sequencing of material. I take the director's view to be tragic, with a focus on the saving grace of artistic inspiration, despite social, historical, and psychological pressures on the artist that nearly stifle his creativity.

Shveitser made *Little Tragedies* for television. First shown in 1980, it was presented as a commemoration of the one hundred fiftieth anniversary of Pushkin's Boldino autumn, and it bears the reverential attitude of commemorative activities. *Little Tragedies* feels like a late Soviet film in its extremely slow pacing (it is 227 minutes long), although, because it was intended for television screenings across three evenings, our perception of the film's pacing if we now watch it in one sitting is a little misleading. Shveitser takes advantage of the intimacy of television viewing in one's own home and the intervals inherent in a screening across several evenings, and he luxuriates in the scenic details, audible silences, and slow changes of impression that mark long films generally. The self-conscious references to Pushkin's greatness, however, do not flow from the form so much as from the subject matter, and they are familiar from all the films studied here, with the possible exception of *Side Whiskers*. (Vladimir Semerchuk has observed that Pushkin films made in the Soviet period were dominated by a "jubilee-ideological" principle.)[84] In *Little Tragedies*, markers include the anniversary dedication, which is inscribed onscreen as the film begins, and a close-up of the Kiprensky portrait of Pushkin with a candle burning before it, used as a transition between the plays. Pushkin's death mask also appears early on, issuing as if supernaturally from an open sky over the sea.

That seascape is the setting for Pushkin's "Scene from *Faust*," which opens the film (it is the first of the framing texts that Shveitser presents). Two actors speak the poem's lines as if they were in conversation. One critic has observed that they seem almost to be in rehearsal, despite the seaside setting.[85] This comment seems apt to me, particularly since the "Scene from *Faust*" rehearses some of the film's themes and technical devices. It draws our attention to the first of many performances in the film, and its Faustian motifs of temptation, self-aggrandizement, greed, and regret will also be repeated.

Next come two scenes from Pushkin's *Egyptian Nights* (*Egipetskie nochi*, 1835).[86] The improvisor from *Egyptian Nights* will seem to perform three of the four little tragedies, after he re-creates one of Pushkin's late lyrics for the benefit of Charsky, a man of Petersburg high society who also fancies himself a writer. The first of the four tragedies, *Mozart and Salieri*, is presented as if Charsky imagines it, suggesting that he feels for the improvisor something like the envy Salieri felt for Mozart.[87] This elaborate lead-in provides a plausible cinematic motivation for the plays and suggests an uncertainty about whether the *Little Tragedies* could stand alone (an anxiety we also find in the critical literature, where attempts to see them as a unified enterprise have often foundered).[88] The framing scenes also reveal Shveitser's boldness in shaping a relationship among the four plays. He has said that he wished to find an external equivalent for the thematic and philosophical links among the plays, and that he hoped to explain their preoccupation with evil.[89] Thus, the Mephistophelian will to destroy a ship full of people (in "Scene from *Faust*") forewarns the murderous impulse to end the lives of Mozart, the baron, Don Carlos, Don Juan, and all who are stricken by the plague. This evil can kill even Pushkin, another reason why the death mask looms over the horizon at the end of the scene from *Faust*.

The use of *Egyptian Nights* as a framing mechanism reveals Shveitser's impulse to provide psychological realism and plausibility.[90] The tragedies' dramatic shifts in style, locale, and scope receive ample motivation from Charsky's and the improvisor's ambitions. Additional inserted material from Pushkin's prose fragments "The guests gathered at the dacha" ("Gosti s"ezzhalis' na dachu," 1828–30), "At the corner of a small square" ("Na uglu malen'koi ploshchadi," 1830–31), and "We were spending the evening at the dacha" ("My provodili vecher na dache," 1835) adds depth to the characters in the audience and creates parallels between one of its members, Zinaida Volskaya, and Cleopatra. Since Pushkin included material from "We were spending the evening at the dacha" in *Egyptian Nights*, Shveitser in a sense merely follows his lead.

Before these salon scenes, the improvisor's private performance of a Pushkin poem, "The poet walks with open eyes" ("Poet idet, otkryty vezhdi," 1835, from *Egyptian Nights*), foregrounds the theme of artistic inspiration. When told that he should write loftier poems, a poet answers with a series of metaphors for the caprice of his choice of material:

—Why does the wind swirl in a ravine,
Raise the leaf and carry off dust,
When a ship in motionless water
Avidly awaits the push of its breath?
Why does the eagle, heavy and fearsome,
Fly down from the mountains and past towers,
Onto a desiccated stump? Ask him.
Why is the Moor loved
By young Desdemona
As the moon loves the darkness of night?
Because no law rules wind or eagle
Or the heart of a maiden.

> The poet is the same: like the cold wind of Aquilon,
> He carries aloft what he chooses.
> Like the eagle, he flies,
> And, asking no one,
> He, like Desdemona, selects
> An idol for his heart.

> —Зачем крутится ветр в овраге,
> Подъемлет лист и пыль несет,
> Когда корабль в недвижной влаге
> Его дыханья жадно ждет?
> Зачем от гор и мимо башен
> Летит орел, тяжел и страшен,
> На чахлый пень? Спроси его,
> Зачем арапа своего
> Младая любит Дездемона,
> Как месяц любит ночи мглу?
> Затем, что ветру и орлу
> И сердцу девы нет закона.
> Таков поэт: как Алвилон,
> Что хочет, то и носит он—
> Орлу подобно, он летает
> И, не спросясь ни у кого,
> Как Дездемона, избирает
> Кумир для сердца своего.[91]

Pushkin treated these lines as an aesthetic manifesto in *Egyptian Nights*, a "polemic against the idealists' elevated view of the poet" in defense of "so-called low subjects," as Leslie O'Bell has put it.[92] Shveitser agrees, as seen in his own mix of high and low in *Little Tragedies*. He also develops a more emotional theme implicit in the poem's tropes. The poet is described by three metaphors: a bitter winter wind, bearing off anything in its path; an eagle flying where it chooses; and the passionate Desdemona, deciding for herself whom to love. All three images emphasize the poet's freedom to choose his destiny, including whom he will love. They involve passionate choices, and Shveitser, in directing Sergei Iursky's performance as the improvisor, has him play up the emotional intensity. Iursky's voice rises precipitously, not with the several images of flight, as we might expect, but with the claim that the eagle will ask "no one" where to fly. Contrasting this Romantic image of creativity, *Egyptian Nights* also presents the artistic product as a commodity, particularly in the improvisor's calculations of how much money he will earn. Monika Greenleaf has noted the tale's image of the "poet as circus performer, and of his poetic product and even process as commodity."[93] One could argue that Shveitser, too, recognizes the commodification of films in Soviet Russia, especially films about Pushkin's legacy. In such a context, he repeats Pushkin's insistence on artistic freedom.

Thus the director urges us to appreciate the mystery and magic of the creative act. He was clearly fascinated by Pushkin's burst of creative energy in the Boldino autumn of 1830, when the *Little Tragedies* were written. At an early stage in his planning, Shveitser intended to include a scene showing Pushkin writing at his desk, the camera peering through a window.[94] Perhaps it is a relief that the film swerved away from this particular form of realism, substituting the creative acts of others, each with its own ideas of inspiration and genius. "The poet walks with open eyes" commences with an image of a poet walking wide-eyed but seeing nothing because he is too absorbed by the ideas of his own imagination. That sightlessness might suggest that the creative act occurs in isolation, without the stimulation of others, but nothing could be further from Pushkin's view of creativity, or Mikhail Shveitser's. In the poem, an audience soon intrudes on this poet: a passerby tugs at his coat and speaks at length about his own observations and aesthetic philosophies (it is the poet's answer to this passerby that I have quoted above). The words of another person stimulate the poet's introspective meditation on his art. For Shveitser, the moment of creation is never private, not in this intensely focused lyric poem, not even in the solitude of Pushkin's Boldino autumn, where his *Little Tragedies* were composed.[95]

The actor playing the improvisor, Sergei Iursky, uses his body to create the spectacle of poetic invention—his body itself seems to find the words of his poem, his hand reaching up as if to pull them into his mind from the air above him.[96] I will return to the question of embodiment in the film in a moment, because it complicates any principle of realism inherent in a filmed performance of the plays. But the cinematic apparatus is important here too, and its presence (obviously) marks the film as distinct from any live theatrical performance. The camera work and editing focus attention on Iursky's hands, for example, as he reaches up toward the ceiling, or on his feet as he taps his foot to gather the momentum of poetic inspiration. His performance has an audience of one, Charsky. The editing cuts in pictures of Charsky's face several times, always rapt with attention. The watching face resembles the passerby who tugs at the poet's coat in the poem, so that the structure of the performance mimics that of the text performed. But Charsky's presence also includes a note of evaluation—he is meant to tell the film's audiences how we should react to the performance on the screen. His stunned response is a single word, "amazing" ("udivitel'no"). The benumbed pleasure forewarns the ecstatic faces of male admirers who later listen to Laura's songs in *The Stone Guest* (*Kamennyi gost'*). Audiences appear often in the film, in fact, always seeming to provide cues to the film's audiences about how to react. The improvisor will perform in a salon; in *Feast in Time of Plague* (*Pir vo vremia chumy*), revelers will listen to Mary's song and then she will listen to the "Hymn to the Plague." These scenes show larger, diverse audiences, some enchanted by what they see, some lost in feelings of frightened confusion.

No one is immune to the visual inspection of the camera or other actors, which means that no one is imagined not to be involved in some sort of performance. Even the audience, then, performs its reaction. In one sense, this proliferation of audiences compensates for the absence of the theatrical audience that Pushkin's *Little Tragedies* would seem to require. No live audience was there to encourage, applaud, laugh, or weep at the actors' work, so the director creates one with his other actors.[97] The layers of performance balance the film's realist inclinations, making it impossible for us to interpret the film as a documentary produced by a still camera recording a theater spectacle. Neither the creative work of filmmaking nor the choices or decisions that go into poetic creativity are meant to be effaced here. *Little Tragedies* goes on to show us many instances of creative performance, beyond the improvisations that effect transitions from one play to the next.[98] Some performances are musical (Laura's and Mary's songs), to very effective melodies by Alfred Schnittke, whose work was crucial to the success of *My Favorite Time*. His melodies are so haunting that they dominate one's memory of *Little Tragedies*. The music also unifies the film: a fragment of the melody for Laura's rendition of "Once there lived a poor knight" ("Zhil na svete rytsar' bednyi," 1829) is strummed much earlier by the improvisor in his private performance for Charsky; the organ music heard at the end of the baron's soliloquy in *The Covetous Knight* (*Skupoi rytsar'*) recurs in *Feast in Time of Plague*.

All these performances, in varying degrees, share two features: an intense moment of anticipatory buildup, just as art is about to be invented before our eyes; and clever camera cross-cutting between performer and audience. Shveitser emphasizes that observers share in the creative act and that reception has its own elements of inspiration. There is nothing fatuous about his self-reference. Salieri listening to Mozart, desperately and demonically, is a frightening measure for the director's filmmaking, especially in the excessive, over-the-top performance of Salieri given by Smoktunovsky. But it is *all* frightening in this film—the deadly willingness of an artist to kill his model in order to better represent a dying body, an exile's surreptitious return to his native city and unexpected wooing of a widow whose husband he killed, and a young man's readiness to send a ship full of people to their death to allay his own boredom.

Shveitser concludes his film with *Feast in Time of Plague*, pushing this terrible association of art with the ecstasy of death to its limit. He moves the famous "Hymn to the Plague" to the end of the play, which gives his film an apocalyptic conclusion: the spectacle of a terrified man speaking words of fear but also pleasure and rage. We quickly lose sight of any "audience" faces that might give meaning to his hymn. As deeply introspective as the baron's soliloquy, this song is heard as speech and as melody, a hoarse and diminished melody that is more terrible than the spoken word.[99] The Master of Revels (Predsedatel') is played by Alexander Trofimov, an actor famous at the time for his work at Moscow's Taganka Theater, where he was Raskolnikov in *Crime and Punishment* and Yeshua in *Master and Margarita*. His association with these roles intensifies his stage presence as the Master of Revels, absorbing into it their defiance, meekness, passion, and compassion. It has been said of Smoktunovsky's performances as Salieri and the baron that he embodied contradictory modes of being,[100] and the same is certainly true of Trofimov.

So I return, in conclusion, to the idea of embodiment. Shveitser chose to have several actors appear in more than one role in *Little Tragedies*, perhaps none so stunningly as Smoktunovsky.[101] These repetitions reveal unexpected similarities between characters, and they unify the film and make it more like a theater performance. It seems the work of a company of actors familiar with one another's work, rather than an unrelated group of trained professionals who disperse when the film is over. To say the same thing in the language of performance theory: the actors embody themselves at the same time that their bodies are meant as vessels for another imagined life.[102] They are, ironically, at once themselves and someone else, and that doubling itself allegorizes the relationship of the performance as a whole to the text on which it is based: "performance reconstitutes the text."[103] Mikhail Shveitser's particular reconstitution of *Little Tragedies* works by means of addition, amplification, and rearrangement. It is not formally self-effacing—in this sense, it is furthest from realism, for we constantly sense the director's immense intellectual and creative work in his film. Its nervousness about realism permeates as well the style of acting, which is excessive, even melodramatic for some of the actors (Smoktunovsky as the baron, for example, Vysotsky in his final scenes in *The Stone Guest*).

Pushkin's *Little Tragedies* also point us toward a different drama of embodiment, for in their tales of sensual passion, avarice, envy, murder, and the pleasure of creating art, they face up to the dangers inherent in these tantalizing experiences, showing the body ever at risk of insult, attack, illness, and exposure. Pushkin's plays, in this Dostoevskian version, contain a very different notion of lived experience from that of the Enlightenment (and, I would say, Soviet) idea of inspiration as a disembodied, spiritual ideal. *Little Tragedies*, to be sure, includes this notion of pure inspiration with its ever-present candles. The flame that burns before a portrait of the poet in the end, however, is the same fire that lights the baron's demented tour of his cellars, the Master of Revels' song praising the ecstasy of coming close to death, Don Juan's walk through a cemetery at night, and Laura's songs of sensual pleasure and knightly honor. Pushkin's creativity, too, seems in equal measure ecstasy and suffering, yet as the last camera frame freezes the image of the candle flame, it remains enigmatic as well, neither extinguished nor entirely understood.

Little Tragedies does not, then, seek to delude us into imagining that we witness Pushkin's lived experiences or even the world in which he lived. The scenes of high society watching the improvisor are the closest that the film comes to this ambition, but these are richly layered as performances within performances and do not work as mere background or sources of historical information. Pushkin's creative work is itself shown to be a kind of performance, an activity for which he had to imagine and internalize an audience, as film must also do. Absorption and theatricality are not mutually exclusive here. The film lets actors play roles from Pushkin's dramas and stories but also play themselves, acting; the motivations for enacting dramas of high emotion and complex ethics are explored in stylized but psychologically compelling ways. As such, Shveitser's film has an ambition we recognize from Pushkin's *Little Tragedies*: to take viewers into distant worlds with few illusions about the demands that distance will make on us; to offer spectacles of creative activity in which material that has already passed through other hands is reworked; and to suggest that creativity absorbs untold energy from the work of others. It occurs in a rich context of influences, examples, and imagined audiences no matter how solitary the creative artist may appear to have been.

All five films treated here, as Soviet films made by at least slightly untraditional directors, passed through many obstacles on their way to completion. None sheds that sense of difficulty more thoroughly than *My Favorite Time*, which covers its many semantic layers with Pushkinian effortlessness. Repetition works variously across these five films. Some of the same actors, composers, and artists appear—Schnittke's music is heard in *My Favorite Time* and in *Little Tragedies*; Smoktunovsky acts in *The Last Road* and *Little Tragedies*, and he reads Pushkin's poetry in *My Favorite Time*; Sergei Iursky reads in *My Favorite Time* and acts in *Little Tragedies*. Viewers come to each film having been taught by the others how to listen for and how to see Pushkin. And they keep this knowledge with them as they return to his writings or encounter representations of him elsewhere in their culture. Films, like museums and anniversaries, are institution builders, and all have shaped the myths of Pushkin that circulate in modern Russian culture.

5 *Anna Akhmatova's Pushkin*

ALLEGORIES, ETHICS, GRIEVING
FOR THE DEAD

> If stories give events an afterlife, it is because they enable the dead to haunt the living; and if that is so, it is essential to understand the relation of life to afterlife, or of those "silent characters" to the poetic speech they nourish.
> —Geoffrey H. Hartman

With this discussion of Anna Akhmatova, I begin several chapters on purely literary texts. Each focuses on a single writer, rather than on the thematic and generic principles that organized Chapters One through Four, but many topics inevitably recur: a concern for the meaning of Pushkin's death matched by an anxiety over whether he can be adequately mourned; a doubt of the authenticity of public rituals and a search for private compensations; a use of Pushkinian material to work out contemporary issues; and a self-conscious wish to contribute to, and to change, Russia's myth of a national poet. In literary material, these themes are explored entirely with words, without the opportunities or distractions of museums, music, landscapes, drawings, or faces. But these words, so skillfully handled by Anna Akhmatova, Marina Tsvetaeva, Andrei Bitov, and Andrei Sinyavsky, conjure up all manner of visual pleasure, re-creating Pushkin's world to engage with it anew.

No poet responded to Russia's myths of Pushkin more personally than Anna Akhmatova (1889–1966), and no one has written so intensely of his death. For Akhmatova, this tragedy was at once universal and individual, a matter for ethical judgment and a path toward self-exploration. In her essays and notes, posthumously collected as *Pushkin* (*O Pushkine*, 1977), Akhmatova appropriates some common myths and demolishes others as sheer nonsense. Her Pushkin was a lonely victim of intrigue who risked his life, a Protean genius who absorbed literary lessons from other cultures, a noble poet who recorded the deaths of friends, including five hanged Decembrists. Oppressed, courageous, original, imitative, proud Russian but critical of his tsar—these contradictions define Akhmatova's Pushkin. No less contradictory was her way of writing about him—by turns legalistic, indirect, aggressive, defensive, mournful, sarcastic, scholarly, and intimate.

Nothing she wrote was definitive, for she continued to revise and add to her essays until she died, yet her every word rings out with utter certainty.

The compulsion to revise and the intonation of certainty are two keys to Akhmatova's Pushkin essays. They assort strangely: the willingness to revise suggests an openness to new ideas and a wish to leave no argument as final, whereas the insistence on the rightness of her ideas conveys an unwillingness to admit another point of view. Similarly, cross-references and repetitions tighten her otherwise disparate essays into a wall of argument. This twofold message of dynamically changing ideas mixed with firm convictions springs from several impulses: Akhmatova's desire to impress readers with the seriousness of her Pushkin writings, her remorseless assessments of the behavior of his contemporaries, and her inclination to write allegorically. To say that she was divided psychologically in these writings is not to weaken them; on the contrary, much of their boldness and lasting value comes from precisely this mix of attitudes, ambitions, and emotions.

One clear sign of Akhmatova's complicated relationship to Pushkin is the sheer quantity of poetry and prose she wrote about him across her long life. She worried over her work, revising her essays with the pattern of obsessive return that marked her long poem *Poem Without a Hero* (*Poema bez geroia*, 1940–62).[1] Some of her planned essays were never written down. We know of them from the memoirs of her friends, and the way in which Akhmatova tried out her ideas on them repeats the combination of tentativeness and certainty that marks her writings. Akhmatova comes to life in memoirs that record her conversations about Pushkin, so much so that Lydia Chukovskaya remarks on her deep sense of kinship—she writes his life as if she had lived it, and her ideas about him are "remembered."[2] The intensity of her attitude toward Pushkin should itself draw our attention—why were her feelings so deep? Something in the work of writing and thinking about Pushkin was psychologically gratifying and necessary to her, hence its inherent incompleteness. She almost always needed the process of writing and publishing about Pushkin, and she derived psychological nourishment from going back to his poems and to memoirs about him.[3]

I believe that her interest in Pushkin was also sustained by personal anguish. First, Akhmatova was uncertain how to think about her dramatically changing fate as a poet and how to regard the equally significant changes in the kind of poetry she wrote. She turned to Pushkin as model and as solace, without imagining that her historical predicament repeated his. She was drawn to texts and biographical details that showed his changing popularity, his relations with his tsar, his reliance on foreign sources, and his efforts to control the way his readers saw him. She sought an image, then, of how Pushkin modeled his career, as others would after her.

Another source of her fascination is more idiosyncratic, and less soothing. Certain details in his writings and reputation provided material through which she could write allegorically about a sense of guilt, most particularly as it related to the death of her first husband, the poet Nikolai Gumilev. More than other losses or separations Akhmatova was to suffer, his execution in 1921 left an open wound. His death was never completely mourned and could not be directly written about in poetry or in prose. The ghost of Gumilev haunts Akhmatova's writings, and although he also has a spectral presence in poems on unrelated themes, it is striking how often subtexts from Pushkin amplify Akhmatova's elegies for Gumilev. His little tragedy *The Stone Guest* (*Kamennyi gost'*, 1830) was crucial for Akhmatova when she wrote indirectly about Gumilev, as evidenced in her essay on that play and in an essay on *The Tale of the Golden Cockerel* (*Skazka o zolotom petushke*, 1834).

Akhmatova maintained her connection to Pushkin in a specific historical context. She lived in an era when the personal was under constant threat, one reason she turned to allegory and indirection to explore personal themes. She also absorbed, repeated, and in some cases transformed specific Pushkin myths. They determined her encoding of autobiographical elements, and they interacted with her own moral intelligence and ethical instincts. In her concern for moral questions, Akhmatova's nearest predecessor among poets was Lermontov. Like him, she writes within a framework of law, justice, and outrage.[4] Her anger is always inflected with a certainty that she bears the responsibility of correcting lies and distortions.[5] Akhmatova's angry intonations have something in common with the search for enemies and saboteurs in the Stalin period, although it probably goes too far to argue that her self-image was "the obverse of Stalinism," as Alexander Zholkovsky has claimed.[6] Yet Akhmatova was a woman of the Stalin age, and we cannot expect her writings to escape the mentality of a people who saw countless examples of unwarranted arrest, imprisonment, and execution. She internalized her era's obsession with right and wrong, and, just as "they" sought out perceived wrongdoers in an effort to purge the new socialist state, so Akhmatova rooted out offending scholars and memoirists, correcting their errors assiduously. She could be merciless in addressing lay readers of Pushkin.

Akhmatova's place in mainstream Pushkin scholarship is thus a complex topic. Because we know that she was marginalized in Soviet literature, blocked from publication for many years, harassed by the arrests and imprisonment of her son, and herself vilified in the press in 1946, it is tempting to see her Pushkin scholarship as peripheral to the ongoing, intense work to canonize Pushkin in Leningrad's Institute of Russian Literature (Pushkin House). But Akhmatova was closely connected to important scholars and to the textological and scholarly work of Pushkin House during the 1930s, the period when her first essays appeared. She shared her Pushkin criticism with these scholars, and sought to buttress her authority by reference to their work and to her connections to them. Her work reveals fundamental similarities in approach, philosophy, and emphasis with that of many of the best-known Soviet Pushkinists. One theme that she takes up more than they is the sexual transgressions that were related to his death, and here we will see her moral arguments forcefully appear. The range of her interest in Pushkin is impressively broad, then, moving from a discussion of his love affairs and his death to detailed studies of individual texts and matters of literary influence. Her Pushkin writings are distinctive for this range from the scholarly and philological to the biographical and speculative, and from the essayistic to the lyrical.

All of these writings, and no small amount of Akhmatova's poetry, bear the mark of an inclination toward judgment and of a fundamentally moral method. For Akhmatova, many of life's activities were inherently moral—writing, friendship, memory, getting friends to memorize her poems, debating the behavior of men and women from Pushkin's age and from her own world. The most prosaic of activities could be imbued with ethical value, like caring for the child of a neighbor whose parents beat him or firmly greeting an old friend on the street at a time when the friend faced political disgrace. Perhaps because of her temperament and the historical circumstances of her life, small matters came to have immense symbolic value to Akhmatova. Her emotions could run deep in arguing the inappropriateness of asking certain questions or in angrily denouncing the inaccuracy of other people's views.

Akhmatova's words are meant to clarify categories of right and wrong, to lay blame for transgressions and harms that will universally seem dreadful, and to make her readers feel that it would be foolish to argue with her. She wrote out of a belief that on these matters there was only one truth, and her research and intuition led her to feel strongly that her views were correct. She wrote at a time when Soviet cultural institutions asserted the moral power of literature, and although she did not share the aesthetic judgments that flowed from these official pronouncements, she did demonstrate fully that she shared a view of writing as a moral act and of poets as tellers of moral truths. Nowhere does this emerge more powerfully than in the poetry cycle *Requiem* (*Rekviem*, 1936–40), as is now universally acknowledged. What is less known is how fully her Pushkin essays also enact arguments about ethics and morality. We will follow Akhmatova's judgments about Pushkin's behavior and that of his contemporaries, about the moral and social implications of his writings, and about his readers. Particularly in her passing comments about how he was read in Russia, we will hear her comment dryly, and slyly, on the effects of myths about Pushkin on scholars and more common readers.

This moral tone has a kind of counter-tone in her Pushkin writings, a sense of grief that makes us chafe less at the moral certainty and feel greater compassion for the author. Akhmatova is not the only modern Russian cultural figure to write about Pushkin from a position of mourning; in the next chapter I will show how Tsvetaeva, too, writes out of a sense of loss. But Akhmatova's reaction is different in quality and intensity, by virtue of her personal experiences and her temperament. The passion in her early love poetry taught her emotional and linguistic lessons that enabled her to respond to future losses. Having begun as a love poet, Akhmatova was to write increasingly of love's underside. Grief floods her writing after the death of Gumilev in 1921 and as the tragedies and separations of the 1930s and 1940s descend on her. She makes the loss of Russia's first poet a testing ground for her theories of what cultures do to themselves when they strike at their best, and of what happens to private individuals when cultural investigations take over the data of their lives and deaths. All of this thinking involved Akhmatova's mind, soul, and spirit, and it meant that she could never lose sight of tangible, visible losses in her writings, nor would she represent as small the costs to the psyche for those who suffered and for those who recorded the suffering. When a woman in a prison line asks her whether she can describe "this," as happens in the prose preface to *Requiem*, her terse, affirmative response becomes the emblem for all that she was willing to take on in her writing. Akhmatova worked across these two intonational ranges—anger at injustice, grief at all that has been lost—in order to explore the meanings for Russian culture and for her own sense of self that Pushkin lived, wrote, and died as he did. Her Pushkin essays sprang from the same impulse as her poetry, I am suggesting; Arkady Belinkov rightly called them a mix of literary scholarship and narrative poetry.[7] I begin with her early poems that show her handling traditional Pushkinian themes. They also demonstrate how she presented a poet's psyche in her lyrics; that is helpful when we turn to the essays, which she says are fundamentally lyrical. The poems will take us to the mid-1930s, where the emerging essays pick up.

Akhmatova's Pushkin Poems: Returns to Tsarskoe Selo

Long before Akhmatova wrote essays about Pushkin, she was reacting to his work in her poetry. Her poems explore the kind of relationship she wanted to have with Russia's national poet. Here is a list of Pushkin-related poems (dates are given according to Akhmatova's datelines, or, in their absence, according to scholars' best estimates):[8]

1910	"The First Return" ("Pervoe vozvrashchenie")
1911	"In Tsarskoe Selo" ("V Tsarskom sele")

1913	"The Last Letter" ("Poslednee pis'mo," published 1918)
1914	"For the last time we met" ("V poslednii raz my vstretilis' togda")
1915	"I keep seeing the hills of Pavlovsk" ("Vse mne viditsia Pavlovsk kholmistyi")
1915	"There is a cherished boundary in intimacy" ("Est' v blizosti liudei zavetnaia cherta")
1916	"Tsarskoe Selo Statue" ("Tsarskosel'skaia statuia")
1916	"Drowsiness takes me over again" ("Vnov' podaren mne dremotoi")
1921	"All the souls of my dear ones are on stars high above" ("Vse dushi milykh na vysokikh zvezdakh")
1923	"New Year's Ballad" ("Novogodniaia ballada")
1925–40	"Fragments from the Tsarskoe Selo poem 'Russian Trianon'" ("Otryvki iz tsarskosel'skoi poemy 'Russkii Trianon'")
1927	"Here began Pushkin's exile" ("Zdes' Pushkina izgnan'e nachalos'")
1929	"The city I have loved from childhood" ("Tot gorod, mnoi liubimyi s detstva")
1936	"Some see themselves in affectionate gazes" ("Odni gliadiatsia v laskovye vzory")
1940	"Cleopatra" ("Kleopatra")
1940	"The Willow" ("Iva")
1940–43	"Northern Elegies" ("Severnye elegii"; some individual lyrics in this cycle are dated as early as 1921, some as late as 1964)
1940–62	*Poem Without a Hero* (*Poema bez geroia*)
1943	"Pushkin"
1945, 1957	"To the City of Pushkin" ("Gorodu Pushkinu")
1946	"Second Anniversary" ("Vtoraia godovshchina")
1950	"In the Pioneer Camp" ("V pionerlagere")
1958	"Primorsk Sonnet" ("Primorskii sonet")
1959	"The Heiress" ("Naslednitsa")
1959	"And it is impossible to take from them" ("I otniat' u nikh nevozmozhno")
1960	"If everyone who had given help" ("Esli b vse, kto pomoshchi dushevnoi")

1961 "Tsarskoe Selo Ode" ("Tsarskosel'skaia oda")
Undated, late "I still hear the fresh spring of freedom" ("Eshche ia slyshu svezhii kliuch svobody")

The first poems on this list come from Akhmatova's earliest published work (she destroyed most of her juvenilia, choosing to fix for generations of future readers the time and nature of her poetic debut), and they treat places associated with Pushkin, principally Tsarskoe Selo (the town renamed Detskoe Selo after the revolution, then Pushkin in 1937). She has her own version of Tsarskoe Selo, diminishing the imperial grandeur described in the poetry of Mikhail Lomonosov, Gavriel Derzhavin, and Pushkin; Roman Timenchik has said that she overcomes "the idyllic chronotope."[9] Akhmatova's stylistic deflating is motivated by the literary challenge of making this place her own. She rose to the challenge so successfully that it is now as much associated with her verse as it is with that of Pushkin. Marina Tsvetaeva called her the "muse of Tsarskoe Selo" in 1916,[10] and the Futurist poet Velimir Khlebnikov's late poem "The Lonely Histrion" ("Odinokii litsedei," 1921) also gave her a proprietary relationship to the place:

> While Akhmatova's singing and tears
> Poured over Tsarskoe Selo,
> I, unrolling my enchanted skein,
> Dragged through the wilderness like a sleepy corpse . . .
>
> А пока над Царским Селом
> Лилось пенье и слезы Ахматовой,
> Я, моток волшебный разматывая,
> Как сонный труп, влачился по пустыне . . . [11]

Pushkin's poem "The Prophet" supplied Khlebnikov's image of the corpse dragging itself through a wilderness, and Khlebnikov likens himself to the prophet. That Pushkin poem was to become important in Akhmatova's later self-definitions, which Khlebnikov could not have known in 1921, when he wrote this poem that recorded how much Tsarskoe Selo seemed a place associated with her.

Something of the weighty intonation of "The Prophet" can already be heard in Akhmatova's earliest poem about Tsarskoe Selo, "The First Return" ("Pervoe vozvrashchenie," 1910), the first poem that I treat in some detail.

> The First Return
>
> On the ground a heavy shroud is placed,
> The bells toll solemnly.
> And once again the spirit is troubled and agitated

By the languid boredom of Tsarskoe Selo.
Five years have passed. Here everything is dead and silent,
As if the end of the world has come.
Like a theme exhausted forever,
The palace reposes in deathly sleep.

Первое возвращение
На землю саван тягостный возложен,
Торжественно гудят колокола,
И снова дух смятен и потревожен
Истомной скукой Царского Села.
Пять лет прошло. Здесь все мертво и немо,
Как будто мира наступил конец.
Как навсегда исчерпанная тема,
В смертельном сне покоится дворец.[12]

Akhmatova chooses an elegant environment, palatial Tsarskoe Selo, for her poem of death. The earth itself appears shrouded in the poem's first line, and in its last image the palace rests in a deathlike sleep. The poet tells us that "everything" is dead in this poem, and we should hear the self-inclusion in that pronoun, given Akhmatova's habits of representing her poetic psyche in architectural terms (for example, in "The Cellar of Memory," "Podval pamiati," 1940). She is the palace stilled to sleep, her imagination is threatened by the exhaustion of the theme she takes up, she is weighted down by the ground's heavy shroud. That is why her spirit is "troubled and agitated," why the dead weight of the iambic pentameter in this double quatrain descends on poet and reader alike.

It is striking that Akhmatova provides five descriptions in this very early eight-line poem that imbue the place with death.[13] A shroud covers the earth, bells toll solemnly, everything is deadly silent, it is as if the world has come to an end, and the palace (always emblematic of Tsarskoe Selo) has fallen into the sleep of death.[14] Here she has in place the patterns of thought that will govern her thinking about Pushkin, including the allusions to death and the imagination of every visitation as a form of return. How odd, after all, that her *first* poem about Pushkin would be presented as a return. The oddity diminishes when we recall its biographical basis: Akhmatova had lived in Tsarskoe Selo with her family from 1891 to 1905, and then with her husband Nikolai Gumilev from 1910 to 1916.[15]

The five-year period mentioned in the poem points to these facts, but Akhmatova's title, "The First Return," alerts us to more than the personal reference. Its two terms, *first* and *return*, suggest that the poet wanted her poem to be both inaugural and an instance of repetition. Many of Akhmatova's later poems will be presented as repeated experiences, where the poet compares an earlier and later example of a person, an emotion, a sight, a site. In "The First Return," that comparison occurs in the observation that "Five years have passed," which breaks the poem into two parts. Following a Romantic pattern, lines 1–3 might be expected to be about the earlier visit, lines 4–8 about the return. But all is equally dead in "The First Return," without the recollected idyll we would find in a Romantic poem. There is little hope of recovering an initial, fresh experience of the place. What is more, that lack of hope pushes into the foreseeable future for the poet, who writes as if this will also be a last visit.[16] Even the theme of an exhausted topic was not Akhmatova's innovation—it had been fully worked out by Innokenty Annensky, and his poem "September" ("Sentiabr'," ca. 1900) also associated Tsarskoe Selo with death.[17] Akhmatova makes the cultural lament found in Annensky into something personal; it is her own deathly enervation that the poem makes so memorable. Akhmatova carefully casts her every word about Tsarskoe Selo as a second word, an echo that itself gets no response.

When Akhmatova writes about Pushkin, she never speaks the first word, but she also always speaks with an air of finality (as if anticipating no next word or no word from another); her words in turn will be subject to her future repetitions and revisions; and her subject will be death, directly or indirectly. All of this happens in a poem that never mentions Pushkin; Akhmatova is confident that she can name a Tsarskoe Selo palace, and readers will catch its allusions to other themes, moods, and poetic legacies.

We see the Pushkin connection more explicitly in Akhmatova's next poem about Tsarskoe Selo, written a year later. "In Tsarskoe Selo" ("V Tsarskom Sele," 1911) has three parts, the first two creating the emblematic setting of garden, lake, swans, marble sculpture, and palace, the third bringing us the sight of a young Pushkin walking through the avenues of trees. The third part of the poem is very famous, but here is the text in full:

In Tsarskoe Selo

1.
The little horses are led along the avenue.
The waves of the combed-out manes are long.
Oh, captivating town of riddles,
I am sad, having fallen in love with you.

It is strange to remember: the soul was melancholy,
It was sighing in the delirium that comes before death.
But now I have become toy-like,
Like my pink friend the cockatoo.

My breast is not tightened with the foreboding of pain,
If you like, look into my eyes.

I dislike only the hour before sunset,
Wind from the sea, and the word "leave."
2.
... But my marble double is there,
Thrown down beneath the old maple,
He has given up his face to the waters of the lake,
It listens to the green rustling.

And light-filled rains wash over
Its caked wound ...
Cold one, white one, wait—
I, too, will become marble-like.
3.
The dark-skinned boy wandered through the avenues,
Felt sad by the shores of the lake,
And for a century now we have cherished
The barely heard rustling of his footsteps.

Thick and prickly, pine needles
Cover the low stumps ...
Here lay his tricorn hat
And his tattered volume of Parny.

1911

В Царском Селе
1.
По аллее проводят лошадок.
Длинны волны расчесанных грив.
О, пленительный город загадок,
Я печальна, тебя полюбив.

Странно вспомнить: душа тосковала,
Задыхалась в предсмертном бреду.
А теперь я игрушечной стала,
Как мой розовый друг какаду.

Грудь предчувствием боли не сжата,
Если хочешь, в глаза погляди.
Не люблю только час пред закатом,
Ветер с моря и слово «уйди».
2.
...А там мой мраморный двойник,
Поверженный под старым кленом,
Озерным водам отдал лик,
Внимает шорохам зеленым.

И моют светлые дожди
Его запекшуюся рану...

> Холодный, белый, подожди,
> Я тоже мраморною стану.
> 3.
> Смуглый отрок бродил по аллеям,
> У озерных грустил берегов,
> И столетие мы лелеем
> Еле слышный шелест шагов.
>
> Иглы сосен густо и колко
> Устилают низкие пни...
> Здесь лежала его треуголка
> И растрепанный том Парни.[18]
>
> 1911

This poem works in a spirit of partition, trying to keep the speaking poet, whose feelings overflow in the first two parts of the poem, out of the third part, where Pushkin is shown to be lost in sadness. I. L. Almi has noted that Akhmatova never imagined a conversation with Pushkin in her poetry and "never put herself into the same frame with him."[19] That spirit of separateness also determines the syntax of "The dark-skinned boy": its eight lines offer four two-line scenes, and although all elements of the poem work to explain why Pushkin wanders in sadness, the elements are discrete— distinctly pictured and syntactically independent. The separations are wishful, however, and our appreciation for the famous lines about Pushkin as a "dark-skinned boy" is diminished if we read the lines out of context. So let us begin at the beginning of "In Tsarskoe Selo," and follow the speaking poet through to the end of the three-part poem.[20] In doing so, we will follow her sadness, for she is nearly swallowed by the pain and anguish associated with this place. The poem's title locates the poet in a place, which unifies the poem's three parts.

The image of Tsarskoe Selo as a toy town, where all is cultivated and excessively perfect, initially defines it. The poet lived here as a child, and coming back reduces her to a childlike state, lessens her in the same way that the horses are rendered as diminutives. She feels none of a child's wonder, only sadness, experienced as a form of delirium that presages death. Then the poem deadens her to such pain, making her like a toy, and again the particular transformation, which could exude innocence and charm, instead feels nightmarish and grotesque. The poet is likened to a pink cockatoo, a change that renders her pretty and silly. The cockatoo is her friend, but not a comforting one. She is not contorted with pain, she claims, but the negation suggests quite the opposite: she remembers psychic anguish, delirious sighs, and forewarnings of death. To whom, then, does she say "If you like, look into my eyes" ("Esli khochesh', v glaza pogliadi")?

Someone is always watching in an Akhmatova poem. Often she is watching herself, a form of self-regard that has struck some as narcissistic; her gaze has more censure and pain than pleasure. The willingness to be examined by another suggests that the poet deserves such scrutiny, and in later poems Akhmatova inevitably condemns herself to suffer guilt for unnamed sins. Here, she confesses to trivial indiscretions, disliked as if uttered in a salon or a tea party.[21] But the small objections are grim in their own way, particularly the last word, "leave." It is the word of another that is at once imperative and abandoning. It suggests a lover with immense power over her or, perhaps, worse, a muse who finds her poems unworthy. Such a dismissal would be sufficient to produce the anguished soul of the previous strophe, as well as the powerlessness of a toy, the weakness of a bird.

The next part of the poem takes up this sense of psychic confusion, belying the claim that the "breast is not tightened" in pain by turning the poet into a cold stone statue. There is nothing classically beautiful about this statue, which lies abandoned, violently thrown down on the ground with a face immersed in water. The statue, bizarrely, is wounded, and although Akhmatova does not explain the wound, she does speak to the statue (which is the marble double announced in the first line), urging it to wait for her as she, too, will turn to marble. There is something of the drowned Ophelia in this image, something suicidal in the statue's having "given up his face" to the water. The final imprecation to the statue to await her as she seeks to join him feels like a promise to die, and the statue with its "caked wound" is as much a corpse as a piece of art. Like the statue, the poet seems a dead object in the landscape, a thing that has been left to listen to nature's sounds and be washed over by its rains.

The appearance of a "dark-skinned boy" in such a landscape sets him up as an innocent wanderer, and we almost worry that he will stumble on the overturned statue or be horrified by the poet's anguish. He is not kept entirely apart from these precedents; for all the ways in which "In Tsarskoe Selo" works in a spirit of separation, images and motifs crisscross three parts of the poem. Akhmatova brings things together in "In Tsarskoe Selo" by transposing qualities between persons or objects. In part three, she recasts earlier images into gentler forms: instead of horses led along the avenue, the boy wanders along the avenue; instead of the "green rustling" grotesquely attended by the statue, "we" cherish the "barely heard rustling" of the boy's steps; instead of the "old maple" beneath which the statue lies, we have pine stumps carpeted over by pine needles. And instead of a toy or a statue, the accompanying aesthetic object is a volume of Evariste Parny, elegant poet of the eighteenth century.[22] This would be an elevated contrast were it not for the tender epithet "tattered." Pushkin is defined by a book of French poetry and a sweetly old-fashioned hat, whereas the poet had imagined for herself only the terrible friendship of a pink bird. The well-thumbed volume of Parny also marks Pushkin as the cosmopolitan, the "Frenchman," as he was known at the lyceum, and it is a worldly image to which the author of "In Tsarskoe Selo" cannot aspire: she is associated with a statue left outside to be dirtied by the weather, with wounds crusted over in neglect.

The poet's sadness in the first two parts of the poem overflows onto Pushkin.[23] We notice the transfer especially because there is no biographical reason for the representation of Pushkin as downcast while at the lyceum.[24] "In Tsarskoe Selo" has emotions pass from thing to person to landscape and on to another person. The poem itself moves among these categories, picturing a person by means of what surrounds him. This is particularly true of the representation of Pushkin. He wanders along avenues and lake in two lines of the poem, represented by the sound of steps, the pine-stump landscape, his hat, and his book. It is a peculiar form of portraiture in which the pictured individual is barely glimpsed, the surroundings shown in greater focus, but in that reversal Akhmatova shows us something of the intense myth-making around Pushkin (note that she says "we have cherished the *barely heard* rustling of his footsteps," my emphasis), where he recedes into a background that is dominated by cultural attributes and a viewer's powerful emotions. Her attitude is one of affectionate reverence, and, although she loses herself in the shared tenderness of "we have cherished," the effect of that merging is an intensification of the poetic quality of this poem, heard in sound repetitions (*l, sl, sh, el, le, st*) that bespeak strong emotions.[25] But a century has passed since Pushkin studied at the lyceum. What place is there for the poet who writes about him one hundred years later?

Akhmatova answers that implicit question with the claim that "we have cherished" the rustle of his footsteps and thus the sounds of his verse. Using footsteps, or feet, to suggest verse recalls the first chapter of *Eugene Onegin*, and Akhmatova reaches for its mix of playfulness and adoration. But there is nothing playful about her poem when read start to finish. The images of toys and delirium in the first part produce the wounded statue and the marble double of the second. The innocent lightness associated with Pushkin offers small consolation after the devastations of the first two parts of the poem, and the anguish is so deep as to weaken the cure. The adoption of Pushkinian poetic patterns is more obvious and perhaps more successful: Akhmatova invokes his poems about Tsarskoe Selo, particularly "Remembrances in Tsarskoe Selo" ("Vospominaniia v Tsarskom Sele," 1814). She substitutes shared memories of Pushkin for his evocations of martial glory and imperial landscape.[26] Perhaps this association with one of his earliest triumphs helped Akhmatova recognize the success of her own poem. She kept "The First Return" out of her first volume of poetry, but she did want her readers to have "In Tsarskoe Selo," for here were her trademark descriptions of landscape and self, the unkind word spoken by a beloved man, the mix of prosaic details with evocative epithets, and the desperate descriptions of stoical suffering. The contemplation of Pushkin from a position of sadness is emblematic of Russia's myth of a national poet, as is the identification with a statue, however idiosyncratically. Akhmatova had begun to make the myth her own.

"Tsarskoe Selo Statue" ("Tsarskosel'skaia statuia," 1916) also studies the poet's relationship to a statue, but it could not differ more from "In Tsarskoe Selo." There, the poet identifies with the pale inertness of a stone object, but here she is intrigued by a mixture of still concentration and implied movement. "Tsarskoe Selo Statue" also has an unusual subject: rather than an image of Pushkin (as in "In Tsarskoe Selo") or a meditation on the problem of writing about Tsarskoe Selo ("Second Anniversary"), this poem looks at a statue of a girl and the poem Pushkin wrote about her:

> Tsarskoe Selo Statue
>
> N.V.N.
>
> Maple leaves are already
> Falling down onto the swans' pond
> And the bushes of slowly
> Ripening rowanberry are bloodstained,
>
> And blindingly lithe,
> Legs that feel no cold are tucked in,
> On the northern stone she
> Sits and looks at the roads.
>
> I felt vague terror
> Before this celebrated girl.
> Rays of thinning light
> Played about her shoulders.
>
> And how could I forgive her
> The ecstasy of your enamored praise ...
> Look, she is happily sad,
> So smartly dressed in her bareness.

> Царскосельская статуя
>
> Н.В.Н.
>
> Уже кленовые листы
> На пруд слетают лебединый
> И окровавлены кусты
> Неспешно зреющей рябины,
>
> И ослепительно стройна,
> Поджав незябнущие ноги,
> На камне северном она
> Сидит и смотрит на дороги.

> Я чувствовала смутный страх
> Пред этой девушкой воспетой,
> Играли на ее плечах
> Лучи скудеющего света.
>
> И как могла я ей простить
> Восторг твоей хвалы влюбленной...
> Смотри, ей весело грустить,
> Такой нарядно обнаженной.[27]

In this poem, where so much is intensely human—jealousy, sadness, aesthetic admiration, and a keen sense of the passage of time—Akhmatova encounters Pushkin as one *poet* meeting another. Her Pushkin, in fact, was always a poet: when she imagines him in the poem "In Tsarskoe Selo," she places a volume of Parny next to him, just as she situates him poring over Apuleius in her fragmentary poem "Russian Trianon" ("Otryvki iz tsarskosel'skoi poemy 'Russkii Trianon,'" 1925–40), and lauds his having written of women's feet in "Pushkin" (1943). She imagines poetry at the center of Pushkin's lived experience, and his lesson to her (and her culture) is how to be a poet in difficult times.

Akhmatova also responds directly to a Pushkin poem. She takes up his four-line lyric from 1830 and enlarges it. She admits that she finds this act of rewriting thrilling. Pushkin had written:

> Tsarskoe Selo Statue
>
> Having dropped the urn filled with water, the maiden broke it against the cliff.
>   The maiden sits sadly, holding the useless bit of pottery.
> It is a miracle! The water will not dry up, pouring from the broken urn;
>   The maiden sits eternally sad, over the eternal stream.
>
> Царскосельская статуя
>
> Урну с водой уронив, об утес ее дева разбила.
>   Дева печально сидит, праздный держа черепок.
> Чудо! не сякнет вода, изливаясь из урны разбитой;
>   Дева, над вечной струей, вечно печальна сидит.[28]

Akhmatova clips the long hexametric line of Pushkin's elegiac distich to iambic tetrameter. She writes four times as many lines, but this lengthening is so formally symmetrical as to seem a drawing in: she gives us four stanzas, four lines each, with four metrical feet per line. The alternating rhymes attract little attention. Poetically self-effacing, the verse has the denuded quality attributed to the statue in the last line, and, like the statue, the poem has its own oxymoronic quality of seeming to be bare but draped in elegance. Akhmatova makes her poem more prosaic than Pushkin's (her binary meter is more conversational, the lexicon down to earth), but she does not empty it of poetic ornamentation. The oxymora of the final two lines are dramatic tropes that the whole poem builds toward, and they are intensified by their position at the end of an otherwise harmonious poem that treats a classical subject. Oxymoron is an ideal trope for conveying religious experience or love's complexity, as we might find in the poetry of Milton and Shakespeare, but Akhmatova uses it to suggest an inner world of emotional conflict. The Pushkin original has its own rhetorical tension when it uses a statue as an emblem of the flight of time.[29] It repeats the word *eternally* (*vechno*) in a poem about ceaselessly moving water, inviting comparison of the water's motion with the still statue.[30] And Pushkin's reliance on repetition in his very short poem suggests lexical immobility, which in turn contrasts beautifully with the flowing lines of the statue itself.

We might expect Akhmatova's "Tsarskoe Selo Statue" to present a similar view of time, given her tendency toward repetition and her fascination with the experience of time passing. Repetition frames her poem, which is already a second instance in a sequence begun by Pushkin's poem. In a limited way, she brings his temporal contrast into her poem: autumn colors give movement to the first quatrain, with falling leaves and ripening bushes, and the stone beneath the statue's figure and her seated position provide the contrast of immobility in the second stanza. But Akhmatova allows neither of the points of this comparison to stand firm—what is still already moves, what changes seems to linger.[31] She has the autumn scene changing in an orderly way, and the statue's figure seeming to have just tucked in her legs and to have the human power of sight as she sits looking out onto the roads (and roads, too, suggest movement and change). When the statue is later said to be happy in her sadness, this suggestion of animation comes as no surprise.

Akhmatova probes the imagined psychology of the statue further than Pushkin does. Her description of rowanberries as staining bushes with blood is extreme, and it prepares us for the strong emotions of the third stanza.[32] She uncovers a feeling of terror that is entirely absent from Pushkin's poem. But terror at what? At the sight of the statue? At the attempt to write a poem about it? Akhmatova behaves as if she had intruded on a lovers' scene (another reason for the suggestion of nudity in the final line), as if she had come across an intimate encounter. She seems to have stumbled on Pushkin with his muse,[33] rather than with some nubile mortal companion, but all the more reason for terror, as Akhmatova's own frightened encounters with her muse suggest (her muse poems include images of torture, of the terror of knowledge, of a grave, of life hanging by a thread, of a feverish delirium, and, in a late poem, of a muse who has been beaten to death).[34]

Putting aside a metapoetic reading of the poem, others have stressed its biographical and personal elements. It is dedicated to Nikolai V. Nedobrovo (1884–1919), for example. He was a poet and critic, author of a perceptive early essay on Akhmatova, and the addressee of several of her poems.[35] David Wells has noted that the statue of the maiden with the broken urn was a frequent meeting place for Nedobrovo and Akhmatova.[36] I. L. Almi claims that the envy is directed toward Nedobrovo, not Pushkin: the infatuation described is his exaltation in aesthetic beauty, and the poetic qualities of the statue cannot be achieved by a live woman.[37] And Roberta Reeder puts aside the dedication to Nedobrovo and places Gumilev at the center of the poem.[38]

None of these allusions to personal information need be ignored in a reading of "Tsarskoe Selo Statue," but none is sufficient to explain the confusion and terror in the poem. When Akhmatova suggests that the statue is happy in her sadness, she shows envy at the capacity to display such deep emotions as if calmly. She resembles the statue in being beautifully adorned for public view but feeling exposed, and the poem stands as a record of her extreme vulnerability and fear. Pushkin was able to write of the statue without having to see himself in it, and his lovely classical lines stand as a form of aesthetic perfection that she cannot reach. Erotic attention intervenes in this poem, where Akhmatova seems so terribly aware of being watched—by the actual men in her life, perhaps, but as if by Pushkin as well. We are used to thinking of her as a Pushkinian poet, but it seems to me that as early as this poem, it was clear to her that she was fated to be a very different kind of poet. To feel, indeed to admit to feeling "vague terror" before an emblem of classical beauty, to believe oneself open to sterner judgments and harsher looks, is not very Pushkinian at all. And the last lines of the poem suggest an incipient moral tone (as if Akhmatova censures the statue for baring her beauty in public), which will intensify in the future.[39]

An unspoken sin is buried in Akhmatova's "New Year's Ballad" ("Novogodniaia ballada," 1923). It draws on Pushkin's *Feast in Time of Plague* (*Pir vo vremia chumy*, 1830) for its image of a toast in dreadful times. Akhmatova situates her own feast among the dead.

New Year's Ballad

And the moon, feeling bored in its cloudy haze,
Cast a dim gaze into the chamber.
There are six places set at the table,
And only one is empty.

My husband, my friends, and I
Await the New Year.
Why do my fingers seem bloody,
And does the wine, like poison, burn?

The host, raising a full glass,
Was serious and still:
"I drink to the earth of our native glades,
In which we all lie!"

And a friend who looked into my face,
Remembering God knows what,
Exclaimed: "And I drink to her songs
In which we all live!"

But the third person, who knew nothing
When he had left this world,
Murmured in answer to my own thoughts:
"We are obliged to drink to him
Who is not yet here among us."

Новогодняя баллада
И месяц, скучая в облачной мгле,
Бросил в горницу тусклый взор.
Там шесть приборов стоят на столе,
И один только пуст прибор.

Это муж мой, и я, и друзья мои
Встречаем новый год.
Отчего мои пальцы словно в крови
И вино, как отрава, жжет?

Хозяин, поднявши полный стакан,
Был важен и недвижим:
«Я пью за землю родных полян,
В которой мы все лежим!»

А друг, поглядевши в лицо мое
И вспомнив Бог весть о чем,
Воскликнул: «А я за песни ее,
В которых мы все живем!»

Но третий, не знавший ничего,
Когда он покинул свет,
Мыслям моим в ответ
Промолвил: «Мы выпить должны за того,
Кого еще с нами нет».[40]

The coupling of New Year's celebrations with spectral intrusions will later occur in Akhmatova's *Poem Without a Hero*, but in 1923 she had something more morbid in mind. Like Dostoevsky's story "Bobok" (1873), "New Year's Ballad" takes place below the earth, where the dead speak as if alive, even as they separate themselves from the living. Dostoevsky's story parodies the pretensions and anxieties of the newly dead, and his characters hilariously discuss the smells of decay. Akhmatova's tone could not be more different, and she has sources elsewhere in Dostoevsky, where the themes of guilt and retribution are taken up with less comic relief.[41] The poet whose fingers are covered with blood in this poem bears the marks of some unmentionable sin, and when she drinks down the wine that ought to drive out such terrible thoughts, it burns its way down as if in punishment.

The mention of wine sets up the poem's three toasts: to the earth, to the poet, and finally, to one who has yet to die. The third oddly revises a more typical toast (to those who are no longer with us), but more important, it corrects the second toast, which embarrassed the poet. Correction is an activity appropriate to moral thinking, and a moral principle partly impels the final toast, which the poet says reflects her own thoughts. Is it, though, still a toast to her? Is she saying that she soon will die? Later in Akhmatova's poetry, such expectations occur, as when she meets her own ghost or when she waits for a representative of the dead to come fetch her (for example, "Has he sent no swan for me," "Ne prislal li lebedia za mnoiu," 1936). Here, in "New Year's Ballad," Akhmatova seems already among the dead and yet awaiting her death, a doubling that intensifies the possibility of punishment—it wholly occupies both present and future, and, for that matter, it must have sprung from the past as a response to some sin. The transgression suggested in the poem is a sin of pride, implicit in the rejected second toast: she had thought of herself as a poet who keeps friends figuratively alive.[42]

These concerns of conscience again link "New Year's Ballad" to Dostoevsky, which puts further pressure on the poem's Pushkinian qualities. They are most significant in the poem's form and subtexts. Again, there is strong contrast. Most of the typical ballad features presented here with complete seriousness—the dark atmosphere, the tripling of events, the sense of fateful secrecy—would have been treated more lightly by Pushkin.[43] But Akhmatova keeps the crucial traits of the Romantic ballad as found in Pushkin: the inclusion of words spoken by the ballad's heroes, the immediacy of the scene, the use of verbal repetition and syntactic parallelism to create such intensity. Elsewhere in her work, Akhmatova took up the ballad form influentially used by Pushkin. As Michael Wachtel has shown, her "Grey-Eyed King" ("Seroglazyi korol'," 1910) repeats the rhythm and rhyme of Pushkin's "Black Shawl" ("Chernaia shal'," 1820), and the form turns up again in the second epilogue to *Requiem*.[44] But Akhmatova does not use the couplets or all-masculine rhyme scheme that Russian poetry drew from "The Black Shawl" in "New Year's Ballad." (She does, however, implicitly use the ballad's theme of revenge, but she turns it into self-punishment: she is at once the instrument and the victim of vengeance.) Unexpectedly, Akhmatova draws on another kind of Pushkin poem here: his lifelong cycle of poems about the lyceum, that is, about Tsarskoe Selo.

One begins to sense that she can never get away from Tsarskoe Selo. Pushkin's mournful 1831 poem that begins "The more one celebrates the lyceum" ("Chem chashche prazdnuet Litsei") provides an important key to "New Year's Ballad"— it gives the exemplary juxtaposition of anniversary celebration with lament for the dead—[45] but in Akhmatova's hands the anniversary becomes a New Year celebration, and lament is transformed into a doleful raising of glasses in anticipation of death. Pushkin's poem provides the tone, however, and in one of its collocations, "the more our celebration / Darkens in its gaiety" ("tem prazdnik nash / V svoem veselii mrachnee"),[46] we see the oxymoronic contrast of sadness with cheer that is typical of Akhmatova's Pushkin poems. "The more one celebrates the lyceum" is also Akhmatova's source for the image of places set around a table and for the number of places associated with the dead or absent. In Pushkin's poem, there are six empty places to mark the six lyceum graduates who died between 1817 and 1831, and Akhmatova holds an empty place (one of six) for the one soon to arrive in the kingdom of the dead. Pushkin's poem mourns several friends, but singles out his dear friend Anton Delvig, who died that year (1831); Akhmatova names no one. In her work we almost always have to supply the names; here they would be Blok, Nedobrovo, and especially Gumilev. Pushkin's poem intimates that he expects to die next. Akhmatova writes in these terms as well in "New Year's Ballad," putting herself among the dead.

The "vague terror" found in "Tsarskoe Selo Statue" recurs here, but from a different cause. Akhmatova is fazed less by her repetition of Pushkin's poetic theme, I suspect, than by the difference in the poems' occasions. He looked back at the lyceum and its friendships in his poem, indeed in all his lyceum anniversary poems, but Akhmatova writes about less well-defined circles of friendship and loss, another reason her poem names no one. The rituals and repetitions of lyceum anniversaries or, for that matter, the New Year, provide no comfort, and as the years wear on, we sense her locked into the repetitions, unable not to observe the anniversaries but unconsoled by any pattern they might offer.

She often wrote poems occasioned by anniversaries, or created datelines that turned her poems into anniversary pieces. My reading of Akhmatova so far would suggest that she did this from a penchant for repetition: it put a poem or experience into a sequence and made a first poem on a given theme or person seem a second or third instance. But another impetus for the creation of anniversary poems has to do with time itself. Akhmatova cast the poem in such a way that it took its meaning from some earlier instantiation, and she held out the possibility of a future poem to come. The temporal perspective of her poetry was layered, but in addition to the "perspective of Time supplied by prosody," as Joseph Brodsky put it,[47] she placed her poems into larger temporal sequences, sometimes history itself, sometimes the memory of an event that her poem is meant to commemorate. These sequences slow down the passage of time, letting the poet appear momentarily to decide whether the events disappear into forgetfulness. What this temporal intervention accomplishes in emotional terms has to do entirely with mourning, with setting up a sequence of events in which loss can be experienced repeatedly; she creates an endless process akin to what Freud would call melancholia.[48] Perhaps for this reason, too, her work is often invoked on anniversary occasions (both the third part of "In Tsarskoe Selo" and her 1961 prose statement on Pushkin, "A Word on Pushkin," "Slovo o Pushkine," have been frequently reprinted), yet these writings derive much of their power from their having been produced outside the official anniversary structures; they preserve an aura of having come from an environment where they risked never reaching a public at all.

"Some see themselves in affectionate gazes" ("Odni gliadiatsia v laskovye vzory," 1936) was such an attempt at staving off oblivion, and it shows Akhmatova's moral imperatives at their strongest. Dedicated to the memory of Nedobrovo when it was first published in 1940, "Some see themselves in affectionate gazes," evokes the Tsarskoe Selo landscape and past festivities there. The poet judges that gaiety severely, as in much of her work from the 1930s onward. Her companion is her stern conscience, described as a relentless two-horned witness who knows nothing of either time or space. The timeless weight of conscience contrasts vividly with the recollected past; the past, as in "New Year's Ballad," has layers of temporal experience (suggested by references to a seasonal festival, Mardi Gras, and to Tsarskoe Selo before the revolution), but the poet gains no release from the temporal flux. She is locked into dialogue with a forbidding interlocutor:

> Some see themselves in affectionate gazes,
> Others drink until the sun's first rays,
> But I conduct negotiations all through the night
> With my indomitable conscience.
>
> I say: "I have been carrying your heavy burden,
> You know, for how many years now."
> But time does not exist for it,
> And for it there is no space in the world.
>
> And again the black, Mardi Gras evening,
> The sinister park, the unhurried trot of the horse,
> And the wind, filled with happiness and gaiety,
> Has flown down on me from the heaven's heights.

And a witness, calm and two-horned,
Stands over me ... oh, to go there, there,
Along the ancient road that passes beneath the Caprice,
Where there are swans and dead water.

Одни глядятся в ласковые взоры,
Другие пьют до солнечных лучей,
А я всю ночь веду переговоры
С неукротимой совестью своей.

Я говорю: «Твое несу я бремя
Тяжелое, ты знаешь, сколько лет».
Но для нее не существует время,
И для нее пространства в мире нет.

И снова черный масленичный вечер,
Зловещий парк, неспешный бег коня,
И полный счастья и веселья ветер,
С небесных круч слетевший на меня.

А надо мной спокойный и двурогий
Стоит свидетель... о, туда, туда,
По древней подкапризовой дороге,
Где лебеди и мертвая вода.[49]

Akhmatova begins by describing other people who are connected to lovers and friends, recalling the mood of "New Year's Ballad" and its celebrations among friends. But she is alone, separated from the pleasures of either late-night drinking or a lover's confirming gaze. Her only companion is her conscience, a silent witness: she speaks when an ambivalent memory descends on her from above and when conscience stands over her in a threatening way. The poet longs for escape to Tsarskoe Selo, although it does not portend any relief. Its images remain contradictory: beautiful swans, but water that is deadly still.

The "dead water" ("mertvaia voda") rewrites Pushkin's description of the Tsarskoe Selo ponds as "these living waters" ("sii zhivye vody"). The description appears in his 1836 lyceum anniversary poem "It was time: our youthful celebration" ("Byla pora: nash prazdnik molodoi").[50] Written in 1936, precisely one hundred years after "It was time," Akhmatova's poem enacts a familiar repetition and commemoration; Pushkin's original was itself an anniversary poem marking his entry twenty-five years earlier into the lyceum. Like him, she looks back with sadness. Significantly, at this moment when it was so difficult to imagine herself in the public role of the poet as it was being recreated in the Soviet Union, she turns to the late Pushkin, to a poem of 1836 in which present and past can be ruefully compared.

Akhmatova condenses Pushkin's poem lexically, intonationally, and formally. His eight-line stanzas are compressed to four, his eight stanzas reduced to four, but she keeps his five-footed iambs and alternating rhymes. His poem has the weighty feel of an ode; indeed its second half turns to historical events and the succession of tsars in ways that remind us of his "Remembrances in Tsarskoe Selo" and of late-eighteenth-century odes more generally. Akhmatova's poem does not move in that direction, although references to Tsarskoe Selo as an alluring place from the past suggest that the odic intonation has tempted her ("oh, to go there, there," she says). She also does not follow Pushkin's movement from personal history to public occasion, instead closing her poem more tightly around two semantic clusters, the recollection of Tsarskoe Selo and the poet's encounter with her conscience. She provides, in effect, a different answer to the exclamation that comes in the fourth stanza of his poem, "What, oh what, have we been witness to!" ("Chemu, chemu svideteli my byli!").[51] Pushkin uses this comment as a transition to the historical events that he and his former schoolmates have been called upon to witness, but Akhmatova invokes a "witness" to her own sins.

The "two-horned witness" presents an unusual collocation. "Two-horned" is a conventionally positive or neutral epithet ("two-horned moon," *dvurogaia luna*, for example, means a crescent-shaped moon), but in her usage we sense a demonic presence. She has taken her epithet from a scene filled with foreboding, the fortune-telling episode in Chapter Five of *Eugene Onegin*: Tatiana is unnerved by the sudden sight of "the two-horned face of the moon" ("dvurogii lik luny").[52] Tatiana offers a rich point of self-comparison as Pushkin's most beloved creation and in some ways his mirror, for example, in the superstitions described in these passages.[53] She is said to tremble and turn pale, and Akhmatova shares this nervousness in "Some see themselves in affectionate gazes." She sees a danger on a path to forbidden territory, like that which stands between Tatiana and the unknown future of her divinations, or between the poet and her past. The danger, though, is as welcome as it is terrifying, just as the "witness" stands as threat and companion, and just as conscience is both burden and moral solace. Akhmatova shares Tatiana's sublime pleasure in her terrors (Tatiana "found a hidden beauty / In fear itself," "Tainu prelest' nakhodila / I v samom uzhase ona").[54]

These fears emerge in many of the poems of 1936, including "Some see themselves in affectionate gazes," one of several poems that marked Akhmatova's return to writing poetry that year. Strictly speaking, she had not fallen into silence, but she wrote little poetry in the early 1930s and saw 1936 as a year of breakthrough, a year when she began *Requiem* and wrote such poems as "Dante," "The Poet" (to Boris Pasternak), "Voronezh" (to Osip Mandelstam), and "Incantation" ("Zaklinanie").[55] Several of these poems respond to grim events. The year 1936 saw the arrests of her son,

Lev Gumilev, and her husband, Nikolai Punin. The tone of "Some see themselves in affectionate gazes" owes as much to her changing self-image. Many of her poems in 1936 are about poetry, and they allow her to identify with the exiled lives of Mandelstam and Dante, and to feel "fear and the Muse" as nighttime guards (in "Voronezh").[56] Pasternak, whom Akhmatova knew to have his own terror at not being able to write,[57] was the subject of "The Poet." It suggests a courageous return to writing and celebrates his unflinchingly childlike enthusiasm for life, but it also puts the poet-hero in a landscape of potential danger and death.[58]

Faced with fears of writing, and of not being able to write, Akhmatova turns to Pushkin's life and works for guidance. Does his example comfort the poet in "Some see themselves in affectionate gazes"? The poem's penultimate quatrain gives an ambiguous answer to that question: the wind is "filled with happiness and gaiety," but the Mardi Gras evening is "black," the park "sinister." The wind falls on the poet from great height, as if it were a weight or a heavy object, rather than a breeze denoting joy and happiness. As before, the poet feels happy memories as a burden; indeed they seem the subject of her nighttime conversations with her conscience. Pushkin may not provide companionship, but his own late solitude, his readiness to write in fragmentary forms ("It was time" is unfinished), and his creation of a solitary, noble heroine like Tatiana stood as inspiring examples of behavior in difficult times.

Akhmatova continued to write poems with Pushkinian themes, subtexts, and locales, as noted above, but in the 1930s she began writing essays as well. The basic pattern of meaning and emotion had been set by 1936: it mixed loss and repetition, mourning and melancholia, conscience and judgment, self-examination and self-reproach.[59] Akhmatova kept at these tasks in the very different material of scholarly prose, and she found greater consolation in Pushkin when she met him on the ground of logic, argumentation, research, and intuition.

Akhmatova's Pushkin Essays: Shape and Design

Akhmatova wrote enough prose about Pushkin that a chronology is helpful as a point of departure. This list shows the timing and sustained nature of her turn to Pushkin, and the emergence of biographical themes out of an early concentration on purely philological matters.

1933	"Pushkin's Last Tale" ("Posledniaia skazka Pushkina")
1936	"Benjamin Constant's *Adolphe* in Pushkin's Writings" ("*Adol'f* Benzhamena Konstana v tvorchestve Pushkina")
1939	Commentary on *The Tale of the Golden Cockerel*

	(*Skazka o zolotom petushke*) for an edition of Pushkin's works
1947	"Pushkin's *Stone Guest*" ("*Kamennyi gost'* Pushkina," published 1958, with additions dated 1958–59)
1958	"Pushkin's Death" ("Gibel' Pushkina," published 1973)
1959	"Pushkin's Two New Tales" ("Dve novye povesti Pushkina," published 1970)
1961	"A Word on Pushkin" ("Slovo o Pushkine")
1962	"Alexandrina" (published 1973)
1963	"Pushkin in 1828" ("Pushkin v 1828 godu," published 1970)
1963	"Pushkin and the Neva Shore" ("Pushkin i Nevskoe vzmor'e," published 1974)
Undated, late	"On Chapter Two, Verse Fifteen, of *Eugene Onegin* . . ." ("O XV strofe vtoroi glavy *Evgeniia Onegina* . . . ," published 1970)
Undated, late	"Boldino Autumn" ("Boldinskaia osen'," published 1970)
1965	"Pushkin and Children" ("Pushkin i deti")

In the 1930s, Akhmatova was concerned with questions of literary influence—in her study of *The Tale of the Golden Cockerel* (Pushkin's last tale, hence the name of her essay), in her commentary on that poem for an edition of his works, and in her essay on the influence of *Adolphe*. "Pushkin's *Stone Guest*" marks a transitional point: it is textual in orientation, but Akhmatova's argument turns on questions of biographical nuance, allegorical expression, and the themes of sex and death. "Pushkin's Death" inaugurates her investigations into Pushkin's life story. Textual analysis continues in "Pushkin's Two New Tales" and in the *Onegin* essay (in both cases, with a subtle admixture of biographical themes), but biographical explorations proliferate thereafter: "Alexandrina," an essay on Natalia Nikolaevna's sister; "Pushkin in 1828," an essay on Pushkin's sexual adventures that year; and "Pushkin and the Neva Shore," a discussion of encoded references to the Decembrists in Pushkin's writings. A late unfinished piece, "Boldino Autumn," beautifully joins these projects, and also brings together themes from earlier writings (literary influence, the Don Juan theme, the psychological dilemmas facing Pushkin as he was about to marry).

"Boldino Autumn" is not the only unfinished essay. As the post-1966 publication dates for several essays show, much of this material was printed posthumously, and in a form far from what Akhmatova had hoped. Plans for more essays were found among her papers, as well as an outline of a book about Pushkin that would unite and expand many of the later essays. The unfinished state of these essays—many are presented as numbered sequences of paragraphs, and some of the paragraphs are aphoristically brief—makes them more open-ended in tone, not unlike her later lyrics. The fragmentary, laconic character of the essays, some of which are called "notes" (*zametki*) by later editors, intensifies the invitation to read the essays as we read Akhmatova's poems, and here I have in mind the special intertextual character of Acmeist writing.[60] The poems are often interpreted as powerfully linked to one another, as almost obsessively repetitive. The same is true of the essays, where many themes are repeated, often to different resolutions. I begin by commenting briefly on two early essays that continue themes we have seen in the poems; after a fuller discussion of what I take to be Akhmatova's central essay, "Pushkin's *Stone Guest*," I conclude with an assessment of "Pushkin's Death."

"Pushkin's Last Tale" and "Benjamin Constant's 'Adolphe'"

Akhmatova's essays on *The Tale of the Golden Cockerel* and Constant's influence on Pushkin are her most finished and focused literary studies.[61] Both are closely argued, with a concerted effort to provide documentation and example. In discussing the way that Pushkin used Washington Irving's 1832 *Alhambra* in the *The Tale of the Golden Cockerel*, Akhmatova sets up parallel columns of text. She tries to let material speak for itself, reserving commentary for observations about intonation and changes Pushkin made in the plot. She cites Irving in the French translation found in Pushkin's library and includes references to the English original and to other supporting matter in English in her notes; in discussing Constant, she draws on Pushkin's marginal comments in his edition of *Adolphe*. When appropriate, she consults his manuscripts to reach conclusions about the process of writing and revising. Her proof of the influence of Irving and Constant is detailed and subtle, based on linguistic similarities or likenesses in plot, pace, and psychological motivation.

Akhmatova provides extensive footnotes for these two essays. She comfortably enters into polemics with other scholars: the first note in "Pushkin's Last Tale" observes that someone else's argument proposing a French text as the source for *The Tale of the Golden Cockerel* is "completely unfounded."[62] She is not overly argumentative, though, and these two essays speak as if to fellow scholars (her desired audience broadens in the later essays). The scholarly apparatus demonstrates that Akhmatova consulted widely with academic experts,[63] and her care in attributing ideas suggested to her by others shows that she wished readers to see her connections to the

Pushkin establishment. The attributions also lend authority to her claims. What I have called the lawyerly aspect of Akhmatova's Pushkin writings appears here as a concern for evidence and argument.

The political and personal themes of the essay on Constant are subtly initiated in Akhmatova's analysis of *The Tale of the Golden Cockerel*. She reads Pushkin's use of the Irving subtext in the *Tale* as the creation of a "stage set" that hides political thoughts in an exotic mix of folklore and satire.[64] Pushkin tells about an astronomer, a ruler who does not live up to his promises, and the astronomer's revenge. Akhmatova reads the revenge as Pushkin's fantasy, for he wished ill of Tsar Nicholas I, who had seemed to promise him freedom and favor in 1826 but instead demeaned him with a low court rank and then blocked the publication of his best work. Akhmatova sees Pushkin as searching for social status and professional success, but she never loses sight of his membership in the hereditary nobility. His historical researches were what he cared about most deeply, and they were threatened by the resignation he tried to submit in 1834 out of frustration and anger at the tsar. Akhmatova pointedly reminds us that when he fled to Boldino in 1834, hoping for another productive autumn, he came back with only *The Tale of the Golden Cockerel* completed.

Akhmatova surely saw the parallels to her own life. She faced daunting obstacles to publication and enormous pressure from the authorities.[65] Pushkin's writings that preserved his integrity but also advanced his professional standing were exemplary to Akhmatova. She quite remarkably characterizes *The Tale of the Golden Cockerel* as a poem designed both to elevate Pushkin's standing and "to return him to the opposition";[66] thus she emphasizes the poem's concluding comments on giving a good lesson to all rulers. By writing about Pushkin she involved herself in prestigious cultural activity, seeming to court the "royal kindness" that so oppressed Pushkin. But Akhmatova also sought to protect herself from its excesses by pursuing topics that expressed her independence—like poetic creativity and poets' relationships with their rulers.[67]

Her essay on *Adolphe* abounds in similarly subtle self-references. Her image of Pushkin's creative process will feel familiar to those who know her poetry. She stresses, for example, the autobiographical elements in Pushkin's prose fragments, but notes that autobiography does not inhibit important literary quotations and debate.[68] She sees his fiction and the translation of *Adolphe* by his friend Prince Viazemsky as the beginning of a Russian fictional prose tradition. They invented a language that had metaphysical potential (which Akhmatova takes to mean a capacity to express abstract ideas, using the word *metaphysical* as Pushkin did), and they present heroes with complicated emotions, repressed feelings, and often a split psyche. Both inclinations should remind us of Akhmatova's innovations in the Russian lyric tradition. Her early poems were famously compared to the Russian nineteenth-century psychological novel.[69] Yet she was writing about Constant and Pushkin at a time of transition in her poetry. Although more ambitious in attempting a personal and national epic (in *Requiem*) and a history of her generation (in *Poem Without a Hero*), her later poems show Akhmatova building on the psychological complexities of her earlier lyrical heroine. She strikingly observes Pushkin's search for a kind of hero whose sufferings can be explored without descending into the autobiographical *mise en abyme* he deplored in the work of Lord Byron. Constant's example offered *Eugene Onegin* a "psychological terminology of love's sufferings,"[70] and here we recognize one of her great themes. Richly experienced in writing about "love's suffering," she was now seeking a language to describe more devastating forms of anguish. She is drawn to the historical moment when great psychological richness and philosophical depth were brought to the Russian tradition. Fascinated with the process of literary innovation, Akhmatova was no doubt eager to import its lessons into her own work. She embeds an allegory of her own creative development in the kinds of discoveries she makes about Pushkin.[71]

Akhmatova ends her study of Constant and Pushkin with reference to *The Stone Guest*, which was to be the subject of her next essay. In these early comments, she is often concerned with genre, and she calls the play a "romantic tragedy."[72] For her, the label "historical tragedy" is inaccurate, for she sees Pushkin's Don Juan as a psychologically modern hero, the play as an exploration of what she calls universal suffering. The self-referential allegory in the two early essays will more fully inform "Pushkin's *Stone Guest*," where she tells a story of loss and endless mourning.

"Pushkin's 'Stone Guest'": On Haunted Writing

Akhmatova begins "Pushkin's *Stone Guest*" by recalling the public's move away from him in 1830. Readers could not keep up with the poet, and understandably so: "All of Pushkin's contemporaries were thrilled to see themselves in the hero of *The Prisoner of the Caucasus*, but would anyone want Evgeny of *The Bronze Horseman* as their self-image?"[73] Readers identify with heroes, according to Akhmatova, but as the heroes change, poetic texts challenge readers to take on new ways of seeing themselves. The reference to mad Evgeny is daring, not least because Pushkin's contemporaries could not have been horrified by the hero of *The Bronze Horseman*, which was not published in his lifetime. Yet her choice makes brilliant sense of a quite revealing sort: she had changed from writing about the beautiful, weeping, and sexual heroines of her youthful verse to the howling, enraged women of *Requiem* (also not published in her lifetime). In *Requiem*, one poem ("The wing of madness," "Uzhe bezumie krylom," 1940) has the same insane feel of Evgeny fleeing at the end of *The Bronze Horseman*.

Akhmatova finds Pushkin's *Little Tragedies* unique in world poetry for the sharpness and complexity with which they pose the "terrifying questions of morality."[74] We will return to what Akhmatova means by morality, but let us stay for a moment with the terror she imputes to the *Little Tragedies*. In a tentative later addition to the *Stone Guest* essay, she exclaimed over the quality of attention Pushkin expected from his readers, how this was a sign of trust: "Perhaps this endless trust, which we cannot help feeling, has proved to be one of the reasons for our love for Pushkin, which has lasted one hundred forty years."[75] These later comments would have humanized the literary, ethical, and professional questions of "Pushkin's *Stone Guest*" had they been included in the essay. Mostly, it proceeds by raising moral questions on literary grounds. Akhmatova begins by comparing Pushkin's play with other dramas about Don Juan, and her comparisons are used less in a philological way than to ground observations about literary reputations and the public response to a poet's words. She insists that Pushkin avoided the direct moralizing of his predecessors, but not by abandoning moral questions. He makes it clear from the start that his hero must perish, she says: the title *The Stone Guest* points not to the don and his adventures (or his sufferings), but to the statue of the commendatore, the instrument of retribution in the play.

We are reminded of Akhmatova's emphasis on the theme of revenge in her discussion of *The Tale of the Golden Cockerel*, and of the imagery of blood in her poems. Why does revenge interest Akhmatova? One grim answer comes from the peculiar logic of criminal justice in Stalin's Russia: relatives of previously arrested or executed people were often taken for fear that they would avenge the wrongs done to their family. That logic would have been partly behind the three arrests of Lev Gumilev, Akhmatova's son. The guilt and blood in her poetry suggest that Akhmatova felt herself implicated in this logic of revenge. A dread of complicity causes her to see the leading characters in *The Stone Guest* as if from the inside. Just as she believes Pushkin to have avoided impersonal moralizing in the play, so she too will not sit mightily above the tragedy she describes.

"Pushkin's *Stone Guest*" also notes his changes in the Don Juan myth: he casts Donna Anna as the commander's widow, not daughter; he has his Don Juan return to Madrid, rather than Seville; and he makes his Don Juan a poet, a composer of the song sung by Laura. Akhmatova reads these changes with reference to Pushkin's life story (thus crossing the two impulses of all her Pushkin essays—the search for source texts and the accretion of a partial biography). Madrid, the capital, is necessary for Pushkin to make Don Juan's crime political, a change that Akhmatova reads as referring to Pushkin's exile (1820–26) and his longed-for return to Petersburg.[76] Don Juan's love for Donna Anna is said to replay Pushkin's anxious love for Natalia Goncharova, to whom he was finally betrothed in 1830, the year in which *The Stone Guest* was written. Pushkin's terror of happiness and his belief that happiness leaves one vulnerable to loss make the ending of *The Stone Guest* tragic, Akhmatova argues, for only if Don Juan loves Donna Anna does his death become a tragedy. She also notes Pushkin's identification with the punishing statue who returns out of jealousy at his widow's infidelity; she cites Pushkin's letters and a similar passage from *Boris Godunov*, where anxieties about a widow's remarriage surface. The essay ends with the extraordinary insight, born of this doubled identification for Pushkin with both Don Juan and the statue who returns to kill him, that "in the tragedy *The Stone Guest* Pushkin punishes himself—himself as young, careless, and sinning; the theme of jealousy beyond the grave (that is, fear of it) resounds as loudly as the theme of revenge."[77]

In this vision of Pushkin as punishing a "young, careless, and sinning" self, we hear echoes of Akhmatova's self-portrayals, including a 1938 poem from *Requiem* that begins, "They should have shown you, mocker, / And the favorite of all your friends, / The gay sinner of Tsarskoe Selo, / What would happen to your life" ("Pokazat' by tebe, nasmeshnitse / I liubimitse vsekh druzei, / Tsarskosel'skoi veseloi greshnitse, / Chto sluchitsia s zhizn'iu tvoei").[78] This poem compares the poet's once carefree life with the lives ending behind a prison wall; a subtle link to the Pushkinian pattern of naïveté recollected in pain is forged by the reference to Tsarskoe Selo, which itself recalls his lyceum anniversary poems and Akhmatova's use of them. A similar self-description, with equivalent subtextual associations, occurs in a later poem, "The Heiress" ("Naslednitsa," 1959), also set in Tsarskoe Selo. Here Akhmatova asks, "Oh, who would have told me then / That I would inherit all this" ("O, kto by mne togda skazal, / Chto ia nasleduiu vse eto"); the inheritance includes "my own shade, / All distorted from terror, / And a hair shirt of repentance" ("sobstvennuiu ten', / Vsiu iskazhennuiu ot strakha, / I pokaiannuiu rubakhu").[79]

These poems create a context for Akhmatova's comments about Pushkin's career in her essay on *The Stone Guest*. We have seen this self-comparison in her Pushkin essays, but here she gives the practice a name, calling it a "lyrical approach" (*liricheskoe nachalo*). She explains that she has shown not that the play is autobiographical, but that it is, at its source, lyrical. She believes that the play remained unpublished in Pushkin's lifetime because of its intense expression of personal experience.[80] No such reluctance to publish affected Akhmatova's attitude toward the equally personal essay "Pushkin's *Stone Guest*," but it may explain why she so heavily reworked the essay with revisions and extensions some ten years later. For her as well, the work at hand has become what she calls "lyrical," and its self-references originate partly in her retrospective glance at the heroines of her earlier poems.

These early poems created myths about the poet's love life, where she is the woman left behind by a man not unlike the legendary Don Juan. Akhmatova built her early poetic reputation on a self-presentation as the woman men loved to leave. Seduced, abandoned, abused, ignored—these epithets are all too appropriate to the speaker in dozens of lyrics. She is the woman who receives no letters, who is fated to experience love's tortures, who forgives her lover's cruel joke, whose lover is arrogant, evil, and in love with other women. Famously, the man she begs not to leave her suggests that she not stand outside in the wind. As songs of a final meeting, these poems remind us of Donna Anna, the woman who has a tragic last meeting with Don Juan.[81] Donna Anna is, Akhmatova claims, truly loved. Similarly, throughout her early love lyrics, there is a peculiar certainty that this man who is so abusive and cold is, in fact, in love with his victim. Akhmatova presents her desolate heroine as fiercely loved. She has "entered into the tragedy so much that she feels herself to be a Pushkinian heroine."[82] One could say that she casts herself as the woman able to capture the heart of even so heartless a man as Don Juan. Given Akhmatova's belief in the magical symbolism of names and numbers, she would have noted the coincidence of her first name with that of Donna Anna.

The role of Don Juan suits Nikolai Gumilev all too well. He won the hand of Anna Akhmatova after six years of relentless wooing, established himself as something of a Don Juan in the two years before their marriage, and represented himself in verse in a parodic version of masculinity ("active, restless, aggressive, 'macho,' an explorer, big-game hunter, pirate captain or warrior, always pursuing").[83] Gumilev's poems often image an erotic relationship as a species of conflict and conquest, particularly when he addresses Akhmatova, and it is worth a brief detour through these poems to substantiate my claim that their relationship informs "Pushkin's *Stone Guest*."

Gumilev's 1914 poem "Holy nights float and melt" ("Sviashchennye plyvut i taiut nochi") opens with scenes of danger and death, but the speaker feels satisfactorily in control: "As if the whole cosmos is feminine / And it is I who govern it entirely" ("Kak budto zhenstvenno vse mirozdan'e / I upravliaiu im vsetselo ia").[84] His bold assertion of erotic power before death recalls Don Juan who, in Julia Kristeva's words, exudes "the pure *jouissance* of a conqueror . . . who knows he has no object, who does not want one."[85] The poem "Holy nights float and melt" gives the poet control over a feminine cosmos, and it describes three specific women. The third is identified as Akhmatova, and the poet puts himself at the center of her poetic world (just as he is the center of the universe in the poem—even the skies tell the stories of his future).[86] He ascribes to her poetry the deadly power of all siren songs.

Women bring death in many of Gumilev's lyrics, often in poems that Akhmatova says were addressed to her.[87] Among these is "Five-Footed Iambs" ("Piatistopnye iamby," 1913), where Akhmatova is concealed as Donna Anna.[88] In another poem, "The Animal Tamer" ("Ukrotitel' zverei," 1912), she seems the source of death. It has an epigraph from her poetry and repeats the sound of her first name almost hypnotically (four times in the final quatrain, where the Russian words are *Fanni, dannyi, kanate*, and *predannyi*).[89] Recalling the bloodied hands in Akhmatova's poems, we might read her guilt partly as an effect of Gumilev's poetic imagery. He predicted that his death would come at her hands, and she in turn created a lyrical persona responsible for his violent demise in her poems. She is also the beast that Gumilev cannot tame, a woman stronger and more resistant than the Donna Anna who faints in Don Juan's arms. The feistiest version of her in his poetry is his shockingly violent poem "This happened more than once" ("Eto bylo ne raz," 1910).[90] The speaker appears to threaten a beating as a way to preserve the cycle of fighting, departure, and submissive return. Acknowledging her strength of will, the poet reveals that one of her battle weapons is silence (Akhmatova is frequently described in his poems as terrifyingly silent, not unlike the beast in "The Animal Tamer").

She was not silent, of course,[91] and she even wrote poems that sarcastically responded to any man's attempt to place her in a submissive role (brilliantly exemplified in the poem "Submissive to you?," "Tebe pokornoi?," 1921).[92] A poem like this one forewarns of the stern, stony self that is the hallmark of Akhmatova's later lyrics, and also of the essays in the middle period, including "Pushkin's *Stone Guest*." Dated 1947, and extended by some fragmentary notes in 1958–59, this essay shows the historical and personal markers we expect. Would that we could place it in the context, for example, of the lyrics from 1947. But there are no poems by Akhmatova from that year, which followed closely on the August 1946 public denunciation of her and Mikhail Zoshchenko.

Implicitly, I have been suggesting that "Pushkin's *Stone Guest*" *is* the lyrical poem from that difficult year, lyrical in its imprint of her painful relationship with Gumilev. Akhmatova dated a typescript of the essay precisely: April 20, 1947, a date that is quite close to the anniversary of her marriage to Gumilev, April 15. She had indicated that her poem "Incantation" ("Zaklinanie") was to and about Gumilev by giving it the dateline April 15, 1936. In "Incantation," Gumilev is cast as the Stone Guest, invited to dinner not with Don Juan's audacity but with the urgency of a woman who has resorted to folk magic to return her beloved to life.[93]

Incantation

From behind the high gates,
From beyond the Okhta swamps,
Along an unmarked path,
Along an uncut meadow,
Through the nighttime cordon,
To the sound of the Easter bells,
Not a guest,
Not a bridegroom,
Come and dine with me.

April 15, 1936

Заклинание

Из высоких ворот,
Из заохтенских болот,
Путем нехоженым,
Лугом некошеным,
Сквозь ночной кордон,
Под пасхальный звон,
Незваный,
Несуженый, —
Приди ко мне ужинать.[94]

15 апреля 1936

This poem, written on the twenty-fifth anniversary of her marriage to Gumilev, is Akhmatova's first recasting of their romance in terms of the myth of Don Juan. Here he is the commendatore, the one who returns as if from the dead. That recasting is intriguing, in part because Akhmatova claimed in 1924 always to have imagined Gumilev as if he were dead—even in her earliest poems about him.[95] The theme of widowhood emerged early in her work and came to be grotesquely literalized after 1921. But in "Incantation" there is another interesting transfer of roles, for Akhmatova also puts herself in the position of the don, the one who invites the statue to dine. Her moral impulse makes her take on this role, for she sees herself as sharing his errant past and thus as vulnerable to similar vengeance. In making Gumilev into the commendatore, she also strikingly creates him as a figure of power and revenge. That 1936 metamorphosis resonates with Akhmatova's interest in the theme of revenge (in *Requiem*, begun in 1936, and in her essay on *The Tale of the Golden Cockerel*).

Significantly, Akhmatova has Pushkin's version of the Don Juan myth in mind, for her commendatore, like his, is a husband, not a father. Gumilev as the Stone Guest is the dead husband to whom one must be loyal. Akhmatova was loyal to him in all senses but that of beyond-the-grave sexual fidelity (or, for that matter, before-the-grave). She took on the role of preserving and promoting his poetic legacy, particularly in the early 1920s.[96] In making him both the commendatore and Don Juan, Akhmatova offers him the same multiplicity of roles she observes in Pushkin's relationship to the play: "it is as if Pushkin divides himself between the commander and Juan."[97] Akhmatova resembles Pushkin in this act of self-division. Her own lyrical insight into his tragedy draws on identifications with Donna Anna, Don Juan, and the commendatore.

Dividing and redistributing roles in this way complicates the moral logic of her essay, just as her poems make it difficult to separate the dead from the mourners. Ghosts disturb the moral clarity of Akhmatova's poems. "Pushkin's *Stone Guest*" incorporates these spectral presences in its analysis of a play in which a statue comes to life. The essay itself is haunted by the ghost of Gumilev. He, like all spectral presences, calls into question the stability of claims about truth, presence, self-certainty, even self. What we have long called Akhmatova's Pushkin "scholarship" is also, then, a form of "haunted writing," to use Avital Ronell's evocative term.[98] What lessons can ghosts teach about right and wrong? The stakes in such questions are unbearably high, for the background of injustice in "Pushkin's *Stone Guest*," as in much of Akhmatova's later writing, is the terror and unpredictability of the Stalinist police state. The ghosts are not meant to lighten the moral fare of her later work, but rather to create scenarios in which one can encounter, as in the haunted houses of Gothic novels, spectral representations of one's own sins. Akhmatova resembles the Gothic heroine, sorting through documents and diversions, determined to get to the true source of the hero's agony and to make clear who has done what to whom.

Like Gothic fiction, Akhmatova's Pushkin scholarship searches for secret knowledge. Leslie O'Bell has seen her method as psychoanalytic, "striving to bring the hidden to light, to get from Pushkin's *tainopis'*, or secret writing, to the *tainy*, or secrets behind it." As she rightly observes, most readers of Akhmatova's Pushkin writings have stressed her political hidden meanings, but O'Bell sees Akhmatova as interested in Pushkin's "riven and unstable psyche, his unresolved conflicts."[99] If we pursue the logic of this claim about psyche and secrecy, then Pushkin becomes a kind of Gothic hero, one whose mysteries are to be explored by Akhmatova as intrepid poet-scholar. We watch her explore his creative processes and repressed wishes as if she were passing through the dark passageways of an ancient castle. Like all Gothic heroines, she sets off to find the story of the hero but then stumbles on truths that are deeply revealing about herself.

In "Pushkin's *Stone Guest*," Akhmatova writes herself into two areas of knowledge that were to ground much of her future poetry, including *Poem Without a Hero*. First, she found that depths of emotion and psychological information could still emerge from her relationship with Gumilev. Even without writing about him directly in this essay, she was able to let her experiences inform new insights into Pushkin's creative methods and his psychological inclinations. The connections among Gumilev, Don Juan, the commendatore, herself, Donna Anna, and Pushkin could be crisscrossed in various ways, and they could show the intensity of her loyalties and her grief. Second, Akhmatova found a moral imagination that was less black and white than her rather legalistic tendencies might have prepared her for. By casting herself as the sinning don (a self-image that recurs in other lyrics and in *Poem Without a Hero*), Akhmatova acts the part of one who is to be judged alongside her already existing capacity to render judgments. Her earlier poetry had fully readied her for both these epistemological positions, as we saw in our small sample of her verse: she knew well the torments of conscience, and the painful experience of being the victim of others' wrongs. In "Pushkin's *Stone Guest*," she discovers a way to occupy both roles at once, adding to them a third and seemingly impartial viewpoint as evaluator or, in her terms, conscience itself. This multiplication of subject positions does not stop Akhmatova from rendering moral judgments, but just as her mournful intonations temper some of her sterner judgments, so here, as she sifts through the felt knowledge of different lives, her attitude softens into something more humane. The true test of her humanity will be in how she judges herself, and beginning in the 1930s, she will have more than thirty years' worth of poems in which to practice forgiveness.

In her ability to think about good, evil, sin, and repentance from more than one perspective, she has truly become the successor of Dostoevsky, which brings us back to our earlier discussion of "Bobok" and the later, wiser novels. In her fullest contemplation of Dostoevsky, the first of the "Northern Elegies," Akhmatova ruefully observes that she has inherited her mother's kindness, which feels like an unneeded gift in her cruel age. But the mix of kindness and cruelty is precisely the inheritance she has needed in order to comprehend what is around her (those are the terms on which the first "Northern Elegy" ends). A further test for this vision of humane ethics was the story of Pushkin's death, which Akhmatova was to write about for the rest of her life. At the risk of jumping ahead of the evidence, I should say at the outset that her humanity and gentleness did not always come to her rescue in this work. For a variety of reasons, some having to do more with the circumstances of her life and her temperament than with the material she unearthed, Akhmatova often inclined to rather stern judgments of Pushkin's contemporaries. But the tales of intrigue, slander, love, loyalty, and loss that emerged from letters and memoirs about Pushkin were endlessly interesting to her. She was compelled to keep writing about Pushkin, and her turn to biography offered endless new material. These essays were even more unfinished and subject to revision than "Pushkin's *Stone Guest*," and they show us her thought processes, as well as the conclusions she reached. She was experimenting with prose forms that could express grief, anger, and sharp judgments at once.

"Pushkin's Death"

Akhmatova begins "Pushkin's Death" by questioning whether she should write such an essay at all. She says that she counts herself as a Pushkinist, and thus among those who think that one should not write about his family tragedy. But the inaccuracies and lies of others' versions impel her to speak out, she says. With these introductory words, she assumes a familiar role: the one who corrects others' mistakes and who speaks out of moral obligation despite an inner conflict about the task at hand. The tone and tempo of this essay are less familiar, though, almost a shock after the deliberate procedures of the other essays. Akhmatova writes in an abbreviated, enigmatic way, assuming that her audience already knows the players in this drama. She embeds her judgments in accounts of their actions. Initially, she focuses on motivation and sketches in characters quickly, recalling Pushkin's own lightning-quick psychological presentation. The level of compression is very high, and Pushkin's fragmentary fictions must have been a model for her style. Leslie O'Bell has observed that we now read the documents relating to Pushkin's death as if they constituted an epistolary novel,[100] but in Akhmatova's hands the letters blossom into psychological novels more like those of the late nineteenth century (again, there is a subtle influence of the methods advanced by Dostoevsky). The focus on motive, the quick movement from one player to another, and the general atmosphere of suspicion give "Pushkin's Death" the feel of Dostoevsky's novels, where crimes are committed, suspects sorted through, and guilt generally spread around to everyone involved. The difficult moment for Akhmatova will be practicing his Christian forgiveness, his compassion for those who sin.

The first chapter of "Pushkin's Death" pursues various crimes of Heeckeren—rumors sown, alliances forged, and slanders perpetuated. Akhmatova's tone mixes outrage with sarcasm: "But even all of this was not enough for Heeckeren," she writes, in transition from one transgression to another.[101] Some of her work is a tale of documents, as in the case of a letter apparently to the Countess Nesselrode from Heeckeren, but, Akhmatova argues, fabricated by both for the benefit of Nicholas I. She discusses at length who actually wrote the anonymous letters that triggered the final duel, insisting that there were several people involved but that one of them must have been the young Prince Pyotr Dolgorukov. She exposes him in clipped, determined paragraphs that read like a legal brief. Her tone remains even as she looks for the truer villains, better known and closer to home. Her underlying motive is to expose the mechanisms by which Heeckeren's version of the events persuaded many in Pushkin's own circle, and here she finds culpability in some of his closest friends.

Akhmatova also analyzes d'Anthès, with more emotion and less detective work about evidence. She asserts that d'Anthès was in love with Natalia Nikolaevna from January 1836 to that fall; she sees him as disenchanted thereafter, to the point that in the end he found her hateful. Only Natalia Nikolaevna and other society ladies believed in his great love, but that was enough to give the legend staying power. It was the more interesting version, simply put. "The elder Heeckeren not only was victorious over Pushkin during his lifetime, to our shame, but he continues to this day to celebrate a diplomatic victory," Akhmatova writes.[102] She is not surprised that it worked in his lifetime, but wonders how Russian society did not unmask the "Cotillion Prince" d'Anthès, how it "allowed a great life to be sacrificed to the vanity of a petty careerist," how, for some 120 years, it could "repeat, make into theatrical adaptations and into a film the slanders of the suspect baron?"[103] She expresses outrage against subsequent generations of Russians who believed the tale of d'Anthès's passionate love. It is not that she expects all Russians to read the documents as well as she does, or even to know where to look for them. But the assumptions that rest beneath the myth of d'Anthès's great love, which some claim to have lasted two years (for example, the influential Pavel Shchegolev), are, she says, ridiculous.[104] That would mean a beginning in 1834, but how could Pushkin have tolerated an affair of two years? Akhmatova's counter-version is that d'Anthès declared himself in January 1836 and received a Tatiana-like response from a pregnant woman. The rumors started in July, when Natalia Nikolaevna began going out again after her confinement.

Akhmatova presents a brilliant set of deductions about Heeckeren's motives, plans, and opinions: he could, she believes, clearly see Pushkin's intention to make d'Anthès look a ridiculous coward and thus end his career. But to make d'Anthès a hero, Heeckeren has him simulate a grand passion in public. Rumors of the homosexual connection between Heeckeren and d'Anthès surfaced in late 1836, and it became all the more imperative to find a suitable wife for d'Anthès. Heeckeren then wanted him married in order to protect d'Anthès's career, and in order to end his liaison with Natalia Nikolaevna, of whom Heeckeren was jealous.[105] All of which made it useful to spread the tales of a grand passion and a jealous husband, transforming d'Anthès into a noble man who marries the ugly sister (Ekaterina Nikolaevna) of the woman he loves, sacrificing himself for her reputation. In the notes to this essay, Akhmatova sharply delineates the conflicting versions of events, but in the text she is satisfied to condemn Natalia Nikolaevna: Heeckeren, she says, used her to transmit his version to Pushkin, making her "Heeckeren's agent."[106]

Akhmatova blames Natalia Nikolaevna, who believed in d'Anthès's great love, for perpetuating this myth. Based on a letter in which d'Anthès reports his love for a lady whose husband is revoltingly jealous, she concludes that Natalia Nikolaevna complained to him about Pushkin's jealousy (this inference is not entirely convincing, one might note: the jealousy and the complaint may as easily have been d'Anthès's fabrication). In passing, Akhmatova attributes various bits of false information to Natalia Nikolaevna, who passed them to Pushkin. His letters (to Heeckeren and to others) then contain them as facts. No less caustic is Akhmatova's view of Natalia Nikolaevna's other sister, Alexandra Nikolaevna, who is said to have known about the duel but did nothing to stop it. (She wrote an entire essay on Alexandra Nikolaevna in 1962, "Alexandrina.")

Some of what is said about Natalia Nikolaevna and her sister is strikingly prejudiced and tendentious in its interpretation of documents. Akhmatova draws conclusions based on the memoirs of Alexandra Arapova, for example, whose exaggerations and inaccuracies were well known; she herself called Arapova's memoirs "hysterical."[107] Also less than fully persuasive is the view that the Tsar's reproach to Natalia Nikolaevna for her behavior helped cause the final duel. Akhmatova suggests that Natalia Nikolaevna did not know how to conduct herself in high society, and that this was widely known, citing memoirs by Countess Vicquelmont and letters from Prince Viazemsky to Natalia Nikolaevna. Again, the evidence is not flawless, particularly Viazemsky's letters. Akhmatova admits that they were unpublished, and thus could not have contributed to public opinion, but she does not tell us that Viazemsky's admonitions to Natalia Nikolaevna might have been affected by his own apparent love for her, and by the role of elder adviser he took on after Pushkin's death.[108]

Viazemsky and Pushkin's friend Vasily Zhukovsky are subsequently seen as blind and inactive by Akhmatova, and in this her interpretation anticipates that of the film *The Last Road*. But their guilt is nothing compared with that of Natalia Nikolaevna: "After the catastrophe, everyone took fright and tried as hard as they could to justify Natalia Nikolaevna, who *alone* could have stopped it all at any moment, but she could not bring herself to believe that d'Anthès did not love her and was making fun of her. How completely alone Pushkin was at this time, and how weak and ineffective was the behavior of his friends (see the two letters by Viazemsky) [and the] behavior of both Heeckerens. . . . Pushkin simply could not take it, and he did not know everything. When he found out, he sent his letter."[109] The sense of the poet alone, betrayed by ineffective friends and a deluded wife, is the core of Akhmatova's interpretation of Pushkin's death. Gone are the cross-identifications and ambiguities of "Pushkin's *Stone Guest*." The solitude seen in Pushkin's last months was also experienced by the author of "Pushkin's Death," at least from her point of view, and she writes as if she alone understands how utterly abandoned Pushkin was.

There is little grief in "Pushkin's Death," which is stuffed with facts and differing interpretations. We hear some sadness in Akhmatova's lament that "Pushkin simply could not take it," and perhaps a sense of loss determines her title, which chooses a word for death (*gibel'*) that suggests an untimely loss, someone perishing or coming to harm. But the dominant emotions of "Pushkin's Death" are anger and indignation, the last manifestation of a grieving process that ought to mark its end, but instead suggests that it cannot end. The self-reproaches are gone. What is left is rage, which is not always the most illuminating emotion. Akhmatova's later Pushkin essays would return to themes of grief and regret, particularly the excellent "Pushkin and the Neva Shore."[110] She would pursue her interest in the origins of rumors in the piece on Pushkin's sister-in-law, "Alexandrina," where the impulse to moral judgment is powerful. But neither these nor the other later pieces would push Akhmatova past the conundrum to which she is brought in "Pushkin's Death." Her wish to find guidance as a poet and public figure had to come to an end when she confronted Pushkin's demise, for the only lessons here were about isolation and betrayal. And so, Akhmatova used her later essays to teach her own readers about the vicissitudes of a life lived in public, the importance of loyal friends and loyal readers, and the confidence that truths will be told. The project of these later, unfinished pieces is tremendously ambitious, but we should expect no less from a poet who, all her life, had found in Pushkin a companion to her most important searches for poetic and personal truth.

6   *Marina Tsvetaeva's Pushkin and the Poet's Identities*

> Pushkin was not one person, but many, and this multiplicity is the poet.
> —Tsvetaeva, 1937

We would be hard put to improve on the poet Marina Tsvetaeva's own characterization of herself. As she aptly put it in 1919: "There are many souls in me."[1] Tsvetaeva (1892–1941) expressed that dynamic, ever-changing identity in imagined encounters with Pushkin. She found inspiration in his poetry, in his biography, in his contemporaries, and in his fictional heroes. In her relationship with Pushkin, she felt a gratifying fullness of self: his confidence and charm helped her invent a charismatic personality of her own.

Most of Tsvetaeva's Pushkin writings were composed after she left Russia in 1922; three earlier poems established the later themes. This short list of poems and essays reflects her typical mix of recollection, fantasy, and idiosyncrasy:[2]

- 1913   "An Encounter with Pushkin" ("Vstrecha s Pushkinym"), a poem
- 1916   "Happiness or sadness" ("Shchastie ili grust'"), a poem
- 1920   "Psyche" ("Psikheia"), a poem
- 1929   "Natalia Goncharova," an essay
- 1931   "Poems to Pushkin" ("Stikhi k Pushkinu"), a cycle of six poems, published 1937
- 1937   "My Pushkin" ("Moi Pushkin") and "Pushkin and Pugachev" ("Pushkin i Pugachev"), two essays

When and where she wrote each item is important, but the poet's capacity to transport herself elsewhere should not be underestimated. The essays are written by an adult in isolated and distressing circumstances, but one who projects an image as a curious and intensely alive child, remembering her first pleasurable encounters with Pushkin.

Distinctively, Tsvetaeva writes from more than one vantage point when she writes of Pushkin: she is child and adult, émigré and Russian, and a curious mix of feminine and masculine as well. Sometimes she offers a vulnerable self in speaking of Pushkin, which makes her early poems about him especially intriguing, but at other moments she speaks with aggressive authority, using him as a weapon against her adversaries and using his struggle against censors and uncomprehending readers to inspire her own battles. After 1922, she writes from the distance of Europe, but also as if from within the experience of Pushkin's own world of imperial Russia.

To prove, then, that Tsvetaeva writes of herself when she writes of Pushkin involves more than the search for self-references in her poems and essays, although these are worth remarking. Harder to grasp is what aspect of the self Tsvetaeva allegorizes—present or past, adult or child, maternal protector or conquering lover, emotional human being or godlike poet— since she frequently suggests that she is all at once. She finds a fascinating alter ego in Pushkin's wife, Natalia Nikolaevna Pushkina. Tsvetaeva came to her fullest understanding of Pushkin by sorting through her feelings about Natalia Nikolaevna; this is among her most important contributions to Russia's myth of Pushkin, and it marks her difference from Akhmatova, for example, very sharply. Through Natalia Nikolaevna, Tsvetaeva faced self-images as a woman that fit uncomfortably with the poetic identity she was fashioning in her encounters with Pushkin. Her use of shifting identities will reappear in the writings of Andrei Bitov, but, rather than his postmodern play with language and subjectivity, where meaning can seem endlessly deferred, Tsvetaeva uses the mobility of self-expression to precise psychological ends.

Which sides of Pushkin does Tsvetaeva illuminate? Often, in true Romantic fashion, the darker, mysterious, even demonic sides. Her writings show her affinity for his poems "Demons" ("Besy," 1830), "Delibash" (1829), "The Vampire" ("Vurdalak," 1834), "The Drowned Man" ("Utoplennik," 1828), "Winter Road" ("Zimniaia doroga," 1826), *Poltava* (1829), *The Gypsies* (*Tsygany*, 1824), and "To the Sea" ("K moriu," 1824). She translated many of these poems into French, as well as more canonical poems like "The Prophet" ("Prorok," 1826)—but not "I have built myself a monument" ("Ia pamiatnik sebe vozdvig nerukotvornyi," 1836), although Tsvetaeva shows an interest in the political Pushkin.[3] She found great pleasure in rejecting a traditional Pushkin canon. In an official questionnaire (the perfect venue for rejecting official views), she proclaimed that she never liked *Eugene Onegin*—a calculated provocation from one who shows in "My Pushkin" that *Onegin* strongly affected her from earliest youth.[4]

When it comes to biography, her attention is caught by the last decade of Pushkin's life.[5] She writes about his death only in the last of her 1931 "Poems to Pushkin" and in her late essays. There she claims the image of

Pushkin lying shot in the snow as a formative vision. Unlike others, for whom his death in a duel was an incomprehensible trick of fate, she saw it as inevitable and dreadfully logical. "Pushkin was killed," she writes, "because he would never have died a natural death, he would have lived forever ... (Pushkin was killed because he was conceived as immortal)."[6] She is actually more interested in the circumstances of his life in the 1830s, including his relationships with his wife and his tsar, and in his turn to history in his writings (this concentration on lived experience will be found in the work of Bitov as well). She also pursues the effects of exile on the writer, so that she can compare her experiences in Europe with Pushkin's confinement to Odessa, Kishinev, and Mikhailovskoe from 1820 to 1826. She takes his poem "To the Sea" as an emblem of the exile, and it becomes emblematic of her own coming of age as a poet; "To the Sea" informs her first utterances to Pushkin as well as her final essay.

I begin with those late essays, somewhat unconventionally presenting her work not in chronological order but according to the self-image she presents in each piece. The sequence tells the story of her progression from child (in the 1937 essays), to teenager (in her first poem to Pushkin), to young adult (in the texts about Natalia Goncharova), to mature poet (in the cycle of poems to Pushkin). This order delineates Tsvetaeva's imagination of her own psychological development, and it shows vividly the different forms her self-creation could take. It also allows this chapter to begin and end with the decisive decade of the 1930s, starting with her fine late essays and ending with her cycle of poems to Pushkin.

The Pushkin Essays

Tsvetaeva's two Pushkin essays are deeply complementary pieces of writing, best treated together. The title "My Pushkin" seems to promise a relatively personal and possessive treatment, whereas "Pushkin and Pugachev" suggests an outward focus, as well as the backward glance of history. Yet both pieces explore personal history, recalling the child who first read and formed ideas of Pushkin and celebrating the insightful errors of those ideas. They also, perhaps surprisingly, interrogate the violence that surrounds her mistakes. Tsvetaeva was not one to revel in childhood's potential innocence. She is attracted to the discoveries that can be born of a child's ignorance, but she imagines herself very much a part of the adult world; the challenges of daily life when she was writing in the 1930s, as well as the harm that came to Pushkin, impose themselves on the evolving identity of the child described in the essays.

"My Pushkin" begins with a visual image: the famous painting by Aleksei Naumov, *Pushkin's Duel with d'Anthès* (*Duel' Pushkina s Dantesom*, 1884; Fig. 21). The dark figure of Pushkin lies mortally wounded in the

FIGURE 21. Oil painting by A. A. Naumov, *Pushkin's Duel with d'Anthès*, 1884. Reproduction from E. V. Pavlova, ed., *A. S. Pushkin v portretakh* (Moscow: Sovetskii khudozhnik, 1989), vol. 1, p. 170. Courtesy National Pushkin Museum, St. Petersburg.

white snow. Tsvetaeva gives a toneless, laconically accurate description of the image: "Snow, black twigs of small trees, two black figures take a third, holding him under his arms, toward a carriage, and there's one more figure, his back turned, who walks away. The one carried is Pushkin, the one walking away is d'Anthès."[7] The contrast of black on white in this painting mesmerizes her, and she will write in "Pushkin and Pugachev" that "my business is to look endlessly at the thing that looms black in the snowstorm."[8] That claim orients Tsvetaeva toward contradiction and danger in Pushkin's writings, with the looming threat of death.

Perhaps because her imagination needs a counter-balancing picture, one that authorizes a more dynamic interpretation of Pushkin, she admits in "My Pushkin" that her favorite portrait of Pushkin shows him as a child, his chin resting on his hand, his skin wonderfully dark: this 1822 engraving by E. I. Geitman (Fig. 22) reveals his "distant African soul," she says, and intimates his future poetic genius. It is a portrait with two spatial realms ("v dve dali") and two temporalities, the present dreaminess of a child and the future brilliance of the poet.[9] Her admiration neatly signifies the split in space and time found throughout her Pushkin texts.

Tsvetaeva achieves a split self-representation in her Pushkin essays by speaking both as the grown-up poet who writes in Parisian emigration and as the little girl in Moscow, Tarusa, and Italy who absorbed Pushkin's poems as if kept alive by them. Irony often informs the views of the adult,

FIGURE 22. Copper engraving by E. I. Geitman, *Pushkin*, 1822. Reproduction from E. V. Pavlova, ed., *A. S. Pushkin v portretakh* (Moscow: Sovetskii khudozhnik, 1989), vol. 1, p. 86. Courtesy of the National Pushkin Museum, Moscow.

who sees the gap between her expectations and her lived experiences, but pathos fills the world of the child. Tsvetaeva divides her childhood between love and abandonment. She was thrilled by her successes but crushed by moments of injury and indifference. She also recreates a general sense of how children read Pushkin, imagining the vulnerabilities of childhood as tangible, physical conditions. She thinks of children "dirty, unfed, blue with cold" for whom one Pushkin anthology that she used might have been intended (it is the same book in which she finds the Geitman drawing of Pushkin as a child).[10] These images of poor urban schoolchildren evoke a sense of psychological need, especially of needs unmet.

That neediness characterizes her self-image as a child, too, but in describing herself Tsvetaeva seems more focused on contrasting knowledge with ignorance. She demonstrates that her erroneous interpretation of the poem "Delibash" at age seven proved truer than that of the Prague students who "corrected" her in 1924. Her first Pushkin memories turn on verbal confusions: near-homonyms, place-names that she took to refer to people, and archaic words that she misread entirely. The child's world, in her memory, is a carnival of language acquisition, a constant curiosity about strange-sounding words and implausible inferences. She remembers her efforts to deduce meanings from context (thus "vampire," because it gnawed at bones, must be a kind of dog; "worn-out," because she had heard it used in her house to describe her mother's winter muffler, meant furry; "sentry" became a clock, etc.). Tsvetaeva cultivates error, we might say, and in so doing she is cultivating the poet within herself; as the contemporary poet Anne Carson has said, "what we are engaged in when we do poetry is error, / the willful creation of error."[11] The inevitability of error in reading was to become a centerpiece of deconstructive poetics, and Tsvetaeva shares that theory's mistrust of rational logic. She embraces error in a contrarian spirit, finding her mistakes to be authentic avenues to meaning because they are castigated by others. In 1911 she had written that "children understand all too well! At the age of seven, they understand Mtsyri and Eugene Onegin much more truly, and more deeply, than at twenty."[12] In "Pushkin and Pugachev," Tsvetaeva makes an adult's argument for the superiority of error when she juxtaposes Pushkin's historical fiction *The Captain's Daughter* (*Kapitanskaia dochka*, 1836) to his essay about the same period, *The History of Pugachev* (*Istoriia Pugacheva*, 1833). She prefers the fictional Pugachev: he seems to make better psychological sense, and he is more appealing (because less terrifying).[13]

Responses to violence appear in both essays. Verbal violence is celebrated, as noted above, but Tsvetaeva is repelled by physical violence. When, in "Pushkin and Pugachev," she quotes Pushkin's explicit and gruesome descriptions, she tells us that a child will naturally find details of eyeballs hanging loose or bodies left to decay to be repugnant. One of these images in fact involves a child, a seven-year-old (we realize with a shock that Tsvetaeva has also repeatedly set her own age at seven in the essay, as if to strengthen her connection to this boy) who is the young brother of a woman Pugachev took to his bed and then had executed. This child is murdered alongside his sister. Tsvetaeva punishingly quotes Pushkin's account of the wounded brother and sister crawling toward each other to die together, and then, as if that were not enough, she reprises the scene in her own words, asserting that no artistic (fictional) work can tolerate the description of the "shooting of a seven-year-old child who crawls to his sister as his blood pours out."[14] We wonder why her own essay has included these violent details, even as she objects to the gore. In copying down, as if obsessively, these scenes of violence, Tsvetaeva is laying the groundwork for the very personal tale her essays will indirectly recount. Here is one reason the essays are so compelling: they encode the tales of her traumas, which is to say, encounters that felt to her like life-and-death experiences. In both essays, the traumas all involve her mother.[15]

"My Pushkin" is structured around tales of her mother's cruelty, expressed when her mother is frustrated with her poor answers to questions about her reading, or when she is irritated by her daughter's ignorance of names like Bonaparte. Tsvetaeva includes these remarks without comment, showing that her mother failed to provide simple, useful facts, that her mother ignored her developing poetic imagination, and that her mother never appreciated the charm—that fateful quality Tsvetaeva will attribute to Pugachev—in her daughter's witty and idiosyncratic notions about Pushkin. These ideas are entrusted to the essay's readers, who are meant to recognize their value and thus see the mother's indifference.

Parent-child relationships are important in both Pushkin essays, often figuratively rather than literally. In "My Pushkin," Tsvetaeva notes Pushkin's gentleness toward his nanny, which she compares with that of Proust toward his mother: both are seen as "monuments to filial emotion."[16] In "My Pushkin," the relationship of daughter to mother, and to substitute mothers, is explored in page after page of recollection and conversation. In "Pushkin and Pugachev," the desired parental figure is always the father, and mothers are made out as unsavory and false alternatives to the genuine pleasures of a father's love. The adult writer, who prefers masculine energy to what she will deride as feminine gentility, has tried to push the mother's image, cruelty and all, firmly to the sidelines in "Pushkin and Pugachev."

"Pushkin and Pugachev" and "My Pushkin" are, I suggest, the same kind of parallel texts that Tsvetaeva finds in *The Captain's Daughter* and *The History of Pugachev*. She writes that *The History of Pugachev* is inferior to *The Captain's Daughter*; indeed the latter is a riposte to the former. "Pushkin and Pugachev" similarly corrects "My Pushkin," completed only a few months earlier; with its inclusion of dialogue and details from childhood, it seems the more accurate account of Tsvetaeva's first encounters with Pushkin's works. And it tries to get past a sense of anger at her mother. She asks in "Pushkin and Pugachev" whether one can forget cruelty. Pushkin, she shows us, essentially did so when he wrote *The Captain's Daughter*. Admiring his historical novella, she tries to emulate his result. Viktoria Schweitzer has perceptively noted that the restrained style of *The Captain's Daughter*, which Tsvetaeva also praised, characterizes "Pushkin and Pugachev." She finds it Tsvetaeva's best work in prose, an artistic breakthrough for a writer not much known for her calm style of writing.[17] To my mind, the aesthetic breakthrough is matched by one in psychology. She no longer paints her family as an obstacle to her encounter with Pushkin; indeed we almost sense that her intense relationship with the poet is helped by her mother's lessons.[18] The acts of risk and idiosyncrasy remain—she renames *The Captain's Daughter*, calling it *The Guide*, and says that some of its characters do not exist for her at all—but they are now drawn into the vortex of her own relationship to the texts. The result is a concentrated reading of the material, a bold account of her attitudes to Pushkin and to herself as a writer. But on its own, "Pushkin and Pugachev" would be a less startling text; with its more chaotic mix of memories and emotions, "My Pushkin" gives us the material with which we can read all that has been restrained in "Pushkin and Pugachev."

In "My Pushkin," Tsvetaeva develops the theme of love as love for Pushkin, showing how he, rather than her family, taught her to express and to know love. Tsvetaeva writes, "Pushkin infected me with love. *With the word*—love."[19] She moves speedily to an emphatic statement about the word for love perhaps out of nervousness in the presence of this strong emotion.[20] The terror of love is specifically a terror of loss. Strikingly, all the examples of love in "My Pushkin," otherwise so dissimilar, confront an experience of loss: an orange cat that disappears; a drummer who goes off to war never to return; a pink Parisian doll that is hidden away forever in a trunk. Now Tsvetaeva can say straight out that Pushkin teaches her something about "love's knowledge."[21] His lessons are retrospectively felt by the adult Tsvetaeva to teach a difficult but necessary truth, that love equals loss. In Freudian terms, this insight is itself formative of identity, to the extent that selfhood is based on fear. Adam Phillips calls it an "originary and constitutive fear—of loss of love," a fear that in Freud is linked "with dependence, and the related question of agency."[22]

How Tsvetaeva handles the question of agency is itself an intriguing and large subject, exemplified in her inquiry into whether expressions of love are a matter of choice. She quite precisely shows her emerging sense of self as a sequence of apparent choices, all of them idiosyncratic, when she is asked by her mother which doll or which poem she likes. There is an equivalence being established here between self and object, where Tsvetaeva the child is judged on the basis of whether she has made a good choice or a bad choice. (The same verb, *nravit'sia*, is used for Tsvetaeva's "wrong" but preferred readings of poems.) The crucial example of a definitive choice is when she is asked to select a favorite Pushkin text. Her preference causes her mother great shame before the school director, yet the child insistently repeats that what she likes most is "Onegin and Tatiana." There is something striking in the urgent repetition of a phrase that must sound like nonsense: it is not the title of a work, not a recognizable scene in *Onegin*; it is a *relationship* ("I didn't fall in love with Onegin, but with Onegin and Tatiana—well, perhaps a bit more with Tatiana—and with them together, with their love").[23] Tsvetaeva is both the child who keeps saying something over and over in the hope of being understood and the poet whose repetitions are the magic words that will be extolled in "Pushkin and Pugachev," the words that one loves before one knows what they mean.

A passionate affection for an incomprehensible object also defines the love relationships in "Pushkin and Pugachev." Tsvetaeva compares love in this essay to a secret fire ("tainyi zhar"), a phrase from the poetry of Alexander Blok, and she finds this fire in Emelian Pugachev as he appears in *The Captain's Daughter* (but emphatically not as he appears in *The History of Pugachev*). Following Pushkin, she calls Pugachev "the guide" (*vozhatyi*), the central syllable of which (*zha*) echoes for her the Russian word for fire or heat (*zhar*), which she hears as a "rhyme."[24] But her chief metaphor in evoking this intense feeling of love is that of charms, *chary*; the sound again echoes *zhar*. In the apt description of Irma Kudrova, "chary" embrace "the spell of an elemental force [*stikhiia*] that knows no fear, the spell of a hero at the edge of an abyss and consigned to death, and the spell of a mutiny," but most centrally Tsvetaeva means the magical power that elicits love for an evil being, in this case the dangerous Pugachev.[25] Tsvetaeva describes *chary* as a spell that "forces you to love someone who has hacked a much-loved young woman to death before your eyes."[26] "Pushkin was spellbound by Pugachev," she writes, using a variant of the noun *chary* to name his feelings ("zacharovan"); "Pushkin fell under Pugachev's spell in *The Captain's Daughter* and did not emerge from it until the last lines of writing."[27]

How odd it must have seemed to her, then, that her mother or teachers imagined she was making a conscious choice in love—choosing a doll, choosing a passage from Pushkin. Such love is not willed, but involuntary, and it is very much the emotion of a child. Pushkin in her rendering is also made childlike by his feeling for Pugachev, and in "My Pushkin" she shows us a further consequence for anyone feeling such intense emotions: this love feels like a loss of self, and it hides a fear that love will vanish and thus itself occasion the feeling of loss. Tsvetaeva has to prefer the scene where there is no love, where Tatiana and Onegin are not together, and this scene in turn determines her own future. She is fated to model her erotic behavior on Tatiana's initiative and her solitude, a fate that comes to her in childhood. She notes that "fear and pity (also anger, longing, and defense) were the main passions of my childhood."[28]

Such a clearheaded diagnosis of sentiment shows Tsvetaeva recognizing that this pain is not entirely negative; it was better to act out of an excess of emotion than to live at the mercy of cold logic, and she projects this standard onto Pushkin without the slightest ambivalence. The self born out of these feelings is that of a poet. She seals the connection to Pushkin when she describes her birth as a poet in "My Pushkin," but the birth is also associated with the impending death of her mother. I turn to a scene that juxtaposes extreme limitation with infinite space and imagination—the sight of the sea.

Tsvetaeva is now ten years old. A journey to the sea is announced, a response to her mother's worsening tuberculosis. Her half-brother, Andriusha, fantasizes that their mother is dying.[29] Tsvetaeva reports these family legends, but insists that, for her, the trip to the sea is more like a journey to a poem by Pushkin, for she has just copied out "To the Sea" into her notebook. This sea means a fullness of emotion and sense of self: "The sea was here, and I would see it tomorrow. *Here* and *tomorrow*. I had never before experienced such fullness of possession and such calm in possession. This sea was made to my measure."[30] It seems unlikely that the sea, once it is before her, can produce the promised "fullness of possession," especially given her general anxiety about water (in 1911, "I am looking at the sea ... and none of it belongs to me, nor I to it"; in 1935, "I don't much like the water. I swim badly and quickly get cold").[31] Tsvetaeva expresses her disappointment in an allegory about the act of writing:

The sea is blue—and salty.
   And suddenly, turning my back to it, I write on the cliff with a broken-off piece of the cliff:
Farewell, free element!
   The poem is long, and I started as high up as my arm could reach, but the poem, I know from experience, is so long that there is no cliff that's big enough, and another one just as smooth is not to be found nearby, and so I keep making my letters smaller and smaller, I crowd and crowd the lines, the last ones are completely minuscule, and I know that any minute now a wave will come and not let me write to the end, and I won't get what I desire—desire?—oh, to *the sea*!—but does that mean I have no desire? well, in any case, even *without* any desire, I have to write to the

end, *before* the wave, write *all of it before* the wave, and the wave is already coming, and just then I manage to sign:
   Alexander Sergeevich Pushkin
—and everything is washed away, as if licked away by a tongue, and everything is wet again, and the slate is clean, it's black again, like *that* granite.[32]

This sublime act of inscription draws its energy from the recollection of the Moscow Pushkin monument ("*that* granite") Tsvetaeva had prized as a child, but refashioned by the experiences of an adult. It uncannily resembles the situation in which Tsvetaeva as a poet found herself in 1937. The act of writing a line of verse in a space where the letters will not fit, the attempt to write faster in order to finish before a wave erases the letters, the rush of emotions causing her to wonder what desire moved her to write in the first place, the repeated determination to write even when she has forgotten her desires, the sight of it all being washed away—this tight sequence enacts precisely the pressures on the mature Tsvetaeva not to write and the possibility that her work would disappear before her eyes. These aspects of her life have been described well by Tsvetaeva's biographers, who detail her increasingly desperate efforts to place her writings, to remain connected to those whom she loved, and to survive amid poverty and political uncertainty. In this essay of 1937, she uses a description of herself as a ten-year-old to convey this emotional atmosphere, and to say how it has shaped her work as a writer.

The two Pushkin essays also show how Tsvetaeva's writing was marked by her gender. This is the last topic I want to address in the essays, and the most complicated. It returns us to experiences of loss and of self-loss, particularly to an adult's understanding of how men and women are imagined to feel loss differently. The topic of gender in Tsvetaeva was raised by scholars as early as the 1970s.[33] It received more sustained attention after 1985, when Simon Karlinsky, who pioneered the study of her work, published his revised biography.[34] Karlinsky's new approach did not treat questions of gender and identity directly, but it facilitated such work by its clear and unalarmed exposition of Tsvetaeva's bisexuality. Others have now written well on the question of how Tsvetaeva's sexual identity informed her poetic identity.[35] Perhaps because relative calm has settled around sexual matters, more anxiety is now concentrated on Tsvetaeva's seeming difficulty in associating feminine identity with writing and her apparent renunciation of maternal identity.[36] "Pushkin and Pugachev," in its sharp swerve away from the world of women toward a violently masculine character, is an excellent text for understanding why Tsvetaeva has been seen in that way. "Pushkin and Pugachev" lets her use wit and irony to air received opinions about the supposed impairments of women writers, and in its performance as strong writing, it offers a counterargument to such beliefs. Its strength, I believe, comes in part from the challenge Tsvetaeva faced in writing about Pushkin: his masculinity challenges her to fashion a poetic identity that will not seem weakly ladylike by comparison.

The essay has several passages in which women and men are compared bluntly. Here, for example, is how Tsvetaeva contrasts Pugachev with Catherine II (she is explaining the magic of Pugachev's charms, his *chary*):

> The contrast between Pugachev's blackness and her whiteness, between his liveliness and her self-importance, his cheerful kindness and her condescending kindness, his peasant ways [*muzhichestvo*] and her ladylike ways [*damstvo*]—all of this could only repel the heart of child from her.[37]

The contrast between black and white appears throughout Tsvetaeva's Pushkin writings, from the opening of "My Pushkin" to her first "Poem to Pushkin," which denounces translations of Pushkin's dark defiance into pallid monumentality. Often, she associates Pushkin with the color black because of his African heritage. In "Pushkin and Pugachev," however, she draws her black-and-white imagery from *The Captain's Daughter*, where Pugachev is first seen as a dark spot in the white snowstorm. She asserts her own connection with that blackness in a memorably telescoped line cited earlier but worth repeating, "My business is to look endlessly at the thing that looms black in the snowstorm."

By contrast, there is Catherine the Great's whiteness, her blankness, her representation as a nothing, an empty space, a sign of lack. In this she is like Masha Mironova, the captain's daughter: "Masha is the blank space of every first love, Catherine is the blank space of every author's non-love."[38] Tsvetaeva has inferred Pushkin's negative attitude toward Catherine the Great to legitimate her own, and a sustained reading of Pushkin's works could well support her view.[39] For example, he wrote in 1822 that "if to rule means to know the weakness of the human soul and how to use it, then on these grounds Catherine merits the amazement of posterity"; a diary entry of 1834 finds "the end of her reign" to be "revolting."[40] But Tsvetaeva's dislike of Catherine is less an explication of Pushkin than her own fantasy of dethroning the empress. She writes, in a complex but lucid chain of figures:

> Against the fiery background of Pugachev—the fires, lootings, snowstorms, nomad tents, feasts—this one, in her nightcap and quilted coat, on a little bench among all the little bridges and leaves,[41] she seemed to me a huge white fish, whitefish. Unsalted. (The basic trait of Catherine is her astonishing blandness. Not a single significant word, not a single word of her own remained after her—except for the successful inscription on Falconet's monument, that is, a signature. Only *phrases*. The Catherine II of the French letters and middling comedies, as a person, is a model of mediocrity.)[42]

Anyone who has doubted that Tsvetaeva has a sense of humor might note her terrific comparison of Catherine II to a huge white fish, and she means for us to enjoy her outrageous comparison. But her crucial point is that what made Catherine mediocre was her linguistic inadequacy.

Throughout the Pushkin essays, Tsvetaeva has shown her love for linguistic magic, for example, in her use of a word like *guide* (*vozhatyi*), a charmed word whose magic inheres in its sound, like *chary*. Such words, Tsvetaeva says, instantly evoke emotion; they are "words that, before they are *spoken*, already signify, words that have significance and sense unto themselves."[43] By comparison, the words associated with Catherine are empty of meaning. Tsvetaeva finds her astonishingly bland because she left behind no words of her own, save her signature on Falconet's monument of Peter the Great (the Bronze Horseman), which was executed during her reign. Even her name seems unable to carry the meaning of her person or identity; in fact we could say that the relation of "Catherine" to Russia's most famous woman ruler reverses the way that *vozhatyi* names Pugachev. Born Sophie Friederike Auguste von Anhalt-Zerbst, Catherine was renamed (in Russian, Ekaterina) when she married. What results is neither the surname of the father, which would have given her a gendered mark of origin, nor a married name marking her as her husband's property, nor even an echo of her original given name, which would have differentiated her among her siblings. The signature on the monument, normally a metaphor of unproblematic paternity,[44] comes to reveal how this ruler lacks authority, whereas *vozhatyi*, for Tsvetaeva, concentrates in its sounds and its magic Pugachev's immense power. The title Catherine II signifies the mighty force of the state; given the preference that Pushkin and Tsvetaeva shared for pretenders over legitimate rulers, her power must be false.[45]

Following Pushkin's lead in *The Captain's Daughter*, Tsvetaeva exposes Catherine II as more illegitimate than the pretender who challenges her. She literally lowers Catherine's historical and personal status when she claims that her single surviving utterance is a signature, for Tsvetaeva first says that Catherine is known by an inscription ("nadpis'") and only then corrects herself to call this a signature ("podpis'"). The move from *nadpis'* to *podpis'* converts a "writing over" to a "writing below," if we focus on the meanings of the prefixes in these otherwise similar words, thus reducing an elevation to a fall. It is a fall expressed with such verbal flair that it recuperates for Tsvetaeva all the verbal authority that Catherine lacks. Tsvetaeva frequently displays verbal pyrotechnics in precisely those instances when she writes about women's silence (although elsewhere, too, of course), making sure that the weakness she describes cannot be hers.

"Pushkin and Pugachev" reinstates an anxiety about women's creativity that had seemed resolved in earlier writings (particularly her 1929 essay, "Natalia Goncharova"). We can read that shift in several ways: the circumstances of Tsvetaeva's life made her more sanguine about the position of women in Western European cultures, and questions that seem resolved in one era of her life are renewed with great intensity at another point. If we turn back to the very beginning of her career, we will find Tsvetaeva asking some of these same questions, but with the uncertainty of a very young writer. Where the late essays ground the multiple and conflicting identities of their author in a sure sense of poetic success and verbal invention, the early poems will leave the conflicts essentially unsettled. Long before the late, great essays, in a poem written when she was twenty years old, Tsvetaeva imagined Pushkin's presence in the Crimean landscape, and she considered what it would be like to meet up with him directly. Which selves would she bring to the encounter? And which new selves would their meeting enable? It is to that poem that I now turn.

A First Encounter

"An Encounter with Pushkin" ("Vstrecha s Pushkinym," 1913) returns us to a moment when Tsvetaeva began to create a poetic identity. In general in 1913, she was leaving the traditional forms and effusive style of her early work for deeper tonalities of passion and irony, and for new rhythms and formal arrangements. "An Encounter with Pushkin" has few of those fresh qualities, but it is a mistake to dismiss the poem as immature.[46] The poet retreats to safer formal and intonational choices because something in the early turn to Pushkin urges her forward and backward at once. This mix of regression with progress is made vertical in the poem's presentation of ascent, then descent.

> An Encounter with Pushkin
>
> I ascend along the white road,
> Dusty, resounding, steep.
> Light-footed, I do not tire
> As I rise high, over heights.
>
> On the left is the steep back of Ayu-Dag,
> A blue abyss is all around.
> I recall the curly-headed Magus
> Of these lyrical places.
>
> I see him on the road and in the grotto …
> A dark-skinned hand at his brow …
> —As if jangled by a glass cart
> At the road's turn … —
>
> A smell—from childhood—vaguely smoky
> Or tribal …
> The enchantment of the Crimea as it used to be
> In Pushkin's lovely times.

Pushkin!—You would have known at a first glance
Who stood in your path.
You would have smiled radiantly, not offering
Your arm to me as we walked.

Not leaning on the dark-skinned arm,
I would have said, as I walked,
How deeply I scorn science
And reject a leader,

How I love names and banners,
Hair and voices,
Old wines and old thrones,
—And every dog that I meet!—

Half-smiles in answer to questions,
And young kings . . .
How I love the cigarette's glow
In the velvet cup of the row of trees,

Actors and the sound of a tambourine,
Gold and silver,
The unrepeatable name: Marina,
Byron and bolero,

Amulets, cards, perfume bottles, and candles,
The smell of nomad camps and furs,
Lying words that go into the soul,
Spoken by enchanting lips.

These words: never and forever,
The rut behind the wheel ...
Dark-skinned arms and blue rivers,
—Ah,—your Mariula!—

The crash of a drum—the master's uniform—
The windows of palaces and carriages,
Groves in the radiant mouth of a fireplace,
The red stars of flares ...

My eternal heart and service
Only to him, the King!
My heart and my reflection
In a mirror ... —How I love ...

Enough ... —I would stop talking,
I would look down below ...
You would be silent, so sadly, so sweetly
Having embraced the thin cypress tree.

We would both be silent for a bit, right?—
Gazing down, where somewhere below

The first light shone
In some charming small hut.

And—since, from the worst sadness
To playfulness, it's only a step—no more—
We would break into laughter, and run
Hand in hand down the mountain.

October 1, 1913

Встреча с Пушкиным
Я подымаюсь по белой дороге,
Пыльной, звенящей, крутой.
Не устают мои легкие ноги
Выситься над высотой.

Слева—крутая спина Аю-Дага,
Синяя бездна—окрест.
Я вспоминаю курчавого мага
Этих лирических мест.

Вижу его на дороге и в гроте...
Смуглую руку у лба...
—Точно стеклянная на повороте
Продребезжала арба...—

Запах—из детства—какого-то дыма
Или каких-то племен...
Очарование прежнего Крыма
Пушкинских милых времен.

Пушкин!—Ты знал бы по первому взору,
Кто у тебя на пути.
И просиял бы, и под руку в гору
Не предложил мне идти.

Не опираясь о смуглую руку,
Я говорила б, идя,
Как глубоко презираю науку
И отвергаю вождя,

Как я люблю имена и знамена,
Волосы и голоса,
Старые вина и старые троны,
—Каждого встречного пса!—

Полуулыбки в ответ на вопросы,
И молодых королей...
Как я люблю огонек папиросы
В бархатной чаще аллей,

Комедиантов и звон тамбурина,
Золото и серебро,
Неповторимое имя: Марина,
Байрона и болеро,

Ладанки, карты, флаконы и свечи,
Запах кочевий и шуб,
Лживые, в душу идущие, речи
Очаровательных губ.

Эти слова: никогда и навеки,
За колесом — колею...
Смуглые руки и синие реки,
— Ах, — Мариулу твою! —

Треск барабана — мундир властелина —
Окна дворцов и карет,
Рощи в сияющей пасти камина,
Красные звезды ракет...

Вечное сердце свое и служенье
Только ему, Королю!
Сердце свое и свое отраженье
В зеркале... — Как я люблю...

Кончено... — Я бы уж не говорила,
Я посмотрела бы вниз...
Вы бы молчали, так грустно, так мило
Тонкий обняв кипарис.

Мы помолчали бы оба — не так ли? —
Глядя, как где-то у ног,
В милой какой-нибудь маленькой сакле
Первый блеснул огонек.

И — потому что от худшей печали
Шаг — и не больше — к игре! —
Мы рассмеялись бы и побежали
За руку вниз по горе.[47]

1 октября 1913

Tsvetaeva sets her imagined encounter with Pushkin near Gurzuf in Crimea, at the foot of the hill Ayu-Dag. The place is sacred yet imbued with pagan magic, and its commanding beauty in the present has rich associations with the past. It conjures up her past, the smells and experiences of childhood, and also the culture's past, both an ancient time of tribes and charms and the time of Pushkin. The description is visual, aural, tactile, and the atmosphere is enchanting, almost tender.

In the second movement of the poem, stanzas 5–16, the poet grows expansive in her list of impressions that she would share with Pushkin, concentrating on what she would say to him were they to meet. The first four stanzas use simple present-tense declarations, but then the poem shifts to conditional verbs, creating an unreal world of enthusiastic speech acts and shared preferences. The poet speaks on and on about what she loves and then stops short, as if remembering the presence of her listener, Pushkin. He seems gentle and attentive in response to her flood of speech. Together their gaze is drawn back to the landscape around them, from which they peer down. This readies their descent from the mountaintop, and in another quick change of mood they playfully run down.

There is no small measure of wish fulfillment in this poem. That mood is sustained partly by Tsvetaeva's use of pairings (up/down, light/dark, speech/silence, what is loved/what is despised), where principally the first term is explored. The poem lets Tsvetaeva enter a magical world where sadness is vanquished and play prevails. Most important, talk about one's inspirations and desires is not regarded as ridiculous or wrong. Her chatter sounds out the topics of Tsvetaeva's poetry, so Pushkin's sympathetic attention fulfills her deepest wish—to be taken seriously as a poet. Tsvetaeva describes herself on an ascending path toward aesthetic achievement. She emphasizes this upward movement in the poem's first stanza, using three words with that connotation; two of them, "vysit'sia" and "vysota," in the stanza's last line (the prosody adds a feeling of harmony as the stress moves from the first syllable of the first word to the last syllable of the last word, "výsit'sia nad vysotói").

The sense of balance is maintained in the poem against considerable odds. A Bloomian poetics of conflict and exaggerated self-assertion would lead us to expect Tsvetaeva to encounter Pushkin defensively, and her work will soon feature self-defense masked as verbal aggressiveness. The emphasis on height and strong contrasts also suggests the sublime, which marks a struggle with a precursor for Bloom.[48] (Height, associated with inspiration since the ancient Greeks, marks aesthetic aims in Tsvetaeva's poetry, which often has many traits of the Romantic sublime.) But this poem submerges agonistic conflict in a fantasy world of joyful play and unimpeded self-expression.

The magical force that lets joy suffuse "An Encounter with Pushkin" is Pushkin himself, whom the poem calls a "Magus." Tsvetaeva's early poetry often pursues a logic of enchantment, and she wrote several encounters (*vstrechi*) with magicians, sorcerers, and the like.[49] Her words for these figures include all the available terms in Russian;[50] one of them, "charodei," the nickname for her onetime suitor, Ellis (L. L. Kobeliansky), soon took on negative associations, particularly in its suggestions of charm that proves deceptive. Ellis drew Tsvetaeva and her sister into a magic circle of poets, but he made the mistake of proposing marriage, and Tsvetaeva renamed him a "former" magician ("byvshii charodei") as a result, although she would rehabilitate a related noun, *chary*, in her essay "Pushkin and Pugachev."[51]

Tsvetaeva's name for Pushkin is not "charodei," but "mag," Magus. Unlike Ellis, he enchants her respectfully. She emphasizes this point by noting that he does not at first offer his arm. She is relieved, we surmise, not to suffer the condescension and subtle sexual subordination the gesture would imply. Pushkin's charms hide none of the deception practiced by Ellis. The term *mag* suggests wizardry of perhaps greater intensity than "charodei," and also sheer power (etymologically it is linked in Russian to the verb *to be able, moch'*).[52] Pushkin as Magus is able to ascend a summit of aesthetic power, and Tsvetaeva seeks to follow his path.

Pushkin's magic is the secret of poetry; another definition of *mag* emphasizes the wizard's access to secret knowledge. To see how he shares that secret with Tsvetaeva, we need one further term for enchantment, *volshebstvo* (the one who performs this kind of magic is a *volshebnik*). More neutral than *charodei* or related terms, *volshebstvo* is a quality Tsvetaeva seeks in poetry from her earliest years, as in her 1910 essay "Enchantment in Briusov's Poetry" ("Volshebstvo v stikhakh Briusova").[53] Tsvetaeva finds enchantment a rare but memorable quality in Valery Briusov's poems. Nearly all her examples are about the maturing of young women, and we surmise that Tsvetaeva identifies with them as they stand on the brink of sexual knowledge.[54] Some of these young women are muses who inspire the erotic poetry of a man like Briusov; for Tsvetaeva they also raise questions about the poet's identity, particularly whether the woman poet must embrace sexual adventure in order to speak wisely of emotional experience.

Perhaps it is no coincidence that Briusov, so emblematic of the mastery of Russian Symbolism for Tsvetaeva, would preside over the 1919 Evening of Poetesses that confirmed her status as a poet and that so angered her by its trivialization of women. Catherine Ciepiela argues that Tsvetaeva's reaction against the Symbolists' (especially Briusov's) creation of "girl-muses" was formative in her poetic identity; it showed her that "the woman poet cannot be a beloved woman."[55] In "An Encounter with Pushkin," when Pushkin does not offer his arm to Tsvetaeva and does not sexualize her, he does not press her to act as his muse. She is free to act as a poet, we might say, and the interesting question in the poem becomes what kind of poet she will make herself out to be—not, it seems, one entirely innocent of sexual knowledge. But there are multiple identities in "An Encounter with Pushkin," and to see them, we need a short detour through the poem's subtexts.

In a poem addressed to Pushkin, we first expect quotations from his work.[56] Alexandra Smith has adduced several subtexts for "An Encounter with Pushkin," including some stylistic and structural aspects of *Eugene*

Onegin and "To Ovid" ("K Ovidiiu," 1821), where the shade of Ovid stands as Pushkin's predecessor as a southern exile.⁵⁷ Pushkin competes with Ovid in that poem, but I do not believe that competition marks Tsvetaeva's references to Pushkin. Particularly in this poem, he is her ally; indeed references to Mariula (from his long poem *The Gypsies*, 1824), or to the cypress tree mentioned by Pushkin in a letter of that year, feel more like friendly echoes than acts of appropriation. But the subtext is a true indicator of tone. There is competition and conflict in this poem, just not with Pushkin. The conflict pits Tsvetaeva against Briusov, who, during the first decade of the twentieth century, was busy establishing himself as an authority on Pushkin. He was poised to collect many of his occasional pieces into the volume *My Pushkin* in 1911, but instead continued writing, and the volume was assembled only after his death.⁵⁸ It is likely that Tsvetaeva read his essays in these years, and that Briusov's essay on Pushkin in Crimea (1908) influenced her choice of this location for her poem.⁵⁹ Her later essay "My Pushkin" would reuse the title of his 1929 collection and take it in an entirely new direction. Envy was an important theme in Briusov's Pushkin writings, as Tsvetaeva devastatingly observes in her 1912 poem to him ("V. Ia. Briusovu"). In "An Encounter with Pushkin," she demonstrates a way that Briusov might appropriately envy her, less by competing with him as an interpreter of Pushkin than by suggesting that Pushkin was her truer teacher, the better "master."⁶⁰ She leaves Briusov behind as an unworthy adversary.

She is not, however, entirely alone on the mountaintop in her communion with Pushkin. She has a more serious rival to vanquish—Anna Akhmatova. Tsvetaeva must have known Akhmatova's poetry in 1913, when she wrote "An Encounter with Pushkin," for she surely saw Akhmatova's 1912 volume of poetry *Evening* (*Vecher*) when it appeared: Mikhail Kuzmin's foreword to *Evening* mentions her, and Tsvetaeva followed reviews of her work keenly.⁶¹ "An Encounter with Pushkin" initiates a lifelong competition with Akhmatova for possession of Pushkin. Akhmatova later said to Lydia Chukovskaya that Tsvetaeva "shouldn't be allowed near Pushkin," so willfully did she misinterpret him.⁶² In "An Encounter with Pushkin," Tsvetaeva tries to show herself more fully in command of Pushkin's imaginative attention, and a powerful poet to boot.

The relevant subtext in *Evening* is "In Tsarskoe Selo," Akhmatova's three-part poem about Pushkin.⁶³ Tsvetaeva establishes a strong contrast in her choice of location for an encounter with Pushkin: rather than the regal Tsarskoe Selo, Tsvetaeva selects Crimea, associated with Pushkin's southern exile. The location lets her "highlight the Romantic landmarks in Pushkin's biography,"⁶⁴ and she pointedly humanizes Pushkin, quite unlike Akhmatova's chosen emblems of a worn book of poetry and old-fashioned tricorn hat. Tsvetaeva invites us to see Pushkin himself, fleetingly, his dark-skinned hand at his brow. Like Akhmatova, she devotes far more attention to the surrounding landscape than to a description of Pushkin, but her concentration on herself is fiercer. Whereas "In Tsarskoe Selo" conjures up entire cultural myths of Pushkin in its reference to all that "we" have felt for him, Tsvetaeva's encounter with Pushkin seems more personal, a tale of two poets recognizing each other as if in private.

Tsvetaeva rewrites another aspect of Akhmatova's poem in her long list of things that she loves. Akhmatova had written in "In Tsarskoe Selo," "I dislike only the hour before sunset, / Wind from the sea, and the word 'leave'"; Tsvetaeva's contrary extensive listing includes lines that remind us of Akhmatova's dislike for a word, for she loves "Lying words that go into the soul, / Spoken by enchanting lips. // These words: never and forever." There is something victorious in Tsvetaeva's self-presentation as able to revel in the deceptions of a lover, to glory equally in vows to stay or to go. She astonishingly reverses the common self-description in early Akhmatova—a woman sadly left by a man. Such sadness permeates the first two poems of "In Tsarskoe Selo," and one can imagine Tsvetaeva exulting in her happier encounter with Pushkin and in her pleasure as a young woman controlling her conquests, rather than the other way around.

The mature Tsvetaeva will project this image often, famously in "An Attempt at Jealousy" ("Popytka revnosti," 1924). It may seem surprising to find this power implied in such an early poem, one that has some sense of relief at *not* being treated sexually by Pushkin. But there are many signs of sexual maturity and knowledge in "An Encounter with Pushkin": the trappings of the theater ("actors and the sound of a tambourine"), jewelry ("gold and silver"), scent ("amulets, . . . perfume bottles, and candles"), and costume ("bolero,"[65] "furs," "uniform"), all with erotic potential; the awareness that words seduce and that there is pleasure in the seduction, even when it is dishonest ("Lying words that go into the soul, / Spoken by enchanting lips"); the pleasurably sighing "Ah" when mentioning Pushkin's Mariula (the mother of Zemfira, fiery heroine of *The Gypsies*, and the first singer of the daring song that leads to her daughter's violent death);[66] and the several references to fire, flames, flares that suggest smoldering passion. These are all things that the poet "loves," along with other items that suggest military and regal might, for example, or movement, or strong emotion. All create an undercurrent of erotic power in the poem that counters its narrative emphasis on childhood's innocent play.

Tsvetaeva implicitly acknowledges, then, what was to be the insidious premise of Briusov's attitude toward her, that she was a woman poet, and that she would never be able to write about poetry itself without reacting to the pervasive eroticization of the woman poet. She successfully excludes Briusov from the narrative logic of "An Encounter with Pushkin," but he can never be banished from its aesthetic logic. There is no failure here, though: she would have taken immense satisfaction from her brilliant substitution of Akhmatova for Briusov in the poem's subtexts. These metapoetic pleasures simmer beneath the surface of the poem, but visible to all readers is a different sort of self-consciousness, the poet's awareness of how she is creating her own self-image.

As the list of objects ends in "An Encounter with Pushkin," the poet's gaze rests on her own reflection in a mirror. The other objects and activities seem absorbed into this last image, as if they have all been mirrors for the self. But rather than cohering a sense of self, the mirror offers up a reflection that cannot be described, and it ruptures the pleasures of the list. The mirror introduces subjectivity as a broken entity, and the mirror itself breaks a trend of thought (as in Lacan's mirror stage).[67] The poem's many dashes are visual and syntactic signs of this sense of rupture; in fact, they are the one formal feature of the poem that is more typical of the mature poetry. Tsvetaeva has succeeded here in re-creating the world of childhood, only to expose it to a dawning awareness of psychological self-division. Pushkin acts as her mirror, we might say, offering back to the poet a more than acceptable self-image. "The ego is outside itself," as one critic of Lacan has put it,[68] and for Tsvetaeva, the discovery of this law is made bearable because it is Pushkin in whom she seeks her reflection. In her next Pushkin poems, self-divisions persist, but the recuperating pleasure of running down the mountain with Pushkin will not be so easily available, nor the recognition of herself as poet. One reason for the change is that gender differences become more daunting as childhood is left further behind.

Facing Beauty: Tsvetaeva's Poems
to Natalia Nikolaevna

Tsvetaeva's next Pushkin poem laconically describes Natalia Nikolaevna Pushkina. It opens with a choice between opposing emotions—happiness or sadness. In "An Encounter with Pushkin," Tsvetaeva had implicitly contrasted her happiness to Akhmatova's malaise, and "Happiness or sadness" (Shchast'e ili grust'") also reflects on the substitution of one emotion for the other and on the unpredictability of love. It dates to 1916 and was untitled.

> Happiness or sadness—
> To know nothing by heart,
> To go out riding in a luxuriant beaver cloak,
> To tug at Pushkin's heart,
> And to be known through the ages
> As long-browed,

Severe toward no one—
Goncharova.

A dream or mortal sin—
To be like silk, like down, like fur,
And, deaf to the sound of a poetic line taking its shape,
To flourish without a wrinkle on the brow.
If one is sad—to bite at the lip
And then, in the grave,
To remember—Lanskoi.

November 11, 1916

Счастие или грусть—
Ничего не знать наизусть,
В пышной тальме катать бобровой,
Сердце Пушкина теребить в руках,
И прослыть в веках—
Длиннобровой,
Ни к кому не суровой—
Гончаровой.

Сон или смертный грех—
Быть как шелк, как пух, как мех,
И, не слыша стиха литого,
Процветать себе без морщин на лбу.
Если грустно—кусать губу
И потом, в гробу,
Вспоминать—Ланского.[69]

11 ноября 1916

Tsvetaeva's poetics have changed in the three years since 1913, and this poem reflects her new sense of compression. It emphasizes rhyme over regular rhythm as an organizing principle and attempts the arch intonation at which she was to excel.[70] Some readers see Natalia Nikolaevna as a heartless and self-absorbed woman in this poem.[71] But the poem's intonational uncertainty and not quite balanced harmonies suggest a more ambivalent attitude, as do Tsvetaeva's subsequent writings about Natalia Nikolaevna. The poet wonders here whether it is luck or misfortune (if we can recast the first line of the poem that way) to be so unfeeling. And *unfeeling* is the key term here, for Natalia Nikolaevna has a face unwrinkled by emotion and a heart unaffected by even that which most deeply sears Tsvetaeva's heart, poetry. Imperviousness to poetic language recurs, near the start of each stanza, and it is the most damning detail; Tsvetaeva repeats it in her 1929 essay.[72]

Is Natalia Nikolaevna, Tsvetaeva wonders, made of a material on which a mark could be left? One notes that the metaphors of the poem all refer to soft substances. Fur, silk, and down (in comparisons that occur in about the same position in each stanza) are associated with the richness and beauty of Natalia Nikolaevna, as is the "luxuriant beaver" of her cloak, but we should also discern in these textiles a resistance to being inscribed in any way. A line of verse, by contrast, is described in terms of its potential for definitive shape: it is poured into its shape, attributing to poetry both the fluidity of a molten substance and the solid shape of a line seen on the page. But Tsvetaeva associates Natalia Nikolaevna with substances neither poured to form nor able to be etched; indeed she says directly that Natalia Nikolaevna bears an unmarked brow (again with parallel references to the brow in the two stanzas). Image, metaphor, word, even acoustical echoes all press us to compare the two stanzas closely; we most note the change to "Lanskoi" (the name of her second husband) from "Goncharova" (her maiden name, given in the instrumental, so that the ending looks like that of "Lanskoi"). Amid such symmetries, Tsvetaeva inserts dramatic signs of incongruity, particularly by shortening the second stanza by one line, which intensifies the surprise of an abrupt end on the name Lanskoi.

Tsvetaeva tries out several names for Natalia Nikolaevna here.[73] In an earlier version, the poem bore the title "Natasha," an astonishingly familiar gesture (does it appropriate the intimate diminutives of Pushkin's letters to his wife, one wonders, or incorporate a note of disdain?). Pushkin's name occurs only in reference to him, although the poem until its final two lines describes Natalia Nikolaevna during the period when her last name was Pushkina. Perhaps to Tsvetaeva, though, she was always Goncharova. As her 1929 essay will make clear, Tsvetaeva associated one trait with the name Goncharova—beauty. And beauty, although not explicitly the descriptive center of this poem, is exuded from its images, from the costly and lovely fabrics, the forehead that never shows the wrinkles of age, and the striking verb "to flourish" (*protsvetat'*). But is the poem meant to convey that Natalia Nikolaevna was, in fact, beautiful? Only one epithet directly describes her: "long-browed" (*dlinnobrovaia*), which draws extra attention to itself as a neologism and as the only word in the poem, besides "Goncharova," to entirely occupy a poetic line. (I have had to render the one-word instrumental form as two words in the English.) To describe a woman as having long eyebrows is not, when one thinks about it, to make her beautiful.

Alexandra Smith has suggested that the image of Natalia Nikolaevna is distorted by some features of Sofia Parnok, Tsvetaeva's lover during the previous year.[74] In "The Girlfriend" ("Podruga," 1916), Tsvetaeva gives Parnok heavy eyebrows that recall those of Beethoven. Smith's observation is ingenious, and it feels true to Tsvetaeva's habits as a poet. Parnok broke off the relationship with Tsvetaeva, which left her in a position like that of

Pushkin, here cast as a victim. Perhaps in any case we would sense Tsvetaeva's identification with Pushkin as poet, but "Happiness or sadness" is also fascinated with Natalia Nikolaevna. In her, I believe, Tsvetaeva wants to understand the mind and heart of a woman who seemed so completely in control of her affections.[75]

Such emotional control is not unrelated to a familiar concern about how women poets fit into a tradition where men speak of their love and women listen as the silent beloved. Resolving this issue can be formative, as feminist analyses of Romantic poetry have shown quite powerfully: the woman poet must overcome the culture's identification of her with the silent object of the male poet's address, and she must speak as poet, not as muse.[76] Tsvetaeva had faced this challenge in "An Encounter with Pushkin," as we have seen, but there, as in many of the earlier poems, she is partly immunized against its deepest threats because the poem's persona is a child. "Happiness or sadness" offers no such protections; in fact there is probably a further complication in Tsvetaeva's bisexuality.[77] The gendered definitions of lover and beloved were less fixed, but the question of what it would feel like to be both beloved and lover at once, or whether one can speak in the tones of vulnerability and power, remains. Tsvetaeva tests that possibility in many poems, not least in the very productive year of 1916 when "Happiness or sadness" was written. To cite one dramatic pair of examples, she describes herself as a female bird of prey (*khishchnitsa*) in March 1916 and as the victim of such predators a month later.[78]

For Tsvetaeva, then, Natalia Nikolaevna is at her most fascinating as a woman in control of her emotions—her brow is unwrinkled by cares, her sadness is contained by the merest effort of biting her lip. Earlier in 1916, in "The Fourth Year" ("Chetvertyi god," dated March 24), she describes herself biting her own lip to stave off repugnance at strong emotions.[79] "The Fourth Year" is addressed to Tsvetaeva's daughter Ariadna, and it is one of many poems in which she balances the dangers of erotic passion against seemingly endless reserves of maternal love. "Happiness or sadness" was written when Tsvetaeva was four months pregnant (her daughter Irina was born April 13, 1917), but one senses little expectation of happiness on the poet's part in this poem; perhaps Tsvetaeva felt emotions more grimly tinged with fear. In a poem written a few days later, "Along roads ringing with frost" ("Po dorogam, ot moroza zvonkim"), Tsvetaeva dreams with dread about her pregnancy: the poem ends with her in the grave, a stunning coincidence with the ending of "Happiness or sadness," where Natalia Nikolaevna is imagined in her grave, remembering her second husband, Pavel Lanskoi.[80] It seems likely to me that the vulnerability Tsvetaeva felt that November had something to do with her expected child. (One must be careful here not to read back into this time the traumas ahead, of revolution in

1917, poverty in 1918–19, and her daughter Irina's death in 1920. In fact Tsvetaeva looked back on 1916 as the last happy time in her life. My point is simply that this happiness was tinged with anxiety, that it was uncertain.) Natalia Nikolaevna's calm facade offers Tsvetaeva a very different way to be a woman. She may deride its superficiality and suspect its beautiful surface as hiding sinful depths, but, just as a measure of wish fulfillment informs her 1913 "Encounter with Pushkin," so in this poem Tsvetaeva lets herself, just for the moment, slip into the "dream" of being soft, lovely, and invulnerable. And she acknowledges the beauty of that invulnerability, its soft allure and tempting surface.

One last biographical detail supports a reading that emphasizes Tsvetaeva's connectedness to this very different heroine. In the fall of 1916, Tsvetaeva was translating the novel *La Nouvelle Espérance* by Anna de Noialle. This work, in which she was passionately involved, took her back to the time of her youth, a time of enthusiasm for Napoleon, Rostand, Sarah Bernhardt, and Marceline Desbordes-Valmore. Beyond its atmosphere, the novel has a pointed similarity to "Happiness or sadness": it opens with a conversation between two young women about whether one of them, the heroine Sabina, is happy or sad. It is entirely possible that the first line of "Happiness or sadness" owes something to this opening meditation on the heroine's state of mind. Sabina says she is happy, but the prose reveals her sadness.[81] She remains unhappy in her marriage to a perfectly kind husband, eventually falling in love with his cousin, who in turn proposes to another. Although the novel's larger narrative has little in common with Pushkin's marriage, the opening gambit, where happiness contrasts a possibly deeper sadness, is very suggestive. In the poem, Natalia Nikolaevna may be expected to be happy in her victorious conquest of Pushkin, but an underlying suggestion of unexpressed sadness persists, not entirely suppressed by a bitten lip. If I am correct in seeing some measure of self-portraiture in Tsvetaeva's description of Natalia Nikolaevna, then it should come as no surprise that this heroine would not, in the end, be able to vanquish every painful emotion.

"Happiness or sadness" might now strike us as a transition to the next, better-known poem about Natalia Nikolaevna, "Psyche" ("Psikheia," 1920). Tsvetaeva herself encouraged this reading when she published both poems, plus "An Encounter with Pushkin," as a single cycle in the Berlin newspaper *Days* (*Dni*, June 8, 1924). "Psyche" dates from a time when Tsvetaeva was living in desperate poverty in Moscow, yet the tone is light and ironic. The poem layers opposing emotions. We hear the rich sound orchestration for which Tsvetaeva's verse is famous. The name Psyche begins with the *p* sound (in Russian it is not a silent *p*) with which the poem creates much of its alliteration and paronomasia. Pushkin's name resounds at the end of the first line, the last of four nouns that, in Russian, start with the letter *p*. The entire poem is a tableau that plays with motifs from Pushkin's acts of self-fashioning, for example, the kiss of the Blackamoor, which draws on his *Blackamoor of Peter the Great* (*Arap Petra Velikogo*, 1827), and the scarecrow-like elderly woman waiting in a carriage in "The Queen of Spades."[82] There is more of a story here than in "Happiness or sadness": it takes place late at night, when Pushkin sees his wife off for a night of dancing.

> Psyche
>
> Punch and midnight. Punch—and Pushkin,
> Punch—and the puffing meerschaum
> Pipe. Punch—and the murmur
> Of ballroom slippers along creaking
> Floorboards. And,—like a specter—
> In the half circle of an arch—like a bird—
> Like a moth—Psyche!
> A whisper: "You're still not asleep?
> I—came in to say good-bye." The gaze is downcast.
> (Maybe she asks forgiveness
> For the impending naughtiness
> Of this night?) Every little finger
> Of her hands that touched your shoulder,
> Every pearl on the smooth little neck
> Has been kissed and kissed again a hundred times.
> And, on tiptoes—like a *peri*!—
> With a pirouette—like a specter—
> She fluttered out of the room.
>   Punch—and midnight.
> She flutters back in: "What a memory I have!
> I forgot my fan!
> I will be late … and I'm to lead off
> The polonaise … "
>   Having thrown a cape
> Over one shoulder—submissively—
> The poet—takes Psyche's arm,
> And accompanies her down the trembling steps.
> He himself tucked the blanket around her,
> Himself draws down the wolf-skin carriage rug.
> —"Godspeed!"
>   And Psyche,
> Leaning over to her female companion—a blind
> Scarecrow in a nightcap—trembles:
> Had the ardent kiss of the Blackamoor
> Burned through her glove …

Punch and midnight. Punch and ashes
Falling onto the straw-colored
Persian dressing gown. And the empty
Froth of a ball gown
In the dusty mirror ...

Психея

Пунш и полночь. Пунш—и Пушкин,
Пунш—и пенковая трубка
Пышущая. Пунш—и лепет
Бальных башмачков по хриплым
Половицам. И—как призрак—
В полукруге арки—птицей—
Бабочкой ночной—Психея!
Шепот: «Вы еще не спите?
Я—проститься...» Взор потуплен.
(Может быть, прощенья просит
За грядущие проказы
Этой ночи?) Каждый пальчик
Ручек, павших Вам на плечи,
Каждый перл на шейке плавной
По сто раз перецелован.
И на цыпочках—как пери!—
Пируэтом—привиденьем—
Выпорхнула.
    Пунш—и полночь.
Вновь впорхнула: «Что за память!
Позабыла опахало!
Опоздаю... В первой паре
Полонеза...»
    Плащ накинув
На одно плечо—покорно—
Под руку поэт—Психею
По трепещущим ступенькам
Провожает. Лапки в плед ей
Сам укутал, волчью полость
Сам запахивает...—«С Богом!»

    А Психея,
К спутнице припав—слепому
Пугалу в чепце—трепещет:
Не прожег ли ей перчатку
Пылкий поцелуй арапа...

Пунш и полночь. Пунш и пепла
Ниспаденье на персидский
Палевый халат—и платья

>   Бального пустая пена
>   В пыльном зеркале...[83]

The puffing rhythm of words reworking combinations with the consonant *p* makes this poem read as a cascade of sounds down the page. The illusion is literalized in the final image of ash falling down upon fabric, as if the weightless sound of words were no more able to mark the air (or page) than the dust that settles on the mirror. Elements of the first two Pushkin poems combine into an entirely new arrangement here: rather than the encounter of young girl with young poet in a symbolic ascent up a mountain followed by a playful descent, and rather than the description of a woman's face as an index of her character, there are suggestions of up-and-down movement, particularly in the sound of steps on the stairs, and attempts to penetrate into the character of both the fluttering Psyche, who introduces so much of the poem's movement, and the deliberate, contemplative poet left behind. The fabrics used as metaphors in "Happiness or sadness" are important here as part of a larger panoply of textures that include a lap rug and a dressing gown, as well as dust, smoke, and ash. That broader range lets the fabrics suggest luxurious and extravagant articles of clothing that show off for an unseen public, as well as comforting rugs and robes meant to protect.

Against what does one need protection in this poem? For most readers, Pushkin looks vulnerable, a Cupid whose Psyche will betray him. (Psyche was a nickname of Natalia Nikolaevna in the 1830s, when it was meant as an allusion to her legendary beauty.)[84] Peter Scotto has suggested that Tsvetaeva "exploits the ironic distance which separates the mythic prototype from the woman who was given her name." For him, Natalia Nikolaevna is "only frightened and alienated by the passion of her Cupid"; she is a "soulless doll who mistakes glamour for beauty and romantic intrigue for love."[85] Yet it is Psyche who seems burned by Cupid, not the other way around. We know that the myth of Cupid and Psyche fascinated Tsvetaeva. Alyssa Dinega has argued that it became the crucial mythological archetype in her idea of artistic genius.[86] Dinega emphasizes transgressive aspects of the myth: "Like Psyche, Tsvetaeva breaks out of an erotic marriage to a potent male divinity who has caused her—by her own acquiescence, if not free will—to sever her ties with her family . . . and indeed with mundane reality itself. Just as Psyche transgresses against Eros's command that she not attempt to look upon him, so too Tsvetaeva breaks her vow of faithfulness to her austere 'genius,' continuing to love and desire the impossible contact with real men (such as Pasternak) that her imaginary muse cannot offer." But Dinega also believes that the myth becomes "the truth of Tsvetaeva's being," infiltrating her "entire sense of her own identity and destiny."[87]

From this argument, which imagines for Tsvetaeva a tormented search for poetic identity that is set fiercely against the pleasures of sexuality, beauty, and *byt* (mundane, daily reality), we would not expect Tsvetaeva to be attracted to aspects of the myth that link it to the beautiful and vitally sexual Natalia Nikolaevna. Dinega sidesteps this difficulty in her brief but insightful discussion of the poem "Psyche," where she sees Natalia Nikolaevna as Pushkin's dangerous muse, effecting his "transition into death" in the poem's final image of garment and ash.[88] But as with "Happiness or sadness," we should recognize that Tsvetaeva also identifies with Natalia Nikolaevna: the burning kiss of passion threatens the poet herself, I want to suggest, even as she identifies with the male poet left behind in the poem's final lines.

The signs of identification are hidden in the poem's images, principally the textures of ash, smoke, and dust, which are distinctive to this poem among the three in the Pushkin cycle. Written in early March 1920, "Psyche" repeats images found in "Attic Writings" ("Cherdachnoe"), a prose description of Tsvetaeva's desperately impoverished life in 1919–20. The texts share references to dust, ash, dresses, and dolls.[89] How extraordinary that, at such a moment, she would conjure up a world of richness and beauty, of social engagements and polite ritual, and not just an escapist fantasy. When Tsvetaeva transforms the poverty and shame that inform "Attic Writings" into Natalia Nikolaevna's airy departure for an evening of dancing, her poem retains an anxious guilt that was deeply her own, showing how complex and productive was her turn to the Psyche myth and to myths of Natalia Nikolaevna.

Guilt and anxiety touch Natalia Nikolaevna in this poem. In ll. 9–10, the shift from *farewell* to *forgiveness*, from *prostit'sia* to *proshchen'e*, presents guilt as a rhetorical question, posed parenthetically as an aside. Tsvetaeva has every reason to try to conceal this suggestion of guilt, especially in its revealing phrasing: it would almost have been a cliché to link the two words, often paired as the verbs *prostit'sia* and *proshchat'sia* on the pages of Russian realist and melodramatic fiction, but in this poem the words have a precise and more painful explanation. I hear an echo here of Tsvetaeva's regret at not having bid farewell to her little girl Irina, as well as her wish to ask forgiveness for her daughter's death, which occurred in February 1920, only a few weeks before this poem was written.[90] In caring for her older daughter, Ariadna, Tsvetaeva had let weeks go by without visiting the children's home where Irina languished; she heard of Irina's death almost by accident and belatedly. The emphasis on Pushkin *himself* having tucked in the departing Natalia Nikolaevna resonates terribly with the farewell that Tsvetaeva missed.

Interpreters of this event have condemned Tsvetaeva, beginning with her husband Sergei Efron's sisters and continuing through a generation of modern scholars, some of whom have argued that she felt no remorse or grief.[91]

Yet the poem about Irina's death makes the sense of guilt entirely clear.[92] So does a letter that begins with an admission of guilt. Its language also points to connections between the imagery of "Psyche" and this event: "Other women forget about their children for balls or love or fancy clothes or the celebration of life. My celebration in life is verse, but I did not forget Irina for verse—in two months I have written nothing!"[93]

The loss of Irina, traumatic for Tsvetaeva in so many ways, also, I believe, deepened her view of Natalia Nikolaevna: it was Tsvetaeva's first experience of not loving enough, an insufficiency that (she felt) brought down a terrible punishment. Mostly we think of Tsvetaeva as loving too much, and she thinks of herself that way, too. The opposite experience must have been psychically almost incomprehensible to her. Although some of her later comments about Irina's death are self-deceiving, the deep pain of Tsvetaeva's first reaction shows a true insight, one that explains the greater sympathy for Natalia Nikolaevna in "Psyche."

This psychological and creative background also helps explain the formal features of "Psyche." Tsvetaeva's poems tended to be experimental in this period. Written in regular lines of trochaic tetrameter (with one line that is broken in half, and a foot missing in the final line), "Psyche" lacks any division into quatrains, presenting a freer flowing narrative. The looseness is in keeping with Tsvetaeva's work in 1920, the strict meter less so. I believe that the return to strict meter is partly an effect of Tsvetaeva's willing herself back to work (we know that she wrote little the previous winter), as if the regular beat of the trochees sounded an irresistible call. The name Pushkin is itself trochaic and was likely the first impulse to the poem and its meter. The trochees' initial stress, like that of the dactyls of "An Encounter with Pushkin," is typical of Tsvetaeva's emphatic lines where first syllables are resonantly heard, and she emphasized these similarities when she published her three Pushkin poems together. In placing "Psyche" third in the cycle, Tsvetaeva closes a metrical circle, and a thematic one as well: the young poet's out-of-doors encounter with a carefree, kind Pushkin in Crimea in the 1913 poem could not contrast more sharply with his preoccupied but caring farewell to an agitated young wife. Set between these two longer poems, "Happiness or sadness" provides the crucial connection in its focus on Natalia Nikolaevna herself—which, for Tsvetaeva, means her face, her memory, her emotions, and her power. What also links the three poems is the image of a mirror. In "An Encounter with Pushkin," the mirror cuts short the poem's list of loved objects. In "Psyche," the mirror is not an interruption but an ending. Its reflection is now shown, but the image produced is entirely unclear: the foamy substance of the ball gown seems already blurry, made more so by the coat of dust on the mirror. Tsvetaeva's encounters with Pushkin, as with Natalia Nikolaevna, come down in the end to a mirror, but still the mirror's power to reflect back to the poet a sense of self is extremely limited. In her next Pushkin writings, she makes the mirror's task more specific but also more difficult, asking it to show an image that is at once woman and poet. The multiple identities offered up must include at a minimum these two, without which the others cannot cohere.

Art and Vision in "Natalia Goncharova"

The essay "Natalia Goncharova" (1929) might never have come into being were it not for the play on names that gives the essay its title. Tsvetaeva principally writes about the Russian émigré artist Natalia Sergeevna Goncharova, whom she met in the late 1920s in Paris and came to admire. The major themes of her essay—artistic expression and vision, the working life of an artist—as well as the coincidence in names motivate digressions about the "other" Natalia Goncharova (whom I will continue to call Natalia Nikolaevna to avoid confusion) and about Pushkin. Scholars have noted that the essay explores how an artist's life is written, and they have acknowledged some measure of self-reference.[94] I want to emphasize a continuity of theme between the essay and the three poems about Natalia Nikolaevna and Pushkin, and not just in passages where Tsvetaeva expresses these themes directly. To that end, I will be discussing many passages that seem merely scenic or transitional, for these apparent digressions allow Tsvetaeva to create telling connections to her earlier works.

The essay begins with a description of the narrow street on which the painter Goncharova lived in Paris.[95] The long search for the street, described with numerous digressions on topics like Blok's house in Moscow, Russian *toska* ("longing" or "anguish"), and the wind, recalls "An Encounter with Pushkin." These pages conjure up the image of a child, one who seeks a house that turns up where one least expects it, and that appears to have magical properties. As Tsvetaeva ascends the staircase to the artist's studio, the steps feel marked by the footsteps of previous visitors, an impression that recalls "Psyche," where much is made of the sound of Natalia Nikolaevna's footsteps. When Tsvetaeva enters the studio, she reacts to its sense of light and space ecstatically. Her prose now sounds familiarly poetic in its density of sound and its short, clipped sentences, much like the opening of "Psyche." She writes: "A desert. A cave. What else? Of course, the deck of a boat!" ("Pustynia. Peshchera. Chto eshche? Da paluba!").[96] The Russian words, which include three nouns alliterative on the letter *p*, bring in the acoustic element that defined Pushkin's presence in "Psyche." In Goncharova's studio, Tsvetaeva has entered a space in which she can contemplate her evolving attitude toward Pushkin, and it is as if she hears the sound of his name long before it is uttered. The coincidence of naming, the fact of two Natalia Goncharovas, will legitimate his presence in the essay, but Tsvetaeva cannot wait for that moment, and she surreptitiously introduces him acoustically.

He will appear four more times before he is formally introduced. He next turns up when Tsvetaeva quotes two lines from "To the Sea." The choice of text recalls the image of the sea in "Encounter with Pushkin" and looks ahead to the powerful use of this poem in "My Pushkin." Here, it instantiates Tsvetaeva's belief in spirits, hinting at a theme the essay will explore, that the creative artist is a kind of god. The first step toward this assertion was taken in "An Encounter with Pushkin," where Pushkin was presented as a Magus, and the pagan element recurs in "Natalia Goncharova" when Tsvetaeva says that paintings in the artist's studio face the walls so their potential for magic power might be hidden.[97]

Tsvetaeva next mentions Pushkin when she discovers that she and Goncharova had lived near each other in Moscow. She is thrilled by the coincidence, which uncovers other similarities and near-meetings in their childhoods. Pushkin's name figures in this charmed reverie because the building where Goncharova had lived also housed a printer who produced Tsvetaeva's and Goncharova's first books, plus Vikenty Veresaev's book on Pushkin. Tsvetaeva calls attention to the Pushkin connection in a note: the printer produced the very edition of Veresaev's *Pushkin in Life* that she was using to write "Natalia Goncharova," she tells us. (In this she resembles her contemporaries, who also relied heavily on Veresaev's book.)

Next, in a passage meant to recreate Goncharova's childhood memories, Tsvetaeva reports that Pushkin helped plant trees on an estate where Goncharova had spent time as a child. The recollection is presented as a discrete, parenthetical paragraph:

(Golubovo, the estate of Baron B. A. Brevsky. "Pushkin took part in planting the orchards and setting up small buildings, according to family legend. His participation was ardent: he laid out the flowerbeds himself and planted many trees, which, as is well known, was one of his passions.")[98]

This passage describes an artist's hard work, and it presents a very human view of the artist, like the perspective offered on Goncharova herself. It also quotes her words, or seems to, something that occurs often in the essay. Such quotations let Tsvetaeva incorporate other voices into her essay. She wonderfully keeps the voices separate, although they often echo with her characteristic intonations. This technique contributes to her creation of a layered identity for herself in the essay.

Tsvetaeva's last reference to Pushkin also has a biographical context, but exudes little confidence about the poet's history. She claims that his childhood and adolescent years are completely incomprehensible to us. Tsvetaeva contrasts this ignorance to her insight into Goncharova's youth and childhood. She will repeat this idea of Pushkin's elusive essence, and she is also asking whether one can locate the source of the artist's identity in childhood.

All of these comments about Pushkin are preliminary and brief. Only in the section of "Natalia Goncharova" titled "Two Goncharovas," when he is formally introduced, does Tsvetaeva sustain her interest in him. Yet even here, she darts from one idea to another. She is interested in topics—his relationship to his wife and his identity as a poet—that cannot be separated. She begins to take up a theme that is important in her later Pushkin writings, Russia's myths of Pushkin, which for her mean its cultural fascination with him at the expense of seeing him as he truly was. But she is not ready for the more abstract pronouncements on this topic that will appear in the 1930s. The intensely personal project of comprehending Pushkin as husband, man, citizen, and poet occupies Tsvetaeva here, keeping her focused on contexts of domestic life, public service, and the private communion between artist and text.

Everything said here about Pushkin is mediated by the life stories of the two Natalia Goncharovas. The section "Two Goncharovas" is roughly one-sixth of the essay, a substantial portion of its length, and it comes at a pivotal moment, about twenty pages in and after Tsvetaeva has finished all the preliminaries of her encounter with Natalia Goncharova.[99] Much of the section is devoted to Pushkin's wife, with extensive quotation from memoirs about her. At first, these descriptions are evaluative: we watch Tsvetaeva criticize, forgive, and sympathize with Natalia Nikolaevna.[100] It is tempting to emphasize her criticism at the expense of her understanding, for Tsvetaeva's harsh words always carry an explosive charge. When she criticizes, her standard emerges from her own deeply symbolic value system, where the beauty of Natalia Nikolaevna, for example, is commensurate with her soullessness, and where the only status imaginable for those who make way for a poet's death is that of the mob (*chern'*). Natalia Nikolaevna, she says, never saw Pushkin on his own terms, only as he was seen at court or created by gossip, Pushkin under surveillance ("Pushkin podnadzornyi").[101] Worse, she saw him as Nicholas I did, through the eyes of fear, and it was fear that motivated her marriage to him, Tsvetaeva writes. Whereas Pushkin entered their marriage with his eyes wide open, so open as to seem lidless and lacerated, she moved blindly, as befits a girl and a beauty. Her blindness, however, protects Natalia Nikolaevna: Tsvetaeva concludes that "from the very beginning, all guilt is removed" from her.[102] Like Pushkin, Natalia Nikolaeva plays a role in a fated drama, and Tsvetaeva is intrigued by parts of her life where she could not exercise control. There is a moving comment about her nonparticipation in so many aspects of her life, including the naming of her children. Given the special quality of naming in Tsvetaeva's own family life and in her work, we suspect that she would have felt this deprivation very keenly.[103] It appears prominently in the essay, no doubt, because of the connection already established between Tsvetaeva's sense of herself as a mother and her incipient sympathy for Natalia Nikolaevna.

Yet when it comes to Natalia Nikolaevna's relationship with Pushkin, Tsvetaeva does not sympathize with her in the least, although she still describes her as helpless. "There was one thing in her: a beauty. Only a beauty, just a beauty, without the corrective of mind, soul, heart, talent. Unsheathed beauty that smites like a sword. And—she smote him."[104] The repetitions, the short sentences, and the intense buildup to a violent conclusion are trademarks of Tsvetaeva's writing style. The point of the violent comparison is not to transform Pushkin's wife into his killer, but to emphasize the immense force buried within her beauty, a force over which she has no control. Tsvetaeva creates an almost inhuman image of Natalia Nikolaevna's beauty commensurate to her idea of Pushkin as a genius ("Just a beauty. Just a genius").

She is reduced to a blank space. We recall that the phrase with which Tsvetaeva joins Catherine II to Masha Mironova in "Pushkin and Pugachev" is "blank space" ("pustoe mesto"), and it is a resonant phrase for its revelation of Tsvetaeva's larger perception that her culture associates women with absence or lack.[105] The same phrase appears here in a description of Natalia Nikolaevna:

Natalia Goncharova is *simply* the fateful woman, that blank space to which one is drawn, around which all forces and passions collide.[106]

And apart from Pushkin, d'Anthès, Lanskoi? In and of herself? She did not exist. Natalia Nikolaevna is totally contained in the day-to-day biography, in the facts (it's a different matter, what kind of facts), as was Helen of Troy in the battle of the Greeks and the Trojans. Helen of Troy, apart from the involuntarily caused events that she suffered simply does not exist. A blank space between the palms of hands enfolded in action. Move the hands apart, and you get air.[107]

This blank emptiness contrasts sharply with the fullness of Pushkin's presence. We get a long, dizzying list of descriptive terms for him that creates a personality as capacious as the language itself.

For everything is here: treachery in love, loyalty in friendship, filial affection to ineffectual and flat-footed parents (of the sort that should completely contradict the possibility of there being a Pushkin), and disloyalty to ideas and people (one minute writing an ode to the Decembrists, the next sending an epistle off to their killer), and the passionate love of a son for Russia—Russia not as mother but as stepmother!—and jealousy in marriage, unfaithfulness in marriage. Pushkin in friendship, Pushkin in marriage, Pushkin in rebellion, Pushkin at the throne, Pushkin in high society,

Pushkin with his nanny, Pushkin writing *The Gavriliad*, Pushkin in church, Pushkin in all of his innumerable faces and appearances—all of this is united and held together by one thing: the poet.[108]

Tsvetaeva goes beyond the cliché of a Protean Pushkin here, for she has her own ideas of what traits make up his many-sided personality, and she stresses the dramatic contrasts, like Pushkin writing the blasphemous *Gavriliad* and then attending church. Pushkin as rebel is a signature detail for Tsvetaeva. Rhetorically, she likes the sound of a list that repeats his name (the same syntax will appear in her "Poems to Pushkin"), as if each trait can hold its own against competing forces of rebellion or jealousy or loyalty, but the force of them all pushing every which way requires a unifying power of equal magnitude, that of the poet himself.

It is striking that a similar grammatical and psychological structure is used to describe Natalia Nikolaevna, despite the claim that she is a "blank space." Tsvetaeva writes:

What is Goncharova according to the testimony of her contemporaries? A beauty. "Nathalie est un ange" (Smirnova). "The stamp of melancholy, renunciation ..." (N.B.—renouncing what? the next ball or dress?). Silent. If words are mentioned, then they are empty. Shockingly wordless. They all note her smile, her walk, her eyes, her shoulders, even her ears—no one notes what she said. For she is nothing but her smiles, eyes, shoulders, ears. Thus she will remain: innocent, wordless—Helen—a doll, an instrument of fate.[109]

Rather than the personality traits and roles attributed to Pushkin, Tsvetaeva details Natalia Nikolaevna's appearance. The final sentence, with its comparison to Helen of Troy, unifies and defines the list: being a poet draws together the strands of Pushkin's being, but being an "instrument of fate" gives meaning to Natalia Nikolaevna's physical beauty. Tsvetaeva asks whether Pushkin and his wife are comprehensible in parallel ways: was her passion for the ball the same as his for poetry? For Tsvetaeva, nothing can really compare to poetry, so the comparison diminishes Natalia Nikolaevna.

One other difference merits note. The first description of Natalia Nikolaevna is given "according to the testimony of her contemporaries." The quotation in French from Smirnova (A. O. Smirnova, née Rosset, 1809–82, a friend of Pushkin's) especially marks this paragraph as containing the words of other people and puts those words under some suspicion. When Tsvetaeva quotes the comment about renunciation, she adds her own gloss meant to trivialize the potentially lofty attribute of self-sacrifice, and concludes with the damning epithet "wordless." I wish to stress, though, that it is the *culture's* description of Natalia Nikolaevna that Tsvetaeva quotes, and that her interpretation hinges repeatedly on interpolated descriptions, on the words of others. With Natalia Nikolaevna, she can never go beyond these accounts. Indeed that is the force of her claim that Natalia Nikolaevna was silent: there are no words of her own with which Tsvetaeva can support or counter the claims of contemporaries. In that imbalance, Tsvetaeva stumbles on a profound truth: because Natalia Nikolaevna's letters to Pushkin were lost, she is known almost entirely through texts about her.[110] Remarkably, throughout "Natalia Goncharova" Tsvetaeva uses others' words not just to describe Pushkin's wife but to create a variegated portrait of the artist Natalia Goncharova.

More than any essay by Tsvetaeva, "Natalia Goncharova" is filled with the words of others. In addition to the interpolated memoirs describing Pushkin and his wife, we read the quoted speech of the painter Natalia Goncharova (including a splendid section entitled "From Our Conversations," "Iz besed"); newspaper comments about the painter and Mikhail Larionov's abjurations to her; and other memoirs about her. Tsvetaeva seems aware that her essay will create yet another text about the painter, and she resists those who would use her words to characterize Goncharova in any simple manner. The broken, repetitive, and uneven movement of her essay seeks to convey the complexity of the artist and the elusiveness of the personality. Tsvetaeva has a broad range of material about Goncharova on which to draw, and she remarkably pulls in details of childhood, art school, emigration, work habits, published reviews, physical appearance, and, of course, aspects of the theme and technique of the art work itself. Tsvetaeva wrote in a letter to a friend that she and Goncharova were "mutually" painting each other.[111] The comment about mutuality hides a fantasy of sorts—that someone might create an account of Tsvetaeva's own "life and work," to quote the subtitle of the essay.

Were someone to write of her in this way, her fantasy is that they would bring to the subject a personality as powerful as she brings to Goncharova. As she writes in a long lovely passage on creativity, "It's always a dialogue, a duel, a skirmish, a struggle, an interaction."[112] If an artist's work is a gesture that answers something commensurate, then the same kind of responsiveness must greet the work itself. It merits an answer, without which the aesthetic act is incomplete, and the psychological experience of creation is potentially devastating. The worst nightmare for Tsvetaeva would be to be only what others made of her, which is the fate of Natalia Nikolaevna.[113] For Tsvetaeva, this amounts to having no biography at all. And that is another point of contrast between the two Natalia Goncharovas. She gives the artist Natalia Goncharova a "purely masculine biography":[114] "*Work*— that is the fate of Natalia Goncharova, a fate that Pushkin would not allow (whom? or what?) to replace, to displace the other Goncharova."[115] Tsvetaeva expands her capacity for multiple acts of identification in this passage: she resembles both Natalia Goncharova and Alexander Pushkin in their dedication to work itself; she experiences work as something she is fated to do; and, it has to be said, she is like, or wishes she could be like, "the other Goncharova," whom a man can never give up even for the sake of treasured work. Not for nothing did Tsvetaeva use that same word *charms* (*chary*) to describe the allure of Natalia Nikolaevna for Pushkin.[116] Against considerable odds, then, Natalia Nikolaevna at times charmed Tsvetaeva herself, not so much that she could not push her away as a "soulless beauty" who was deaf to the more important beauty of poetry, but enough that she would allow all too human aspects of Pushkin's wife to show through, indeed to reflect some of Tsvetaeva's own very human traits. By including Goncharova, Pushkin, and Pushkin's wife in this essay, Tsvetaeva creates one of her richest explorations of the identities she lived, as poet, wife, émigré, and critic. But in addition to showing us a great deal of herself, she also, wonderfully, takes us deeply into the lives of her subjects. The non-response she so feared for her own work is the opposite of what she offers to Natalia Goncharova, the painter, and also Natalia Nikolaevna, the wife of the poet, whose efforts to come into being ("vyiavlevnie") she traces. The painter, we might say, is at last that external ego or mirror in whom the poet can stabilize an image of herself, and in whose presence connections to both Pushkin and his wife can be explored richly and rewardingly.

Poems to Pushkin, Poet to Poet

Tsvetaeva's life in 1931, when she worked on the six-poem cycle "Poems to Pushkin," seems little changed from 1929, the year of "Natalia Goncharova." Still struggling to find her place in émigré literature and thus some support, however meager, for her family, Tsvetaeva lived at the edge of desperation.[117] She wrote less poetry, and to an ever more indifferent audience. No one understood *Poem of the Air* (*Poema Vozdukha*, another long poem written in 1927, published 1930), and no one would publish *Perekop* (1929). Estrangement and loneliness were certainly not manufactured, although some would say that Tsvetaeva exaggerated, even cultivated them. She had found brief solace in her intense connection with Goncharova in 1929, and she sought similar friendships in her remaining years in France.

More and more, the poetic record of such connections shows her communing with the dead. The first poem to move in this direction was "New Year's Greeting" ("Novogodnee," 1927), which mourned the death of Rilke. The readers who found it "incomprehensible" would not have found much to admire in "To Mayakovsky" ("Maiakovskomu," 1930), given his hostile reception by most émigrés.[118] Both poems prepared Tsvetaeva to write her Pushkin cycle.[119] Similarities in language, rhetoric, and tone are important, particularly the discursive self-examinations that show a poet ever dissatisfied with her own formulations. Joseph Brodsky, writing about "New Year's Greeting," aptly described this quality of Tsvetaeva's poetry: "the author subjects every word of hers, every thought of hers, to the sharpest rebuke: that is, she comments upon herself. More precisely, though: the ear comments upon the content."[120] In "Poems to Pushkin," Tsvetaeva writes as if in dialogue with herself, listening to her lines for words, sounds, and details that might be imprecise or insufficient, then propelling the poem forward by means of correction, addition, and minute alteration. This conversation with herself might also be understood as the logical extension of that wish for dialogue in "Natalia Goncharova." She is, the poem suggests, her own interlocutor of last resort.

The many selves of her poetry are well accommodated in "Poems to Pushkin," where she speaks as literary historian, cultural critic, and fellow poet. The mood is more highly charged than in her earlier Pushkin texts: the intonations are clamorous, the metaphors militaristic, and the fundamental relationship of the poem, of poet to tsar, is inherently more antagonistic and competitive than the domestic arrangements of the earlier texts. Let me give an overview of the six "Poems to Pushkin," with special attention reserved for a strange middle poem, "(The Lathe)" ("[Stanok]"), and for the final poem, on Pushkin's death.

In the first poem, "Scourge of the gendarmes" ("Bich zhandarmov"), Tsvetaeva lists Pushkin's many identities, which, unlike the positive attributes listed in "Natalia Goncharova," here become a précis for argument. Nine times the poem will mockingly describe "Pushkin, in the role of . . . ," always as a riposte to an exaggerated description of some official image of the poet. A tight sequence of densely allusive contrasts and neologisms results. The poem balances four-line stanzas with two-line questions or exclamations, the four lines in alternating rhyme, the two lines a couplet, creating a bold dynamic that feels unstoppable. The meter is trochaic tetrameter, with all four beats dramatically heard in many of the lines. It is seventy-three lines long, beginning in this way:

> Scourge of gendarmes, god of students,
> Bile of husbands, delight of wives,
> Pushkin—in the role of a monument?
> Of the stone guest?—He,
>
> Teeth-bared, rudely staring
> Pushkin—in the Commendatore's role?
>
> The critic, whining, the whiner repeating:
> "Where is Pushkin's (sob)
> Feeling of measure?" Did they forget the feeling—
> Of the sea—beating

Against granite? That salty
Pushkin—in the role of a dictionary?

Stretching out his two legs—to warm himself—
And jumping onto the table
Before the Autocrat,
The self-authorizing African—

The one who killed our ancestors with laughter—
Pushkin—in the role of a tutor?

Бич жандармов, бог студентов,
Желчь мужей, услада жен,
Пушкин—в роли монумента?
Гостя каменного?—он,

Скалозубый, нагловзорый
Пушкин—в роли Командора?

Критик—ноя, нытик—вторя:
«Где же пушкинское (взрыд)
Чувство меры?» Чувство—моря
Позабыли—о гранит

Бьющегося? Тот, солёный
Пушкин—в роли лексикона?

Две ноги свои—погреться—
Вытнявувший, и на стол
Вспрыгнувший при Самодержце
Африканский самовол—

Наших прадедов умора—
Пушкин—в роли гувернера?[121]

Tsvetaeva counters these offensive versions of Pushkin with evocations of his passions, dynamism, and creative energy. She seems to quote her antagonists at times (for example, "Where is Pushkin's (sob) / Feeling of measure?"), and her words also anticipate hostile reaction to her own poem. She imagines that, after reading the first six lines of her poem, readers will wonder what has happened to Pushkin's appreciation for harmony and balance in her stormy description of him, but she derides their piety by inserting a parenthetical sob of emotion and by calling the critic a "whiner."[122] Catherine Ciepiela has rightly described these critics, in Tsvetaeva's opinion, as "philistine admirers who insult him with their praise," and she pinpoints the devastating effects of Tsvetaeva's mockery when she notes that the poet does not just quote her opponents' words, but also "mimics the manner in which they are spoken."[123]

Tsvetaeva attacks misguided views of Pushkin for their violence in creating false images of him. Violence as such is not Tsvetaeva's objection; indeed the conflict-ridden imagery of her poem and her forceful language and rhythms appropriate this violence easily (a similar paradox is at work in "Pushkin and Pugachev"). Her very first characterization of Pushkin invokes violence—he is "scourge of gendarmes." The word for "scourge" is *bich*, a term for whip or lash that is related to the verb *bit'*, meaning "to beat." Words with this root recur in the poem, often in prominent positions, like the description of water beating against granite where a strong enjambment makes "beating" (*b'iushchegosia*) especially noticeable. Another example occurs in the third poem, "(The Lathe)": "—Do not beat us with Pushkin! / For I am beating you—with him!" ("—Pushkinym ne beite! / Ibo b'iu vas—im!").[124] Just before these lines, she uses the root meaning *to beat* in two other ways, one in a reference to broken glass ("bokal / Bityi"), the other in commenting on a battle ("bitva"). Tsvetaeva does something similar with other words and phonetic groupings in the poem, often in ways related to themes of violence, struggle, and unexpected action, but I stress this particular semantic cluster because it so defines her tone in the cycle, and because it marks such a change from her earlier writings about Pushkin.[125]

The metaphor of violence also permits Tsvetaeva to write about harm done to the body and thus about Pushkin's physical presence in the world, a topic sufficiently important that it occupies the fourth poem entirely. In this poem, "Overcoming" ("Preodolen'e"), Tsvetaeva turns his body inside out, opening its limbs to reveal the bone, blood, and tissue that keep the poet moving. She describes the muscles and veins of the body, concentrating on the connective tissues and means of blood circulation that enable movement; her choices also create a metonymy of connection, of ropelike materials inside the body that produce linkages of body to thing, of self to other. Tsvetaeva gives a body to all that surrounds this poet, later comparing his might to the strength of an oar as it cuts through muscular sea waves.

This imagery of the body informs the other five poems with an extraordinarily dynamic image of Pushkin, who seems always to be moving in energetic and surprising ways. We see him jumping onto a table, galloping like the Bronze Horseman, striding along as mightily as the gigantic Peter the Great, racing from the ballroom to the solitude of his writing table, escaping imprisonment as if along the rope of his own powerful veins, and lying stretched out with the powerful muscles of an athlete even when he has died. These images displace the figure of Pushkin as monument, even a monument that comes to life like his own Stone Guest, as Tsvetaeva announces in the opening of "Scourge of gendarmes." Pushkin is the "most living and most alive" ("Vsekh zhivuchei i zhivee!") man imaginable.[126] His body, however, is constantly invoked by synecdoche or the fleeting impressions of his active movements; we see the former in the jaw and gaze of the poet in line 5 of

"Scourge of gendarmes," for example, or the two legs of line 13. This is the same technique that creates a feeling of bodily presence in "Psyche," making us feel as if we see the poet and his departing wife, just as an avant-garde artist might suggest a face by drawing a nose or the outline of an ear. Pushkin himself was adept at giving the impression of a complete picture with only a few details, but Tsvetaeva does this in a more modernist way by her weird choices of physical detail and her extreme minimalism.[127] (I believe it is one reason she truly appreciated the work of Natalia Goncharova, despite others' claim that she was too near-sighted to find much of value in art.)

Tsvetaeva also uses this technique of synecdoche in "Scourge of gendarmes" when she refers to the police or the censorship to mean the larger power structures Pushkin encountered. That topic deeply interests her in "Poems to Pushkin," in contrast to her earlier Pushkin works, although her resistance to false, official views about art informs the essay "The Poet on the Critic" ("Poet o kritike," 1926). She sees these false views as more extensive in "Poems to Pushkin," attributing them to the contemporaries who wrote misleading memoirs about him, to the officials who put obstacles in his path, and to later critics. All are guilty of turning him into a pallid tutor, an apologist for extreme nationalism, a gravedigger, a mausoleum, and a lookalike for Tatiana, his heroine in *Eugene Onegin*. The range of this list, like the vast number of metaphors used throughout "Poems to Pushkin," creates a dazzling number of Pushkins—of *false* Pushkins, to be sure, but of competing versions of the poet that make his name heard twenty-one times in "Scourge of gendarmes." The repetition beats into the imagination of a listener the trochaic meter of the poem, repeating the metrical logic of "Psyche."

The theme of power is taken up in a more precise way in the cycle's two poems about Pushkin's relationship to the tsar: the second poem, "Peter and Pushkin," and the fifth, one of two poems bearing the parenthetical title "(Poet and Tsar)." The two poems are graphic opposites of one another, "Peter and Pushkin" a lengthy poem with long (amphibrachic trimeter) lines in heavy repetitive quatrains, "(Poet and Tsar)," lightning quick, again with quatrains but of dactylic dimeter with many truncated feet, and one significant lengthening—in the final stanza, where the tsar is named. These are variations on a theme that Tsvetaeva would explore in her later essays on Pushkin. There, too, she juxtaposes historical facts about Pushkin's difficulties with Nicholas against fantasized alternative relationships. In the "Poems to Pushkin," the alternative is an imagined relationship between Pushkin and Peter the Great. Tsvetaeva builds this fantasy on Pushkin's own fascination with Peter and on her sense that they were equivalent in their importance to Russia. Each founded an aspect of Russia's modernity, and, she intuits, had they been tsar and subject, their relationship would have been based on mutual respect, rather than on the antagonism and suspicion of Nicholas I's view of Pushkin.

Tsvetaeva's rising interest in Pushkin's relationship with various rulers shows a shift away from her view that his family life was the most important context for his creative acts. This might seem an effect of Pushkin's own example: from at least 1825, when he was writing *Boris Godunov*, he produced a number of important texts in which he sought to increase his authority as a poet by writing to and about Russian rulers. Tsvetaeva generally preferred rebels and pretenders as topics for historical writing, and the figures who loomed largest in her imagination were other poets. But in the last decade of her emigration, she was working on a long poem about the Romanov family, and she completed *Perekop* (1929), which recounts a White Army defeat at Perekop and propelled Tsvetaeva toward her poem about the murder of the imperial family.[128] These poems focus on defeat and tragedy; Nicholas II is not the poet's powerful alter ego but a victim of violent death. "Poems to Pushkin," however, explores a stronger sense of the tsar as an agent of violence and as a source of life: it refers to Peter's having murdered his son—for his "masculine timidity" ("robost' muzhskaia"), in Tsvetaeva's phrase—and it establishes Peter as a progenitor for Pushkin, the "genuine great-grandson" who can stand alongside him as an equal.[129] Just as Pushkin makes a better son to Peter, so Peter makes a more appropriate tsar for Pushkin; unlike Nicholas, he would have let Pushkin travel, made it easier for him to write, and, most intangibly, respected in Pushkin precisely the free spirit that Nicholas punished. These images all come from the second poem in the cycle, but in the fifth poem, where Peter is not present as the preferable alternative tsar, Nicholas I is a murderer. He is the savage butcher of Poland ("Pol'skogo kraia—/ Zverskii miasnik") and the killer of Pushkin himself: Tsvetaeva calls him an assassin of the singer (*pevtsoubiitsa*), basing her neologism on the word for a killer of the tsar (*tsareubiitsa*).[130] Her neologism suggests that killing a poet has the symbolic social and cultural resonance of regicide.

The result of this image of tsar as killer (and poet as victim) comes in the sixth and last of the "Poems to Pushkin," which begins "No, the drum was beating" ("Net, bil baraban"; in some versions this is part two of poem number five). It re-uses the word for beating or striking (*bit'*), so important throughout the "Poems to Pushkin," also at the root of the word for killer of the poet (*pevtsoubiitsa*). Maintaining the sarcasm of its predecessors, this poem interrogates the connection between seemingly incommensurate metaphors for the poet: how can one be understood as the recipient of all the actions connoted by the verb *bit'* (beating, striking, and, as *ubit'*, killing) at the same time that one is comparable to a tsar? One answer, for Tsvetaeva, is to make the poet the agent of the verb *bit'*, to have him strike the tempo of his own poetry (or, as in the fourth poem, to have his powerful muscles beat with a life force). Although appealing, this possibility is inadequate, as the metaphor of the beating drum (at the poet's burial) in this poem suggests. The drum, meant to do honor to the dead poet, turns into a ghastly tapping of the tsar's teeth ("To zuby tsarevy nad mertvym pevtsom / Pochetnuiu drob' vyvodili").[131] Tsvetaeva suggests that the ruler was horrified at the public tribute paid the poet; hence the infamous decisions that substituted police guards for most of the friends who wished to accompany his body to Sviatogorsk Monastery (this is one biographical detail that links the scene of burial—in which no dead person is named—to Pushkin).

As in all the poems of this cycle, the rhythmic line is strikingly heard (alternating tetrameter and trimeter in amphibrachs), and a single word, *pochetnyi*, is repeated a number of times, reiterating the rhythmic foot and repeating the poem's theme, honor. In the penultimate stanza, that word, *honor*, is heard as an adverb (*pochetno*) five times, and echoed by a sixth word (a verb, *pechetsia*, that mockingly describes the Tsar's "worrying over" the poet). In the stanza before that, both adverb and noun are heard, preceded by the *cho* sound remade into the word *something* (*chto-to*), a word that dilutes any possible honor with its semantic vagueness: "The something, something, something that this honor resembles / Honorably—all too honorably!" ("Na chto-to, na chto-to, na chto-to pokhozh / Pochet sei, pochetno—da slishkom!").[132] Tsvetaeva searches here for something to compare the "honor" to, but she finds nothing because it is no honor at all. The poetry stutters over impossible substitutions, again in a phrase ("na chto-to") that echoes the amphibrachic rhythmic unit of the poem. We fear that the poet has reached the limits of language's ability to find equivalences, but in the phonic wizardry of this poem, Tsvetaeva succeeds in demonstrating that it was the political and social world that failed Pushkin, not language. We recall the repeated "Pushkin" of the first poem, said there to echo like the mindless call of a parrot, so that the false honors of the last poem bring us back full circle to the ludicrous opinions of the critics in "Scourge of gendarmes" (the police are here, too, as inappropriate witnesses to the poet's burial). Tsvetaeva repeats one further technique from "Scourge of gendarmes," where she had mockingly quoted the critics' views of Pushkin, when she ends with the italicized line "*The smartest man in Russia*" ("*Umneishego muzha Rossii*"), a well-known description of the poet uttered by the Tsar after their meeting in 1826.

A tsar who takes a true estimation of a great poet's mind will at the least respect him as an equal, creating the "conspiracy of equals" described in "Peter and Pushkin." Such a tsar can be a muse to the poet, and Peter inspired Pushkin in ways that Tsvetaeva discerned well. The living Tsar who spoke the words "The smartest man in Russia," though, inflects them with contempt: he gives the dead poet the funeral of a criminal or a traitor, Tsvetaeva writes. Tsars differ, however, and Tsvetaeva emphasizes the difference when she concludes the fifth poem in "Poems to Pushkin" with "Tsar Nicholas / The First" ("Tsar' Nikolai / Pervyi"). The epithet "the First" adds a fifth line to the last quatrain, and it makes an incomplete metrical unit (the poem is in dactylic dimeter, often with truncations in the second foot; *pervyi* would be a truncated foot in the initial position). These irregularities draw attention to the epithet and hint at another tsar who shadows this reference, not "the First" Nicholas, but the Second.

Tsar Nicholas II (and his family) were denied even the empty honors done to Pushkin in 1837, since they received no religious ceremony of interment after they were murdered. Tsvetaeva stresses Pushkin's inappropriate funeral rites in the sixth of the "Poems to Pushkin" with this similarity in mind, I believe, for she was also working on her long poem about the family of Nicholas II in the early 1930s. The consistent metaphorical and thematic mix in the "Poems to Pushkin" puts tsars next to poets, and politics next to inspiration. Tsvetaeva directs the poem toward a scene of burial, where mourning is overshadowed by more pressing questions: who controls the rites of passage? do rites honor or insult the dead? and is the deceased characterized by his intelligence and creativity or by his "criminal" acts?[133] Tsvetaeva's sense of a connection between the two burials also explains her idiosyncratic representation of Pushkin's death: whereas other poets have used Pushkin's death as a setting for expressing grief, venting rage against his killer, and allegorically writing of their own mortality or their uncertain positions as poets, Tsvetaeva grieves over something more universal. Her "Poems to Pushkin" are not without rage or allegory, but her real target is a culture that has permitted the false farewells to a dead poet (and a dead tsar) and in the process made him seem a degraded, traitorous victim.

The reason the poet has a power comparable to a tsar's is given in the third poem in the cycle, "(The Lathe)," to which I now turn. The title is odd, with its metaphor of a machine used to shape wood—a metaphor little related to other tropes in the cycle—and its parentheses, as if the title were a tentative alternative (but to what? no other title is offered).[134] These idiosyncrasies are not unique. Tsvetaeva uses parenthetical titles elsewhere, and in this poem she even says that she knows what it means to open a parenthesis. We know the metaphor of the lathe from her discussions of creative labor in "Natalia Goncharova," and Peter the Great was also known to enjoy using just such a machine tool. Here, she imagines the scene where creative work takes place, along with other sites—the natural world, the ballroom, the salon—that attract, distract, and inspire the poet:

(The Lathe)
All of his learning—
Is might. In the light—I see this:
I shake Pushkin's hand,
I do not lick it.

To his great-grandfather—a chum:
In this same workshop!
Every stroke of writing—
Made as if with his hand.

Put a free man—beneath this pile?
No, put me there. In this cauldron of miracles—
I know the heft
Of an open parenthesis,

I can imagine the slips of the pen—
The meaning—in a word, all of it.
For there is no probe
More searching than that of kinship!

This is how they sang—one sings
This way even now.
We know, how it "comes easily"!
How it hovers just above, "a trifle,"

We know—how one sweats
Because of you, a stroke of the brush,
I know—what it means to long
For forest—for the ball—for a ride in the sleigh …

And how one wants to sleep!
Over the little flower of love—
I know, how the Negro's teeth
Clamp down hard!

Quills sharpened—
I know, how he repaired them!
Fingers never had the chance to dry
From stains of his ink!

And yet—among the wax
Candles, the battles over cards—
I know—how it happened!
Away from mirrors, bare

Shoulders, wine glasses
Broken on the floor—
I know, what it means to run
To the bare desk!

To battle where there is no wrongdoing:
Self—with self!
—Do not use Pushkin to give a beating!
For I beat you—with him!

(Станок)
Вся его наука—
Мощь. Светло—гляжу:
Пушкинскую руку
Жму, а не лижу.

Прадеду—товарка:
В той же мастерской!
Каждая помарка—
Как своей рукой.

Вольному—под стопки?
Мне, в котле чудес
Сём—открытой скобки
Ведающей—вес,

Мнящейся описки—
Смысл, короче—всё.
Ибо нету сыска
Пуще, чем родство!

Пелось как—поется
И поныне—та́к.
Знаем, как «дается»!
Над тобой, «пустяк»,

Знаем—как потелось!
От тебя, мазок,
Знаю—как хотелось
В лес—на бал—в возок...

И как—спать хотелось!
Над цветком любви—
Знаю, как скрипелось
Негрскими зубьми!

Перья на востро́ты—
Знаю, как чинил!
Пальцы не просохли
От его чернил!

А зато—меж талых
Свеч, картежных сеч—
Знаю—как стрясалось!
От зеркал, от плеч

Голых, от бокалов
Битых на полу—
Знаю, как бежалось
К голому столу!

В битву без злодейства:
Самого́—с самим!
—Пушкиным не бейте!
Ибо бью вас—им!¹³⁵

Intonationally, "(The Lathe)" is built around exclamations and parallelisms, like "Scourge of gendarmes." But the polemic with contemporaries is heard here only in the last lines. Tsvetaeva instead returns to a plot from her earliest Pushkin poem, the wish to set the terms of their relationship and to write of him as an equal.¹³⁶ Her words bespeak knowledge and familiarity: five times she repeats "I know" (six times in my translation), and twice, "we know." The object of knowledge is poetic creativity: "in this cauldron of miracles— / I know the heft / Of an open parenthesis." Her connection to Pushkin, however, is also a relationship of kin (*rodstvo*). She knows his experiences cognitively and also in her bones. The poem offers several bodily metaphors to suggest the sweat of a poet's hard work: the exhausted longing for sleep, the gnashing of teeth, the feel of wet ink on fingers.

A scene for Pushkin's creativity is well imagined in the second stanza, where the hereditary work space recalls descriptions from "Natalia Goncharova," both of Goncharova's own studio and of the study in which Pushkin worked in Polotniany Zavod, but Tsvetaeva balks at placing Pushkin in such confinement. Instead, *she* belongs in the cauldron of creativity. Yet the cauldron remains his world of work and life: later stanzas, with their images of ballroom, sleigh, gambling, and bared shoulders, recreate the Pushkin period, not Tsvetaeva's life in European exile. Tsvetaeva collapses temporalities in the poem, as when she has Pushkin and his great-grandfather seem to work together in a room both had visited decades apart. She, too, works alongside them. Her lathe creates the artifact of this poem, which takes some of its slender visual appearance from what a sculptor or woodworker might make with a turning wheel. Tsvetaeva creates the lovely look of this poem in part with the magic of meter: she chooses a trochaic trimeter rhythm, used in a traditional way with four-line stanzas and feminine-masculine, feminine-masculine rhymes. This meter is typically pegged to journeys, nature scenes, or domestic details, and her poem might suggest that last topic.¹³⁷ Such poems can also be about work, often peasant work, and it is to this theme that Tsvetaeva would also seem to adhere, but the product of labor in this poem is more narrowly the poem itself, and perhaps to some extent the poetic persona as well. The poem sculpts a self, we might say, particularly in its concluding lines that record a struggle of self with self as the center of the creative process. In such a battle, there can be only one winner, and Tsvetaeva concludes the poem with an insistence that it is she who will use Pushkin as a weapon, both in the struggle she has represented as creative work and in the struggle for suitable recognition of him in the culture more generally.

In her next poem to Pushkin, which begins "Overcoming / Russian torpor" ("Preodolen'e / Kosnosti russkoi"), the same struggle occurs, but now all lines lead to escape. More than any other poem in the cycle, Tsvetaeva confronts here the presence of the body, both alive and dead. Here are stanzas seven and eight of the twelve-stanza poem.

> The heavier the load—
> The more beautifully he bears it—
> The muscle of a gymnast
> And prisoner,
>
> Who on the rope
> Of his own veins
> Made it out of the casemate—
> Like a falcon!
>
> Больше балласту—
> Краше осанка!
> Мускул гимнаста
> И арестанта,
>
> Что на канате
> Собственных жил
> Из каземата—
> Соколом взмыл![138]

When Tsvetaeva compares Pushkin to a prisoner, she invokes themes of limitation and tragedy, both of which will dominate the last two poems in this cycle. This poem also includes an image of the poet's corpse, which, hefted, seems more appropriate for an athlete than a poet. But the final comparison will be to a seraphim, and the final musculature is that of the wings, lending a more hopeful and transcendent conclusion to the fourth poem. Russian torpor, so to speak, has been overcome, and when the poet says that this body is not burdened by the illnesses of Russian blood (in stanza five), she reveals that the success has come because it is Russia that the poet, in this fantasy, escapes.

Is Pushkin's dead body, then, that of mortal, human remains (does it have flesh and blood?), or is his the body of an angel? Tsvetaeva in some sense never resolves that question, but we can conclude this discussion of her myths of Pushkin with a fantasy that brings her before the body of the poet. In this story, he is dying but not yet dead, and in speaking with him at this highly symbolic moment, Tsvetaeva says and thinks all the things that fill her poems and essays about Pushkin. The story appeared to her in a dream, published in 1997 in Elena Korkina's edition of Tsvetaeva's notebooks.

Tsvetaeva's Dream

When she was writing her "Poems to Pushkin" in July 1931, Marina Tsvetaeva had a dream about him. She recorded it, with interpolated commentary and explanation, some of it later, and gave it the title "A Dream About Pushkin."

Before the dream about Pushkin, a long conversation with Nicholas I, very much mine, very much his. I remember only one of his sentences:
"You can't be both Russia's premier poet and the husband of the most beautiful woman in the land!"
"But she didn't love him!"
(My response utterly lacked logic, but its intonation and conviction, it's *but* are entirely mine.) (Now, in 1938, I would explain it this way: you are talking about two problems, but Goncharova's beauty is no problem for him since she did not love him.)
And I remember one more thing: "You send him no blessing?"
"No."(Clearly I was trying to persuade him to go to Pushkin and bid him farewell.)
Then:
A hospital. A French attendant tells me that no one is with him now and I can go in. A corridor. Wards. Which one? The attendant points to the third open door on the left. I ask her, "But how will I recognize him?" I can't see anything. I go in. There are no windows, the only light comes through the doorway. It's dim. Visitors are along the walls. I see Volodya Sosinsky (already!) drawing a picture. Directly across from the entrance in the middle of the room stands a bed. Pushkin lies on it. On the left is another bed, empty. Someone, seeing me, says, "And this is M. Ts., our best poet." I get down on my knees in the space between the beds, and he offers—I take it—his hand. "Well, *Masetochka,* did you come to see how one dies? Farewell, Masetochka?" "Farewell, my countryman!" (The country of poetry, of course, but right away I remember that he's from Petersburg, not Moscow.) The resemblance is *very* strong, it's *him* as he really was. A small face and body. Huge rolling whites of his eyes, blue-*green* in color from his fever. *His* forehead, hair, side whiskers. *His* mouth. I don't know which portrait this comes from, it's *not* an image from one portrait but a pastiche of them all.
The voice—I can't put it any other way—elegant, playful, light, with a *barely* ironic intonation—even on his deathbed—of play.[139]

Tsvetaeva transposes Pushkin's death from his apartment at Moika 12 to an anonymous French hospital, giving him the life in a foreign land that she suffered. Other aspects of her own life experience are transferred to him as well. When she fears that she will not recognize him, she imposes on him the anonymity of her life in the 1930s, not his in the 1830s. The French attendant accentuates this strangeness and marks the transfer from home to hospital, Russia to France.

Tsvetaeva, who opens her essay "My Pushkin" with a portrait of Pushkin, here emphasizes the way in which Pushkin's face was recorded by artists. She has one of her contemporaries, Sosinsky, drawing a premature impression of the dead man's face, and she compares her own visual imagination of Pushkin's appearance to known portraits. That it is *his* face is what matters finally to her, and she uses the emphatic possessive (as in the conversation with Nicholas I that opens the dream) to assert the identity of the poet. She writes in her essay of *her* Pushkin (the reverse, she noted in a draft letter to Pasternak, is not true: Pushkin would never have said "my" to her, she insists).[140]

Pushkin calls her Masetochka in this dream, and it is so wonderfully a child's name that we cannot but marvel at the contrast with the words that introduce her to him as "our best poet." This doubled identity, as child and as poet, reprises a multiplication of selves seen throughout her Pushkin writings. And of course Goncharova, with her beauty, appears as well. Pushkin in the dream seems to know her in all her aspects. She, who was worried whether she would be able to pick him out, is mysteriously, deeply familiar to him. He speaks to her with the knowledge that his death has something to teach her, and he speaks as the adult. Tsvetaeva stands in the space between two beds (her word is *promezhutok*) to mark a difference (thus she stresses that he is from Petersburg, she from Moscow). The divide of generations is benign, as is everything in this dream. Even death is not frightening, to her or to him.

Why does Tsvetaeva's dream of Pushkin come as a dream of his death? The question seems almost superfluous, given all that we know of the culture's tendency to think about Pushkin as a man who died a symbolic death, and given Tsvetaeva's claim in "My Pushkin" that her first knowledge of Pushkin was that he died. She has every reason to use this scene of death and parting as an occasion to think through its symbolism for Russian culture and its private meanings to her as a poet—hence her valediction to him as a fellow citizen of the land of poetry. But surely she gets the idea of this scene from Pushkin's own works, specifically Grinev's dream in *The Captain's Daughter*, parts of which here appear out of sequence (the blessing, for example, that Nicholas refuses to send). Grinev's dream ends in violence, presaging the uprising that Pugachev will lead, but Tsvetaeva's dream turns instead toward playfulness. She emphasizes the oddity of this turn, making it a sign of Pushkin's nobility of spirit—he can be playful even as he faces death.

Tsvetaeva will have more traditional observations on the tragedy of Pushkin's death when she writes her two essays later in the 1930s, and it is with those essays that this chapter began. I have chosen to end with this less well-known instance of her Pushkin writings and one that emphasizes the iconoclastic side of her approach to him, which has been much in evidence throughout this chapter. Tsvetaeva's rebelliousness, like his, turns up in places when we little expect it, for example, in her more complicated approach to Natalia Nikolaevna. She never challenges the primacy of Pushkin's place in Russian culture; indeed her greatest contempt is heaped on those who underestimate Pushkin, or who try to narrow his identity or make it less dynamic. Tsvetaeva also seems fixed on an idea of bidding Pushkin farewell, an event that reverberated through many of her Pushkin writings, linking a poem in which Pushkin bids his wife farewell, the missed farewell between Tsvetaeva and her daughter Irina, the inadequate burials of Pushkin himself and Tsar Nicholas II. One cannot but wonder whether Tsvetaeva, who so felt the impending doom of life around her in Europe in the 1930s, feared that an entire culture's relationship with Pushkin was coming to an end. Would her Pushkin writings be a last word? That was not to be, as later history shows, and the two writers still to be discussed here, Andrei Bitov and Andrei Sinyavsky, happily find new ways to write about Pushkin in part because of the lessons they learned from Tsvetaeva.

7 Andrei Bitov and the Mystifications of Self and Story

> Without Pushkin we cannot conceive of ourselves, without Pushkin we have nothing.
> —Andrei Bitov

The contemporary fiction writer Andrei Bitov (b. 1937) has invented an intriguing set of fictionalized relationships to Pushkin, all of them endless quests for the great man. He spins stories about the preservation of distance from Pushkin, although his tales are filled with love without any of the self-dissolving idealism of first love. He acknowledges that Pushkin is adored by Russian culture, and he celebrates his having invented a harmonious and free way to think about life, but Bitov never forgets himself when he looks at Pushkin. The patterns of self-referential digression are web-like and dense, catching any reader who might come close to Bitov himself. The man who "long ago learned not to look in the mirror" finds his reflection in the objects on which he casts his gaze, but readers must beware the inevitable distortions.[1] Bitov's mystifications inevitably also catch us up, and can replicate the frustrations Bitov exudes in searching for Pushkin.

I begin with those mystifications, which Bitov most fully presents in his three major essays on Pushkin. These essays are hybrid texts, part fiction and part scholarly argument. The parts resist separation, and I will look at how the fictional characters and ironic self-references shape the essays' arguments. Mystification is Bitov's central rhetorical device in writing about Pushkin, but it works hand in hand with the device of quotation, which figures most intriguingly in the novel *Pushkin House* (*Pushkinskii dom*, 1978).[2] The second part of the chapter turns to that novel's playfulness with others' words and plots. The distance created between the author and his text covers over several kinds of transgressions. The view of evil in *Pushkin House* is surprisingly ambiguous. Indeed Bitov is that rare writer about Pushkin for whom the terms of right and wrong do not organize his thinking about Pushkin's death. He remarkably resists the tragedy of that theme, and he does so by transforming Pushkin's last year into a time of new life. He writes about the cycles of renewal in ways that parallel his own career, making him yet another writer who eventually writes about himself when he writes about Pushkin. Finally, in the concluding section of the chapter, I suggest that Bitov has been wrongly interpreted as the proponent of a kind of "museum" approach to Russian culture; rather, I argue that the metaphor of a museum is helpful only if we think in terms of the "house-museums" that honor many writers, Pushkin among them. Both *Pushkin House* and the remarkable short story "Pushkin's Photograph (1799–2099)" ("Fotografiia Pushkina [1799–2099]," 1987) are pertinent here. Bitov's love of cultural quotation and literary allusion has distracted readers from seeing that he lacks the sensibility of a collector. By mystifying his authorial personality with layers of irony, he has nearly masked his love for Pushkin, which needs to be reinstated as the prime impulse for his digressions and divagations.

Bitov's earliest stories struck readers as intensely lyrical.[3] Even without first-person narration, more common in the later stories, these tales brought readers into the world of a boy growing up in recognizable Leningrad surroundings. The delicate psychological insights of a story like "The Leg" ("No-ga," 1962) draw their simplicity from the young innocence of the hero; as the hero moves through adolescence and manhood, Bitov makes him less attractive and more worldly in stories like "The Door" ("Dver'," 1962) and "Penelope" ("Penelopa," 1962). The motivations of the hero remain intriguing, but Bitov increases his distance from the hero; seeming autobiographical references work more to suggest clearheaded perspective and maturity. Distance, in my view, defines the narrator and often the hero of Bitov's mature writings, whether it is the psychological remove of a traveler's account of a strange land or the rhetorical distance created when a story pauses over a choice of words. Bitov's narrative positions shift, but behind the blur of movement always rests a relationship of obliqueness, a slant of remote connection that links him to the subject at hand. To have that distance on Pushkin in Russian culture is truly remarkable.

"It is not I who writes ..."

Bitov has written three essays on Pushkin: the undated "Three 'Prophets'" ("Tri 'Proroka'"),[4] "The Intention to Live" ("Predpolozhenie zhit'"), and "Take Away the Hare: Three Variants" ("Vychitanie zaitsa: Tri varianta"). The most controversial of these essays is the earliest, "Three 'Prophets,'" which was lifted out of the novel *Pushkin House* to be published first, in 1976, in a scholarly journal. The three prophets are Pushkin, Lermontov, and Tiutchev, whose poems are discussed: one each by Pushkin and Lermontov called "The Prophet," and a third poem by Tiutchev called "Madness" ("Bezumie," 1830). The essay prints the poetic texts alongside one another. The play of reading works both vertically and horizontally is a visual device that Bitov likes—the epigraphs to his essay are positioned this way as well.[5] "Three 'Prophets'" argues that a conversation and a competition occurred among these three poets, with Tiutchev in the unhappy role of jealous last speaker. The essay is not divided up into smartly titled sections, although it embeds potential section titles in its prose—the most striking is "Tiutchev, Pushkin's Murderer" ("Tiutchev kak ubiitsa Pushkina").

"Three 'Prophets'" is presented as something written by a fictional hero of Bitov's invention—Lev Nikolaevich Odoevtsev, or Lyova for short, the protagonist of *Pushkin House*. The novel was not publishable in Soviet Russia in 1976, so the link to *Pushkin House* receives small notice in the version of the essay that appeared in the scholarly journal. Were the essay read only in *Pushkin House* (where it appears as an addendum to Part Two of the novel), it would serve as a means of character development, showing us Lyova's literary sensibilities. Bitov includes comments about Lyova's level of skill and intuition in the essay, but he also adds a different layer of self-consciousness, explaining to an audience of fellow scholars his decision to speak in someone else's voice.[6]

These observations were dropped in the published novel, but they remain valuable as an early rehearsal of Bitov's logic of ventriloquism. He first compares the device to a scientific experiment: "The conditions of the experiment are these: it is not I who writes, but the hero. I am laying out my impressions of what I have read." The choice of a scientific experiment to describe the project of this essay increases the distance between Bitov and Lyova. This is not messy and emotional art, which is associated with Lyova; it is cold, clear science (a world Bitov knows firsthand, having attended a geological institute). In the world of science, one sets up artificial experimental conditions to prove hypotheses.[7] But this metaphor of the scientific experiment is something of a feint. Far from proving any hypothesis, Bitov proceeds to "lay out his impressions" of Lyova's essay.

The narrative split keeps the one who writes (Lyova) apart from the one who reports on the writing (Bitov). This split will appear in all of Bitov's essays about Pushkin. The explanation continues: "I am laying out my impressions of what I have read, and I am separated from the hero by the distance of the present and of my own life. L. N. Odoevtsev is a beginning literary scholar at the time of the action, the 1960s. The hero is young enough to try to express himself passionately and immediately, and sufficiently inexperienced that the immediacy is what gets expressed, indeed it expresses him much more than what he tries to say."[8] Bitov's irony and cool clarity about his hero are straight out of Pushkin's novel in verse, *Eugene Onegin*, mixing the narrator's friendly tolerance of Onegin with some of the gentle disdain reserved for the Romantic poet Vladimir Lensky. The kind of "immediacy" that Lyova indulges in in his essay is not for Bitov.

He next summarizes the argument of Lyova's essay (called "Tiutchev's Duel" in the journal version and "Three Prophets" in the novel), and says when he is persuaded and when he is not. Notes end the text, some supporting Lyova's ideas with references to other scholars. The notes participate fully in the mystification; many are discursive or chatty, and some were incorporated into the essay when the novel appeared.[9] They maintain the essay's tone, mixing gentle disagreement with enthusiasm at Lyova's successes. I emphasize the kind tone of those notes to make sure there can be no impression of competition between Bitov and his imagined hero. This is in direct contrast to the actual subject matter of "Three 'Prophets,'" where jealousy and bitterness mark relations among the poets.[10] It emphasizes the powerful influence of Pushkin on his successors. That focus accords well with the intertextuality so prominent in Bitov's fiction, especially in *Pushkin House*, and it seems almost a natural question for him to raise.

A more charged topic, however, is the nature of Pushkin's inner world. It is taken up in Bitov's most ambitious piece of writing about Pushkin, "The Intention to Live" ("Predpolozhenie zhit'," 1980–84, published in 1986).[11] One hundred pages long, the essay slowly poses questions of biography and textual sequencing, of aesthetic judgment and canon formation.[12] It moves in many directions, and Bitov stresses the separateness of the sections, giving them riddle-like titles. He pauses at one point to reproduce "mail" received in response to a preceding section. What unifies the huge undertaking is the focus on Pushkin's intense inner world during the last year of his life. Bitov attempts to read 1836 as something other than a prelude to death, and thus he finds texts and memoirs and bits of historical trivia that reveal Pushkin's intention to live. Bitov takes an equally revisionist approach to the year 1825 in the essay "Take Away the Hare: Three Variants" ("Vychitanie zaitsa: Tri varianta," 1982, 1986, published in 1990). A triptych, "Take Away the Hare" offers three approaches to one historic moment: a hare crossed Pushkin's path in December 1825, and this sign of bad luck caused him to stop his journey.[13] The exiled Pushkin was illegally setting off for Petersburg, where he would have been caught up in the Decembrist uprising. Instead he returned to his exile in Mikhailovskoe and continued writing with the same remarkable productivity that had marked all of 1825. Bitov treats the year as a turning point, like 1836; and in both cases, he bases his argument on the chronology of Pushkin's writings. He insists on changed dates for several important Pushkin texts (pushing some to the time after the hare crossed the road, for example). Written more or less at the same time as "Intention to Live," although published later, "Take Away the Hare" resembles it thematically, and both essays interweave their explorations of Pushkin's imagined inner life with fictions about the authorship of ideas. I am most concerned to understand how Bitov fashions his argument as a form of authorial mystification and thus extends the device that shapes "Three 'Prophets.'" His rhetorical performances make arguments of their own, and he will often take rhetoric as his point of departure when he looks at Pushkin.[14]

The rhetorical trope most used in these essays is that of ventriloquism. It emerges in "The Intention to Live" about one-third of the way in, in Part Three, "Sword of the Punctilious Nobleman" ("Shpaga shchekotlivogo dvorianina"; the intriguing title is a citation from Pushkin),[15] beginning with supposed letters from readers. The letter writers have fantastic, obviously invented names: Comrade Boberov from Mytishchy (who also appears in "Take Away the Hare") and d'Ash. Bitov has special fun with the name d'Ash. A cross-linguistic pun (dash), the word is often put in the genitive case, where it becomes a woman's name (Dasha). Because the Pushkin text under discussion is about Joan of Arc, d'Ash also becomes a visual forewarning of that name (in Russian, d'Ark). And it reminds us of the name of Pushkin's killer, d'Anthès. The distance from d'Ash to d'Anthès is further than for the puns just cited, so Bitov puts extra effort into showing us the link; for example, when he discredits the fake aristocratic flourishes in the letter from d'Ash by associating them with the man who killed Pushkin—he incorporates paraphrases of the insulting letter to Heeckeren that Pushkin used to provoke his duel with d'Anthès. When Bitov calls d'Ash's letter a "challenge" (*vyzov*), he ensures that readers will note the similarity.[16]

The letters from Boberov and d'Ash also occasion play with the idea of quotation. As supposed letters from readers, Bitov cites them as if they were evidence. But they are inventions masquerading as quotation, made all the more apparent by contrast to the essay's many interpolated passages of actual quotation and paraphrase.[17] What is gained by the impersonation is a multiplication of voices in "The Intention to Live," a chance for Bitov to speak as if he were a barely educated Pushkin enthusiast and a boastful and pretentious man of noble descent. But because each letter takes a different point of view about Pushkin, the text also dramatizes how fiercely Russians are willing to argue about their national poet, and how even Bitov might be unsettled by a reader who tells him that he does not know what he is talking about. An especially disturbing reproach from d'Ash charges that he does not know which finished text really was Pushkin's last.

Bitov has thus gone to elaborate lengths to motivate a major point in "Intention to Live," the question of Pushkin's last written words. He sifts through the late writings, querying the assumed chronology: maybe the dates are incorrect, and what we have taken to be a work from November 1836 was in fact finished in January 1837? This willed fluidity of chronology lets Bitov engage in a bit of imaginative and very pleasurable work (which he also enjoys when he rearranges time in "Pushkin's Photograph [1799–2099]" and lets plot variants proliferate in *Pushkin House*). In

"Take Away the Hare," Bitov moves the composition of "Scene from *Faust*" later in 1825 in order to place it immediately after *Boris Godunov*.[18] His impetus is more than a scholar's wish to establish provenance. He eagerly moves sequences of time in order to deny death's inevitability; he creates a context in which he can turn over in his mind the nature of Pushkin's work at the precise moment when he was about to stop writing. He slows the forward movement of time, in effect, putting off the endpoint as long as he can.

When he does finally propose a candidate for the final finished text by Pushkin, Bitov comes up with a choice predicted by a quotation in the letter. He has d'Ash cite "What wretched times! What a wretched people!" ("Zhalkii vek! zhalkii narod!") from Pushkin's long-acknowledged mystification, "Joan of Arc's Last Relative" ("Poslednii iz svoistvennikov Ioanny d'Ark," 1836).[19] Bitov argues that in Pushkin's last months, such essays came to occupy the space previously taken up by poems and fiction, absorbing all their attendant artistic complexity and rich intentionality. He finds them to be allegorical with the reference to Pushkin's own situation, arguing for stunning parallels between "Joan of Arc's Last Relative" and Pushkin's letter to Heeckeren in the shared theme of an innocent woman's honor.

Bitov also invites us to read him as he is reading Pushkin, saying—just as he is about to argue that the Joan of Arc essay is an allegory—that all writing is autobiographical: "It is said: 'Every writer writes about himself.' What is meant is: one way or another."[20] The specific context for this comment is how Pushkin's writing changed, a topic Bitov considers in some detail. He organizes Pushkin's development as a writer into periods bounded by crises. In the years 1825, 1830, and 1836, Pushkin reinvented himself, Bitov claims, or at least he tried to: 1836 became a tragedy because renewal failed. Bitov, too, has reinvented himself. When he wrote "The Intention to Live," he was producing little narrative fiction but many pieces in experimental, borderline, and mystified genres, examples of which we are considering here.[21] Such work remained his central achievement well past the 1980s.[22] When Pushkin is said to have put his creative energies into texts like "Joan of Arc's Last Relative," Bitov describes a pattern found in his own oeuvre.

In reading "The Intention to Live," we have given d'Ash more than his share of attention, and it is only fair that we now look at the other invented persona of the essay, Comrade Boberov, who shows a more transgressive side of Bitov's relationship to Pushkin. His letter to the author is quoted in part, then Bitov summarizes it, preserving its abstruse theorizing. Comrade Boberov proposes the unfinished essay on the medieval epic *The Lay of Igor's Campaign* (*Slovo o polku Igoreve*, 1187) as Pushkin's last piece of writing. He uses mathematical formulas involving word and letter frequency to argue his case. Bitov presents the suggestion as parody, replete with a distant, distorted source (Ivan Bunin, not the writer, but an American professor and Harvard graduate known for his biblical word counts).

If Comrade Boberov were then to disappear, this might seem distracting entertainment, but he has a fuller life in Bitov's work, especially in "Take Away the Hare."[23] He appears as a poet in the first part of the essay, subtitled "Faust and the Hare (Confession of a Hack Writer)" ("Faust i zaiats [Ispoved' grafomana]").[24] In the course of the essay, Bitov gives us the confessions of a hack writer, the poetry of a metalworker, the logical arguments of a learned writer. These generic variants are a virtuoso writing exercise meant to stimulate the writer's thinking. As Bitov has noted, "Changing genres is a way to help along one's creative energies. Pushkin changes not only genres, but also, so to speak, authors."[25] Can one cross, though, from prose to poetry, as Pushkin did so freely? That is the question Comrade Boberov seems designed to explore. The essay opens with an enigmatic imperative about broken vows and transgressive acts: "Either hurry up and finish, or don't make any pledges to yourself … (Which, by the way, is also a pledge.) The author (in this case, myself) from his very first feeble steps in prose strongly announced to himself that he would never write verse and never write about great men."[26] But the vow was broken by Bitov's hero, Lyova Odoevtsev, who wrote about Pushkin, "the most forbidden of all great men," Pushkin.[27]

"Take Away the Hare" also breaks the taboo on poetry. Bitov confesses to having written an acrostic to an Armenian lady, a trivial sin that makes a joke of the confession, but the presentation of bits of a poem, "Faust and the Hare," suggests a more serious transgression. Whose transgression? The essay begins with the imagined author poised over a sheet of paper, considering the possibility of writing a line of verse. The poetry emerges as if from the mind of Comrade Boberov, which Bitov suggests in a scene shift to Mikhailovskoe. Boberov is found among the members of an excursion group:

What a wonderful idea! This could be a certain Boberov, one not too distant provincial Pushkin lover, and it's he who is right now composing these feeble verses, and not I, whereas I, you see, am not myself, but I'm writing him, as he writes … Boberov, my savior! The literary hero, rushing in to rescue the author who has gotten bogged down—isn't this some union!—a deserved reward for creative efforts.[28]

Bitov wavers on ceding creative control to Boberov once he sees the tour guide, a pretty young woman. He hardly wants to impersonate a metalworker on a prepaid group tour before this attractive woman, so he decides to get rid of Boberov: "I look around ironically, and as a devotee amid an uninitiated throng, I want to distinguish myself in the eyes of the tour guide. The image of the author splits in two: the master craftsman has faded into the background."[29] But the split is not just because of a wish to flirt. Bitov makes it central to the act of composing poetry and of being an admirer of Pushkin: "This desire for a kind of ignorance—receding into the shadows, hiding behind Boberov, but also for a kind of erudition—to put oneself forward, pushing him into the background—unfortunately, it characterized not only me but also the poet who was composing the verses about Pushkin."[30]

A sense of wrongdoing has reemerged as an ambivalence about showing off one's knowledge. As a result, Bitov needs two authorial doubles in "Intention to Live," so he can contrast their education as much as their social class (d'Ash is a parody of the upper-class know-it-all, Boberov an ignoramus with better manners but a "provincial's love of Pushkin").[31] They are born of the inherent uncertainty in Bitov's authorial persona whenever he writes about Pushkin: that is an important point, since Bitov spins fictions of imagined identity in Pushkinian contexts more than in others, not, for example, when he addresses other writers in essays or interviews.[32] Bitov seems to fear transgression more when he speaks of Pushkin, thus to need the cover of a double. As he says, it is they who write, not he.

In "Take Away the Hare," the creation of poetry becomes as risky as the turn to Pushkin. We are correct to suspect that writing a poem, for this prose writer, produces anxiety. Bitov told an interviewer in 2001, "I have always had a complex about poetry because I thought this was something I couldn't do."[33] A further problem occurs when the poems quote Pushkin: the appropriation of his words seems more charged than other acts of quotation in which Bitov readily indulges. When, for example, his poem cites "He lived among us" ("On mezhdu nami zhil") from a poem Pushkin wrote about Adam Mickiewicz, Bitov panics at the sight of it, and once again, the problem is who precisely has produced these words:

> But it is not he, not I, I mean, who wrote this! Pushkin wrote it! And, it seems, not about himself, but about Mickiewicz. A poet, so to speak, writing about a poet ... It turns out that if I introduce Pushkin's words, then can I justify them only because they belonged to *Pushkin*? ... All the more so since they were addressed not just to anyone but to another poet and a genius. Therefore, continuing Pushkin's words, I was writing about Pushkin himself, which in reality I would not dare in belles-lettres, still less in verse![34]

As the passage continues, Bitov appears equally disturbed by the intrusion into someone else's consciousness, especially Pushkin's consciousness.

As lyrical poetry, the cited line seems to come from Pushkin's own point of view. That impersonation carries a terrible taboo. Early on in the essay, Bitov asks whose point of view he is speaking from ("ot ch'ego litsa"). But when he repeats this question, wondering about some of the words in the poem, his confusions of perspective run deeper. Consider the following passage, where the line of verse at issue—"The old woman beyond the wall rustles, murmurs, and mumbles" ("Starushka za stenoi shurshit, murshit i miamlit")—refers to Pushkin's nanny, Arina Rodionovna.

So the little picture has turned into a little scene. The house has become inhabited. The poet went to bed, but Arina Rodionovna is still bustling about on the other side of the wall. The erudite has visibly won out: "the old woman" was crossed out and replaced by Arina. "Rustles, murmurs" rests with the conscience of the author like a relic of the not so bright tourist-craftsman.... But as an erudite I suddenly close ranks with my craftsman-repairman: Pushkin would hardly have called his nanny Arina, that's our schoolboy speech that used to leave out the teacher's patronymic ...
So maybe I am both men, the metalworker and the erudite? After all, didn't I do repair work once upon a time? For whose benefit do I hide behind him, then come out of hiding? To whom do I wish to appear? Alexander Sergeevich, of course.[35] There's the whole motive. I'm afraid for him to see me stupid—isn't that stupid?[36]

Such circumnavigations continue as the poem develops, leaving a tired Bitov to sigh, "Wouldn't it be simpler just to be oneself?"[37] But he perseveres, carried along by the energy of the poem and by a tingle of doing something forbidden.[38] He assumes alternative identities in order to enable writing (about Pushkin) that would otherwise be too risky. When these writings bring him up against the temptation to write as if he were Pushkin, Bitov tries to stop short, and yet keeps on writing.

He pushes toward the writing of poetry itself, several pages of which are interpolated into "Take Away the Hare" (in Part Two of the essay, "Grateful Russia," we read the poem "The Year 1825," sent to the author by Comrade Boberov). The siren lure of writing poetry is irresistible. It is an identity the writer within Bitov might wish to inhabit whether via impersonation, as in this essay, or with the courage of his own voice (the latter has led to the publication of dozens of poems beginning in the late 1990s, many of them dated earlier).[39] The poem in "Take Away the Hare" is a pastiche of quotations from Pushkin, with none of the urgency or linguistic flair of the originals. Many lines are brilliantly inept, compared by one scholar to Dostoevsky's hilarious writing for Captain Lebyadkin in *Demons*.[40] The side of Bitov that fears appearing "stupid" before Pushkin has made sure that this poem seems not to spring from his pen.

The poetry is perhaps most interesting as a rhetorical device that calls attention to its own presence. We may read that as an intrusion of a higher literary form, a reading that many of Bitov's comments about the supreme value of poetry would support, but we might also consider its intrusion as an interpolation of a different form of language use. Because the quoted poem, in all its three parts, is iambic, with couplet rhyme, it introduces a rhythmic and phonically repetitive form of language into the essay. Rhythmic consciousness, as the psychoanalyst Nicolas Abraham has described it, stops time with its repetitiveness and fixed intervals, and it produces what he calls "a *fascinated* consciousness."[41] An alternative, slower contemplation of ideas is enabled, and thus it is no surprise that the poem has essentially the same narrative as the essay—a description of Pushkin's life in 1825 in exile, focused on what he was writing, then the attempt to flee that is stopped by a hare crossing his path. The poem ends with the proposal to erect a monument to that hare, which we know to have been one of Bitov's pet projects. The essay's odd title, "Take Away the Hare," points toward an alternative reality where there was no Pushkin as national poet: take away the hare, Bitov imagines, and you let Pushkin continue on to Petersburg just in time for the Decembrist uprising and all the repressions that its aftermath brought to like-minded noblemen. A monument to the hare celebrates the moment when Pushkin swerved back onto the path that let him become Russia's national poet. It lets Bitov create a point of origin for that myth, in a way that is whimsical, irreverent, and again slightly transgressive.

Bitov writes much less whimsically in his novel *Pushkin House*, to which I now turn. There, the interpolations tend toward scholarly prose, not poetry. The trope of quotation remains important in this novel; in fact Bitov here began unfolding his notion of what quoted speech can do in a literary text. He also set the question of transgression onto moral and ethical grounds more familiar from Soviet history.

Quotations of Word and Plot

Pushkin House is neither a novelized version of Pushkin's life nor a focused meditation on the themes from his works. It tells a rambling tale of family romance, a first love, and a jealous friendship, with a stunning final scene involving Pushkin's dueling pistols and drunken destruction in a literary museum. Plots from Pushkin's writings mix with allusions to his life. Pushkin also appears in verbal embellishments like chapter titles, epigraphs, and quotations. Allusions to Pushkin are typically contextualized by references to other writers, Dostoevsky, Lermontov, Turgenev, and Chernyshevsky among them.[42] Quoted words work only secondarily as referential pieces of a narrative puzzle: for Bitov, they are first units of sound that can be remixed to comic or poignant effect.

Pushkin's significance in the novel is encoded in its title. Pushkin House (Pushkinskii dom), as we know, is the common name for Petersburg's Institute of Russian Literature, not a house in which Pushkin lived. Bitov uses a generally accepted metonymy that describes Russian culture as a house

Pushkin taught Russians how to inhabit. Bitov has said that he intended this larger sense in naming his novel *Pushkin House*,⁴³ and indeed the novel has less to do with the Institute of Russian Literature than with cultural norms of growing up in post-Stalinist Russia.

Bitov accentuates the choice of title in one of his two epigraphs to the novel.⁴⁴ He quotes part of Alexander Blok's poem "To Pushkin House" ("Pushkinskomu domu," 1921), where the title "Pushkin House" resounds familiarly. But Blok's claim for fullness of meaning and passionate belief no longer holds true.⁴⁵ This contrast shows us that, in Bitov's novel, the name Pushkin House is unavoidably ironic. Bitov cites this quatrain from Blok's poem:

Имя Пушкинского Дома
В Академии Наук!
Звук понятный и знакомый,
Не пустой для сердца звук!..⁴⁶

The translator Susan Brownsberger, in her admirable version of *Pushkin House*, succeeds in condensing into two lines the essential point Bitov wants to make in citing Blok:

Pushkin House! A name apart,
A name with meaning for the heart!⁴⁷

Bitov's novel shows how little meaning this name has to most of his characters (the exceptions are older men with significantly non-Russian sounding names—Uncle Dickens and Blank). Indeed, rather than remaining "a name apart," Pushkin House is rife with the betrayals of day-to-day Soviet life. Thus the novel's crisis, a drunken duel between Mitishatyev and Lyova, takes place within its walls, and it uses and endangers relics from the Pushkin period (a death mask and his dueling pistols).

In addition to the irony Bitov brings before us in the name Pushkin House, he is drawing our attention to how the name functions, making us notice and think about the name rather than just using it to denote a place. When Bitov cites Blok's locution of saying "Puskhin House" and then talking about it as a name, he is giving us an example of what will be a frequent habit of speech in his novel. Bitov repeatedly puts words before the reader as something to be noticed and talked about, rather than as cooperative participants in the onrush of narrative meaning. In that sense, he writes prose as a poet would, calling attention to sounds, words, and syntactical patterns.(That habit also reflects his wish to write poetry.)

The way Bitov most commonly draws attention to words is to set them off in quotation marks. The prologue contains several instances of this usage, but in the novel proper the first quoted phrase is taken from Pushkin's poem to the Decembrists, "In the abyss of Siberian mines" ("Vo glubine sibirskikh rud," 1827). The quotation comes in a sentence that establishes multiple points of origin for the hero, Lyova Odoevtsev. Bitov places him in the contexts of family, history, literature, and geography with these few words: "His infancy, it is true (Lyova was conceived in a 'fateful' year), had brought some disagreeable relocations for him, or rather for his parents, to the land of their notable ancestor—'deep into the Siberian mines,' as it were."[48] The point of the Pushkin quotation is in one sense purely informational: by referring to Siberia, especially after mentioning the "fateful" year (which all Russian readers will recognize as 1937, conventionally taken as the height of Stalin's campaign of mass arrests and deportations), the narrator establishes the fact that Lyova's grandfather had been arrested and exiled.

Bitov uses the quoted words to convey that fact, that is, he brings in words from another context, depends on our knowledge of that other context for the point to be clear, and sets the cited words off from his sentence with framing quotation marks. The word for quotation marks in Russian is *kavychki*, and the term has historical links to expressions that mean obstacles or barriers.[49] Bitov uses them in precisely this way, as visual separations that frame a word for us to study it. In the passage just cited, the English translation makes a tiny and perceptive addition of quotation marks to the Russian original: it refers to the "fateful" year in which Lyova was conceived. Susan Brownsberger no doubt meant to draw the non-Russian reader's attention to this word, which a Russian would quickly know to be significant, but in fact the quotation marks separate the word *fateful* in a way that is like the demarcation of the quotation from Pushkin: the translator is asking us to linger for a moment on its meanings, and she suggests that there are ironies in the multiple meanings we will find. There is a derisiveness in Bitov's use of the word, a resentment at the way this year, 1937, proved fateful to so many.

The translator draws this idea from Bitov himself. In the next few paragraphs of *Pushkin House*, a number of words are placed in quotation marks—and, as was the case with "fateful," they all bitterly denote events of arrest and exile. We read about people who "were actually lucky" ("eshche povezlo"), of measures that were "milder" than they could have been ("miagkikh"), of those who were taken ("vziali") or left alone ("ne trogali"), of events that happened "at just the right moment" ("vovremia"). There are those who did not manage as well ("ne tak oboshlis'"), who lived "beyond the boundary" ("zakordonnykh"). And through it all, there is the appalling belief that "it could have been worse" ("moglo byt' khuzhe") and the lie that, for the young hero, these arrests and exiles were part of a "wartime childhood" ("voennoe detstvo"). I have given here nearly all the expressions that Bitov highlights in quotations marks in this recapitulation of the hero's childhood. The translator of *Pushkin House* duplicates Bitov's choices throughout, sometimes in more telescoped form than my word-for-word translations suggest. In one case she, like Bitov, precedes an adjective with the phrase "so-called."[50] That, too, makes sense, since all of Bitov's words given in quotation marks work as cited material (these were the expressions families like the hero's used to refer to events of arrest and exile), but also to mark the falseness of the naming. This framing action of quotation marks, like the warning action of the epithet "so-called," marks a word as inadequate. The quotation marks reveal an inauthenticity in language, and they disclose a psychological authenticity in their euphemistic coyness, letting us see the fearful psyche that the Terror created.

This irony is a key feature of narration in *Pushkin House*: distancing himself from the words with which he writes, the narrator also sets himself apart from his story. And Bitov sets words apart from the story they tell. We are invited to examine the words in and of themselves, as if they were on exhibit in a museum. Surely this is one sense of the claim that *Pushkin House* is a "museum-novel,"[51] which returns us to the novel's title and the question of Pushkin's presence in its telling. In the quotation from Pushkin's poem, Bitov uses both quotation marks and an expression of warning that works just like the epithet "so-called": Lyova's relative was sent, we were told, "'deep into the Siberian mines' as it were" ("'vo glubinu sibirskikh rud,' tak skazat'"). The English "as it were" (Russian "so to speak," "tak skazat'") doubly draws our attention to the quotation and introduces some further distance or a doubtful intonation. Why would the quotation be ironic? Perhaps Bitov reminds us that the circumstances of arrest and exile during the Pushkin period were better than those of the Stalin years (this is a point Andrei Sinyavsky will also make, with some sadness).

Bitov may also be alluding to the fact that the citation from Pushkin's epistle to the Decembrists was already ironic. The poem was perceived as false in its day and earned a stinging poetic response from one of the Decembrists, Prince Alexander Odoevsky (1802–39).[52] Bitov often invokes the doubleness of meanings, for example, in the words cited above where euphemisms conceal violent social acts and reveal the reluctance of speakers to mention these things at all. Bitov points toward a doubled meaning where *both* terms contain some falseness. The characters in his novel do not speak literally (they do not have Pushkin or the Decembrists in mind), and Pushkin himself did not speak with successful sincerity. Is the latter point fair? Bitov at least wants us to wonder about it. The fact that the sarcastic answer to Pushkin was penned by an *Odoevsky* would not be lost on him: this is the name that gives rise to his hero's surname Odoevtsev, and it is also the surname of Prince Vladimir Odoevsky (1803 or 1804–69), one of Bitov's favorite writers.[53]

I stress the possible falseness of Pushkin's poem, then, because I believe it is crucial. Citations are not, for Bitov, a way to get back to some more authentic language.[54] One can see how rebelliously he uses quoted speech by contrasting his techniques with those of literary norms. One version of these norms, persuasively formulated by the critic of English literature Susan Stewart, is particularly relevant:

> The quotation lends both integrity and limit to the utterance by means of its "marks." In detaching the utterance from its context of origin, the quotation marks textualize the utterance, giving it both integrity and boundary and opening it to interpretation. The quotation appears as a severed head, a voice whose authority is grounded in itself, and therein lies its power and its limit. For although the quotation now speaks with the voice of history and tradition, a voice "for all times and places," it has been severed from its context of origin and of original interpretation, a context which gave it authenticity.[55]

Stewart's analysis is innovative in claiming that quoted words lose some of their original authenticity. But Bitov would push this insight still further, resisting the opposition between authentic and inauthentic contexts, and he also does not see the boundary between contexts as so firmly drawn. What he would share with Susan Stewart is the sense that no point of origin can ever be fully recovered. That does not mean that he will not praise the quests some of his characters launch, or make such attempts himself—this is one way to read the story "Pushkin's Photograph (1799–2099)"—but it does mean that the search will never succeed, that, as in "Pushkin's Photograph," the hero will return from his journey through time with no photograph of Pushkin, no record of his voice, just a button torn off from his coat as some sort of pitiful relic.

Bitov, for all his praise of Pushkin's supreme achievements and incomparable status in defining Russian culture, is suggesting that Pushkin cannot stand as some recoverable, authentic point of origin for Russia's sense of itself. Throughout *Pushkin House*, the references to Pushkin tend to bring him into all-too-human contexts. Even his name has no special aura. Lyova uses it as a presumed "Semite" to quell an argument about Jews.[56] A minor character at another point is named Pushkin, and he is a common man, a metalworker (prefiguring the occupation of Comrade Boberov, perhaps).[57] Nor is the name a required signal for important comments about literature, as in the narrator's discussion of literary quotation.

In a passage entirely italicized and introduced with a parenthetical self-reference—"*(The italics are mine—A.B.)*"— the narrator draws attention to puns on literary or film titles in newspaper headlines. Such phrases are re-accentuated in their new context, he finds, often by means of slight word changes. The theories of Mikhail Bakhtin come to mind here, and Bakhtin is certainly not irrelevant to this novel, as Bitov indicates in a note about the similarities between his character Uncle Dickens and Bakhtin.⁵⁸ The best examples of re-accentuated phrases in *Pushkin House* are Bitov's own chapter titles, as when Dostoevsky's *Poor People* crosses with Pushkin's *Bronze Horseman* to produce "The Humble Horseman" and "Bronze People."⁵⁹ The narrator criticizes journalists for doing violence to titles, and he calls the re-accentuation a form of "distortion."⁶⁰ But he stresses that what is cited and changed around is typically itself a citation, and his examples draw on epigraphs from previous centuries. Epigraphs being themselves a form of citation, we realize that we are in a moment of *mise en abyme*—a citation of a citation of a citation—and that no source, not the Bible (which Bitov discusses in this passage) or the poetry of Pushkin, can stop this endless chain of motion.⁶¹

Bitov draws his meditation to a close by recalling the indirect learning of quoted names and titles in a typical Soviet school education, and Pushkin is noticeably absent from his list: "Sometimes it seems that only through quotation do well-read people know the names of 'Christ, Mohammed, Napoleon' (Maxim Gorky), or Homer, Aristophanes, Plato, or Rabelais, Dante, Shakespeare, or Rousseau, Sterne, Pascal … and a few of their popular sayings."⁶² As if Bitov senses the omission of Pushkin, and as if he knows his readers are making connections between these comments and his own writing practices in *Pushkin House*, he continues:

The title of this novel is stolen, too. Why that's an institute, not a title for a novel! With nameplates for the departments: *The Bronze Horseman, A Hero of Our Time, Fathers and Sons, What Is to Be Done*? And so on, through the school curriculum … A tour of a museum-novel …

The nameplates guide us, the epigraphs remind.⁶³

And so we are returned to the novel's title, to Pushkin himself, to the idea of a novel as a (Pushkin) museum. Thinking about Bitov is filled with such circular journeys that leave us in a place that looks like where we started, but the result is to change the way we see that point of origin. That is certainly what he does with Pushkin, in taking us on a journey that seems to be designed to bring us closer to him. Bitov shows how the distance can never be covered or covered up, but we can learn to see Pushkin differently.

We are taught to see him differently by one other device: Bitov does not just quote words; he also quotes plots, which is to say that he uses plots that repeat the events of other lives and other fictions. In *Pushkin House*, the repeated plot is that of the duel. It comes from Pushkin's life, as well as from his writings (including *Eugene Onegin*, "The Shot" ["Vystrel," 1830], *The Bronze Horseman*, "The Queen of Spades" ["Pikovaia dama," 1833], and *The Captain's Daughter*) and from other writers' works, like *A Hero of Our Time*. The duels, in Pushkin as in Bitov, are both literal and figurative. Moreover, dueling supplies the main metaphor in the embedded essay on Pushkin, Lyova's essay "Three 'Prophets,'" and Bitov sets up tensions among these forms of dueling.

The duel between Lyova Odoevtsev and his friend Mitishatiev unites the novel's beginning with its end. *Pushkin House* opens in the museum, where the duel has just been fought, and Lyova appears to lie dead. The novel backtracks to tell everything that led to the duel: Lyova's childhood, his family history, his love affairs at the university, his training as a literary scholar, and his frustrations in all these realms. Mitishatiev emerges as his inevitable rival. His surface is too smooth, his movements through life are too untroubled for him to be anything but Lyova's opposite. The Russian writer and critic Yuri Karabchievsky characterized him as a little devil ("bes," an image suggested by the novel itself) or a serpent who slithers up to Lyova at every opportunity.[64] But Ellen Chances has more perceptively identified the devilment of *Pushkin House* in pointing out that Mitishatiev and Lyova are both devils.[65] As she notes, Lyova is no innocent victim, for all his powerlessness in the face of Mitishatiev's manipulations. Lyova, like everyone of his post-Stalinist generation, has been reared in an atmosphere of duplicity and falseness. He imbibes these values even as he fights them. We especially see this in the first part of *Pushkin House*, where Lyova meets his grandfather and wants to create an impression of brave integrity. The crucial point here, as we advance toward an understanding of Lyova's and Mitishatiev's duel as a rewriting of Pushkin's and d'Anthès's encounter, is that Lyova commits transgressions of his own, some of which lead directly to the duel.

When Lyova challenges Mitishatiev to the duel, it seems that Pushkin is at the root of the problem. Lyova is already irritated with Mitishatiev, but he grows exasperated when Mitishatiev plays with Pushkin's death mask, jumps around with it to antagonize him, and tries it on. They struggle for possession of the mask, and Mitishatiev drops it, to shatter into pieces. "I will not forgive you *him*," Lyova says. At this moment, Lyova sees Mitishatiev as "evil, a geometrical volume of evil."[66] In their competitive friendship earlier in the novel, they engage in a more predictable form of competition, jealousy over a woman. Lyova rightly suspects that Mitishatiev has been carrying on with Faina, whom he loves unrequitedly. Yet the duel is not caused by Faina, but by a betrayal of far more significance to these men. And the responsibility for the betrayal does not rest solely with Mitishatiev. Lyova, in their drunken spree, insults his much loved older friend Blank and causes him to leave; he blames Mitishatiev for this, because Lyova was so drunk that he remembered none of it and has to hear it from Mitishatiev. But the sin—against friendship and, more important, against those very values of loyalty and honesty that Blank, along with Uncle Dickens and

Lyova's grandfather, represents—is Lyova's, and the revelation that he cannot incarnate these values pushes him toward the duel in anger.[67]

The idea of a duel in which evil is complexly distributed is also found in Lyova's supposed essay, "Three Prophets."[68] That essay, whose framing devices were discussed above, now needs our attention for its substantive argument. It does, as its title promises, discuss three poems (by Pushkin, Lermontov, and Tiutchev), but Lermontov makes a comparatively brief appearance, and one can safely say that the intensity of the essay's argument comes in the discussion of Tiutchev (in an earlier version, it was titled "Tiutchev's Duel"). Tiutchev's poem "Madness" is read as an aggressive answer to the apparent social slights inflicted by Pushkin. The jealousy and anger are barely concealed by the claim of love in his poem about Pushkin's death (a poem this essay treats as pedestrian and unconvincing except for its lines about first love). Tiutchev's poem provokes a reaction of equal anger from Lyova. Bitov, in reporting on Lyova's argument, establishes a chain of figurative duels: Tiutchev with Pushkin, Lyova with Tiutchev. He judges Lyova's reaction to Tiutchev as extreme, an unjustified form of hatred that reveals more in its exaggerations than Lyova might have intended:

What had Tiutchev, for example, done to Lyova? And what, after all, had he done to Pushkin? Even if Lyova was right about everything, what was Tiutchev guilty of? Of feeling jealous over Pushkin and of Pushkin? Of preserving, throughout his life, a peculiar and secret relationship with him? That's no crime.[69]

We cannot miss the similarities to the duel Lyova actually fights, especially as Bitov goes on to lament Lyova's shortsightedness and his anger caused by painful self-recognitions:

Tiutchev is to blame that Faina happened to Lyova, Grandfather happened; he is to blame for being born too late and emerging too late like Lyova (each in his own epoch); and Lyova the latecomer, with his heart turned to another epoch, cannot forgive Tiutchev for having been its "contemporary," as Lyova desires to be and cannot ... Oh, if only it had been Lyova! *He* would have embraced Pushkin, *he* would have pressed him to his heart ... but enough; he has already embraced his grandfather once.[70]

Bitov wants us to see that Lyova has marked his reading of Tiutchev with his own jealousies and frustrations. The duels of both essay and novel, in a sense, do not take place. In the essay, earlier on, Lyova had described Tiutchev's rancor at Pushkin's never seeming to notice him:

Next Lyova names the word "duel" and rides it, long and beautifully, from sentence to sentence, stitching them together, like the bobbin in a sewing machine. We well remember that oscillating motion. A duel—a duel that was not—a duel that was—it was indeed a duel. A secret duel, because nobody knew about it except one of the duelists.[71]

The same question mark hangs over the duel fought between Mitishatiev and Lyova, since Bitov gives alternative endings to *Pushkin House* meant to leave one wondering if the duel was fought at all. Bitov's passion for variants, evident in *Pushkin House* every time an interpolated passage called "The Version and the Variant" appears, in effect undoes every plot choice he makes, including the climactic scene of dueling with Pushkin's pistols in the museum room devoted to Pushkin's death.[72]

The two duels match contestants who are not so starkly legible as good vs. evil. Bitov is free to undo fatal duels between fictional characters or between writers who barely know each other, but he is constrained by the historical fact that d'Anthès killed Pushkin (although he expends considerable effort trying to imagine a variant here as well). The ethics of the duel remain open to interpretation. By putting Tiutchev in the role of Pushkin's antagonist, Bitov powerfully unseats the image of Pushkin as martyr familiar from Lermontov's poem "The Death of the Poet." And by making the duel between Mitishatiev and Lyova a contest between two whirling devils, one of whom is sympathetic but neither of whom is wholly innocent, Bitov asks his readers to consider a battle in which evil has lost much of its potency. Bitov stops short of using these allegories to offer a reinterpretation of Pushkin's duel in *Pushkin House*, although he strongly suggests that the tragedy that killed Pushkin is not merely the morality tale of good and evil that we have taken it to be.

Pushkin Lives!

Bitov can write of Pushkin as an "eternal loss" ("Pushkin—eto vechnaia utrata"),[73] but he defines Pushkin in terms of his passion for life. Bitov moves around the passion of Pushkin's death as if it were an obstacle, always keeping it in view, but denying it the power to define the Pushkin myth. He begins one text about Pushkin by quoting Maria Osipova from 1835: "He was so alive!" ("Kakoi on byl zhivoi!").[74] Even the comment about eternal loss just quoted comes from an essay called "The Intention *to Live*." Its first section has two epigraphs from Pushkin's poetry. One reads, "I, all of me, soon will die" ("Ia skoro ves' umru," 1825); the other reads, "No, all of me will not die" ("Net, ves' ia ne umru," 1836). Readers will know which one is truer. The first comes from a dramatic monologue on André Chénier, set on the eve of his execution; the second from "I have built myself a monument not made by human hand" ("Ia pamiatnik sebe vozdvig nerukotvornyi"), which became an emblem in official celebrations of Pushkin's legacy. In the course of the essay, Bitov will displace this poem's centrality, making a powerful case for *The Bronze Horseman* as Pushkin's more authentic statement of artistic credo, but here he uses the line to unseat the inevitability of death. He describes Pushkin's death as the end of a life that was personal, short, immensely alive, and utterly Pushkin's own ("kogda konchilas' ego lichnaia, ego kratkaia, ego takaia sobstvennaia, takaia edinstvennaia, takaia ego, takaia zhivaia, takaia odna, takaia zhizn'"), as the moment when "the fortress of his life was falling" ("kogda krepost' ego zhizni pala").[75] The expressive intensity of the second formulation is all the greater after the jagged, lurching motion of the first. So typical of Bitov's penchant for variants, this doubled description shows him searching for a rhetorical effect that can adequately convey the enormity of the event but also deny its force as an endpoint to a life.

Thus death is not vanquished from "The Intention to Live"; Bitov pushes at its intrusive presence, trying to shape it into something else and to read its hidden signs of life.[76] The essay's sections take up this desire in different ways. In the first part, "The Contemporary and the Descendant" ("Sovremennik i potomok"), Bitov recalls how Pushkin's contemporaries thought he had written himself out in the 1830s. Succeeding generations, despite greater access to Pushkin's later work, repeat that mistake, in Bitov's view. They bury Pushkin alive ("Pushkin was written off as dead [lit., buried during his lifetime] more than once, like no one before or after him"; "Pushkina khoronili pri zhizni neodnodratno, kak nikogo do i nikogo posle").[77] The trope of burial also occurs in a tale Bitov tells about how others once treated him (in "Notes from the Corner," "Zapiski iz-za ugla," 1963). We might resist being deflected quickly onto an autobiographical or allegorical reading, however, for the trope not only directs us back to the author; it points us to the rhetorical figure itself. Throughout the first few pages, "The Contemporary and the Descendant" uses a metaphorical language of death, as if to vanquish the literal fact of Pushkin's death. Here is another example, taken from a passage where Bitov describes how different editions of Pushkin feel to the reader:

All of our editions, right down to today, are in some sense, perhaps even mainly, *posthumous*. "Who was he really? and whom did we lose!"—this is a never-ending sigh. And maybe precisely for this reason, like an unconscious desire to ease the loss, the tradition brought down to us from his contemporaries has not died—we, too, bury him alive.[78]

The metaphors used when Bitov writes of book editions and traditions are meant to displace the literal death of Pushkin. Lacking the grotesque imagination of a writer like Sinyavsky, for example (Sinyavsky had noted the prominence of dead bodies in Pushkin's writings in his *Strolls with Pushkin*), Bitov prefers images like books, editions, footnotes, and quotations. Something about the very idea of death, of a soon-to-be-dead body, cannot be fully admitted into his writing world, a world in which Pushkin, if only in his words, must live.

Bitov reports a telling fantasy in "Intention to Live," one that he attributes to Marina Tsvetaeva: a man who has been abroad for many years returns to Russia in the 1880s, sees a graying general in the theater, and thinks it is Pushkin. Bitov envies this momentary lapse in memory, when a man can actually think he has seen "Pushkin *alive*" ("*zhivogo* Pushkina").[79] Bitov cites memoir testimony of Pushkin's energetic and elusive behavior in public, which he reads as evidence of Pushkin's resistance to being forced into a predictable or fixed role. Again, the point is to emphasize the life force Pushkin represents, but this part of the essay cannot avoid the nearness of death. Bitov admits a desire to see the life as having some kind of unified shape, confessing that this desire forces him to accept, even wish for, the final hours of duel and death. He matches memoir accounts of Pushkin's readiness for death with claims that he was preparing for many years of productive life.

Bitov sides with the latter: Pushkin was ready for more life; what he was fed up with was the old life he had been living during 1836. This choice lets Bitov explain the urgent liveliness of the acknowledged final text that Pushkin wrote, just hours before he went off to his duel with d'Anthès—a letter to the writer Alexandra Ishimova. In the letter, Pushkin applauds Ishimova's work with the exclamation, "That's how one should write!," and Bitov stresses the enthusiasm of this sentence. More important, he reads the generosity of the letter as a superstitious token: a text produced so as to ensure that he would come back safely from the duel.[80] This "last" text, then, receives a reading that denies it any intentional finality on Pushkin's part, in fact turns it into a marker of the desire for life itself.[81] The final year emerges as a time of a sudden, necessary, but never to be reached state of ripeness; and particularly when we put this passage into the context of Bitov's speculation elsewhere about which text really was Pushkin's last, the finality is further diminished. In Part Three of "The Intention to Live," "Sword of the Punctilious Nobleman," discussed above for its mystifications of authorship, Bitov asks which text was Pushkin's last. As new candidates are proposed for Pushkin's "last" text, Bitov keeps holding off the moment of death, offering up further possibilities for those last words.[82] The resistance to an ending also appears in a later section of the essay that fantasizes a future for Pushkin beyond 1837 (Part Six, "Between the Victim and the Cathedral").

Those fantasies also inform Part Four, "Boldino 1836" ("Boldinskaia 36-go"), which, at nine pages, seems the slightest section of "The Intention to Live." Once again, Bitov contemplates chronological rearrangements, proposing changes in the dating of individual texts that invite readers to rethink the time line of Pushkin's last months.[83] He speculates how 1836 might have become a year of splendid poetic harvest,[84] as happened when

Pushkin was detained in Boldino in the fall of 1830 and when he returned there in 1833 (the Boldino fall of 1834 was less successful). Pushkin did not succeed in getting out of Petersburg in the fall of 1836, even to Mikhailovskoe, and wrote comparatively little. This disappointing lack of a Boldino-like autumn in 1836, Bitov argues, was the central fact that led to his death. Bitov notes important work dated October 19, 1836; in many years, October 19 (the anniversary of the founding of the Tsarskoe Selo lyceum) elicited poems of commemoration from Pushkin, as well as becoming a symbolic date for him more generally (not unlike December 14, as Bitov observes). Works associated with the lyceum founding date are typically about the past; among those Pushkin dated October 19, 1836, was *The Captain's Daughter*. Bitov argues that Pushkin felt an increasing distance from the past and an eagerness to look ahead to a new period in his life. The next few pages are devoted to clarifying some details about other texts dated October 19, like the letter to Pyotr Chaadaev and a poem that some say is about Voltaire but one that Bitov connects to Chaadaev. He has made many of these substantive points already in the essay, admittedly about different texts, so one is led to ask what work these pages are doing for his essay. That question in and of itself might be inappropriate to Bitov, who digresses constantly and at considerable length.

Yet in this case, I believe, the delays are strategic. These details point toward Bitov's own career and his growth as a man; it is here that the autobiographical underpinnings of this large essay almost show through. The epigraphs to this section raise questions about how people change their views (and are charged with waffling) and about aging. There is also a long interesting note about the psychology of aging, on how generations get divided by things like whether one remembers a war (true of Bitov's contemporaries, he notes, as of Pushkin's). Bitov may want to show us Pushkin starting to feel old, as he is, although he makes the point with hesitation and ambivalence: "On October 19, 1836, he was at once young and old, his own son as well as his own father; the younger self could not fight down the older, and the older self wanted no easy victory over the younger...."[85]

The more interesting point has to do with the rhythm of Pushkin's autumn retreats, mentioned repeatedly. For Bitov, too, especially early in his career, periods of writing in the countryside were important, and many of his stories feature a writer who has sought refuge and inspiration in the countryside. Such a writer is the hero of Bitov's best-known story, "Life in Windy Weather" ("Zhizn' v vetrenuiu pogodu," 1963), and he appears in "A Man in the Landscape," "Pushkin's Photograph (1799–2099)," and elsewhere. At times, a palpable fear of not being able to write emerges, with reference to Pushkin's frustrations in Boldino in 1834 or in Petersburg in 1836. Some stories or essays simply present a writer at his desk, trying to write. In "Take Away the Hare," a writer sits before a blank page, slightly horrified as lines of poetry, not prose, begin to appear. Other stories and essays record narratives of writing. Bitov even constructed a companion piece to "Life in Windy Weather," his "Notes from the Corner," which purports to annotate the composition of that story. Bitov gives primacy in his fictional world to the scene of writing, as many modernists do (to undermine the apparent realism of the text), and because writing grounds his means of apprehending the world.[86] He told one interviewer, "I overcome the condition of confused loss, on paper I start to understand. A writing person apprehends the world at the moment when he writes. I have no doubt that I do not err when I write. In life, yes, all over the place, but in the text, never."[87]

Bitov seems most fully alive at the moment of writing, which yields a further insight into his reading of Pushkin. He suggests that Pushkin's "Intention to Live" was expressed in his writing. Pushkin *was* his writing; thus a narrative about his death cannot be silent on this point. Bitov's writings necessarily repudiate biographical speculation or even explanation, for example, in *Pushkin House*, when a conversation about Pushkin's sexual adventures and Natalia Nikolaevna's fidelity can occur only during drunken revels among barely coherent participants. Bitov sees that Russians are curious about Pushkin's life, but their curiosity merits parody. What Pushkin wrote matters, and thus to dream of an alternative ending to Pushkin's life is to dream about what he might have written, not about how his love life might have been different. Bitov writes, late in the essay, "But no! he's alive! at this minute, at this desk!..."[88] The scene of writing thus recurs as a scene of conjuration. Would that it could bring back Pushkin, Bitov wishes, so that he could keep on writing.

Bitov is fascinated by the things that Pushkin *did not* write (and, similarly, he has talked of his own unwritten texts).[89] "The Intention to Live" begins with the observation that Pushkin wrote no final will and testament, leaving us unusually free to edit and organize his works. He returns this freedom bequeathed to readers back to Pushkin himself—not an original idea, but Bitov turns it into an insight into what Pushkin did not write and what he crossed out:

For me, as for many others, Pushkin stands for the utmost freedom. Not because he called us to the barricades, quite the opposite. Our ideology has always tried to declare Pushkin a revolutionary, someone close to the Decembrists. But this is not so: his sense of feeling for the government is complicated, as is his closeness to the Tsar. These are different parameters for understanding life.

Pushkin is also a genius because he had a very strong inner editor. To our ears, the words "inner editor" have been discredited, sounding like a system of slavery that internalizes something foreign. But there is another inner editor: what you can and cannot say. I have long dreamed of writing about the excised passages in

Pushkin. No one will ever figure it out—why did he cross out wonderful passages in *Eugene Onegin*, or the continuation of "Autumn"?[90]

The paradox of Pushkinian discipline as the source for a greater freedom appeals to Bitov, makes more mysterious a creative process that includes decisions not to allow phrases or whole sections of writing. Bitov imagines Pushkin's legacy as a vast body of work whose borders we cannot finally determine, a nod at the voluminous publication of drafts and omitted passages. He reaps enormous advantages for the freedom of his own idea of Pushkin; he can fantasize different sequences for the writings, rearrange them so as to defer the final moment when writing comes to an end. That fantasy produces a lyric of frustrated love in "The Intention to Live," where Bitov reads the last year as a time when renewal, not death, was in the air. Bitov's description of an unwritten essay about deleted passages in Pushkin becomes an imagined extension of "The Intention to Live," an unpaid debt to a poet whose death left him with many texts incomplete.

Bitov prefers coincidence to causation, fantasy to fact, variant to fixed outcome. Thus his essay's final section opens and closes in the world of numerical coincidence.[91] It begins with comments about the number twenty-seven, a repeatedly fateful number in Bitov's writings. He has his hero Lyova explain the number as a turning point in life, after which your fate is decided. A minimal amount of detective work reveals that the number twenty-seven recurs in *Pushkin House*: it is the age at which Lyova writes "Three Prophets," the age at which all three poets composed the poems discussed in "Three Prophets," the age at which Lyova reads his grandfather's stories, the age at which his grandfather wrote his stories. The number has relevance to Bitov's own life: he was born on May 27, 1937, and he was twenty-seven years old when Joseph Brodsky was put on trial (in 1964—an event Bitov experienced as decisive, he reports) and when he began to write *Pushkin House*.[92] "The Intention to Live" claims that twenty-seven is a fateful number in Pushkin's life. Pushkin fought his fatal duel with d'Anthès on January 27, 1937. Bitov thus puts January 27 alongside more familiar dates (December 14 and October 19). He adds a footnote that exaggerates the numerical coincidence to the point of burlesque. Comrade Boberov is brought back for a tour-de-force performance in numerology, where 27, 37, and 99 become the 3, 7, and ace of Pushkin's life. "The Queen of Spades" has usurped the text of biography, but before all grows too wild, Bitov notes that Boberov's demented calculations have the Queen of Spades falling precisely on January 27, 1837, a coincidence where things "stop being merely amusing."[93] Still less amusing is the turn to Alexander Blok, who worked on his poem "The Twelve" ("Dvenadtsat'," 1918) on January 27–29, 1918. Bitov grimly reminds us of Blok's age (thirty-seven) at the time. He calls "The Twelve" a "duel in which he will die" and concludes with an image drawn from that poem, although not only from that poem, of red and white, blood on snow.

The end of "The Intention to Live" turns away, then, from magical coincidences and an urgent wish to live. Its last section bears an epigraph that has editorial markings by Bitov meant to emphasize this change:

> That's how one should write!
> *Pushkin,*
> *Last sentence*
> *Last letter,*
> *Last point.*[94]

The italicized lines that Bitov adds read like a poem, with anaphora replacing rhyme and something of a pun on the word *point* (*tochka* can also mean the period that ends a sentence). The actual argument of this final section has to do with parallel texts, Zhukovsky's account of Pushkin's death and Pushkin's outline for a history of Peter the Great. It lets Bitov play with side-by-side textual comparisons again, and with the idea of texts as variants of one another. But by the end, Bitov notes that there are no variants to the documents of death, no parody of the letter to Heeckeren. His choice of Blok's image of red blood on white snow has Bitov ending with a death no variant can vanquish. Worse, the parallel between Pushkin and Blok makes a familiar but no less moving point—that tragic deaths pursue Russia's poets. The autobiographical elements of "The Intention to Live," especially as they are interwoven with *Pushkin House*, show us how Bitov is placing himself into the same contexts of life, work, and writing that shaped Pushkin's life. For all the life force his essay generates, he comes against a seeming truth about violence and suffering in Russian history. Bitov takes great pleasure in the games of language and thinking that grace all his writings, but as a writer he is grounded in realities of politics and history as well. Now we have only to examine the way those realities shape his impressions of Pushkin's legacy in Russia today.

Repudiating Museum Culture

Bitov's novel *Pushkin House* and his short story "Pushkin's Photograph (1799–2099)" offer us excellent material for summarizing his contribution to Russia's myth of Pushkin. The science-fiction fantasy "Pushkin's Photograph" has everything to recommend it: a compelling, inventive plot, splendid humor, an idealistic and insightful hero. The humor begins with the title, where the parenthetical dates transform an author's conventional dates of birth and death into the markers of a future anniversary celebration. The story includes two narrative frames: a writer writes in 1985;

and, in the year 2097, anniversary planners decide to send a time traveler to record a photograph of Pushkin's face and a tape of his voice.[95]

The idea of the story is a flash of genius. Nothing reveals the fetishizing of Pushkin paraphernalia more candidly than this plot, especially since the quest is in vain: the hero returns with a blurred image and no audiotape.[96] The experience makes him crazy; he is left muttering in an insane asylum about threes, sevens, and aces, like Hermann in "The Queen of Spades." Bitov works that parallel as a quotation in plot, as he had done in *Pushkin House*. It makes plain his view that the mission for Pushkin's photograph is base and embarrassing: like Herman greedy for money, this future world seeks to possess objects merely in order to have them.

First published in a Pushkin anniversary issue of *The Banner* (*Znamia*, January 1987), this story ridicules those who plan jubilee celebrations, particularly the way they seek a pièce de résistance. The narrative just catches the weighty phrases of official discourse, its exaggerations and clichés: "We have before us no more noble task than to mark appropriately on the pages of our publications the three hundredth anniversary of Alexander Sergeevich Pushkin's birth. Pushkin's whole life, his activity, his titanic labor are near and dear to hundreds of millions of those who dwell on our planet. The name of Pushkin rings out everywhere."[97] The hyperbole of these words, and the ludicrous scene in which they are spoken, might lead one to think that Bitov despises anniversary commemorations. But he has revealed mixed sentiments about jubilees: he criticized "the huge gypsum figures of our literature," but noted that jubilees usefully provide a structure for repeated reevaluations of writers and artists.[98] What makes reevaluation possible, he suggests, is when an anniversary does not trumpet a writer's greatness, and instead enables quiet contemplation and assessment. But the frame story of "Pushkin's Photograph (1799–2099)" shows the opposite, where the participants raise high stakes in a noisy and shallow act of celebration.

The story opens in the strange world of the future, for all its obvious parallels to Soviet daily life (Bitov wrote the story before the collapse of the Soviet Union). In this future, travel is easily interplanetary, and domes cover cities like Petersburg, Paris, and Beijing, making them into gigantic museums where life is preserved rather than lived. One speaker proclaims that, as the twenty-first century closes, "The epoch of the successful preservation of nature and monuments has arrived!"[99] In the museum of Pushkin's apartment on the Moika, domes cover exhibited objects, and these domes are dwarfed by the larger dome over the whole city, a dizzying *matryoshka* effect that will cause a delirious reaction in Igor, the hero. He reacts with considerable estrangement to everyday events, for example, when he listens to dull jubilee speeches and then fantasizes removing his head from his shoulders, whirling it around like an apple, having it roll down the aisles to the presidium. It is a marvelous touch on Bitov's part, a metaphor for the extreme boredom of sitting through such proceedings mixed with fear that one will reveal the boredom.

The separable head also offers up a vision of the face. The hero's head is presented as if for the photographic record, just before it is decided that he will undertake the mission to travel back in time and photograph Pushkin. Bitov has already turned the tables on these delegates, imagining what would happen if the photographers were to try to fix an image of their deliberations:

These people are not obliged to look attentive or to applaud in the necessary places—they're busy. With foreshortening, catching an essential delegate—and then a new pale blue flash illumines first of all the photographers themselves, and the print of this moment will always signify that the moment has passed, but will comfort those caught in the picture with the idea that the moment allegedly existed.... And we, like a camera lens, will fumble in the aisles and take a close-up of this one and that one—totally arbitrarily (we might need one of them for a hero later in the story—what a clumsy maneuver!).[100]

The description of delegates too busy to pose for pictures foreshadows what the hero will find when he pursues Pushkin. Photographs are meant to provide comfort that a moment existed even though it quickly passes, but our maneuvers to take the picture are clumsy, Bitov notes, and the picture is necessarily imprinted with our awkwardness.

Bitov wants to produce a photograph-like mental image that includes its own frame. He tells us this directly (I cite his words below), and he also shows us indirectly in the narrative frame for "Pushkin's Photograph (1799–2099)." The outer frame story (of a writer writing in 1985) connects representation, photography, and reversible time, which also characterize the second frame story (the scene of the jubilee meeting), as well as the innermost narrative (the story of Igor's trip back to the age of Pushkin). Here is how the writer-narrator speaks in the outermost frame (he describes the view from the attic window):

In the foreground a fly is crawling on the glass, and my thought crawls off after the fly.... Look at that, I think, it's not a painting or a photograph—there's no way to describe what was framed for me by someone who built this house long before I was around and who naturally did not think about planning the view from my window, but nonetheless sentenced me to this landscape. You couldn't photograph it to catch the frame of the window—like the frame of a painting—and the fly crawling on the picture, and a pole in the foreground with wires like a music staff lining the landscape in advance so that the fence is on the bottom line, on the middle one they're turning hay, and on the top two are the distant forest and the sky.[101]

Bitov claims that photography cannot capture the layers he wishes to include: window frame, fly crawling on window, wire pole, wires, fence, hay, and sky. The sense of photography's failure, like the author's prediction that he will fail to describe the view from his window, is false (just as a false fear that the story will never be completed turns up in "Pushkin's Photograph"). Words succeed in conjuring up for the reader a powerful impression of fractured images, pieces of frame, layers of depth, and profound visual pleasure. Bitov's words make these impossible pictures work, and it is an achievement he repeats elsewhere, for example, in "View of the Sky at Troy" ("Vid neba Troi," 1988), where one impossible snapshot after another drives the plot and forever changes the hero.[102]

Bitov works with photographs (rather than paintings or drawings), and not just in "Pushkin's Photograph (1799–2099)": his images invoke the limits of mechanical reproduction and the frustrations of a form that wishes to imprint the original features of a face or a landscape.[103] In "Pushkin's Photograph," Bitov exposes the desire to know and produce copies of Pushkin's face while effacing the selfhood and experiences of the photographer. These traces of the photographer's sense of self are like depth effects that the photographed image, as his narrative describes it, inevitably preserves. Thus Igor returns with these evocative images of his journey to Pushkin's life:

But only a shadow, like the wing of a bird flying up before the lens, came out. One was struck, however, by the unusual senseless beauty of individual shots, especially in relation to the notes of the insane time traveler: The storm that preceded the cloud that had inspired the poet to write the line "The last cloud dispersed by the storm . . ."; the portrait of the cook Vasily slamming the door; the remarkable portrait of the rabbit in the snow—in a drift, ears erect, front paws folded under; the cart harnessed to the bullocks covered with the tarpaulin with Abreks prancing all around it; the hand with the candle and a piece of someone's beard; the waves carrying coffins . . . and all the rest of the shots were of water and waves.[104]

The only two images that represent Pushkin are the shadow "like the wing of a bird flying up before the lens" and "the hand with the candle and a piece of someone's beard": these are abruptly fragmentary images, catching the movement that resists still photography. The "unusual senseless beauty" is not senseless at all; these photographs substitute it for the scientific precision Igor was sent to capture.

Accuracy is always an illusion in this story. Igor learns that the more closely he imitates inhabitants of 1836 Petersburg, the more readily he gives himself away: "The more exactly they had reconstructed a detail from the past, the more suspicious it was."[105] But these words, spoken with the narrator's authority, are mild condemnation when compared with an eloquent digression about the imprecisions of writing history:

You will find nothing in a past epoch that the epoch did not leave you *itself*. And even of that you will not find everything. Humanity also lives its *private* life, hidden from the eyes of outsiders—that is what history is. It is inaccessible. You take a look at an epoch—and you're too late, sir.[106]

Even Igor, in some ways an ideal observer of this earlier age, cannot produce scientific truths, for observing is never one-sided: "Some observer! He wasn't doing the looking at all, he was being looked at."[107] He can recognize as significant what he has been trained to search out. He sees "only quotations from what he knew."[108]

As he begins to live fully in the time he visits, Igor cannot transmit his experience in the documentary records that the authorities have sent him to make. He becomes passionately involved in Pushkin's life:

Like an unlucky lover, he kept track of Pushkin's hours and routes, he would steal after him—just to catch a glimpse of him ... mentally help him into his carriage, hand him his cane, and sit down next to him ... and thus he would remain, gazing after the carriage, spattered with mud from the wheels. Pushkin would turn around and laugh.[109]

Igor compares himself to Pushkin in this devotion to the beloved, giving examples from Pushkin's writing to prove the comparison. He feels keenly how much this love has become his whole life, his identity: "without Pushkin he himself was gone."[110] The story embodies his love, as reflected in the penultimate paragraph: "And here we place our final period, like a monument, a monument to an utterly selfless and unreciprocated love."[111] Love drives Igor crazy, produces beautiful but vague photographs, makes the story itself into an endless quest.

The opposite of love, we are asked to imagine, is the acquisitive urge of those who sent Igor time-traveling. They seek proof of Pushkin's existence, emblems that can celebrate their skills in organizing jubilees. Bitov, like Igor, values the imagined, lived experience of Pushkin as he might have been; thus his story catches bits of Pushkin's spoken conversation and glimpses of his physical presence. These moments give readers the pleasure of imagining Pushkin alive. It is no accident that Igor loses consciousness as the duel nears—he cannot bear the scene of Pushkin's death, although he uselessly brought penicillin along in hopes of saving his life. The vial of medicine becomes another motif of impossible desire. Instead, Igor's time travels yield scenes like these: "Yes, the candle was burning ... yes, a man lay on a tiny little cot and was writing something so fast that it was as if he were just pretending to write line after wavy line like a child.... How strangely he was dressed! In a woman's bed jacket, a nightcap, wrapped in a scarf."[112] Bitov makes the by-now predictable scene of the writer at work somewhat comic by dressing Pushkin in women's clothes and later giving him a beard (which, as he only half-jokingly explains, is "how such a brilliant work as *The Bronze Horseman* was written . . . tugging and nibbling his beard").[113] More endearingly, Bitov turns Pushkin's writing into the quick wavy lines penned by a child. We also see Pushkin close up in a scene where Igor fixates on Pushkin's long fingernails (the fixation is prompted by Orest Kiprensky's 1827 portrait of Pushkin with its prominent fingernails; see Fig. 13). Pushkin plucks grapes, and has a conversation with Igor that comes close to the perilous subject of cuckoldry. Here, and in another encounter in 1829 on the road near Tiflis, Pushkin precipitously disappears from Igor's view, making the scenes all the more tantalizing and also ensuring their success, since Bitov never has to link these vignettes into a connected narrative. His story has its own logic, a reversal of Pushkin's life where 1836 leads back to 1833, then to 1829 and 1825, and finally to the scene of the Petersburg flood of 1824. Bitov has transformed the fantasy of time travel into a biography of the age of Pushkin, its narrative sequence turned backwards so that the final scene, the flood of 1824, also lets Bitov repeat a belief expressed in "The Intention to Live"—that *The Bronze Horseman* was Pushkin's most significant literary achievement. He presents both the scene of its composition in 1833 and the 1824 flood it describes. And he has Igor experience the terrors of its hero, Evgeny. His travails in recording Pushkin's life make him resemble Evgeny—a simple, working man struggling with Russia's history, a mad survivor of its catastrophes.

Igor is not a scholar or a scientist or even much of a writer (he tries to pass off Blok's lyrics as his own). He is not an intellectual, and thankfully so, since Bitov indicts intellectuals because they know nothing for themselves.[114] But Igor's experiences are completely his own: he comes to know something unique to him, and he lives it, as Bitov would say. What Bitov disdains is not thought (how could he?), but those who think the same thoughts as everyone else around them. Earlier in "Pushkin's Photograph," he describes the jubilee planners as a mass of conformists. Petersburg, he says, is "the room in the public library that requires a special pass," and, he continues, "to get through all this you need rather to blend in than to stand out."[115] In this culture no one even suspects anyone of difference, so completely has it atrophied. Bitov here situates the desire for Pushkin's photograph as an urge to collect and gather evidence of the past, an emotionless wish for knowledge.

In the novel *Pushkin House*, Bitov gives a chilling example of this kind of quest. Here is Lyova's grandfather, trying to tell his grandson how knowledge, clouded by emotions, lets evil happen. The man he is describing is his former prison guard.

Right this moment, your version of the facts is at work accommodating your feeling, right this moment you're explaining the origin of his gaze by its convenient consequences, precisely by its consequences. You're explaining it to yourself as goodness, attentiveness, understanding—that's what you need right now. All you f—ing humanists—people are supposed to understand you! But he really does understand you, he's got you figured. Because he has a flawless *method*, and it's all he uses, it makes him sharp and clear; he's not looking at you—he's reading you, he's a professional.[116]

Bitov puts an angry condemnation of soft humanists into the grandfather's speech, but, although he admires Lyova's grandfather, he does not side with his view. The "professional" who knows everything in advance is repugnant to him. This is not knowledge but surveillance, the acquisition of knowledge used in order to harm.

Less malevolent but equally chilling is Bitov's representation of other forms of knowledge based on "method," rather than on emotional connection to the subject at hand. A mistrust of museums, as cultural institutions and as ways of apprehending the past, is embedded in *Pushkin House* and "Pushkin's Photograph (1799–2099)." It is a "time-honored museum tradition" for novels to welcome allusions and cultural repetitions,[117] but Bitov is offering us a brilliant feint when he says his novel is like a museum. The idea of a museum operates as a fiction within the novel.[118] Among critics, Alla Latynina has said the most forthrightly that *Pushkin House* is itself not a museum, and she is right to caution against excessive literalness.[119] Bitov's contemporary Viktor Erofeev may have run that risk: he suggests that the "creation of a museum-novel" in *Pushkin House* fails to "domesticate" culture and thus free the author from a "literariness" he disdains.[120] What is useful in Erofeev's comment is the imagined opposition between home and museum, between private domestic space and an official cultural institution.[121] *Pushkin House* rearranges the relationship between official cultural space and the scene of the hearth, and in the process Bitov redefines the museum in a salutary, hopeful way.

The dominant cultural institution in Russia's veneration of Pushkin, as we saw in Chapter Two, is the museum-house ("dom-muzei"), typically a home in which Pushkin lived or visited, now furnished with period decor and glass display cases. One of the most remarkable things about Andrei Bitov's contribution to the Pushkin myth is that, without writing about any of these museum-houses, he manages in *Pushkin House* to cast them in an entirely new light, to reveal to us how much the idea of the museum and the idea of the home are embedded in Russia's cultural appropriation of Pushkin's life and work. The novel's title signals this concern: Pushkin House, in addition to its preeminence as an institute and archive of Russian literature, is a conventional literary museum. (Recall that the building in question here is not Moika 12, where Pushkin died, but the Institute of Russian Literature, across the Neva on Vasily Island.) It houses on its second floor a sequence of museum rooms, including a room about Pushkin's death, that display original items or manuscript replicas meant to illustrate the life and work of various classical Russian and Soviet writers. (In the 1990s, the literary museum closed to the public, a victim of financial collapse in Russia's cultural institutions; when Bitov was writing *Pushkin House*, it was a functioning museum, although, as friends reminded me when I inquired whether the museum had reopened, it was usually closed even during the Soviet period; as of this writing, it has reopened.) Bitov uses this museum space in *Pushkin House* as a stage set for the duel between Lyova and Mitishatiev. It contains, significantly, props: the revelation that the death mask on display was a copy lets their tragic duel be rewritten in the novel's last variant as a silly misunderstanding. Museum space is theatrical for Bitov, especially the literary museum, which collects items genuine and fake, splendid and insignificant, and jumbles them up in a way that does nothing but make visitors feel that they have been in a museum. In one of the plot sequences that concludes *Pushkin House*, Lyova escorts a foreign visitor around Petersburg on a day when all the literary museums are closed. They cannot find the site of Pushkin's duel on Chernaia Rechka. Both are moments of great verisimilitude, of course: the museums close often, both regularly and unpredictably, and the site of Pushkin's duel is extremely difficult to find—in my experience, local inhabitants give confused directions, and some look at inquiring visitors with incomprehension. But Bitov does more than record a fact of daily life. He suggests that visiting the literary museums of Petersburg is inherently frustrating. They are, in a sense, closed even when they are open. His view also applies to rural Pushkin museums. As Bitov exclaims in "Take Away the Hare," "I have never visited Mikhailovskoe. Oh, this is a separate subject altogether, how many times I have never been in Mikhailovskoe!"[122]

We might suspect that Bitov prefers museums where someone once actually lived, the "museum-houses" whose domestic space conveys the life of a family. *Pushkin House* is in various senses a domestic novel, one whose themes and locations convey an atmosphere of familiarity and intimacy. The idea of the family home is fundamental to the novel's plot, but Bitov never idealizes home or hearth. The Odoevtsev family is the many-generationed nest of Russian culture, and it is not a scene of happiness and comfort. The parents have concealed the grandfather's arrest and exile; the son has grown up in "an atmosphere of secret treachery."[123] The novel has elements of family romance, resembling Freudian patterns in its ability to conceal disturbing, even traumatic shared memories. For Bitov, as for nearly all Russians alive today, domestic space is not cozy. Even the word for a house or home, *dom*, can signify a block of apartments, as if the separateness of private space could have no name. (As others have remarked, Russian has no word for privacy.)[124] Home in Bitov's fiction is complex and divided space, only a partial refuge from the outside world.[125] But domestic chaos, if it turns destructive, is for Bitov always reversible: the novel opens with a picture of the hero lying dead, the literary museum in shambles, but it ends with harmony restored, the hero alive, his *family* having helped him clean up the mess in the museum.

Bitov suggests that Russian culture is akin to this emotion-laden scene of the home, rather than to any official institution like the museum. This is not just because the architecture or symbolism of the home appeals to Bitov, although it is obvious from his writings that it does;[126] he also prefers the narrative logic of the home, where generations advance to reverse patterns of dominance, and where relationships shift and settle, shaping the way family members see themselves and the world. In museum logic, such changes are much harder to explore. One room leads to another, as if in natural sequence. Museums make time seem to stand still, freezing the past and preserving it "as it was." (The best emblem of this wish to stop time is the stopped clock in the Moika 12 apartment.) But Bitov shows us that time can never be made to hold still—he says as much in "Pushkin's Photograph": "If you put a dam on time in an effort to store the past or accumulate the future, you will be flooded through the tiny little hole called 'now,' and you will choke in the flood of the present."[127] Stopping up the flow of time can have mortal results, Bitov warns, but it is culture that dies when time is stopped still.

Bitov's qualification of museum culture also emerges in a spatial metaphor that he uses often. If museum space works horizontally, pushing visitors from one room to the next, then Bitov insists that genuine culture proceeds vertically as well. Recall his own frequent recourse to images of height. The attic location for more than one fictional writer's study comes to mind (in "Pushkin's Photograph," among other stories).[128] These elevated perspectives may have let some find a kind of elitism in Bitov, as if he wanted to be above the world he describes. But he descends deep into architectural spaces, just as he climbs up over an expansive view. The story "A Man in the Landscape" offers a particularly good example of both patterns in its alternation of broad, open landscapes with journeys through frightening passageways that seem only to go deeper and deeper down. But it is in *Pushkin House* that Bitov gives his most passionate account of this urge to dig deeply, and in this novel the result always leads to a recovery of cultural value. Lyova's grandfather, for example, uses the image of the mine to criticize a culture fixated on preserving the past. He says this to Lyova:

Russia, homeland, Pushkin ... the word, the nation, the spirit ... all these words will be heard again as if in their first, natural, unofficial meaning, they'll strip naked—and that will be the end of these concepts. Next will come an era of "new" concepts, which you will have tracked down among those long forgotten. This will be a kind of industry—the "mining" of the word (one poet has already put it that way, I think). Exhausted words will be dumped in slag heaps. Like in a mine ... Ever work in a mine, Lyova? ... Now you're going through Tsvetaeva and Pushkin, next you'll go through Lermontov and somebody else, and then you'll stumble on Tiutchev and Fet: you'll make the one a genius, the other a great man. You'll drag up Bunin ... This inflating and devouring of reputations will pass for the growth of contemporary culture.[129]

The grandfather speaks with angry frustration at the falsity around him, offering Lyova no image with which to save himself. In fact, he tells him that what looks like it will save you is your ruin. The apparent renewal of culture, the descent into mines where values have been preserved, is an empty and repeating ritual, a substitution of the old for insight into the real.

The ingeniousness of this passage, like the one about his prison guard, is that the grandfather actually *is* talking about what matters. He speaks out of sadness that names like Tsvetaeva, Tiutchev, Fet, Bunin, and even Pushkin rise up from the depths of the past like newly tantalizing commodities. The grandfather sees them treated with the same greed that motivates the desire for a photograph of Pushkin in the year 2099, but this is the dystopian present, not some fanciful intergalactic future. Bitov's rejection of the phenomenology of the list and the cult of the collection includes a suspicion of those who compulsively dig, like archeologists who participate in the project of the museum. That is, he does not simply contrast vertical imagery to horizontal; he shows that all forms of movement may be emptied of meaning and abused for offensively ambitious purposes.[130]

Thus, in the end, Bitov looks not just at Pushkin himself, but at what Russians do with Pushkin. He has much of substance to say about Pushkin's writings, as we have seen, but his writings always also address the question of an attitude toward Pushkin. As Bitov himself once noted: "It is not so much that Pushkin is our national poet as our relationship with him that has become constituent of us as a nation."[131] In *Pushkin House*, he says something similar:

People always took a more personal attitude toward Pushkin than Pushkin took toward anyone else, and since his death this has even become a kind of Russian tradition—one-sided personal relationships with Pushkin (Pushkin established this kind of relationship only with Peter the Great).[132]

Bitov's mystifications and digressions appear to separate him from Russians who take a "more personal attitude" toward Pushkin, but they make it possible for him to contemplate Pushkin's legacy from many vantage points. His fictional relationships mediate the closeness between Pushkin and himself, and his quotations from the writings intensify the self-consciousness of that mediation. Bitov is neither an "official" adherent of the Pushkin cult nor a rebel against sanctioned Pushkin celebrations. He writes bracing criticisms of jubilee celebrations and museum sites, but also creatively transforms these fixations on time and place into new narratives for looking at Pushkin. He wittily parodies the idea that Pushkin generated a national self-definition for Russia, but he also transforms the Pushkin story into a national narrative of identity by relocating its themes of betrayal and self-loathing into the Stalin years (in *Pushkin House*). Finally, Bitov's insistence on recreating a Pushkin who is alive challenges the dominant narrative of martyrdom, and evokes for readers a changing, elusive poet whose works continue to fascinate Russian readers, including Bitov himself. When Bitov comments on the way Russians have subjected Pushkin to "eternal examination," when he marks Pushkin's uniqueness as one who "has been put before the glance of the other like no one else,"[133] he is celebrating the pleasures and lessons of that gaze, and joining in its fixations himself.

Afterword
ENDING / BEGINNING WITH
ANDREI SINYAVSKY / ABRAM TERTZ

> Art is not a better, but an alternative existence; it is not an attempt to escape reality but the opposite, an attempt to animate it. It is a spirit seeking flesh but finding words.
> —Joseph Brodsky

Before Bitov, there was Andrei Sinyavsky, writing defiantly as Abram Tertz. Sinyavsky's fate (prison, internal exile, emigration) meant a life more directly imprinted with the tragedies of Soviet history than Bitov's, and his Pushkin texts took greater risks. The scandal that he created remains instructive, although it receded, finally, when he died in 1997. He seems at last to have gained some acceptance as a contemporary prose writer: a two-volume edition of his writings appeared in 1992, and the anthology *Pushkin: pro et contra* included an excerpt from *Strolls with Pushkin* (*Progulki s Pushkinym*, 1975) in 2000 with a short account of its controversial reception in the commentary.[1] The writings themselves, including *Strolls with Pushkin*, as some Russians are discovering, merit rereading, for they respond innovatively to long traditions of writing about Pushkin. Sinyavsky was one of the last writers in the twentieth century to contribute to and debunk Russia's myth of Pushkin, and he thus offers a fine endpoint for this study. He also points the way to the future.

Sinyavsky and Bitov share much in common. Having resisted Soviet cultural norms, both were later seen as men of the 1960s.[2] They led the way for Russian literature's encounter with postmodernism. But Sinyavsky paid a dear price for coming to postmodernism before Russians were ready for it, whereas Bitov's path to respect, at least in post-Soviet Russia, has been in general comparatively smooth. Bitov has become an important cultural figure in Moscow, heading prize committees, sitting on editorial boards, publishing fiction and essays to polite reviews. He participated fully in the 1999 Pushkin anniversary. His distanced but loving writings about Pushkin typify attitudes of his generation: they value irony so long as it is gentle, and their affection for Pushkin conforms to an essentially traditional view of Russian culture. Sinyavsky did not gain this degree of cultural acceptance before his death in 1997, in part because, in Paris, the role of post-Soviet *intelligent* was less available, but also because doubts that he loved Pushkin persisted, and it was thought that he mourned Pushkin's death with insufficient piety and seriousness.

To turn, then, to Sinyavsky's views of Pushkin and to the controversy surrounding them is to reopen fundamental questions about Russia's elevation of Pushkin to the status of national poet. The Sinyavsky/Tertz story demonstrates that a commitment to love and be loyal to Pushkin remains a quintessential moment in Russian self-definition; that the tone in which one shows that love is as important as the demonstration of the emotion; that various and shifting constituencies of the Russian public, as well as official institutions, feel free to judge the loyalties of others; and that the judgments can be pernicious and surprisingly long-lived.

Others have chronicled the controversies surrounding Sinyavsky, and they have begun the process of evaluating his distinctive contribution to late-twentieth-century Russian culture.[3] After summarizing the controversies briefly, my goal is to look at Sinyavsky's Pushkin writings in the post-Soviet context, to see what they show us about the immediate past and what they might predict about the future. His writings are freshly compelling in their paradoxical contribution to Russia's myth of a national poet and their insights into the cult of Pushkin itself. He was able, as Sergei Bocharov put it admiringly, to light sparks in the Pushkinian text that would have eluded a calmer and more scholarly approach.[4] His writings address two highly charged themes, sex and death, and he treats them with a familiarity and lack of inhibition that finally grew less shocking to Russians after the demise of the Soviet Union. The 1990s was also a time of immense vulgarity, as I am not the first to note, but Sinyavsky lithely escapes this charge—in a way that can only be called Pushkinian.

The Controversy

Sinyavsky, writing as Abram Tertz, first scandalized the Soviet elite with his Jewish, low-brow pseudonym and subversive theories in the 1960s.[5] *Strolls with Pushkin* was written in a Soviet labor camp and published abroad. It outraged émigré critics. Roman Gul attacked his originality, integrity, and intelligence, and Alexander Solzhenitsyn later followed suit.[6] The outcry paradoxically echoed official Soviet denunciations of the 1960s, when Sinyavsky was put on trial and sentenced to a labor camp. When a substantial portion of *Strolls* appeared in Russia in 1989, the scandal was repeated in more bitter tones.[7] The name-calling of the early 1990s was fueled by a new and fairly hysterical form of nationalism.[8] Sinyavsky was said to have transgressed in writing too familiarly of Pushkin, and his errors were judged as moral flaws. Gul had insinuated that Sinyavsky's release from the labor camps a year early was a KGB favor to one of its own; indeed the fact that Sinyavsky had written in the camps at all, he said, made him suspect.[9] In 1990, Dmitri Urnov again claimed that he could not have written *Strolls with Pushkin* while in the camps.[10] Dishonesty was a first step toward something worse, however: Sinyavsky was said to hate Pushkin and Russian culture.[11] Igor Shafarevich signaled these political implications in a bizarre footnote to his infamous essay "Russophobia."[12] Sinyavsky responded vigorously to the fascist and anti-Semitic allegations of this essay and of *Pamiat* more generally.[13]

The politics of the old controversy never went away, then. Sinyavsky continued to represent a subversive, anti-establishment position against official culture that, although it included former dissidents in the post-Soviet era, still had a powerful stake in conserving fixed notions of Russian national identity. So it is unsurprising that some members of the younger generation of literary and cultural figures newly embraced Sinyavsky after his death, particularly during the run up to the 1999 Pushkin bicentennial. The young were drawn, I believe, to Sinyavsky's comfort in criticizing Russia's cult of Pushkin. This had freed him to write about erotic themes in Pushkin's work and about the erotic aspects of his creativity, which also inspired younger readers, as did his claims about Pushkin's attraction to the theme of death and his insistence that the poet's own death was not merely the morality play for which official myths have taken it.

Beginning with the Cult

Sinyavsky opens *Strolls with Pushkin* by questioning the status and affection accorded Pushkin in Russian culture:

Despite all our love for Pushkin, a love that borders on worship, we for some reason find it difficult to explain why we consider him such a genius and why Pushkin and no one else always comes in first in Russian literature.[14]

An audacious opening sentence, by any standard. It issues a challenge to readers even as it suggests a note of confession or self-criticism. The love and worship for Pushkin come first, but the subordinate clause comments that Russians cannot easily account for his greatness. Sinyavsky implicitly tells us that his book will take up the question of Pushkin's greatness, that he will offer his own explanation of why Russians adore him and why they consider him a genius. The opening also hints that the adoration might be blind, the genius overrated, as a later sentence says quite directly: "We have the right to ask, to express our doubts (and many have doubted): is your Pushkin really so great, what's he so famous for anyway, once you take away a dozen or so skillfully cut-out pieces, about which you can't say anything except that they are skillfully stitched together?"[15]

By insisting on a right to ask this question and to express doubts, Sinyavsky acknowledges that his approach may offend. He speaks not with belligerence, though, but with a lightness he attributes to Pushkin himself. Sinyavsky says that we need to bypass the grand front entrance to the house of Pushkin's fame, with its statuary and laurels, because "he's our Charlie Chaplin, a contemporary ersatz Petrushka, who spiffed himself up and got the hang of strutting his stuff in rhyme," and, still more daringly, "he learned to write badly, any old way, worrying not about perfecting his 'winged epistles' but only about writing them on air—thoughtlessly and fast, without exerting himself."[16] Sinyavsky cares little whether this is a pose or genuine laziness: "If Pushkin (let's assume!) was only pretending to loaf, it means that he needed that pretense to free his tongue . . . and without it he couldn't have written anything good."[17]

To say that Pushkin concentrated on "unpolished verse" attributes to it a "rough-hewn" quality that Sinyavsky also sees in his popular image,[18] and it also lends Pushkin the informality, lightness, and friskiness (his term) that Sinyavsky strives for in his book. We have found this kind of mirroring in the writings of Akhmatova and especially Tsvetaeva, who wrote in terribly difficult circumstances in emigration. Sinyavsky's light tone, incredibly sustained in *Strolls with Pushkin* (although *Strolls* was composed in bits and pieces), is countered by the dateline, given on its last page: "1966–1968, Dubrovlag." Despite this reference to the labor camp, Sinyavsky's tone little resembles Tsvetaeva's plangent meditations in her Pushkin essays, but its mix of playfulness with ironic reality is remarkably like her poetry. In general, poetic models are exceptionally pertinent to Sinyavsky's Pushkin writings, even though he never published a line of verse, to my knowledge. Sergei Bocharov intimates the same thing when he sees Sinyavsky's Pushkin writings as direct contact between two poets.[19] The jabbing indictment of official "Pushkinolatry" in Tsvetaeva's "Poems to Pushkin" is, then, a fine antecedent to Sinyavsky's pointed humor, and both he and Tsvetaeva owe a great deal to Mayakovsky's 1924 "Anniversary Poem." Sinyavsky wanted to write a book on Mayakovsky during his last years (it had been the subject of one of his long-running Sorbonne seminars), and, as we can tell from his fine essay on the poetry of Boris Pasternak, futurist and modernist poetry generally sparked his imagination.[20] I will return to the impact of poets on Sinyavsky in a moment, but his own work, I would argue, remains a valuable resource for contemporary writers' access to modernist poetics, refracted through his lens of postmodernism. In that revision, he has been enormously influential.[21] He shows how to respond deeply to the literary tradition without following the Soviet stereotype of praise for Russian classics.[22] Contemporary writers appreciate the sense of freedom in Sinyavsky's writing—we recall that the rubric *Freedom to Pushkin!* often contained his work in the journal *Sintaksis* (a point of contact with Bitov, whose work appeared there as well).

That insistence on freedom includes an ease in writing about the body and its pleasures that turned some older conservatives against him.[23] The presentation of Pushkin as lazing about in bed to toss off his verse effortlessly was a shock: critics have long insisted that the lightness and ease were studied, that they came at the price of great effort.[24] The revisions in manuscripts are thought to prove this point conclusively, as do the later historical writings, with all their efforts in collecting what we would now call oral histories. Sinyavsky, however, sees writing as a pleasure, not as a labored effort (perhaps because, in a labor camp, writing was the very opposite of one's oppressive daily work). The emphasis on pleasure shapes Sinyavsky's canon of Pushkin writings as well: his starting point is not late but early Pushkin, where the verse is often short, occasional, and frivolous. Sinyavsky also writes of later works, but chooses problem pieces, *The Stone Guest* and *Boris Godunov*. In his 1994 essay "Journey to Chernaia Rechka" ("Puteshestvie na Chernuiu rechku"), he focuses on *The Captain's Daughter*, but eschews topics like realism or historical fidelity, instead producing a fantasy on motivation and desire more like the fantastic realism he urged in his other critical writings. *Strolls with Pushkin*, too, typically takes an unusual approach to traditionally beloved texts, as in the explication of the foot digression in *Eugene Onegin*.

Strikingly familiar from others' writings about Pushkin are the themes of love and loss, although they are deftly transformed by Sinyavsky. He tells us that Pushkin taught himself to write, for example, with erotic verse, and his pose as a poet was ever after to be influenced by the lover's need for variability, responsiveness, and speed: "Erotica was his school—above all a schooling in nimbleness."[25] Love is turned into something changeable and experimental, rather than steadfastly loyal, as is more typical of Russia's approach to Pushkin. "Pushkin ran into great poetry on thin erotic legs and created a commotion,"[26] writes Sinyavsky (a sentence that enraged his critics).

Sinyavsky later (in "Journey to Chernaia Rechka") pursued the theme of love in Pushkin in ways that continued to link Pushkin's psychology and creativity with the erotic adventures of his characters. Pushkin was "long tortured by trying to figure out what precisely this strange state of marriage, so enjoyable for everyone, could mean"; this curiosity became a theme of his writing in the early 1830s and, Sinyavsky notes happily, accompanied a substantial creative flowering in Pushkin's work.[27] He continues the parallel between Pushkin's life and his writings when he discusses *The Captain's*

Daughter. The young hero Grinev learns about life by learning about love ("love opens his eyes, it nourishes and breathes life into his mind").[28] His approach to this text, indeed his very choice of it as a template through which to explore a loving relationship to Pushkin and the role of love in one's life, remarkably follows the model of Marina Tsvetaeva in "Pushkin and Pugachev."[29] Like her, he finds it a secret text, a secret that is initiated by its title. And, like Tsvetaeva, he notes the unimportance and passivity of the heroine, Masha Mironova, although he does so in order to establish a contrast to his own wife, Maria Vasilevna, making sure that we note the ironic identity of their names (Masha is the diminutive of Maria).[30] He again resembles Tsvetaeva in taking the occasion to comment on Pushkin's relationship to his wife. But unlike Tsvetaeva, who has complex fears about identifying with Pushkin's wife and with Pushkin, Sinyavsky simply identifies with Pushkin's love for Natalia Nikolaevna, because he in an entirely uncomplicated way says he loves his own wife and muse:

> Pushkin permitted no bad thoughts about his wife. Not because she was beyond reproach, but we ought to remember Natalia Nikolaevna not in some fabric store but in Pushkin's consciousness and in his comprehension of her. He admitted in a letter that he loved her soul more than her face but that he could find no suitable comparison in the world for that face. It was not without his help, one has to say, that she was nicknamed Psyche. She really was Psyche, the soul of Pushkin's soul. She colors the atmosphere of *The Captain's Daughter* with her breath.[31]

Sinyavsky's likeness to Tsvetaeva in writing about Pushkin is easier to see in "Journey to Chernaia Rechka" because it is thematic, but the provocations of *Strolls with Pushkin* are intonationally similar to her "Poems to Pushkin," and he shares her motive for the sharp rhetoric: a wish to criticize the culture of monuments and to argue that it creates misreadings of Pushkin. But the result was a misreading of Sinyavsky himself, perhaps because his essay is more accessible than Tsvetaeva's poetry and thus seemed less an aesthetic artifact, less a careful use of figurative language than her work so obviously is. Sinyavsky's language is figurative, however, as I will illustrate more fully in a moment, but it is also telling that we would find his best antecedent in the work of Tsvetaeva. His fiction and essays owe a tremendous amount to the Russian poetic tradition; indeed Silver Age poetry in particular nourished the growth of Soviet and émigré literature in and after the 1960s. The poetry of Mandelstam, Tsvetaeva, and Khodasevich (Nabokov's particular favorite), among many others, offered a psychological and spiritual authenticity that renewed novel writing in Russian, not unlike the way in which disfavored fiction energized many poets (Dostoevsky and Platonov for, say, Joseph Brodsky and Elena Shvarts). My point is not to ignore the equally valuable influences of poets on poets, fiction writers on fiction, but to emphasize the cross-fertilization that also occurred. In the narrower field of writing about Pushkin, as my choices in this book suggest, it is the poets who have wielded the greatest influence, even on those who write in prose. Sinyavsky remains a valuable and not entirely understood contributor to this tradition, and to the traditions of essay writing in Russian (his beloved predecessor here is Vasily Rozanov), one of the culture's great and underappreciated traditions, a place for generic experimentation and, as Sinyavsky's example shows well, radical innovation with ideas as well.[32]

A Death Beyond Good and Evil

Strolls with Pushkin ends with an interpretation of Pushkin's death that is also experimental. It fueled the reaction to the book as much as the theme of eroticism did. This is not the tragic murder of an innocent victim, as has been paradigmatic since Lermontov's poem "Death of the Poet" in 1837, but instead an elaborately theatrical event where Pushkin played both a directorial and a performing role. The comparison implied in this passage is to a poet like Lord Byron, "forced to take part in a spectacle not even of his own conception":

It was even more impossible for Pushkin to leave this life quietly and unnoticed, as he would have liked. . . . His photogenic personality had already become a topic of gossip. Everyone knew for a fact from his own words—with whom, when, where, and about whom—they were au courant, kept him in their sights, and waited to see what would happen next. "The folk demand strong sensations, for them even an execution is a spectacle." He had to die in public, in the street [because] it was the poet who first started the rumor that drove him to his grave. It was he who organized and arranged everything.[33]

The theatrical metaphor behind these observations was unnerving, since it seemed to suggest that the death, far from being a fated historical event, was a work of art.[34] It helps little that Sinyavsky quotes Pushkin to make his point, since the quoted words have Pushkin irreverently commenting that the passion for popular spectacles is so strong that even executions seem a form of entertainment. Sinyavsky catches Pushkin being impious about "the people" (*narod*), another taboo gesture, and finds his "photogenic personality" a source of entertainment. Entertainment here has a light, frivolous quality, emphasized by the references to gossip, entirely unsuitable from an official perspective to describe the relentless tragedy of the poet's death.

Still worse, the implication that Pushkin created the setting for his death, and thus exercised some agency, tears away at another crucial myth in Russian culture, that there are those who do evil and those who are its victims, and that these are two quite distinct groups. Lermontov first articulated this view in the context of Pushkin's death; in the twentieth century, Akhmatova most strongly repeats it, although some of her work does so in a revisionist manner. Writers and thinkers from all political positions have had a stake in this belief, which is very generally behind much of Russian and Soviet history, including thousands of people who perpetrated an idea like "enemies of the people," and those who wrote in moving testimony against this lie (for example, Alexander Solzhenitsyn). Sinyavsky subverts this division elsewhere, perhaps most memorably at the end of his autobiographical novel, *Goodnight!* (*Spokoinoi nochi*, 1984), when he tells the story of his own entrapment as a collaborator with Soviet spies. The refusal to divide all the world into "us" and "them" follows from his political liberalism, but for many Russians, even some who think they share Sinyavsky's liberalism, it was a shock to see this thinking in the context of Pushkin's death, which was so typically seen as a martyr's death.[35] This rejection of conventional morality was also suited to postmodern thinking, and thus another element in the text that was poorly timed for its first and second generation of readers, but suddenly quite welcome in Russia in the 1990s.

Sinyavsky did something still more extreme when he noted that there were an awful lot of dead bodies in Pushkin's writings, which had the jolly effect of livening things up. Such irreverence about death was disturbing, as was any thought that Pushkin himself might have shared in the irreverence. The sympathetic critic Leonid Batkin found the claim about Pushkin's pleasure in describing "unburied bodies" shocking and false.[36] But Sinyavsky meant to shock: dead bodies do not just energize Pushkin's fiction and drama, he writes; they are the necessary sustenance of Pushkin's own body and soul. He compares Pushkin's creative energies with those of Don Juan. Both suck life from their victims just like a vampire:

> Passion transformed Juan into an angel and Pushkin into Pushkin's creation. But don't get too carried away: what we see before us is a vampire.
>
> Something of the vampire was hidden in so heightened a susceptibility. That's why Pushkin's images have such a luster of eternal youth, of fresh blood, high color, that's why the present manifests itself in his works with such unprecedented force: the whole fullness of existence is crammed into the moment when blood is transfused from random victims into the empty vessel of the one who in essence is no one, remembers nothing, does not love, but only declares to the moment: "You're beautiful! (You're full of blood!) Stop!"—guzzling until he slides off.[37]

Sinyavsky likens Pushkin's capacious imagination to the vampire's passionate need for fresh blood. Heightened receptivity means sucking life out of all that is around. But Sinyavsky principally describes the image itself as vampiric. It absorbs the vital energy of a victim's blood, only to fall back in satisfaction.

The trope of vampirism is an intriguing, significant choice. One anthropologically informed interpretation of vampires suggests that they allow cultures to think through the physiological processes of death and to establish narratives about what happens to dead people.[38] The figure of the vampire also facilitates a fantasy about what happens after death to the human desire for nourishment and for connection to others. Using a similarly anthropological but also rigorously linguistic approach, Jan Perkowski has argued that the vampire becomes a site for all that a culture imagines as evil.[39] Sinyavsky, then, broke several taboos with this reference: he associated Pushkin with the parasitic and murderous behavior of vampires, and with the evil they symbolize. Critics responded, predictably, by turning that image against Sinyavsky himself.[40] Among the implications of this attack was the suggestion that Sinyavsky had no respect for Pushkin, which is demonstrably false (although, admittedly, his respect is based on familiarity, camaraderie, and affection, not blind adulation). But the attack also suggests that Sinyavsky has no respect for Pushkin's death, or for death more generally.

Readers of Sinyavsky know how much he enjoyed grotesque disproportions and fantastic exaggerations, and he could lampoon death as easily as any form of life. (The meditation on whether Gogol was buried alive in *In Gogol's Shade, V teni Gogolia*, 1981, is a good example of this daring pleasure, as are the pertinent passages in *Strolls with Pushkin*.) But it does not follow that Sinyavsky had no respect for death itself, or that he did not know what it is to mourn. Again, it is useful to look ahead to his final Pushkin text. In "Journey to Chernaia Rechka," he sets out for the famous site of Pushkin's duel and also makes it a site of contemplation. It is his own pilgrimage to a Pushkin shrine, repeating the destination of so many Russians before him, a journey he represents as fraught with danger (imaged in the essay's opening pages as a terrifying thunderstorm in Paris, where the journey begins). This essay, which so amply responds to the critics of *Strolls with Pushkin*,[41] contemplates journeys of various kinds—returns to Russia, Pushkin's travels in search of historical material, tourists' journeys in search of diversion, and the metaphorical journey of any person from life to death. Sinyavsky firmly refuses to give up the outrageous imagery from *Strolls with Pushkin*, but some of what is said about death in this text is more sober without being any the less figurative. There is a lovely passage where Sinyavsky imagines himself walking among the gravestones of all the great writers of the past in some fantastic Elysian Fields of philology. He says that he would like to go up to each monument and whisper in the imagined ear of the dead inhabitant, "Wake up! Your time has come!"[42] Pushkin, he says, would surely stand up and eagerly walk across the boundary into Sinyavsky's world, tapping his cane as he walked.

That verbal image beautifully renders the visual image from the cover of both the Russian and the English edition of *Strolls with Pushkin*, where Sinyavsky is seen walking with Pushkin, Sinyavsky shorter and broader, dressed in his rough prison-camp garb, Pushkin in his top hat and frock coat.[43] It affirms the independent spirit of that book, while subtly disproving the criticism of those who claimed that Sinyavsky did not "love" Pushkin (in fact, love is a central topic in "Journey to Chernaia Rechka": Pushkin's love for Natalia Nikolaevna, Grinev's love for Masha, Sinyavsky's love for Maria Rozanova). The images create the fantasy of Pushkin as a living, walking, companion, a fantasy that can be found in countless places in Russian culture of the present as well as the past. Sinyavsky continues that tradition, but he never loses sight of how dramatically he has revised it. In that graveyard scene, for example, he asks rhetorically whether he would take the opportunity to mourn all these dead writers. No, he answers, they are already well mourned—his commitment is to bringing them back to life. As one of his best critics, Jane Grayson, has observed, Sinyavsky "conceives of art as a free play of the imagination which is at one and the same time a powerful instrument of intellectual and spiritual inquiry."[44] How Pushkinian, of course, to emphasize art's freedom but to insist on the serious work that art and the imagination can yet perform. And, following Pushkin's canny awareness of the impact of political forces on his own career, let us not imagine this emphasis on imagination or free inquiry was apolitical: reaction against Sinyavsky was fueled by political and ideological passions, against which he spoke with equal passion.

As a new era begins in Russian culture, Pushkin still has a role to play. Not, Sinyavsky says, as monumental poet or object of blind veneration, but rather as a model for intellectual and imaginative inquiry, as an example of how to forge a writer's life with playfulness and integrity in equal measure. The 1999 anniversary showed that Pushkin could be a pretext for mediocre artistic work and empty slogans, as he was for much of the Soviet period, and that he could serve all too well the needs of a commercial culture. But Sinyavsky himself, a man of gentleness and thoughtfulness in the face of harsh personal experiences and public vilification, offered the hope that Russia could yet produce writers and thinkers worth profound admiration, and he reminded us that the arguments swirling around such figures could be defining moments for the nation's culture. To have had a national poet, he demonstrated, was to have had an inspiring example in the past of how to be a writer in public and in private. One could commemorate him, which is to say remember and honor him, without turning him into a monument.

REFERENCE MATTER

Notes

Unless otherwise noted, all quotations from Pushkin rely on A. S. Pushkin, *Polnoe sobranie sochinenii* (10 vols. Leningrad: Nauka, 1977–79), abbreviated as *PSS* throughout. I have faithfully used suspension points (...) in all the Russian passages, as opposed to ellipses (. . .) for true excisions. For clarity, I have everywhere added "my ellipses" for my omissions. Absent that phrase, the typography is as in the original.

INTRODUCTION

Portions of the Introduction and of Chaps. 2–5 appear in "The Pushkin Myth in Russia," in David M. Bethea and Alexander Dolinin, eds., *Alexander Pushkin: A Handbook* (Madison: University of Wisconsin Press, 2004).
EPIGRAPH: Lidiia Ginzburg, "Iz zapisei 1950–1970-kh godov," *Literatura v poiskakh real'nosti* (Leningrad: Sovetskii pisatel', 1987), p. 331.
  1. Stanislav Rassadin, "Bez Pushkina, ili nachalo i konets garmonii," *Znamia*, no. 6, 1991, pp. 216–29; quoted passage from p. 220; emphasis in the original.
  2. "Coldness and Rationality: An Interview with Elena Shvarts," in Valentina Polukhina, ed., *Brodsky Through the Eyes of His Contemporaries* (London: St. Martin's Press, 1992), pp. 215–36, cited from p. 226.
  3. The quotation is from one of the best essays on Pushkin's death: Irina Surat, "'Da pristupliu ko smerti smelo ...': O gibeli Pushkina," *Novyi mir*, no. 2, 1999, pp. 166–81; cited from p. 166. Surat goes on to explain: "The mighty and tragic finale exposes the genuine weight of his 'effortless' life. But the meaning of the finale remains concealed from us."
  4. Nina Tumarkin, *Lenin Lives! The Lenin Cult in Soviet Russia* (Cambridge, Mass.: Harvard University Press, 1983), p. xii.
  5. An extravagant example of the first approach is found in the claim that Pushkin founded the modern Russian literary language. See esp. V. V. Vinogradov, *Iazyk Pushkina: Pushkin i istoriia russkogo literaturnogo iazyka* (Moscow-Leningrad: Academia, 1935).
  6. For an argument that there has been an evolution from "our" Pushkin to "my" Pushkin, which also castigates inappropriately personal attitudes toward the poet, see O. S. Murav'eva, "Obraz Pushkina: istoricheskie metamorfozy," in M. N. Virolainen, ed., *Legendy i mify o Pushkine* (Petersburg: Akademicheskii proekt, 1994), pp. 109–28; see esp. p. 127.
  7. F. I. Tiutchev, *Sochineniia*, 2 vols. (Moscow, 1980), vol. 1, p. 92.
  8. Adam Phillips, *Promises, Promises: Essays on Psychoanalysis and Literature* (New York: Basic Books, 2001), p. 19. My ellipses.

9. Some of this material is discussed in Chaps. 3 and 4. See also Jeffrey Brooks, "Russian Nationalism and Russian Literature: The Canonization of the Classics," in Ivo Banac et al., eds., *Nation and Ideology: Essays in Honor of Wayne S. Vucinich* (Boulder, Colo.: Westview, 1981), pp. 315–34; and Marcus C. Levitt, "Pushkin in 1899," and Greta N. Slobin, "Appropriating the Irreverent Pushkin," in Boris Gasparov, Robert P. Hughes, and Irina Paperno, eds., *Cultural Mythologies of Russian Modernism: From the Golden Age to the Silver Age* (Berkeley: University of California Press, 1992), pp. 184–203, 214–30.

10. For an essay that catches the urgency of this intonation but offers remarkably well-informed and sane arguments, see Irina Surat, "Biografiia Pushkina kak kul'turnyi vopros," *Novyi mir*, no. 2, 1998, pp. 177–95.

11. The discussion of myth here draws on anthropological as well as humanistic treatments of the topic, including Thomas A. Sebeok, ed., *Myth: A Symposium*, (Bloomington: Indiana University Press, 1965); Roland Barthes, *Mythologies*, tr. Annette Lavers (New York: Hill & Wang, 1972); and the cultural semiotics work of Yuri Lotman and others in the Tartu school, well exemplified among American Slavists by Irina Reyfman, *Vasilii Trediakovsky: The Fool of the "New" Russian Literature* (Stanford, Calif.: Stanford University Press, 1990); and Irina Paperno, *Chernyshevsky and the Age of Realism: A Study in the Semiotics of Behavior* (Stanford, Calif.: Stanford University Press, 1988). This is not the same thing as Roman Jakobson's notion of an individual poet's "mythology," as in his study of Pushkin's "sculptural myth" (taken up below in the analysis of Pushkin's monument poem).

12. Reidar Th. Christiansen, "Myth, Metaphor, and Simile," in Sebeok, ed., *Myth*, pp. 64–80; quotation from p. 65.

13. As in Roland Barthes's *Mythologies*.

14. An excellent statement of the view of Pushkin's "elastic ambiguity" (to use Roman Jakobson's term) remains Victor Erlich, *The Double Image: Concepts of the Poet in Slavic Literatures* (Baltimore, Md.: Johns Hopkins University Press, 1964), pp. 16–37. See also pp. 1–15, for an astute contextualization of the image of the poet in Romantic and post-Romantic culture and its classical antecedents.

15. My argument, which sees the idea of the nation as a community imagined by its inhabitants, has been shaped by Benedict Anderson, *Imagined Communities: Reflections on the Origin and Spread of Nationalism* (London: Verso, 1983). See esp. p. 32, for a discussion of a scene in a Filipino novel, *Noli me tangere*, where an event is described as simultaneously experienced by an entire nation.

16. Commenting not on the political, but on the cultural and historical, significance of Pushkin's burial, Irina Surat writes, "Pushkin's funeral, although perhaps not unique in our barbaric history, is, for a great artist and national genius, nonetheless unbelievable." Surat, "'Da pristupliu ko smerti smelo,'" p. 173.

17. Others have commented on the juxtaposition of the jubilee celebration with Stalin's Terror, among them Marcus Levitt, *Russian Literary Politics and the Pushkin Celebration of 1880* (Ithaca, N.Y.: Cornell University Press, 1989), pp. 162–66. The poet Alexander Kushner noted that "the arrests and tortures of 1937 took place even as Pushkin's poetry resounded from every stage." Kushner, "Protivostoianie," in *Apollon v snegu* (Leningrad: Sovetskii pisatel', Leningradskoe otdelenie, 1991), p. 505.

18. L. Rassovskaia and S. Agranovich, "Vokrug Pushkina," *Oktiabr'*, no. 6, 1990, pp. 189–96; see p. 196.

19. One might also contend that monuments have displaced the Russians' capacity to imagine Pushkin as having a body in the first place. As Natalia Ivanova eloquently argues, thinkers may still not have overcome a rhetoric that disembodies Russianness. Natal'ia Ivanova, "Russkii vopros," *Znamia*, no. 1, 1992, pp. 191–204. Ivanova also suggests that the myth of love for country displaces any actual erotic imagination in its fiercest proponents (pp. 200ff).

20. An edition of *Gavriiliada* was prepared by Boris Tomashevsky and published by Pushkin House in 1921. Long unavailable, it was reissued by the Moscow publishing house Khudozhestvennaia literatura in 1991. I follow Tomashevsky (p. 46) in dating the poem 1821, not 1822, as had been commonly believed.

21. Elena Rabinovich, "Kto?—Pushkin?," in *Ritorika povsednevnosti: Filologicheskie ocherki* (St. Petersburg: Izdatel'stvo Ivana Limbakha, 2000), pp. 123–31, argues that this expression refers to the Moscow monument to Pushkin.

22. Osip Mandelstam, "Pushkin and Scriabin," in Mandelstam, *The Complete Critical Prose and Letters*, ed. Jane Gary Harris (Ann Arbor, Mich.: Ardis Press, 1979), p. 90. A revised edition of this volume appeared in 1997. For the Russian original, see Osip Mandel'shtam, *Sobranie sochinenii*, 3 vols., ed. G. P. Struve and B. A. Filippov (New York: Inter-Language Literary Associates, 1971), vol. 2, pp. 313–19. The phrase was the title of the obituary for Pushkin in the journal *Literaturnye pribavleniia k Russkomu Invalidu*, no. 5 (Jan. 30, 1837), p. 48. It is thought to have been written by V. F. Odoevsky, even though the journal's editor, A. A. Kraevsky, was a close enough acquaintance of Pushkin's to have helped to carry his coffin out of his house. See L. A. Chireiskii, *Pushkin i ego okruzhenie* (Leningrad: Nauka, 1988), pp. 212, 302.

23. Apollon Grigor'ev, "Vzgliad na russkuiu literaturu so smerti Pushkina," in V. V. Kunin, ed., *Svetloe imia Pushkina*, pp. 70–95; quotation on p. 78.

24. Andrew Wachtel, *The Battle for Childhood: Creation of a Russian Myth* (Stanford, Calif.: Stanford University Press, 1990); Gregory Freidin, *A Coat of Many Colors: Osip Mandelstam and the Mythologies of Self-Creation* (Berkeley: University of California Press, 1987).

25. Levitt, *Russian Literary Politics*; Gasparov et al., ed., *Cultural Mythologies of Russian Modernism*; R. A. Gal'tseva, ed., *Pushkin v russkoi filosofskoi kritike* (Moscow: Kniga, 1990); M. N. Virolainen, "Kul'turnyi geroi Novogo vremeni," in Virolainen, ed., *Legendy i mify o Pushkine* (St. Petersburg: Akademicheskii proekt, 1994), pp. 321–41. See also S. A. Kibal'nik, *Pushkin i sovremennaia kul'tura* (Leningrad: Znanie, 1989), a short study of the cult of Pushkin at the end of the Soviet era.

26. Paul Debreczeny, *Social Functions of Literature: Alexander Pushkin and Russian Culture* (Stanford, Calif.: Stanford University Press, 1997).

27. E. I. Vysochina, *Obraz, berezhno khranimyi: Zhizn' Pushkina v pamiati pokolenii* (Moscow: Prosveshchenie, 1989); O. Murav'eva, "Pushkinist, sovremennaia professiia," *Voprosy literatury*, no. 2, 1987, pp. 75–109. See also L. Rassovskaia and S. Agranovich, "Vokrug Pushkina"; Stanislav Rassadin, "Pochitaem Pushkina," *Oktiabr'*, no. 6, 1988, pp. 181–89; Rassadin, "Bez Pushkina"; and Svetlana

Boym, "Inscriptions on the Poet's Monument," *Harvard Review*, vol. 1, no. 1 (Fall 1986), pp. 64–81.

28. Many such essays and books are mentioned in later chapters; among the most recent is Angela Brintlinger, *Writing a Usable Past: Russian Literary Culture, 1917–1939* (Evanston, Ill.: Northwestern University Press, 2000). An interesting work in progress is Monika Greenleaf's study of Gogol, Tsvetaeva, and Nabokov. As reviewed by Abram Reitblat, M. V. Zagidullina, *Pushkinskii mif v kontse XX veka* (Cheliabinsk: Cheliabinskii gosudarstvennyi universitet, 2001), also seems an important if limited treatment of the Pushkin myth (I have not been able to read the book). See Reitblat, *Novoe literaturnoe obozrenie*, no. 59 (2003), pp. 600-603.

29. "The Prophet" and "I have built myself a monument" have also often been discussed together in support of the claim that Pushkin was not a partisan of "pure art." See *Pushkin: Itogi i problemy izucheniia* (Moscow-Leningrad: Nauka, 1966), p. 114.

30. Major studies of Pushkin that emphasize this approach include William Mills Todd III, *Fiction and Society in the Age of Pushkin* (Cambridge, Mass.: Harvard University Press, 1986); Boris Gasparov, *Poeticheskii iazyk Pushkina kak fakt istorii russkogo literaturnogo iazyka*, Wiener Slawistischer Almanach, vol. 27 (1992); and Monika Greenleaf, *Pushkin and Romantic Fashion: Fragment, Elegy, Orient, Irony* (Stanford, Calif.: Stanford University Press, 1995).

31. For a lucid account of Pushkin's poems about the poet, see Victor Erlich, "Sacred Play," in Erlich, *Double Image*, pp. 16–37. The poems ranged from exhortation and advice to an imagined poet to conversations between poet and bookseller, and poet and crowd. There are exalted descriptions of the poet transformed by inspiration or, in the long, lovely fragment "Autumn" ("Osen'," 1833), of the poet awaiting and then welcoming the muse. Especially inspiring for later poets was "The Poet" ("Poet," 1827). All of the poems are well known, and many come close to being contradictory. These differences cannot be explained away by Pushkin's own changes over time: in 1836, the same year as Pushkin's calmly Horatian vision of the future discussed below, he also wrote "(From Pindemonte)," "(Iz Pindemonti)," which repeats the themes of popular indifference and poetic independence found in "To the Poet" ("Poetu," 1830).

32. This is not to say that the theme is entirely absent. See Lensky's death in *Eugene Onegin* and the lyric poem "André Chénier." For a brief but sensitive treatment of Pushkin's image of the poet's death, see Surat, "'Da pristipliu ko smerti smelo,'" pp. 168–74. An insightful discussion of the treatment of death more generally in Pushkin's poetry is S. A. Kibal'nik, "Smert' u A. S. Pushkina kak poeticheskaia i religioznaia tema," in V. A. Kotel'nikov, ed., *Khristiianskvo i russkaia literatura* (St. Petersburg: Nauka, 1994), pp. 157–84. On the influence of Pushkin's death on the theme of the poet's death in Russian literature, see E. S. Lebedeva, "'… Slukh obo mne …': Smert' poeta kak siuzhet russkoi liriki i narodnoi legendy," *Pushkinskaia epokha i khristianskaia literatura*, no. 2, 1994, pp. 66–73, which also discusses Pushkin's death as popular legend.

33. A possible early exception is "The Youth's Coffin" ("Grob iunoshi," 1821); the poem was long taken as a lament for his lyceum friend Nikolai Korsakov, who died in Italy. As with Delvig, Pushkin seemed to be writing about a specific death. The poem was not, though, about the death of a poet, although it bespeaks an anx-

iety over who will remember the dead youth that reminds one of topoi typically found in poems on dead poets. On such poems as a genre, see Lawrence Lipking, *The Life of the Poet: Beginning and Ending Poetic Careers* (Chicago: University of Chicago Press, 1981), pp. 138–79.

34. For an argument that Küchelbecker's "Prorochestvo" ("Prophecy," 1822) was also an intermediary text, see S. Kibal'nik, *Khudozhestvennaia filosofiia Pushkina* (St. Petersburg: RAN, 1993), pp. 73–75.

35. Several other translations are available. See, for example, Alan Myers, *An Age Ago: A Selection of Nineteenth-Century Russian Poetry* (New York: Farrar, Straus & Giroux, 1983), p. 37; and D. M. Thomas, *The Bronze Horseman: Selected Poems of Alexander Pushkin* (New York: Viking, 1982), p. 57.

36. *PSS*, vol. 2, p. 304.

37. The operating table appears in Gennadii Rossosh's discussion of the poem in "Pushkin i svoboda: Prevratnosti i otkroveniia," *Oktiabr'*, no. 2, 1996, pp. 168–76; see p. 174.

38. S. A. Fomichev, former head of the Pushkin Commission in Pushkin House, states the official position in describing "The Prophet" as Pushkin's first answer to the Decembrist uprising. See Fomichev, *Poeziia Pushkina: Tvorcheskaia evoliutsiia* (Leningrad: Nauka, 1986), p. 113. His source is M. A. Tsiavlovskii, ed., *Letopis' zhizni i tvorchestva Pushkina 1799–1826*, 3d ed. (Leningrad: Nauka, 1991[1951]), p. 631. We lack the textual material to resolve questions surrounding supposed original versions of "The Prophet," including strophes that were said to judge Nicholas as the murderer of the Decembrists. See D. D. Blagoi, *Tvorcheskii put' Pushkina* (Moscow-Leningrad: Izd. AN SSSR, 1950), pp. 533–42, 579; the discussion in *Pushkin: Itogi i problemy izucheniia*, pp. 202, 214–15; and (definitively, in my view), Viktor Esipov, "'K ubiitse gnusnomu iavis' ... ,'" *Voprosy literatury*, no. 1, 1998, pp. 205–25.

39. Most readers see "The Prophet" as referring to a spiritual crisis. A central work of criticism on the poem is Vladimir Solov'ev, "Znachenie poezii v stikhotvoreniiakh Pushkina," variously reprinted in Russia after 1987, for example, in R. A. Gal'tseva, ed., *Pushkin v russkoi filosofskoi kritike* (Moscow: Kniga, 1990), pp. 41–91. Solovyov emphasizes the "crossroads" at which the poet stands to indicate a moment of spiritual choice, and he denies that the prophet derives from the Koran, as others claimed. See also B. A. Vasil'ev, *Dukhovnyi put' Pushkina* (Moscow: Sam & Sam, 1994), pp. 103–10.

40. The lack of a specific prophecy is also emphasized by Solov'ev, "Znachenie poezii."

41. Any affinity between the prophet and his audience would be denied by Maxim Gorky, who used the last line of "The Prophet" to argue that Pushkin's fate was that of any great man who must live among petty, vulgar, and self-seeking people. See Gor'kii, *Istoriia russkoi literatury* (Moscow: Goslitizdat, 1939), p. 102, cited in *Pushkin: Itogi i problemy izucheniia*, p. 115.

42. In 1929, Valery Briusov offered a powerful demonstration of the poem's phonic brilliance, but only after strangely claiming that it initially seems aurally unimpressive. V. Ia. Briusov, "Prorok. Analiz stikhotvoreniia," *Moi Pushkin: Stat'i, issledovaniia, nabliudeniia*, ed. N. K. Piksanov (Munich: Fink, 1970), pp. 279–97.

43. N. V. Gogol', *Sobranie sochinenii*, 7 vols. (Moscow: Khudozhestvennaia literatura, 1984–86), vol. 6, p. 56.

44. Dostoevsky's speech is available in English in Sona Stephan Hoisington, ed., *Russian Views of Pushkin's 'Eugene Onegin'* (Bloomington: Indiana University Press, 1988), pp. 56–67. Dostoevsky calls Pushkin a "prophetic phenomenon" and (in a different phrase, a "singular manifestation of the Russian spirit") uses Gogol as his point of departure (p. 56). For the Russian original of Dostoevsky's speech, see F. M. Dostoevskii, *Polnoe sobranie sochinenii*, 30 vols. (Leningrad: AN SSSR, 1972–90), vol. 26, pp. 136–49.

45. Solovyov also stresses this aspect of the poem in his reading (in "Znachenii poezii").

46. Also noted in Rossosh, "Pushkin i svoboda," p. 175, and elsewhere.

47. Mikhail Epshtein, "Like a Corpse I Lay in the Desert," in *Mapping Codes: A Collection of New Writing from Moscow to San Francisco* (*Five Fingers Review* 8/9) (San Francisco: Five Fingers Press, 1990), pp. 162–67, esp. 166–67.

48. For an English translation, see Joseph P. Clancy, tr., *The Odes and Epodes of Horace* (Chicago: University of Chicago Press, 1960), p. 154. The ode that begins "Exegi monumentum" is III, 30. Assumptions about Pushkin's supposedly deep knowledge of Horace have been reassessed in Rabinovich, "Eshche raz o Pushkine i Goratsii," in *Ritorika povsednevnosti*, pp. 141–55.

49. A sign of the poem's status is the appearance of parodies. For a selection, see Viktor Shenderovich, "Iz tsikla parodii 'Ia pamiatnik sebe vozdvig ... ,'" *Voprosy literatury*, no. 6, 1995, pp. 358–60.

50. Surat, "'Da pristupliu ko smerti smelo,'" p. 172.

51. For another translation, see Thomas, *Bronze Horseman*, p. 92.

52. *PSS*, vol. 3, p. 340.

53. For a comparison of all source texts and subsequent imitations, see M. P. Alekseev, *Stikhotvorenie Pushkina "Ia pamiatnik sebe vozdvig..."* (Leningrad: Nauka, 1967). It is a fitting testimony to the importance of this poem in the canon that it has an entire book devoted to it.

54. Subsequent poets and critics have echoed the ironical politics of joining these two "Alexanders." See, for example, Osip Mandelstam's poem "I have not sought in the blossoming moments" ("Ia ne iskal v tsvetushchie mgnoven'ia," 1917), briefly discussed by Boris Gasparov, "Introduction," in Gasparov et al., *Cultural Mythologies of Russian Modernism*, p. 11.

55. Renate Lachman, *Memory and Literature: Intertextuality in Russian Modernism*, tr. Roy Sellars and Anthony Wall (Ann Arbor: University of Michigan Press, 1997), p. 209. Without reference to Lachman, Murianov briefly disputes the relevance of Alexandria to the name choice (unconvincingly, to my mind) but adds an intriguing further possibility: Nicholas I spent time in a dacha named Aleksandria, which would make the epithet a double reference to two tsars, Nicholas and Alexander. See M. F. Mur'ianov, "Iz nabliudenii nad tekstami Pushkina," *Moskovskii pushkinist*, vol. 1 (1995), pp. 122–50, esp. p 129.

56. In an essay in 1919, Mikhail Gershenzon argued that this evaluation was what the people would care about, not Pushkin. He contrasted the praise Pushkin valued (l. 8: "so long as . . . / Lives even a single poet") with the vulgar appreciation

of the masses who take a utilitarian and moralizing view of poetry (stanza 4). See M. Gershenzon, *Mudrost' Pushkina* (Ann Arbor, Mich.: Ardis Press, 1983), pp. 49–68. Gershenzon underestimated the rhetorical complexity of these lines, but he rightly predicted the dominant interpretation of the poem for the Soviet period.

57. So accepted is the interpretation that it appears in the very brief commentary in the Academy edition. See *PSS*, vol. 3, p. 469.

58. V. Nepomniashchii, "Uderzhivaiushchii teper': fenomen Pushkina i istoricheskii zhrebii Rossii," *Novyi mir*, no. 5, 1996, pp. 162–90.

59. Much work has been done on this particular epithet and, since the collapse of the Soviet Union, on other Russian Orthodox and biblical references in the poem. See M. Mur'ianov, "Dva etiuda o slovoupotreblenii Pushkina: I. Epitet nerukotvornyi," *Voprosy literatury*, no. 4, 1989, pp. 206–14; Irina Surat, *Zhizn' i lira* (Moscow: Knizhnyi sad, 1995), pp. 150–58; and V. V. Ivanov, "K issledovaniiu arkhaizmov v *Pamiatnike* Pushkina," in *Lotmanovskii sbornik* (Moscow: Izdatel'stvo "ITs-Garant," 1995), pp. 415–19.

60. Compare the comments of Lachmann, *Memory and Literature*, p. 212, on the iconoclastic nature of the sign produced in this poem.

61. Ol'ga Sedakova, "'Ne smertnye tainstvennye chuvstva': O khristianstve Pushkina." Paper presented at the Andreevskie chteniia, Bibleisko-bogoslovskii institut Sv. Apostola Andreiia, Moscow, Dec. 12–13, 1999. A version titled "V glubine tainstvennykh chuvstv: Pushkinskaia nauka poezii—eto nauka chtit' svobodu" appeared in *Nezavisimaia gazeta, Kulisa NG*, March 26, 1999, pp. 9, 13. For an English translation, see Olga Sedakova, "'Non-Mortal and Mysterious Feelings': On Pushkin's Christianity," in Joe Andrew and Robert Reid, eds., *Two Hundred Years of Pushkin III: Pushkin's Legacy* (Amsterdam: Rodopi, 2003).

62. Writing about this poem in 1999, the poet Sergei Gandlevsky commented on the epithet "liubeznyi" as a sign of the poet's humility. See his "Nichei Pushkin," in Gandlevskii, *Poriadok slov* (Ekaterininburg: Izd-vo "U-Faktoriia," 2000), p. 374.

63. Vl. Dal', *Tolkovyi slovar' zhivogo velikorusskogo iazyka*, 4 vols. (Moscow: Russkii iazyk, 1979), vol. 2, p. 282. Compare *Slovar' iazyka Pushkina*, 4 vols. (Moscow: Gosudarstvennoe izdatel'stvo natsional'nykh i inostrannykh slovarei, 1957), vol. 2, p. 518, where four meanings are adduced from Pushkin's writings—(1) predupreditel'nyi, uchtivyi; (2) liubimyi, dorogoi, priiatnyi; (3) dorogoi, milyi; (4) vozliublennyi, liubimyi—and this example falls into the second category.

64. The placement of the poem as a summation of the poet's life and works, which would seem an accident of Pushkin's biography, is also, as it were, borrowed from Horace, who placed this poem last in his third and final volume of odes. Pushkin of course did not live to see the poem published, but it comes late in any chronological sequence of his writings, having been written in August 1836.

65. M. F. Mur'ianov, "Iz nabliudenii," p. 126.

CHAPTER 1

An earlier version of this chapter appeared as "The Law, the Body and the Book: Three Poems on the Death of Pushkin," *Canadian-American Slavic Studies*, vol. 23, no. 3 (Fall 1989), pp. 281–311.

EPIGRAPH: V. K. Kiukhel'beker, "19 oktiabria 1837 goda," *Izbrannye proizvedeniia*, 2 vols. (Moscow-Leningrad: Sovetskii pisatel', 1967), vol. 1, pp. 295–96.

1. Tributes to Pushkin's greatness began as soon as he died. For a survey of 19th-century poems about him, see R. V. Iezuitova, "Evoliutsiia obraza Pushkina v russkoi poezii XIX veka," *Pushkin: Issledovaniia i materialy*, vol. 5 (1967), pp. 113–39. An excellent anthology of 19th-century poems to Pushkin is V. Kallash, ed., *Russkie poety o Pushkine: sbornik stikhotvorenii* (Moscow: tip. G. Lissnera i A. Geshelia, 1899). Poems from the first third of the 20th century through the 1937 jubilee are included in the anthology S. Fomin, ed., *Pushkin v russkoi poezii* (Moscow: Khudozhestvennaia literatura, 1937). The Soviet period is covered fully in *Rossii pervaia liubov': pisateli o Pushkine, poety—Pushkinu* (Moscow: Sovetskii pisatel', 1989).

2. V. A. Manuilov and L. N. Nazarova, *Lermontov v Peterburge* (Leningrad: Lenizdat, 1984), pp. 112–27; I. S. Chistova, "'Smert' poeta,'," in V. A. Manuilov, ed., *Lermontovskaia entsiklopediia* (Moscow: Sovetskaia entsiklopediia, 1981), pp. 511–13. The latter includes an excellent list of scholarly works on the poem. Among the essays that have appeared since Chistova's article, the work of David Powelstock deserves special mention. See his "Living into Language: Mikhail Lermontov and the Manufacturing of Intimacy," in Monika Greenleaf and Stephen Moeller-Sally, eds., *Russian Subjects: Empire, Nation, and the Culture of the Golden Age* (Evanston, Ill.: Northwestern University Press, 1998), pp. 297–324; and his monograph in progress, *The Framing of Mikhail Lermontov: Poetics and the Semiotics of Behavior*. Also of considerable interest is V. M. Markovich, "Mif o Lermontove na rubezhe XIX–XX vekov," in Markovich, *Pushkin i Lermontov v istorii russkoi literatury* (St. Petersburg: Izdatel'stvo S.-Peterburgskogo universiteta, 1997), pp. 157–84.

3. The point has been made by many, including G. P. Makogonenko, "Naslednik Pushkina," in Makogonenko, *Lermontov i Pushkin* (Leningrad: Sovetskii pisatel', 1987), pp. 3–12. On p. 10, Makogonenko quotes an apt comment from Alexander Herzen: "The pistol shot that killed Pushkin awakened the soul of Lermontov."

4. M. Iu. Lermontov, *Sobranie sochinenii*, 4 vols. (Moscow: Khudozhestvennaia literatura, 1975), vol. 1, pp. 23–25. I have capitalized "God" ("Bozhii"). The epigraph found in some versions (beginning "Otmshchen'ia, gosudar', otmshchen'ia!") is of doubtful provenance (see p. 516). For a verse translation of the entire text, see *From the Ends to the Beginning: A Bilingual Anthology of Russian Verse*, max.mmlc.northwestern.edu/~mdenner/Demo/texts/death_poet.html, a version from which I have borrowed a number of locutions; and David Rigsbee's translation in Christine Rydel, ed., *The Ardis Anthology of Russian Romanticism* (Ann Arbor, Mich.: Ardis Press, 1984), p. 88.

5. Lermontov's use of the epithet "nevol'nik chesti" in the first line of the poem has reference to Pushkin, who had applied it to the prisoner in his long poem *The Prisoner of the Caucasus* (*Kavkazskii plennik*, 1823). Makogonenko, *Lermontov i Pushkin*, p. 6, corrects the *Lermontovskaia entsiklopediia* on this point. The lines beginning "Like that other singer, unknown but dear" ("Kak tot pevets, nevedomyi, no milyi"), recall both the death of Lensky in *Eugene Onegin* and, more significant for this poem, the death of the French poet André Chénier, the inspiration for a long elegy by Pushkin in 1825. Lermontov also uses the death of Chénier as an emblem of an unjust society's destruction of a poet of genius; see V. B. Sandomirskaia, "'An-

drei Shen'e,'" in N. V. Izmailov, ed., *Stikhotvoreniia Pushkina 1820–1830-kh godov* (Leningrad: Izdatel'stvo "Nauka," 1974), pp. 31–33. For an excellent account of Lermontov's echoes of various poets and a new reading of one source, see Walter Vickery, "Kyukhel'beker's *On the Death of Chernov* and Lermontov's *The Death of a Poet: The Foreigners*," in Julian W. Connolly and Sonia I. Ketchian, eds., *Studies in Russian Literature in Honor of Vsevolod Setchkarev* (Columbus, Ohio: Slavica, 1984), pp. 255–73.

6. In part, Lermontov's poem is making the same point as Alexander Blok's famous assessment of 1921: "And it absolutely was not d'Anthès's bullet that killed Pushkin. He was killed by the absence of air." Blok, "O naznachenii poeta," in Blok, *Sobranie sochinenii*, 6 vols. (Leningrad: Khudozhestvennaia literatura, 1982), vol. 4, p. 419. Like Lermontov, Blok opposes Pushkin's holy gifts to the murderous demands of the mob.

7. In his poem about Pushkin's death, Evgeny Baratynsky also used the terms of slander and verbal abuse, referring to literary critics who misunderstood and unfairly dismissed Pushkin's late work. The poem is "When your voice, O poet" ("Kogda tvoi golos, o poet," 1841), discussed in Stephanie Sandler, "Baratynskii, Pushkin, and *Hamlet*: On Mourning and Poetry," *Russian Review*, vol. 42, no. 1 (Jan. 1983), pp. 73–90.

8. Thus Lermontov shapes the discourse about Pushkin's death with the view that words have a potentially deadly impact in the world. His choice proved ironic, since his poem produced an order for his exile; his life was to end in a duel within four years.

9. For a provocative discussion of how moral discourse separates itself from history, see Jacques Derrida, "Devant la loi" (tr. Avital Ronell), in Alan Udoff, ed., *Kafka and the Contemporary Critical Performance: Centenary Readings* (Bloomington: Indiana University Press, 1987), pp. 128–49.

10. Robert M. Cover, "Violence and the Word," *Yale Law Journal*, vol. 95 (1986), pp. 1601–29. Cover's comments on the importance of martyrdom in understanding the violence hidden in the law are especially appropriate to my reading of Lermontov. He writes: "Precisely because it is so extreme a phenomenon, martyrdom helps us see what is present in lesser degree whenever interpretation is joined with the practice of violent domination. Martyrs insist in the face of overwhelming force that if there is to be continuing life, it will not be on the terms of the tyrant's law" (p. 1604). The language of martyrdom is found throughout "Death of the Poet," both in the descriptions of the poet's persecutions (the crown of thorns is the most obvious instance, suggesting as it does the death of Jesus) and in the avowed belief, in the final stanza, in divine retribution and in a higher law than that of the "tyrants."

11. I have been influenced here by Elaine Scarry, *The Body in Pain: The Making and Unmaking of the World* (New York: Oxford University Press, 1985), which was also important to Cover's essay "Violence and the Word." See also Scarry, ed., *Literature and the Body: Essays on Populations and Persons*, Selected Papers from the English Institute 1986 (Baltimore, Md.: Johns Hopkins University Press, 1988), pp. vii–xxvii.

12. Lermontov might well have used the duel's injuries to Pushkin's body as his

point of departure in "Death of the Poet," for he knew Pushkin had been mortally wounded. As Chistova, "'Smert' poeta,'" p. 513, and Manuilov and Nazarova, *Lermontov v Peterburge*, p. 112, note, Lermontov was being treated for a cold between the date of the duel and the date of Pushkin's death (Jan. 26–29, 1837, o.s.) by Dr. N. F. Arendt, who was also in attendance on Pushkin. Both add that Lermontov would have known of Pushkin's condition in any case, since it was the talk of Petersburg.

13. For a comparison of the letter to S. L. Pushkin with the poem to Pushkin, see V. N. Toporov, "Iz issledovanii v oblasti poetiki Zhukovskogo," *Slavica Hierosolymitana*, vol. 1 (1977), pp. 33–38. From lexical similarities in the poem and the letter, Toporov infers that Zhukovsky was working toward developing a unified literary lexicon. For the notes that Zhukovsky made for himself, see P. E. Shchegolev, *Duel i smert' Pushkina*, 4th ed. 2 vols. (Moscow: Kniga, 1987), vol. 2, pp. 10–12; or *Pushkin v vospominaniiakh sovremennikov*, 2 vols. (Moscow: Khudozhestvennaia literatura, 1974), vol. 2, pp. 339–41.

14. After a first line in perfectly rendered anapestic pentameter, Zhukovsky switches to the elegiac distich, and uses it with a freedom that is unusual for his poetry.

15. V. A. Zhukovskii, *Sochineniia*, ed. I. M. Semenko. 3 vols. (Moscow: Khudozhestvannaia literatura, 1980), vol. 1, pp. 316–17. When the poem was first published, in the newspaper *Russkii* (1867), the editors added the title "To the Deceased" ("Pokoiniku"). Since at least the 1959 four-volume edition of Zhukovsky, Soviet editors put that title and their own choice, "A. S. Pushkin," in brackets to indicate that they were not part of the original text. See Iezuitova, "Evoliutsiia obraza Pushkina," p. 126, n. 27.

16. Sarah Webster Goodwin and Elisabeth Bronfen, eds., *Death and Representation* (Baltimore, Md.: Johns Hopkins University Press, 1993), p. 12.

17. Maurice Blanchot, *The Space of Literature*, tr. Ann Smock (Lincoln: University of Nebraska Press, 1982).

18. See Zhukovsky's memoir in *Pushkin v vospominaniiakh sovremennikov*, vol. 2, pp. 353–54. Compare the recollections of Pushkin's second in the duel, Konstantin Danzas, who noted that Pushkin and Zhukovsky had a long conversation, alone, shortly before Pushkin died. Ibid., pp. 332–33. See also R. V. Iezuitova, *Zhukovskii v Peterburge* (Leningrad: Lenizdat, 1976), p. 267.

19. The birthday coincidence is noted by A. I. Turgenev in his diary and by Zhukovsky in his letter to Sergei Lvovich Pushkin. *Pushkin v vospominaniiakh sovremennikov*, vol. 2, pp. 176, 354. For the letter to Dmitriev, see Zhukovskii, *Sochineniia*, vol. 3, p. 526.

20. See I. Eiges, "Pushkin i Zhukovskii," in D. D. Blagoi and V. Ia. Kirpotin, eds., *Pushkin. Rodonachal'nik novoi russkoi literatury* (Moscow-Leningrad: Izdatel'stvo Akademii nauk, 1941), pp. 195–96, 199; and R. V. Iezuitova, "Zhukovskii i Pushkin (K probleme literaturnogo nastavnichestva)," in D. S. Likhachev, R. V. Iezuitova, and F. Z. Kanunova, eds., *Zhukovskii i russkaia kul'tura* (Leningrad: Izdatel'stvo "Nauka," 1987), pp. 229–43. Eiges asserts that Zhukovsky and Pushkin grew into a more mature relationship, although he does not describe how it came about; Iezuitova carefully traces their complicated friendship through letters, poetry, and memoirs.

21. See I. Semenko, *Zhizn' i poeziia Zhukovskogo* (Moscow: Khudozhestvennaia literatura, 1975), pp. 19–22. Semenko sees Zhukovsky's behavior as the older, protective, and instructing male as an imitation of the modes of behavior found in sentimental literature, although she also mentions possible "Freudian" patterns in his behavior.

22. The most important crises were Pushkin's plea for a foreign visa in order to escape from exile in 1825; his attempt to retire from government service in 1834; and his reactions to the anonymous, insulting letters of 1836–37 that led to the fatal duel. The crises, and Zhukovsky's efforts on Pushkin's behalf, may be followed in their correspondence, reprinted in *Perepiska A. S. Pushkina*, 2 vols. (Moscow: Khudoszhestvennaia literatura, 1982), vol. 1, pp. 86–133.

23. Ibid., p. 97.

24. For a good discussion of the differences in their poetry, see I. M. Semenko, "Pushkin i Zhukovskii," *Filologicheskie nauki*, no. 4, 1964, pp. 118–30.

25. William Mills Todd III, *Fiction and Society in the Age of Pushkin* (Cambridge, Mass.: Harvard University Press, 1986), pp. 106–9.

26. His secrecy was motivated in part by fears that friends would intervene to prevent the duel, as had occurred in November 1836. Pushkin also apparently wished to keep Zhukovsky out of a scandal that could damage the reputation of someone so highly regarded at court. For their interpretations of Pushkin's actions, see the memoirs of Danzas and Zhukovsky in *Pushkin v vospominaniiakh sovremennikov*, vol. 2, pp. 332–33, 339–55.

27. See Jahan Ramazani, *Poetry of Mourning: The Modern Elegy from Hardy to Heaney* (Chicago: University of Chicago Press, 1994), pp. 1–31.

28. I. Brodskii, "Ob odnom stikhotvorenii," in *Sochineniia Iosifa Brodskogo*, 8 vols. projected (St. Petersburg: Pushkinskii fond, 1999–), vol. 5, pp. 142–87, translated into English as "Footnote to a Poem," in Brodsky, *Less Than One* (New York: Farrar, Straus & Giroux, 1986), pp. 195–267; see especially the opening pages. See also Lawrence Lipking, *The Life of the Poet* (Chicago: University of Chicago Press, 1981), pp. 140ff; and Peter Sacks, *The English Elegy: Studies in the Genre from Spenser to Yeats* (Baltimore, Md.: Johns Hopkins University Press, 1985), pp. 1–37.

29. *Pushkin v vospominaniiakh sovremennikov*, vol. 2, pp. 355–68.

30. Ibid., p. 353.

31. Zhukovskii, *Sochineniia*, vol. 1, p. 249. It is worth recalling that Zhukovsky initiated conventions for the sentimentalization of death in Russian culture with his translation of Gray's "Elegy Written in a Country Churchyard" (1801; he retranslated the poem in 1839). On the importance of his translation for Russian literary culture, see V. N. Toporov, "'Sel'skoe kladbishche' Zhukovskogo: K istokam russkoi poezii," *Russian Literature*, vol. 10 (1981), pp. 207–86; and Catherine Ciepiela, "Reading Russian Pastoral: Zhukovsky's Translation of Gray's Elegy," in Stephanie Sandler, ed., *Rereading Russian Poetry* (New Haven, Conn.: Yale University Press, 1999), pp. 31–57.

32. Zhukovsky is relatively specific about the religious vision he supposed the dying Pushkin to have had in the letter to S. L. Pushkin, as opposed to the poem, where he contents himself with asking vaguely what Pushkin sees, having described it oxymoronically as a "deep, lofty thought." An argument could be made that Pushkin's later lyrics grew more religious, though many of those poems were not

known to Zhukovsky until he began sorting through Pushkin's papers. For an excellent discussion of the later lyrics' pattern of intertextuality, see Sergei Davydov, "Poslednii liricheskii tsikl Pushkina: opyt rekonstruktsii," *Revue des Études Slaves*, vol. 59 (1987), pp. 151–71. The theme of Pushkin's Christian beliefs has become an important topic among post-Soviet Pushkin scholars, as discussed in the Introduction. See, for example, V. Nepomniashchii, "Setovaniia i nadezhdy," *Voprosy literatury*, no. 4, 1989, pp. 189–90.

33. Ramazani, *Poetry of Mourning*, p. 4.

34. See the memoirs of V. A. Nashchokina and V. I. Dal', in *Pushkin v vospominaniiakh sovremennikov*, vol. 2, pp. 207–8, 225, 230. See also Iezuitova, *Zhukovskii v Peterburge*, pp. 265–70; and Shchegolev, *Duel i smert' Pushkina*, vol. 1, pp. 236–37.

35. In a shortened form that omitted any reference to the duel, Zhukovsky published it as "Pushkin's Last Minutes" ("Poslednie minuty Pushkina"); this detailed description of the time between Pushkin's duel and the moment of his death, many images of which coincide with the poem to Pushkin, was published in 1837 in the fifth volume of Pushkin's journal *The Contemporary (Sovremennik)*. A fuller but still incomplete text of the letter appeared in 1864, allowing words like *duel* and *wound*. Further nuances were added by Pavel Shchegolev in his *Duel i smert' Pushkina*; see esp. vol. 1, pp. 177–220. This sequence is significant for Pushkin's image in 20th-century Russian literature. Shchegolev's book, which went through three editions between 1916 and 1928, had an enormous impact on readers and provided much new information about the duel.

36. V. V. Kunin, ed., *Druz'ia Pushkina: Perepiska; Vospominaniia; Dnevniki*, 2 vols. (Moscow: Izdatel'stvo Pravda, 1984), vol. 1, p. 615: "Like other materials by Zhukovsky, this letter is one of the original sources for all information about Pushkin's death. In addition this is an artistic document, whose equal is rare among the memoir and epistolary sources about Pushkin."

37. Such loyalties were quite in keeping with Zhukovsky's sentiments. For example, he wrote that Pushkin asked him to tell the tsar that he was sorry to be dying; his will would have been to serve his tsar ("byl by ves' ego"). The tsar responded with conciliatory, generous sentences; and Zhukovsky concludes by citing Pushkin's answer, again as if verbatim, an exclamation of how consoled he is and an extended wish for the tsar's long and happy reign. Zhukovskii, *Sochineniia*, vol. 3, p. 505. He also notes, "His Highness the Emperor received news from Dr. Arendt (who checked on the sick man six times a day and several times in the night); Her Highness the Grand Princess, who had so loved Pushkin, sent me several notes, in response to which I provided a detailed report to Her Highness about the course of the disease. Such concern was touching, but natural; natural in a Sire, to whom the nation's glory was dear." Ibid., p. 507.

38. Rostopchina sets her encounters with Pushkin in the daily life of men and women of their class; her descriptions were regarded as trivializations by Vissarion Belinsky. See Belinskii, "Stikhotvoreniia grafini E. Rostopchinoi," in V. G. Belinskii, *Polnoe sobranie sochinenii*, 20 vols. (Moscow: Izdatel'stvo Akademii nauk, 1953–59), vol. 3, p. 458: "The entire poetic corpus of Countess Rostopchina, so to speak, is limited to the ball: even her meeting and acquaintance with Pushkin, as something

that occurred at a ball, is essentially a description of the ball, which would have been more appropriate to a letter or essay in prose than to poetry."

39. Evdokiia Rostopchina, *Stikhotvoreniia. Proza. Pis'ma*, ed. Boris Romanov (Moscow: Sovetskaia Rossiia, 1986), pp. 95–96.

40. Rostopchina makes sure the reader will know this by adding a footnote to her poem, identifying the man she sees as "Alexander Sergeevich Pushkin."

41. Rostopchina, *Stikhotvoreniia*, p. 95.

42. Ibid., pp. 92–93.

43. As executor of Pushkin's literary estate, Zhukovsky came into possession of a blank notebook that Pushkin had ordered. He wrote nine poems in the notebook or, as he called it, album; the poem about Pushkin discussed above is the last. Inscriptions in albums were typically light, flattering bits of verse, often commenting on the occasion of their inscription or on the owner of the album. Frequently impromptu, or apparently improvised, album verses could be serious and even melancholy, yet they were almost always self-consciously occasional. Zhukovsky's album poems, for example, show the range of possibilities: he addressed one to the daughter of the historian Nikolai Karamzin centering on her beautiful soul; in another he wrote a remembrance of happy times to the sister of Masha Protasova; and in still another, he told the fable of a "beautiful death." See Zhukovskii, *Sochineniia*, vol. 1, pp. 275–78, 283. Pushkin's album poems, by comparison, include everything from the obscene and juvenile to serious elegiac verse. For a fine history and analysis of album poetry in this period, see Justyna Beinek, "The Album in the Age of Russian and Polish Romanticism: Memory, Nation, Authorship." Ph.D. dissertation, Harvard University, 2001.

44. Margaret Homans, *Women Writers and Poetic Identity: Dorothy Wordsworth, Emily Bronte, and Emily Dickinson* (Princeton, N.J.: Princeton University Press, 1980), p. 29.

45. Barbara Heldt, *Terrible Perfection: Women and Russian Literature* (Bloomington: University of Indiana Press, 1987), pp. 104–15 (Heldt does not discuss Rostopchina's poetry, but gives extended analyses of works by Anna Bunina and Karolina Pavlova); Catriona Kelly, *A History of Russian Women's Writing, 1829–1992* (Oxford: Oxford University Press, 1994), pp. 19–78, 93–107 (again, with little mention of Rostopchina); Wendy Rosslyn, *Anna Bunina (1774–1829) and the Origins of Women's Poetry in Russia* (Lewiston, N.Y.: Edwin Mellen Press, 1997); Judith Vowles, "The 'Feminization' of Russian Literature: Women, Language, and Literature in Eighteenth-Century Russia," in Toby W. Clyman and Diana Greene, eds., *Women Writers in Russian Literature* (Westport, Conn.: Praeger, 1994), pp. 35–60 (this essay, although on the 18th century, is pertinent to the study of 19th-century Russian women poets; see also the essay by Diana Greene in the same volume, pp. 95–110); Judith Vowles, "The Inexperienced Muse: Russian Women and Poetry in the First Half of the Nineteenth Century," in Adele Barker and Jehanne Gheith, eds., *A History of Russian Women's Writing* (Cambridge, Eng.: Cambridge University Press, 2002), pp. 62–84.

46. As cited in Rostopchina, *Stikhotvoreniia*, pp. 412–13.

47. V. Khodasevich, "Grafinia E. P. Rostopchina," in Khodasevich, *Sobranie sochinenii*, 4 vols. (Moscow: Soglasie, 1996), vol. 2, pp. 17–39; see p. 24. Khoda-

sevich, who sees Rostopchina's poetry as a lyrical diary, provides a great deal of biographical data. For further information on her life, see the introduction by Boris Romanov to Rostopchina, *Stikhotvoreniia*, pp. 5–27; the essay by her brother, Dmitri Sushkov, in E. Rostopchina, *Sochineniia*, 2 vols. (Petersburg: Tip. I. N. Skorokhodova, 1890), vol. 1, pp. iii–xlviii; and the fascinating collage of documents, letters, and memoirs appended to E. P. Rostopchina, *Talisman* (Moscow: Moskovskii rabochii, 1987), pp. 261–311.

48. E. A. Gan, "Sud sveta," in V. Uchenova, ed., *Dacha na Petergofskoi doroge: Proza russkikh pisatel'nits pervoi poloviny XIX veka* (Moscow: Sovremennik, 1986), p. 152. Gan makes these words doubly ironic by putting them into the mouth of a "perspicacious" and "great" male poet. "Sud sveta" was first published in 1840.

49. Rostopchina, *Stikhotvoreniia*, p. 134. As Rostopchina's popularity waned, she wrote bitterly in a letter to Mikhail Pogodin (1853): "I am a woman writer perhaps, but first and foremost I am a woman, rather empty but very kind, open, a bit bristling from excessive displays of openness." Cited in Rostopchina, *Talisman*, p. 300.

50. Representations of women's social position in Rostopchina's work merit separate treatment. She can praise the glittering world of the ball and hinge her preference on being a "mere woman" (in "The Temptation" ["Iskushen'e"], 1839); she can fill a woman's life with sadness worthy of exile (in "Remembrance" ["Vospominan'e"], 1839). Several poems value women's contemplative moments: "Stars at Midnight" ("Zvezdy polunochi," 1840); "Unfinished Embroidery" ("Nedokonchennoe shit'e," 1839); "At the Window on a Moonlit Night" ("U okna, v lunnuiu noch'," 1840). Rostopchina conveys a complex view of Russian noblewomen; she is particularly insightful into the strange combinations of passivity and moral authority, of social grace and preference for solitude that were expected of intelligent and sensitive aristocratic women.

51. *PSS*, vol. 7, p. 38. The aphorism comes from Pushkin's "Extracts from Letters, Thoughts and Observations" ("Otryvki iz pisem, mysli i zamechaniia," 1827). The published selections also contained a provocative comment on women's prudery as the sign of an impure imagination (p. 43).

52. At least one woman poet, Anna Gotovtsova (d. 1871), took offense at these lines, and perhaps at similar sentiments found in Pushkin's poem "Women" ("Zhenshchiny," 1827). Gotovtsova's criticism comes after 21 lines of high praise for "the glory of our age" in her poem "To A. S. Pushkin" ("A. S. Pushkinu"). Her reluctance to scold Pushkin is both a sign of how women poets had been taught timidity and a sign of how they used irony to express their rage: "Your judgment is unfair—/ But we do not dare to reprimand you: / We know how to forgive genius—/ Silence will express the reproach." For the Russian original, see N. V. Bannikov, ed., *Russkie poetessy XIX veka* (Moscow: Sovetskaia Rossiia, 1979), p. 78. The poem was published in *Northern Flowers* (*Severnye tsvety na 1829 g.*), with a response from Pushkin. He professed not to know what he had done to arouse her wrath in "Response to A. I. Gotovtsova" ("Otvet A. I. Gotovtsovoi," 1828); see *PSS*, vol. 3, p. 83.

53. To give one example of a text with complicated modulations of tone: "A lady was saying to me that if a man starts to talk to her about empty things as if adapt-

ing himself to the weak powers of feminine comprehension, then he instantly uncovers to her eyes his ignorance of women. As a matter of fact, is it not ridiculous to consider women subordinate beings in comparison to us, when they so often astound us with the speed of their comprehension and subtlety of emotions and perceptions? This is particularly odd in Russia, where Catherine II reigned, and where women in general are better educated, read more, follow the course of events in Europe more than do we, the 'proud' (so named, God knows why)." *PSS*, vol. 8, p. 67. The passage comes from his *Table-talk*.

54. Letter, S. N. Karamzina to A. N. Karamzin, Dec. 30, 1836, in N. V. Izmailov, ed., *Pushkin v pis'makh Karamzinykh 1836–1837 godov* (Moscow-Leningrad: Izdatel'stvo Akademii nauk, 1960), p. 149. (For the French original, see p. 289.)

55. Letter, E. P. Rostopchina to P. A. Pletnev, April 21, 1841, excerpted in Rostopchina, *Talisman*, p. 278. In a letter to Victor Hugo meant to accompany Rostopchina's poem to Hugo, E. P. Meshchersky wrote that she was "one of the most beautiful women of Petersburg society and one of the best Russian poets." Ibid., p. 274.

56. On Rostopchina's salons in Petersburg (1836–45) and Moscow (1847–58), see M. Aronson and S. Reiser, *Literaturnye kruzhki i salony* (St. Petersburg: Akademicheskii proekt, 2001 [1921]), pp. 219–24.

57. Rostopchina, *Talisman*, p. 301.

58. Sergei Ernst, "Karolina Pavlova i gr. Evdokiia Rostopchina," *Russkii bibliofil*, no. 6, 1916, p. 22.

59. Rostopchina, "Gde mne khorosho" (1838), in *Talisman*, p. 49.

CHAPTER 2

Part of this chapter was published in an earlier version as "Remembrance in Mikhailovskoe," in Boris Gasparov, Robert P. Hughes, and Irina Paperno, eds., *Cultural Mythologies of Russian Modernism: From the Golden Age to the Silver Age* (Berkeley: University of California Press, 1992), pp. 231–50.

EPIGRAPH: John R. Gillis, ed., *Commemoration: The Politics of National Identity* (Princeton, N.J.: Princeton University Press, 1994), p. 17.

1. In Moscow alone, there are six plaques, varying from simple markers with engraved text ("Pushkin frequented this house where his uncle, the poet V. L. Pushkin, lived") to more elaborate medallions and sculptures in bas-relief. See O. Peskov, N. Nizkovskaia, and L. Adadurova, *Pamiat, vysechennaia v kamne: Memorial'nye doski Moskvy* (Moscow: Moskovskii rabochii, 1978), pp. 158–60. For the list of 291 monuments, see A. D. Gdalin, G. A. Drovenikov, and I. L. Popeliukher, "Pamiatniki A. S. Pushkinu (Materialy k annotirovannomu katalogu)," *Vremennik pushkinskoi komissii*, no. 25 (1993), pp. 74–92. The catalogue includes foreign monuments, and those destroyed or rebuilt. Some places that figured in his writings now memorialize Pushkin, like the "Pushkin cliff" ("Pushkinskaia skala") near Alushta in Crimea, from which it is imagined that he bid farewell to the south as described in his poem "To the Sea" ("K moriu," 1824), or the station master's house in Vyra, outside Petersburg, recreated as a museum about horse and carriage travel, but based on the posting station of the literary character Samson Vyrin in "The Station Master" ("Stantsionnyi smotritel'," 1830).

2. As Andrei Bitov has said about the name Pushkin, one can say about Boldino and Mikhailovskoe that they are not just names, but words to which something distinct and knowable is linked in our consciousness. Their symbolic value has largely taken them over. Bitov, "Bitva," *Zhizn' v vetrenuiu pogodu* (Leningrad: Khudozhestvennaia literatura, 1991), p. 571.

3. *Pushkinskie mesta Rossii: Putevoditel'* (Moscow: Profizdat, 1984), p. 157; V. Bozyrev, *Po Pushkinskomu zapovedniku* (Moscow: Profizdat, 1977), p. 7. An expanded version is Bozyrev, *Muzei-zapovednik A. S. Pushkina* (Leningrad: Lenizdat, 1979), which I cite below for its more explicit patriotism.

4. See K. A. Timofeev, "Mogila Pushkina i selo Mikhailovskoe," *Russkaia starina*, vol. 98 (May 1899), pp. 267–76; and S. Bobin, "Pushkinskie 'Torzhestva' v Mikhailovskom v 1899," *V nashi dni*, no. 3–4, 1937, pp. 74–81. One visitor claimed that few brave souls made it to Mikhailovskoe before 1914. See "Garris," *Ugolok Pushkina* (Moscow-Petrograd: Gos. izdatel'stvo, 1923), p. 53. Garris, the pseudonym of the journalist Maria Kallash (1866–1918), writes that Mikhailovskoe "had become still further removed from the center and more forgotten in the past decades, because the estate house was empty, life had deserted it. It seems as if you'll never get there, never reach it. In fact it was rare that anyone set off for Mikhailovskoe, and few made it there. After the noisy celebrations of the Centennial Jubilee, when there were flags, wreaths, and garlands here, speeches were heard, and the surging crowd made noise from every side, the Pushkin nook was again buried in silence, and it has been forgotten. Visitors more often head for the monastery to pray, whereas Mikhailovskoe (or, as it is called here, Zuevka or Zuevo), is almost never asked about." Despite such claims, a number of written accounts about trips to Mikhailovskoe survive, in striking contrast to Boldino, on which there are virtually no published or archival sources before the Soviet period.

5. In a fascinating study of early-19th-century American tourism, John Sears has linked the emerging interest in sites like Niagara Falls, Yosemite, and Yellowstone with rising national self-awareness. See John F. Sears, *Sacred Places: American Tourist Attractions in the Nineteenth Century* (Oxford: Oxford University Press, 1989).

6. Keats's house in Hampstead was saved from destruction in 1920–21; the Wordsworth Trust (Dove Cottage) was founded in 1890; Wordsworth House in Cockermouth was bequeathed to the National Trust in 1939 after a campaign that began in 1896. Christina M. Gee, *Keats House, Hampstead* (London: Jarrold Publishing, 1990); *Wordsworth House, Cumbria* (London: National Trust, 1985).

7. On the affinities between religious motifs and myths of Pushkin, see Paul Debreczeny, *Social Functions of Literature: Alexander Pushkin and Russian Culture* (Stanford, Calif.: Stanford University Press, 1996), pp. 223–30. I also recall a comment by Boris Kozmin, the director of Petrovskoe, when asked whether the name of the town Pushkinskie gory (Pushkin Hills) was likely to be changed back to its pre-Soviet name of Sviatye gory (Holy Hills): "Why bother? The names mean the same thing in our culture; Pushkin means holy." Conversation, Oct. 12, 1991, in Petrovskoe.

8. G. Ia. Esipovich, *Na rodine poeta A. S. Pushkina. Putevye ocherki* (Simferopol': tip. S. B. Sinani, 1902), p. 5. The internal quotations come from Pushkin's

poem "… Once again I visited" ["…Vnov' ia posetil"], 1835); it was common for visitors to cite Pushkin's poetry to articulate and justify their emotions on seeing this hallowed place.

9. P. M. Ustimovich, "Po Pushkinskim mestam," *Istoricheskii vestnik*, no. 109 (March 1908), p. 1036. Evgeny Shreder begins similarly: "To spend some time in the 'Pushkin Nook,' in Mikhailovskoe, Trigorskoe, in Sviatye Gory, in the places closely associated with the name of the great poet, had been my long-standing wish." Evgenii Shreder, "V Pushkinskom ugolke," *Voskhody*, Sept. 1907, p. 665.

10. Robert Burns's poems taught his readers to see a shared history in the Scottish landscape (as did the novels of Sir Walter Scott), and it is this status as a national bard that likely prompts the reference to Burns. It reminds us of the importance of foreign models for constructing national poets' shrines. Wordsworth's Lake District is the more pertinent model for Pushkin's Mikhailovskoe: in 1810 Wordsworth was already imagining it as a "national property." David McCracken, *Wordsworth and the Lake District* (Oxford: Oxford University Press, 1984), p. 4.

11. Timofeev, "Mogila Pushkina," p. 271.

12. See F. A. Vasil'ev-Ushkuinik, *Pushkinskie ugolki Pskovskoi gubernii* (Moscow: Izd. T-va "V. V. Dumnov, n-ki br. Salaevykh," 1924), pp. 62–63. The fate of the three trees was reported elsewhere. For example, the journal *Niva* reported in 1913: "But the poet's prediction did not come true: carelessness and ignorance had their way with Pushkin's old friends. In the 1880s, the sad bare hull of one of the famous Pushkin pines still jutted out of the earth, but later it was removed, and only a small cutting from it is still preserved in Mikhailovskoe." "Pushkinskie mesta," *Niva*, no. 26 (1913), p. 510. A 1901 visitor was taken past the site of the pines, and he took comfort from the young grove of pines now there; see Esipovich, *Na rodine poeta A. S. Pushkina*, pp. 34–35.

13. V. V. Timofeeva-Pochinkovskaia, "Mikhailovskoe zatochen'e (Stranitsy iz nedavnego proshlogo)," 1924, in L. S. Ginzburg, Kollektsiia al'bomov, Manuscript Division, Saltykov-Shchedrin Public Library, St. Petersburg, f. 886, op. 2, no. 2, ll. 8–11; citation from l. 9.

14. Ibid., l. 10.

15. Ibid.

16. Ibid., ll. 10–11.

17. *Pushkinskii dom pri Rossiiskoi Akademii Nauk. Istoricheskii ocherk i putevoditel'* (Leningrad: Rossiiskaia Akademiia Nauk, 1924), pp. 157–58.

18. V. V. Timofeeva-Pochinkovskaia, "Sredi pamiatnikov bylykh vdokhnovenii," *Vestnik literatury*, no. 1 (25), 1921, pp. 16–17.

19. "Pushkinskii ugolok," *Vestnik literatury*, no. 1 (25), 1921, p. 8, and reported elsewhere. Some histories of Mikhailovskoe omit this information. Bozyrev, *Po Pushkinskomu zapovedniku*, p. 8, for example, lists the destructive fires of 1918 alongside the fire of 1908 (or, in some records, 1907) as if both had natural causes. *Pushkinskie mesta Rossii*, p. 182, reported the loss of the billiard set and carriage in the 1908 fire. This rewriting of history is discussed below.

20. Letter, Mariia Nikolaevna Stoiunina to Nestor Aleksandrovich Kotliarevskii, March 31, 1918, Manuscript Division, Pushkin House (IRLI), f. 244, op. 30, no. 7.

21. Vasil'ev-Ushkuinik, *Pushkinskie ugolki*, p. 52.

22. Letter, Elizaveta Aleksandrovna Sadova to Mariia Iakovlevna Maikhrovskaia, Aug. 7, 1921, Manuscript Division, Saltykov-Shchedrin Public Library, St. Petersburg, f. 666, op. 2, ed. khr. 24, Arkhiv Sadovykh A. I., E. A., M. A. My ellipses. Sadova also wrote about a famous contemporary, the jurist A. F. Koni (whose 1921 speech about Pushkin is considered in Chap. 3) in her memoirs. Her archive includes an essay about the disrepair of Koni's grave (1946–47).

23. Ibid., p. 2. My ellipses.

24. Ibid., pp. 3–4. My ellipses.

25. Near the end of her letter, Sadova writes: "A. F. Koni often said that we are a people who have no 'yesterday,' that we lack 'gratitude as well as curiosity.' ... At Pushkin's grave, in the lands of Mikhailovskoe that were so dear to his heart, these sad words were proven true. Both his children and society felt indifference to Pushkin's memory." Ibid., p. 4.

26. P. M. Ustimovich, "Pushkinskie ugolki," *Zapiski peredvizhnogo teatra*, no. 68 (Jan. 1, 1924), p. 6.

27. Lunacharsky's essay "Na mogile Pushkina" was published in *Krasnaia gazeta*, Sept. 6–8, 1926 (no. 206–8), evening ed. Substantial portions appear in F. V. Volkov, "Lunacharskii v Pushkinskom zapovednike," in *A. V. Lunacharskii: Issledovaniia i materialy* (Leningrad: Nauka, 1978), pp. 233–39.

28. Volkov, "Lunacharskii," pp. 235–36.

29. A. M. Gordin, *Pushkin v Mikhailovskom* (Leningrad: Lenizdat, 1989), pp. 419–20.

30. Bozyrev, *Po Pushkinskomu zapovedniku*, p. 12.

31. Ibid., pp. 12–13; Gordin, *Pushkin v Mikhailovskom*, pp. 428–29.

32. Most recent publications about Mikhailovskoe include descriptions of Trigorskoe and Petrovskoe, where fuller information about their histories and present state can be found. See, for example, Bozyrev, *Muzei-zapovednik A. S. Pushkina*, pp. 143–210.

33. The poetry festival now occurs in dozens of venues, with Mikhailovskoe as the featured site. For an account of one, see "'Ia chislius' po Rossii,'" *Literaturnaia gazeta*, June 4, 1986 (no. 23 [5089]), pp. 1, 4 (p. 4 lists the itinerary for that year's festival).

34. "Rech' V. P. Semenova-Tian-Shanskogo v sele Mikhailovskom," *Voprosy literatury*, no. 6, 1979, pp. 154–58; quotation from p. 155. Semyonov-Tian-Shansky also gives an alternative to Timofeeva's claim that Switzerland's William Tell National Preserve was the relevant model: he names Ulysses S. Grant Park in the United States (p. 156). Presumably he refers not to Grant Park in Chicago but to Grant's Tomb in New York. Ulysses S. Grant also signed the federal bill creating the world's first national park (Yellowstone) in 1872, according to the entry on national parks in the *Encyclopedia Americana*, 30 vols. (Danbury, Conn.: Grolier, 1982), vol. 19, pp. 766–81. Among many other possible models is Stratford-upon-Avon, with its association with the English national poet.

35. "Rech' V. P. Semenova-Tian-Shanskogo v sele Mikhailovskom," p. 156. My ellipses.

36. Ibid., p. 157.

37. A more moderate approach to the act of preservation was taken by the director of Petrovskoe, Boris Kozmin. See his "Muzei-usad'ba 'Petrovskoe' (Novyi dom i staryi park)," in V. A. Koshelev, ed., *Pushkin i drugie* (Novgorod: Novgorodskii gos. universitet, 1997), pp. 108–12.

38. "Rech' V. P. Semenova-Tian-Shanskogo v sele Mikhailovskom," p. 157.

39. These dates are gleaned from *Pushkinskii dom*, pp. 5–40, 156–63; *50 let Pushkinskogo doma* (Moscow-Leningrad: Izd. AN SSSR, 1956), pp. 5–16; and N. M. Volovich, *Pushkinskie mesta Moskvy i Podmoskov'ia* (Moscow: Moskovskii rabochii, 1979).

40. See S. L. Abramovich and N. I. Goller, "Iz istorii sozdaniia muzeia-kvartiry A. S. Pushkina na Moike (1922–1927)," *Muzeinoe delo v SSSR*, issue 27 (1977), pp. 131–41.

41. O. A. Iatsenko has updated the early history of the museum; see "Posledniaia kvartira A. S. Pushkina: sud'ba muzeia i ego sozdatelia," in *Muzei v sovremennoi kul'ture: sbornik nauchnykh trudov* (St. Petersburg: Akademiia kul'tury, 1997), pp. 120–27. The essay is especially valuable for its history of the arrest of the curator M. D. Beliaev and the subsequent destruction of his exhibit; as Iatsenko points out, the emphasis on emotion so important to Beliaev was replaced in the 1930s with an emphasis on facts and information.

42. Timofeeva-Pochinkovskaia, "Mikhailovskoe zatochen'e," l. 11.

43. Michel de Certeau has argued that histories of cultural institutions and most other discourses of authority exclude reference to the conditions that produced them. See his "History: Science and Fiction," in de Certeau, *Heterologies: Discourse on the Other*, tr. Brian Massumi (Minneapolis: University of Minnesota Press, 1986), pp. 200–207.

44. Most scholars agree that "To the Sea" was begun in Odessa and finished in Mikhailovskoe. See, for example, N. L. Stepanov, *Lirika Pushkina* (Moscow: Sovetskii pisatel', 1974), p. 277. Boris Tomashevsky, however, claims that the whole poem was written in Mikhailovskoe. Tomashevskii, *Pushkin: Kniga vtoraia* (Moscow-Leningrad: Izd. AN SSSR, 1956), p. 9. In either case, all or part of the poem works as a remembered farewell to the sea.

45. *PSS*, vol. 8, p. 17.

46. Fuller information about Pushkin's trip to Mikhailovskoe from September to mid-October 1835 can be gleaned easily from his letters to his wife during that period. He went in order to write, but he had trouble setting to work. Scholars have surmised that he worked on *Egyptian Nights* (*Egipetskie nochi*) during these six weeks.

47. Most readings of the poem emphasize its philosophical content, seen as a perception of nature's law of constant change and renewal. For an authoritative account of this reading, see Ia. L. Levkovich, "Vnov' ia posetil ... ," in N. V. Izmailov, ed., *Stikhotvoreniia Pushkina 1820–1830-kh godov* (Leningrad: Nauka, 1974), pp. 306–22, esp. p. 308.

48. *PSS*, vol. 3, p. 313.

49. Ibid.

50. This process also receives a nice formulation in Levkovich, "Vnov' ia posetil ... ," p. 310: "Instead of his own memories, a memory about the process of

remembrance in the past rises forth. This create a temporal perspective, a sense of depth, and an uninterrupted chain of the stages in one's life."

51. The very poetic language is also a kind of recollection. Compare "Remembrance" ("Vospominanie," 1809), by Konstantin Batiushkov, an important model for Pushkin in matters of genre, tone, and rhetoric. In that poem, he, too, remembers himself in the act of remembering. See K. N. Batiushkov, *Opyty v stikhakh i proze* (Moscow: Nauka, 1977), p. 210.

52. *PSS*, vol. 3, p. 314.

53. I have put aside the obvious question of how the image of a future visitor is a poetic convention. Compare similar endings, for example, in Pushkin's "To Ovid" ("K Ovidiiu," 1821) and Baratynsky's gloomy and revisionist "Planting a Wood" ("Na posev lesa," 1842?). In a fuller treatment of the poetic tradition surrounding " ... Once again I visited," relevant texts would include Pushkin's other poems about landscapes suffused with recollections, such as "Remembrances in Tsarskoe Selo" ("Vospominaniia v Tsarskom Sele," 1814). There is a brilliant reading of this poem, particularly in the context of its antecedents, in Andrew Kahn, "The Poetics of Reminiscence in Pushkin: A Reading of Four Elegies." Senior Honors Thesis, Amherst College, Amherst, Mass., 1984.

54. One reading of the poem goes so far as to suggest two differently perceiving consciousnesses in the text, relying on Bakhtin to turn this into an interesting argument about lyric polyphony. See E. V. Slinina, "Vospominanie v lirike A. S. Pushkina (1826–1836)," *Boldinskie chteniia*, 1987, pp. 41–50, esp. pp. 46–47.

55. A similar observation about verbs is made in S. E. Shatalov, "Obrazets filosofskoi liriki (O stikhotvorenii Pushkina 'Vnov' ia posetil')," *Uchenye zapiski Tadzhikskogo gosudarstvennogo universiteta*, vol. 19, no. 2 (1958), pp. 25–36; as cited in Levkovich, "Vnov' ia posetil," p. 311.

56. I offer a detailed reading of this poem in *Distant Pleasures: Alexander Pushkin and the Writing of Exile* (Stanford, Calif.: Stanford University Press, 1989), pp. 25–39.

57. *Pushkinskie mesta Rossii*, p. 158. The identical text appears in an expanded two-volume version, *Pushkinskie mesta. Putevoditel'* (Moscow: Profizdat, 1988), vol. 1, p. 225. In these guides, the elliptical reference to earlier fires recurs when rebuilding in 1949 is discussed. See *Pushkinskie mesta. Putevoditel'*, p. 178; and Bozyrev, *Muzei-zapovednik A. S. Pushkina*, p. 36.

58. Bozyrev, *Muzei-zapovednik A. S. Pushkina*, p. 12. A similar formulation appears in S. S. Geichenko, *Pushkinogor'e* (Moscow: Molodaia gvardiia, 1981), p. 16. Geichenko fails to mention any destruction or fire at Mikhailovskoe before the Second World War, implying in a terse statement that the Germans were wholly responsible for the damage: "The original house was not preserved. After the Hitlerites destroyed the museum built in 1937, the house was rebuilt in its historical form in 1949" (p. 18).

59. A. M. Savygin, *Pushkinskie gory*, 3d ed. (Leningrad: Lenizdat, 1989), p. 23.

60. In a conversation in Amherst, Mass., in the mid-1980s, Mikhail Nikolaev suggested to me that it was not the Germans but the Soviet Army's bombardments that did the most damage (military maps from the Pskov-area battles proved this to him).

61. See Bozyrev, *Muzei-zapovednik A. S. Pushkina*, pp. 15–17; *Pushkinskie mesta Rossii*, p. 160; S. S. Geichenko, *U lukomor'ia* (Leningrad: Lenizdat, 1981), pp. 142, 196–99; Geichenko, *Pushkinogor'e*, pp. 81–99, which includes photographs of war damage, liberating Soviet troops, and a map of the line of defense.

62. The prose in the museum guides is bland. See Bozyrev, *Muzei-zapovednik A. S. Pushkina*, pp. 36–52, for example (and compare the comments about Boldino later in this chapter). In a parody of this reticence to delineate between copies and authentic displays, Sergei Dovlatov's fictional hero in *The Preserve* (*Zapovednik*, 1983) presses the curator on the issue; the best she can do is point to the trees. See Dovlatov, *Zapovednik* (Ann Arbor, Mich.: Ermitazh, 1983), p. 34.

63. My argument about memorials and temporality has profited from Gary Saul Morson, "The Reader as Voyeur: Tolstoi and the Poetics of Didactic Fiction," *Canadian-American Slavic Studies*, vol. 13, no. 4 (1979), pp. 465–80.

64. Geichenko, *U lukomor'ia*, pp. 393–95. The same metaphor appears in Iu. Osipov, "Vechnost' Mikhailovskogo," in Osipov, ed., *'Minuvshee menia ob"emlet zhivo ... ,'* (Moscow: Sovremennik, 1989), pp. 113–26; see p. 113. Geichenko worked for over 30 years as the director, or the *khranitel'*, of Mikhailovskoe. He originated many of the ideas that structure Mikhailovskoe, added to its collection, and wrote about the place extensively. On his efforts, see Osipov, "Vechnost' Mikhailovskogo"; L. Ageeva and V. Lavrov, *Khranitel'* (Leningrad: Sovetskii pisatel', 1980); and, for a poetic appreciation, Mikhail Dudin, "Pis'mo v Mikhailovskoe," in *Rossii pervaia liubov'* (Moscow: Sovetskii pisatel', 1989), pp. 420–21.

65. Stephen J. Greenblatt, ed., *Allegory and Representation*, Selected Papers from the English Institute, 1979–80, n.s. no. 5 (Baltimore, Md.: Johns Hopkins University Press, 1981), p. viii.

66. I use allegory in the sense developed in Paul de Man, *Allegories of Reading* (New Haven, Conn.: Yale University Press, 1979).

67. Well argued in Iakov Gordin, *Pravo na poedinok* (Leningrad: Sovetskii pisatel', 1989).

68. John Rennie Short, *Imagined Country: Society, Culture, and Environment* (London: Routledge, 1991), pp. 28–39; quotation from p. 31.

69. Ibid.

70. For useful summaries of the pastoral mode, see Alex Preminger, ed., *The Princeton Encyclopedia of Poetics* (Princeton, N.J.: Princeton University Press, 1974), p. 603–6; and J. A. Cuddon, *A Dictionary of Literary Terms* (Garden City, N.Y.: Doubleday, 1977), pp. 476–82. See also *Literaturnyi entsiklopedicheskii slovar'* (Moscow: Sovetskii entsiklopediia, 1987), p. 59, for a short entry on "Bucolic poetry" by M. L. Gasparov.

71. William Empson, *English Pastoral Poetry* (New York: Norton, 1938), p. 11.

72. See N. A. Savvin, *Boldino i A. S. Pushkin* (Nizhnii Novgorod: Izd. Nizhegorodskoi arkheologo-etnologicheskoi komissii, 1929), pp. 14ff; A. I. Zvezdin, *O Boldinskom imenii A. S. Pushkina v Nizhegorodskoi gubernii i o prebyvanii v nem poeta v 1830-kh godakh* (Nizhnii Novgorod, 1912), pp. 5–7; and Arsenii D'iakonov, "Boldino," *Literaturnyi sovremennik*, no. 1, 1937, pp. 197–204.

73. According to "Pushkinskie ugolki," *Leningrad*, June 6, 1924 (no. 11 [27]), p. 7, everything had been destroyed, but nearly all popular writing about Pushkin's

Boldino cites the minutes and official written record of the 1918 meeting, where a decision was made to protect the house and its park. See, for example, *Muzei-zapovednik A. S. Pushkina v s. Bol'shom Boldine (v pomoshch' ekskursantu)* (Bol'shoe Boldino, 1954), p. 10; Iu. Levina, *Pushkinskoe Boldino* (Gorky: Volgo-Viatskoe knizhnoe izd-vo, 1974), p. 64; and *Pushkinskie mesta: Putevoditel'*, vol. 1, p. 316.

74. T. N. Kezina, *Boldino* (Gorky: Volgo-Viatskoe knizhnoe izdatel'stvo, 1989), p. 3.

75. The question of whether the house at Boldino had been built on the foundation of the original house was answered when it was gutted and reconstructed. Excavation in the 1980s showed that portions of the frame dated from 1830s, the 1840s, and the 1870s. See ibid., pp. 4–5. Tamara Kezina also pointed out to me that the engineers found two foundations, one built into the other (conversation, Oct. 3, 1991, in Boldino). This would explain why earlier publications talk about a second house but assume that it is in a different spot from the one in which Pushkin lived in the 1830s.

76. Ibid., p. 5. I draw details about the planned effect of the museum from this source, and from what Ms. Kezina and others told me during my visit to Boldino in 1991.

77. For Pushkin's drawing of his desk, see *Boldinskie risunki A. S. Pushkina* (Gorky: Volgo-viatskoe knizhnoe izdatel'stvo, 1988), unpaginated; and Kezina, *Boldino*, p. 23.

78. Kezina, *Boldino*, p. 61.

79. Ibid.

80. Kezina's guide to the museum is structured as a kind of imaginative journey, where the reader is asked to imagine Pushkin as he first arrived in Boldino, or during his horseback rides, etc.

81. See Kezina, *Boldino*, p. 66, on the portrait, and p. 84 for the text of the letter. As we will see, the Moika 12 exhibit that opened in 1987 is also newly generous to Natalia Nikolaevna.

82. Kezina, *Boldino*, provides a full explication and detailed description of this part of the museum, but in the largest guide to Pushkin shrines, these rooms are not mentioned. See *Pushkinskie mesta. Putevoditel'*, vol. 1, pp. 324–30. Publications in the *Boldino Symposia* (*Boldinskie chteniia*) series also occasionally include material about the history of the museum and the region. See, for example, Iu. I. Levina, "Mezhevye plany Boldina," *Boldinskie chteniia*, 1981, pp. 182–91; and N. F. Filatov, "Pushkiny i Boldino v pervoi polovine XVII veka," *Boldinskie chteniia*, 1986, pp. 166–74.

83. *PSS*, vol. 3, p. 179. The critic of the first line was identified as Faddei Bulgarin in Boris Meilakh, *Khudozhestvennoe myshlenie Pushkina kak tvorcheskii protsess* (Moscow-Leningrad, Izd. AN SSSR, 1962), pp. 151–57. The poem suggests that the described landscape is enough to make even this disputatious and mocking critic feel sad. Pushkin also notes the impoverished conditions in Boldino in "History of the Village Goriukhino" ("Istoriia sela Goriukhino," 1830).

84. A few lines from "My ruddy-faced critic" appear in some official publications about Boldino. In *Pushkinskie mesta. Putevoditel'*, vol. 2, p. 320, local conditions are described so as to emphasize Pushkin's awareness of social inequality and

sense of kinship with peasants; the guidebook also suggests that he turned to historical writing to get his mind off the dismal conditions around him.

85. The dating of "Autumn" has been disputed. Some Pushkinists assert that it was composed in 1830 and recopied in 1833; others say the 1833 differences argue that those who dated the poem to 1830 confused it with "My ruddy-faced critic." For details, see N. V. Izmailov, "*Osen'* (Otryvok)," *Stikhotvoreniia Pushkina 1820–1830-kh godov*, pp. 222–54; see pp. 224–28. Sergei Fomichev calls "Autumn" Pushkin's lyrical confession for 1833; he finds special meaning in the poem's "poeticizing of simple and natural existence" as life's norm, and emphasizes its spiritual dimension. See S. A. Fomichev, *Poeziia Pushkina: Evoliutsiia tvorchestva* (Leningrad: Nauka, 1986), p. 198.

86. *PSS*, vol. 3, p. 247.

87. Ibid.

88. The paradox is noted by Nikolai Izmailov, who reminds us of lines from *Eugene Onegin* where autumn trembles pale and victim-like (chap. 7, verse 29; *PSS*, vol. 5, p. 131). He joins others in reading Pushkin's attitude toward the autumn landscape as largely positive. Izmailov, "*Osen'*," p. 238.

89. See, for example, N. L. Stepanov, *Lirika Pushkina* (Moscow: Sovetskii pisatel', 1959), p. 388: "Pushkin feels ecstasy at the sight of Russian nature, her autumn extravagance and beauty, which he takes as a sign of eternally renewing life." Stepanov, whose book was reissued in 1974 with a preface by Yuri Mann, represented mainstream Soviet scholarly views; his essay unifies the poem on thematic grounds. Another authoritative view of the poem is Izmailov's "*Osen'*," where the poem is described as radiant and life-affirming ("svetlye, zhizneradostnye tona"; p. 252), and as a sole instance of optimistic creativity in Pushkin's later work. Readings that discuss the inner polyphony of "Autumn" do so in terms of language and style. See especially L. Ginzburg, *O lirike*, 2d ed. (Leningrad: Sovetskii pisatel', 1974), pp. 224–25 (she shares Stepanov's assumption about the supreme value invested in the Russian natural setting in this poem). Iu. N. Chumakov, "*Osen'* Pushkina v aspekte struktury i zhanra," *Pushkinskii sbornik, Uchenye zapiski LGPI*, vol. 483 (Pskov, 1972), pp. 29–42, sees the central achievement of the poem as its inclusion of fundamentally opposing elements joined seamlessly (as compared with Baratynsky's "Autumn"). See esp. pp. 32–33.

90. *PSS*, vol. 3, p. 248.

91. For example, Izmailov, "*Osen'*," p. 232, argues that "the main theme of the poem is the awakening of poetry in the poet's consciousness."

92. *PSS*, vol. 3, p. 248.

93. On the manuscript of the final stanza, Pushkin penned a few more lines listing geographical destinations for the ship. See Stepanov, *Lirika Pushkina*, p. 397; and for a fuller textual history, Izmailov, "*Osen'* (Otryvok)," pp. 222–23. See also Pushkin's drawings in the margins of his manuscript, which include a small boat among the waves, reproduced in *Boldinskie risunki A. S. Pushkina*, unpaginated.

94. Chumakov, "*Osen'* Pushkina," pp. 41–42, appropriately comments that the first complete edition of *Onegin* was also published in 1833. ("Autumn" was not published during Pushkin's lifetime.) See also V. A. Grekhnev, "O liricheskikh finalakh Pushkina," *Boldinskie chteniia*, 1986, pp. 77–93, for a fine discussion of

semantic patterns in the endings of Pushkin's meditative lyrics; the ending of "Autumn" is analyzed on pp. 88–93 as a conflict between the openness of the last question and the barriers to such an imaginative voyage in Pushkin's daily life. A longer version of this essay appears in Grekhnev, *Etiudy o lirike A. S. Pushkina* (Nizhnii Novgorod: Volgo-Viatskoe knizhnoe izdatel'stvo, 1991), pp. 139–60.

95. The topic of fragmentary structures and themes in Pushkin has attracted excellent critical attention, especially in the work of Monika Greenleaf. See Monika Dudli, "'V malen'koi ramke': Fragmentary Structures in Pushkin's Poetry and Prose, Ph.D. dissertation, Yale University, 1982; and Monika Greenleaf, *Pushkin and Romantic Fashion: Fragment, Elegy, Orient, Irony* (Stanford, Calif.: Stanford University Press, 1994).

96. Kezina, *Boldino*, pp. 76–78.

97. This interpretation also appears in *Pushkinskie mesta. Putevoditel'*, vol. 1, p. 323.

98. See, for example, S. Orlov, "Pushkin i Boldino," *30 dnei*, no. 2, 1937, pp. 92–93; and Al. Gol'd, "Pushkin v Boldine," with photographs by Gushchin, *Traktorist kombainer*, no. 3, 1937, p. 17.

99. Among the most frequently cited statements by Pushkin about Boldino is his suggestion in an 1834 letter to Natalia Nikolaevna that he was thinking about leaving Petersburg altogether and settling in Boldino. See A. S. Pushkin, *Pis'ma k zhene*, ed. Ia. L. Levkovich (Leningrad: AN SSSR, 1986), p. 58. In her commentary, Ianina Levkovich rightly links this statement to others by Pushkin from the time about his desire to resign his position as a Gentleman of the Bedchamber (p. 163).

100. I cite only a few of many examples: A. Gladkii, "Pushkinskii ugolok," *Novaia zhizn'*, no. 4, 1922, p. 41; A. Gordin, "'Vnov' ia posetil tot ugolok zemli ... ' (Pushkin v Mikhailovskom v 1835 godu)," *Na beregakh Velikoi: Pskovskii literaturnyi al'manakh*, no. 2, 1949, p. 163.

101. Consider, for example, Vasil'ev-Ushkuinik, *Pushkinskie ugolki*, p. 54: "Arina Rodionovna played an enormous role in the poet's life. She replaced the poet's mother. The poet had a joyless childhood. Both his mother and father loved high society and were indifferent to home and family."

102. Pushkin presents a kinder view of his exile in the poem that also mentions Arina Rodionovna fondly, "... Once again I visited," although the poem explicitly refers to the visit as a period of exile.

103. See the 1924 memoir of Varvara Timofeeva-Pochinkovskaia, "Mikhailovskoe zatochen'e," cited above.

104. This conflict can be traced in the archival records of Mikhailovskoe, held in the Manuscript Division, Pushkin House (IRLI), f. 244, op. 30, nos. 20, 44–49, 55, 56. The documentation is extensive, including hundreds of pages of correspondence among local farmers, Pushkin House representatives, and party officials. The intensity and length of this epistolary exchange suggest that the conflict over land use was not unlike Russia's larger history of collectivization, and peasant resistance was fierce.

105. In most accounts, the tale is told as if all decisions were reached easily with local support. See A. M. Gordin, *Pushkin v Mikhailovskom*, pp. 418–36. This book is especially valuable for its reproduction of extensive photographs of Mikhailovskoe and Trigorskoe from earlier in the 20th century.

106. For an appreciation of the symposia and a short history of them, see G. V. Krasnov, "Pod znakom Pushkina (Iz istorii Boldinskikh chtenii)," *Boldinskie chteniia* (Novgorod: Idz. NNGU, 1998), pp. 3–12.

107. The figure cited in a 1988 publication is over 600,000. See *Pushkinskie mesta. Putevoditel'*, vol. 1, p. 229. An essay from 1984, Iu. Osipov's "Vechnost' Mikhailovskogo," put the figure at 1,000,000 (p. 124). I have been unable to find reliable statistics for the number of visitors in the post-Soviet period. But as of 2003, the existence of more than a dozen tourist organizations with websites offering bus tours to Mikhailovskoe suggests to me that the numbers may still be quite high. Geography remains important here: the Pskov region is accessible to Russians living in and around Petersburg, and to tourists from Scandinavia and other parts of northern Europe.

108. It has become common to complain about Mikhailovskoe, even for those who were involved in its layout and design. See Gordin, *Pushkin v Mikhailovskom*, pp. 434–35.

109. Andrei Bitov, "Predpolozhenie zhit'," in Bitov, *Chelovek v peizazhe* (Moscow: Sovetskii pisatel', 1988), p. 221.

110. I take my etymological information from *Webster's New World Dictionary of the American Language*, 2d college ed. (New York: World Publishing Co., 1972), p. 1373. For Russian meanings, see Vladimir Dal', *Tolkovyi slovar' zhivogo velikorusskogo iazyka*, 7th ed. 4 vols. (Moscow, "Russkii iazyk," 1978), vol. 1, pp. 503–4.

111. Arguments about preserving the landscape in Mikhailovskoe were revived in the 1990s, causing the director to speak out unsentimentally about the deleterious effects of keeping rotting and diseased trees. See Georgii Vasilevich, "… Priiut zadumchivykh driad … ," *Novyi mir*, no. 10, 1998, pp. 226–29.

112. Geichenko, *U lukomor'ia*, p. 12. My ellipses.

113. Ibid., p. 14.

114. N. I. Popova, "Kvartira Pushkina na Moike, 12," *Panorama iskusstv*, vol. 11 (1988), pp. 266–81; see p. 266.

115. For other photographs of this room, see N. I. Popova, *Muzei-kvartira A. S. Pushkina na Moike* (Moscow: Sovetskaia Rossiia, 1989), pp. 61, 73, 75.

116. Objections to the reconstruction of walls within the building were also raised. For a charged account, see S. S. Landa, "Chto proiskhodit na Moike, 12?" *"Ia vizhu nekii svet …"* (St. Petersburg, 1999), pp. 260–71. The objections were also repeated to bolster a new controversy over changes at Mikhailovskoe. See V. Eliseeva, "O 'vkuse k podlinnosti' i 'restavratsii' Mikhailovskogo," *Novyi mir*, no. 10, 1998, pp. 224–25.

117. The gesture also risked historical inaccuracy if it suggested that Pushkin sold books out of his apartment, which he certainly did not. Nina Popova, the museum director at the time, made it clear that the books were present because Pushkin had taken possession of unsold copies of his work and stored them, but she admitted that it had not been documented that he stored them in the apartment.

118. On the website of the museum at Moika 12, one can see images of those books (they are duplicates, actually; Pushkin's own books are housed in Pushkin House's rare books section) and read a short supporting text that emphasizes the symbolic importance of his library. See www.pushkin.ru/museum4.html.

119. One visitor, writing in 1966, found that the objects produced in her a sense

of distance and disappointment. See Bella Akhmadulina, "Vstrecha," in Akhmadulina, *Zimniaia zamknutost'* (St. Petersburg, Pushkinskii fond, 1999), pp. 107–11.

120. Boris Groys, "The Struggle Against the Museum; or, The Display of Art in Totalitarian Space," in Daniel J. Sherman and Irit Rogoff, eds., *Museum Culture: Histories, Discourses, Spectacles* (Minneapolis: University of Minnesota Press, 1994), pp. 144–62; citation from p. 148.

121. For accounts of the reconstruction at Moika 12, see Popova, "Kvartira Pushkina na Moike"; Angelina Minina and Nina Popova, "Chto takoe *kvartira na Moike?*," *Dekorativnoe iskusstvo*, no. 6, 1987, pp. 18–21; and Popova, *Muzei-kvartira A. S. Pushkina na Moike*.

122. As noted by Osipov, "Vechnost' Mikhailovskogo," p. 113.

123. Yasnaya Polyana elicited such a reaction from the journalist Alessandra Staley. In her article "At Tolstoy's Retreat, Bones of Contention," *New York Times*, March 7, 1994, p. CII, she wrote: "At Tolstoy's vast country estate, Yasnaya Polyana, everything is just as it was when the great writer died. His pen lies on his writing table. The simple peasant blouse he always wore hangs from a peg in his bedroom. His beloved birch-lined drive still thrives."

124. Cited from Popova, *Muzei-kvartira A. S. Pushkina*, p. 71.

125. Ibid.

126. Viktor Bokov, "Stikhi o Pushkine," in *Rossii pervaia liubov'*, p. 526; Raisa Akhmatova, "Blagoslovi menia, blagoslovi," in ibid. p. 386. Both poems are set in Mikhailovskoe.

127. *Rossii pervaia liubov'* contains many examples, including, for Mikhailovskoe, Elena Serebrovskaia, "Pushkin v Mikhailovskom" (pp. 264–65), Vladimir Sokolov, "Gusinye per'ia na ptich'em dvore" (p. 338), Konstantin Vanshenkin, "Kolokol'chik," (p. 368), and Vsevolod Azarov, "Dom Gannibalov" (p. 507); and for Boldino, Margarita Aliger, "Osen' v Boldine" (pp. 214–16), Iuliia Drunina, "Boldinskaia osen'" (pp. 476–77), and Ovidii Liubovnikov, "Pushkin v Viatke" (pp. 611–12). The list is by no means exhaustive.

128. Lev Ozerov, in V. I. Baranov, ed., *Ochei ocharovaniia: Pushkinskoe Boldino v sovetskoi literature* (Gorky: Volgo-Viatskoe Knizhnoe izdatel'stvo, 1980), p. 26. My ellipses.

129. These places have generated an unbelievable amount of poetry, a result of the system of "sotsial'nyi zakaz" that governed Soviet literature until the early 1990s. Particularly after special poetry festivals were instituted in Mikhailovskoe and, later, Boldino, the numbers of poems grew substantially. For astute comments on how a class of poets who could turn out such poetry was produced, see G. S. Smith, "Russian Poetry Since 1945," in Neil Cornwell, ed., *Routledge Companion to Russian Literature* (London: Routledge, 2001), pp. 197–208. Because the poems are generally not particularly interesting as aesthetic artifacts, I tend to cite only my English translations.

130. *Ochei ocharovan'e*, pp. 107–8.

131. Ibid., pp. 153–54.

132. Ibid., p. 155. Many poets similarly compare themselves with the greatness of Pushkin, for example, Aleksei Ivanov-Klassik, "Pamiati Pushkina," in *Rossii pervaia liubov'*, p. 155; and Petrus' Brovka, "Slovo na prazdnike v Mikhailovskom,"

in ibid., p. 358. It is hard to believe that there have not been more parodies of these poems. In one such example, "Boldino. Autumn" ("Boldino. Osen'"), Viktor Kumakshev paints a satirical portrait of poets wandering around in Boldino looking for inspiration. *Ochei ocharovaniia*, p. 282.

133. Ibid., p. 108.

134. Sears, *Sacred Places*, p. 6.

135. Ibid., p. 7.

136. Benedict Anderson, *Imagined Communities: Reflections on the Origin and Spread of Nationalism* (London: Verso, 1983), p. 20.

137. My former Amherst College colleague and the biographer of Marina Tsvetaeva, Viktoria Schweitzer, drove home my point one day. When I told her that the little signs with Pushkin's poetry had irritated me when I was in Mikhailovskoe, she was surprised, because she hadn't even noticed them.

138. Andrei Bitov, "Vychitanie zaitsa," in Bitov, *Vychitanie zaitsa 1825* (Moscow: Nezavisimaia gazeta, 2001), p. 19.

139. For a picture of Dovlatov working as a tour guide in Mikhailovskoe in 1977, see the website: www.dovlatov.km.ru/mikh2.html.

140. In one conversation, when Dolatov's hero is trying to prove that he can handle the job, he says he's been to Mikhailovskoe three times. This conversation ensues:

—That's not much.

—I agree, that's why I've come again ...

—But one must prepare thoroughly. Study the method. In Pushkin's life so much remains uninvestigated.... Some things have changed since last year....

—In Pushkin's life?, I said with surprise.

Dovlatov, *Zapovednik*, p. 13. Dovlatov uses this exchange to suggest that Mikhailovskoe's organizers change their versions of Pushkin from year to year to suit their needs.

141. Ibid., p. 16.

142. Ibid., p. 75. Compare p. 84, where another invention (the Kern walk, said to be the linden alley where Pushkin walked with A. P. Kern) is denounced as fanciful.

143. The would-be guide goes on:

I was ready to cry, although I could still understand that this was the effect of the alcohol. Obviously, harmony was hiding itself at the bottom of a bottle....

I said to myself: "Pushkin also had debts and bad relations with the government. And trouble with his wife. To say nothing about his difficult personality" ...

So what? They opened the preserve anyway. Forty guides. And all of them madly in love with Pushkin....

Ibid., pp. 97–98. One interesting aspect of this meditation is the way the hero manages to bring his reveries around to Pushkin and identifies with him, then backs away by joking about the preserve. In an analysis of *The Preserve*, Jekaterina Young has suggested that Pushkin's laconic prose style is the model for Dovlatov's tale, a tale that she rightly contrasts to the more typically idealized, not to say rhapsodic, Soviet writing about the countryside. See Young, "Dolotov's *Sanctuary* and Pushkin," in Joe Andrew and Robert Reid, eds., *Two Hundred Years of Pushkin*, vol. 1: *'Pushkin's Secret': Russian Writers Reread and Rewrite Pushkin* (Amsterdam: Rodopi, 2003), pp. 135–52.

CHAPTER 3

EPIGRAPH: Carol Jacobs, *Telling Time: Lévi-Strauss, Ford, Lessing, Benjamin, de Man, Wordsworth, Rilke* (Baltimore, Md.: Johns Hopkins University Press, 1993), p. 6.

1. For reports of the Odessa commemorations, see "Istoriko-literaturnaia rabota v Odesse," *Atenei*, no. 1-2, 1924, pp. 190–91; and *Literaturno-khudozhestvennoe prilozhenie, Izvestiia Odesskogo Gubispolkoma*, July 15, 1923 (no. 1084), esp. p. 1. The 1926 commemorative booklet, *Pushkinskii al'manakh*, was published by the Pushkinskoe obshchestvo druzei knigi (Moscow) in an edition of 300 copies. The celebration was held in the Bolshoi Theater, a traditional site for these gatherings, on April 12, 1926. The booklet is composed of typical short sections: speeches by Pushkin scholars (in this case, M. A. Tsiavlovsky, L. P. Grossman, V. V. Veresaev); texts by Pushkin read that evening (including excerpts from *Eugene Onegin*) and poems to Pushkin by Akhmatova, Blok, Kuzmin, and Esenin; and comments about the exhibit in the theater foyer.

2. This concentration on the dates of birth and death suggest a parallel between Pushkin and royalty. As John R. Gillis has noted, the enduring popular commemorations in France among conservatives were observances of the death or birth of a king. Gillis, ed., *Commemorations: The Politics of National Identity* (Princeton, N.J.: Princeton University Press, 1994), p. 8. Gillis cites Eugen Weber, *Peasants into Frenchmen: The Modernization of Rural France, 1870–1914* (Stanford, Calif.: Stanford University Press, 1976), on this point.

3. Some examples are cited below. See also Konstantin Fedin, "Aleksandr Blok," *Kniga i revoliutsiia*, no. 1 (13), 1921, pp. 23–25, esp. p. 24, for a comparison of Blok's speech in 1921 to Dostoevsky's 1880 speech; and A. Pleshcheev, "Pushkinskii prazdnik v Moskve (1880 g.)," memoirs about the 1880 celebration that appeared in a commemorative special edition of the Paris émigré journal *Vozrozhdenie*, Feb. 6, 1937 (no. 4064), p. 16.

4. A. D. Gdalin, G. A. Drovenikov, and I. L. Popeliukher, "Pamiatniki A. S. Pushkinu (Materialy k annotirovannomu katalogu)," *Vremennik pushkinskoi komissii*, no. 25 (1993), pp. 77–93, lists 34 monuments erected in Russia between 1817 and 1917, and 20 in foreign countries.

5. Pierre Nora, "Between Memory and History: Les Lieux de mémoire," *Representations*, no. 26 (Spring 1989), pp. 7–25; I have quoted from p. 12.

6. Marcus C. Levitt, *Russian Literary Politics and the Pushkin Celebration of 1880* (Ithaca, N.Y.: Cornell University Press, 1989), p. 4.

7. Marcus C. Levitt, "Pushkin in 1899," in Boris Gasparov, Robert P. Hughes, and Irina Paperno, eds., *Cultural Mythologies of Russian Modernism: From the Golden Age to the Silver Age* (Berkeley: University of California Press, 1992), pp. 183–203.

8. F. M. Dostoevsky, "Pushkin," in Sona Stephan Hoisington, ed., *Russian Views of Pushkin's 'Eugene Onegin'* (Bloomington: Indiana University Press, 1988), p. 56.

9. Ibid., p. 66, translation slightly modified; compare F. M. Dostoevskii, *Polnoe sobranie sochinenii*, 30 vols. (Leningrad: Nauka, 1984), vol. 26, p. 148.

10. By March 1, 1921, the list of participating organizations reached 24, in quite marked contrast to the centralized cultural planning of the 1930s. See "Pushkinskie dni v Dome Literatorov," *Vestnik literatury*, no. 3 (27), 1921, p. 18, which also lists all the events. Although I note when a particular speech was given, I treat the month of events as a single, extended celebration. One participant, Vladislav Khodasevich, goes further, pointing to origins in 1920 plans and forward to celebrations as late as 1927. See Vladislav Khodasevich, *Sobranie sochinenii*, 2 vols., ed. Robert Hughes and John Malmstad (Ann Arbor, Mich.: Ardis Press, 1983), vol. 2, pp. 520–22, for sources that chronicle the sequence of events and for Khodasevich's 1927 account of the 1921 commemorations.

11. "Deklaratsiia o ezhegodnom vserossiiskom chestvovanii pamiati Pushkina v den' ego smerti," *Vestnik literatury*, no. 3 (27), 1921, pp. 17–18; quotation from p. 17.

12. Other projects: the government publishing house, Gosizdat, would continue publishing Pushkin's works and would issue a portrait of Pushkin suitable for use in schools; and participants in Proletkult would produce a Pushkin play each year and organize a contest in his name. Another publishing house, Vsemirnaia literatura, promised to produce an album of Pushkin drawings. "Obshchenatsional'nye Pushkinskie pominki," *Vestnik literatury*, no. 2 (26), 1921, p. 15.

13. One review called Blok's speech "brilliant" and a "key and explanation of his poetic worldview and, in part, of his death." See the article signed "Knizhnyi chelovek" in *Nachalo* (Ivanovo-Voznesensk), no. 2-3, 1922, p. 165.

14. I differ slightly, then, with Robert P. Hughes's suggestion that it set the pattern for subsequent anniversaries. Hughes, "Pushkin in Petrograd, February 1921," in Gasparov et al., *Cultural Mythologies of Russian Modernism*, pp. 204–13.

15. Others who did not speak in 1921 held the same view. A good example is Mikhail Gershenzon, *Stat'i o Pushkine* (Moscow: Academia, 1926), p. 111, as cited in Brian Horowitz, "M. O. Gershenzon and the Intellectual Life of Russia's Silver Age" (Ph.D. dissertation, University of California–Berkeley, 1993), p. 428 (translation mine): "My generation is probably the last to see even the faint traces of the living Pushkin before their eyes. We knew people who had seen Pushkin...."

16. Hughes, "Pushkin in Petrograd," p. 208.

17. "Rech' A. F. Koni," *Vestnik literatury*, no. 3 (27), 1921, p. 18.

18. Ibid. My ellipses.

19. Ibid.

20. Other examples of serious scholarly work presented on this occasion include Yuri Tynianov's "New Pages from 'Egyptian Nights,'" ("Novye stranitsy iz 'Egipetskikh nochei'"), Pavel Shchegolev's "Pushkin's Duel" ("Duel' Pushkina"), and Pyotr Guber's "Pushkin and Russian Culture" ("Pushkin i russkaia kul'tura").

21. B. Eikhenbaum, "Problemy poetiki Pushkina," in *O poezii* (Leningrad: Sovetskii pisatel', 1969), pp. 23–34; quoted from p. 23.

22. Ibid.

23. Ibid. The poem that Mikhail Kuzmin read on several Pushkin evenings also insists that Pushkin is alive (that is its opening sentence: "On zhiv!"). For an analysis of the repetition of this theme in Kuzmin's poem as a rejoinder to Lermontov's "Death of the Poet," see Hughes, "Pushkin in Petrograd," pp. 205–6.

24. Eikhenbaum, "Problemy poetiki Pushkina," p. 23.

25. Ibid. The metaphors of nearness and distance, and a second mention of the statuette, reappear in the essay's concluding remarks (p. 34).

26. See Svetlana Boym, "Inscriptions on the Poet's Monument," *Harvard Review*, Fall 1986, pp. 64–81; on monuments, see pp. 71–75.

27. See Vladimir Markov, ed., *Manifesty i programmy russkikh futuristov* (Munich: Fink, 1967), for the manifesto, "Poshchechina obshchestvennomu vkusu," pp. 50–51.

28. See the first paragraph of D. Lukhotin, "Novinki 'Pushkiniany,'" *Vestnik literatury*, no. 10 (22), 1920, pp. 4–5; and Iurii Slezkin, "Literatura v provintsii (Pis'mo iz Vladikavkaza)," *Vestnik literatury*, no. 1 (25), 1921, pp. 12–13. Slezkin observes that the young writer Mikhail Bulgakov had the courage to argue on Pushkin's behalf, but paid the price the next day, when he was accused in *The Communist* of virtual counterrevolutionary action.

29. See *Vestnik literatury*, no. 2-3, 1922, pp. 7–8.

30. See "Deklaratsiia o ezhegodnom vserossiiskom chestvovanii," p. 17.

31. John E. Malmstad, "Khodasevich and Formalism: A Poet's Dissent," in Robert Louis Jackson and Stephen Rudy, eds., *Russian Formalism: A Retrospective Glance. A Festschrift in Honor of Victor Erlich* (New Haven, Conn.: Yale Center for International and Area Studies, 1985), pp. 68–81, esp. pp. 68–70.

32. What Khodasevich says about *The Bronze Horseman*, for example, summarizes what others said long before him. See also his essay "Pushkin's Petersburg Tales" ("Petersburgskie povesti Pushkina," 1915).

33. The "Pushkinian" quality of Khodasevich's work is described with precision in David Bethea, *Khodasevich: His Life and Art* (Princeton, N.J.: Princeton University Press, 1983), esp. pp. 69–79. A splendid study of Khodasevich's Pushkin essays has also appeared: Irina Surat, *Pushkinist Vladislav Khodasevich* (Moscow: "Labirint," 1994). Surat convincingly shows the originality of Khodasevich's thinking about Pushkin, as well as the breadth of his scholarship (she cites dozens of journal articles that have never been republished).

34. In "Gershenzon" (1925), Khodasevich writes: "His book *Pushkin's Wisdom* turned out to a certain degree to be the 'wisdom of Gershenzon'" and "in a certain sense his errors are more valuable and more profound than many truths." See Vladislav Khodasevich, *Sobranie sochinenii*, 4 vols., ed. I. P. Andreeva and S. G. Bocharov (Moscow: Soglasie, 1996), vol. 4, p. 104 (unless otherwise indicated, citations from Khodasevich come from this edition). For a full discussion of Khodasevich's and Gershenzon's intellectual relationship, see Surat, *Pushkinist Vladislav Khodasevich*, pp. 24–35; and Brian Horowitz, *The Myth of A. S. Pushkin in Russia's Silver Age: M. O. Gershenzon, Pushkinist* (Evanston, Ill.: Northwestern University Press, 1996), passim.

35. Khodasevich, *Sobranie sochinenii*, vol. 2, p. 80.

36. Ibid.

37. Ibid.

38. See Irina Paperno, "Pushkin v zhizni cheloveka Serebrianogo veka," in Gasparov et al., eds., *Cultural Mythologies of Russian Modernism*, pp. 19–51.

39. For a nuanced discussion of Khodasevich's views of time, see Bethea, *Khodasevich*, pp. 206–8.

40. Khodasevich, *Sobranie sochinenii*, vol. 2, pp. 83–84. My ellipses. The reference to the "eclipse of Pushkin" engages the imagery of Pushkin's death as an eclipse of the sun, first articulated at the time of his death in an obituary notice (as discussed in the Introduction).

41. Ibid., pp. 84–85.

42. This has been famously discussed in Roman Jakobson, "The Statue in Pushkin's Poetic Mythology," in Jakobson, *Pushkin and His Sculptural Myth*, tr. John Burbank (The Hague: Mouton, 1975), pp. 1–44.

43. Khodasevich, *Sobranie sochinenii*, vol. 2, p. 85.

44. His recollections about the evening come in his essay on Blok and Gumilev, written a decade later (1931) and commemorating both the 1921 gathering and their deaths that August. The essay shows Khodasevich's mixed feelings toward both men, but it evokes their deaths as painfully symbolic of the death of the poet and of genuine Russian culture.

45. Khodasevich, *Sobranie sochinenii*, vol. 4, p. 84.

46. The similarity also reinforces the general sense of loss that, for Khodasevich, marks the gatherings.

47. Aleksandr Blok, "O naznachenii poeta," in Blok, *Sobranie sochinenii*, 6 vols. (Leningrad, 1982), vol. 4, pp. 413–20; quoted from pp. 413–14.

48. Ibid., p. 414. My ellipses.

49. Ibid., p. 419.

50. Ibid., pp. 416, 417.

51. Ibid., p. 420.

52. A. Lunacharskii, "Pushkin," *Krasnaia gazeta*, June 8, 1924 (no. 129), morning ed., p. 5.

53. *Leningradskaia pravda*, June 8, 1924 (no. 129), p. 3 (unsigned and untitled article, headlined "125 Years Since the Birth of Pushkin").

54. Jeffrey Brooks, *When Russia Learned to Read* (Princeton, N.J.: Princeton University Press, 1985), p. 97. On the pre-Soviet period, see Brooks, "Russian Nationalism and Russian Literature: The Canonization of the Classics," in Ivo Banac et al., eds., *Nation and Ideology: Essays in Honor of Wayne S. Vucinich* (Boulder, Colo.: Westview, 1981), pp. 315–34; and B. S. Meilakh, "Pushkin v vospriiatii i soznanii dorevoliutsionnogo krest'ianstva," *Pushkin. Issledovaniia i materialy*, vol. 5 (1967), pp. 61–111.

55. A. Kraiskii, "Pushkin v 1924 godu," *Krasnaia gazeta*, June 8, 1924 (no. 129), morning ed., p. 5.

56. Ibid. See also Lunacharskii, "Pushkin," p. 5, for a less eagerly political reading of Pushkin but one that predicts his rising popularity; and, in that same issue of the newspaper, A. Men'shoi, "Pushkin—Protest," for an interpretation of several instances in Pushkin's life and writings as acts of protest against the conservative pieties of his time.

57. "A. S. Pushkin. K 125–letiiu so dnia rozhdeniia," *Pskovskii nabat*, June 5, 1924 (no. 124), p. 2.

58. L. Sosnovskii, "Za chto liubil Pushkina Lenin," *Krasnaia gazeta*, June 8, 1924 (no. 129), morning ed., p. 2.

59. V. I. Lenin, *O literature i iskusstve* (Moscow: Gosudarstvennoe izdatel'stvo politicheskoi literatury, 1957), pp. 521, 534.

60. The books include "Garris" (pseud. Maria Kallash), *Ugolok Pushkina* (Moscow-Petrograd: Gos. izdatel'stvo, 1923); and F. A. Vasil'ev-Ushkuinik, *Pushkinskie ugolki Pskovskoi gubernii* (Moscow: Izd. T-va "V. V. Dumnov, n-ki br. Salaevykh," 1924).

61. One 1924 collection of essays from the region included a short piece titled "Two Pushkin Jubilees." Its author, A. Gladky (soon to be named director of the Mikhailovskoe preserve), claimed that "not a single Russian poet of the last century is as close to revolutionary contemporary life in spirit or in the content of his works as is Pushkin," sounding the theme of Pushkin's primacy in the new post-revolutionary culture. He also observed that even though Pushkin was born in Moscow, his name was closely connected to Pskov and the Pskov region. A. Gladkii, "Dva Pushkinskikh iubileia," *Poznai svoi krai*, Sbornik Pskovskogo Obshchestva kraevedeniia, no. 1, 1924, pp. 22–25; quoted material from pp. 22, 24.

62. "Pushkinskie torzhestva u mogily poeta," *Leningradskaia pravda*, June 13, 1924 (no. 133), p. 5; "Pushkinskie dni," ibid., June 7, 1924 (no. 128), p. 3.

63. "Pushkinskie torzhestva (Po sluchaiu 125–letiia so dnia rozhdeniia)," *Pskovskii nabat*, June 14, 1924 (no. 134), pp. 2–3.

64. Garris, *Ugolok Pushkina*, p. 7.

65. Vasil'ev-Uskuinik, *Pushkinskie ugolki*, pp. 52–53.

66. N. V. Izmailov, "Iz vospominanii o Pushkinskom dome," *Russkaia literatura*, no. 1, 1981, pp. 89–106; see pp. 95–97.

67. Mstislav Tsiavlovskii and Tat'iana Tsiavlovskaia, *Vokrug Pushkina: dnevniki, stat'i 1928–1965*, ed. K. P. Bogaevskaia and S. I. Panov (Moscow: NLO, 2000), p. 282.

68. M. Tsiavlovskii, "Poezdka v Mikhailovskoe," in Tsiavlovskii and Tsiavlovskaia, *Vokrug Pushkina*, p. 153.

69. Tsiavslovskii and Tsiavlovskaia, *Vokrug Pushkina*, pp. 284–85.

70. The name change was widely reported, for example, in "Pushkinskii muzei v sele Mikhailovskom," *Krasnaia gazeta*, June 10, 1924 (no. 130), morning ed., p. 1.

71. "K chestvovaniiu stoletiia ssylki Pushkina," *Krasnaia gazeta*, Aug. 27, 1924 (no. 193 [583]), evening ed., p. 4.

72. "Na Pushkinskie torzhestva," *Krasnaia gazeta*, Sept. 9, 1924 (no. 205 [595]), evening ed., p. 2. I have been unable to find additional confirmation that Akhmatova actually went on the trip, although the newspaper account is not implausible, given her contribution to the 1921 celebrations and her friendships with Pushkin scholars, including Boris Tomashevsky, who was also named.

73. "Pushkinskie torzhestva," *Krasnaia gazeta*, Sept. 13, 15, 16, 1924 (nos. 208–10 [598–600], evening ed., pp. 2, 1, 1, respectively.

74. "Vozvrashchenie delegatsii iz Mikhailovskogo," *Krasnaia gazeta*, Sept. 17, 1924 (no. 211 [601]), evening edition, p. 3.

75. "Otkliki Pushkinskikh chestvovanii," *Krasnaia gazeta*, Sept. 23, 1924 (no. 216 [606]), evening ed., p. 2.

76. Different plans had been stated in public from the beginning, for example, the demand for a Pushkin museum in Pskov, in Gladkii, "Dva Pushkinskikh iubileia," p. 25; a plan for a free university in Pushkinskie Gory, in "Po povodu zakrytiia shkoly im. Pushkina," *Krasnaia gazeta*, Sept. 12, 1924 (no. 207 [597]), evening ed., p. 2; a plan to erect a monument to Pushkin on the precipice overlooking the Sorot River, in "Pamiatnik Pushkinu v Mikhailovskom," *Krasnaia gazeta*, May 17, 1924 (no. 110), evening ed., p. 3). In the last connection, the deadline for the monument was extended to August, with new instructions that it represent Pushkin as aged 24–26; and the inclusion of his nanny was now thought desirable. See "Pamiatnik Pushkinu v sele Mikhailovskom," *Krasnaia gazeta*, July 23, 1924 (no. 165 [555]), evening ed., p. 2.

77. "Pushkinskie dni," *Krasnaia gazeta*, June 7, 1924 (no. 127), evening ed., p. 1.

78. Ivanov's inclusion is discussed briefly in John E. Malmstad, "Silver Threads Among the Gold: Andrei Belyi's Pushkin," in Gasparov et al., eds., *Cultural Mythologies of Russian Modernism*, p. 431.

79. An invitation to the Academy of Sciences' Pushkin celebration gives little more information than was found in the newspapers. It lists three speeches: Academician M. N. Rozanov, "Pushkinskie otzvuki ital'ianskoi poezii"; Honorary Academician A. F. Koni, "Zhiznennaia drama Pushkina"; and B. L. Modzalevskii, "Pushkinskii Dom, kak pamiatnik Pushkinu." See RGALI (Rossiiski gosudarstvennyi arkhiv literatury i isskusstva, formerly TsGALI), f. 384, no. 2, op. 57, item 5.

80. Victor Erofeyev, "Dying for the Party," *Times Literary Supplement*, Jan. 7, 1994, p. 9.

81. Iurii Karabchievskii, *Voskresenie Maiakovskogo* (Moscow: Sovetskii pisatel', 1990), p. 23.

82. For a discussion of this manifesto and Mayakovsky's role in it, see Edward J. Brown, *Mayakovsky: A Poet in the Revolution* (Princeton, N.J.: Princeton University Press, 1973), pp. 54–55.

83. V. V. Maiakovskii, *Polnoe sobranie sochinenii*, 13 vols., (Moscow: Khudozhestvennaia literatura, 1957), vol. 6, p. 47.

84. Svetlana Boym has suggested that the poem has lines spoken by Pushkin, but the lines she cites seem to me much more plausibly spoken by Mayakovsky to himself. See her *Death in Quotation Marks: Cultural Myths of the Modern Poet* (Cambridge, Mass.: Harvard University Press, 1991), p. 135.

85. Maiakovskii, *Polnoe sobranie sochinenii*, vol. 6, pp. 52, 55. The list that follows the second comment is confined to acceptably revolutionary male poets, so Mayakovsky omits Mandelstam, Akhmatova, and Tsvetaeva but also, remarkably, Boris Pasternak (the spelling of whose name would indeed have placed him between Mayakovsky and Pushkin). Any of these poets would disprove his claim that Russia had an impoverished poetic tradition in 1924.

86. On Mayakovsky's self-fascination as part of the myth of the poet he created for himself, and for a good discussion of his use of his own name in "Anniversary Poem," see Boym, *Death in Quotation Marks*, pp. 120–37.

87. Maiakovskii, *Polnoe sobranie sochinenii*, vol. 6, p. 48.

88. Ibid., p. 50.

89. Compare Gary Saul Morson, *The Boundaries of Genre: Dostoevsky's "Diary of a Writer" and the Traditions of Literary Utopia* (Austin: University of Texas Press, 1981), p. 110.

90. We know from Lilia Brik that Mayakovsky often cited these lines from *Onegin*. She wrote that "*these* lines corresponded to his spiritual state for his entire life." L. Iu. Brik, "Chuzhie stikhi (Glava iz *Vospominanii*)," in V. V. Grigorenko et al., eds., *V. Maiakovskii v vospominaniiakh sovremennikov* (Moscow: Khudozhestvennaia literatura, 1963), pp. 328–54; citation from p. 331. Mayakovsky also quoted the lines during a 1924 debate. "Vystuplenie na dispute o zadachakh literatury i dramaturgii, 26 maia 1924 goda," in Maiakovskii, *Polnoe sobranie sochinenii*, vol. 12, pp. 263–66, esp. p. 265; he says they represent a supreme example of an emotion expressed as thought, and they merit constant study and repetition. He also says in this debate that his relationship to Pushkin can best be found in "The Anniversary Poem" (p. 266).

91. Maiakovskii, *Polnoe sobranie sochinenii*, vol. 6, p. 55. Emphasis in the original.

92. A. K. Zholkovskii, "O genii i zlodeistve, o babe i vserossiiskom masshtabe (Progulki po Maiakovskomu)," in Zholkovskii and Iu. K. Shcheglov, *Mir avtora i struktura teksta: Stat'i o russkoi literature* (Tenafly, N.J.: Hermitage, 1986), pp. 255–78; see p. 273.

93. Maiakovskii, *Polnoe sobranie sochinenii*, vol. 6, p. 55. The characterization of d'Anthès recapitulates Lermontov's poem "The Death of the Poet," which Mayakovsky also cites.

94. Ibid., p. 53.

95. Ibid., p. 55.

96. N. Khardzhiev and V. Trenin discuss the reference to "Koopsakh" as typical linguistic play for Mayakovsky. See their *Poeticheskaia kul'tura Maiakovskogo* (Moscow: Iskusstvo, 1970), pp. 254–55.

97. Maiakovskii, *Polnoe sobranie sochinenii*, vol. 6, p. 47.

98. Ibid., p. 51. Mayakovsky's stairstep line breaks have the effect of isolating him further from his contemporaries, placing the words "I" and "alone" in lines all to themselves. For a discussion of the loneliness found in much of Mayakovsky's poetry, see Brown, *Mayakovsky*, esp. the early chapters.

99. Maiakovskii, *Polnoe sobranie sochinenii*, vol. 6, p. 54.

100. Other writers and poets have performed similar gestures of completion with regard to Pushkin's writings. Some used Pushkin's fragments as their point of origin—like *Egyptian Nights* (*Egipetskie nochi*, 1835), which Briusov attempted to complete. Zoshchenko added to the open-ended Belkin Cycle ("Sixth Belkin Tale," "Shestaia povest' Belkina," 1937). On Zoshchenko's tale, see Irina Reifman, "Shestaia povest' Belkina: Mikhail Zoshchenko v role Proteia," in Gasparov et al., eds., *Cultural Mythologies of Russian Modernism*, pp. 393–414. The same volume contains an essay on Briusov's approach to Pushkin, with some commentary about his completion of *Egyptian Nights*: Joan Delaney Grossman, "*Moi Pushkin*: Briusov's Search for the *Real* Aleksandr Sergeevich," pp. 73–87. Other poets had tried their hand at completing these same lines, including A. Maikov and G. Shengeli. See Khodasevich, *Sobranie sochinenii*, vol. 1, p. 525.

101. Shorter and less well known than the Mayakovsky poem, Khodasevich's "Romance" is here given in full:

Romance
Across the Ethereal blue field
The gold Evening Star glides.
The old Doge sails in his gondola
With the young Dogaressa.

The young Dogaressa
Does not look at her spouse,
Her white breast does not sigh,
And nothing does she say.

The long silence weighs heavy,
But, gathering courage in the end,
The gondolier starts to sing to them
About a lofty legend past.

And hearing Tasso's octaves
The old man lives as if anew,
And he takes his wife's hand
With languor, and by rights.

But the young wife
Gazes into the distant sea.
Without complaint, without a sigh,
Nothing does she say.

Cooling his ardor unwillingly,
The Doge drooped his head.
The night is quiet. In the heavenly field
The gold Evening Star glides.

A warm breeze blows from the Lido,
And the master will command
That the singer who has grown silent
Now return to the palace.

Романс
В голубом Эфира поле
Ходит Веспер золотой.
Старый Дож плывет в гондоле
С Догарессой молодой.

Догаресса молодая
На супруга не глядит,
Белой грудью не вздыхая,
Ничего не говорит.

Тяжко долгое молчанье,
Но, осмелясь наконец,
Про высокое преданье
Запевает им гребец.

И под Тассову октаву
Старец сызнова живет,
И супругу он по праву
Томно за руку берет.

Но супруга молодая
В море дальнее глядит.
Не ропща и не вздыхая,
Ничего не говорит.

Охлаждаясь поневоле,
Дож поникнул головой.
Ночь тиха. В небесном поле
Ходит Веспер золотой.

С Лидо теплый ветер дует,
И замолкшему певцу
Повелитель указует
Возвращаться ко дворцу.

Khodasevich, *Sobranie sochinenii*, vol. 1, p. 307. Here, quotation marks do not appear around the first five lines. They are found in earlier Soviet editions of the poem, for example, Khodasevich, *Stikhotvoreniia* (Leningrad: Sovetskii pisatel', 1989), pp. 249–50. As I. P. Andreeva and N. G. Bogomolov point out in their commentary to Khodasevich, *Sobranie sochinenii* (vol. 1, p. 525), Khodasevich's "quotation" is inaccurate when compared with published texts of the Pushkin poem, but remarkably close to a draft found subsequently.

102. Here is the Pushkin lyric that Khodasevich takes as his point of departure:

The night is quiet, in the heavenly field
The gold Evening Star shines.
The old Doge sails in his gondola
With the young Dogaressa.
The air is filled with the wafting of laurel.
The flags on the Bucintoro slumber.
The dark sea is silent.
. . . .

Ночь тиха, в небесном поле
Светит Веспер золотой.
Старый дож плывет в гондоле
С догарессой молодой.
Воздух полн дыханьем лавра.
Дремлют флаги бучентавра.
Море темное молчит.
. . . .

PSS, vol. 3, p. 360. The subject has been assumed to be the Venetian doge Marino Faliero (14th century); the *Bucintoro* was a large decorated boat for Venice celebrations (see ibid., p. 471). Khodasevich keeps Pushkin's trochaic tetrameter rhythm, with its melodic lilt; he also repeats most of Pushkin's images and some of his words, in a rearranged sequence.

103. In an analysis of "Romance," I. A. Balashova has argued that Pushkin would not have introduced song imagery into a poem so close to its end. I. A. Balashova, "V. L. Khodasevich, soavtor Pushkina (Stikhotvorenie 'Romans')," in Balashova, *Istochniki plenitel'nykh obrazov: Traditsii v russkoi romanticheskoi literature* (Rostov-na-Donu: Izdatel'stvo Rostovskogo pedagogicheskogo instituta, 1996), pp. 131–39.

104. See *Russkaia gazeta,* May 3, 1924, for the attack by A. I. Kuprin; *Poslednie novosti,* May 22, 1924, for Khodasevich's response; and Khodasevich, *Sobranie sochinenii,* ed. Hughes and Malmstad, vol. 1, p. 381, for a discussion of the polemic.

105. Khodasevich, *Sobranie sochinenii,* vol. 1, p. 350.

106. S. L. Abramovich, *Pushkin. Poslednii god. Khronika* (Moscow: Sovetskii pisatel', 1991), pp. 215–19.

107. I have in mind poems like "In Front of the Mirror" ("Pered zerkalom," 1924), with its epigraph from Dante and ending that has the speaker bereft of any companion, staring only at the image of his face in a mirror. See Khodasevich, *Sobranie sochinenii,* vol. 1, p. 277. For a fine reading of "In Front of the Mirror" and of Khodasevich's later poetry, see Alexandra Kirilcuk, "The Estranging Mirror: The Poetics of Reflection in the Late Poetry of Vladislav Khodasevich, *Russian Review,* vol. 61, no. 3 (2000), pp. 377–90.

108. Khodasevich, "O chtenii Pushkina," in Khodasevich, *Sobranie sochinenii,* vol. 2, pp. 114–20; Khodasevich, *Poeticheskoe khoziaistvo Pushkina* (Leningrad: Mysl', 1924). Khodasevich's autobiographical readings were controversial. See, for example, Boris Tomashevsky's review of *Poeticheskoe khoziaistvo Pushkina* in *Russkii sovremennik,* no. 3, 1924, pp. 262–63. Khodasevich's defense and reexplanation of his views also repay rereading: Khodasevich, "V sporakh o Pushkine," *Sovremennye zapiski,* vol. 37 (1928), pp. 275–94. For an excellent discussion of Khodasevich's views and of the subsequent polemics, see Surat, *Pushkinist Vladislav Khodasevich,* pp. 41–60.

109. Several of these rituals, including the Pushkin jubilees, are well studied in Karen Petrone, *Life Has Become More Joyous, Comrades: Celebrations in the Time of Stalin* (Bloomington: Indiana University Press, 2000). For a discussion of Soviet ritual celebrations through Brezhnev's rule, see Christel Lane, *The Rites of Rulers: Ritual in Industrial Society—The Soviet Case* (Cambridge, Eng.: Cambridge University Press, 1981).

110. David Brandenberger, "Russocentric Populism During the USSR's Official 1937 Pushkin Commemoration," *Russian History,* vol. 26, no. 1 (Spring 1999), pp. 65–73; quotations from pp. 72, 73. For a post-Soviet revisionist view of the 1937 Pushkin jubilee, see Iu. A. Molok, *Pushkin v 1937 g.: materialy i issledovaniia po ikonografii* (Moscow: NLO, 2000).

111. A. V. Blium, "'Sniat' kontrrevoliutsionnuiu shapku ... ': Pushkin i leningradskaia tsenzura 1937 g.," *Zvezda,* no. 2, 1997, pp. 209–15; quotation from p. 209.

112. Quoted material from Levitt, *Russian Literary Politics,* p. 165. My ellipses.

113. See, for example, B. Meilakh, "Nasledie Pushkina i sotsialisticheskaia kul'tura," *Krasnaia nov',* no. 1, 1937, pp. 111–27, esp. pp. 125–26.

114. Nikolai Tikhonov, speaking at the Bolshoi Theater, was among those who

performed this sleight of hand: "Rech' poeta N. Tikhonova," *Literaturnaia ucheba*, no. 3, 1937, p. 16.

115. For a fine discussion of the contradictions inherent in the preference for a triumphant narrative in Stalinist art, with particular reference to film, see Mikhail Iampolski, "Censorship as the Triumph of Life," in Thomas Lahusen and Evgeny Dobrenko, eds., *Socialist Realism Without Shores* (Durham, N.C.: Duke University Press, 1997), pp. 165–77.

116. Among many examples, see N. Svirin, "Sozdatel' russkogo literaturnogo iazyka," *Leningradskaia pravda*, Feb. 8, 1937. (Here and in subsequent notes, the lack of page numbers for newspaper articles in this period means that I cite clippings held in the Pushkiniana collection of Pushkin House [IRLI].)

117. A. V. Blium, *Sovetskaia tsenzura v epokhu total'nogo terrora. 1929–1939* (St. Petersburg: Akademicheskii proekt, 2000), pp. 170–72. An especially interesting example cited here is the objection to the claim in memoir accounts that Pushkin composed his ode on liberty ("Vol'nost'. Oda," 1817) in an impromptu, salon setting. Blium takes his material from the censorship records in the party archives in St. Petersburg. The incidents described in this book are also recounted in Blium, "'Sniat' kontrrevoliutsionnuiu shapku.'"

118. To cite three intrinsically interesting examples of academic and journalistic writing, from a vast literature: N. Stepanov, "Put' Pushkina k realizmu: stat'ia tret'ia, Realizm Pushkina," *Literaturnyi Leningrad*, Feb. 11, 1937 (no. 7 [212]), pp. 2–3; N. Svirin, "Pushkin i nasha sovremennost'," ibid., p. 1; L. Ginzburg, "Put' Pushkina k realizmu, ibid., June 6, 1936 (no. 26 [171]), p. 2. This Leningrad literary newspaper was soon to be shut down.

119. *PSS*, vol. 2, p. 240.

120. Petr Zaichenko, "'Russkii bunt.' 1998 god," *Iskusstvo kino*, no. 6, 1999, p. 5. Zaichenko, an actor, attributes this observation to the writer Andrei Bitov. The same sentiment was behind a headline in *Literaturnaia gazeta*, "On sterpel nashe vse," June 9, 1999, p. 9.

121. As reported in Catriona Kelly and David Shepherd, eds., *Constructing Russian Culture in the Age of Revolution: 1881–1940* (Oxford: Oxford University Press, 1998), p. 314.

122. Such statements were quoted repeatedly. I take these words from the flyleaf of the Leningrad journal *Zvezda*, no. 1, 1937 (as shown in Fig. 9).

123. See Lane, *Rites of Rulers*, pp. 204–20, on the proliferation of heroes in the Soviet period (the examples given are chiefly political, with an extended analysis of the cult of Lenin).

124. As noted in E. N. Mastenitsa, "Iz istorii muzeinoi pushkiniany, 1937 g.," *Peterburgskaia pushkiniana* (St. Petersburg: SpbGUKI, 2000), pp. 113–20; see p. 116.

125. "Pushkinskie iubilei v XX veke: ot mifologii k khristianstvu," interview with N. I. Granovskaia, *Pushkinskaia epokha i khristianskaia literatura*, vol. 7 (1995), pp. 3–6; see p. 3.

126. My favorite example of this unity of attention to Pushkin is the report of a train that was traveling between Rtishchevo and Bekovo on the anniversary day. The Rtishchevo library organized Pushkin readings for the length of the train trip. "Passazhiry poezda slushaiut stikhi Pushkina," *Kommunist* (Saratov), Feb. 11, 1937.

127. As reported in "V Sovnarkome Soiuza SSP," *Literaturnyi Leningrad*, Jan. 5, 1937 (no. 1 [206]), p. 1.

128. The 1899 centennial festivities also tried to push the celebration outward across the country, to synchronize multiple sites for commemoration, and to imprint "Pushkin" on objects of everyday life, from lamps and perfume to postcards and toys. Levitt, "Pushkin in 1899." Such commercialization occurred in 1937, too (rugs, tea service, faience vases, cookies, stamps, etc.). See "Kovry na pushkinskie temy," *Kommunist* (Saratov), Feb. 9, 1937; *Trud*, Feb. 11, 1937; *Vechernaia Moskva*, Feb. 14, 1937; and *Khar'kovskii rabochii*, Feb. 4, 1937. And it recurred in 1999, as discussed below.

129. *Pravda*, Feb. 10, 1937, p. 1.

130. In December 1936, complaints in provincial newspapers escalated, perhaps as anxiety about the nearness of the jubilee brought intensifed pressure from Moscow. Among many examples, see "Nakanune Pushkinskikh dnei: Usilit' tempy podgotovki," *Rabochii* (Minsk), Dec. 21, 1936; and "'Ochered' eshshe ne doshla,'" *Novyi put'* (Zaluch'e), Dec. 20, 1936.

131. For a striking example, see the report on a conference for representatives from all "Pushkin villages" (collective farms in places where Pushkin had lived). The discussion topics included increased flax production, electrification, anti-illiteracy campaigns, the lack of books and pictures of Pushkin, and the absence of leadership from Pushkin scholars. "Konferentsiia pushkinskikh sel," *Krest'ianskaia pravda*, Jan. 6, 1937.

132. "'Nachalos' s mertvykh petel',' ili kak prazdnovali Pushkina v 1936 godu," published by M. V. Stroganov, *Novoe literaturnoe obozrenie*, no. 37 (1999), pp. 173–79; see p. 176. The eyewitness is N. V. Zhuravlev (1901–1957).

133. "700 tysiach slushatelei na lektsiiakh o Pushkine," *Literaturnyi Leningrad*, Feb. 11, 1937 (no. 7 [212]), p. 4.

134. For a vivid description of the participation of factory workers, school groups, labor organizations (couched as criticism of the Writers' Union for not providing leadership for these amateurs), see "Bez pomoshchi i rukovodstva: Na soveshchanii litkritikov v Dome pisatelia" (unsigned), *Literaturnyi Leningrad*, Jan. 20, 1937 (no. 5 [210]), p. 4. In its next issue, the newspaper criticized the amateurish nature of such evenings: R. Villemson, "Ptichka bozhiia ne znaet," *Literaturnyi Leningrad*, Feb. 5, 1937 (no. 6 [211]), p. 4.

135. Iv. Tkhorzhevskii, "Cherez sto let," *Vozrozhdenie*, Feb. 6, 1937 (no. 4064), pp. 9–10; see p. 9.

136. "V Sovnarkome Soiuza SSR," *Literaturnyi Leningrad*, Jan. 5, 1937 (no. 1 [206]), p. 1.

137. *Pravda*, Feb. 4, 1937 (the entire front page was given to Pushkin-related material); *Izvestiia*, Feb. 4, 1937; *Leningradskaia pravda*, Feb. 4, 1937; *Trud*, Feb. 6, 1937; *Krasnaia zvezda*, Feb. 3, 1937.

138. Two of the more incongruous examples: an essay on Pushkin's poetry by Professor Doranov in *Sovetskaia torgovlia*, Feb. 10, 1937; and a piece by Professor Spassky on Russia's national poet in the newspaper of the food industry the same day.

139. "O poriadke provedeniia pushkinskikh iubileinykh dnei," *Literaturnaia gazeta*, Feb. 5, 1937 (no. 7 [643]), p. 1.

140. "Strana gotovitsia k pushkinskim dniam," ibid., Feb. 1, 1937 (no. 6 [642]), p. 4.

141. For the full list, see "Postanovlenie Tsentral'nogo Ispol'nitel'nogo Komiteta SSSR," *Literaturnyi Leningrad*, Feb. 11, 1937 (no. 7 [212]), p. 4. Except for the town of Pushkin, where he had indeed been a lyceum student and spent the first months of his marriage, none of these places had the slightest thing to do with Pushkin, which was not unusual in revolutionary renamings.

142. One such exhibit was a display of Pushkin's original manuscripts (or so it was claimed) in the Hermitage, the first such public showing. "Vystavka v Ermitazhe," *Literaturnaia gazeta*, Feb. 5, 1937 (no. 7 [643]), p. 1.

143. One cannot underestimate the repetitiveness in newspaper publications during this period—anything printed in *The Literary Gazette* or *Izvestiia* was reprinted many times in provincial newspapers.

144. M. A. Zoshchenko, "V pushkinskie dni," in Zoshchenko, *Sobranie sochinenii*, 2 vols. (Leningrad: Khudozhestvennaia literatura, 1986), vol. 2, pp. 416–21. The two speeches appeared in *Krokodil* in 1937, nos. 3 and 5.

145. On nervousness in Zoshchenko, see A. K. Zholkovskii, *Mikhail Zoshchenko: poetika nedoveriia* (Moscow: Shkola "Iazyki russkoi kul'tury," 1999). Zholkovsky also comments on "During the Pushkin Days" from a different point of view: the speaker's musing about which of his ancestors might have provided care for Pushkin, which one might have carried him in his arms, recalls one of Zoshchenko's invariant characters (the nanny) here "transformed into an ironic interpretation of the theme of literary fathers and sons, not unlike the formalist theory of literary evolution and its Bloomian variants" (p. 175).

146. Three examples. Pp. 3–4 of the journal *Krasnaia nov'*, no. 1, 1937, dealt with the show trials, under the headline "Bditel'nost', eshche i eshche raz bditel'nost'," with the following pages given to Pushkin: a full page with only a centered caption, "100 let so dnia gibeli velikogo russkogo poeta A. S. Pushkina 1837–1937," with an engraving of Pushkin on the next page. The four-page newspaper *Literaturnyi Leningrad*, no. 5 (210) devoted the first three pages of its Jan. 20, 1937, issue to the coverage of the trials, including calls for the death sentence; only the last page went to Pushkin-related articles. Finally, and perhaps most bizarrely, the lead article in the journal *Literary Studies* (a publication of the Soviet Writers' Union) combined both themes: it raised larger ideological questions, rehearsed the history of the Soviet Union since Lenin's death, praised the strength of a nation able to wipe out the "spies, murderers, diversionary tacticians, and servants of Fascism" now threatening it, and then placed the importance of the forthcoming Pushkin celebrations into this context. "Pod znamenem Lenina," *Literaturnaia ucheba*, no. 1, 1937, pp. i–iii.

147. Blium, *Sovetskaia tsenzura*, p. 169.

148. "Literaturnoe zaveshchanie Pushkina," *Literaturnaia ucheba*, no. 4, 1937, p. 5. My ellipses.

149. As one historian of Pushkin literary museums noted, despite all the vigilance and centralization, there were numerous examples of innovation and creativity in museum expositions. See Mastenitsa, "Iz istorii muzeinoi pushkiniany," p. 119. Historians have begun more generally to study Soviet citizens' less compliant forms of behavior in the Stalin period. See, for example, Lynne Viola, ed., *Con-*

tending with Stalinism: Soviet Power and Popular Resistance in the 1930s (Ithaca, N.Y.: Cornell University Press, 2002).

150. L. Ia. Ginzburg, "'I zaodno s pravoporiadkom...,'" *Tynianovskii sbornik: Tret'i tynianovskie chteniia* (Riga: Zinatne, 1988), pp. 218–30; quoted from p. 219.

151. Ginzburg, "Put' Pushkina k realizmu."

152. As an example of the approach to Pushkin's death in the 1930s, see B. Kazanskii, "Gibel' poeta," *Literaturnyi sovremennik*, no. 3, 1937, pp. 219–43. The article gives an account of previous approaches and reviews the relevant documents in the final duel. In its language and its attitude toward evildoers and martyred innocents, it is similar to the denunciations of enemies of the people that were appearing in the newspapers at the time, and Kazansky's essay was itself widely excerpted and reprinted.

153. See A. G. Rabiniants, "Iz tvorcheskoi istorii p'esy M. Bulgakova *Aleksandr Pushkin* (Bulgakov i pushkinistika 1920–1930 gg.)," *Problemy teatral'nogo naslediia M. A. Bulgakova* (Leningrad: LGITMiK, 1987), pp. 76–86.

154. See A. Colin Wright, *Mikhail Bulgakov: Life and Interpretations* (Toronto: University of Toronto Press, 1978), p. 213; and "Stenogramma zasedaniia Khudozhestvennogo soveta pri direktsii MKhAT 24.X.1939," *Russian Literature Triquarterly*, no. 15 (1978), p. 324.

155. For well-argued praise, see Ia. L. Levkovich, "Pushkin v sovetskoi khudozhestvennoi proze i dramaturgii," *Pushkin: Issledovaniia i materialy*, vol. 5 (1967), pp. 140–79, esp. pp. 177–79. More measured but still positive is A. Gozenpud "'Poslednie dni' ('Pushkin') (Iz tvorcheskoi istorii p'esy)," in *M. A. Bulgakov— dramaturg i khudozhestvennaia kul'tura ego vremeni* (Moscow: Soiuz teatral'nykh deiatelei RSFSR, 1988), pp. 154–67. Least enthusiastic is Wright, *Mikhail Bulgakov*, pp. 210–22, who finds "considerable craftsmanship" but no mastery.

156. Susan Larsen, "'I'm an Actor, Not a Writer'—Acting and Authorship in Bulgakov's Works," *Theater*, vol. 22, no. 2 (Spring 1991), pp. 40–46; see p. 46.

157. As reported in Elena Sergeevna Bulgakova's diaries. See J. A. E. Curtis, *Manuscripts Don't Burn: Mikhail Bulgakov: A Life in Letters and Diaries* (Woodstock, N.Y.: Overlook Press, 1992), p. 185.

158. Wright, *Mikhail Bulgakov*, pp. 215–16.

159. The poem begins:

A storm covers the sky in darkness,
Spiraling whirlwinds of snow;
It will howl like a wild beast,
Then start to cry, like a small child,

Буря мглою небо кроет,
Вихри снежные крутя;
То, как зверь, она завоет,
То заплачет, как дитя,

PSS, vol. 2, p. 258.

160. Mikhail Bulgakov, *P'esy* (Moscow: Sovetskii pisatel', 1986), p. 251.

161. The aside to Saltykova is suggestive in two other directions. Her name and patronymic, Alexandra Sergeevna, are used repeatedly as a form of address in this

scene (this was also noticed by O. Esipova, "Pushkin v p'ese M. Bulgakova," *Boldinskie chteniia*, 1985, pp. 183–90; see p. 185), giving her the role of a double for Pushkin. (There are other doubles in the play, like the Negro who stands guard in the fountain scene and the Kamer-junker who approaches the tsar with a message.) Saltykova also bears the brunt of her husband's misogynistic comments, which find many echoes in the play, as when Vorontsova's defense of Pushkin is dismissed as the chatter of a society woman, Natalia Nikolaevna is called "the Blackamoor's wife" ("arapskaia zhena"), and Heeckeren says that he hates women.

162. See Curtis, *Manuscripts Don't Burn*, p. 186.

163. As noticed by A. Gozenpud, "'Poslednie dni,'" p. 163.

164. Gozenpud sees the concern as typical of the age in which Bulgakov lived (ibid.).

165. Bulgakov, *P'esy*, pp. 284–85. My ellipses.

166. "Vast Pushkin Fete Is Held in Soviet," *New York Times*, Feb. 11, 1937.

167. Illuminating studies of trauma and nation include Paul Antze and Michael Lambek, eds., *Tense Past: Cultural Essays in Trauma and Memory* (New York: Routledge, 1996); Shoshana Felman and Dori Laub, *Testimony: Crises of Witnessing in Literature, Psychoanalysis, and History* (New York: Routledge, 1992); and Cathy Caruth, *Unclaimed Experience: Trauma, Narrative, and History* (Baltimore, Md.: Johns Hopkins University Press, 1996).

168. Pushkin was made a symbol of the motherland's salvation in 1949, noted one museum worker. See "Pushkinskie iubilei v XX veke," p. 4.

169. Daniil Kharms, *Polnoe sobranie sochinenii*, ed. V. N. Sazhin, 3 vols. (St. Petersburg: Akademicheskii proekt, 1997), vol. 2, p. 356.

170. For a discussion of the motif of falling more generally in "Incidents," without reference to the Pushkin tales, see Robin Aizlewood, "Towards an Interpretation of Kharms's *Sluchai*," in Neil Cornwell, ed., *Daniil Kharms and the Poetics of the Absurd: Essays and Materials* (New York: St. Martin's Press, 1991), pp. 97–122, esp. pp. 109–11. Falling is also the subject of one chapter of Mikhail Iampol'skii, *Bespamiatstvo kak istok* (Moscow: Novoe literaturnoe obozrenie, 1998), pp. 74–105. Iampolski's psychoanalytic and postmodern approach to Kharms has been exemplary for my thinking about Kharms's Pushkin texts.

171. Daniil Kharms, *Polet v nebesa* (Leningrad: Sovetskii pisatel', 1988), p. 531. The citation comes from the archives of the Institute of Russian Literature (IRLI), note the editors, giving no further details. I assume, though, after comparing the two extant versions of Kharms's 1936 children's tale, "Pushkin," that this is a trial run or discard from that text. See Kharms, *Polnoe sobranie sochinenii*, vol. 3, pp. 190–95, 305–8.

172. Anthony Anemone, "The Anti-World of Daniil Kharms," in Cornwell, ed., *Daniil Kharms*, pp. 71–96, esp. p. 79.

173. Pushkin, "Derzhavin," in *PSS*, vol. 8, p. 48.

174. Daniil Kharms, *Gorlo bredit britvoiu*, published as issue 4 of *Glagol*, 1991, p. 128.

175. Anthony Anemone suggests the possibility of such a reading when he persuasively sets out the terms for a moral and ethical interpretation of Kharms's later work: "Kharms gradually becomes aware that his role, as an artist, was one of com-

plicity in the creation of a monstrous social order." Anemone, "The Anti-World of Daniil Kharms," p. 81.

176. Iampol'skii, *Bespamiatstvo kak istok*, p. 89.

177. Likhachev gave the opening speech at the Pushkin House commemorative conference on Feb. 9, 1987. Other speakers over the three days included the filmmaker Andrei Khrzhanovsky, the historian Natan Eidelman, the writer Daniil Granin, and the film historian Neia Zorkaia. Not a group of radicals, to be sure, but all stalwarts of the liberal intelligentsia. The January issues of some journals ran items worthy of note, including Andrei Bitov, "Fotografiia Pushkina (1799–2099)," and Fazil' Iskander, "Motsart i Sal'eri," in *Znamia*, no. 1, 1987, pp. 98–120, 125–31; and Natan Eidel'man, "Ukhod," and V. Nepomniashchii, "Prorok," in *Novyi mir*, no. 1, 1987, pp. 98–125, 132–52.

178. *Ogonek*, Feb. 1987 (no. 6).

179. "The Poet of the People," *Boston Globe*, June 2, 1999, p. 1.

180. Celestine Bohlen, "Nobody Doesn't Like Aleksandr Sergeyevich," *New York Times*, June 2, 1999, pp. B1–B2. Bohlen also commented on the "crass commercialization" of the jubilee that "shamelessly put his name on everything from chocolates to vodka."

181. V. Nepomniashchii, "Iubileinye obryvki," *Iskusstvo kino*, no. 1, 2000, p. 61.

182. V. Radzishevskii, "Orden dlia Pushkina," *Literaturnaia gazeta*, Jan. 13, 1999 (no. 1-2 [5728]), p. 1.

183. Both cited by Evgenii Bunimovich, "Lichnaia zhizn'," *Literaturnaia gazeta*, June 1, 1999 (no. 22 [5745]), p. 13.

184. *Vozvrashchennye relikvii: Pushkiniana russkogo zarubezh'ia* (Moscow: Dom-muzei Mariny Tsvetaevoi, 1999).

185. Lev Rubinshtein, "Pushkin kak ob"ekt kitcha," *Itogi*, April 27, 1999. (Here, and subsequently for 1999 newspapers, the absence of a page number indicates an item read on the Internet through the Universal Database of Russian Newspapers.) The vodka label seems to have been particularly alarming: a photomontage on the front page of *The Literary Gazette* as early as January 1999 showed a (dreadful) bust of Pushkin atop two leather-bound volumes next to a vodka bottle, with a picnic spread in the foreground and a lake and birch tree in the background. The caption wished Pushkin courage: "Muzhaites', Aleksandr Sergeevich!" *Literaturnaia gazeta*, January 13, 1999, p. 1 (no. 1-2 [5728]). The accompanying article, V. Radzishevskii, "Orden dlia Pushkina," lamented the vodka bottle as well. Serious treatment of the Pushkin/Goethe connection also appeared. See Sergei Averintsev, "Gete i Pushkin (1749–1799–1999)," *Novyi mir*, no. 6, 1999, pp. 189–98; and Iurii Arkhipov, "'Pokoi i volia . . .': Pushkin i Gete," *Moskva*, no. 5, 1999, pp. 196–207.

186. Evgeniia Shcheglova, "Mifologiia obyvatelia, ili Evgenii Onegin—terminator: polemicheskie zametki," *Neva*, no. 7, 1999, pp. 193–202. Shcheglova's lengthy review has perhaps its best line in the title and risks breaking a cardinal philological rule that she herself restates: when arguing with force, choose a worthy opponent.

187. Andrei Turkin, "Sredi iubileinogo 'sora,'" *Iskusstvo kino*, no. 11, 2000, pp. 34–37.

188. V. Nepomniashchii, "Poor boy Onegin," *Iskusstvo kino*, no. 2, 2000, pp. 65–67. To his credit, Nepomniashchii temporarily avoids the xenophobic trap in which Shcheglova, in her repeated references to Druzhnikov as a California professor, languishes: he justly notes that most of *Onegin*'s failures are familiar from Russian film and stage versions. But he writes off the offensive image of Tatiana dreamily abed, slightly vampiric and sexualized as she reads Onegin's letter, as requisite eroticism destined for a Western audience—as if Russian speakers had shown no preferences of their own in the post-Soviet period for eroticized images of women.

189. Nepomniashchii, "Iubileinye obryvki," p. 61.

190. Anatolii Rubinov, "Pushkinskii iubilei sto let nazad…," *Novye izvestiia*, June 4, 1999, p. 6.

191. "Pushkin v medi(a)," *Ex libris NG*, June 1999 (no. 21 [93]), p. 1. The film was written by Andrei Bitov and Igor Klekh, based on an idea of Mikhail Gasparov, and was directed by M. Gureev. On the production of the film, see Igor' Klekh, "Pushkinskii prazdnik," www.guelman.ru/slava/writers/kleh4.htm.

192. Natal'ia Ivanova, "V Peterburge, s Pushkinym," *Znamia*, no. 9, 1999, pp. 238–39; quotation from p. 239, where Ivanova also reported that the night before she left for Petersburg, she received a note that the whole event was to be cancelled because the funding had fallen through. Money worries never really ended, apparently. Ivanova did note that a few too many poets read in Petersburg, as if collectively trying to fill in the void of Pushkin's absence (p. 238). More charitable toward the 200 poets was A.L., presumably Alla Latynina, "'Severnaia Pal'mira' i 200 poetov," *Literaturnaia gazeta*, June 9, 1999 (no. 23 [5746]), p. 9; the author also notes that the large crowds came to hear the poets.

193. The last two gaffes were noted by Nepomniashchii, "Iubileinye obryvki," p. 59.

194. As reported in Anna Gessen, "Pushkin Not Flooded: Toward a History of the Pushkin Myth and Anti-Myth," unpublished paper, 2001.

195. Irina Petrovskaia, "Iurskii chitaet *Onegina*," *Izvestiia*, June 5, 1999 (no. 101), preferred the TV-Tsentr channel's version of one reader, Sergei Iursky, reciting the entire text.

196. Ibid.

197. Andrei Novikov, "Ia ustal ot slova 'kul'tury'! O Mednom vsadnike kak glavnom geroe Pushkinskogo iubileia," *Znamia*, no. 7, 1999, pp. 208–12; see p. 208. This is a diatribe by one very angry critic, identified in the journal as a member of the Writers' Union and the Moscow Journalists' Union.

198. Dmitrii Abaulin, "On sterpel nashe vse," *Literaturnaia gazeta*, June 9, 1999 (no. 23 [5746]), p. 9.

199. "… I v nashi dni," *Novye izvestiia*, June 4, 1999, p. 6.

200. *Ex libris NG*, June 1999 (no. 21 [93]); my comments concern articles on pp. 1–2. The issue concludes with its own form of questionnaire, asking Petr Vail, Timur Kibirov, Eduard Limonov, Dmitri Prigov, Genrikh Sapgir, and Igor Yarkevich, among others, why they are not Pushkin. Predictably, only Limonov rises to the occasion: "In the first place, I don't want to be Pushkin. To be him means to be a poet of calendars, a poet who founds cities, rivers … I would not want to be this monument-monster" (p. 4).

201. Andrei Zorin, "Moi Pushkin," *Neprikosnovennyi zapas*, no. 2 (4), 1999, p. 40.

202. *Literaturnaia gazeta*, June 9, 1999 (no. 23 [5746]), p. 1.

203. Andrei Zorin, "Bezopasnyi seks," in *Shinel' Pushkina: Sbornik k 200-letnemu iubileiu A. S. Pushkina* (Moscow and St. Petersburg: Pentagraphic, Ltd., 2000), p. 6.

204. "Anketa 'LG,'" *Literaturnaia gazeta*, June 1, 1999 (no. 22 [5745]), pp. 1, 9.

205. "'Idi, kuda vlechet tebia svobodnyi um ... ,'" *Znamia*, no. 6, 1999, pp. 172–78.

206. "'Na fone Pushkina,'" *Iskusstvo kino*, no. 6, 1999, pp. 101–7.

207. Genrikh Sapgir, "Chernoviki Pushkina," *Druzhba narodov*, no. 5, 1999, pp. 110–15; for "I ia by mog kak shut na [...]," see p. 111.

208. *Faksimil'noe vosproizvedenie samodel'noi knigi Dmitriia Aleksandrovicha Prigova 'Evgenii Onegin Pushkina'* (St. Petersburg: Mitkilibris and "Krasnyi matros," 1998).

209. D. A. Prigov, "Pop-geroi," an interview conducted by Sergei Shapoval, *NG—Figury i litsa*, June 5, 1999 (no. 11 [32]). Prigov also noted that he was inspired to recopy *Onegin* in the first place by an anecdote that circulated in the late Soviet period, about a mother whose son would only read *samizdat* literature, so she copied out *War and Peace* for him on a typewriter.

210. The two films were praised by Zhanna Vasil'eva, "Na boikom meste 'Kinotavra' lidiruet 'Na-Na,'" *Literaturnaia gazeta*, June 9, 1999 (no. 23 [5746]), p. 9.

211. The first is *A Lullaby for Cricket* (*Kolybel'naia dlia sverchka*), an homage to the Italian writer Tonino Guerra filmed during his visit to Petersburg. Nearly half the film is devoted to a poem Guerra wrote about Pushkin, read in Russian translation by Bella Akhmadulina. Guerra is seen at several Petersburg Pushkin shrines (including the apartment on the Moika and the duel site at Chernaia rechka).

212. On the exhibit opening, see *Obzor dzhazovoi zhizni*, Oct. 30, 1998 (no. 2), at www.jazz.ru/mag/2/longarms.htm. The event also featured literary talent, including Andrei Bitov and Lev Rubinshtein.

213. Mary Russo has also linked flight to the grotesque. See Russo, *The Female Grotesque: Risk, Excess and Modernity* (New York: Routledge, 1994), pp. 17–52.

214. Another promising Pushkin film of 1999 was never made. Marlen Khutsiev intended to make a movie about Pushkin, the result of which was a documentary about his unrealized plan, plus a published excerpt from *Pushkin*, a "film-novel." The documentary was made for television, under the title *Marlen Khutsiev. Istoriia zamysla* (1997); see *Pushkinskii kinoslovar'* (Moscow: Sovremennye tetradi, 1999), p. 181. For the text, see Khutsiev, "Pushkin: Kinoroman, otryvki," *Tainy pushkinskogo slova* (Moscow: Moskovskii detskii fond and Kontinent-Press, 1999), pp. 251–64.

215. The scene also ludicrously proves the truth of Shvabrin's earlier slanders, as is noted in Anastasiia Arkhipova, "Pushkin i Proshkin," *Nezavisimaia gazeta, Religii*, Nov. 15, 2000, p. 7.

216. George Faraday, *Revolt of the Filmmakers: The Struggle for Artistic Autonomy and the Fall of the Soviet Film Industry* (University Park: Pennsylvania State

University Press, 2000), p. 138. He adds that filmmakers began to target festival audiences as a way to garner artistic prestige. Although writing of the early 1990s, Faraday offers insights into the economics of post-Soviet filmmaking that were still keenly felt by Proshkin later in the decade.

217. A producer's objection to the image of a slain wolf in *The Russian Uprising* is tellingly to the point: "We're making a movie for Europe," he said, where groups like Greenpeace would never stand for such cruelty. Petr Zaichenko, "*Russkii bunt*. 1998 god," *Iskusstvo kino*, no. 6, 1999, pp. 5–15, quotation on p. 14.

218. Arkhipova, "Pushkin i Proshkin." A less acerbic reviewer in *Iskusstvo kino* also found the historical logic of the uprising absent and, strangely, saw the film itself as timid. See V. Matizen, "Russkii bunt: istoki i smysl," *Iskusstvo kino*, no. 5, 2000, pp. 18–24, esp. p. 22.

219. Aleksandr Proshkin, "'Eto nasha beda, chto my sdelali iz razboinikov natsional'nykh geroev,'" an interview conducted by Anzhelika Artiukh, *Iskusstvo kino*, no. 5, 2000, pp. 24–29, quotation from p. 26.

220. Vladimir Krakovskii, "Odin nad nami rok," *Oktiabr'*, no. 8, 1999, pp. 3–51; quotation from p. 4.

221. Ibid., p. 18.

222. Ibid., p. 12.

223. Ibid., p. 43.

224. Il'ia Foniakov, "Svershilos'!.. Nakonets vyshel pervyi tom akademicheskogo Pushkina," *Literaturnaia gazeta*, June 9, 1999 (no. 23 [5746]), p. 9.

225. "Sluzhenie muz," *Iskusstvo kino*, no. 6, 1999, p. 169. The journal published excerpts from the dictionary in its Pushkin issue. For the volume, see *Pushkinskii kinoslovar'.*

226. For example, O. S. Murav'eva, "Geroi" and "Napoleon," *Zvezda*, no. 1, 1999, pp. 233–38; M. Virolainen, "Andrei Shen'e," and O. S. Murav'eva, "Voobrazhaemyi razgovor s Aleksandrom I," *Zvezda*, no. 2, 1999, pp. 233–37; and I. S. Chistova, "Oda. Vol'nost'," *Zvezda*, no. 7, 1999, pp. 235–38. A popular version of an encyclopedia, unrelated to this project, was printed for the jubilee, on fancy paper with lots of illustrations: *Pushkinskaia entsiklopediia 1799–1999* (Moscow: Izdatel'stvo AST, 1999). No editors' names appear in the volume.

227. A. S. Pushkin, *Polnoe sobranie sochinenii*, CD-ROM (Moscow: MtsF, 1999), for the second and fuller edition (with illustrations and some criticism).

228. N. V. Kolosova, ed., *Boldinskaia osen': Stikhotvoreniia, poemy, malen'kie tragedii…* 1st, 2d eds. (Moscow: Molodaia gvardiia, 1974, 1982), 3d ed. (Gorky: Volgo-Viatskoe knizhnoe izdatel'stvo, 1990).

229. *Letopis' zhizni i tvorchestva Aleksandra Pushkina*, 4 vols. (Moscow: Slovo, 1999). The portion prepared by Tsiavlovsky (1799–1826) was revised and reissued in 1991 as well.

230. Tsiavlovskii and Tsiavlovskaia, *Vokrug Pushkina*.

231. B. L. Modzalevskii, *Pushkin: vospominaniia, pis'ma, dnevniki* (Moscow: Agraf, 1999). This is a reprint of the 1929 edition, mistakes uncorrected. See B. Radzishevskii, "Viazemskii vmesto Kiukhel'bekera," *Literaturnaia gazeta*, June 16–23, 1999 (no. 24 [5747]), p. 10, for a review. See also B. L. Modzalevskii, *Pushkin i ego sovremenniki: Izbrannye trudy 1898–1928* (St. Petersburg: Iskusstvo-SPB,

1999); L. I. Vol'pert, *Pushkin v roli Pushkina* (Moscow: Iazyki russkoi kul'tury, 1998); Natan Eidel'man, *Stat'i o Pushkine* (Moscow: NLO, 2000); and V. E. Vatsuro, *Pushkinskaia pora* (St. Petersburg: Akademicheskii proekt, 2000). Vatsuro's large study of the Gothic novel was also later published: *Goticheskii roman v Rossii* (Moscow: NLO, 2002).

232. Vladimir Nabokov, *Kommentarii k romanu A. S. Pushkina "Evgenii Onegin"* (St. Petersburg: Iskusstvo-SPB and Nabokovskii fond, 1998). *The Literary Gazette* called the release of this book in February 1999 a significant publishing event. See "Nabokov, oruzhenosets Pushkina," *Literaturnaia gazeta*, March 17, 1999 (no. 11 [5736]), p. 10.

233. Oleg Proskurin, *Poeziia Pushkina, ili Podvizhnyi Palimpsest* (Moscow: Novoe literaturnoe obozrenie, 1999). See "Piat knig nedeli," *Ex libris NG*, June 1999 (no. 21 [93]), p. 1, for the praise.

234. See the photograph accompanying Maria Sedykh's interview with Kama Ginkas, "Igrai, da ne zaigryvaisia!" *Literaturnaia gazeta*, June 2, 1999 (no. 22 [5745]), p. 12.

235. Celestine Bohlen, "Wily Gamester Keeps Theater Alive in Russia," *New York Times*, July 25, 2000, pp. B1–B2; Liubov' Oves, "Kama Ginkas. 'Pushkin. Duel'. Smert',''' *Peterburgskii teatral'nyi zhurnal*, March 2000 (no. 20), www.theatre.ru/ptzh/2000/20/064.html.

236. I cannot judge Ginkas's play, not having seen it, but I can tell that it fits well with traditions for celebrating Pushkin: it focuses on his death, like so much work earlier, and it does so in a deeply moral way. The production used black and white as its constant colors, meant to suggest good vs. evil and to turn the play into an ethical contemplation of the nature of Pushkin's demise. The drama's website is www.theatre.ru/maska/2000/drama/pushkin. For a thorough account of the play, see Oves, "Kama Ginkas."

237. See www.guelman.ru/actions/dantes and, for more on Irina Waldron, www.guelman.ru/artists/waldron.html.

238. See www.geocities.com/SoHo/8070/pushpics.htm.

239. "S Natal'ei Nikolaevnoi ... ," *Literaturnaia gazeta*, June 9, 1999 (no. 23 [5746]), p. 9.

240. Mikhail Kuraev, "Ganichev i drugie na fone Pushkina," ibid., Feb. 17, 1999, p. 9. The design and execution of the monument for 1937 is fairly well documented. For a short history of the site, see V. K. Zazhurilo, L. I. Kuz'mina, and G. I. Nazarova, *Pushkinskie mesta Leningrada* (Leningrad: Lenizdat, 1974), pp. 203–12, slightly updated in the 1989 ed., retitled *Liubliu tebia, Petra tvoren'e* (pp. 222–30).

241. Sedykh and Ginkas, "Igrai, da ne zaigryvaisia!" Ginkas draws the collocation from the 1988 American film *The Unbearable Lightness of Being*, without mentioning Milan Kundera's novel.

CHAPTER 4

Part of an earlier version of this chapter appeared as "Pushkin as a Sign in Russian Culture: The Example of Film," in Robert Reid, Joe Andrew, and Valentina Polukhina, eds., *Structure and Tradition in Russian Society* (Helsinki: Slavica Helsigiensia, 1994), pp. 138–52. Another part has been published as "*Little Tragedies* on Film: Cinematic Realism and Embodied Inspiration," in Svetlana Evdokimova, ed., *The Poetics of Brevity: Pushkin's Little Tragedies* (Madison: University of Wisconsin Press, 2003), pp. 290–301.

EPIGRAPH: Iurii Lotman and Iurii Tsiv'ian, *Dialog s ekranom* (Tallinn: Aleksandra, 1994), p. 213.

1. Svetlana Boym, "Estrangement as a Lifestyle: Shklovsky and Brodsky," in Susan Rubin Suleiman, ed., *Exile and Creativity: Signposts, Travelers, Outsiders, Backward Glances* (Durham, N.C.: Duke University Press, 1998), pp. 241–62; quoted from p. 241. See also Boym, *The Future of Nostalgia* (New York: Basic Books, 2001).

2. See N. N. Efimov, "Biograficheskie fil'my o Pushkine," in *Pushkin. Issledovaniia i materialy*, vol. 5 (1967), pp. 305–15. Efimov also discusses *The Poet and the Tsar* (*Poet i tsar'*, 1927), *Journey to Arzrum* (*Puteshestvie v Arzrum*, 1937), *The Poet's Boyhood* (*Iunost' poeta*, 1937), and two films in which Pushkin appears as a minor character: *Glinka* (1946) and *Glinka the Composer* (*Kompozitor Glinka*, 1952).

3. For the statistics, see Vladimir Semerchuk, "Mezhdu poetikoi i ideologiei: Pushkin v igrovom kino: Dve strategii ekranizatsii," *Pushkinskii kinoslovar'* (Moscow: Sovremennye tetradi, 1999), p. 246. Semerchuk counts 50 Pushkin films (against 43 for Chekhov, 24 for Tolstoy, and 10 for Dostoevsky). A few details about the screening history of *Boris Godunov* appear in *Pushkinskii kinoslovar'*, p. 15. The film was made in the studio of A. Drankov and not preserved.

4. Yuri Tsivian, *Early Cinema in Russia and Its Cultural Reception*, tr. Alan Bodger (New York: Routledge, 1994), p. 6.

5. Bill Nichols, *Representing Reality: Issues and Concepts in Documentary Film* (Bloomington, Ind.: Indiana University Press, 1991), pp. 12–31. Nichols defines documentary films, after Foucault, as a set of institutional practices, as a corpus of recognizable work, and as films with a community of viewers.

6. On Vorontsova, see L. A. Chereiskii, *Pushkin i ego okruzhenie* (Leningrad: Nauka, 1988), p. 78. G. P. Makogonenko has argued that the legendary love of Pushkin for Vorontsova is almost entirely baseless, and that theirs was a typical society infatuation, more playful than serious, and extremely short-lived. See his *Tvorchestvo A. S. Pushkina v 1830-e gody (1830–1833)* (Leningrad: Khudozhestvennaia literatura, 1974), pp. 53–79. He also disproves the idea, put forth in P. K. Guber's *Don-Zhuanskii spisok Pushkina* (1923; reprinted in *Liubovnyi byt pushkinskoi epokhi*, 2 vols. Moscow: Izd. Vasanta, 1994, vol. 1, pp. 11–185) that the name Tatiana on Pushkin's Don Juan list refers to Vorontsova (Makogonenko, *Tvorchestvo A. S. Pushkina*, p. 74). I mention this, however, because it is possible that the filmmakers knew Guber's work, and that it motivated their choice of a name for Aleksei Petrovich's wife (as much as the more obvious association with the heroine of *Eugene Onegin*).

7. For the poem, see *PSS*, vol. 2, p. 230.

8. A still from this scene was used in two bits of criticism, both clearly meant to promote the film. See *Sputnik kinozriteli*, Oct. 1986, p. 8; and *Iskusstvo kino*, no. 11, 1986, p. 35.

9. One critic found these seemingly unscripted scenes wonderfully informal and spontaneous, so much so that it seemed to infect the more clearly "acted" parts of the film with an unimpeachably real and conversational feel. B. Runin, "Na fone Pushkina," *Iskusstvo kino*, no. 11, 1986, pp. 25–32; see p. 26. The director has said that this air of spontaneity and lightness is very important to him on all his film sets, no less so here. Roman Balaian, "Kak sochetat' nesochitaemoe" (an interview conducted by Zara Abdullaeva), *Literaturnoe obozrenie*, no. 4, 1987, pp. 88–94; see p. 88.

10. Films that refuse to let an actor play Pushkin resemble Bulgakov's play *The Last Days*, which Kozakov soon mentions in a slightly different context.

11. Kraval's views did begin to find their way into print in the 1980s, for example in a short piece, "Providcheskii risunok Pushkina?," in *Iunost'*, no. 6, 1984, pp. 102–5. But a book-length study of her interpretations did not appear until the late 1990s: L. Kraval', *Risunki Pushkina kak graficheskii dnevnik* (Moscow: Nasledie, 1997).

12. Okudzhava makes a further point: that one reads the arguments between Pushkin scholars with amazement and a little disbelief. For himself, he says, he believes them all, at least in part. This idea, too, speaks to a valuable multiplicity of perspectives on Pushkin, even as it very gently ridicules the scholars who would seek to control Pushkin's legacy.

13. G. S. Smith, "Okudzhava Marches On," *Slavonic and East European Review*, vol. 66, no. 4 (Oct. 1988), pp. 553–63; quotations from p. 554. Smith also argues persuasively that "guitar poetry was probably the most characteristic artistic expression of the generation of Soviet intellectuals that matured after the 1956 Thaw" (p. 558), which suggests to me that the film, in associating itself with Okudzhava's work, also associates itself with this generation, thus broadening and complicating its exploration of the moral crisis of a member of the intelligentsia.

14. Okudzhava, *Chaepitie na Arbate: Stikhi raznykh let* (Moscow: PAN, 1995), p. 267. This volume shows well Okudzhava's interest in Pushkin over the years. It includes "Aleksandr Sergeich" (pp. 117–18); "Schastlivchik Pushkin" (pp. 157–58); "Byloe nel'zia vorotit', i pechalit'sia ne o chem" (pp. 167–68); "Dom na Moike" (pp. 318–19); and "Stalin Pushkina listal" (pp. 330–31).

15. Cited from the film. The poem does not appear in any of Okudzhava's books, but it must have had some currency at the time. The author of the film's scenario takes two lines from it as the epigraph to his script: "While all is not yet lost, / Keep me safe, my talisman" ("Poka eshche ne vse poteriano, / Khrani menia, moi talisman." Rustam Ibragimbekov, "Khrani menia, moi talisman," *Iskusstvo kino*, no. 4, 1986, pp. 149–74; quoted on p. 151.

16. Balaian's plural "we" is his signal for social commentary, an element that in many Pushkin films, as in this one, emerges as a claim that "we" have lost something valuable that existed in the Pushkin period. Balaian, "Kak sochetat' nesochitaemoe," p. 89.

17. V. Demin, "V nadezhde na talisman," *Iskusstvo kino*, no. 11, 1986, pp. 32–40; see p. 38.

18. Runin, "Na fone Pushkina," p. 27.

19. Ibid.

20. The director defends this silly behavior both as an aspect of the light atmosphere he wished to create in the film and as a psychologically plausible response to a situation where Klimov knows unerringly that he does not risk being killed. Balaian, "Kak sochetat' nesochitaemoe," p. 89.

21. Runin, "Na fone Pushkina," pp. 30–31.

22. Peter Brooks, "Melodrama, Body, Revolution," in Jacky Bratton, Jim Cook, and Christine Gledhill, eds., *Melodrama: Stage Picture Screen* (London: BFI Publishing, 1994), pp. 11–24; quoted from p. 19.

23. Oleg Iankovskii, introductory remarks, in Ibragimbekov, "Khrani menia, moi talisman," p. 151.

24. Ibid., p. 150.

25. Ibid., p. 172. Earlier in the film script, Kirill also dreams that he duels with d'Anthès (p. 167).

26. Runin, "Na fone Pushkina," p. 30. More critical of the film in its entirety is the Pushkin scholar Sergei Kibalnik, who reported that others shared his irritation with the vulgarity of the end result, despite their high hopes that a film drawing on such talented people would be successful. S. A. Kibal'nik, *Pushkin i sovremennaia kul'tura* (Leningrad: Znanie, 1989), p. 23.

27. Brooks, "Melodrama, Body, Revolution," pp. 11–12, 18.

28. For a reading of this scene as a sign of Aleksei Petrovich's moral inadequacy, see Demin, "V nadezhde na talisman," p. 40.

29. An excellent analysis of Russian dueling practices is Irina Reyfman, *Ritualized Violence Russian Style: The Duel in Russian Culture and Literature* (Stanford, Calif.: Stanford University Press, 1999). Reyfman observes that literary duels often violated conventions and norms of honor, which is also true in this latter-day example.

30. In the film script, Briantsev (the prototype for Klimov) asks for forgiveness during the duel. He says, "If you forgive me, I'll disappear. I'll swear on whatever you want, I'll disappear forever, as if I'd never been." Ibragimbekov, "Khrani menia, moi talisman," p. 171. The film keeps only the moment when the "demon" disappears.

31. Iankovsky is not without interest, of course—although one cannot agree with Balaian, who praises exclusively his face. "Kak sochetat' nesochetaemoe," p. 88. The enthralled reactions to Tatiana Drubich's performance as Tanya seem excessive, if not implausible. See ibid., p. 91. Demin adores the performance as "human responsiveness itself, a miracle of the feminine dissolved into her beloved, unconditional, unlimited, and great in its sense of ease." "V nadezhde na talisman," p. 35.

32. Ibragimbekov, "Khrani menia, moi talisman," p. 158.

33. Balaian, "Kak sochetat' nesochetaemoe," p. 88.

34. Demin, "V nadezhde na talisman," pp. 32–33.

35. Both claims were made to me in conversations with Leonid Menaker and Iakov Gordin in Petersburg, Oct.–Nov. 1991. I take this occasion to thank both for meeting with me, and to thank Mr. Menaker for making me a copy of his film and giving me the film script.

36. Iu. N. Tynianov, "Kino—slovo—muzyka," in Tynianov, *Poetika, istoriia literatury, kino* (Moscow: Nauka, 1977), pp. 320–45; see p. 321.

37. Among consultants for the film was the excellent Pushkin scholar Vadim Vatsuro. For a full listing of actors and technical staff, see *Pushkinskii kinoslovar'*, p. 62.

38. The later image of Pushkin's wounded body being carried into the Moika apartment by his servant Nikita Kozlov may recall E. E. Moiseenko's much-praised painting *In Memory of the Poet* (*Pamiati poeta*, 1985). The one-year interval between the painting and the film gives me pause in asserting a connection, although it is entirely possible that the painting was quickly seen by Leningrad intellectuals. Another source for this image is the production of Bulgakov's play *The Last Days* in Moscow in the 1950s, when an exception to the general exclusion of Pushkin from the action was the moment when Nikita Kozlov was seen carrying him (as described to me by Viktoria Schweitzer).

39. In the film script there are several occasions where the technical remarks call for facsimile documents from the period, and the notes stress the importance of using specially prepared paper, ensuring that their appearance conformed to the originals. Some furnishings for the sets and other props are indicated as originals from the period.

40. The presentation of both men, I would argue, is somewhat slanted. Particularly in the case of Viazemsky, who appears in a less important role in the film, there are large assumptions about his distance from Pushkin in these years. Iakov Gordin's writings make clear that he feels quite strongly on this point. See "Gibel' Pushkina," his 1973 quasi-chronicle of Pushkin in the 1830s, in Gordin, *Tri povesti* (Leningrad: Sovetskii pisatel', 1983), pp. 120–288. Gordin stresses the enmity between Viazemsky and Pushkin (pp. 153, 179–80) and has Viazemsky note that Pushkin was not understood by his friends (pp. 287–88). In a review of L. A. Chereiskii's *Pushkin i ego okruzhenie*, Gordin faults his portrayal of Viazemsky for not taking into account the difficulties between him and Pushkin in the 1830s. See Gordin, "Sud'ba sredi sudeb," *Voprosy literatury*, no. 9, 1977, pp. 265–71, esp. pp. 267–68.

41. This interpretation is amply supported by Gordin's other writings about Pushkin, especially "Gibel' Pushkina." Gordin radically diminishes the importance of Pushkin's family life in the 1830s, noting that Pushkin's marriage was not a factor in his newfound sense of happiness in the early 1830s (p. 152) and only briefly commenting on Natalia Nikolaevna's attractiveness to the tsar (pp. 196–97). He also has d'Anthès make only the briefest appearance (p. 283). See also Gordin, *Pravo na poedinok* (Leningrad: Sovetskii pisatel', 1989), on the historical-political context of dueling in the 1830s and on dueling as a metaphor in Pushkin's struggles as a public figure.

42. See William Mills Todd III, *The Familiar Letter as a Literary Genre in the Age of Pushkin* (Princeton, N.J.: Princeton University Press, 1976); and Iu. M. Lotman, "Dekabrist v povsednevnoi zhizni (Bytovoe povedenie kak istoriko-psikhologicheskaia kategoriia)," *Literaturnoe nasledie dekabristov* (Leningrad: Nauka, 1975), pp. 25–74, esp. pp. 64–69, translated by C. R. Pike as "The Decembrist in Everyday Life," in Ju. M. Lotman and B. A. Uspenskij, *The Semiotics of Russian Culture*, ed. Ann Shukman (Ann Arbor: University of Michigan Press, 1984), pp. 71–124. The cult of male friendship, so typical of the 1810s and early 1820s, was much diminished by the 1830s, but when Pushkin died, some evocation of these bonds occurred. *The Last Road* suggests this in the scene when Zhukovsky uses a

reference to Arzamas to try to remind S. S. Uvarov of his onetime friendly relationship with Pushkin.

43. Vera Viazemskaia tries to warn her husband of the impending disaster, but elicits only his famous comment that he turns his face away from the doings in Pushkin's house (the scene has him repeat the rumor that Pushkin is in love with Aleksandra Nikolaevna, to his wife's disbelief and horror that he would repeat it); Viazemsky and Zhukovsky discuss the behavior of all concerned with mild disgust and no inclination to intervene. After the duel, Turgenev asks Danzas why he did not prevent the duel; Natalia Nikolaevna accusingly asks her sister, Aleksandra Nikolaevna, if she knew about the duel (and the film, in betraying Aleksandra Nikolaevna's nervousness, suggests that she did); and Viazemsky is seen falling down in despair in the snow, lamenting to his wife that he could have saved Pushkin.

44. Natal'ia Ivanova, "Russkii vopros," *Znamia*, no. 1, 1992, pp. 191–204. For the controversy, see "'Fallichnost' natsii' i russkii vopros," *Literaturnaia gazeta*, Jan. 29, 1992 (no. 5 [5382]), p. 4; Ivanova's response, "'Davaite snachala uchit'sia...,'" *Literaturnaia gazeta*, March 4, 1992 (no. 10 [5387]), p. 5; and Igor' Zolotusskii, "'Oni ne zhelali oboniat' *dukh*,'" *Literaturnaia gazeta*, March 4, 1992 (no. 10 [5387], p. 5.

45. This comment undoubtedly stems from Zhukovsky's memoir of Pushkin's death, written in the form of a letter to Pushkin's father. He writes, "In general, from the beginning to the end of his sufferings (except for two or three hours the first night, when the suffering exceeded all bounds of human endurance), he was remarkably strong. 'I participated in 30 battles,' said Dr. Arendt, 'I have seen many dying men, but few who were like this.'" See Zhukovskii, "Pis'mo k S. L. Pushkinu," in V. E. Vatsuro et al., eds., *Pushkin v vospominaniiakh sovremennikov*. 2 vols. (Moscow: Khudozhestvennaia literatura, 1974), vol. 2, pp. 346–47.

46. This is the order of the conversation in the film script, but it is reversed in the final version of the film.

47. See K. K. Danzas, "Poslednie dni zhizni i konchina Aleksandra Sergeevicha Pushkina v zapisi A. Amosova," in *A. S. Pushkin v vospominaniiakh sovremennikov*, vol. 2, p. 331.

48. Compare a Petersburg documentary television program aired in 1992, also called *The Last Road*, which retraced the path of Pushkin's dead body and showed various sites as they are now. There, the title's metaphor is more fully the structuring narrative.

49. Interestingly enough, the television script that Yuri Lotman wrote about Pushkin also ends with the death mask, an original of which is held at Tartu University, where Lotman taught. He adds that the sight of the mask involuntarily calls to mind Zhukovsky's poem on Pushkin's death, where he wanted to ask the dead Pushkin what he sees. See Iu. M. Lotman, "V mire pushkinskoi poezii," *Versii: Televizionnye stsenarii* (Moscow: Iskusstvo, 1989), pp. 32–33. Lotman uses this question, how Pushkin saw the world, to unify his presentation of visual imagery in Pushkin's writing, whereas I am suggesting that the film omits entirely the question of how Pushkin saw the world.

50. Karen Swann, "The Strange Time of Reading," *European Romantic Review*, vol. 9, no. 2 (1998), pp. 275–82; quotation from p. 275. For all the differences between Keats, the subject of this essay, and Pushkin, Swann's essay has many perti-

nent observations, including her comment on the obligations to the dead felt by the poet's friends, and her more general project of analyzing the rhetoric and temporality of the poet's writings that seem to speak across the bounds of death.

51. For the poem, see *PSS*, vol. 2, pp. 16–17. On the vast influence of "The Black Shawl" on the Russian ballad, see Michael Wachtel, *The Development of Russian Verse: Meter and Its Meanings* (Cambridge, Eng.: Cambridge University Press, 1998), pp. 20–58. Wachtel's reading is especially pertinent to my argument here because he traces the confluence of theme (revenge, betrayal) with meter in later ballads.

52. Mamin's two previous films, both well received, are treated as successful satires in Andrew Horton, "Carnivals Bright, Dark, and Grotesque in the Glasnost Satires of Mamin, Mustafayev, and Shakhnazarev," in Horton, ed., *Inside Soviet Film Satire: Laughter with a Lash* (Cambridge, Eng.: Cambridge University Press, 1993), pp. 138–48, esp. pp. 138–44.

53. See Mikhail Bakhtin, *Tvorchestvo Fransua Rable i narodnaia kul'tura srednekov'ia i renessansa* (Moscow: Khudozhestvennaia literatura, 1965), translated as *Rabelais and His World* by Helene Iswolsky (Cambridge, Mass.: MIT Press, 1968). Mamin's comments about the film suggest that the carnival model found in the films of Fellini was especially pertinent to him. See Andrew Horton, "'One Should Begin with Zero': A Discussion with the Satiric Filmmaker Yuri Mamin," in Horton, ed., *Inside Soviet Film Satire*, p. 155.

54. The sex scenes, such as they are, are entirely theatrical: rather than Capella members engaged in sexual contact, the film shows them playing at sex, with a ritualized burying of a young woman's maidenhead, for example.

55. A similar image begins Alfred Hitchcock's film *Vertigo* (1958), and in the same precise way: a facial close-up where the eyes look to one side, then the other, then straight ahead. For Hitchcock, the face introduces the film's fascination with a woman's identity. Mamin parodies the tragic atmosphere of Hitchcock's film, mocking Victor in the scene where he claims that his resemblance to Pushkin is a remarkable coincidence of fate.

56. Capella members use walking canes as weapons, having filled them with lead; Pushkin's walking cane was also said to have been weighted, so he could strengthen his arm for dueling. This is a good example of how the film uses minor details from Pushkin's life for new ends.

57. One scholar found the ending too gloomy and deemed the film "a very bitter and unsubtle diatribe against the rise of antisemitism and dangerous right-wing political movements." See Vida T. Johnson, "Laughter Beyond the Mirror: Humor and Satire in the Cinema of Andrei Tarkovsky," in Horton, ed., *Inside Soviet Film Satire*, p. 103.

58. Catharine Theimer Nepomnyashchy, review of *Side Whiskers*, *Slavic Review*, vol. 51, no. 3 (1992), p. 566. As Michael Cooke once noted with regard to the long poems of the Romantic period, satire, elegy, and prophecy are often found in combination, which gives us another reason for this film's having used Pushkin's "Prophet" as its point of departure. Cooke, *Acts of Inclusion: Studies Bearing on an Elementary Theory of Romanticism* (New Haven, Conn.: Yale University Press, 1979), pp. 1–54.

59. For a more psychoanalytical reading of the situation of film viewers than I

offer here that has been very influential in film studies, see Jean-Louis Baudry, "The Apparatus: Metapsychological Approaches to the Impression of Reality in the Cinema," originally published in 1975 and reprinted in Philip Rosen, ed., *Narrative, Apparatus, Ideology: A Film Theory Reader* (New York: Columbia University Press, 1986), pp. 299–318.

60. For a description of each short film (the titles are "I k vam lechu vospominan'em...," "I s vami snova ia...," and "Osen'"), see *Pushkinskii kinoslovar'*, pp. 105–7.

61. Khrzhanovsky had used Pushkinian themes in some of his earlier works, including *V mire basen* (1973), based on Krylov's fables but with some animation of Pushkin's drawings; and *Den' chudesnyi* (1975), a film that animates children's drawings of Pushkin's characters in his fairytales. On both films, see *Pushkinskii kinoslovar'*, pp. 103–4.

62. See A. V. Ivashkin, ed., *Besedy s Al'fredom Shnitke* (Moscow: RIK 'Kul'tura,' 1994), pp. 121–25. The volume includes a list of Schnittke's compositions, including those for the 63 films on which he worked (pp. 295–97). For an affectionate memoir written after Schnittke's death, see Andrei Khrzhanovskii, "Prodolzhenie zhizni," *Iskusstvo kino*, no. 2, 1999, pp. 72–85, esp. pp. 80–85 on the Pushkin trilogy.

63. It is interesting that the filmmakers do not focus on Pushkin's drawings of himself as much as we might expect, given the film's concentration on Pushkin's psyche and the general agreement that the self-portraits are of supreme importance. Pushkin was hardly the only Russian writer to leave an interesting legacy of artwork, and was probably not even the most interesting artist among Russian writers. See the remarkably interesting self-portraits of Konstantin Batiushkov, for example, in *Risunki russkikh pisatelei* (Moscow: Sovetskaia Rossiia, 1988).

64. Quoted in E. O. Vysochina, *Obraz, berezhno khranimyi* (Moscow: Prosveshchenie, 1989), p. 212.

65. Ibid., p. 214.

66. Yuri Lotman has noted that cartoons can thrill us with their improbable animation of still images in just the same way as a statue or other work of art would when it is made to come alive. Iurii Lotman, "O iazyke mul'tiplikatsionnykh fil'mov," in Lotman, *Izbrannye stat'i*, 3 vols. (Tallinn: Aleksandra, 1993), vol. 3, pp. 323–24.

67. For a discussion of the theories of animated films, see Edward S. Small and Eugene Levinson, "Toward a Theory of Animation," *The Velvet Light Trap*, no. 24, 1989, pp. 67–74.

68. Compare Monika Greenleaf, "Tynianov, Pushkin and the Fragment: Through the Lens of Montage," in Boris Gasparov, Robert P. Hughes, and Irina Paperno, eds., *Cultural Mythologies of Russian Modernism* (Berkeley: University of California Press, 1992), pp. 264–92. See esp. p. 170, for a discussion of stylistic and semantic density alongside an "intimate, occasional quality."

69. The opening sequence shows a foot inscribing an arabesque as if onto ice (we hear skates cutting across the ice), setting up this moment when a drawing is produced as prologue to many sequences in which poetry will be produced. The best scholar of Pushkin's drawings, Abram Efros, noted that they appear in the manu-

scripts as a kind of pause in the writing process, but the film avoids suggesting that these activities were sequential or in any way separate. Abram Efros, *Avtoportrety Pushkina* (Moscow: Goslitmuzei, 1945), p. 14.

70. Efros remarks that Pushkin shared his drawings with virtually no one, and in that sense they were among his most intimate creations. Ibid., p. 12.

71. *Pushkinskii kinoslovar'*, p. 108; www.film.ru/process/article.asp?ID=23. The working title of the project was "Hardworking Pushkin" ("Trudoliubivyi Pushkin"). *Autumn Has Arrived* was shown at the Gatchina festival in 1999 and at the Vyborg festival of animated film in 2000.

72. See A. Bitov and R. Gabriadze, "Svobodu Pushkinu!," *Sintaksis*, no. 27, 1990, pp. 167–75. A limited edition of *Pushkin in Spain* (*Pushkin v Ispanii*, 1989) was released as part 1 of a proposed five-part series. As announced in *Pushkin zagranitsei* (Paris: Sintaksis, n.d.), parts 2–4 would take Pushkin to Paris, New York, and China; and part 5 would deal with "Pushkin and Dumas." Fragments of *Pushkin Abroad*, including a section on Pushkin in Georgia, appear in M. N. Virolainen, ed., *Legendy i mify o Pushkine* (St. Petersburg: Academicheskii proekt, 1994), pp. 303–18. Gabriadze has also illustrated several of Bitov's Pushkin texts.

73. The two voices switch off at times, to splendid tonal effect. For example, at the end of a stanza from *Eugene Onegin*, one voice gives way to another for the recitation of the final couplet, signaling its more ironic tone; in passages where Pushkin wrote dialogue, the two voices can simulate these different personae.

74. In interpreting the drawing (not the film, which came much later), Abram Efros argues that the Moor was indeed a more subservient Pushkin, if impatiently so. He links this figure to Pushkin's humiliatingly failed attempts to end his exile, a linkage based on the dating of the figure (early Nov. 1823, Odessa); unlike other interpretations by Efros, this one is not based on the juxtaposition of figure with text (the *arap* appears in the margins of *Eugene Onegin*, chap. 2, verse 21, which is about Lensky). Efros, *Avtoportrety Pushkina*, p. 94. For other details about the manuscript page and interpretations of Pushkin's views of his black ancestry, see T. G. Tsiavlovskaia, *Risunki Pushkina* (Moscow: Iskusstvo, 1986), p. 341–43, 441.

75. This scene uses the conversation as told by A. O. Rosset to Ia. K. Grot, who recorded it. See Sergei Gessen and Lev Modzalevskii, eds., *Razgovory Pushkina* (Moscow: Politizdat, 1991 [1929]), p. 71. For a thorough account of all the documentation of Pushkin's meeting with the tsar on Sept. 8, 1826, see N. Eidel'man, *Pushkin: Iz biografii i tvorchestva, 1826–1837* (Moscow: Khudozhestvannaia literatura, 1987), pp. 9–50.

76. *PSS*, vol. 3, pp. 275–76.

77. *PSS*, vol. 2, p. 233.

78. The very final image of the film, in fact, is a horseback rider trotting off. The music switches to an even tick-tock sound, there is a blur of light across the dark screen that resembles snow, and the music continues as the credits roll.

79. The spoken text comes from a diary of an Opochka merchant, I. I. Lapin; cited in V. V. Veresaev, *Pushkin v zhizni*, 2 vols. (Moscow: Sovetskii pisatel', 1936), vol. 1, p. 272.

80. Norshtein's affinities with folklore imagery are also apparent in an earlier film, *A Tale of Tales* (*Skazka skazok*, 1979), coauthored with Liudmila Petru-

shevskaia. For an interesting and extended conversation with Norshtein, see M. Vasil'eva and Iu. Norshtein, "Ia prosto sdelal kino...," *Literaturnoe obozrenie*, no. 3-4, 1992, pp. 90–100 (the first page of the interview is on the inside cover). At the time of the interview, he had been working for nearly a decade on an animated version of Gogol's story "The Overcoat," which he discusses here; he also talks about his work on a never-completed film about Mayakovsky.

81. This sequence is emphatically *not* realistic, not meant to diminish the artifice of the images even prior to their animation. Again, to refer to Lotman's brief essay on animated film, this is a marvelous potential of cartoons, since they so often use paintings or drawings that are already ironic or deliberately primitive and childlike. See Lotman, "O iazyke," p. 324. The inclusion of *lubok* serves this end well, but so does the film's basis in Pushkin's own schematic, often ironic drawings. This point is made by Efros, *Avtoportrety Pushkina*, pp. 20–22, where he suggests that the goal of all Pushkin's drawings was irony.

82. For a list of Shveitser's films through the mid-1980s, see *Kino: Entsiklopedicheskii slovar'* (Moscow: Sovetskaia entsiklopediia, 1986), p. 497. His later work included *How Are You, Crucians? (Kak zhivete, karasi?*, 1991).

83. This is not to say that his adaptations were removed from the concerns of the contemporary world, or that his filmmaking decisions ignored the requirements of Soviet cinema. Shveitser's 1987 film *The Kreutzer Sonata (Kreitserova sonata)* took advantage of early glasnost's looser restrictions on sexual expression in cinema, as noted in David Gillespie, "New Versions of Old Classics: Recent Cinematic Interpretations of Russian Literature," in Birgit Beumers, ed., *Russia on Reels: The Russian Idea in Post-Soviet Cinema* (London: I. B. Tauris, 1999), p. 118.

84. Semerchuk, "Mezhdu poetikoi i ideologiei," p. 246. He praises *Little Tragedies* as "brilliant" (p. 252), notable in a brief essay that otherwise disparages nearly all Soviet Pushkin films.

85. Ia. Varshavskii, "Est' upoenie v boiu...," *Teatr*, no. 12, 1980, pp. 55–60; see p. 57.

86. A part of Pushkin's 1830 short story "Grobovshchik" is interpolated into one of these scenes.

87. Yuri Liubimov, who directed a performance of *Little Tragedies* in the late 1980s, used a similar framing device: the performance opened with *Feast in Time of Plague*, broken up as if it were the *Decameron*, with feasting revelers "telling" each of the other three plays.

88. Among the more successful efforts, see Vladimir Alexandrov, "Correlations in Pushkin's *Malen'kie tragedii*," *Canadian Slavonic Papers*, vol. 20 (1978), pp. 176–93; Lorraine Wynne, "The Multiple Unity of Pushkin's *Little Tragedies*," Ph.D. dissertation, New York University, 1984; and Michael Shapiro, "Journey to the Metonymic Pole: The Structure of Pushkin's *Little Tragedies*," in Vladimir Markov and Dean S. Worth, eds., *From Los Angeles to Kiev* (Columbus, Ohio: Slavica Press, 1983), pp. 169–206.

89. L. Rybak, *Kak rozhdalis' fil'my Mikhaila Shveitsera* (Moscow: Soiuz kinematografistov SSSR, 1984), pp. 135–41.

90. The scenes from *Egyptian Nights* also explore a social ethic as a basis for individual identity and self-worth. For a valuable reassessment of the ethics of com-

munity inherent in realist poetics, see Elizabeth Cheresh Allen, *Beyond Realism: Turgenev's Poetics of Secular Salvation* (Stanford, Calif.: Stanford University Press, 1992), esp. pp. 18–34.

91. *PSS*, vol. 6, p. 250.

92. Leslie O'Bell, *Pushkin's 'Egyptian Nights': The Biography of a Work* (Ann Arbor, Mich.: Ardis Press, 1984), p. 104; she in turn refers her readers to the solid treatment of this topic in L. Ginzburg, "Pushkin i liricheskii geroi russkogo romantizma," *Pushkin: Issledovaniia i materialy*, vol. 4 (1962), pp. 140–54.

93. Monika Greenleaf, *Pushkin and Romantic Fashion: Fragment, Elegy, Orient, Irony* (Stanford, Calif.: Stanford University Press, 1995), p. 209.

94. Rybak, *Kak rozhdalis' fil'my Mikhaila Shveitsera*, p. 145.

95. The film abounds in moments of seeming seclusion (e.g., the baron underground, Don Juan and Donna Anna in her extraordinary chambers, the end of *Feast in Time of Plague*). The paradox of solitude and observation is maintained even in these scenes, perhaps most powerfully in the baron's soliloquies, which are self-consciously addressed to the camera.

96. The camera's fascination with the improvisor's body and the wonderful suppleness of the actor Iursky's body urge us to focus on a different aspect of embodiment in Iursky's performance—the gentle but splendid eroticism of the body as it performs before us. Compare the comments about Colin Firth's performance as Mr. Darcy in the 1995 BBC version of *Pride and Prejudice*, in Esther Sonnet, "From *Emma* to *Clueless*: Taste, Pleasure, and the Scene of History," in Deborah Cartmell and Imelda Whelehan, eds., *Adaptations: From Text to Screen, Screen to Text* (London: Routledge, 1999), p. 58.

97. On audiences within film, see Roger Manvell, *Theater and Film: A Comparative Study of the Two Forms of Dramatic Art, and of the Problems of Adaptation of Stage Plays into Film* (Cranbury, N.J.: Associated University Presses, 1979), p. 53.

98. These improvisations include the songs Laura sings in *The Stone Guest* (Shveitser uses two Pushkin poems, "I am here, Inez" ["Ia zdes', Inezil'ia," 1830] and "There lived a poor knight" ["Zhil na svete rytsar' bednyi," 1829]), as well as those that Mary and Walsingham sing in *Feast in Time of Plague*, Don Juan's declaration of love to Donna Anna, Mozart's performance of his *Requiem* for Salieri and supervision of other performances, and the baron's soliloquies in *The Covetous Knight*.

99. Compare an observation that Shveitser, the brother of Tsvetaeva's biographer Viktoria Shveitser, would certainly have known: "What does *Feast in Time of Plague* leave us (in our ears and souls)? Two songs—Mary's and Walsingham's. A love-song and a plague-song." Marina Tsvetaeva, "Iskusstvo pri svete sovesti" (1933), in Tsvetaeva, *Sobranie sochinenii*, 7 vols. (Moscow: Ellis-Lak, 1994), vol. 5, p. 349.

100. Varshavskii, "Est' upoenie v boiu ... ," p. 58.

101. We also see Nikolai Kochegarov as Faust, as a reveller in Laura's admiring band and then around the feast table in *Feast in Time of Plague*; Natalia Danilova as Zinaida Volskaia and also in the group scenes in *Feast*; and Ivars Kalnynsh as Faust and Don Carlos. Interestingly, Trofimov, Smoktunovsky, and Nikolai Burliaev (Albert in *The Covetous Knight*) fleetingly appear in the audience for the improvi-

sor's second performance. For a full roster of the actors and the technical team and a summary of the film, see *Pushkinskii kinoslovar'*, pp. 57–59.

102. See Barbara Hodgdon, "Replicating Richard: Body Doubles, Body Politics," *Theatre Journal*, vol. 50, no. 2 (May 1998), pp. 207–26; and W. B. Worthen, "Drama, Performativity, Performance," *PMLA*, vol. 113, no. 5 (Oct. 1998), pp. 1093–1107. Both essays are about Shakespeare performances, which would have the same status for English-speaking audiences as the performance of Pushkin plays has for Russian theatergoers.

103. Worthen, "Drama, Performativity, Performance," p. 1097.

CHAPTER 5

Part of this chapter appeared in an earlier form as "The Stone Ghost: Akhmatova, Pushkin, and Don Juan," in Edward J. Brown, Lazar Fleishman, Gregory Freidin, and Richard D. Schupbach, eds., *Literature, Culture, and Society in the Modern Age: In Honor of Joseph Frank* (Stanford Slavic Studies, vol. 4, part 2 [1992]), pp. 35–49.

EPIGRAPH: Geoffrey H. Hartman, *The Unremarkable Wordsworth* (Minneapolis: University of Minnesota Press, 1987), p. 63.

1. Khodasevich's vast body of work on Pushkin also bears the marks of repetition and reconsideration, but without Akhmatova's obsessiveness and moral certainty. He more precisely might be said to come back to similar topics because he has not finished thinking about them; his was an analytical and endlessly clarifying attitude.

2. L. K. Chukovskaia, *Zapiski ob Anne Akhmatovoi*, 2 vols. (Paris: YMCA Press, 1976, 1980), vol. 2, pp. 7–8. Similarly, Pavel Luknitsky observed in his diary that Akhmatova always spoke of Pushkin, Dante, or any other genius "in an intonation of familiarity and with diminutives." For him, it was "as if she were speaking about a good friend with whom she had just been talking, as if he had just gotten up and left the room and would be right back, . . . and as if there were no separations of space and time, as if he were a member of her family." Quoted in Vera Luknitskaia, *Pered toboi zemlia* (Leningrad: Lenizdat, 1988), p. 314. My ellipses. Lydia Ginzburg noted the same familiarity in "Akhmatova (Neskol'ko stranits vospominanii)," in Ginzburg, *O starom i novom* (Leningrad: Sovetskii pisatel', 1982), p. 332.

3. I would disagree, then, with the comparison of Akhmatova's Pushkin writings to her translations of other poets, as is suggested in David N. Wells, *Akhmatova: Her Poetry* (Oxford: Berg Publishers, 1996), pp. 14, 20.

4. Akhmatova studied at the Faculty of Jurisprudence in Kiev, which led Eduard Babaev to observe that she could read and understand documents of accusation. Babaev, "Pushkinskie stranitsy Akhmatovoi," *Novyi mir*, no. 1, 1987, p. 156.

5. Akhmatova writes out of adult anger, one might add, whereas Tsvetaeva's Pushkin writings rely on the buried sense of childhood rage. See Paul Debreczeny, *Social Functions of Literature: Alexander Pushkin and Russian Culture* (Stanford, Calif.: Stanford University Press, 1997), pp. 65–67. (We will return to the point in Chap. 6.)

6. See Alexander Zholkovsky, "Strakh, tiazhest', mramor (Iz materialov k zhiz-

netvorcheskoi biografii Akhmatovoi)," *Wiener Slawistischer Almanakh*, vol. 36 (1996), pp. 119–54; and Zholkovsky, "The Obverse of Stalinism: Akhmatova's Self-Serving Charisma of Selflessness," in Laura Engelstein and Stephanie Sandler, eds., *Self and Story in Russian History* (Ithaca, N.Y.: Cornell University Press), pp. 46–68.

7. "Akhmatovskii motiv v pis'makh A. V. Belinkova k Iu. G. Oksmanu," *Znamia*, no. 10, 1998, pp. 139–47; see p. 143.

8. This list is necessarily partial, not least because what constitutes a "Pushkin-related" poem in Akhmatova's work is an open question. I have included, in addition to poems about Pushkin, poems that invoke themes and places Akhmatova associated with Pushkin (e.g., Tsarskoe Selo, the Decembrists) and were written about in ways that advert specifically to him. I have also included poems that have Pushkinian epigraphs or that scholars have seen as relying on discrete Pushkin subtexts, when they also illuminate Akhmatova's attitude toward Pushkin.

9. Roman Timenchik, "On Akhmatova's Tsarskoe-Selo Code," in Lev Loseff and Barry Scherr, eds., *A Sense of Place: Tsarskoe Selo and Its Poets* (Columbus, Ohio: Slavica, 1993), p. 365. See the essay by Andrei Ariev in the same volume: "'The Splendid Darkness of a Strange Garden': Tsarskoe Selo in the Russian Poetic Tradition and Akhmatova's 'Ode to Tsarskoe Selo,'" pp. 51–87, esp. p. 79, where Ariev writes that "the signs of Tsarskoe Selo's 'past' are not in its 'wondrous breathing' (Tiutchev) but in the fact that it breathes horror."

10. Marina Tsvetaeva, "Stikhi k Akhmatovoi" (poem no. 3), *Stikhotvoreniia i poemy* (Leningrad: Sovetskii pisatel', 1990), p. 119.

11. Velimir Khlebnikov, *Sobranie sochinenii*, 3 vols. (St. Petersburg: Akademicheskii proekt, 2001), vol. 1, pp. 423–24; quoted from p. 423. My ellipses. On this poem, see A. E. Parnis, "The Futurist Khlebnikov as a Successor to the Tsarskoe Selo Tradition," in Loseff and Scherr, eds., *A Sense of Place*, pp. 367–68.

12. Anna Akhmatova, *Ia—golos vash* (Moscow: Knizhnaia palata, 1989), p. 21. Although all translations here are my own, I have consulted other versions and incorporated locutions from *The Complete Poems of Anna Akhmatova*, tr. Judith Hemschemeyer, ed. Roberta Reeder, 2 vols. (Somerville: Zephyr, 1990); and *Poems of Akhmatova*, tr. Stanley Kunitz with Max Hayward (Boston: Little, Brown, 1973).

13. Roman Timenchik has suggested that the imagery of death in this poem effectively sets up the reanimating activities of Akhmatova's later Tsarskoe Selo lyrics; he sees the cycle of death and rebirth as a structure through which Akhmatova would imagine Tsarskoe Selo. R. D. Timenchik, "Akhmatova i Pushkin: Zametki k teme," in *Pushkinskii sbornik*, vol. 2 (Riga, 1974), p. 47. In a footnote on that page, Timenchik describes later citations from Pushkin as Akhmatova's animation of a dead text; he reminds us of her phrase in a later Pushkin essay, "Alexandrina": "the citation had hardened to stone" ("tsitata okamenela").

14. No more memorable image of her associations of Tsarskoe Selo with death occurs than in her cycle "Wreath to the Dead" ("Venok mertvym," 1938–57), where she writes that every flower bed looks like a fresh grave ("Kazhdaia klumba v parke / Kazhetsia svezhei mogiloi"). Akhmatova, "*Ia—golos vash*," p. 210.

15. Biographical details are given in V. Vilenkin, *V sto pervom zerkale* (Moscow: Sovetskii pisatel', 1987), p. 181. He also cites the memoirs of Valentina Sreznev-

skaya to show that in the summer of 1910, Akhmatova and her friends were suddenly struck by the boredom of the palatial architecture in Tsarskoe Selo and began to prefer walking in the open fields (pp. 183–84). For a biographical reading of the poem, see Sonia I. Ketchian, "Returns to Tsarskoe Selo in the Verse of Anna Akhmatova," in Loseff and Scherr, eds., *A Sense of Place*, pp. 121–22. Ketchian reads the poem as an "artistic embodiment" of the beginning of the end of Akhmatova's relationship with Gumilev.

16. Of course, Akhmatova was to return to Tsarskoe Selo a number of times, but there is an uncanny prediction in the lines. She claimed not to have returned after 1944, although Aleksei Batalov remembered otherwise. See Ariev, "Splendid Darkness," p. 75.

17. On Annensky's Pushkin, see V. V. Musatov, *Pushkinskaia traditsiia russkoi poezii pervoi poloviny XX veka* (Moscow: Izdatel'skii tsentr RGGU, 1998), pp. 167–240; the book also has a very good chapter on Akhmatova, pp. 321–72. On Akhmatova's debt to Innokenty Annensky, see Ariev, "Splendid Darkness," pp. 64–69.

18. Akhmatova, *Ia—golos vash*, p. 22.

19. I. L. Al'mi, "O liricheskikh siuzhetakh Pushkina v stikhotvoreniiakh Anny Akhmatovoi," *Tainy remesla*, Akhmatovskie chteniia, vol. 2 (Moscow: Nasledie, 1992), pp. 5–19; quoted from p. 9. As Almi notes, this sense of distance marks a difference between the representations of Pushkin found in Tsvetaeva on the one hand and Mayakovsky on the other.

20. I will be treating "In Tsarskoe Selo" as a single poem, in three parts. For others, these are three separate poems, published together as a cycle. Roman Timenchik, who discusses the third part of the poem separately, gives some textual evidence to support his decision when he observes that the first two parts are dated February 1911, the third Sept. 24, 1911 (in a typescript of an unpublished collection of Akhmatova's verse; he gives no date for the typescript). See Roman Timenchik, "Akhmatova i Pushkin (Razbor stikhotvoreniia 'Smuglyi otrok brodil po alleiam ...'), " in *Pushkinskii sbornik* (Riga: Redaktsionno-izdatel'skii otdel Latviiskogo gosudarstvennogo universiteta, 1968), pp. 124–31; see n. 6, p. 126. My argument shows how the third poem makes a different kind of sense after the images and meanings of the first two. Moreover, we have no reason to suppose that the poet wanted the texts to be read apart from one another.

21. Only a year earlier, Akhmatova had written "He liked ..." ("On liubil ... ," 1910), with its famous account of the three things he liked and the three he did not like (crying children, raspberry tea, and women's hysterics). The syntax here is precisely the same, and we would be right to assume that the man imagined in "He liked ..." has some role in the imperative "leave" that ends the last sentence in "The little horses." There is every reason to see Gumilev as inspiring the terrified report of "He liked ...," not just because the timing would be right but also because the description of psychic violence that informs the poem is central to Akhmatova's way of describing him, as discussed below.

22. For a fine analysis of Pushkin's response to Parny, focusing on his "Persephone" ("Prozerpina," 1824), see Monika Greenleaf, *Pushkin and Romantic Fashion: Fragment, Elegy, Orient, Irony* (Stanford, Calif.: Stanford University Press, 1994), pp. 96–107.

23. It recalls the mournful attitude imposed on Pushkin by Khodasevich in "He left his carriage at the gate" (discussed in Chap. 3).

24. Yuri Lotman rightly observes that, although the atmosphere at the lyceum was not so perfect as Pushkin would later claim in his October 19 poems, it was a refuge for friendship and a kind of Enlightenment, humanistic spirit. See Iu. M. Lotman, *Aleksandr Sergeevich Pushkin: Biografiia pisatelia* (Leningrad: Prosveschenie, 1981), pp. 12–23.

25. Neither of the first two parts of the poem has anything like the marvelous sound orchestration of the third. See E. V. Dzhanzhakova, "'Smuglyi otrok brodil po alleiam . . .'," *Russkaia rech'*, no. 5, 1976, pp. 16–19; and Timenchik, "Akhmatova i Pushkin" (1968), for close readings of the sounds, images, semantics, and rhythm.

26. In the barely audible rustle of Pushkin's steps, Akhmatova surely echoes his lines, "Here every step gives birth in the soul / To the remembrance of years past" ("Zdes' kazhdyi shag v dushe rozhdaet / Vospominan'ia prezhnikh let"). See Pushkin, "Vospominaniia v Tsarskom Sele," in *PSS*, vol. 1, p. 70.

27. Akhmatova, *Ia—golos vash*, p. 78.

28. *PSS*, vol. 3, p. 171. Pushkin describes a statue placed in the Catherine Garden in 1810, not far from the lyceum where he studied, P. P. Sokolov's *Milk Maiden* (*Molochnitsa*). See A. I. Kuz'min, "'Tsarskosel'skaia statuia' A. Akhmatovoi," *Russkaia rech'*, no. 1, 1979, pp. 44–49, esp. p. 45.

29. S. A. Kibal'nik, *Russkaia antologicheskaia poeziia pervoi treti XIX v.* (Leningrad: Nauka, 1990), gives an account of texts that Pushkin might have drawn on for this poem, including Derzhavin's translation of Herder's "Der Warme Quelle," the first Russian treatment of the theme of the moment stopped in time (p. 204).

30. Pushkin changes the Lafontaine fable "Pierette," on which the Sokolov statue was based, by having his maiden sit over a stream of water, not the puddle of spilled milk in Lafontaine. A succinct account of Pushkin's interpretation of the fable is given in Lev Loseff, "The Toy Town Ruined," in Loseff and Scherr, eds., *Sense of Place*, pp. 40–41.

31. She begins with the word *already* (*uzhe*), which signals that what this poem is doing has already been done, as in the theme of exhaustion in "Second Anniversary." The adverb *uzhe* also suggests that things are happening faster than the poet expects, which makes the observation of time's unhurried passage ("okravavleny kusty / Nespeshno zreiushchei riabiny") a strong moment of contrast.

32. The sadness of "In Tsarskoe Selo" is also present in "Tsarskoe Selo Statue," in the final stanza's description of the statue as happy in her sadness. As in the earlier poem, Akhmatova here attributes the sadness to the thing or person she describes, not to the speaking poet, but in contrast to her transfer of sadness to Pushkin, in this case the emotion is entirely motivated (by the statue's posture, and by Pushkin's description of the sculpted woman as well).

33. A. I. Kuzmin suggests that Pushkin's maiden is also a muse (muses are often found near sources of water in classical myth). Kuz'min, "'Tsarskosel'skaia statuia' A. Akhmatovoi," p. 45

34. See "To the Muse" ("Muze," 1911), "The muse left along the road" ("Muza ushla po doroge," 1915), "The Muse" ("Muza," 1924), and "Shards" ("Cherepki," late 1940s, 1950).

35. On Nedobrovo, see the essays and publications in *Shestye tynianovskie chteniia* (Riga-Moscow, 1992), pp. 82–152. His 1914 essay "Anna Akhmatova" is reproduced in M. M. Kralin, ed., *O Anne Akhmatovoi* (Leningrad: Lenizdat, 1990), pp. 49–68.

36. David Wells, *Akhmatova and Pushkin: The Pushkin Contexts of Akhmatova's Poetry*. Birmingham Slavonic Monographs no. 25 (Birmingham: Birmingham University, Department of Russian Language and Literature, 1994), p. 50.

37. Al'mi, "O liricheskikh siuzhetakh Pushkina," p. 8.

38. Roberta Reeder, *Anna Akhmatova: Poet and Prophet* (New York: St. Martin's Press, 1994), p. 103.

39. In the journal *Apollon*, on the page just after "Tsarskoe Selo Statue," Akhmatova offers her readers a less frightening version of the poem: "Once again drowsiness gives me its gift" ("Vnov' podaren mne dremotoi"). This untitled poem, also dated 1916, takes us to a second place associated with Pushkin, Bakhchisarai. Timenchik has observed that this doubled act of placement is typical of Akhmatova's topograph. Timenchik, "Akhmatova i Pushkin" (1974), p. 35n.

40. Akhmatova, *Ia—golos vash*, p. 141.

41. For an illuminating discussion of Akhmatova's engagement with Dostoevsky, based on a later poem, "Prehistory" ("Predystoriia," 1940–43), see Susan Amert, *In a Shattered Mirror: The Later Poetry of Anna Akhmatova* (Stanford, Calif.: Stanford University Press, 1992), pp. 73–80.

42. Elsewhere in her poetry, and to some extent in this poem, too (which has a husband among the dead, conjuring up the shade of Gumilev), Akhmatova sins more as a woman, as if early sexual adventures had caused her suffering in later, harsher times.

43. Al'mi, "O liricheskikh siuzhetakh Pushkina," p. 13. For a discussion of Akhmatova's innovative work with various genres and her violations of what the author calls "communicative logic," see I. Gurvich, "Anna Akhmatova: traditsiia i novoe myshlenie," *Russian Literature*, vol. 41, no. 2 (Feb. 15, 1997), pp. 121–96; see p. 167 for a comment on this poem and its ballad form.

44. Michael Wachtel, *The Development of Russian Verse: Meter and Its Meanings* (Cambridge, Eng.: Cambridge University Press, 1998), chap. 1.

45. Al'mi, "O liricheskikh siuzhetakh Pushkina," pp. 14–16.

46. *PSS*, vol. 3, p. 215.

47. Joseph Brodsky, Introduction to Anna Akhmatova, *Poems*, tr. Lyn Coffin (New York: Norton, 1983), p. xxvi, reprinted as "The Keening Muse," in Brodsky, *Less Than One* (New York: Farrar, Straus & Giroux, 1986), pp. 34–52; quotation on p. 47, where the capital letter on "Time" is gone.

48. Sigmund Freud, "Mourning and Melancholia," *General Psychological Theory*, ed. Philip Rieff (New York: Macmillan, 1963), pp. 164–79.

49. Akhmatova, *Ia—golos vash*, p. 147.

50. The subtext was identified by Roman Timenchik, "Akhmatova i Pushkin: Zametki k teme," in *Pushkinskii sbornik* (Riga: Uchenye zapiski Latviiskogo gos. universiteta, 1974), pp. 32–55, esp. pp. 33–36. Timenchik insists that Akhmatova's poetics of quotation mix multiple sources, but in a hierarchy of sources, with Pushkin the poet of first position (p. 32).

51. *PSS*, vol. 3, p. 341.

52. *PSS*, vol. 5, p. 88. The subtext was also noticed by Timenchik, "Akhmatova i Pushkin," p. 46. He concludes that Akhmatova can invoke Tatiana's world of popular belief alongside imperial Tsarskoe Selo without her readers feeling any particular opposition between the two.

53. For a review of scholarship about Pushkin's attitude toward Tatiana and an intriguing argument about what she calls Tatiana's "poeticity," see Caryl Emerson, "Tatiana," in Sona Stephan Hoisington, ed., *A Plot of Her Own: The Female Protagonist in Russian Literature* (Evanston, Ill.: Northwestern University Press, 1995), pp. 6–20. A fine full-length study of Pushkin's heroine is Olga Peters Hasty, *Pushkin's Tatiana* (Madison: University of Wisconsin Press, 1999).

54. *PSS*, vol. 5, p. 88.

55. See Amert, *In a Shattered Mirror*, p. 200, n. 12.

56. Akhmatova, *Ia—golos vash*, p. 149.

57. Reeder, *Anna Akhmatova*, p. 204. For a description of Pasternak's state of mind, see Elena Pasternak, *Boris Pasternak: Materialy dlia biografii* (Moscow: Sovetskii pisatel', 1989), p. 514. Akhmatova had seen him in Leningrad in the summer of 1935; she went to Voronezh in February 1936 to see Mandelstam.

58. Akhmatova, *Ia—golos vash*, p. 148.

59. In *Pushkin and Romantic Fashion*, Monika Greenleaf argues that repetition and loss provide the emotional and linguistic structure of Pushkin's elegies. Drawing on the work of Paul de Man and Peter Sacks, she writes: "The elegiac poet experiences selfhood amid the random array of his experiences only when the configuration which he has come to regard as his leitmotiv is repeated. Non-repeating experience is dead, meaningless—a theme we will encounter in Pushkin time and again" (p. 49). Her point is thus both general (about the elegy) and specific (about Pushkin), and raises the question of why Akhmatova did not find greater similarity between her poetic practices and Pushkin's. One answer to that question has to do with her sense of guilt, not a prominent part of the Pushkinian model, whereas in her poems it is the source of the most dramatic imagery (the blood, for example, in nearly all the poems considered here) and emotional experiences.

60. On Acmeist poetics, see Justin Doherty, *The Acmeist Movement in Russian Poetry: Culture and the Word* (Oxford: Oxford University Press, 1995). David Wells has used Doherty's book in particular to construct readings of the individual volumes of Akhmatova's poetry based on Acmeist principles. See Wells, *Anna Akhmatova*, pp. 44–63.

61. Her first essay may in fact have seemed *too* finished to Akhmatova. In the 1950s she began to rework it, intending to publish a revised version in her planned book about Pushkin. The final plan for the book, however, suggests that she decided not to include the essay.

62. Akhmatova, *O Pushkine* (Leningrad: Sovetskii pisatel', 1977), p. 8. Her negative attitudes toward some Pushkin scholars were recorded as early as the 1920s. See, for example, Pavel Luknitsky's diary in Luknitskaia, *Pered toboi zemlia*, pp. 346–48.

63. See, for example, Akhmatova, *O Pushkine*, pp. 14, 15.

64. Ibid., p. 25.

65. Reeder, *Anna Akhmatova*, p. 226, makes a similar point, and David N. Wells has observed that Akhmatova "frequently 'encodes' personal and political messages into her work which are similar to Pushkin's satirical 'encoded' statements in *The Tale of the Golden Cockerel* and *The Stone Guest*, which she noted in her critical essays." Wells, *Akhmatova and Pushkin*, p. 111. Amanda Haight succinctly treats Akhmatova's turn to Pushkin as an exploration of the nature of poetic inspiration and isolation. She observes that Akhmatova's study of Pushkin was "closely relevant to her own life." Haight, *Anna Akhmatova: A Poetic Pilgrimage* (Oxford: Oxford University Press, 1976), pp. 82–83.

66. Akhmatova, *O Pushkine*, p. 32.

67. Akhmatova suggests a further parallel between her work and Pushkin's when she dates his acquaintance with Washington Irving to 1833, then presents and publishes her essay "Pushkin's Last Tale" in 1933. The 100-year span would have appealed to her love of anniversary commemorations, as seen in the same time span between Pushkin's "It was time" and her "Some see themselves in affectionate gazes." In effect, she suggests the centennial return that Silver Age poets had often used in their evocations of the Golden Age, although she was writing in what felt like the Iron Age of the 1930s. On the connections between the Silver Age and the Golden Age, see Boris Gasparov, Robert P. Hughes, and Irina Paperno, eds., *Cultural Mythologies of Russian Modernism: From the Golden Age to the Silver Age* (Berkeley: University of California Press, 1992), particularly two essays: Irina Paperno, "Pushkin v zhizni cheloveka Serebrianogo veka," pp. 19–51; and Boris Gasparov, "Tridtsatye gody—zheleznyi vek (k analizu motivov stoletnego vozvrashcheniia u Mandel'shtama," pp. 150–82. A translation of Gasparov's essay appears in Stephanie Sandler, ed., *Rereading Russian Poetry* (New Haven, Conn.: Yale University Press, 1998), pp. 78–103.

68. Akhmatova, *O Pushkine*, p. 66.

69. Osip Mandel'shtam, "Pis'mo o russkoi poezii"(1922), in Mandel'shtam, *Slovo i kul'tura* (Moscow: Sovetskii pisatel', 1987), pp. 173–76; see p. 175; Boris Eikhenbaum, *Anna Akhmatova: opyt analiza* (Paris: Lev, 1980 [1923]), p. 127.

70. Akhmatova, *O Pushkine*, p. 80.

71. Other embedded allegories occur in these early essays, for example the way in which Akhmatova shows the satire of the new aristocracy in *Eugene Onegin* and in Pushkin's prose fragments. She was likely to have felt similar contempt toward the rising social classes in the new Soviet Union. All her examples from Pushkin's writings are filled with indignation at what seems to her an inappropriate assumption of privilege and power.

72. Akhmatova, *O Pushkine*, p. 81.

73. Ibid., p. 90.

74. Ibid., p. 91. In a later revision, Akhmatova wrote that nowhere else were the terrifying questions of morality "posed so sharply or resolved with such secrecy." Ibid, p. 234.

75. Ibid., pp. 234–35.

76. "Secret return from exile was an agonizing dream for Pushkin in the 1820s": ibid., p. 92.

77. Ibid., p. 108.

78. Anna Akhmatova, "Ia—golos vash," p. 158.

79. Ibid., p. 278. In his analysis of "Naslednitsa," Roman Timenchik adds that the poem's first lines, "pesnia speta / Sred' etikh opustelykh zal" ("a song sung / Among these deserted chambers"), have a Pushkinian subtext, "Among magnificent, deserted chambers" ("Sred' pyshnykh opustelykh zal," from *Fragments from Onegin's Journey, Otryvki iz Puteshestviia Onegina*). R. D. Timenchik, "Avtometaopisanie u Akhmatovoi," *Russian Literature*, no. 10-11, 1975, pp. 213–16; see p. 219.

80. Akhmatova, *O Pushkine*, pp. 103–4.

81. In a footnote in an essay on Akhmatova's first name, Mikhail Meilakh writes more tentatively: "It is not impossible that Akhmatova's conception of *The Stone Guest*, according to which love for Donna Anna awakens Juan to a new life, is to a certain degree autobiographical." M. B. Meilkah, "Ob imenakh Akhmatovoi: 1. Anna," *Russian Literature*, no. 10-11, 1975, p. 55. Meilakh's point has principally to do with Gumilev's "Five-footed iambs" ("Piatistopnye iamby," 1913), discussed below.

82. E. A. Obukhova and L. G. Frizman, "Kniga o Pushkine—neosushchestvlennyi zamysel Anny Akhmatovoi," *Vremennik Pushkinskoi komissii*, no. 23 (Leningrad, 1989), p. 172.

83. See Roman Timenchik, "'Ostrov iskusstva': Biograficheskaia novella v dokumentakh," *Druzhba narodov*, no. 6, 1989, pp. 244–53; Haight, *Akhmatova*, pp. 8–15 (on Gumilev's relentless wooing); Earl D. Sampson, *Nikolay Gumilev* (Boston: Twayne, 1979), p. 22 (on his premarital affairs); Sheelagh Graham, "Amor fati: Akhmatova and Gumilev," in Wendy Rosslyn, ed., *The Speech of Unknown Eyes: Akhmatova's Readers on Her* Poetry. 2 vols. (Nottingham: Astra, 1989), vol. 2, pp. 247–56; see pp. 250–51 on his masculinity (source of quotation).

84. Nikolai Gumilev, *Stikhotvoreniia i poemy* (Leningrad: Sovetskii pisatel', 1988), p. 403. Dates given for Gumilev's poetry are dates of first publication, although many of the poems are thought to have been composed earlier; see the notes in this edition.

85. Julia Kristeva, "Don Juan, or Loving To Be Able To," *Tales of Love*, tr. Leon S. Roudiez (New York: Columbia University Press, 1987), p. 193. My ellipses.

86. The lines about Akhmatova read:

And in the nighttime sky, ancient and lofty,
I see the notations of my fates
And I know that the siren verses of Akhmatova
Sing of my distant self.

А ночью в небе, древнем и высоком,
Я вижу записи судеб моих
И ведаю, что обо мне, далеком,
Звенит Ахматовой сиренный стих.

Gumilev, *Stikhotvoreniia i poemy*, p. 403.

87. Nineteen of these lyrics are conveniently collected in E. G. Gershtein, ed., "Stikhi i pis'ma. Anna Akhmatova. N. Gumilev," *Novyi mir*, no. 9, 1986, pp. 196–227. To them I would add two poems, not because I claim that they are addressed to Akhmatova, but because I see them as vivid extensions of the themes I am work-

ing out here: "The Duel" ("Poedinok," 1908), where the poet is killed by a woman who loves him in death; and "Beyond the Grave" ("Za grobom," ms. 1907), where lying in the coffin makes the poet eternally subject to the sharp-toothed kiss of a horrifying woman. For an interesting account of the gendered erotics of Gumilev's poetry, see Taras Koznarsky, "Myth as a Model of Realization: N. Gumilev's Poetic Biography," unpublished seminar paper, Harvard University, 1996.

88. Akhmatova says that this poem was about her. See Chukovskaia, *Zapiski ob Anne Akhmatovoi*, vol. 2, pp. 179, 443.

89. Here is the final quatrain from "Animal Tamer":

Fanny, the flower you gave has wilted,
But you, as always, are happy on your leash.
My beast is drowsy at your bedside,
He looks into your eyes, like a faithful Great Dane.

Фанни, завял вами данный цветок,
Вы ж, как всегда, веселы на канате.
Зверь мой, он дремлет у вашей кровати,
Смотрит в глаза вам, как преданный дог.

Gumilev, *Stikhotvoreniia i poemy*, p. 176.

90. This poem is seen as a concentrated version of their relationship by Gershtein, "Stikhi i pis'ma," p. 198. It addresses a beloved woman as a "warring friend":

This happened more than once, it will happen more than once,
    In our deaf and stubborn struggle:
As always, you have now renounced me,
    Tomorrow, I know, you will return submissive.
But for that reason do not be surprised, my warring friend,
    My enemy, seized by this dark love,
If groans of love become groans of pain,
    If kisses are colored by blood.

Это было не раз, это будет не раз
    В нашей битве, глухой и упорной:
Как всегда, от меня ты теперь отреклась,
    Завтра, знаю, вернешься покорной.
Но зато не дивись, мой враждующий друг,
    Враг мой, схваченный темной любовью,
Если стоны любви будут стонами мук,
    Поцелуи—окрашены кровью.

Gumilev, *Stikhotvoreniia i poemy*, p. 145.

91. Akhmatova's use of the word *silence* to name her poetic work has been noted. An eloquent example appears in the seventh poem of her "Northern Elegies," which begins "And I am silent, I have been silent for thirty years" ("A ia molchu, ia tridtsat' let molchu"), quoted from *Ia—golos vash*, p. 297. The poem is well discussed in these terms in Amert, *In a Shattered Mirror*, pp. 112–17.

92. This poem is from a cycle usually traced to her relationship with Vladimir Shileiko, but it also offers a resilient answer to "The Animal Tamer," its obvious subtext. It uses the image of blood (a bird's blood spotting the white wing), but it is the blood of a self-inflicted wound. Written in the month of Gumilev's arrest and execution, the poem shows Akhmatova making peace with their warring relationship, although her starting point is a polemical, challenging refusal to submit to him, even in his death.

93. On Akhmatova's use of folklore generally, see N. Iu. Griakalova, "Fol'klornye traditsii v poezii Anny Akhmatovoi," *Russkaia literatura*, no. 1, 1982, pp. 47–63. See also Mikhail Meilakh, "Anna Akhmatova's Poem 'Zaklinanie,'" in Rosslyn, *Speech of Unknown Eyes*, vol. 2, pp. 173–82.

94. Akhmatova, *Stikhotvoreniia i poemy*, 3d ed. (Leningrad: Sovetskii pisatel', 1984), p. 365.

95. Noted by Pavel Luknitsky in his diary, Dec. 19, 1924. P. N. Luknitskii, "Ob Anne Akhmatovoi," *Nashe nasledie*, no. 6, 1988, pp. 57–58, as quoted in T. M. Nikolaeva, "Smert' vlastelina na okhote ('Okhota' N. Gumileva i 'Seroglazyi korol'' Akhmatovoi," *Russian Literature*, vol. 30, no. 3 (1991), pp. 343–56; quotation on p. 347.

96. See Anna Akhmatova, "Avtobiograficheskaia proza" (ed. R. D. Timenchik and V. A. Chernykh), *Literaturnoe obozrenie*, no. 5, 1989, p. 13: "In 1924 I dreamed of X [Gumilev] three times in a row, for six years collected his 'Works and Days' and other material: letters, drafts, memoirs. In general, I have done everything for his memory that is possible. It is striking that no one is doing this work. The so-called pupils have acquitted themselves shamefully. The role of Georgy Ivanov. They have all renounced him abroad."

97. Akhmatova, *O Pushkine*, p. 168.

98. Avital Ronell, *Dictations: On Haunted Writing* (Bloomington: Indiana University Press, 1986). Two other important influences on my thinking here are Kenneth Gross, "Moving Statues, Talking Statues," *Raritan*, vol. 9, no. 2 (Fall 1989), pp. 1–25; and Jacques Derrida, *Of Spirit: Heidegger and the Question*, tr. Geoffrey Bennington and Rachel Bowlby (Chicago: University of Chicago Press, 1989).

99. Leslie O'Bell, "Akhmatova and Pushkin's Secret Writing," in Sonia Ketchian, ed., *Anna Akhmatova, 1889–1989* (Berkeley, Calif.: Berkeley Slavic Specialities, 1993), pp. 136–48; quotation from p. 136.

100. Leslie O'Bell, "Writing the Story of Pushkin's Death," *Slavic Review*, vol. 58, no. 2 (Summer 1999), pp. 393–406.

101. Akhmatova, *O Pushkine*, p. 113.

102. Ibid., p. 115.

103. Ibid.

104. In the conclusion of her essay, Akhmatova takes on Shchegolev once again, presenting a long sequence of events and documents that he ignored (ibid., pp. 131–33). This attack differs from her earlier polemics with scholars, where she amplified her own authority by reference to others' work. Now Akhmatova assumes the power to speak the truth, and she assails Shchegolev with the same intensity that she

turns on Pushkin's contemporaries. Her target is P. E. Shchlegolev, *Duel' i smert' Pushkina*, 2 vols. (Moscow: Kniga, 1987), based on the third edition, 1928, the one she knew (see Akhmatova, *O Pushkine*, p. 228).

105. Although laws against male homosexual conduct were made stricter after 1832, it is not clear that they were enforced, particularly against prominent men; the historian Sergei Solovyov later said that in 19th-century Russia homosexuality was treated "as a joke." See Simon Karlinsky, "Russia's Gay Literature and Culture: The Impact of the October Revolution," in Martin Bauml Duberman, Martha Vicinus, and George Chauncey, Jr., eds., *Hidden From History: Reclaiming the Gay and Lesbian Past* (New York: NAL, 1989), pp. 347–64, esp. pp. 349, 353 n.3. Akhmatova's claim about the motive of jealousy is thus better founded.

106. Akhmatova, *O Pushkine*, p. 118.

107. Ibid., p. 142. Arapova's memoirs have been republished in *Iz semeinoi khroniki: A. S. Pushkin* (Moscow: Izd. "Tri veka istorii," 2000), pp. 393–468, with useful commentary and introductory material by G. A. Galin.

108. I. Obodovskaia and M. Dement'ev note Viazemsky's love for Natalia Nikolaevna, in *Natal'ia Nikolaevna Pushkina*, 2d ed. (Moscow: Sovetskaia Rossiia, 1987), pp. 241ff. I treat the relationship in "Pushkin's Last Love—Natal'ya Nikolaevna in Russian Culture," in Marianne Liljestrom, Eila Mantysaari, and Arja Rosenholm, eds., *Gender Restructuring in Russian Studies* (Helsinki: Slavica Tamperensia, 1993), pp. 209–20, esp. p. 216.

109. Akhmatova, *O Pushkine*, p. 133. My ellipses.

110. Inna Chechelnitsky, "Akhmatova and Pushkin: *Apologia Pro Vita Sua*," in Ketchian, ed., *Anna Akhmatova*, pp. 29–42.

CHAPTER 6

Part of an earlier version of this chapter was published in "Embodied Words: Gender in Tsvetaeva's Reading of Pushkin," *Slavic and East European Journal*, vol. 34, no. 2 (Summer 1990), pp. 139–57.

EPIGRAPH: Marina Tsvetaeva, fragments of a draft for "Pushkin i Pugachev," RGALI f. 1190, op. 2, ed. khr. 16, l. 1; cited in Elena Korkina, "'Pushkin i Pugachev': Liricheskoe rassledovanie Mariny Tsvetaevoi," in *Marina Tsvetaeva: One Hundred Years / Stoletie Tsvetaevoi*, ed. Viktoria Schweitzer et al. (Oakland, Calif.: Berkeley Slavic Specialties, 1994), p. 223.

1. Marina Tsvetaeva, "O Germanii" (1919), in Tsvetaeva, *Sobranie sochinenii*, 7 vols. (Moscow: Ellis Lak, 1994), vol. 4, p. 549.

2. Tsvetaeva's Pushkin writings also include her translations of his poems in 1936–37, and many references to him in other essays and in her letters; I will concentrate, however, on the major texts listed here.

3. She also translated some splendid emotional lyrics, like the two songs from *Feast in Time of Plague* (*Pir vo vremia chumy*, 1830), "As I wander down noisy streets" ("Brozhu li ia dvol' ulits shumnykh," 1829), "What is my name to you?" ("Chto v imeni tebe moem?," 1830), and "I loved you" ("Ia vas liubil," 1829). For a complete list of the Pushkin poems she translated, see Tsvetaeva, *Sobranie sochinenii*, vol. 7, pp. 826–27. Alexandra Smith shows how Tsvetaeva's translations re-

shaped the poems to express her own poetic self-mythology in *Song of the Mocking Bird: Pushkin in the Work of Marina Tsvetaeva* (Berne: Peter Lang, 1994), pp. 151–82. Among the political lyrics she translated are "To Russia's Slanderers" ("Klevetnikam Rossii," 1831) and "The Hero" ("Geroi," 1830). She devotes her essay "Pushkin and Pugachev" to political as well as psychological questions.

4. The 1926 questionnaire is reprinted in Tsvetaeva, *Sobranie sochinenii*, vol. 4, pp. 621–24; see esp. p. 622.

5. Tsvetaeva was writing her Pushkin essays in what turned out to be her own last decade of creative work, exactly a century later; her Silver Age contemporaries Mandelstam, Akhmatova, and Kuzmin were more taken by the symbolism of this centennial return than she was. See Boris Gasparov, "The Iron Age of the 1930s: The Centennial Return in Mandelstam," in Stephanie Sandler, ed., *Rereading Russian Poetry* (New Haven, Conn.: Yale University Press, 1999), pp. 78–103; and Irina Paperno, "Dvoinichestvo i liubovnyi treugol'nik: Poeticheskii mif Kuzmina i ego pushkinskaia proektsiia," in J. E. Malmstad, ed., *Studies in the Life and Works of Mixail Kuzmin, Wiener Slawistischer Almanach*, vol. 24 (1989), pp. 57–82.

6. Marina Tsvetaeva, *Neizdannoe. Svodnye tetradi*, ed. E. B. Korkina and I. D. Shevelenko (Moscow: Ellis Lak, 1997), pp. 442–43.

7. Tsvetaeva, *Sobranie sochinenii*, vol. 5, p. 57. I give my own translations of Tsvetaeva's prose; for complete translations of the two Pushkin essays, see Marina Tsvetaeva, *A Captive Spirit: Selected Prose*, tr. J. Marin King (Ann Arbor, Mich.: Ardis Press, 1983), pp. 319–64, 372–403.

8. Tsvetaeva, *Sobranie sochinenii*, vol. 5. p. 511.

9. Tsvetaeva, *Sobranie sochinenii*, vol. 5, p. 73. I am pleased to use this account of visual representations to launch my discussion of Tsvetaeva, as an indirect challenge to those who have claimed that she had no visual imagination herself. See the discussion of "Natalia Goncharova" below.

10. Ibid. She also recalls the "sober-minded pupils of Soviet Russia" who would be reading him in the 1930s, when she is writing her essay from the distance of emigration in France. That description figures a different sort of deprivation—the failure of imagination and the lack of pleasure in reading. Ibid., p. 74.

11. Anne Carson, "Essay on What I Think About Most," *Raritan,* vol. 18, no. 3 (Winter 1999), pp. 49–54; quotation from p. 53.

12. Tsvetaeva, *Sobranie sochinenii*, vol. 6, p. 46. The quotation comes from a letter to Maksimilian Voloshin. *Mtsyri* refers to Lermontov's 1833 poem about a novitiate monk.

13. In a searching commentary on the ethics and psychology of her own generation, Lydia Ginzburg uses Tsvetaeva's delineation of Pushkin's two Pugachevs to try to understand how one can be charmed by violent revolutionary figures. Ginzburg, "Iz zapisei 1950—1970-kh godov," *Literatura v poiskakh real'nosti* (Leningrad: Sovetskii pisatel', 1987), pp. 312–22.

14. Tsvetaeva, *Sobranie sochinenii*, vol. 5, p. 515.

15. Although I am concentrating on the relationship to her mother here, Tsvetaeva's other important emotional connections are also encoded in "Pushkin and Pugachev." Elena Korkina has read the essay's description of a violent leader who charms a young man as a rewriting of Pasternak's infatuation with Stalin; she sees

Pugachev's surprising tenderness toward the young man as a parallel to the forgiveness seemingly expressed toward Tsvetaeva's family members as they returned to the Soviet Union, beginning in 1937. Korkina, "'Pushkin i Pugachev.'" Korkina also fundamentally argues that the two themes of the essay are the nature of the poet and the possibility that the poet can be politically engaged, and she shows how these themes are especially well developed in variants and fragments that were excluded from the final text.

16. Tsvetaeva, *Sobranie sochinenii*, vol. 5, p. 81. By mentioning Proust in an essay so much about her memories, Tsvetaeva also suggests a resemblance between her own project and that of Proust, and, like him, she presents her relationship with her mother as formative in literal as well as symbolic ways.

17. Viktoriia Shveitser, *Byt i bytie Mariny Tsvetaevoi* (Fontenay-aux-Roses: Syntaxis, 1988), pp. 400–401.

18. Remarkably, Tsvetaeva attributes to her mother the capacity to make Pushkin's texts mysterious to her. At one point in "My Pushkin," she calls a series of poems a row of enigmatic pictures, made mysterious by the questions posed by her mother. Tsvetaeva, *Sobranie sochinenii*, vol. 5, pp. 82–83.

19. Ibid., p. 68.

20. Paul Debreczeny, in *Social Functions of Literature: Alexander Pushkin and Russian Culture* (Stanford, Calif.: Stanford University Press, 1997), p. 66, comments that "the kind of love she thought she found in Pushkin always had connotations of pain and disillusionment," but he concludes, in terms I would not use, that "her childhood libido was attached to pain" (p. 67).

21. The term comes from the evocative title of Martha Nussbaum, *Love's Knowledge: Essays on Philosophy and Literature* (New York: Oxford University Press, 1990). See especially her chapters on Proust and Henry James for discussions of love, words, and knowledge that are pertinent to my reading of Tsvetaeva.

22. Adam Phillips, *Terrors and Experts* (Cambridge, Mass.: Harvard University Press, 1995), pp. 50–51.

23. Tsvetaeva, *Sobranie sochinenii*, vol. 5, p. 71.

24. Ibid., p. 501.

25. Irma Kudrova, "'Zagadka zlodeianiia i chistogo serdtsa' (Chelovek i stikhiia v tvorchestve Mariny Tsvetaevoi)," in *Marina Tsvetaeva: Stat'i i teksty*, Wiener Slawistishcher Almanach, vol. 32 (1992), pp. 201–15; see p. 202. Although she begins her essay by asserting that the central theme of "Pushkin and Pugachev" is love, Kudrova links the dangerous, transforming love described there to "The Swain" ("Molodets," 1922–23, pub. 1924), with its tale of passionate love for a vampire. I would stress the essay's autobiographical sources as well: Tsvetaeva's love for her mother, as shown in "My Pushkin," is a love for someone felt to be harmful. Elena Korkina has suggested that this description also fits Tsvetaeva's husband, Sergei Efron, and that a further allegory in the essay is Boris Pasternak's infatuation with Stalin (see n. 15 above).

26. Tsvetaeva, *Sobranie sochinenii*, vol. 5, p. 508.

27. Ibid., pp. 506, 508.

28. Ibid., p. 79.

29. Debreczeny, *Social Functions of Literature*, p. 69, also comments on the im-

portant fact that it is the impending loss of her mother that will take Tsvetaeva to the sea. Peter Scotto perceptively notes that the loss of her mother is Tsvetaeva's first step toward autonomy of the self. See Scotto, "The Image of Pushkin in the Works of Marina Cvetaeva," Ph.D dissertation, University of California–Berkeley, 1987, p. 228.

30. Tsvetaeva, *Sobranie sochinenii*, vol. 5, p. 89.

31. Ibid., vol. 4, pp. 44 (letter to M. Voloshin), 427 (letter to A. Teskova).

32. Ibid., vol. 5, p. 90. Compare the ambivalence about a sea-cliff inscription in a letter to Voloshin of 1911; ibid., vol. 4, p. 45.

33. Anya Kroth, "Androgyny as an Exemplary Feature of Marina Tsvetaeva's Dichotomous Poetic Vision," *Slavic Review*, vol. 38, no. 4 (1979), pp. 563–82; Antonina Filonov Gove, "The Feminine Stereotype and Beyond: Role Conflict and Resolution in the Poetics of Marina Tsvetaeva," *Slavic Review*, vol. 36, no. 2 (1977), pp. 231–55.

34. Simon Karlinsky, *Marina Tsvetaeva: The Woman, Her World, and Her Poetry* (Cambridge, Eng.: Cambridge University Press, 1985).

35. See, for example, Svetlana Elnitskaya, "Dve 'Bessonitsy' Mariny Tsvetaevoi," in Schweitzer et al., eds., *Marina Tsvetaeva: One Hundred Years*, pp. 91–110; Diana Burgin, "After the Ball Is Over: Sophia Parnok's Creative Relationship with Marina Tsvetaeva," *Russian Review*, vol. 47 (1988), pp. 425–44; Sibelan Forrester, "Bells and Cupolas: The Formative Role of the Female Body in Marina Tsvetaeva's Poetry," *Slavic Review*, vol. 51, no. 2 (Summer 1992), pp. 232–46; and Sibelan Forrester, "Wooing the Other Woman: Gender in Women's Love Poetry in the Silver Age," in Pamela Chester and Sibelan Forrester, eds., *Engendering Slavic Literatures* (Bloomington: Indiana University Press, 1996), pp. 107–34.

36. David Bethea, *Joseph Brodsky and the Creation of Exile* (Princeton, N.J.: Princeton University Press, 1994), pp. 187–90; Catriona Kelly, *A History of Russian Women's Writing, 1820–1992* (Oxford: Oxford University Press, 1994), pp. 308–9; Alyssa Dinega, "Exorcising the Beloved: Problems of Gender and Selfhood in Marina Tsvetaeva's Myths of Poetic Genius," Ph.D. dissertation, University of Wisconsin–Madison, 1998. A revised version of Dinega's dissertation has been published as *A Russian Psyche: The Poetic Mind of Marina Tsvetaeva* (Madison: University of Wisconsin Press, 2001). For an astute discussion of critics' tendencies to blame the poet, see Catherine Ciepiela, "The Demanding Woman Poet: On Resisting Marina Tsvetaeva," *PMLA*, vol. 111, no. 3 (1996), pp. 421–34.

37. Tsvetaeva, *Sobranie sochinenii*, vol. 5, p. 510.

38. Ibid., p. 512.

39. For a good account of Pushkin's comments about Catherine II, see Roman Jakobson, "The Statue in Pushkin's Poetic Mythology," in John Burbank, ed., *Pushkin and His Sculptural Myth* (The Hague: Mouton, 1975), pp. 15–18. Scholars have long noted Pushkin's preference in *The Captain's Daughter* for the rebel Pugachev over the reigning Catherine. See D. D. Blagoi, *Masterstvo Pushkina* (Moscow: Sovetskii pisatel', 1955); and Iurii Lotman, "Ideinaia struktura *Kapitanskoi dochki*," in *Pushkinskii sbornik* (Pskov, 1962), pp. 3–21, reprinted in Lotman, *Pushkin* (St. Petersburg: Iskusstvo-SPB, 1995), pp. 237–52.

40. *PSS*, vol. 8, pp. 39, 91.

41. Tsvetaeva's description here—the nightcap, the quilted coat, the leaves and bridges—is taken from *The Captain's Daughter*, where Pushkin depends on a 1791 painting by Vladimir Borovikovsky of the empress walking in her garden. Pushkin knew of the painting from an 1827 engraving. See M. I. Gillel'son and I. B. Mushina, *Povest' A. S. Pushkina 'Kapitanskaia dochka.' Kommentarii* (Leningrad: Izdatel'stvo "Prosveshchenie," 1977), pp. 164–67.

42. Tsvetaeva, *Sobranie sochinenii*, vol. 5, p. 510.

43. Ibid., p. 498. These are, in fact, the words that open the essay: "Есть магические слова, магические вне смысла, одним уже звучанием своим— физически-магические—слова, которые, до того как *сказали*—уже значат, слова—самознаки и самосмыслы, не нуждающиеся в разуме, а только в слухе, слова звериного, детского, сновиденного языка."

44. Nancy Miller, "The Text's Heroine: A Feminist Critic and Her Fictions," *Diacritics*, Summer 1982, pp. 48–53; see p. 50. Although making her own, explicitly feminist point, Miller depends in her reading of signatures on the work of Jacques Derrida, for example, "Signature Event Context," in *Glyph*, no. 1, 1977, pp. 172–97.

45. Much has been written on Pushkin's relationship to his pretenders. See, for example, Caryl Emerson, "Grinev's Dream: *The Captain's Daughter* and a Father's Blessing," *Slavic Review*, vol. 40, no. 1 (1981), pp. 60–76.

46. Most studies pass over the poem in silence. Exceptions include Jane A. Taubman, *A Life Through Poetry: Marina Tsvetaeva's Lyric Diary* (Columbus, Ohio: Slavica, 1988), pp. 49–50, although she sees little of interest in the poem's singsong meter and self-indulgent tone; Anna Saakiants, *Marina Tsvetaeva: Zhizn' i tvorchestvo* (Moscow: Ellis Lak, 1997), pp. 48–49, who calls the poem naive; and Simon Karlinsky, in his influential biographical study, *Marina Tsvetaeva*, p. 49. He sees the poem as a holdover of Tsvetaeva's earlier romantic manner. More sustained attention informs Alexandra Smith, *Song of the Mocking Bird*, pp. 14–17, 23–28, discussed below.

47. Tsvetaeva, *Sobranie sochinenii*, vol. 1, pp. 187–88. For some textual variants and a fuller publication history, see Tsvetaeva, *Stikhotvoreniia i poemy*, 5 vols. (New York: Russica, 1980–90), vol. 1, p. 294.

48. See Harold Bloom, *Agon: Towards a Theory of Revisionism* (New York: Oxford University Press, 1982), esp. pp. 91–118, 224–45; and Bloom's earlier, better-known books on influence.

49. Many of the early poems are about a child's world of magical events, several with the feel of fairy tales. See, for example, "Skazochnyi Shvartsval'd," "Nashi tsarstva," "El'fochka v zale." Tsvetaeva, *Sobranie sochinenii*, vol. 1, pp. 41, 42–43, 54–55. Some scholarship on this topic exists, although it concentrates on Russian folkloric sources for later long poems. See, for example, E. B. Korkina, "Liricheskii siuzhet v fol'klornykh poemakh Mariny Tsvetaevoi," *Russkaia literatura*, no. 4, 1987, pp. 161–68. Also pertinent are poems structured as encounters, for example two entitled "Vstrecha": the first is a vision of a dead woman, the second about an accidental encounter on the streets of the Arbat that ends with the monument to Gogol nodding from his pedestal. Tsvetaeva, *Sobranie sochinenii*, vol. 1, pp. 52, 66. As will be obvious to readers who know Russian, my translation of *vstrecha* as "encounter" is unsatisfactory. The word in Russian can connote a particular kind of encounter or meeting, one with a magical force or demon or sign of impending evil; it

also is used in expressions of greeting, as in "vstretit' khlebom-sol'iu." Tsvetaeva invokes both these connotations.

50. Including (1) *koldun'ia* or *koldun*: "Kolduni'a," ibid., vol. 1, 33–34 (all page numbers in this note are from this volume), "Dobryi koldun," pp. 70–71, "Nedoumenie," pp. 72, "V subbotu," p. 102, "'Kurlyk,'" p. 103, and "Neravnye brat'ia," p. 113; (2) *ved'ma*: "Utomlen'e," p. 47; (3) *volshebnik*: "Skazki Solov'eva," pp. 77–78, "Volshebnik," pp. 107–8, "Mal'chik-bred," p. 110, "Dekabr'skaia skazka," pp. 134–35, and "Volshebstvo," p. 149; (4) *volshebnitsa*: "Nashi dushi, ne pravda l'," pp. 84–85. This list of examples is not meant to be complete, although once all volumes of the concordance have appeared, it will be simple to compile such a list. See O. G. Revzina, *Slovar' poeticheskogo iazyka Mariny Tsvetaevoi*, 4 vols. to date (Moscow: Dom-muzei Mariny Tsvetaevoi, 1996–).

51. Ellis (1879–1947) knew Tsvetaeva and her sister, Anastasia Ivanovna (Asya), beginning in 1909. On their close relationship and its literary dimensions, see Karlinsky, *Marina Tsvetaeva*, pp. 28–31; and Viktoria Schweitzer, *Tsvetaeva*, tr. Robert Chandler and H. T. Willetts, ed. Angela Livingstone (New York: Farrar, Straus & Giroux, 1993), pp. 54–57. The word *charodei* appears in "Pervoe puteshestvie," "Oshibka," "Byvshemu Charodeiu," "Charodeiu," and the long poem *Charodei* (1914). Tsvetaeva, *Sobranie sochinenii*, vol. 1, pp. 21–22, 64, 66–67, 67–68; vol. 3, pp. 6–15.

52. M. Vasmer, *Etimologicheskii slovar' russkogo iazyka*, 4 vols. (Moscow: Progress, 1967), vol. 2, p. 554; *Slovar' sovremennogo russkogo literaturnogo iazyka*, 17 vols. (Moscow-Leningrad: AN-SSSR, 1957), vol. 6, p. 466. The latter equates *charodei* with *mag* in its second meaning, the first being a priest of ancient Eastern religions, with an example from the poetry of Baratynsky. Tsvetaeva, who sets her encounter with Pushkin in Crimea and always associated it with the ancient world, probably has this context in mind as well, which would further explain the religious connotations of imagery in the first stanza. *Belaia doroga* has a secondary meaning of church road. Tsvetaeva clearly uses that meaning in "A poka tvoi glaza" (1917) and "Konsuela!—Uteshen'e!" (1919). The "ringing" of l. 2 is also presumably the ringing of church bells.

53. Tsvetaeva, *Sobranie sochinenii*, vol. 5, pp. 226–29. This piece, an extraordinarily interesting text for understanding Tsvetaeva's image of poetry at this early stage, was published only in 1979; it was a response to Briusov's 1908 collection *Puti i pereput'ia*. Briusov was an important figure in Tsvetaeva's imagination and poetic growth at this time, although scholars emphasize their later, more embattled relationship. See Karlinsky, *Marina Tsvetaeva*, pp. 29, 34; Schweitzer, *Tsvetaeva*, pp. 60–61; Saakiants, *Marina Tsvetaeva*, pp. 40–41; and, for an astute comparison of Tsvetaeva's and Khodasevich's essays on Briusov, I. Andreeva, "Dva Briusova," in Schweitzer et al., eds., *Marina Tsvetaeva: One Hundred Years*, pp. 202–20.

54. In her study of Pasternak and Tsvetaeva, *The Same Solitude* (forthcoming from Cornell University Press), Catherine Ciepiela sets this essay in the little explored context of Tsvetaeva's encounter with Symbolism. Her reading of Tsvetaeva's selections from Briusov's poetry and their implicit self-revelations is especially astute: "Tsvetaeva's sexual yearnings and fears blossomed in the Symbolist hothouse, and she found a language for them in Briusov's poetry" (ms. chap. 3, p. 11).

55. Ibid., p. 16. John Malmstad has suggested to me that Tsvetaeva's use of *mag*

to describe Pushkin reflects her close reading of the Symbolists, for whom the term was common in describing their elevated notion of the poet.

56. Or we might expect a poet to take on the poetic voice of an addressee in order to speak to him in familiar tones. So argues Lawrence Lipking in *The Life of the Poet: Beginning and Ending Poetic Careers* (Chicago: University of Chicago Press, 1981).

57. See Smith, *Song of the Mocking Bird*, p. 23. I would add that Tsvetaeva writes with none of Pushkin's elegiac spirit, nor does she speak as directly to Pushkin as he does to Ovid (his poem is filled with apostrophe). I have written about modulations of voice in "To Ovid," in *Distant Pleasures: Alexander Pushkin and the Writing of Exile* (Stanford, Calif.: Stanford University Press, 1989), pp. 39–56.

58. V. Briusov, *Moi Pushkin: Stat'i, issledovaniia, nabliudeniia*, ed. N. K. Piksanov (Munich: Wilhelm Fink Verlag, 1970 [1929]), p. 3.

59. See Smith, *Song of the Mocking Bird*, p. 11, although she goes on to say that Tsvetaeva's "Pushkin myth . . . in many ways matches the vision of Pushkin of Valerii Briusov." My ellipses. I see her as more hostile to Briusov.

60. Compare the very interesting comments on Tsvetaeva's idea of teaching in O. Ronen, "Chasy uchenichestva Mariny Tsvetaevoi," *Novoe literaturnoe obozrenie*, no. 1, 1992, pp. 177–90. Ronen uses as a prime example for his argument one of her poems from the cycle "The Pupil" ("Uchenik," 1921), which he holds to be directed against Briusov's "The Sower" ("Seiatel'," 1907).

61. Schweitzer, *Tsvetaeva*, p. 117, and Saakiants, *Marina Tsvetaeva*, p. 41, note that she certainly read *Vecher* when it appeared; Taubman, *Life Through Poetry*, p. 95, thinks it more likely that she knew the poetry of *Chetki* (1914). Mikhail Gasparov emphasizes that Tsvetaeva was well acquainted with contemporary poetry as early as 1910–12, despite others' claims for her cultural innocence. See his essay "Marina Tsvetaeva: Ot poetiki byta k poetike slova," in Gasparov, *Izbrannye stat'i* (Moscow: Novoe literaturnoe obozrenie, 1995), pp. 307–15, esp. pp. 307–8. On Tsvetaeva's and Akhmatova's relationship across the course of their lives, see Irma Kudrova, "Sopernitsy (Tsvetaeva i Akhmatova)," in Kudrova, *Posle Rossii: O poezii i proze Mariny Tsvetaevoi* (Moscow: ROST, 1997), pp. 201–17.

62. Lidiia Chukovskaia, *Zapiski ob Anne Akhmatovoi*, 2 vols. (Paris: IMKA Press, 1976, 1980), vol. 2, p. 283. Interestingly, Akhmatova in the same passage criticizes Tsvetaeva's essay on Briusov as "insufficiently hostile" ("Briusova ona rugaet nedostatochno"), which I read less as an assessment of Tsvetaeva's mildness than a revelation of Akhmatova's still deeper antipathy.

63. Akhmatova's 1910 poem "The First Return," also about Tsarskoe Selo, seems less pertinent since it was published only in 1960.

64. Smith, *Song of the Mocking Bird*, p. 25.

65. "Bolero" can mean both the Spanish dance by that name and an item of clothing worn during the dance (a short, rounded vest). Since this is the only usage in Tsvetaeva's poetry (as per *Slovar' poeticheskogo iazyka Mariny Tsvetaevoi*, vol. 1, p. 93), and nothing in the context tells us whether she means the dance or the vest, I include it here with the clothing. But the reference to the dance would of course be equally erotic, perhaps more so.

66. *PSS*, vol. 4, p. 159. Tsvetaeva associates Mariula with her own name,

Marina, as shown in a poem she published by her daughter, Ariadna Sergeevna Efron. See Tsvetaeva, *Stikhotvoreniia i poemy*, 5 vols., vol. 2, p. 321. Tsvetaeva herself wrote a cycle of poems titled "Mariula," some of which were destined for the volume *Psyche* (which included her daughter's poems). See ibid., pp. 347–48, for a discussion of the cycle and notes on the poems that appeared in *Psyche*. Some of those *Psyche* poems were subsequently published in *Versty II*.

67. Jacques Lacan, "The Mirror Stage as Formative of the Function of the I as Revealed in Psychoanalytic Experience," *Ecrits: A Selection*, tr. Alan Sheridan (New York: Norton, 1977), pp. 1–7. An immense amount has been written on Lacan's mirror stage, first described in 1937 and presented as a lecture in 1949. I have found these writings particularly stimulating: Mikkel Borch-Jacobsen, "The Statue Man," in Borch-Jacobsen, *Lacan: The Absolute Master*, tr. Douglas Brick (Stanford, Calif.: Stanford University Press, 1991), pp. 43–96; Cynthia Chase, "Desire and Identification in Lacan and Kristeva," in Richard Feldstein and Judith Roof, eds., *Feminism and Psychoanalysis* (Ithaca, N.Y.: Cornell University Press, 1989), pp. 65–83, esp. pp. 69–71, for a pertinent discussion of recognition; and, although it treats identification only in passing, Shoshana Felman, *What Does a Woman Want? Reading and Sexual Difference* (Cambridge, Mass.: Harvard University Press, 1993).

68. Borch-Jacobsen, "Statue Man," p. 46.

69. Tsvetaeva, *Sobranie sochinenii*, vol. 1, p. 325.

70. The poem lacks the exuberant sense of accomplishment that marks the 1916 poems to Blok, Akhmatova, and Mandelstam. Anna Saakiants, *Marina Tsvetaeva*, p. 114, sees the poems of the fall of 1916 as generally less interesting than those from earlier in the year.

71. Peter Scotto finds Natalia Nikolaevna "an empty-headed flirt with no sympathy or understanding for either her husband or his poetry," with "no more substance than the gauze which decorates her dresses." Scotto, *Image of Pushkin*, p. 171. He contends that the poem "Psyche" is written "much in the same vein" (ibid.).

72. The source for this comment is easily traced to Vikenty Veresaev's compendium of material about Pushkin, although Tsvetaeva misinterprets the source. See the excerpt from the memoirs of L. N. Pavlishchev in V. Veresaev, *Pushkin v zhizni* (Moscow: Moskovskii rabochii, 1984), p. 292. For Tsvetaeva's elaboration of her error, see "Natal'ia Goncharova," in Tsvetaeva, *Sobranie sochinenii*, vol. 4, p. 82.

73. The other poem Tsvetaeva wrote on the same day as "Happiness or sadness," which begins "Like wind above the cornfield, like / The first bell—this name" ("Slovno veter nad nivoi, slovno / Pervyi kolokol—eto imia"), is a meditation on the Aramaic name Eloim, meaning "O my God." Its concern with naming is shared with "Happiness or sadness," but its subject matter, a midnight meeting of lovers opening out to the infinite expanse of the divine universe, is entirely different.

74. Smith, *Song of the Mocking Bird*, pp. 17–18.

75. It is possible that the verb used to describe Natalia Nikolaevna's "tugging at" Pushkin's heart (*terebit'*) unexpectedly renders Natalia Nikolaevna herself vulnerable to such strong feelings. In a September 1833 letter to her, Pushkin worried that she was being pulled every which way by men to whom he owed money ("Zhivo voobrazhaiu pervoe chislo. Tebia terebiat za dolgi"). *PSS*, vol. 10, p. 344, cited in

Slovar' russkogo literaturnogo iazyka, vol. 15, p. 322. Tsvetaeva would have found this portion of the letter in V. Veresaev, *Pushkin v zhizni*, 3d ed. (Moscow: Nedra, 1928), p. 101.

76. Barbara Johnson, "Gender and Poetry: Charles Baudelaire and Marceline Desbordes-Valmore," in Johnson, *The Feminist Difference: Literature, Psychoanalysis, Race, and Gender* (Cambridge, Mass.: Harvard University Press, 1998), pp. 101–28. The topic is much written about, but I choose to cite Johnson's essay for its elegant clarity, and for its excellent analysis of Desbordes-Valmore, whom the young Tsvetaeva passionately absorbed as a poetic model. See her early poem "V zerkale knigi M. D.-V." (probably 1910), an intriguing meditation on poetic identity and the dangers of feeling too much. The poem ends "These lines—are mine! This heart—is mine! / Who is Marceline—you or I?" ("Eti stroki—moi! Eto serdtse—moe! / Kto zhe, ty ili ia—Marselina?"). Tsvetaeva, *Sobranie sochinenii*, vol. 1, p. 99.

77. A powerful argument that Tsvetaeva's deepest attachments were to other women is made by Diana Burgin in "Mother Nature Versus the Amazons: Marina Tsvetaeva and Female Same-Sex Love," *Journal of the History of Sexuality*, vol. 6, no. 1 (1995), pp. 62–88; and in Burgin, *Marina Tsvetaeva i transgressivnyi eros* (St. Petersburg: Inapress, 2000). See also Elnitskaya, "Dve 'Bessonitsy' Mariny Tsvetaevoi," who persuasively shows that Parnok remained important in Tsvetaeva's poetic imagination, and that Parnok informs the presentation of other women in "Bessonitsa."

78. Respectively, "Kanun Blagoveshchen'ia," in Tsvetaeva, *Sobranie sochinenii*, vol. 1, p. 263; "Ia prishla k tebe chernoi polnoch'iu," ibid., p. 301.

79. Ibid., p. 264. She revels in her identification with Marina Mniszech in poems written that spring. The Polish aristocrat Mniszech was implicated in the rise of the False Dmitry during the Time of Troubles.

80. Ibid., p. 326.

81. Anna de Noialles, *Novoe upovanie*, tr. Marina Tsvetaeva, in ibid., vol. 5, p. 527.

82. To this list, we might add the following from Smith, *Song of the Mocking Bird*, p. 32: "images such as 'pipe,' 'punch,' 'insomnia' appear in Pushkin's poetry of the 1810s and 1820s in relation to dreaming, escapism, and the tragic vision of his own life. In the poem 'Sleza' (written in 1816), the imagery described above signals an elegiac mood."

83. Tsvetaeva, *Sobranie sochinenii*, vol. 1, pp. 508–9.

84. Two motifs from the Greek myth also appear in the poem: the butterfly and bird as emblems of Psyche; and plot details from Apuleius's version of the Cupid and Psyche story, including the drop of hot oil Psyche spills on Cupid and Cupid's appearances to Psyche only at night (all reversed, as discussed below).

85. Scotto, *Image of Pushkin*, p. 172.

86. Dinega, "Exorcising the Beloved." Psyche appears in a two-poem cycle of 1918, in the poem before us (1920), in a scene in the 1919 play *The Adventure* (*Prikliuchenie*), and as the name of Tsvetaeva's 1923 volume of verse. She is also mentioned in letters at the time, including two to Boris Pasternak.

87. Dinega, "Exorcising the Beloved," pp. 127–28, 129. My ellipses. The first

quotation, very slightly revised to tie it more closely to Tsvetaeva's relationship with Pasternak, also appears in Dinega, *A Russian Psyche*, pp. 94–95. There Dinega notes that "the myth of Psyche perfectly encapsulates the basic paradox of female creativity as Tsvetaeva understands it."

88. Dinega, "Exorcising the Beloved," pp. 138–39.

89. To mention only a few of the pertinent images in "Attic Writings": Tsvetaeva comments on the dust (from wood shavings needed to make a fire) that fills her room (compare the dusty mirror that closes "Psyche," as well as the ash in the poem, a metonym); she describes her one dress as burnt through with holes from coal or cigarettes, and her hands as constantly burned by her impatient picking up of live coals (compare the burning kiss of the Blackamoor, and also Psyche's luxurious ball gown, with his straw-colored dressing gown); elsewhere she mentions a luxuriant and frightening pink dress that is more than 70 years old, with a bonnet to match. Tsvetaeva, *Sobranie sochinenii*, vol. 4, pp. 534–42. This account of Tsvetaeva's life in Moscow can now be read in a fine English translation: Marina Tsvetaeva, *Earthly Signs: Moscow Diaries, 1917–1923*, ed. and tr. Jamey Gambrell (New Haven, Conn.: Yale University Press, 2002).

90. Smith, *Song of the Mocking Bird*, p. 33, also notes that this is the first poem Tsvetaeva wrote after Irina's death but does not otherwise link it to that loss.

91. See Schweitzer, *Tsvetaeva*, pp. 186–93. Harsher accounts appear in Bethea, *Joseph Brodsky*, pp. 187–90; and Kelly, *History of Russian Women's Writing*, pp. 308–9.

92. Tsvetaeva's poem on Irina's death, "Two hands" ("Dve ruki," 1920), includes a line where she states flatly that, although she saved one daughter from death, she failed to protect the other ("Snatching the elder away from the darkness— / I failed to save the younger"; "Starshuiu u t'my vykhvatyvaia— / Mladshei ne uberegla"). Tsvetaeva, *Sobranie sochinenii*, vol. 1, p. 518.

93. Ibid., vol. 6, p. 154. These comments appear in a long letter where all else concentrates on details of illness and death, of Irina and Ariadna. They thus stand out for their passing generalization about women as a category, and for their seemingly inappropriate gesture of self-defense, as if Tsvetaeva would have been *more* guilty of her daughter's death had she been busy writing poems while Irina was starving in an orphanage. Compare her comment in a 1935 letter to Boris Pasternak: Robert Schumann, she tells him, "*forgot* that he had children, forgot how many, forgot their names ..." Ibid., vol. 6, p. 277. Tsvetaeva insists that she is not capable of such forgetting, but one senses an underlying fear that her neglect contributed to her child's death.

94. The essay has perhaps seemed marginal. One of the few large prose texts not to exist in an English translation (another is "Tale About Sonechka" ["Povest' o Sonechke"], 1937), it was regarded as a failure by Karlinsky, *Marina Tsvetaeva*, p. 198. But others have seen it as valuable. Liza Knapp writes that "Goncharova was an interesting subject not so much because of her painting but because she appeared to Tsvetaeva to have found some solution to the duel between life and art that tormented Tsvetaeva herself." Knapp, "Tsvetaeva and the Two Natal'ia Goncharovas: Dual Life," in Gasparov et al., *Cultural Mythologies of Russian Modernism*, p. 89. Scotto argues, in *The Image of Pushkin*, that Tsvetaeva is working out a new rela-

tionship between the life and works of her subtitle, one that moved beyond contemporary polemics about a poet's biography (pp. 148–84, where he also provides a good discussion of the cultural context in which the essay was written). Also pertinent is Svetlana Boym, *Death in Quotation Marks* (Cambridge, Mass.: Harvard University Press, 1991), pp. 210–11, which mentions the essay to advance a larger point about poetic identity. Boym's argument is particularly valuable because she concentrates on Tsvetaeva's refutation of traditional gender arrangements.

95. A perceptive reading of these pages appears in Aleksandar Flaker, "Avangard slovesnyi i avangard izobrazitel'nyi: Tsvetaeva o Goncharovoi," *Russian Literature*, no. 36 (July 1, 1994), pp. 1–12. Flaker observes the spatial arrangements of these descriptions, of closed space opening out into larger but not unlimited space, and correlates them to Tsvetaeva's evaluations of Goncharova's paintings. He values Tsvetaeva's insights, suggesting that her own avant-garde poetics led her to comprehend deeply Goncharova's work.

96. Tsvetaeva, *Sobranie sochinenii*, vol. 4, p. 68. Olga Peters Hasty has noted the way in which this description of Goncharova's studio places the creative act near death. See Hasty, *Tsvetaeva's Orphic Journeys in the Worlds of the Word* (Evanston, Ill.: Northwestern University Press, 1996), pp. 184–85.

97. Tsvetaeva, *Sobranie sochinenii*, vol. 4, p. 68.

98. Ibid., p. 76.

99. Tsvetaeva begins the section "Two Goncharovas" this way: "'What are you writing these days?' 'Natalia Goncharova.' 'This one or that one?'" Ibid., p. 80. The imagined curiosity of a reader who hears the essay title and wonders which Goncharova she means propels Tsvetaeva forward into the substantive part of the section.

100. The most balanced assessment of Tsvetaeva's point of view appears in Knapp, "Tsvetaeva and the Two Natal'ia Goncharovas."

101. Tsvetaeva, *Sobranie sochinenii*, vol. 4, p. 81.

102. Ibid., p. 83.

103. See Schweitzer, *Tsvetaeva*, pp. 83, 247, 249.

104. Tsvetaeva, *Sobranie sochinenii*, vol. 4, p. 84.

105. To say that what women lack defines them is to travel a path explored in many of Freud's writings and embellished by Lacan. The Freudian observation may now sound crude (that nothing makes such a difference for the "configuration of femininity" as the "lack of a penis"; Sigmund Freud, "Femininity," in James Strachey, tr., *New Introductory Lectures on Psychoanalysis* [New York: Norton, 1965], pp. 99–119; see p. 117). But it enabled Lacan and later feminist theorists to explain the social marginalization of women. Jacques Lacan, "The Signification of the Phallus," *Ecrits*, pp. 281–91. The territory that I map out here has been surveyed by many others. A feminist perspective on the transition from Freud to Lacan can be found in the first chapter of Jane Gallop, *The Daughter's Seduction: Feminism and Psychoanalysis* (Ithaca, N.Y.: Cornell University Press, 1982).

106. Tsvetaeva, *Sobranie sochinenii*, vol. 4, p. 84.

107. Ibid., p. 88.

108. Ibid., p. 84.

109. Ibid., p. 85.

110. Tsvetaeva would not have had the benefit of reading Natalia's letters to her brother, found and published only in the 1980s. See I. Obodovskaia and M. De-

ment'ev, *Natal'ia Nikolaevna Pushkina* (Moscow: Sovetskaia Rossiia, 1987). I discuss the complex myth that has grown up around Pushkin's wife in "Pushkin's Last Love: Natal'ya Nikolaevna in Russian Culture," in Marianne Liljestrom, Eila Mantysaari, and Arja Rosenholm, eds., *Gender Restructuring in Russian Studies* (Helsinki: Slavica Tamperensia, 1993), pp. 209–20.

111. Letter to Anna Teskova, Feb. 19, 1929, in Tsvetaeva, *Sobranie sochinenii*, vol. 6, p. 376.

112. Ibid., vol. 4, p. 107.

113. This would be doubly awful for Tsvetaeva, who found responses to her nearly always inadequate. Critics typically blame Tsvetaeva for neediness and overwhelming intensity in this regard, but Catherine Ciepiela has exposed logical inconsistencies in many of these accounts and shown how Tsvetaeva's poetry effectively uses the linguistic structure of apostrophe and anticipated response. See Ciepiela, "The Demanding Woman Poet." She also covers the matter in her forthcoming book on Pasternak and Tsvetaeva, *The Same Solitude*.

114. Tsvetaeva, *Sobranie sochinenii*, vol. 4, p. 88.

115. Ibid., p. 102. Tsvetaeva also claims that Natalia Goncharova resembles Pushkin himself more than she resembles Pushkin's wife (her great-aunt after whom she was named). Ibid. p. 114. The artist's genealogy is thus reduced to (male) artists.

116. Ibid., p. 85.

117. Simon Karlinsky notes that "from 1931 to 1933, Tsvetaeva lived in the worst poverty she was ever to experience." Karlinsky, *Marina Tsvetaeva*, p. 212. Not a small claim, when we think of her dreadful hope for a job as a dishwasher in Elabuga in 1941. For confirmation of Karlinsky's view, see Taubman, *A Life Through Poetry*, pp. 245–247; and Saakiants, *Marina Tsvetaeva*, pp. 539–41.

118. Karlinsky, *Marina Tsvetaeva*, p. 188 (on reactions to "Novogodnee").

119. The context of poems on a poet's death is also suggested in Il'ia Kukulin, "'Russkii bog' na rendez-vous (O tsikle M. I. Tsvetaevoi 'Stikhi k Pushkinu')," *Voprosy literatury*, Sept.–Oct. 1998 (no. 5), pp. 122–36, esp. p. 136.

120. Brodsky continues, "Tsvetaeva's verse is dialectical, but it is the dialectics of dialogue: between meaning and meaning, between meaning and sound. It is as though Tsvetaeva were constantly struggling against the *a priori* authority of poetic speech." Joseph Brodsky, "Footnote to a Poem," in Brodsky, *Less Than One: Selected Essays* (New York: Farrar, Straus & Giroux, 1986), p. 215.

121. Tsvetaeva, *Sobranie sochinenii*, vol. 2, p. 281.

122. In *The Image of Pushkin*, Peter Scotto has thoroughly researched the identities of these critics and traced relevant patterns in émigré writing about Pushkin. He also clarifies which memoirs about Pushkin Tsvetaeva might have objected to; see esp. pp. 7–41, 65–82.

123. Catherine Ciepiela, "Lyric's Fatal Lure: Politics and the Poet in Tsvetaeva's 'Krysolov,'" Ph. D. dissertation, Yale University, 1992, pp. 14–15.

124. Tsvetaeva, *Sobranie sochinenii*, vol. 2, p. 287.

125. The image of violence directed against Pushkin's body derives not just from his death in a duel, but undoubtedly from the rumor that he was beaten by the police. The history of this rumor and Bulgakov's fascination with it were discussed in Chap. 3.

126. Tsvetaeva, *Sobranie sochinenii*, vol. 2, p. 282. The announcement that

Pushkin "lives" owes much to Mayakovsky's "Anniversary Poem" (discussed in Chap. 3) and to his "Vladimir Ilich Lenin" (1924), as Kukulin shows in "'Russkii bog' na rendez-vous," pp. 126–30.

127. Much has been written on the dualism of body and soul, of *byt* and *byt'e*, in Tsvetaeva's writings, often suggesting that she denies the value or symbolic meanings of the body. See S. Elnitskaia, "O nekotorykh chertakh poeticheskogo mira M. Tsvetaevoi," *Wiener Slawistischer Almanach*, no. 3, 1979, pp. 59–73; Ieva Vitins, "Escape from Earth: A Study of Tsvetaeva's Elsewheres," *Slavic Review*, vol. 36, no. 4 (1977), pp. 644–57; and Shveitser, *Byt i byt'e Mariny Tsvetaevoi*. This is not a position that I would share.

128. For an excellent reading of *Perekop*, see M. S. Smith, "Marina Tsvetaeva's Perekop: Recuperation of the Russian Bardic Tradition," *Oxford Slavonic Papers*, n.s. vol. 32 (1999), pp. 97–126. On the long poem about the tsar's family, see Elena Korkina's efforts at reconstructing the text: "Poema o Tsarskoi Sem'e," *Wiener slavistischer Almanach: M. Tsvetaeva. Stat'i i teksty*, vol. 32 (1992), pp. 171–200.

129. Tsvetaeva, *Sobranie sochinenii*, vol. 2, p. 285.

130. Ibid., p. 289. Peter Scotto, *Image of Pushkin*, p. 112, observes that the ending of this poem is meant to repeat the rhythm of a revolutionary slogan.

131. Tsvetaeva, *Sobranie sochinenii*, vol. 2, p. 289.

132. Ibid.

133. Tsvetaeva continues that focus in the "seventh" poem to Pushkin, "It's for the sovereign people who have toppled the throne" ("Narodopravstvu, svalivshemu tron"), which is included in *Sobranie sochinenii* as part of the cycle but given as a separate poem in other editions, including the authoritative *Stikhotvoreniia i poemy* prepared by Elena Korkina. I share Korkina's view that Tsvetaeva did not intend to have this poem in the final version of the cycle (Tsvetaeva prepared a fair copy of poems 1–6 in 1939, confirming them as the final text of the cycle); in her notebooks, Tsvetaeva wrote "dubious" ("somnitel'noe") above the text of poem 7; see *Stikhotvoreniia i poemy*, pp. 652, 764. I suspect that it was important for Tsvetaeva to maintain the coherence of the six poems, written in one month in 1931, as opposed to the "seventh" poem, written in 1933, and I also imagine that she preferred the defiant conclusion of *"the smartest man in Russia"* that ends poem 6 to the grotesque ending of poem "7," briefly discussed below.

134. The last two poems of the cycle together also have a parenthetical title, "(Poet and Tsar)."

135. Tsvetaeva, *Sobranie sochinenii*, vol. 2, pp. 286–87.

136. Relations of equals are important to her more generally: compare the "conspiracy of equals" ("zagovor ravnykh") that defines Pushkin's relationship with Peter, as she imagines it in "Peter and Pushkin." Ibid., p. 287.

137. Mikhail Gasparov has carefully studied the thematics of this meter in poems from 1890 to 1925, and traced the origins of the form in Russia to Lermontov's "Mountain summits" ("Gornye vershiny," 1840, a transposition of Goethe). M. L. Gasparov, *Russkie stikhi 1890-kh–1925-go godov v kommentariiakh* (Moscow: Vysshaia shkola, 1993), pp. 222, 256; for a fuller discussion of trochaic trimeter, see pp. 221–56.

138. Tsvetaeva, *Sobranie sochinenii*, vol. 2, p. 288.

139. Tsvetaeva, *Neizdannoe*, p. 451.
140. Ibid., p. 443.

CHAPTER 7

EPIGRAPH: Andrei Bitov, "Raznye dni cheloveka," in Bitov, *My prosnulis' v neznakomoi strane. Publitsistika* (Leningrad: Ogonek, 1991), p. 37.

1. Andrei Bitov, "Blagodat' bezvremen'ia," an interview conducted by Liubov' Paikova, *Iskusstvo kino*, no. 5, 2001, pp. 73–81; quoted from p. 75.

2. In the commentary to the novel (which I take as part of it), Bitov says he completed the novel in 1971 and the commentary in 1978, and he adds the dates 1971, 1978, at the end of the commentary. *Pushkinskii dom* was published in the West in Russian in 1978. I have used the first Soviet edition (Moscow: Sovremennik, 1989). I shall cite from both that Russian edition and the 1987 English translation: *Pushkin House*, tr. Susan Brownsberger (Ann Arbor, Mich.: Ardis Press, 1987).

3. Bitov's work began appearing in Russia and abroad in the 1960s. Besides his novel *Pushkin House*, he published several cycles of stories, two long travel essays on Armenia and Georgia, literary critical pieces on classical and contemporary Russian literature, and a spate of what Russians call "publicistic" writings: essays and interviews offering opinions on a range of topics, from censorship and pornography to cultural politics. Bitov states his views forthrightly, avoiding the more circuitous paths of his fiction.

4. The section title is taken from this work. Bitov, "Tri 'proroka,'" *Voprosy literatury*, no. 7, 1976, p. 152.

5. Bitov notes that positioning "side by side, parallel," is significant for content and for method. *Pushkinskii dom*, p. 227.

6. The critical apparatus did not make it into the novel version of "Three 'Prophets'" (although a note sends readers to the *Voprosy literatury* essay for the notes). See Bitov, *Pushkinskii dom*, p. 381. But much of their substance was retained, either made into foot-of-the-page notes or incorporated into the text itself. The direction to *Voprosy literatury* appears in the commentary at the end of *Pushkin House*, also presented as a mystification with a disquisition on whether it was the author or Lev Odoevtsev who wrote the notes. Ibid., p. 355. The commentary goes in many different directions, recounting historical details and fascinating stories about the writing and publishing of the novel.

7. Bitov contrasts science with humanism in "Pushkin's Photograph (1799–2099)," in Sergei Zalygin, ed., *The New Soviet Fiction: Sixteen Short Stories* (New York: Abbeville Press, 1989), pp. 15–59; see p. 42. The translation is by Priscilla Meyer, and I cite it below, with occasional slight changes; I have used the Russian version in Bitov, *Chelovek v peizazhe* (Moscow: Sovetskii pisatel', 1988), pp. 417–54. Compare also the mention of theoretical physics in *Vychitanie zaitsa 1825* (Moscow: Nezavisimaia gazeta, 2001), p. 17.

8. Bitov, "Tri 'proroka,'" p. 146.

9. Some scholars see the notes as written straightforwardly from Bitov's point of view. See, for example, V. V. Kozhinov, *Kniga o russkoi liricheskoi poezii XIX veka: Razvitie stilia i zhanra* (Moscow: Sovremennik, 1978), p. 115, who argues with the

findings in the essay and seeks to address Bitov, not Lyova. The essay occasioned other disputes when it appeared in *Voprosy literatury*. See Ellen Chances, *Andrei Bitov: The Ecology of Inspiration* (Cambridge, Eng.: Cambridge University Press, 1993), p. 220.

10. Later comments contain some mock elements of competitiveness, for example, in an interview, where Bitov recalls the polemics occasioned by Lyova's "Three 'Prophets,'" whereas a later piece of his own was barely noticed. See Bitov, *My prosnulis' v neznakomoi strane: Publitsistika* (Leningrad: Ogonek, 1991), p. 37.

11. The essay has seven parts; the first four appeared in the January 1986 issue of the Leningrad literary journal *The Star* (*Zvezda*), and later that same year, Bitov published a book, *Stat'i iz romana* (Moscow: Sovetskii pisatel', 1986), with a full and slightly amended version. A beautiful edition appeared for the Pushkin jubilee, *Predpolozhenie zhit' 1836* (Moscow: Nezavisimaia gazeta, 1999), with Bitov named as "editor." The volume contains several hundred pages that reproduce Pushkin's writings from his last year of life, including a facsimile edition of *The Captain's Daughter*.

12. For a cogent analysis of the arguments and ironies of "Intention to Live," see Ronald Meyer, "Andrei Bitov's Memoir of Pushkin," *Studies in Comparative Communism*, vol. 21, no. 3-4 (Autumn-Winter 1988), pp. 379–87.

13. This hare also appears in "Pushkin's Photograph (1799–2099)," where the hero, Igor, takes credit for scaring the hare out of the woods onto Pushkin's path and comes back from his journey through time with only one truly splendid photograph, that of the hare.

14. Bitov notes, in a discussion of Pushkin's journal articles, that "image is more important than their information" and "the material serves as a pretext for Pushkin's pronouncements" ("Predpolozhenie zhit'," in Bitov, *Stat'i iz romana*, pp. 244–45). I cite "Predpolozhenie zhit'" throughout from this *Stat'i iz romana* version, unless otherwise noted.

15. The title comes from the text Bitov is talking about ("Poslednii iz svoistvennikov Ioanny d'Ark"), although it is not a phrase he discusses. See *PSS*, vol. 7, p. 350.

16. Bitov, "Predpolozhenie zhit'," p. 233. Later, he wonders whether d'Ash has the letter to Heeckeren in mind as the final finished text authored by Pushkin (pp. 235–36).

17. One quotation comes from Tolstoy's play *The Living Corpse* (*Zhivoi trup*, published 1911), surely chosen for the paradox of its title, which compares nicely with the juxtapositions of life and death in "The Intention to Live." An example of paraphrase is the use of Pushkin's letter to Heeckeren, which (like the quotation from Tolstoy) appears in the letter from d'Ash.

18. "Scene from *Faust*" had been dated Summer 1825, and Bitov moves it to November. Shortly after Bitov published "Take Away the Hare," scholars placed "Scene" in June-July. See Irina Surat, "Pamiatnik zaitsu" [1994], in *Pushkin: biografiia i lirika* (Moscow: Nasledie, 1999), pp. 225–30; see p. 229.

19. *PSS*, vol. 7, p. 352. The lines recall syntactically the last line of *The Covetous Knight* (*Skupoi rytsar'*, 1830), "What dreadful times, what dreadful, evil hearts" ("Uzhasnyi vek, uzhasnye serdtsa!"). *PSS*, vol. 5, p. 305.

20. Bitov, "Predpolozhenie zhit'," p. 246.

21. Bitov notes this aspect of his work in several interviews, for example, "So-

protivlenie kul'tury," in Bitov, *My prosnulis' v neznakomoi strane*, p. 101. See also his comments about the reception of "A Teacher of Symmetry" ("Prepodovatel' simmetrii," 1987, revised and expanded 1988), which he compares to Pushkin's contemporaries' failure to understand him. Bitov, "Vozniknovenie kul'tury," in ibid., p. 57.

22. See, for example, Bitov, *Neizbezhnost' nenapisannogo: Godovye kol'tsa 1956–1998–1937* (Moscow: Vagrius, 1999).

23. This essay might seem slight compared with the voluminous "Intention to Live," but Bitov has signaled its importance by republishing it twice after its original journal appearance in 1990. See the two book versions, both with illustrations by Rezo Gabriadze, *Vychitanie zaitsa* (Moscow: Olimp, 1993) and *Vychitanie zaitsa 1825*, the 2001 edition I cite. A few addenda appear in the 1993 volume, but the beautiful 2001 edition is much fuller, including short pieces on related themes Bitov had published in the 1990s, as well as the short story "Pushkin's Photograph (1799–2099)." The 2001 volume also contains lengthy commentary by the excellent Pushkin scholar Irina Surat, and a substantial appendix of Pushkin texts mentioned by Bitov (the juxtaposition of Pushkin's writings with Bitov's similarly structures the 1999 republication of *Predpolozhenie zhit' 1836*, which also bears a longer title to include the pertinent year of Pushkin's life). In this format, the scholarly side of Bitov's work bears more weight, although it is balanced by Gabriadze's wonderfully quick drawings.

24. Part Two of "Take Away the Hare," subtitled "Grateful Russia. An Explanatory Note about the Proposal for a Roadside Monument" ("Blagodarnaia Rossiia. Poiasnitel'naia zapiska k proektu pridorozhnogo pamiatnika"), gives Boberov's poem in full; like the essay that contains it, the poem is a three-part text with fulsome commentary. One note, longer and more substantive, advances an argument about the dating of Pushkin's "Scene from *Faust*" ("Stsena iz Fausta," 1825), which then becomes the point of Part Three, subtitled "The Hare and the World's Road. The Scholarly Variant" ("Zaiats i mirovaia doroga. Uchenyi variant"). This part of the essay proposes that a monument be erected to the hare that crossed Pushkin's path in 1825. Such a monument was put up in 2000, at the initiative of Bitov and others, as mentioned in the editorial introduction to Bitov, "Vychitanie zaitsa," *Zvezda*, no. 12, 2000, pp. 3–13 (see p. 3); and "Vechnyi zaiats," *Literaturnaia gazeta*, June 6–12, 2001 (no. 23 [5836]), p. 9. The publication in *Zvezda* is an addendum to the essay "Vychitanie zaitsa" discussed here: it includes the documentary drama "Zanaves" and "Pushkinskii leksikon," also in the 2001 book, *Vychitatnie zaitsa*, pp. 129–49. The hare makes several appearances in these short texts, prompting Pushkin during the play to wish he were a Russian wolfhound so he could kill it (p. 147).

25. Bitov, *Vychitanie zaitsa*, p. 52. A similar comment emerged in a 1998 interview: "I have been changing genres not because it's a fashionable thing to do but simply because there was no other means of moving forward in my work." Andrei Bitov, "Izobretenie kamennogo topora," interview with Anton Kuznetsov, *Voprosy literatury*, Jan.-Feb. 1998, pp. 281–97; quotation from p. 290.

26. Bitov, *Vychitanie zaitsa*, p. 13.

27. Ibid.

28. Ibid., p. 22.

29. Ibid. The tense shift is in the original.

30. Ibid., pp. 22–23.

31. Ibid., p. 22.

32. See, for example, an essay about Iuz Aleshkovsky: Bitov, "Povtorenie neproidennogo," *Znamia*, no. 6, 1991, pp. 192–206. In another essay, on Gogol, he uses fragmentary, evocative structures rather than any psychological impersonation: Bitov, "Being Buried Alive, or Gogol in 1973," in Susanne Fusso and Priscilla Meyer, eds., *Essays on Gogol: Logos and the Russian Word* (Evanston, Ill.: Northwestern University Press, 1992), pp. 14–18. In reserving his ventriloquism for Pushkin, Bitov's practice is unlike Andrei Sinyavsky's, whose invention, Abram Tertz, also appears as the author of books about Pushkin and Gogol, prison memoirs, and short stories. For Bitov, as he says in "Take Away the Hare," Pushkin is a forbidden topic, in fact the most forbidden topic.

33. Bitov, "Blagodat' bezvremen'ia," p. 75.

34. Bitov, *Vychitanie zaitsa*, p. 15.

35. In an addendum to "Take Away the Hare," Bitov again confessed that it was Pushkin to whom he wished to make himself understood. Ibid., p. 131.

36. Ibid., p. 23. My ellipses.

37. Ibid., p. 25.

38. When the poem comes to a line about Pushkin's urge to surpass Goethe's achievements as a writer (this is the argument about Pushkin's writings in 1825 that Bitov later makes in "Take Away the Hare"), Bitov seems stunned by his own daring: "Here I have crossed into completely impermissible territory, one that for me is puzzling. As if from nowhere Pushkin's own stream of consciousness has started up. These characteristics could belong only to him or only to me. No banal set of opinions about Pushkin contained them. It is unbecoming, as if Pushkin thinks about himself in such a bragging fashion...." Ibid., p. 28.

39. Bitov has published a number of experiments in verse. In 1970 he wrote a parodic outline of a novel called "The Twelve" ("Dvenatsat'"), where the procession from Blok's poem of the same name is interwoven with references to *The Bronze Horsemen* and *Eugene Onegin*, and to Lyova from *Pushkin House*, who is chased through the drafts of the novel by a truck full of soldiers. See "Dvenadtsat'," in Bitov, *Zhizn' v vetrenuiu pogodu*, pp. 528–29. He began to publish some poems in journals in the glasnost period. For example, three poems appeared in *Druzhba narodov*, no. 12, 1988, pp. 105–7; the third of them, "Otkrytoe okno, Peredelkino," parodies Pushkin's "The Prophet." In the post-Soviet period, many more poems have appeared. See Bitov, *V chetverg posle dozhdia (Dnevnik prozaika): Sbornik stikhov* (St. Petersburg: Pushkinskii fond, 1997). Poems mix with prose in *Derevo 1971–1997* (St. Petersburg: Pushkinskii fond, 1998); and *Neizbezhnost' nenapisannogo*.

40. Surat, "Pamiatnik zaitsu," p. 227.

41. Nicolas Abraham, *Rhythms: On the Work, Translation, and Psychoanalysis*, tr. Benjamin Thigpen and Nicholas T. Rand (Stanford, Calif.: Stanford University Press, 1995), p. 23.

42. For an account of the novel's literary allusions, see Alice Stone Nakhimovsky, "Looking Back at Paradise Lost: The Russian Nineteenth Century in Andrei

Bitov's *Pushkin House*," *Russian Literature Triquarterly*, no. 22, 1989, pp. 195–204. On Bitov's dialogue with Dostoevsky, see Ellen Chances, "The Island and the Ocean: Andrei Bitov and His 'Allusions' to Dostoevsky: The Significance of Dostoevsky for Bitov's Writings," in Edward J. Brown, Lazar Fleishman, Gregory Freidin, and Richard D. Schupbach, eds., *Literature, Culture, and Society in the Modern Age: In Honor of Joseph Frank. Stanford Slavic Studies*, vol. 4, no. 2 (1992), pp. 461–77.

43. See "Raznye dni cheloveka," in Bitov, *My prosnulis' v neznakomoi strane*, pp. 36–37: "I did not have this institution [Pushkin House] in mind, honestly I did not spend time there when I was writing the novel. I understand that there can be various criticisms on my ignorance of the literary critic's life and my distortion of the image of this House. But I can assure you that I have Pushkin House in mind in a symbolic sense." Bitov continues, citing the novel's characterization of all of Russian literature as Pushkin's house and citing Pushkin's last spoken words, "Il faut que j'arrange ma maison." He adds, "I wanted to sketch out this house of Pushkin's without Pushkin. Although without Pushkin we cannot conceive of ourselves, without Pushkin we have nothing."

44. The other epigraph is from Pushkin himself, part of a rejected epigraph to his *Tales of Belkin* (*Povesti Belkina*, 1830): "And this is what will be—that we will not be" ("A vot to budet, chto i nas ne budet"). Bitov, *Pushkinskii dom*, p. 3.

45. The novel's story charts behaviors and attitudes that radically depart from all Pushkinian values. As Natalya Ivanova has argued, Bitov's attitude toward Pushkin always involves an ethical argument. See Natal'ia Ivanova, "Sud'ba i rol': Andrei Bitov," in Ivanova, *Tochka zreniia: O proze poslednikh let* (Moscow: Sovetskii pisatel', 1988), pp. 194–201.

46. Bitov, *Pushkinskii dom*, p. 3.

47. Bitov, *Pushkin House*, unnumbered page. Typically, in subsequent citations of this translation, when I have made some change or am making a specific point about the Russian phrasing, I give the Russian text citation as well. Throughout, I use Bitov's suspension points rather than the ellipses of the English edition.

48. Ibid., p. 11. Compare Bitov, *Pushkinskii dom*, p. 13: "В младенчестве, правда (Лева был зачат в роковом году), случились с ним, вернее, с его родителями кое-какие неприятные перемещения в сторону их замечательного предка, так сказать, «во глубину сибирских руд»."

49. Vladimir Dal', *Tolkovyi slovar' zhivogo velikorusskogo iazyka*. 4 vols. (Moscow: Russkii iazyk, 1978), vol. 2, p. 71.

50. Bitov, *Pushkin House*, p. 12.

51. Bitov, *Pushkinskii dom*, p. 9; the phrase is repeated on p. 131. For a discussion of the metaphor of the museum in Bitov's work, see Sven Spieker, *Figures of Memory and Forgetting in Andrej Bitov's Prose* (Frankfurt am Main: Peter Lang, 1996), pp. 101–15.

52. For Pushkin's poem "Vo glubine sibirskikh rud" in full, see *PSS*, vol. 3, p. 7. For Odoevsky's answer, "Strun veshchikh plamennye zvuki," see ibid., p. 434.

53. Bitov's narrator in *A Teacher of Symmetry* also names Odoevsky as his favorite writer, just before quoting from Odoevsky's works. Bitov, *Chelovek v peizazhe*, p. 311. As is pointed out in Spieker, *Figures of Memory and Forgetting*, pp. 158–59, Odoevsky's fragment "The Year 4388: Petersburg Letters" ("4388-i god: Peter-

burgskie pis'ma") is an important subtext for "Pushkin's Photograph (1799–2099)." For an excellent account of Odoevsky's life, see M. A. Tur'ian, *'Strannaia moia sud'ba...': O zhizni Vladimira Fedorovicha Odoevskogo* (Moscow: Kniga, 1991).

54. One seeming counter to this argument can be found in the novel. It is the incident with Faina and the ring, when Lyova must replace Faina's ring with one he truly believes she will accept as the same as the original. She does not. This plot rhyme is in some ways like the use of quoted speech, but it depends more heavily on a contrast between the real thing and its substitute. The substitute is false, and the urge to substitute is false. We are meant to see it as evidence of Lyova's dishonesty.

55. Susan Stewart, *On Longing: Narratives of the Miniature, the Gigantic, the Souvenir, the Collection* (Durham, N.C.: Duke University Press, 1993), p. 19.

56. Bitov, *Pushkinskii dom*, p. 197.

57. Ibid., p. 86. Compare the false Pushkins encountered by Igor in his time travels in "Pushkin's Photograph (1799–2099)": he meets up first with someone named Apushkin, then with a Nepushkin.

58. Ibid., p. 370. In addition to Bakhtin, Bitov mentions the writer Yuri Dombrovsky and Count Igo Stin, a geologist and writer who suffered arrest and exile, as relevant to his creation of Uncle Dickens. I have not really brought a Bakhtinian view of quotation into this discussion, which would emphasize how the different voices bring polyphony into *Pushkin House*. I believe Bitov cares more about the visual marking of the quotations and the presentation of literal quotations than about the voices they represent. Bakhtin would in fact see the quotation marks as a matter of degree, as Gary Saul Morson and Caryl Emerson point out in *Bakhtin: Creation of a Prosaics* (Stanford, Calif.: Stanford University Press, 1990), pp. 325–26. Ellen Chances has interpreted the usefulness of Bakhtinian theory in reading *Pushkin House* differently by focusing on the relationship between author and hero. See Chances, *Andrei Bitov*, pp. 232–33.

59. Ellen Chances has observed that these titles encode a deeply moral failure: "In the false world of *Pushkin House* shaped by Stalin, cultural monuments are distorted. 'Poor People' become 'Bronze People.'" See Chances, "Keeping the Lies Alive: Case Studies of the Psychology of Stalinism in Contemporary Soviet Literature and Film," *Harriman Institute Forum*, vol. 4, no. 4 (April 1991), pp. 1–8; quoted from p. 7.

60. Bitov, *Pushkinskii dom*, p. 130.

61. Another example of this *mise en abyme* occurs in the description of Lyova's upbringing. For his family, we are told, the external world was also a book, a citation, a style; it was in quotation marks. Ibid., p. 98. Bitov in this sense resembles Vladimir Nabokov. On similarities and differences between the two, see Spieker, *Figures of Memory and Forgetting*, pp. 153–56.

62. Bitov, *Pushkinskii dom*, p. 131.

63. Ibid.

64. Iurii Karabchievskii, "Tochka boli: O romane Andreia Bitova *Pushkinskii dom*," *Grani*, no. 103 (1977), pp. 141–203; see p. 171.

65. Ellen Chances, "The Island and the Ocean," p. 467.

66. Bitov, *Pushkin House*, p. 308.

67. Karabchievskii, "Tochka boli," pp. 196ff, also sees Lyova's offense against Blank as the climax of *Pushkin House*. He argues that this is no duel (no ritualized settling of scores between noblemen), but a brutal fight between enraged, inebriated men.

68. In the novel, the quotation marks around "prophets" were removed.

69. Bitov, *Pushkin House*, p. 241.

70. Ibid., pp. 241–42.

71. Ibid., p. 231.

72. See the discussion of shadow narratives in Gary Saul Morson, *Narrative and Freedom: The Shadows of Time* (New Haven, Conn.: Yale University Press, 1994), pp. 117–72.

73. Bitov, "Predpolozhenie zhit'," p. 221. Bitov used bits of this essay in his short piece "K slovu o Pushkine," *Chelovek i priroda*, no. 6, 1987, pp. 73–76, with some changes. Many of his other writings show this habit of transposition, rewriting, and accretion.

74. Bitov, "K slovu o Pushkine," p. 73. This passage also appears in the longer version of "Predpolozhenie zhit'," in its opening section (p. 211).

75. Bitov, "Predpolozhenie zhit'," p. 212.

76. When Bitov must give details about Pushkin's duel, he makes his reluctance to do so quite clear: "Despite my passionate desire not to sift through these tragic circumstances yet again, for the sake of my argument I will have to emphasize one detail nonetheless …" Ibid., p. 211.

77. Ibid., p. 214.

78. Ibid., p. 215.

79. Ibid., p. 221. Compare the sentiments of Igor in "Pushkin's Photograph (1799–2099)," as he walks through the streets of Petersburg reveling in a sense that Pushkin is, at that moment, still alive.

80. We might note how strongly "The Intention to Live" is at this point linked to the essay "Take Away the Hare," which also focuses on the role of signs (*primety*) in Pushkin's life.

81. Bitov's idea that such finality, when achieved, will always have a fictional source, can also be seen in a provisional epigraph for this part of the essay (later changed): "Gentlemen, let's go: let those be his final words" (Pushkin's comment at the deathbed of his uncle Vasili Lvovich Pushkin). Without someone else to mark the actual closure, Bitov suggests, it remains undefined and imprecise. See Bitov, "Predpolozhenie zhit'," journal version, p. 157.

82. In an interview, Bitov emphasized an idea found in "The Intention to Live"—that Pushkin's last conversation with the son of his friend Prince Viazemsky was most like a final testament. See Bitov, *My prosnulis' v neznakomoi strane*, p. 99.

83. One could make much more of this point about chronology, especially given the reversed sequencing in "Pushkin's Photograph (1799–2099)" and the digressive narrative of *Pushkin House*. Bitov wants to clarify actual sequences of time (thus he wishes there were a completely chronological edition of Pushkin's works; "Predpolozhenie zhit'," p. 217), but he also offers his own willful ordering of Pushkin's writings.

84. Bitov likes this metaphor, although it is a cliché. He uses it to nice verbal ef-

fect in the start of this section: "The poet and the peasant are essentially similar, they even sound the same: they write and reap, toil and suffer, harvest and sacrifice" ("poet i krest'ianin sushchestva po prirode skhodnye, dazhe sozvuchnye: pishut i pashut, strada i stradanie, zhatva i zhertva"). Ibid., p. 248. He adds that one does not know how successful the work of either the farmer or the poet is until harvest time, and both depend on the weather.

85. Ibid., p. 257.

86. In a different interview, Bitov observed that, when reading, a writer takes in fully the process of creation, experiencing a deeper pleasure than other readers do. Bitov, *My prosnulis' v neznakomoi strane*, p. 76.

87. Ibid., p. 89.

88. Bitov, "Predpolozhenie zhit'," p. 273.

89. Most explicitly in *Neizbezhnost' nenapisannogo*, as the title suggests.

90. Bitov, *My prosnulis' v neznakomoi strane*, p. 67. This essay on what Pushkin crossed out also makes a fleeting appearance in *Pushkin House*, mentioned in the final drinking bout.

91. Titled "Behavior as a Text (Period)" ("Povedenie kak tekst [tochka]"), the "period" of the title suggests an insistence on closure, which for Bitov is always ambivalent. As one scholar has noted, every time Bitov republished *Pushkin House*, he added something to the ending. See Rolf Hellebust, "Fiction and Unreality in Bitov's *Pushkin House*," *Style*, vol. 25, no. 2 (Summer 1991), pp. 265–79; see p. 273–74.

92. Bitov, *My prosnulis' v neznakomoi strane*, p. 14.

93. Bitov, "Predpolozhenie zhit'," p. 291.

94. Ibid., p. 290.

95. More frames for "Pushkin's Photograph (1799–2099)" were added in subsequent publications. See the versions in the collection *Chelovek v peizazhe* (1988), where the story appeared as a part of "A Teacher of Symmetry" ("Prepodavatel' simmetrii"); and *Life in Windy Weather* (*Zhizn' v vetrenuiu pogodu*, 1991), where it is a part of "After *Pushkin House*" ("Posle *Pushkinskogo Doma*").

96. Bitov also finds the words of his contemporaries about Pushkin wanting. See his comments in "Predpolozhenie zhit'," p. 226, where the optical and acoustical imagery remind one of "Pushkin's Photograph (1799–2099)."

97. Bitov, "Pushkin's Photograph," pp. 18–19.

98. Bitov, *My prosnulis' v neznakomoi strane*, p. 97.

99. Bitov, "Pushkin's Photograph," p. 20.

100. Ibid., p. 21.

101. Ibid., pp. 17–18.

102. The photographs include the view named in the story's title and Urbino in the future, but the tale also uses photographic images as symbolic details and motivations of the plot, for example in a list of impossible visual images, in a moment when Dika/Helen compares photographs of herself to her actual face, and in the hero's quest for a story of coming disaster that will explain the look on his future face. The story has not yet been translated into English; it appears in Bitov, *Chelovek v peizazhe*, pp. 311–45.

103. For an account of photography in this story as a source of psychosis and as a form of simulacrum, see Spieker, *Figures of Memory and Forgetting*, pp. 141–64.

104. Bitov, "Pushkin's Photograph (1799–2099)," p. 59.
105. Ibid., p. 37.
106. Ibid., p. 39.
107. Ibid., p. 34.
108. Ibid., p. 37.
109. Ibid., p. 33.
110. Ibid., p. 44.
111. Ibid., p. 59.
112. Ibid., p. 44.
113. Ibid., p. 45. The image of a bearded man in a dress comes from Pushkin's *House in Kolomna* (*Domik v Kolomne*, 1830).
114. Bitov, "Pushkin's Photograph (1799–2099)," p. 49.
115. Ibid., p. 21.
116. Bitov, *Pushkin House*, p. 55. The passage continues: "He has just a single flaw—he's gone mad, like Hermann: three, seven ... he keeps running through it." And, later: "For you, understanding is already sympathy. You're accustomed to think so because, in your life, understanding is an accident, or indeed not an accident, but a kind of functional, periodic misquote of the situation—like a physical function, only not so honorable or necessary...." For the Russian version, see *Pushkinskii dom*, p. 57. The ending of "Queen of Spades" is used differently from what one finds in "Pushkin's Photograph (1799–2099)": rather than its tale of madness as pure feeling, this is a presentation of madness as icy rationality.
117. Bitov, *Pushkinskii dom*, p. 7.
118. One could argue that the characters of *Pushkin House* are shown to us as exhibits. At one point, Faina and Mitishatiev look at Lyova as if he is a museum exhibit, with Faina as the museum guide. Ibid., p. 157.
119. Alla Latynina, "Duel' na muzeinykh pistoletakh (Zametki o romane Andreia Bitova *Pushkinskii dom*)," in Latynina, *Za otkrytym shlagbaumom* (Moscow: Sovetskii pisatel', 1991), pp. 260–68.
120. Viktor Erofeev, "Pamiatnik proshedshemu vremeni," *Oktiabr'*, no. 6, 1988, pp. 203–4; quoted from p. 204. Erofeev tries to compensate for this criticism by saying that the failure marks the novel as having been written by a member of the 1960s generation. For a scholarly essay that takes the metaphor of the museum seriously to read its cultural and literal allusions, see Nakhimovsky, "Looking Back at Paradise Lost."
121. As I will suggest, Bitov would disagree with this opposition of Erofeev's. See his 1987 interview: "My House is settled not just by contemporary heroes, but also literary heroes. The latter, by the way, also gave the novel its compositional form: a museum-novel." Bitov, *My prosnulis' v neznakomoi strane*, p. 36.
122. Bitov, *Vychitanie zaitsa*, p. 19.
123. Bitov, *Pushkin House*, p. 96.
124. See, for example, Svetlana Boym, *Common Places: Mythologies of Everyday Life in Russia* (Cambridge, Mass.: Harvard University Press, 1994), pp. 73–88, 92–95.
125. Home turns out to be at once restorative and threatened. We find this out in the first narrative sequences of *Pushkin House*, where Uncle Dickens (not literally the hero's uncle) returns home and claims most of the family's possessions. Home

turns out not to have been home at all, and Uncle Dickens further disrupts the security of family relations when Lyova starts to fantasize that Uncle Dickens is his father. No sooner does he come to terms with the truth than another family member returns, his father's father, Lyova's grandfather.

126. Bitov comments, in *My prosnulis' v neznakomoi strane*, p. 33: "Everything that I write, it seems to me, is a single house [and] I know all too well which rooms aren't finished, where and on which floor I need more bricks." Referring to the unfinished quality of Bitov's work, Ronald Meyer has compared him to an architect who keeps building the same house. Meyer, "Andrei Bitov's Memoir of Pushkin," p. 379.

127. Bitov, "Pushkin's Photograph (1799–2099)," p. 56.

128. In "View of the Sky at Troy," we get a nice parody of this preference for heights when we learn that the invented author, Urbino Vanoski, is an elevator operator. See Bitov, *Chelovek v peizazhe*, p. 312.

129. Bitov, *Pushkinskii dom*, pp. 66–67; *Pushkin House*, p. 65. See also "Dve zametki perioda zastoia" on dictionary entries for outmoded but much-needed ethical expressions, in Bitov, *My prosnulis' v neznakomoi strane*, pp. 23–24.

130. Bitov trusts metaphors of depth and height more fully in the psychology of his characters, and journeys down into the mind are always valued. Bitov's plots frequently rely on dreams that reveal unconscious wishes and drinking bouts that permit the articulation of unspeakable desires. He recognizes the mind's capacities for denial, repression, internal reversals, and the like. To study this aspect of his work is beyond the scope of this chapter, but I bring it up because scholarship about Bitov has looked less at psychology than at semiotics, intertextuality, and philosophy. Exceptions include Kurt Shaw, "Chasing the Red Balloon: Psychological Separation in the Early Fiction of Andrei Bitov," Ph.D. dissertation, University of Kansas, 1988; Ivanova, *Tochka zreniia*, pp. 182–83; and Chances, *Andrei Bitov: The Ecology of Inspiration*. Compare M. Lipovetskii, "Razgrom muzeia: Poetika romana A. Bitova 'Pushkinskii dom,'" *Novoe literaturnoe obozrenie*, no. 11, 1995, pp. 230–44. Lipovetsky says the scholarship has been too psychological, and offers a more philosophical and literary theory–driven account of the novel, fascinating on its own terms.

131. Bitov, "Predpolozhenie zhit'," p. 210. He sees this relationship as including worship ("poklonnichestvo").

132. Bitov, *Pushkin House*, p. 241.

133. Bitov, "Predpolozhenie zhit'," p. 211.

AFTERWORD

Parts of the Afterword were published in "Sex, Death and Nation in the *Strolls with Pushkin* Controversy," *Slavic Review*, vol. 51, no. 2 (Summer 1992), pp. 294–308.

EPIGRAPH: Joseph Brodsky, "A Child of Civilization," in Brodsky, *Less Than One: Selected Essays* (New York: Farrar, Straus & Giroux, 1986), p. 123.

1. Abram Terts / A. D. Siniavskii, *Sobranie sochinenii*, 2 vols. (Moscow: SP "Start," 1992); *Pushkin: pro et contra*, 2 vols. (St. Petersburg: Izdatel'stvo Russkogo Khristianskogo gumanitarnogo instituta, 2000), vol. 2, pp. 491–504, 628–30. Pro-

gulki s Pushkinym is also reprinted in Abram Terts (Andrei Siniavskii), *Puteshestvie na Chernuiu rechku* (Moscow: Zakharov, 1999), pp. 6–120; this posthumous collection emphasizes the polemical side of Terts's legacy and describes him in its jacket blurb as "an adventurer, a criminal, a rule-breaker, and an escapee—that is, a writer."

2. For a brief, compelling description of Sinyavsky's prominence in Soviet culture in 1965 just before he was arrested, see Sergei Bocharov, "Chistoe iskusstvo i sovetskaia istoriia: v pamiat' Andreia Donatovicha Siniavskogo," in *Siuzhety russkoi literatury* (Moscow: Iazyki russkoi kul'tury, 1999), pp. 551–56, esp. p. 551.

3. See Catharine Theimer Nepomnyashchy, "Andrei Sinyavsky's 'Return' to the Soviet Union," *Formations*, vol. 6, no. 1 (Spring 1991), pp. 24–44; and Jane Grayson, "Back to the Future: Andrei Siniavskii and *Kapitanskaia dochka*," in Arnold McMillin, ed., *Reconstructing the Canon: Russian Writing in the 1980s* (Amsterdam: Harwood Academic Publishers, 2000), pp. 147–72, esp. pp. 147–52, for good discussions of the controversy. On Sinyavsky more generally, see Catharine Theimer Nepomnyashchy, *Abram Tertz and the Poetics of Crime* (New Haven, Conn.: Yale University Press, 1995).

4. Bocharov, "Chistoe iskusstvo i sovetskaia istoriia," p. 554.

5. The attacks on Sinyavsky and some letters written in his defense can be read conveniently in *Tsena metafory, ili prestuplenie i nakazanie Siniavskogo i Danielia* (Moscow: Kniga, 1989), pp. 16–56.

6. Roman Gul characterizes Abram Tertz generally as an infectious disease, as less talented than Dmitry Pisarev, from whom he says Tertz took his title (compare Pisarev's 1865 "Progulka po sadam rossiiskoi slovesnosti"). Gul fails to mention other pertinent antecedents, like Rousseau's "Rêveries d'un promeneur solitair," Batiushkov's two "Progulki," and the peripatetic teachings of Socrates. Solzhenitsyn writes with sarcasm and wit, but his criticisms seem disproportionate, particularly when he tediously disproves Sinyavsky's claim about emptiness by arguing that Pushkin's writings were rich in philosophical content. Roman Gul', "Progulki khama s Pushkinym," *Novyi zhurnal*, vol. 124 (1976), pp. 117–29; Aleksandr Solzhenitsyn, "... Koleblet tvoi trenozhnik," *Vestnik Russkogo Khristianskogo dvizheniia*, vol. 142 (1984), pp. 133–52. Roman Gul's essay was partly reprinted by the right-wing *Literaturnaia Rossiia*, June 30, 1989 (no. 26), pp. 18–19, a good example of how the earlier controversy was recycled the second time around.

7. Abram Terts, "Progulki s Pushkinym. Fragment," *Oktiabr'*, no. 4, 1989, pp. 192–99. *Voprosy literatury* subsequently published *Strolls with Pushkin* in full in the seventh, eighth, and ninth "1990" issues of the journal that appeared late in 1991, followed by a discussion forum that well represents the responses within Russia, including several defenders of Sinyavsky. For the forum, see "Obsuzhdenie knigi Abrama Tertsa *Progulki s Pushkinym*," *Voprosy literatury*, no. 10, 1990, pp. 77–153.

8. For a good discussion of the Sinyavsky controversy in the context of Russian nationalism, see Wendy Slater, "The Patriots' Pushkin," *Slavic Review*, vol. 58, no. 2 (Summer 1999), pp. 407–27. Sinyavsky himself called attention to the similarity between these two stages in branding him an "enemy of the people"—first anti-Soviet, then anti-Russian. See Andrei Siniavskii, "Dissidentstvo kak lichnyi opyt," *Sintak-*

sis, no. 15, 1986, pp. 131–47, esp. pp. 146–47; the essay is reprinted in Siniavskii, *Puteshestvie na Chernuiu rechku*, pp. 398–416. It first appeared in English as "Dissent as a Personal Experience" (tr. Maria-Regina Kecht), *Yearbook of Comparative and General Literature*, no. 31 (1982), pp. 21–29.

9. The charge of collaboration or switching sides continued to haunt Sinyavsky till his death. See, for example, the pointed question about whether he served his full prison sentence in an interview conducted by Feliks Medvedev, "Besedy s Andreem Siniavskim i Mariei Rozanovoi o Pushkine, i ne tol'ko o nem," *Knizhnoe obozrenie*, Jan. 26, 1990 (no. 4), pp. 8–9; see p. 8.

10. Dmitrii Urnov, contribution to "Obsuzhdenie knigi Abrama Tertsa *Progulki s Pushkinym*," p. 142.

11. Some of Sinyavsky's other writings also elicited considerable hostility. For a furious review of his Gogol book, see R. Pletnev, "O zlom suemudrii knigi Abrama Tertsa," *Novyi zhurnal*, no. 121 (1975), pp. 72–80.

12. Igor' Shafarevich, "Rusofobiia," *Nash sovremennik*, no. 6, 1989, pp. 167–92; the reference to Sinyavsky is on p. 185.

13. See Andrei Siniavskii, "Russkii natsionalizm," *Sintaksis*, no. 26, 1989, pp. 91–110; translated by Dale E. Peterson as "Russian Nationalism," *Massachusetts Review*, vol. 31, no. 4 (Winter 1990), pp. 475–94. For the best-known instance of Solzhenitsyn's statements against the liberal tolerance Sinyavsky represents, see his "Nashi pliuralisty," *Vestnik Russkogo Khristianskogo dvizheniia*, no. 139 (1983), pp. 133–60; translated into English as "Our Pluralists," *Journal of East and West Studies*, vol. 29, no. 2 (Summer 1985), pp. 1–28. In "Nashi pliuralisty," Solzhenitsyn repeats Gul's insinuation that Sinyavsky obtained an early release from the labor camps (p. 150, Russian text).

14. Abram Tertz (Andrei Sinyavsky), *Strolls with Pushkin*, tr. Catharine Theimer Nepomnyashchy and Slava I. Yastremski (New Haven, Conn.: Yale University Press, 1993), p. 49.

15. Ibid.

16. Ibid., pp. 50, 51.

17. Ibid., p. 54. My ellipsis.

18. Ibid., p. 50.

19. Bocharov, "Chistoe iskusstvo i sovetskaia istoriia," p. 554.

20. For the essay on Pasternak, see A. D. Siniavskii, "Poeziia Pasternaka," in Boris Pasternak, *Stikhotvoreniia i poemy* (Moscow-Leningrad: Sovetskii pisatel', 1965), pp. 9–62; translated as Sinavsky, "Boris Pasternak," in Donald Davie and Angela Livingstone, eds., *Pasternak* (London: Macmillan, 1969), pp. 154–219. A different English version, which contains some material Sinyavsky added that does not appear in the Russian original, is "Pasternak's Poetry," tr. Elizabeth Henderson, in Victor Erlich, ed., *Pasternak: A Collection of Critical Essays* (Englewood Cliffs, N.J.: Prentice-Hall, 1978), pp. 68–109.

21. As noted by Aleksandr Zholkovskii, "Vospominaia Siniavskogo," *Sintaksis*, no. 36, 1995, p. 25. In that same issue of *Sintaksis*, published in Sinyavsky's memory, Mikhail Epshtein argues for the proto-deconstructionist elements in *Strolls with Pushkin*. Epshtein, "Siniavskii kak myslitel'," pp. 87ff. See also Viacheslav Kurytsyn, *Russkii literaturnyi postmodernizm* (Moscow: OGI, 2001), pp. 178–79; and

Aleskandr Genis, "Andrei Siniavskii: estetika arkhaichnogo postmodernizma," *Novoe literaturnoe obozrenie*, no. 7, 1994, pp. 277–84.

22. For a short and very intelligent piece that discusses the "new épatage" of contemporary Russian writing, see (no author), "Dialog chitatelia s kul'turoi: russkaia literatura v tekstakh Igoria Iarkevicha," netmarginal.narod.ru/yarkevitch.htm. Igor Yarkevich is the principal example here, but he is placed in the context of Victor Pelevin, Venedikt Erofeev, Sergei Dovlatov, and others, and Sinyavsky is given as an important antecedent to their rebellions against literary and other conventions.

23. I treat this subject in "Sex, Death and Nation in the *Strolls with Pushkin* Controversy," *Slavic Review*, vol. 51, no. 2 (Summer 1992), pp. 294–308.

24. An early proponent of this view was Vasily Zhukovsky, in the letter to Pushkin's father discussed in Chap. 1.

25. Tertz, *Strolls with Pushkin*, p. 55.

26. Ibid., p. 55; compare Abram Terts, *Progulki s Pushkinym* (London: Overseas Publication Interchange, 1975), p. 17.

27. Abram Terts, "Puteshestvie na Chernuiu rechku," in Terts/Siniavskii, *Puteshestvie na Chernuiu rechku*, pp. 437–38.

28. Ibid., p. 441.

29. He praises Tsvetaeva's essay, quoting her description of Pugachev as a wolf (in order to motivate his own comparison of him to a werewolf, repeating a word he had used in *Strolls* to the great ire of his critics). Ibid., p. 458.

30. Sinyavsky calls his wife "Masha" in the text at one point (ibid., p. 461), a pointed departure from his and other close friends' practice of calling her by a different diminutive, Maia.

31. Ibid., pp. 442–43.

32. A worthy successor to this tradition is the contemporary writer Olga Shamborant. See her *Priznaki zhizni* (St. Petersburg: Pushkinskii fond, 1998).

33. Sinyavsky, *Strolls with Pushkin*, p. 140.

34. Urnov called this the "scandalous posing of a serious question" in "Obsuzhdenie knigi Abrama Tertsa," p. 139. Sinyavsky similarly observes theatrical aspects of a tragic situation in his essay about Stalin: "Stalin—geroi i khudozhnik stalinskoi epokhi," *Sintaksis*, no. 19, 1987, pp. 106–25.

35. For a cogent reading of the religious dimensions in the rhetoric of Pushkin's martyrdom, and of the Pushkin myth more generally, see Paul Debreczeny, *Social Functions of Literature: Alexander Pushkin and Russian Culture* (Stanford, Calif.: Stanford University Press, 1997), pp. 223–46.

36. Leonid Batkin, "Siniavskii, Pushkin—i my," *Oktiabr'*, no. 1, 1991, p. 177. The quotation from *Strolls with Pushkin* is from p. 84 (original p. 67).

37. *Strolls with Pushkin*, p. 83. For the original of this metaphorically charged passage, see Siniavskii, *Progulki s Pushkinym*, p. 66. Critics who do not fall into the trap of reading these images literally risk taming the images excessively. One sympathetic critic claims that "'Emptiness' or 'vampirism'—these are just metaphors for conveying paradoxically, provocatively, exaggeratedly, the thought that Pushkin was unusually able to place all the fullness of existence into himself, into his lines of verse." Vozdvizhenskii, "Progulki s Shafarevichem i bez … ," p. 169. The metaphor has been rendered innocuous, the vampire has lost its bite.

38. I am adding a bit to the intriguing argument found in Paul Barber, *Vampires, Burial, and Death: Folklore and Reality* (New Haven, Conn.: Yale University Press, 1988).

39. See Jan L. Perkowski, *The Darkling: A Treatise on Slavic Vampirism* (Columbus, Ohio: Slavica, 1989), esp. pp. 18–36. Perkowski traces the origins of the vampire myth to specifically Slavic cultures (note the Russian words *vampir, upyr'*). Pushkin contributes to the vampire vocabulary in his poem no. 13, "Vurdalak," in "Songs of the Western Slavs" ("Pesni zapadnykh slavian"), *PSS*, vol. 3, pp. 282–83. For a Russian vampire folktale, see "Upyr'," in *Biblioteka russkogo fol'klora: Skazki* (Moscow: Sovetskaia Rossiia, 1989), vol. 2, pp. 421–24.

40. See, for example, Solzhenitsyn, "... Koleblet tvoi trenozhnik," p. 137, for a figurative and indirect (and thus more interesting) example of this attack. Valentin Nepomniashchy simply asserts that it is not Pushkin who is the vampire, but Sinyavsky. "Obsuzhdenie knigi Abrama Tertsa," p. 150.

41. For a thorough account of the essay as a response to critics, see Grayson, "Back to the Future," pp. 155–67.

42. Terts, *Puteshestvie na Chernuiu Rechku*, p. 444.

43. A persuasive study of the ways in which visual imagery and word pictures complement verbal artistry in Sinyavsky's writings is Jane Grayson, "Picture Windows and the Art of Andrei Siniavskii," in Catriona Kelly and Stephen Lovell, eds., *Russian Literature, Modernism, and the Visual Arts* (Cambridge, Eng.: Cambridge University Press, 2000), pp. 88–118.

44. Ibid., p. 89.

Index

Abdulov, Alexander, 142
Abraham, Nicolas, 275
Abramovich, S. L., 106
Acmeism, 200
Akhmadulina, Bella, 123
Akhmatova, Anna, 15, 16, 39, 90, 95, 99, 100, 119, 175–213, 307–8; anniversary poems by, 194–96; "Benjamin Constant's 'Adolphe'" (1936), 200–202; commentary on *The Tale of the Golden Cockerel* (1939), 200–201; and death, 182, 191–94; "The First Return" (1910), 181–83; and Gumilev, 205–9; "Incantation" (1936), 206–7; interest in Pushkin of, 176–77; "In Tsarskoe Selo" (1911), 183–88; love lyrics of, 205; and morality, 178, 209; and mourning, 179; "New Year's Ballad" (1923), 191–94; Pushkin essays of, 198–213; Pushkin poems of, 179–98; "Pushkin's Death" (1958), 210–13; "Pushkin's *Stone Guest*" (1947), 202–10; scholarship of, 177–78; "Some see themselves in affectionate gazes" (1936), 195–98; and Tsarskoe Selo, 181–97, 204; "Tsarskoe Selo Statue" (1916), 188–91; Tsvetaeva and, 233–34
Akhmatova, Raisa, 80
Alexander II, 35
"Alexandrina" (Akhmatova, 1962), 199, 212, 213
Alhambra (Irving, 1832), 200
Allegory, 60–62, 79
All-Union Pushkin Museum, 55
Almanacs, poetry, 7, 8, 10, 11
Almi, I. L., 185, 191
"Along roads ringing with frost" (Tsvetaeva, 1916), 238
Amelin, Maxim, 123
Anderson, Benedict, 88
Anemone, Anthony, 117
"Animal Tamer, The" (Gumilev, 1912), 206

Anisimov, Grigory, 120
Annensky, Innokenty, 183
Anniversary celebrations, *see* Celebrations, of Pushkin
"Anniversary Poem, The" (Mayakovsky, 1924), 100–104, 304
Anniversary poems, by Akhmatova, 194–96
Apuleius, 189
Arapova, Alexandra, 212
Arkhipova, Anastasia, 129
"Attempt at Jealousy, An" (Tsvetaeva, 1924), 234
"Attic Writings" (Tsvetaeva, 1920), 243
Autumn Has Arrived (film), 160
Avvakumov, Yuri, 132–33

Bakhtin, Mikhail, 102, 150, 279–80
Balaian, Roman, 141, 143, 144, 167
Ballad form, 193
Banner, The (*Znamia*, journal), 122, 290
Baratynsky, Evgeny, 7, 17
Batkin, Leonid, 308
Belinkov, Arkady, 179
Belinsky, Vissarion, 92, 97
Benckendorff, Aleksei, 32, 36
"Benjamin Constant's 'Adolphe'" (Akhmatova, 1936), 200–202
Berdiaev, Nikolai, 6
Bernhardt, Sarah, 239
Bicentennial celebration, *see* Celebrations, of Pushkin: of 1999
Bisexuality, 224, 238
Bitov, Andrei, 7, 15, 16, 75, 83–84, 119, 122, 131, 160–61, 266–99, 305; compared to Sinyavsky, 301–2; "The Intention to Live" (1980–84), 131, 269–72, 283–89; Pushkin essays of, 267–75; *Pushkin House* (1978), 275–83, 289, 294–99; "Pushkin's Photograph (1799–2099)" (1987), 289–90; "Take Away the Hare: Three Variants" (1982, 1986), 272–75; "Three 'Prophets'" (1976), 267–69

Blanchot, Maurice, 34
Blium, Arlen, 107, 111
Blok, Alexander, 10, 14, 90, 91, 95–97, 194, 222, 245, 276, 288–89
Bloom, Harold, 231
"Bobok" (Dostoevsky, 1873), 192–93, 209
Bocharov, Sergei, 302, 304
Body, *see* Embodiment
Bokov, Viktor, 80
Boldino, 13, 48, 62–71; Bitov on, 285–86; historical interpretation at, 64–65, 70–71, 73; in *Keep Me Safe, My Talisman*, 138; pastoral aspects of, 62–64, 73; poems about, 80–81; Pushkin on, 66–70
"Boldino Autumn" (Akhmatova, 1970), 199
"Boldino Autumn" (Sokolov), 80
Bondarchuk, Sergei, 167
Boris Godunov (film), 137, 167
Boym, Svetlana, 136
Brandenberger, David, 107
Brezhnev, Leonid, 127
Brik, Lilia, 101
Briusov, Valery, 232, 233, 234–35
Brodsky, Joseph, 4, 6, 12, 36, 123, 195, 252, 288, 301, 306
Bronze Pushkin, The: Seven Jubilees or the Holy Week (film), 120
Brooks, Peter, 141, 142
Brownsberger, Susan, 276, 277
Bulgakov, Mikhail, 14, 112–16, 132, 143, 146
Byron, George Gordon, Lord, 202, 307

Carson, Anne, 219
Catherine II, Empress, 16, 23, 225–26
Celebrations, of Pushkin, 13–14, 85–136; of 1880, 87–89; of 1899, 49, 88; of 1921, 89–97; of 1923, 87; of 1924, 53, 97–107; of 1926, 87; of 1937, 9, 38, 53, 107–16, 127; of 1949, 53, 116; of 1987, 118–19; of 1999, 5, 119–35, 310; art exhibitions and, 132–35; false versus authentic, 87, 88; media and, 120–23; publications and, 90, 123–25, 341n12; "Pushkin's Photograph (1799-2099)" and, 289–90
"Cellar of Memory, The" (Akhmatova, 1940), 182
Centennial celebration, *see* Celebrations, of Pushkin: of 1899

Chaadaev, Pyotr, 151, 286
Chances, Ellen, 280
Chechnya, 129
Chénier, André, 30, 283, 320n5
Chernov, Andrei, 123
Chernyshevsky, Nikolai, 93
Chistova, Irina, 131
Christianity, 5, 23–24, 210, 323n32
Chukovskaya, Lydia, 176, 233
Ciepiela, Catherine, 232, 253
Citizens of the Night (*Grazhdane nochi*, poetry almanac), 11
Class, 107
Constructivism, 134
Contemporary, The (*Sovremennik*, journal), 43, 76, 106
Cover, Robert, 31
Creative process, 156–60, 165, 167, 170–72, 174, 287–88, 305
Cultural Mythologies of Russian Modernism (Gasparov, Hughes, and Paperno, 1992), 7

Dangerous Liaisons (film), 128
"Dante" (Akhmatova, 1936), 197
Dante Alighieri, 198
d'Anthès, Georges, 36, 103, 112, 115, 139–40, 146–47, 211–12
Danzas, Konstantin, 147
Days (*Dni*, newspaper), 239
"Death of the Poet, The" (Lermontov, 1837), 26–32, 115, 144, 146, 283, 307
Debreczeny, Paul, 12
Decembrists, 23, 123, 160, 175, 199, 269, 275, 276, 278
Defamiliarization, 137, 160, 164, 166
Delvig, Baron Anton, 17, 194
Demons (Dostoevsky, 1872), 274
Derzhavin, Gavriel, 23, 24–25, 117, 181
Desbordes-Valmore, Marceline, 239
Dinega, Alyssa, 242–43
Dmitriev, Andrei, 123
Dmitriev, Ivan, 35
Dolgorukov, Pyotr, 210
"Door, The" (Bitov, 1962), 267
Dostoevsky, Fyodor, 6, 7, 20, 88–89, 96, 192–93, 209, 210, 274, 280, 306
Dovlatov, Sergei, 84
"Dream About Pushkin, A" (Tsvetaeva, 1931), 263–64
Druzhnikov, Yuri, 120
Duels, 141–44, 147–48

"During the Pushkin Days" (Zoshchenko, 1937), 110–11

Efron, Sergei, 243
Eidelman, Natan, 131, 132
Eikhenbaum, Boris, 90, 91–93, 97
Eisenstein, Sergei, 167
Elegies, for Pushkin: by Lermontov, 26–31; by Rostopchina, 38–46; by Zhukovsky, 31–38
Embodiment: in elegies of Pushkin, 31, 38; in *Little Tragedies*, 173; martyrdom and, 147; in "Poems to Pushkin," 254–55; in "The Prophet," 21; and Pushkin's death, 9; in *Side Whiskers*, 150–51
Empson, William, 64
"Enchantment in Briusov's Poetry" (Tsvetaeva, 1910), 232
Enclosed in Winter (Akhmadulina, 1999), 123
"Encounter with Pushkin, An" (Tsvetaeva, 1913), 227–35, 238, 244
Encyclopedia, Pushkin, 131
Erlich, Victor, 7
Erofeev, Viktor, 295
Esenin, Sergei, 100
Estrangement, *see* Defamiliarization
Eugene Onegin, Nabokov's commentary on, 132
Eugene Onegin (film), 120
Eugene Onegin (opera), 120
Eugene Onegin (Prigov, 1992), 123
Evening (Akhmatova, 1912), 233
Evening of Poetesses (1919), 232
Ex libris (literary supplement), 121, 132

Falconet, Étienne-Maurice, 225, 226
Favorsky, Alexander, 125
Fiennes, Martha, 120
Figaret, Alexander, 80
Film Art (*Iskusstvo kino*, journal), 120, 123
Films: and 1999 celebrations, 125–29; encyclopedia of, 131; Pushkin, 136–74 (*see also individual films*); and representation of Pushkin, 137, 139, 144, 147–48, 153
"First Return, The" (Akhmatova, 1910), 181–83, 187
"Five-footed Iambs" (Gumilev, 1913), 206
Fomichev, Sergei, 139
Formalism, 91, 93, 136

"Fourth Year, The" (Tsvetaeva, 1916), 238
Freidin, Gregory, 12
Freud, Sigmund, 37, 195, 221
Futurists, 92, 93, 97–98, 100, 304

Gabriadze, Rezo, 160–61, *161*
Galberg, S. I., 78
Gan, Elena, 44
Ganichev, Valery, 134
Gannibal, Abram, 48, 161
Geichenko, S. S., 60, 76, 84, 122
Geitman, E. I., 217–19
Gershenzon, Mikhail, 93
Gillis, John R., 47
Ginkas, Kama, 132, 135
Ginzburg, Lydia, 1, 4, 112
"Girlfriend, The" (Tsvetaeva, 1916), 237
Glasnost, 119, 131
Goethe, Johann Wolfgang von, 119–20
Gogol, Nikolai, 20, 89, 120
Golden Calf, The (film), 167
Golovachevsky, S., 104
Goncharova, Natalia Nikolaevna, *see* Pushkina, Natalia Nikolaevna
Goncharova, Natalia Sergeevna (artist), 245–51, 255
Goodnight! (Sinyavsky, 1984), 308
Gordin, Iakov, 144
Gorky, Maxim, 109
Gorodetsky, Sergei, 100
Grant's Tomb, New York, 330n34
Grayson, Jane, 310
Greenblatt, Stephen, 61
Greenleaf, Monika, 170
"Grey-Eyed King, The" (Akhmatova, 1910), 193
Grigoriev, Apollon, 10–12, 120, 153
Gromov, Pavel, 108, 126, 127–28
Grot, Yakov, 45
Groys, Boris, 79
Guelman, Marat (gallery), 132
Gul, Roman, 302–3
Gumilev, Lev, 198, 203
Gumilev, Nikolai, 90, 95, 177, 179, 182, 191, 194, 205–9

"Happiness or sadness" (Tsvetaeva, 1916), 235–39, 244
Hartman, Geoffrey H., 175
"Has he sent no swan for me" (Akhmatova, 1936), 193

Heeckeren, Baron Louis Borchard, 147, 210–12, 270, 271, 289
"Heiress, The" (Akhmatova, 1959), 204
Heldt, Barbara, 43
"He left his carriage at the gate" (Khodasevich, 1924), 104–7
"Holy nights float and melt" (Gumilev, 1914), 205
Homosexuality, 211
Horace, 21, 23, 24–25
"How Women Are Supposed to Write" (Rostopchina, 1840), 44
Hughes, Robert P., 90, 96

Iampolski, Mikhail, 118
Iankovsky, Oleg, 142
Ibragimbekov, Rustam, 142, 143
"Incantation" (Akhmatova, 1936), 197, 206–7
"Incidents" (Kharms, 1939), 117–18
Independent Gazette, The (*Nezavisimaia gazeta*, newspaper), 121
In Gogol's Shade (Sinyavsky, 1981), 309
Institute for the Study of Books, 90
Institute of Russian Literature (Pushkin House), 51, 55, 131, 177, 275–76, 295–96
"Intention to Live, The" (Bitov, 1980–84), 131, 269–72, 283–89
Internet, art on, 132, 134
"In Tsarskoe Selo" (Akhmatova, 1911), 100, 183–88, 195, 233–34
Irving, Washington, 200–201
Ishimova, Alexandra, 285
Iskander, Fazil, 119
Istomina, Evdokia, 159
Iursky, Sergei, 156, 170, 171, 174
Ivanov, Viacheslav, 100
Ivanova, Natalia, 120, 122, 147
Ivory, James, 136

Jacobs, Carol, 85
Jakobson, Roman, 6
"Journey to Chernaia Rechka" (Sinyavsky, 1994), 305–6, 309
Juan, Don, 203–9, 308
Jubilees, Pushkin, *see* Celebrations, of Pushkin

Kapnist, Vasily, 24
Karabchievsky, Yuri, 100, 101, 280
Karadzhova, Elena, 145

Karamzin, Nikolai, 45
Karamzina, Sophia, 45
Karlinsky, Simon, 224
Keep Me Safe, My Talisman (film), 63, 138–44, 149–50, 165
Kelly, Catriona, 43
Kharms, Daniil, 14, 90, 117–18
Khlebnikov, Velimir, 4, 90, 181
Khodasevich, Vladislav, 14, 43, 90, 91, 93–96, 104–7, 119, 306
Khomutiansky, Yuri, 145
Khrushchev, Nikita, 127
Khrzhanovsky, Andrei, 69, 125, 127, 138, 156, 158, 160, 164–167
Kibirov, Timur, 7, 123
Kinotavr film festival, 121
Kiprensky, O. A., 152, 168, 294
Kistenyovo, 64
Klimov, Elem, 143
Kliuev, Nikolai, 100
Kobeliansky, L. L., 231–32
Koliagin, Alexander, 145
Koni, Anatoly, 90–91, 95
Korkina, Elena, 263
Kozakov, Mikhail, 139, 141
Kozlov, A. A., 79
Kozmin, Boris, 74
Krakovsky, Vladimir, 130
Kraval, Liubov, 140
Kristeva, Julia, 205
Küchelbecker, Wilhelm, 26
Kultura (television station), 120
Kupchenko, Irina, 145
Kushner, Alexander, 122, 123
Kuzmin, Mikhail, 90, 95, 100, 119, 233

Lacan, Jacques, 235
Lachman, Renate, 23
Lanskoi, Pavel, 237, 238
Larionov, Mikhail, 250
Last Days, The (Bulgakov, 1934–35), 112–16, 146
Last Road, The (film), 113, 137, 139, 144–50, 154, 155, 165, 212
"(Lathe, The)" (Tsvetaeva, 1931), 258–62
Latin Quarter (*Latinskii kvartal*, poetry almanac), 7, 8
Latynina, Alla, 295
Lay of Igor's Campaign, The (medieval epic), 271
Lef (journal), 103

Legends and Myths About Pushkin (Virolainen, 1995), 7
"Leg, The" (Bitov, 1962), 267
Lenin, V. I., 98, 108, 109, 127
Leningrad, *see* St. Petersburg
Lermontov, Mikhail, 8–9, 13, 115, 121, 144, 146, 177, 267, 282, 283, 307; elegy for Pushkin of, 26–32
Let's Fly Away! (film), 125–27
Levitt, Marcus, 12, 88
Lifar, Serge, 119
Life and Death of Pushkin, The (film), 136
"Life in Windy Weather" (Bitov, 1963), 286, 287
Likhachev, Dmitri, 119, 122
Literary Gazette, The (*Literaturnaia gazeta*, newspaper), 109, 111, 122
"Little leaves again have droplets, The" (Pilnik), 81
Little Tragedies (film), 127, 137–38, 154, 167–74
Lomonosov, Mikhail, 24, 181
"Lonely Histrion, The" (Khlebnikov, 1921), 181
Lotman, Yuri, 7, 121, 132, 136
Luknitsky, Pavel, 119
Lunacharsky, Anatoly, 53, 97, 98

"Madness" (Tiutchev, 1830), 267, 282
Maikov, A. N., 104
Makovetsky, Sergei, 128
Malmstad, John, 93
Mamin, Yuri, 150, 154–55, 167
Mandelstam, Osip, 4, 10, 12, 90, 115, 197, 198, 306
"Man in the Landscape, A" (Bitov), 286
Marx, Karl, 108
Mashkov, Vladimir, 128
Master and Margarita (Bulgakov, 1928–40), 115, 143
Mayakovsky, Vladimir, 10, 14, 96, 100–104, 109, 134, 251, 304
Media, and Pushkin celebrations, 120–23
Melikhov, Lev, *133*, 134–35
Melodrama, 141–42
Memory, *see* Remembrance
Menaker, Leonid, 137, 144, 167
Merchant, Ismail, 136
Mickiewicz, Adam, 273
Mikhailovskoe, 13, 60; as allegory, 60–62; and death, 55; in Dovlatov's *The Preserve*, 84; early history to preserve, 48–53; historical interpretation at, 59–60, 73–74; 1937 celebration at, 109; 1924 celebration at, 98–99; pastoral aspects of, 71–75; as preserve, 51–55, 58, 61–62, 72, 98, 99–100; Pushkin on, 56–60
Modernism, 304–5
Modzalevsky, Boris, 90, 132
Moika 12 (museum), 32, 33, 48, 55, 74, 77, 80, 108, 118, 297; theatricality in museum presentation at, 76–79
Monuments, to Pushkin, 7, 8, 9–10, 47, 88, 126, *133*, 134–35. *See also* Shrines, Pushkin
Moscow, 100, 108, 109, 119, 121
Museums, 47–84; Bitov's approach to Pushkin and, 267, 295–99; death memorabilia in, 9. *See also* Shrines, Pushkin
My Favorite Time (film), 69, 138, 156–67
My Pushkin (Briusov, 1929), 233
"My Pushkin" (Tsvetaeva, 1937), 215, 216–27, 233
Myths: and poets' lives, 2; types of, 5–6. *See also* Pushkin, Alexander: mythologizing of

Nabokov, Vladimir, 132, 306
Na-Na (pop group), 121
Napoleon, 239
"Natalia Goncharova" (Tsvetaeva, 1929), 226, 245–51, 252, 258
Nationalism, 6, 49, 150. *See also* Pushkin, Alexander: as national symbol
Nature: at Mikhailovskoe, 50–51, 54–55; and the pastoral, 62–64; Pushkin on Mikhailovskoe, 56–60
Naumov, Aleksei, 216–17
Nedobrovo, Nikolai V., 191, 194, 195
Nepomnyashchy, Valentin, 23, 120
Nesselrode, Countess Maria, 210
Neva (journal), 120
New Literary Review (*Novoe literaturnoe obozrenie*, journal), *133*
"New Year's Ballad" (Akhmatova, 1923), 191–94, 196
"New Year's Greeting" (Tsvetaeva, 1927), 251–52
New York Times (newspaper), 116
Nicholas I, 9, 146, 163, 201, 210, 255–58
Nicholas II, 256, 258
Nichols, Bill, 137

Nizhny Novgorod, 64
Noialle, Anna de, 239
Nora, Pierre, 88
Norshtein, Yuri, 156, 160
"Northern Elegies" (Akhmatova, 1940–43), 209
Nostalgia, 136. *See also* Remembrance
"Notes from the Corner" (Bitov, 1963), 287
Nouvelle Espérance, La (Noialle), 239
NTV (television station), 121

O'Bell, Leslie, 170, 208, 210
October (*Oktiabr'*, journal), 130
Odoevsky, Alexander, 278
Odoevsky, Vladimir, 278
Okudzhava, Bulat, 134, 139–40, 141, 144
One Fate for Us All (Krakovsky, 1999), 130–31
"On the Death of Goethe" (Baratynsky, 1832), 17
ORT (television station), 121
Osipova, Maria, 283

Panfilov, Gleb, 123
Paperno, Irina, 94
Parnok, Sofia, 237
Parny, Evariste, 186–87
Pasternak, Boris, 197, 198, 242, 264, 304
Pastoral, 62–64, 71–75
Pelevin, Victor, 121
"Penelope" (Bitov, 1962), 267
Penkin, Sergei, 121
Penkovsky, Iosif, 65
Peoples' Friendship, The (*Druzhba narodov*, journal), 123
Perekop (Tsvetaeva, 1929), 251, 256
Perestroika, 7, 118, 150
Perkowski, Jan, 309
Peter I, ("The Great"), 91, 226, 256, 258, 289
Petrograd, *see* St. Petersburg
Petrovskoe, 74
Phillips, Adam, 4, 221
Piast, Vladimir, 100
Pilnik, Boris, 81
Pisarev, Dmitri, 93
Platonov, Andrei, 306
Pochinkovskaia, O., *see* Timofeeva, Varvara
Poem of the Air (Tsvetaeva, 1927), 251

"Poems to Pushkin" (Tsvetaeva, 1931), 215, 225, 251–63
"Poems about Pushkin" (Bokov), 80
Poem Without a Hero (Akhmatova, 1940–62), 192, 202, 208–9
"Poet, The" (Akhmatova, 1936), 197, 198
"Poet on the Critic, The" (Tsvetaeva, 1926), 255
"Poet's Calling, The" (Blok, 1921), 95–97
Pogodin, Mikhail, 45
Poor People (Dostoevsky, 1846), 280
Popov, Evgeny, 122
Popova, Nina, 76
Postmodernism, 305, 308
Pravda (newspaper), 109
Preserve, The (Dovlatov, 1983), 84
Prigov, Dmitri Aleksandrovich, 7, 12, 123
"Problems in Pushkin's Poetics" (Eikhenbaum, 1921), 91–93
Proletarian poets, 98, 99
"Prophet, The," (Lermontov), 267
Proshkin, Alexander, 128–29, 167
Proskurin, Oleg, 132
Protasova, Maria, 35
Proust, Marcel, 220
Pskov region, 119
"Psyche" (Tsvetaeva, 1920), 239–45
Pugachev, Emelian, 16
Punin, Nikolai, 198
Pushkin, Alexander: African heritage of, 23, 161, 217, 225; autobiographical writings, 17–25; burial of, 9, 52, 61, 257–58; death mask of, 78, 79, 148, 163–65, 168; death of, 2, 8–9, 10, 25, 26–42, 32, 61, 79, 112–13, 163, 210–13, 216–17, 257–58, 263–64, 283–85, 289, 293–94, 307–8, 364n45; drawings by, 124, 156–65, *157*, *158*, *162*; and duel, 8, 211–12, 216–17, 217, 270, 280–83, 285, 296; evocation through objects of, 75–76, 78–79, 145–46, 149, 163; and exile, 19, 48, 204, 216, 269; as "Frenchman," 187; grave of, 52, 53, 55, 60, 61, 98; love of, 3–4, 303–4, 310; marriage of, 247–48, 306; and modernity, 5; mythologizing of, 1–3, 5–13, 107–8, 165, 289–99; as national symbol, 1–9, 81–82, 88, 122, 149, 188, 275, 298, 302–3, 310; perspectives on, 4, 5–7, 10–12, 255, 270,

361n12; on the poet, 17–21, 68–70, 171, 316n31; political significance of, 9, 23, 61, 93, 98; portrait of, *152*, 168, 294; possessions of, 75–76; and religion, 37, 323n32; and Russian literature, 89–90, 91–93, 313n5; self-mythologizing of, 17–25; Soviet interpretation of, 107–8, 111–12; tragic view of, 6–7; and tsar, 37–38, 255–58, 324n37; on women and poetry, 44–45

Pushkin, Alexander (works): "André Chénier" (1825), 165; "Arion" (1827), 159, 160; "At the corner of a small square" (1830–31), 169; "Autumn" (1833), 19, 67–70, *157*; "Bacchic Song" (1825), 98, 107–8; *Blackamoor of Peter the Great* (1827), 240; "Black Shawl, The" (1820), 149, 155, 193; *Boris Godunov* (1825), 7, 17, 49, 204, 305; *The Bronze Horseman* (1833), 95, 98, 134, 158, 163, 202, 280, 283; *The Captain's Daughter* (1836), 7, 128, 129, 131, 219–22, 225, 226, 264, 280, 286, 305, 306; "The Countryside" (1819), 56, 59, 61, 72; "Delibash" (1829), 215, 219; "Demons" (1830), 159, 215; "The Drowned Man" (1828), 215; *Egyptian Nights* (1835), 168–70; "Elegy" (1830), 159; *Eugene Onegin* (1823–31), 17, 48, 70, 101, 102, 120, 122, 124, 151, 159, 162, 187, 197, 202, 215, 222, 232–33, 255, 268, 280, 305; *Feast in Time of Plague* (1830), 191; "(From Pindemonte)" (1836), 140, 316n31; *Gavriliad* (1821), 10, 249; "God grant that I not go out of my mind" (1833), 159; "The guests gathered at the dacha" (1828-30), 169; *The Gypsies* (1824), 7, 159, 215, 234; *History of Pugachev* (1834), 76, 128, 219–22; "I have built myself a monument" (1836), 17, 21–25, 215, 283; "Imagined Conversation with Alexander I" (1825), 161; "In the abyss of Siberian mines" (1827), 276–77; "I remember the wondrous moment" (1825), 56; "It was time: our youthful celebration" (1836), 196–97; "Joan of Arc's Last Relative" (1836), 271; "Keep Me Safe, My Talisman" (1825), 138, 155; "Lines Composed During a Night of Insomnia" (1830), 159; "Love, hope, and quiet fame" (1818), 127, 151; "The more one celebrates the lyceum" (1831), 194; "My ruddy-faced critic" (1830), 66–67, 107; "…Once again I visited" (1835), 56–58, 61, 74, 105–6; "Once there lived a poor knight" (1829), 172; "The Poet" (1827), 17; "The Poet walks with open eyes" (1835), 169, 171; *Poltava* (1829), 215; "The Prisoner" (1822), 127; *The Prisoner of the Caucasus* (1822), 202; "The Prophet" (1826), 7, 17–21, 89, 151, 154–55, 181, 215, 267; "Queen of Spades, The" (1833), 240, 280, 290; "Remembrances in Tsarskoe Selo" (1814), 117, 187, 197; *Ruslan and Liudmila* (1820), 35; "Scene from *Faust*" (1825), 159, 168–69; "Songs of the Western Slavs" (1834), 163; *The Stone Guest* (1830), 95, 177, 202–10, 305; *The Tale of the Golden Cockerel* (1834), 70, 177, 200–201; "To Ovid" (1821), 233; "To the Poet" (1830), 17; "To the Sea" (1824), 56, 215, 216, 223, 246; "Tsarskoe Selo Statue" (1830), 189; "The Upas Tree" (1828), 98; "The Vampire" (1834), 215; "We were spending the evening at the dacha" (1835), 169; "Winter Evening" (1825), 113; "Winter Road" (1826), 215

Pushkin. Duel. Death (Ginkas, 1999), 132
Pushkin, Grigory Aleksandrovich (son), 53
Pushkin, Lev (brother), 48
Pushkin, Olga (sister), 48, 138
Pushkin, S. L. (father), 32, 37, 64, 165, 323n32
Pushkin, Vasily Lvovich (uncle), 64
Pushkina, Natalia (daughter), 106
Pushkina, Natalia Nikolaevna (née Goncharova)(wife), 15, 65, 77, 106, 134, 199, 204, 211–12, 287, 306; Tsvetaeva and, 215, 235–45, 247–51
Pushkin Academy Theater, 110
"Pushkin Again" (exhibition, 1998), *125*, 126
Pushkin (Akhmatova, 1977), 175
"Pushkin" (Akhmatova, 1943), 189
Pushkin and His Wife Before a Looking-glass at a Court Ball (Ulyanov, 1945), 145

"Pushkin and Pugachev" (Tsvetaeva, 1937), 216–27, 382n25
"Pushkin and the Neva Shore" (Akhmatova, 1963), 199, 213
"Pushkin as an Object of Kitsch" (Rubinshtein, 1999), 119–20
Pushkin (engraving), 217–19, *218*
Pushkin (helicopter), *125*, 126
Pushkin House, *see* Institute of Russian Literature
Pushkin House (Bitov, 1978), 16, 267–68, 275–83, 289, 294–99
"Pushkin in 1828" (Akhmatova, 1963), 199
Pushkin in Life (Veresaev, 3d ed., 1928), 246
Pushkin in Spain (Bitov and Gabriadze, 1989), 160
"Pushkin's Birch Trees" (Figaret), 80
"Pushkin's Death" (Akhmatova, 1958), 199, 210–13
Pushkin's Duel and Death (Shchegolev, 1927), 112
Pushkin's Duel with d'Anthès (Naumov, 1884), 216–17, *217*
Pushkinskie Gory (Sviatye Gory), 99
"Pushkin's Notebook" (Rostopchina, 1838), 38–43, 45–46
Pushkin's Overcoat (anthology, 2000), 122
"Pushkin's Photograph (1799-2099)" (Bitov), 279, 286, 289–94
Pushkin's Poetic Economy (Khodasevich, 1924), 106
"Pushkin's Realism" (Ginzburg, 1937), 112
"Pushkin's *Stone Guest*" (Akhmatova, 1947), 199, 202–10
Pushkin Street (Bolshaia Dmitrovka), 110
Pushkin's Wisdom (Gershenzon, 1919), 93
Pushkin (town), *see* Tsarskoe Selo

Quotation, Bitov's use of, 276–79

Radio Russia, 120
Ramazani, Jahan, 37
Rassadin, Stanislav, 1, 3, 6, 10, 94, 155
Realism, 107, 144, 155, 172
Reeder, Roberta, 191
Remembrance, 25, 56–58, 62. *See also* Nostalgia

Requiem (Akhmatova, 1936–40), 178, 197, 202–3, 204
Revolution, Russian, 58
Rilke, Rainer Maria, 251
"Romance" (Khodasevich, 1924), 104, 347n101
Romanticism, 7–8, 21, 34, 38, 49, 231, 238
Ronell, Avital, 208
Rosslyn, Wendy, 43
Rostand, Edmond, 239
Rostopchina, Evdokia, 13, 37; elegy for Pushkin of, 38–43, 45–46; as poet, 43–46
Rozanova, Maria Vasilevna, 306, 310
Rubinshtein, Lev, 119–20, 123
Russia (*Rossiia*, journal), 104
Russian Idea (Berdiaev), 6
Russian Myths (Druzhnikov), 120
"Russian Trianon" (Akhmatova, 1925–40), 189
Russian Uprising, The (film), 128–29, 167
"Russophobia" (Shafarevich, 1989), 303

Sadova, Elizaveta, 52, 58
Sapgir, Genrikh, 123
Satire, 155
Savygin, Alexander, 59
Sazontiev, Sergei, 145
Schnittke, Alfred, 156–57, 159, 166, 172, 174
Scholarship, Pushkin, 12–13, 131–32, 177–78, 361n12; Akhmatova's, 200–213
Schweitzer, Viktoria, 221
Scotto, Peter, 242
Scriabin, Alexander, 10
Sears, John F., 80–81
Second World War, 59–60, 116
Sedakova, Olga, 23
Semerchuk, Vladimir, 168
Semyonov-Tian-Shansky, Benjamin, 54, 59, 81, 330n34
"September" (Annensky, ca. 1900), 183
Sexuality: Akhmatova on Pushkin's, 199; Bitov on Pushkin's, 287; Pushkin's, 10; in Rostopchina's depiction of Pushkin, 39–40; Sinyavsky on Pushkin and, 305–6; Tsvetaeva and, 232, 234. *See also* Bisexuality; Homosexuality
Shafarevich, Igor, 303

Shakespeare, William, 330n34
Shcheglova, Evgenia, 120
Shchegolev, Pavel, 90, 95, 112, 211
Short, John Rennie, 63
Shrines, Pushkin, 47–84; author's experiences at, 82–83; Boldino, 62–71; display of objects in, 75–76, 78–79; historical interpretation at, 79–80; Mikhailovskoe, 48–63, 71–75; poems about, 80–82, 338n129; *Pushkin House* and, 295–97; visitor experiences at, 82–83. *See also* Monuments, to Pushkin
Shvarts, Elena, 1–3, 7, 306
Shveitser, Mikhail, 127, 137, 154, 167, 169–74
Side Whiskers (film), 20, 137, 147, 150–55
Sintaksis (journal), 161, 305
Sinyavsky, Andrei (pseudonym Abram Tertz), 7, 10, 15, 16, 121, 278, 284, 301–10
Smirnova, A. O. (née Rosset), 249
Smith, Alexandra, 232, 237
Smith, Gerald, 140
Smoktunovsky, Innokenty, 144, 145, 156, 172–174
Sokolov, Vladimir, 80
Sokolova, Ekaterina, 160
Solzhenitsyn, Alexander, 302–3, 308
"Some see themselves in affectionate gazes" (Akhmatova, 1936), 195–98
Sosnovsky, L., 98
Spark, The (*Ogonek*, journal) 119
Stalin, Joseph, 9, 108, 127
Star, The (*Zvezda*, journal), 86, 131
Stewart, Susan, 278
Stone Island, 106
St. Petersburg (Petrograd, Leningrad), 89–90, 100, 109, 119
Stratford-upon-Avon, 330n34
Strolls with Pushkin (Sinyavsky, 1975), 10, 284, 301–10
Sublime, 231
"Submissive to you?" (Akhmatova, 1921), 206
Sukhorukov, Viktor, 153
Surat, Irina, 21
Sviatogorsk Monastery, 52, 53, 60, 98, 257
Sviatye Gory (Pushkinskie Gory), 99
"Swaying Tripod, The" (Khodasevich, 1921), 93–96, 104, 119

Switzerland, 51
Symbolism, 96, 100, 232

"Take Away the Hare: Three Variants" (Bitov, 1982, 1986), 269, 271, 272–75, 287, 296
Tasso, Torquato, 104
Tchaikovsky, Piotr Ilich, 120
Tell, William, 51
Terror, 108, 111–16, 277–78
Tertz, Abram, *see* Sinyavsky, Andrei
Theatricality, in museum presentations, 76–79
"This happened more than once" (Gumilev, 1910), 206
"Three 'Prophets'" (Bitov, 1976), 267–69, 282
Three Songs of Lenin (film), 127
Three Songs of Pushkin (film), 108, 126–28
Timenchik, Roman, 181
Timofeeva, Varvara (pseudonym O. Pochinkovskaia), 50–52, 55, 58
Tiutchev, Fyodor, 3, 26, 267–69, 282–83
Todd, William Mills, III, 36
Tolstoy, Leo, 12, 88, 97, 98, 109
"To Mayakovsky" (Tsvetaeva, 1930), 251
"To Pushkin House" (Blok, 1921), 276
Trigorskoe, 49, 52, 53, 56, 72, 74, 98, 99
Trofimov, Alexander, 173
Trotsky, Leon, 112
Tsarskoe Selo, 55, 110; Akhmatova and, 181–97, 204
"Tsarskoe Selo Statue" (Akhmatova, 1936), 188–91
Tsiavlovsky, Mstislav, 132
Tsivian, Yuri, 136, 137
Tsvetaeva, Marina, 10, 15, 39, 90, 96, 181, 214–65, 285, 304, 306; bisexuality of, 224, 238; and childhood, 216–27; "A Dream About Pushkin" (1931), 263–64; "An Encounter with Pushkin" (1913), 227–35; and gender, 224–26, 238, 248; and identity, 214–15, 221–24, 227–35, 250–51, 252; "(The Lathe)" (1931), 258–62; and love, 221–23; "Natalia Goncharova" (1929), 245–51; and Natalia Nikolaevna Pushkina, 215, 235–45, 247–51; "Poems to Pushkin" (1931), 251–63; Pushkin essays of, 216–27; relationship to mother of, 220–22

Tumarkin, Nina, 2
Turgenev, Andrei, 36, 88
Turkin, Andrei, 120
"Twelve, The" (Blok, 1918), 288–89
"Two Meetings" (Rostopchina, 1838, 1839), 39–40
Tynianov, Yuri, 145

Ulyanov, N. P., 145
Union of Russian Writers, 134
Urnov, Dmitri, 303
Ustimovich, P. M., 49, 53
Utkin, Anton, 123

Vaginov, Konstantin, 100
Vampirism, 308–9
Vatsuro, Vadim, 132
Ventriloquism, Bitov and, 268, 270
Veresaev, Vikenty, 112, 246
Vertov, Dziga, 127
VGIK film institute, 167
"V. Ia. Briusovu" (Tsvetaeva, 1912), 233
Viazemsky, Pyotr, 36, 146–47, 212
Vicquelmont, Countess Daria, 212
"View of the Sky at Troy" (Bitov, 1988), 292
Virolainen, Maria, 131
Vneshekonombank, 131
Volpert, Larisa, 132
Voltaire, 56, 286
"Voronezh" (Akhmatova, 1936), 197
Vorontsova, Countess Elizaveta, 138, 360n6
Vostokov, Alexander, 24

Vowles, Judith, 43
Vysotsky, Vladimir, 123

Wachtel, Andrew, 12
Wachtel, Michael, 193
Waldron, Irina, 132
Wells, David, 191
"What's in My Name?" (Anisimov, 1999), 120
"When your voice, o poet" (Baratynsky, 1843), 17
Women, literary role of, 43–45
"Word on Pushkin, A" (Akhmatova, 1961), 195
Wright, Colin, 113
Writers' Union, 100, 109, 111

XL Gallery, 132

Yeltsin, Boris, 120
Yakovleva, Arina Rodionovna, 61, 72, 106, 274

Zholkovsky, Alexander, 177
Zhukovsky, Vasily, 13, 112, 146–47, 212, 289; drawing of Pushkin by, 32; drawing of Pushkin's apartment by, 32, 33; elegy for Pushkin of, 32–38; letter to Pushkin's father from, 32, 37–38, 165, 323n32, 364n45; and Pushkin's death, 31–38; relationship with Pushkin of, 35–38; and Rostopchina's elegy, 43
Zilbershtein, Ilya, 119
Zorin, Andrei, 121–22
Zoshchenko, Mikhail, 110–11, 117, 206